Yale Language Series

Japanese: The Spoken Language

PART 1

Eleanor Harz Jorden
with Mari Noda

Yale University Press
New Haven and London

Published with assistance from the
foundation established in memory of
Philip Hamilton McMillan
of the Class of 1894, Yale College.

Designed by Sally Harris
and set in Baskerville type by
Brevis Press, Bethany, Connecticut.
Printed in the United States of America by
Murray Printing Co., Westford, Mass.

Library of Congress Cataloging-in-Publication Data

Jorden, Eleanor Harz.
    Japanese, the spoken language.

    (Yale language series)
    Includes index.
    1. Japanese language—Text-books for foreign
speakers—English. 2. Japanese language—Spoken
Japanese. I. Noda, Mari. II. Title. III. Series.
PL539.3.J58 1987   495.6′83421   86–15890
ISBN 0–300–03834–8 (pbk. : v. 1 : alk. paper)
ISBN 0–300–04188–8 (pbk. : v. 2 : alk. paper)
ISBN 0–300–04191–8 (pbk. : v. 3 : alk. paper)

The paper in this book meets the guidelines for
permanence and durability of the Committee on
Production Guidelines for Book Longevity
of the Council on Library Resources.

20   19   18   17   16   15   14   13   12   11   10

To
William Seike Jorden
and
Michael Tadashi Noda
who bring our two worlds together

Contents

Acknowledgments

In 1962–63, *Beginning Japanese,* Part 1 and Part 2, written with the assistance of Hamako Ito Chaplin, was published by Yale University Press. In the years that have followed, the book has been reprinted 30 times, for a total of more than 135,000 copies. But the time has come for *Beginning Japanese*'s retirement. Video is now a language-learning tool that offers marvelous opportunities to see the Japanese language in action, and it should be an integral part of a language course. In addition, the author has long been eager both to introduce modifications in her grammatical and sociolinguistic analysis and her pedagogical approach, and to introduce currently valid situations. Much that was the underlying philosophy of *Beginning Japanese* remains as the basis for this new book, but much of the surface is changed. One point must be stressed: every modification that has been made results from direct observation of language use by Japanese in Japan and of foreigners' successes and failures with the Japanese language.

To express my gratitude adequately to all who helped in the preparation of this book would really require that I go back to the day *Beginning Japanese* was published, for it was then that I began planning for the current volumes. But the list would be too long, so I limit myself to those more directly involved with this actual book and the tapes that accompany it.

I am particularly indebted:

to the Japanese language teaching staffs and students—particularly the FALCONS—at Cornell University, whose questions and answers over the years constantly affected my thinking. Several "long-termers" deserve special mention: Elizabeth Hengeveld, Emiko Konomi, Reiko Ochi, Polly Szatrowski, Reiko Yamada, Patricia Wetzel;

to members of the first elementary Japanese-language class at Williams College, who patiently and uncomplainingly coped with cumbersome draft copies of this text for an entire year as I used it as a classroom text for the first time;

to Robert Sukle, of Cornell University, for sharing his valuable insights into the Japanese language, not to mention his skill and conscientiousness in "minding the store" during my absence from Cornell to complete this book;

to A. Ronald Walton of the University of Maryland for many years of fruitful collaborations in pedalinguistics, our area of special concern; I am deeply indebted to him for his continuing enthusiastic support;

to James Noblitt, of Cornell University, for his invaluable assistance in providing his glossary program, and to Roberta Valente, also of Cornell, for preparing and formatting the data base from which the glossaries were generated;

to Yoshio Kasugai, Makoto Koizumi, Giichi Ito and associates of Tower Television, the actors' and actresses' group, and the staff of Kunihiro Jimusho/IMAC for the filming of the Core Conversations on location in Tokyo and for their preparation of the master videotapes. Their imagination and skill in bringing the conversations to life and their devotion to the project will never be forgotten;

to the audiovisual staff of Cornell University, particularly Neil Jacobs, Gordon Webb, and Jon Hilton, for their patience and fortitude—to say nothing of their expertise—in the preparation and editing of accompanying audio and videotapes;

to Takamasa Itoh, Ryo Ochiai, and the staff of the Sony Corporation, for the preparation of video disks, which moved the video material into a new age of technological advancement. Their important contribution to the project is deeply appreciated;

to Masashi Orishima of Tokyo Medical and Dental University, and Kyoko Saurer of the Cornell Japanese Language Program, assisted by Nobukazu Shibahata and Mariko Sheldon, for their cheerful cooperation in the initial filming of video drill tapes, a task that would have exhausted all but the most steadfast;

to Taichi Hori of ELEC, Tokyo, for his careful audiorecording of the Core Conversations;

to the many native speakers of Japanese who cheerfully and cooperatively participated in the recording of countless hours of drill material;

to Osamu Mizutani of Nagoya University, and to Hisao Akashi and Junko Akashi for their careful checking of the manuscript of the Core Conversations;

to Ellen Graham and Nancy Woodington of Yale University Press, for their invaluable assistance and constant encouragement during the lengthy process of preparing the manuscript for publication. The interest and care they demonstrated were particularly appreciated;

to the International Research and Studies Division of the Department of Education, for grants that helped support the preparation of accompanying audio and videotapes;

to the typists who struggled with a difficult manuscript and with temperamental word-processors and printers—in particular, Roberta Valente, Angela Menitto, Sarah Pradt, Lynn Miller, and Corinne Vanchieri—for their skill, patience, and determination to see the job through.

In addition, there are several individuals in special categories to whom I owe a lasting debt. My mentor, the late Bernard Bloch of Yale University, continues to influence my work in ways that are increasingly obvious to me. My unending debt to Hamako Ito Chaplin of Yale for her guidance and help over the years will never be forgotten. And to Samuel Martin, also of Yale, I am indebted for discussions and suggestions that have always been invaluable.

To my children—Tem, Tabi, and Telly—I am deeply grateful for their constant encouragement, support, and patience—and for their tolerance of an extremely variant specimen of the genus "kyoiku-mama."

And finally, I come to Mari Noda, without whose collaboration this particular text could never have been written. Her thorough understanding of the methodological and linguistic foundations on which it was conceived, combined with her unique ability to translate that understanding into a Japanese-language corpus that met the challenging requirements posed, was truly awesome. Her extraordinary talent both as a linguist and as a language teacher is evident in everything she produces. My gratitude and my debt to her for joining me in the production of this text are impossible to express adequately. Any inadequacies or inaccuracies in the final product are my responsibility, not hers.

Eleanor Harz Jorden

How to Use This Book

You are now about to begin learning the Japanese language following a carefully developed system. Assisting you in this endeavor—along with your instructors—are the textbook and accompanying video and audiotapes. But in order for the textbook to be as effective as possible, it should be used in the manner intended. It was designed on the basis of a particular approach to foreign-language learning, and in order to gain the greatest possible benefit from using it, following the recommended procedures is important.

The following are basic underlying assumptions which have affected the construction of this textbook:

1. The order of the lessons is of crucial importance.

Each lesson presumes control of what has been introduced previously. Only Lesson 1 is completely new; each later lesson consists of a limited amount of new material combined with material introduced earlier that is already familiar. Thus, each lesson serves both to add new knowledge and to review old.

2. No lesson can be omitted.

Each lesson is heavily dependent on all preceding lessons. Since explanations of vocabulary, structural patterns, and usage are regularly included within the lesson where they first occur in the textbook, the failure to cover every lesson carefully will result in persisting problems.

3. No part of any lesson can be omitted.

Developing a skill involves the forming of new habits, and new habits are acquired only through extensive practice. In addition to explanatory material, each lesson in this text includes a variety of practice material aimed at developing fluent oral control of the language. To omit reading the explanations is to fail to take advantage of the shortcuts to learning provided by systematization. To omit any of the recommended drill procedures is to stint on the skill side of language learning and run the risk of becoming able only to talk *about* Japanese.

4. Developing speaking and listening skills in a foreign language cannot be done through the eye.

For memorization and drill practice, oral models are absolutely necessary. Romanized Japanese (i.e., Japanese written with the letters of our alphabet) should serve only to remind you of what you have already heard—and heard many, many times. The letters used in romanization are all familiar to English speakers, but when used to represent Japanese, they represent a completely different set of sounds. If you have studied French, or German, or Spanish—or even Vietnamese—this will not surprise you. 'Six' as an English word and 'six' as a French word stand for totally different pronunciations. You must not attempt to read any of the Japanese material that follows until you first become familiar with Japanese sounds, and next learn the spelling code according to which familiar symbols represent those sounds in a completely regular and predictable fashion. You may be surprised to learn the native pronunciation of familiar Japanese place names like 'Tokyo,' 'Kyoto,' and 'Osaka'; and of cultural borrowings like 'kimono,' 'sake,' and 'sukiyaki.'

The Japanese, of course, use a completely different writing system, but they, too, postpone using their written code until they have already learned to speak. For foreigners who are interested in learning to read Japanese, it is most efficient to study the special written symbols *after* acquiring at least some familiarity with the material being read. In other words, if you are told that a particular symbol in the Japanese writing system stands for **X** at a time when you also have to be instructed as to what **X** means, 'reading' in its usual sense is impossible; you will undoubtedly proceed to decode—to move directly from Japanese symbols to your own native language, bypassing the Japanese language completely. To avoid this, we recommend that beginning readers start out by reading only material in which they have already acquired oral competence.[1]

Always listen to an utterance first; *after that* you may check to see how it is represented in a written code, but *do not let the written form become a crutch* for your understanding or speaking. Remember that most conversations in the real world proceed free of any connection with the written language. Listening and speaking are very different from reading and writing; they are totally different kinds of skills and are best acquired through different approaches. The ability to speak and understand a language is much more significant as an aid to learning to read than the reverse.

The lessons that follow the Introduction are organized in the following way:

SECTIONS A AND B

Each of these sections contains **Core Conversations** (which may be single exchanges between two people or longer conversations), their **English Equivalents, Breakdowns** with **Supplementary Vocabulary, Miscellaneous Notes, Structural Patterns, Drills,** and **Application Exercises**.

Core Conversations are to be *memorized,* using the accompanying video and audiotapes. Note that new vocabulary and new patterns are thus acquired in context with appropriate pronunciation and intonation. While supplementary vocabulary is included (with the Breakdowns), even these items should be practiced within a familiar context; they should not be memorized or practiced as isolated items. A word means what it means *in context*.

The English Equivalents and Breakdowns will assist you in comprehending the Core Conversations. The Miscellaneous Notes and Structural Patterns should be read carefully as soon as the Core Conversations have at least become familiar. The Japanese language is totally unrelated to English: unless you understand in depth how the language is put together, you will continue to encounter seemingly baffling examples which actually should not be at all surprising. It is important to strive for thorough understanding of the building blocks of the language and to take advantage of its regularity as an independent system.

Drills are to be practiced with the tapes. Your performance in these drills must not be

---

1. For those interested in reading, see the forthcoming *Japanese: The Written Language* for a systematic introduction, and *Japanese: The Spoken Language—Supplement* for the written Japanese version of all the Japanese-language material included in this text.

considered satisfactory until you can participate promptly and accurately according to the models, without reference to the textbook. For each stimulus in these drills, there is only one correct answer, which follows the model of the first example of the drill. (For example, one drill may require you to answer every stimulus question in the negative [Stimulus: 'Are you hungry?' Response: 'No, I'm not.'] regardless of your actual condition.) All the drills are response drills, which means that each stimulus + response is actually a short conversation.

Application Exercises, on the other hand, suggest practice that utilizes reality—provided by either visual aids or your general knowledge—as the basis for correct responses.

SECTION C

Eavesdropping (devoid of any negative connotations!) involves listening in on Japanese conversations on tape, and answering questions about their content. Note that (a) only the questions are printed in the textbook; and (b) the language of both the questions and answers is English. This section represents a kind of situation that commonly occurs in real life: imagine that you are being questioned by an English-speaking friend, who doesn't understand Japanese as well as you do, about the meaning of a Japanese conversation that you have both overheard. This portion of the lesson involves processing from Japanese to English, a competence distinct from operating within the foreign language alone, but one which is also important to develop.

Utilization presents typical situations in which the Japanese you have learned might be utilized. A situational orientation of this kind is intended to emphasize the importance of speaking a foreign language according to what is grammatically and culturally appropriate in a given setting, rather than through direct translation of what would be appropriate in your native language in a similar setting. Again, the ease with which you produce accurate answers will be a clear signal of the degree to which you have mastered the material. Slow, hesitant, mistake-ridden answers—produced only after constant checking back to earlier explanatory material—clearly signal the need for further study and practice before moving to the next lesson. Remember that each lesson presupposes good control of everything that has already been introduced. And remember too that the acquisition of a skill like speaking takes *time* and *practice*. If the foundation is weak, ultimate collapse becomes a worrisome possibility; but if each lesson is systematically mastered, increment by increment, a solid proficiency can be acquired.

The **Check-up** is intended to check your control of the 'fact' component of the lesson. We assume that the foreign language student can learn a foreign language more quickly if the patterns of the language are explained systematically. While learning *about* a language will never produce foreign language proficiency unless supplemented by hours of active practice, it can speed the process by guiding you to accurate, extended usage of the patterns that are being drilled.

The Check-up section can be covered outside of class. The relevant notes should be carefully checked if there are questions that present difficulties. The questions themselves serve to emphasize the most important structural features that have been introduced in each lesson.

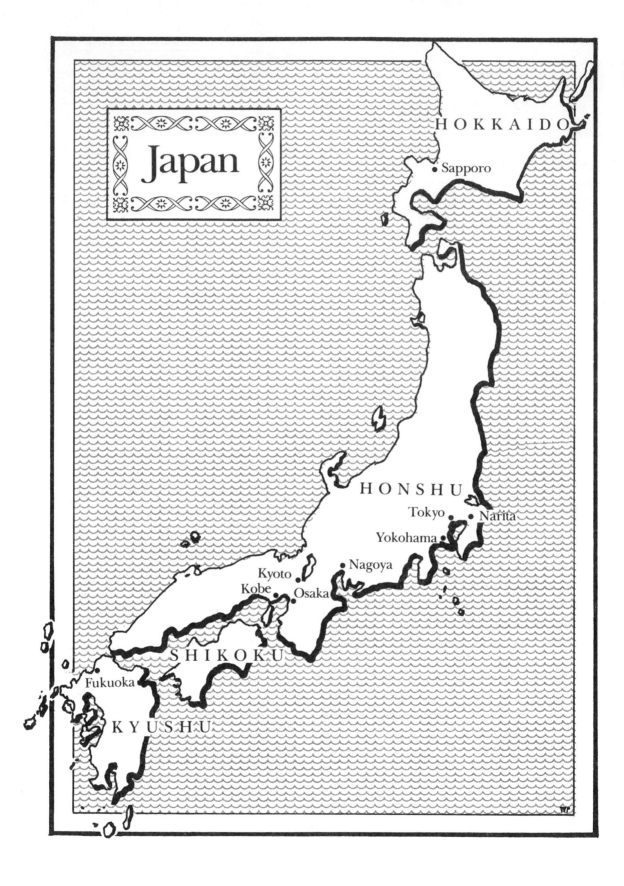

Introduction

I. PRONUNCIATION

Mora is the term we will use to refer to the syllable-like unit of Japanese: each mora represents one beat and occupies roughly the same unit of time (a 3-mora word takes three times as long to pronounce as a 1-mora word).

The so-called 'standard' dialect of Japanese (spoken by educated natives of Tokyo) can be described in terms of 113 distinct mora of the following kinds:

5 single vowel
67 consonant + vowel
36 consonant + **y** + vowel
5 single consonant

Your first task is to learn (1) how the sounds of Japanese are pronounced and (2) how the Japanese sounds—which are different from the sounds of English—are represented in this text with the letters of our alphabet. For (1), you will need as a model a native speaker of Japanese and/or a recording made by a native speaker.[1] For (2), you must study the chart and notes below, always bearing in mind that the letters are no more than arbitrary symbols which are meant to *remind* you of the actually occurring Japanese sounds. Although the symbols may seem unnecessarily arbitrary at the beginning, while the structure of Japanese is still unknown, you will become accustomed to them very quickly as you become familiar with the language.

The Mora of Japanese

1	2	3	4	5	6	7	8	9	10	11	12	13	14	15	16	17
a	ka	ga	ğa	sa	za	ta	da	na	ha	pa	ba	ma	ya	ra	wa	k
i	ki	gi	ği	si	zi	ti	—	ni	hi	pi	bi	mi	—	ri	—	s
u	ku	gu	ğu	su	zu	tu	—	nu	hu	pu	bu	mu	yu	ru	—	t
e	ke	ge	ğe	se	ze	te	de	ne	he	pe	be	me	—	re	—	p
o	ko	go	ğo	so	zo	to	do	no	ho	po	bo	mo	yo	ro	—	ñ

	2	3	4	5	6	7	8	9	10	11	12	13	14	15	16
	kya	gya	ğya	sya	zya	tya	—	nya	hya	pya	bya	mya	—	rya	—
	kyu	gyu	ğyu	syu	zyu	tyu	—	nyu	hyu	pyu	byu	myu	—	ryu	—
	kyo	gyo	ğyo	syo	zyo	tyo	—	nyo	hyo	pyo	byo	myo	—	ryo	—

1. The practice drills that follow are available on audiotape.

(In the following discussion, row numbers correspond to the numbers of the vertical rows in the chart above. IN THIS SECTION ONLY, mora within a word are separated by hyphens to show mora division, and capital letters represent a pitch level higher than that represented by lower-case letters.)

Row 1	The symbol:	stands for a sound approximately like:	but the Japanese sound:
a	'a' in 'father'	is short and clipped
i	'i' in 'machine'	is short and clipped
u	'u' in 'put'	is short, clipped, and without lip-rounding
e	'e' in 'bet'	is short and clipped
o	'o' in 'horse'	is short and clipped

When two or more Japanese vowels follow each other directly, each one retains its original quality and length, but the sequence is regularly pronounced as a continuum. The occurrence of the same vowel symbol twice indicates a long vowel: e.g., **aa** represents **a** + **a** pronounced without a break.

A word in Japanese has at least as many mora as it has vowels: thus, **a-O-i** is a 3-mora word; **E-e** is a 2-mora word.

Practice 1[2]

a 'oh!'	**A-o** 'blue'	**u-E** 'top'	**e** 'picture'
A-a 'oh!'	**I-i** 'is good'	**o-I** 'nephew'	**E-e** 'yes'
A-i 'love'	**i-E** 'house'	**o-O-i** 'are many'	**o-U** 'owe'
A-u 'meet'	**i-I-E** 'no'	**a-O-i** 'is blue'	**o-O-U** 'conceal'

Row 2	The symbol:	stands for a sound approximately like:	but the Japanese sound:
k before **a, u e, o**	'c' in 'coot'	has less aspiration[3]
ky, and **k** before **i**	'c' in 'cute'	has less aspiration[3]

The values of the vowel symbols remain the same as in Row 1 above.

Practice 2

ka-U 'buy'	**a-KA-I** 'is red'	**ka-I-KE-E** 'account'
ka-O 'face'	**o-O-KI-i** 'is big'	**KYA-a** 'eek!'
i-KE 'pond'	**KE-e-ko** 'practice'	**KYO-o** 'today'
ko-KO 'here'	**ku-U-KO-O** 'airport'	**KYU-u** 'grade'

---

2. All the practice drills that follow are for pronunciation practice only. Do not try to remember the meanings of these items.

3. The corresponding English sound is followed by a strong puff of breath.

Row 3	The symbol:	stands for a sound approximately like:	but the Japanese sound:
	g before **a, u, e, o**	'g' in 'begone'	in initial position is more fully voiced than the corresponding English initial[4]
	gy, and **g** before **i**	'g' in 'regular'	in initial position is more fully voiced than the corresponding English initial[4]

Practice 3

GA-i 'injury'   **gi-KO-O** 'art'   **GU-ke-e** 'my elder brother'
GE-e 'craft'   **GI-ka-i** 'the Diet'   **GYA-ku-i** 'traitorous mind'
GO-i 'vocabulary'   **go-KA-I** 'misunderstanding'   **gyo-O-KO-O** 'good fortune'
gi-KE-E 'brother-in-law'   **gu-U-I** 'a moral'   **GYU-u** 'beef'

ROW 4

The symbol **ḡ** represents a sound like the 'ng' of 'singer'[5]—that is, it is a sound made with the tongue in position for a **g** but with the air escaping through the nasal passages. In Japanese, this sound never occurs at the beginning of an utterance.

Like **gy** and **g** before **i**, **ḡy** and **ḡ** before **i** are pronounced with the tongue raised in a 'y' position, somewhat like the 'ngy' of 'bring you.'

The occurrence of **ḡ** is a matter of dialect. While it is usually considered a feature of Tokyo Japanese, there are many Tokyo speakers who regularly use **g** instead, and there are still others who alternate freely between the two. The situation, as far as this text is concerned, is as follows:

Where **g** is written, **ḡ** is NOT to be substituted.

Where **ḡ** is written, **g** can ALWAYS be substituted.

Example:

GA-i: G occurs in the speech of all speakers of Japanese.

KA-ḡu: Some speakers say **KA-ḡu** (with the nasal **ḡ**) consistently, others say **KA-gu** consistently, and still others alternate freely between the two pronunciations.

Whichever pronunciation you use, you must be able to understand both.[6]

Practice 4

E-e-ḡa 'movie'   **KA-ḡe** 'shadow'   **KA-i-ḡi** 'conference'
i-KA-ḡa 'how?'   **GO-ḡo** 'afternoon'   **ka-I-ḠYA-KU**[7] 'a jest'
KA-ḡu 'furniture'   **ko-O-ḠO** 'spoken language'   **ka-I-ḠYU-U** 'sea-cow'
a-O-ḡu 'look up'   **ku-ḠI** 'nail'   **KO-o-ḡyo-o** 'industry'

4. A voiced sound is one accompanied by vibration of the vocal cords. In English, a voiced consonant at the beginning of a word begins without voice (vibration); in Japanese an initial voiced consonant is voiced throughout its articulation.

5. This is a valid comparison only for those speakers of English who distinguish between the medial sounds of 'singer' and 'finger,' with the latter containing the medial sound of 'singer' + 'g.'

6. Accordingly, examples of **g** substitution for **ḡ** have been included on the tapes that accompany this text.

7. See the section on whispered mora below.

Row 5	The symbol:	stands for a sound approximately like:	but the Japanese sound:
	s before **a, u, e, o**	's' in 'see'	is pronounced further forward in the mouth
	sy, and **s** before **i**	'sh' in 'she'	

Practice 5

A-sa 'morning'	**o-SA-KE** 'rice wine'	**SYA-ka-i** 'society'
a-SU 'tomorrow'	**SU-ḡu** 'right away'	**HA-i-sya** 'dentist'
A-se 'perspiration'	**ko-O-SU-I** 'perfume'	**KYU-u-syu-u** 'Kyushu'
a-SI 'leg'	**o-I-SI-I** 'is delicious'	**sya-SYO-O** 'conductor'
a-SO-KO 'there'	**o-KA-SI-i** 'is funny'	**syu-U-SYO-O** 'grief'

Row 6	The symbol:	stands for a sound approximately like:	but the Japanese sound:
	z before **a, u, e, o**	'z' in 'bazaar' or 'dz' in 'old zebra'	is pronounced further forward in the mouth and is regularly fully voiced[4]
	zy, and **z** before **i**	'j' in 'reject'	

Practice 6

za-I-KA 'inventory'	**GO-zi** 'five o'clock'	**ZYU-u** 'ten'
KA-zu 'number'	**KA-zi** 'a fire'	**KA-zyu** 'fruit tree'
ki-ZU 'a cut'	**zi-E-E** 'self-defense'	**zyo-O** 'feeling'
ZE-e 'a tax'	**ZYA-a** 'well then'	**zyo-SE-E** 'woman'
ZO-o 'elephant'	**zya-KO-O** 'musk'	**ko-O-ZYO-o** 'factory'

Row 7	The symbol:	stands for a sound approximately like:	but the Japanese sound:
	t before **a, e, o**	't' in 'tip'	is pronounced with the tongue touching the teeth and with little aspiration
	ty, and **t** before **i**	'ch' in 'cheap'	is pronounced further forward in the mouth
	t before **u**	'ts' in 'tsetse fly'	is pronounced further forward in the mouth

Practice 7

ka-TA 'person'	**TI-zu** 'map'	**o-SI-ḠO-TO-TYU-U** 'in the middle of work'
ta-KA-i 'is high'	**ti-I-SA-i** 'is small'	**ko-O-TYO-O** 'director'
ki-I-TE 'listening'	**o-TYA** 'tea'	**TYO-o-me-e** 'long life'
to-O-KA 'ten days'	**ko-O-TYA** 'black tea'	**TU-i-te** 'concerning'
si-ḠO-TO 'work'	**TYU-u-i** 'warning'	**tu-ZU-KI** 'continuation'

Row 8	The symbol:	stands for a sound approximately like:	but the Japanese sound:
	d	'd' in 'redeem'	is pronounced with the tongue touching the teeth and is regularly fully voiced[4]

Practice 8

e-DA 'branch'	**DE-te** 'leaving'	**KA-do** 'street corner'
o-KA-DA (family name)	**i-SO-i-de** 'hurrying'	**DO-ko** 'where?'
ku-DA-SA-i 'give me'	**de-KI-ḡo-to** 'occurrence'	**do-O-ḠU** 'tool'

Row 9	The symbol:	stands for a sound approximately like:	but the Japanese sound:
	n before **a, u, e, o** **ny,** and **n** before **i**	'n' in 'deny' 'n' in 'menu,' 'avenue,'[8] etc.	is pronounced with the tongue touching the teeth and is regularly fully voiced[4]

Practice 9

NA-ka 'inside'	**o-KA-NE** 'money'	**NYA-o** 'meow'
KI-nu 'silk'	**so-NO** 'that'	**gyu-U-NYU-U** 'milk'
te-NU-ḠU-I 'towel'	**NA-ni** 'what?'	**nyu-U-ZYO-O** 'entrance'
NE-ko 'cat'	**ni-KA-I** 'second floor'	**NYO-o-ḡo** 'court lady'

8. Applicable only for those speakers who use a 'nyu' pronunciation in English.

Row 10	The symbol:	stands for a sound approximately like:	but the Japanese sound:
	h before **a, e, o** **hy,** and **h** before **i**	'h' in 'hot' 'h' in 'humid'	has more friction
	H before **u** is made by bringing the upper and lower lips together and then puffing air out between them. Unlike English 'f,' which is the closest English sound, Japanese **h** before **u** does not involve the lower teeth in its production.		

Practice 10

HA-i 'yes' **hi-ḠE** 'beard' **HYO-o** 'hail'
HA-ha 'mother' **ko-O-HI-i** 'coffee' **HU-u** 'manner'
he-E 'wall' **HYU-u-zu** 'fuse' **HU-ne** 'boat'
HO-o 'direction' **hya-KU-DO** '100 times' **HU-zi** 'Fuji'

Row 11	The symbol:	stands for a sound approximately like:	but the Japanese sound:
	p before **a, u, e, o** **py,** and **p** before **i**	'p' in 'poor' 'p' in 'pure'	has less aspiration

Practice 11

PA-a-zi 'purge' **PU-u-pu-u** (noise of a horn) **PO-o-zu** 'a pause'
a-PA-a-to 'apartment' **pe-E-ZI** 'page' **PYU-u-pyu-u** (noise of a whistle)
de-PA-a-to 'department store' **PO-ka-po-ka** 'repeatedly' **pi-A-NO** 'piano'

Row 12	The symbol:	stands for a sound approximately like:	but the Japanese sound:
	b before **a, u, e, o** **by,** and **b** before **i**	'b' in 'rebel' 'b' in 'rebuke'	is regularly fully voiced[4]

Practice 12

BA-ta-a 'butter' **ka-BE** 'wall' **sa-BI-SI-i** 'is lonely'
ta-BA-KO 'cigarette' **bo-O** 'stick' **BYA-ku-e** 'white robe'
a-SO-BU 'play' **o-BO-e-te** 'remembering' **BYU-u-byu-u** (noise of wind)
a-BU-NA-I 'is dangerous' **e-BI** 'shrimp' **byo-O-BU** 'screen'

Row 13	The symbol:	stands for a sound approximately like:	but the Japanese sound:
m before **a, u, e, o** **my,** and **m** before **i**	'm' in 'remind' 'm' in 'amuse'	is regularly fully voiced[4]

Practice 13

MA-e 'front' **mu-SU-ME** 'daughter' **KYO-o-mi** 'interest'
ma-TA 'again' **ME-e-zi** 'Meiji' **mya-KU-DO-O** 'pulse'
NO-mu 'drink' **I-tu mo** 'always' **MYU-u-zu** 'muse'
mu-KO-O 'over there' **MI-se-te** 'showing' **ko-O-MYO-O** 'great deed'

Row 14	The symbol:	stands for a sound approximately like:	but the Japanese sound:
y	'y' in 'year'	is regularly fully voiced[4]

Practice 14

ya-O-YA 'vegetable store' **o-YU** 'hot water' **yo-SI-DA** (family name)
NA-ḡo-ya 'Nagoya' **yu-KI-yo** 'snowy night' **sa-YO-O** 'that way'
o-YA-SU-MI-NA-SA-i **yu-U-ME-E** 'famous' **o-HA-YO-O** 'good morning'
  'good night'

ROW 15

The Japanese **r** is a flap-**r**, made by flicking the tip of the tongue against the alveolar ridge (area behind the upper teeth). This sound closely resembles the 'r' in the British English pronunciation of 'very.' To speakers of American English, it often sounds like a **d**, but there are two main differences: (1) the Japanese **r** is shorter than **d**; and (2) in the production of **r**, the tip of the tongue makes contact with the alveolar ridge, whereas in the production of **d**, it is the area of the tongue immediately behind the tip that makes contact against the upper teeth. When **r** is immediately followed by **i** or **y**, the **r** articulation just described is accompanied by palatalization—that is, the back part of the tongue is in position to make a **y** sound, while the tip makes the flap-**r**.

Practice 15

ra-KU 'comfortable' **o-HU-ro** 'bath' **rya-KU-ZI** 'simplified character'
sa-YO-NA-RA 'goodbye' **o-MO-SI-RO-i** 'is interesting' **ka-I-RYU-U** 'ocean current'
BI-ru 'building' **ri-KO-O** 'clever' **ryu-U-KO-O** 'fashion'
RU-u-ru 'rule' **ko-O-RI** 'ice' **RYO-o-zi** 'consul'
KI-re-e 'pretty' **a-RI-ḡa-to-o** 'thank you' **ryo-O-RI-ya** 'restaurant'

Row 16	The symbol:	stands for a sound approximately like:	but the Japanese sound:
w	'w' in 'want'	is regularly fully voiced[4]

Practice 16

wa-KA-i 'is young'	**wa-KA-ru** 'understand'	**wa-RE-WA-RE** 'we'
he-E-WA 'peace'	**yu-BI-WA** 'ring'	**wa-SU-RE-RU** 'forget'

Row 17	The symbol:	occurs as a mora by itself immediately preceding a mora having initial:	and the Japanese sound:
	k	k (cf. English 'bookkeeper')	
	s	s (cf. English 'less sleep,' 'horse-show')	lasts for a full mora beat
	t	t (cf. English 'hot tip')	
	p	p (cf. English 'top part')	

All double (long) consonants in Japanese are characterized by tenseness. A following mora beginning with **k, t,** or **p** is pronounced without aspiration—that is, without a puff of breath following the consonant.

Practice 17a

mi-K-KA 'three days'	**a-S-SA-ri** 'briefly'
yu-K-KU-ri 'slowly'	**ma-S-SU-ğu** 'straight'
NI-k-ko-o 'Nikko'	**i-S-SO-O** 'more'
ha-K-KI-ri 'clearly'	**za-S-SI** 'magazine'
se-K-KYO-o 'sermon'	**ma-S-SI-ro** 'all white'
ha-K-KYU-U 'small salary'	**i-S-SYU-U** 'one round'
ka-T-TA 'bought'	**i-P-PA-I** 'full'
i-T-TE 'going'	**i-P-PU-U** 'somewhat'
TYO-t-to 'a bit'	**ri-P-PO-O** 'legislation'
ma-T-TI-ba-ko 'matchbox'	**ha-P-PI** 'workman's coat'
ko-MA-t-tya-t-ta '[I]'m upset'	**ha-P-PYA-KU-ME** '800 momme'
yo-T-TU-ME 'fourth thing'	**ha-P-PYO-O** 'announcement'

ROW 17 (CONTINUED)

Ñ represents a nasal sound which always has a full mora beat of its own—that is, it constitutes a mora—and is always pronounced with the nasal passages open; but its pronunciation varies depending on the sound that immediately follows in the same word or a following word.

Row 17 (continued)	The syllable:	before:	represents:
	ñ	(1) **p, b,** or **m**	a full-mora **m**[9]
		(2) **z, t, d, n,** or **r**	a full-mora **n**[9]
		(3) **k, g,** or **ğ**	a full-mora **ğ**[9]
		(4) **s, h, y, w,** a vowel, or pause	full-mora nasalization; pronounced by raising the tongue toward the roof of the mouth but not making contact anywhere, and at the same time releasing the flow of air through the nasal passages and vibrating the vocal cords
		(4) **o**	**ñ + w + o**
		(4) **e**	**ñ + y + e**

Practice 17b

(1) **sa-Ñ-PO**
'a walk'
SA-ñ-ba-i
'three cupfuls'
a-Ñ-MA-RI
'too much'

(2) **be-Ñ-ZYO**
'toilet'
ke-Ñ-TO-o
'a guess'
KO-ñ-do
'this time'
da-Ñ-NA-SA-ma
'master'
BE-ñ-ri
'convenient'

(3) **be-Ñ-KYO-O**
'study'
ni-HO-Ñ-GI-ñ-ko-o
'Bank of Japan'
ni-HO-Ñ-ĞO
'Japanese language'

(4) **te-Ñ-I-Ñ** 'store clerk'
ni-HO-ñ o 'Japan (as direct object)'
ni-HO-ñ e 'to Japan'
sa-Ñ-SE-E 'approval'
HA-ñ-ha-ñ 'half and half'
HO-ñ-ya 'bookstore'
de-Ñ-WA 'telephone'
a-RI-MA-SE-ñ 'there isn't any'

WHISPERED MORA

The Tokyo dialect of Japanese is characterized by the frequent occurrence of whispered (that is, voiceless[10]) mora. Whenever an **i** or **u** vowel[11] occurs between any two voiceless

9. It constitutes a full mora and is longer than the related sound which occurs as the initial part of a mora.
10. A voiceless sound is one which is not accompanied by vibration of the vocal cords.
11. Other vowels are less commonly affected.

consonants (**k, s, t, p,** or **h**), the vowel automatically becomes voiceless or, in some cases, is lost.[12] This happens whether the two consonants come in the same word or in consecutive words.

Practice 18

In the following practice drills, the lighter letters represent whispered (i.e. voiceless or lost) vowels.

ki-SYA 'train'	**su-SU-MU** 'advance'	**hi-SYO** 'secretary'
ki-TE 'coming'	**su-TE-RU** 'throw away'	**hi-TO** 'person'
ki-T-TE 'stamp'	**na-SU-t-te** 'doing'	**hi-P-PA-ru** 'pull'
ku-SYA-mi 'sneeze'	**ti-KA-i** 'is close'	**hu-KA-i** 'is deep'
NA-ku-te 'not being any'	**ti-T-TO mo** '[not] a bit'	**hu-SI-ĠI** 'strange'
si-TE 'doing'	**tu-KI-MA-si-ta** '[I] arrived'	**hu-TO-i** 'is big around'
si-T-TE 'knowing'	**tu-TO-me-te** 'being employed'	**hu-T-TO-BO-o-ru** 'football'
su-KI-i 'skiing'	**hi-KI-MA-si-ta** '[I] pulled'	**hi-HA-Ñ** 'criticism'

In the phrases in the left-hand column below, the final vowel of the first word is preceded AND followed by a voiceless consonant and accordingly is itself voiceless. In the phrases in the right-hand column, the final vowel of the first word is preceded but not followed by a voiceless consonant and accordingly has its full, voiced value—that is, it is accompanied by vibration of the vocal cords.

Practice 19

DO-t-ti ka 'either one'	**DO-t-ti ġa** 'which one (as subject)?'
DE-su kara 'therefore'	**DE-su ġa** 'however'
I-tu kara 'since when?'	**I-tu ma-de** 'until when?'
hi-KO-o-ki to 'with an airplane'	**hi-KO-o-ki no** 'of an airplane'

When an **i** or **u** vowel preceded by a voiceless consonant comes at the end of an utterance, the vowel either has its full voiced value or is whispered. There is variation depending on the speaker, the occasion, and the word in question. Alternants like the following occur commonly:

Practice 20

hi-TO-tu *or* **hi-TO-tu** 'one unit'

SO-o de-su *or* **SO-o de-su** 'that's right'

o-HA-YO-O GO-ZA-I-MA-su *or* **o-HA-YO-O GO-ZA-I-MA-su** 'good morning'

Accent

The rhythm of Japanese, unlike that of English, is regular and even: each mora is given moderate, approximately equal stress, and has approximately equal length.[13] However, some

---

12. When it is lost, the first of the two consonants has a full-mora beat.

13. Measurements of the mora with sophisticated machinery seem to produce different results for different researchers. Some claim that all mora do indeed have the same length with a very limited range of variation. Others claim greater variation. But from the point of view of a listener's perception, all mora *sound* as if they occupy the same time frame.

mora seem more prominent than others. This prominence—or accent—is primarily a matter of higher pitch in Japanese, and only secondarily a matter of stress (loudness).

Any continuous Japanese sequence of one or more words is said to be accented if it contains at least one example of a single high-pitched mora, or an uninterrupted series of high-pitched mora, followed by an abrupt drop to a low-pitched mora; and the accent is said to occur on the last (or only) high-pitched mora, which is slightly stressed and slightly higher than an immediately preceding high mora. Thus, an utterance that sounds like this:

a^{merikaryoozi}_{kañ} 'American consulate'

is an accented utterance, and the accent occurs on the mora **zi**, which is slightly stressed (louder) and higher.

For the purposes of this text, we recognize three significant pitch levels: one accented level (high) and two unaccented levels (neutral and low). These are not absolute pitch levels but are relative to each other within a given utterance.

Some Japanese utterances are accented and some are unaccented. The first mora of an unaccented sequence of more than one mora is automatically pronounced with low pitch, and the following mora all have neutral pitch. An unaccented sequence that follows a pause (that is, which occurs at the beginning of a sentence, or within a sentence after a pause), or which follows a comma or semicolon (see below), appears in this text without any special accent marks and assumes the automatic rise.

koko is pronounced **ko**^{ko} 'here'

asoko is pronounced **a**^{soko} 'there'

ano sakana is pronounced **a**^{no sakana} 'that fish'

akai kuruma o katta is pronounced **a**^{kai kuruma o katta} 'I bought a red car'

However, when an unaccented word or phrase having the above pitch contour occurs in the middle of a sequence, it is preceded by a prime mark /ʹ/ which indicates a rise in pitch from low level to neutral level. Thus:

kore wa ʹasoko e is pronounced **ko**^{re wa}**a**^{soko e} 'this one, over there'

An accented sequence contains one or more of the following superscript symbols:

Symbol	Meaning
´	Rise from neutral or low to high pitch on the marked mora.
`	Drop from high to neutral or low pitch after the marked mora.
^	Only the marked mora is high pitched.

The accent mark is regularly written on the final or only symbol of a mora. Thus:

dôozo is pronounced **do**^{ozo} 'please'

anâta is pronounced **a**^{na}**ta** 'you'

aôi is pronounced **a**^o**i** 'is blue'

wakárimasèñ is pronounced **wa**^{karimase}**ñ** 'it isn't clear'

daízyòobu is pronounced **da**^{izyo}**obu** 'safe'

moó iti-do itte kudasài is pronounced **mo⁰ iti-do itte kudasaᵢ** 'please say it again'

When a sentence contains more than one accented sequence, each successive sequence tends to be pitched lower than the preceding one to the point where some normally accented sequences lose their accent, unless there is special interest or focus on a later sequence, in which case that sequence is pitched as high as or higher than the preceding. Except for loss of accent, this kind of variation will not be marked, since so many variations in focus— and relative pitch—are possible.

Thus **kîree na ozyôosañ** is pronounced:

(1) **ki̇ree na o^{zyo}osañ** *or*

(2) **ki̇ree na ₒzyoₒosañ** 'a pretty girl'

In (1) there is more focus on **ozyôosañ** 'girl' than in (2).

A single accented word never has more than one high-pitched sequence, and therefore, under ordinary circumstances, cannot have more than /ʹ/ or /ʺ/ plus /ʹ/. The occurrence of anything more signals *not* two accented sequences but rather *alternate* accents. In particular, the accent patterning of the Japanese adjectival is currently undergoing change, with even some individual speakers vacillating between two alternates. Thus:

nâg̃âku is pronounced **na^{g̃}aku** *or* **nag̃^{a}ku**

omósìròku is pronounced **o^{mosi}roku** *or* **o^{mosiro}ku**

tîísàku is pronounced **ti̇isaku** *or* **ti^{isa}ku**

Note the following rules and conventions:

1. Only a word which contains /ʹ/ or /ʺ/ is said to be accented, and the accent is on the mora where the accent mark occurs.
2. Actually, the rise in pitch symbolized by /ʹ/ is automatic, given the boundaries of the accent phrase. It always occurs on the second mora of the accent phrase, unless the accent itself falls on the first mora, in which case only the first mora is high-pitched.[14]
3. Accented words or elements which regularly form a single high sequence in combination with a preceding unaccented word or phrase will be cited with the /ʹ/ accent only. Thus, **dà** indicates that /**sore + dà**/ > **soré dà**; /**Yokohama + dà**/ > **Yokóhama dà**. (But note: /**Kyôoto + dà** > **Kyôoto da**/.)

Whispered mora in Japanese cannot be distinguished by pitch. Their position within the pitch contour is determined by other linguistic criteria. In some cases, the accent of an item moves to an adjoining mora if regular patterning would place it on a whispered mora (cf. **kitê** 'coming,' from **kûru**); but in other cases, the position of the accent remains constant, with the vowel of an ordinarily whispered mora either becoming voiced or remaining voiceless, depending on the speaker.

Since accent in Japanese is a matter of high pitch relative to a following low pitch, it is impossible to hear accent without a following low mora. The occurrence of /ʹ/ or /ʺ/ at the end of a single word in this text means that the word ordinarily has that accent when a

---

14. Symbols for the rise are included here to simplify reading the transcription for the beginning student. It is possible to represent Japanese accent by using an accent mark on the last high syllable (where this text has ʹ), with no symbol to indicate the automatic rise—provided the boundaries of the accent phrase are identified.

following low mora occurs. For example, **hasi** 'edge' and **hasî** 'bridge' sound alike in isolation—but when they are followed by a neutral or low mora, they contrast with each other:

hasi wa (ha$^{\text{si wa}}$) 'as for the edge,' *but* **hasî wa** (ha^{si} wa) 'as for the bridge';

Similarly, **ki** 'spirit' and **kî** 'tree' are alike in isolation, but compare:

ki wa (ki ^{wa}) 'as for the spirit,' *but* **kî wa** (^{ki} wa) 'as for the tree.'

Accordingly we do speak of Japanese words that are accented on the final mora, although we recognize that the accent can be heard in only some occurrences.

When a word is accented on its next-to-last mora and the final mora has a whispered alternate, the accent is regularly marked. For example, **ikímàsu** means either

$_{\text{i}}$**kima**$_{\text{su}}$[15] *or* $_{\text{i}}$**kima**$_{\text{su}}$.

Accent presents difficulty for a foreign student of Japanese largely because of accent variation.[16] This variation is of the following kinds:

1. *Variation in basic word accent.* Many words have alternate accents within the Tokyo dialect. This is increasingly true as Japan becomes a more mobile society. Many—but by no means all—alternate standard accents are noted in this text. Thus, the accepted pronunciation of the word for '(electric) train' is **deñsya** or **dêñsya**.

2. *Gain and loss of accent in particular environments.* Many basically unaccented words sometimes acquire an accent, and many accented words sometimes lose their accent. For example, accented **kudásài** regularly loses its accent following an accented **-te** word:

hanâsite kudasai 'please talk'

An unaccented **-te** word acquires an accent before **mo** and **kara**:

itte 'going,' *but* **ittè kara** 'after going'

When cited in isolation, such words will, of course, be marked with their basic accent.

In addition there is the variation in the relative pitch level of multiple high-pitched sequences within a sentence that has already been noted. In some cases variation extends to loss of accent. It is as if a basically accented Japanese utterance has an infinite number of degrees, from "clearly accented" to "no accent." Often the dividing line between "accented" and "accent lost" is extremely difficult to determine.

Also, as an indication of animation or emphasis, the interval between pitch levels increases. Sometimes the interval between low and neutral pitch within one emphatic unaccented phrase may be as great as, or greater than, that between neutral and high pitch in a following unemphatic accented phrase.

Superimposed on these kinds of variation is dialectal variation. The accent of Tokyo Japanese is different from that of other parts of Japan. Students working with a Japanese instructor who is not a native of Tokyo will find that the pitch contours marked in this text often do not match those used by the instructor.

Doesn't this mean, then, that the student of Japanese might just as well ignore accent? Not at all! The fact that two different accents are sometimes acceptable does not mean that any accent at all is permitted. (Some native speakers of English say 'dry cléaning' and others

15. This is the more common alternate in Tokyo speech.

16. The accents and intonations marked in this text generally follow those of the tapes that were recorded to accompany it for all the material that was recorded.

say 'drý cleaning,' but no speaker says 'dry cleaníng.') Further indication of the importance of accent is the fact that many pairs of utterances with different meanings are distinguished only by their accent.

INTONATION

The following intonation symbols are used in this text:

1. Period   /./: A period ending a sentence indicates that the final mora and all immediately preceding unaccented mora are pronounced with low pitch level, with the final mora—if it is not whispered—lowest of all. In the event that the sentence, or its final accent phrase, contains no accent—that is, if the final or only pitch contour of the sentence is low + neutral—a final period indicates only the onset of silence, again with the final mora (of a sequence of two or more) pronounced with slightly lower pitch.

   Period intonation, indicating finality, occurs most commonly at the end of statements, suggestions, rhetorical questions, and questions asked indirectly. At the end of direct questions, it often indicates abruptness, stiffness, aloofness, etc. Examples:

   Wakárimasèñ desita.   'I didn't understand.' is pronounced $\mathbf{wa^{karimase}_{ñ}\,desi_{ta}}$

   Asoko e iku.   'I'm going to go there.' is pronounced $\mathbf{_{a}soko\,e\,i_{ku}}$

2. Question mark   /?/: A question mark ending a sentence indicates a rise in pitch on the final mora,[17] usually with lengthening of that mora. Question-mark intonation regularly changes a statement into a question, and is typical of relaxed style. Examples:

   Wakâru?   'Is it clear?' is pronounced $\mathbf{wa^{ka}_{ru}{}^{u}}$

   Kore?   'This one?' is pronounced $\mathbf{ko^{ree}}$

3. Rising hook   /↰/: A rising hook ending a sentence indicates a slight rise in pitch on the final mora, usually without lengthening of that mora. The final mora may start on a low or neutral or on a high pitch.[18] This intonation usually occurs with certain sentence particles and implies empathy, friendliness, and interest in the reaction of the person addressed. Where a rising hook occurs, one can usually substitute a period as an alternate intonation without changing the meaning, beyond making the sentence less empathetic. Examples:

   Wakárimàsita ka↰ 'Did you understand?' is pronounced

   $\mathbf{wa^{karima}_{sita}\,ka}$↰ *or* $\mathbf{wa^{karima}_{sita}{}^{ka}}$↰

   Îi desu yo↰   'It's all right!' is pronounced

   $\mathbf{^{i}_{i}\,desu\,yo}$↰ *or* $\mathbf{^{i}_{i}\,desu\,{}^{yo}}$↰

   Kore yo↰   'It's this one!' is pronounced

   $\mathbf{ko^{re}\,yo}$↰ *or* $\mathbf{ko^{re}\,{}^{yo}}$↰

4. Reversed question mark   /ʕ/: A reversed question mark occurs only in combination with sentence-particle **ne**, and represents an intonation similar to that indicated by a rising hook /↰/ (cf. 3, immediately preceding). However, (1) /ʕ/ represents a high-pitched start much more frequently, and (2) alternating another intonation in place of /ʕ/ results in a

---

17. With this intonation, the final mora is never whispered.
18. A high-pitched start is more common in women's speech.

meaning change more significant than affect, as in the case of /↗/. Neʔ is a request for confirmation: 'right?' 'isn't that correct?' Example:

Wakárimàsita neʔ 'You understood—right?'

5. Exclamation point /!/: An exclamation point ending a sentence indicates that the final mora starts high and has slightly falling pitch. Articulation may end abruptly, and there is no significant lengthening of the final mora. This is an intonation of animation. Example:

Ano ne! 'Say there!' is pronounced a^{none}↘

6. Double periods /. ./: Double periods ending a sentence indicate that the final mora has neutral pitch. It often is lengthened, and there is a gradual fading into silence. This intonation denotes incompleteness. Examples:

Kamáwànakereba . . 'If it doesn't matter . . .' is pronounced

    ka^{mawa}nakerebaa

Sôo desu ğa . . 'That's so, but . . .' is pronounced

   ^{so}o desu ğaa

7. Comma /,/ and Semicolon /;/: A comma within a sentence indicates a break within the utterance: **X, Y** means that there is a slight slowing down of articulation and/or pause at the end of **X;** that unaccented mora at the end of **X** have a low alternate of neutral pitch; and that **Y** starts a new accent phase.[19] In many utterances, the occurrence of comma intonation is optional.

    A semicolon marks the same general kind of division as a comma, but in sentences containing more than one such division, the semicolon is used to indicate a division of major rank. Examples:

Supéiñğo wa yamemàsita ğa, nihóñğo wa màda beńkyoo-site imàsu.

'Spanish I gave up, but Japanese I'm still studying.'
is pronounced

    peiñğo wa yamema $^{hoñğo\ wa\ ma}$ ñkyoo-site ima
su   sita ğa ^{ni} $_{da\ be}$ $_{su}$

Zikáñ ğa nài kara, supéiñğo wa yamemàsita ğa; nihóñğo wa màda beńkyoo-site imàsu.

'Spanish I gave up, because I have no time; but Japanese I'm still studying.'
is pronounced

kañ ğa na   peiñğo wa yamema $^{hoñğo\ wa\ ma}$ ñkyoo-site ima
zi   i kara $_{su}$ sita ğa ^{ni} $_{da\ be}$ $_{su}$

8. Dash /—/: A dash occurs within inverted sentences (cf. Lesson 5B, Structural Pattern 2), indicating that what follows is pronounced as an add-on to what would ordinarily constitute a sentence ending. The pitch level within the add-on is lower than a corresponding phrase within the initial portion. Examples:

---

19. This means that if the first two mora of **Y** have unaccented pitch, the first is low and the second neutral.

Îi desu nêe—sore wa. 'Isn't it nice—that.' is pronounced

ⁱi desu ^{ne}e sore wa

Ikímàsita yo↗[20]—Kyôoto e. 'I went—to Kyoto.' is pronounced

ⁱkima_{sita} yo↗ Kyo_{oto e}

Pronunciation may seem discouragingly complicated at the beginning, but with perseverance, it will soon become surprisingly easy. After all, it is a finite system that can be learned much more quickly than all the structural patterns and vocabulary that must be mastered—and once learned will affect *everything* you say in Japanese—FOREVER! Faulty pronunciation will strain the imagination and grate on the ears of every Japanese who must listen to you. Accurate pronunciation, on the other hand, will contribute immeasurably to smooth communication. Efforts expended on pronunciation are well rewarded!

Supplementary Pronunciation Drills

1. VOWEL COMBINATIONS

aráimàsu 'wash' (distal-style)	**hiatari** 'exposure to the sun'	**huañ** 'uneasiness'
arau 'wash' (direct-style)	**iu (yuu)**[21] 'say'	**huite** 'wiping'
aráòo 'let's wash'	**sumie** 'ink drawing'	**suehiro** 'folding fan'
	kikíòku 'hear (and keep in mind)'	**huoñ** 'unrest'

deasi 'start'	**dôa** 'door'
deiri 'going in and out'	**hirôi** 'is wide'
neuti 'value'	**omôu** 'think'
neoki 'lying down and getting up'	**kôe** 'voice'

2. SHORT AND LONG VOWELS

obasañ 'aunt'	**hâ** 'tooth'	**ozisañ** 'uncle'
obâasañ 'grandmother'	**hâa** 'yes'	**ozîisañ** 'grandfather'
kitê 'coming'	**kûroo** 'trouble'	**husetu** 'construction'
kiite 'listening'	**kûuro** 'air route'	**huusetu** 'rumor'
kirê 'cloth'	**seğyoo** 'management'	**tôtte** 'taking'
kîree 'pretty'	**sêeğyo** 'control'	**tôotte** 'going through'
mûko 'bridegroom'	**tori** 'bird'	**oki** 'open sea'
mukoo 'beyond'	**toórì** 'avenue'	**oókìi** 'is big'

20. This intonation symbol, which ordinarily occurs only at the end of a sentence, occurs in the middle of an inverted sentence.

21. The combination /i + u/ is regularly pronounced **yuu**.

3. SHORT AND LONG CONSONANTS

maki 'firewood'	**ite** 'being'	**Masao** (proper name)
mâkki 'the last years'	**itte** 'going'	**maśsào** 'deep blue'
konâ 'flour'	**nisi** 'west'	**kono boosi** 'this hat'
koñna 'this kind'	**nîssi** 'diary'	**kôñ no boosi** 'navy-blue hat'
matî 'town'	**Supêiñ** 'Spain'	
mâtti 'match'	**súppài** 'is sour'	

4. su ~ tu CONTRAST

masu 'increase'	**sûri** 'pickpocket'	**sukî** 'liking'
mâtu 'wait'	**turi** 'fishing'	**tukî** 'moon'
sûmi 'corner'	**suḡî** 'past'	**susumu** 'advance'
tûmi 'crime'	**tuḡî** 'next'	**tutûmu** 'wrap'

5. d ~ r CONTRAST

dôo 'how?'	**hodo** 'extent'	**muda** 'useless'
rôo 'prison'	**hôro** 'hood'	**mura** 'village'
dañboo 'heating'	**mâde** 'until'	**sode** 'sleeve'
rañboo 'rough'	**marê** 'rare'	**sore** 'that thing'

6. n ~ ḡ ~ ñ ~ ñḡ CONTRAST

kani 'crab'	**kaneñ** 'a combustible'	**sâni** 'in what follows'
kaḡî 'key'	**kaḡeñ** 'moderation'	**sâḡi** 'fraud'
kâñi 'severe cold'	**kâñeñ** 'hepatitis'	**sañi** 'approval'
kâñḡi 'Korean singing girl'	**kañḡeñ** 'restoration'	**sâñḡi** 'participation in government'

7. EVEN-RHYTHM PRACTICE

a 'oh!'

are 'that one'

asoko 'there'

tokídokì 'sometimes'

ano sakana 'that fish'

ano tomodati 'that friend'

anó tomodati dà 'it's that friend'

asoko no tomodati 'a friend from that place'

Amerika no tomodati 'an American friend'

Amérika no tomodati dà 'it's an American friend'

8. ACCENT CONTRASTS

Îma desu. 'It's now.'
Imâ desu. 'It's a living room.'

Mâiniti desu. 'It's every day.'
Maíniti dèsu. 'It's the Mainichi (a newspaper).'

Yôñde kudasai. 'Please read [it].'
Yoñde kudasài. 'Please call [him].'

Tuyú dèsu. 'It's the rainy season.'
Tûyu desu. 'It's broth.'

Âtuku simasu. 'I'll make it hot.'
Atúku simàsu. 'I'll make it thick.'

Soré o kìru kara . . 'Since I'm going to cut it . . .'
Soré o kirù kara . . 'Since I'm going to wear it . . .'

Hâsi desu. 'They're chopsticks.'
Hasí dèsu. 'It's the edge.'
Hasî desu. 'It's a bridge.'

9. INTONATION CONTRASTS

Dekîru. 'It's possible.'
Dekîru? 'Is it possible?'

Sôo desyoo. 'That's probably so.'
Sôo desyoo? 'That's so, isn't it?'

Sore. 'That one.'
Sore? 'That one?'

Isóg̃asìi. 'I'm busy.'
Isóg̃asìi? 'Are you busy?'

Sôo desu ka. 'Oh.'
Sôo desu ka⤹ 'Oh?'

Tig̃áimàsu yo. 'They're different.'
Tig̃áimàsu yo⤹ 'They're different⤹'[22]

Owárimàsita yo. 'I've finished.'
Owárimàsita yo⤹ 'I've finished⤹'[22]

22. Differences in the English equivalents are also differences of intonation.

Ikímàsu ka 'Are you going?'
Ikímàsu ḡa . . 'I'm going, but . . .'

Onázi dèsu yo. 'They're the same.'
Onázi dèsu ḡa . . 'They're the same, but . . .'

II. SPECIAL SYMBOLS AND CONVENTIONS

1. ( ), [ ]

In a Japanese sequence, material enclosed in parentheses ( ) may be omitted. In every case, the shorter utterance is more casual and/or less polite. Thus, **a(b)** means that **ab** and **a** both occur with the same meaning except that **a** is more casual and/or less polite than **ab**.

Square brackets [ ] in the English equivalent of a Japanese sequence introduce material necessary in the English but not specifically corresponding to anything in the Japanese sequence. Conversely, parentheses in the English equivalent enclose explanatory material or something literally translated from the Japanese which is not needed in the English. Compare:

Ikímàsita ka 'Did [you] go?'
Êe, ikímàsita. 'Yes, [I] did (go).'

'You' and 'I' are needed for natural English but do not specifically correspond to anything in Japanese. 'Go' in the second sentence corresponds to something in the Japanese that is usually omitted in the English equivalent.

Square brackets and parentheses are used more frequently in the earlier lessons, as an aid to the beginning student.

2. | |

Vertical lines enclose hesitation noises and linguistic fillers, comparable to English 'uh,' 'you know,' etc.

3. ↑, ↓, +

In explaining Japanese, there will be frequent references to 'in-group' and 'out-group,' and an understanding of this distinction is crucial to understanding how the culture and its language work.

Japanese society is group-centered, not individualistic, in its basic orientation. An individual Japanese belongs to a number of different groups—the family, school, workplace, clubs, etc.—and depending on the context of the moment, the appropriate group-membership becomes the speaker's in-group and everyone else the out-group. On those occasions when the speaker is indeed representing only him/herself, it is perhaps most accurate to regard that individual as a 'minimal in-group.'

The in-group/out-group membership then is constantly shifting. For example, if Ms. Suzuki is speaking to a friend about her own mother, she and her mother form an in-group vis-à-vis the friend, who becomes out-group. But in speaking to her office manager about herself alone, she is now the minimal in-group and the manager the out-group. Even the manager can become a member of her in-group, on those occasions when she speaks to someone having no connection with her or her company. A great deal more will be said about this in-group/out-group differentiation in connection with individual structural patterns as they are introduced and explained.

A raised arrow pointing upward / ↑ / following a Japanese word or phrase indicates that the word or phrase is honorific-polite—that is, it exalts the person(s) to whom it refers. Such a word is used only in reference to persons other than the speaker, who are members of the out-group within the given context. Example:

> **nasáimàsita** ↑ 'you (alone or including members of your—not my—in-group) did [it]' or 's/he/they (of our out-group) did [it]'—and I am being polite in reference to the person(s) referred to.

A raised arrow pointing downward / ↓ / following a Japanese word or phrase indicates that the word or phrase is humble-polite—that is, it humbles the person(s) to whom it refers in deference to the person to whom it is directed. Such a word is used only in reference to a member/members of the in-group—most commonly the speaker alone. Example:

> **itásimàsita** ↓ 'I or we (including members of my in-group) did [it]'—and I am being polite to the person affected.

A raised plus sign / + / following a Japanese word or phrase indicates that the word or phrase is neutral-polite—that is, it is polite and deferential to the person addressed without any notion of exalting or humbling its referent. Example:

> **gozáimàsu** + '[it] is [here]' or '[I] have [it]'—and I am being polite to you, the addressee.

4. MAJOR SENTENCES; MINOR SENTENCES AND FRAGMENTS

In this text, utterances which are regarded as complete, standard sentences ending in specially designated, final inflected forms, with or without following sentence-particles, are called MAJOR SENTENCES. All others are MINOR SENTENCES. Within the latter category are FRAGMENTS, which are utterances that end in noninflected words (words with one form only) with or without following particles. Using a parallel approach adapted for English, we would say that in the exchange:

> (1) 'Are you coming here tomorrow?'
> (2) 'Tomorrow?' (3) 'If it doesn't snow.'

Item (1) is a major sentence, (2) and (3) are minor sentences, and (2) is also a fragment.

5. MISCELLANEOUS

/*lit.*/ is used throughout the text as an abbreviation for 'literally.'

In the Japanese material, only the first word in a sentence and names of persons and places are capitalized.

Hyphens are used within Japanese words to separate meaningful parts of longer words, when such marking makes them easier to handle.

A raised dot separates elements of a sequence having a close semantic and phonologic connection but an accent pattern different from that of a single compound word. Example: **mâa·mâa** 'so-so.'

III. ROMANIZATION

Various systems of romanization—representation of the Japanese language by letters of the Roman alphabet—are in use in Japan today. The system used in this book is an adaptation of the Shin-kunrei-shiki 'New Official System' and will be designated as JSL Romanization.[23] Other common romanizations are Hepburn (Hebon-shiki, also called Hyōjun-shiki 'Standard System') and Nippon-shiki 'Japanese System.' The differences among them are slight and can be learned with little difficulty. For example, the word for 'romanization' is variously represented as follows:

JSL:	**roomazi**
Shin-kunrei-shiki:	**rômazi**[24]
Hepburn:	**rōmaji**[24]
Nippon-shiki:	**rōmadi**[24]

Hepburn romanization is the system most familiar to Westerners; but there are three cogent reasons for not using it in a Japanese textbook.

1. JSL, Shin-kunrei-shiki, and Nippon-shiki bear a direct relation to Japanese structure, whereas Hepburn has no such connection. Thus, in describing Japanese inflection, many statements become unnecessarily complicated and parallelism is obscured if Hepburn romanization is used. For example, compare the following:

To form the stem of consonant verbals:	
Using JSL, Shin-kunrei-shiki, or Nippon-shiki:	Using Hepburn romanization:
change final **-u** to **-i**	change final **-u** to **-i**, but if **-u** is preceded by **ts**, change the **ts** to **ch**, and if **-u** is preceded by **s**, add **h** after the **s**.

The complexity of the second statement results not from special cases in Japanese verbal structure, but only from the fact that Hepburn romanization is based on languages of the West (its vowels have values roughly as in the Romance languages, its consonants as in English) rather than on the Japanese language.

2. For the student who plans to learn the native Japanese writing system, the transition from Hepburn is more difficult than from the other systems.

3. The Japanese themselves do not adhere consistently to any single system; in fact, they sometimes use a mixture of several within the same word! It therefore becomes necessary for foreign students to familiarize themselves with the symbols used in all the systems. JSL, Shin-kunrei-shiki, and Nippon-shiki romanizations take a little longer for English-speaking students to master (though only slightly longer); but once they have learned one, they can switch to Hepburn with no trouble. Students who have used only Hepburn, however, may find the conversion a bit difficult.

The minor differences between JSL on the one hand and Shin-kunrei-shiki and Nippon-shiki on the other result from an attempt to avoid certain inconsistencies and ambiguity in

---

23. However, Japanese words appearing throughout the book as nonquoted parts of English sentences (as in this explanatory paragraph) are spelled in Hepburn romanization.

24. The long mark over the **o** is sometimes omitted.

the latter systems. For example, in JSL, **ee** and **ei** consistently represent different and distinct sequences of sounds of Tokyo Japanese. The spelling of these sequences in all the other romanizations (including Hepburn) is inconsistent, so that it is often impossible for a student to be certain which value a given occurrence of **ei** represents. This destroys the regularity we expect of romanization.

The most important difference between JSL and the other romanization systems described above is that only JSL includes a system for marking accent, which is viewed as an intrinsic and essential feature of the language that should be represented in romanization.

A final reminder: In dealing with romanization—or any kind of writing system—we are working with a new code, and only the speech of a native speaker (and/or recordings of a native speaker) can provide us with an authentic code breaker. Without the specific code breaker for the language we are dealing with, we are totally in the dark as to how the language really sounds. No writing system—native or romanized—can serve as a substitute. Remember the order: *first,* the sound; *then* the written symbols we use to represent them.

CONVERSION TABLE OF ROMANIZATION[a]

Symbol in another romanization	Corresponding symbol in JSL
ā[b]	aa
ū[b]	uu
ē[b]	ee
ci	ee (*or* ei)[c]
ye	e
ō[b]	oo
wo	o
-g-	-ḡ- (*or* -g-)[c]
shi	si
sha	sya
shu	syu
sho	syo
ji	zi
ja	zya
ju	zyu
jo	zyo
di	zi
dz	z
chi	ti
cha	tya
chu	tyu
cho	tyo
tsu	tu
fu	hu
-n'-	-ñ-
-n (final)	-ñ
-n + consonant other than y-	-ñ-
-mp-	-ñp-
-mb-	-ñb-
-mm-	-ñm-

[a]The left-hand column includes symbols and combinations which either do not occur in JSL romanization, or else they correspond to more than one JSL symbol, so that their interpretation is ambiguous.

[b]A circumflex (ˆ) over a vowel in non-JSL romanizations has the same meaning as a macron (ˉ)—length.

[c]Which alternate is used conforms to the actual pronunciation of the Japanese.

IV. CLASSROOM INSTRUCTIONS[25]

1. **Kiíte (ite) kudasài.** *or*	Please listen.
Kiítè te kudasai.	
2. **Itte kudasài.**	Please say [it].
3. **Moó iti-do itte kudasài.**	Please say [it] once more.
4. **Miñnà de itte kudasài.**	Please say [it] all together.
5. **Hitó-ri-zùtu itte kudasài.**	Please say [it] one (person) at a time.
6. **Môtto hâyâku hanâsite kudasai.**	Please speak more quickly.
7. **Môtto haḱkìri hanâsite kudasai.**	Please speak more clearly.
8. **Môtto ôoki na kôe de hanâsite kudasai.**	Please speak in a louder voice.
9. **Suzúki-sañ ni kiite kudasài.**	Please ask Mr/s. Suzuki.
10. **Kotâete kudasai.**	Please answer.
11. **Hôñ o mînai de kudasai.**	Please don't look at your book.
12. **Eéḡo o tukawanài de kudasai.**	Please don't use English.

V. GREETINGS AND USEFUL PHRASES

1. **Oháyoo (gozaimàsu)** +.	Good morning.
2. **Koñniti wa.**	Good afternoon.
3. **Koñbañ wa.**	Good evening.
4. **Oyasumi-nasai.**	Goodnight.
5. **Sayo(o)nara.**	Goodbye.
6. **Arîḡatoo (gozaimasu)** +.	Thank you.
7. **Arîḡatoo (gozaimasita)** +.	Thank you (for what you did).
8. **I(i)e.**	No. *or* Not at all.
9. **Dôo itasimasite** ↓.	Don't mention it.
10. **Su(m)ímasèñ.**	I'm sorry. *or*
	Thank you for your trouble.
11. **Su(m)ímasèñ desita.**	I'm sorry (for what I did). *or*
	Thank you (for the trouble you took).
12. **Sitûree(-simasu).**	Excuse me (on leaving).
13. **Sitûree(-simasita).**	Excuse me (for what I did).
14. **Onéḡai-simàsu.** ↓	Please (speaker requesting something).
15. **Dôozo.**	Please (speaker offering something).
16. **Moósiwake arimasèñ.** *or*	
Moósiwake gozaimasèñ. +	Forgive me.
17. **Otúkaresama (dèsita).**	(You must be tired!)

25. These sentences are primarily for use by an instructor in giving classroom directions. It is suggested that introductory drill on them be conducted only for the purpose of aural recognition.

18. **Suzuki-sañ.**   文庫   Mr/s. Suzuki.
19. **Hâi.; Êe.; Hâa.**   Yes.
20. **Dôo mo.**   (In every way).

MISCELLANEOUS NOTES[26]

1. **Ohayoo** is used when addressing a family member or friend or colleague or inferior casually. **Oháyoo gozaimàsu** is a formal greeting used in addressing a superior, or in any situation requiring formality. Basically these are initial greetings of the day which may occur at any hour.

2, 3. Like their English equivalents, these Japanese greetings are never used within the family.

4. **Oyasumi-nasai** is a rather informal expression used within the home or among friends or close associates who are going separate ways. The abbreviated **oyasumi** is extremely casual.

5. **Sayonara** is the contracted, less formal equivalent of **sayoonara.** Neither alternate is ever used when leaving one's own home, or when leaving on an errand with an intention of returning soon. (See Lesson 7A).

7. **Ariĝatoo (gozaimasita)** is the perfective (i.e., finished) equivalent of **ariĝatoo (gozaimasu)** and expresses gratitude for an activity already completed.

8. **Iie** (or more casual **ie**) is used in negative replies to questions, in contradictions and denials, and as an informal reply to apologies, expressions of thanks, and compliments.

9. **Dôo itasimasite** is used alone, or with **i(i)e**, as a polite, formal reply to apologies, expressions of thanks, and compliments. In form, it is humble-polite (↓).

10, 11. **Suímasèñ** is the contracted, less formal equivalent of **sumímasèñ.** Unlike **ariĝatoo** expressions, the use of **su(m)ímasèñ** as a 'thank you' always includes a note of apology for troubling the addressee. **Su(m)ímasèñ desita** is the perfective equivalent of **su(m)ímasèñ** and refers to an action already completed. It is commonly used to apologize or say thank you by someone who is on the point of leaving. However, the imperfective form without **desita** is used in expressing regret and/or thanks for something immediate or in the future.

12. **Sitûree-simasu** means literally 'I [am about to] commit a rudeness.' It is a polite way of excusing oneself from someone's presence, sometimes in the sense 'Excuse me for a moment' and sometimes as 'Excuse me—goodbye.' A number of other uses will be introduced later. **Sitûree** is a casual, informal alternate.

13. **Sitûree-simasita** is the perfective equivalent of the preceding and means literally 'I committed a rudeness.' It is an apology for something that has already been done. **Sitûree**, again, occurs as a casual, informal equivalent.

14. Among the more common English equivalents of **onéĝai-simàsu** are such expressions as: 'Would you please do it?' 'Please take care of things'; 'Please do'; 'May I have it?' 'I'd like to have it'; etc. The equivalent differs depending upon the context, but the basic meaning is always the same— 'I make a request'—and the word is humble-polite (↓).

15. **Dôozo**, which occurs by itself as an expression of offering or invitation ('Please have some'; 'Go ahead'; 'Here you are'; etc.), also occurs within sentences of request or invitation, making the utterance softer and less abrupt.

16. **Moósiwake gozaimasèñ** is a more polite equivalent of the alternate with **arimasèñ.** These are polite apologies, meaning literally 'I have no excuse,' which may occur in any kind of situation where it is appropriate to express regret for an action or situation.

17. **Otúkaresama (dèsita)** occurs much more commonly in Japanese than its English equivalent. It comments ritualistically on the addressee's tiredness, whether or not the speaker has been the cause. For example, it is used in greeting a traveler at the end of a journey, or a student at the end of an

---

26. Numbers in this section correspond to the numbers of the items in the Greetings and Useful Phrases section above.

exam, or a participant at the end of a conference, or anyone who has come to the end of a long, hard day.

18. **-Sañ** is added to a family name (as in **Suzuki-sañ**), a given name (as in **Târoo-sañ**), or a family name plus a given name (as in **Suzuki Târoo-sañ**), but it is NOT added to one's own name or to that of members of one's own family or household when speaking to outsiders. Thus, Mr. Yamamoto calls Mr. Suzuki **Suzuki-sañ**, but Mr. Suzuki identifies himself simply as **Suzuki**.

19. **Hâi** and more casual **êe** and more polite **hâa** are used in affirmative replies to questions. **Hâi** is also the regular response to a knock at the door or the calling of one's name.

20. The literal meaning of **dôo mo** ('in every way') does little to suggest the countless situations in which this expression occurs. When used alone, it implies the emphatic assertion of the appropriate remark of the moment—which is left unsaid! The basic meanings tend to relate to gratitude and/or regret. Thus: '[Thanks] very much'; '[I'm] very [sorry]'; '[I'm] very much [obliged to you].' It may also be repeated: **Dôo mo dôo mo**. Within longer utterances, it intensifies the meaning.

PRACTICE

(In each example, the utterance on the right is a response to the one on the left. Keep in mind the special implications if both are not of a similar politeness or formality level: for example, a difference in rank of two speakers immediately shows up in this way. A student would speak politely to a professor, but the professor would have the option of replying in a less polite or formal style. As you practice these exchanges, always visualize an appropriate situation. Repeated drilling will be required before you develop automatic control—a worthwhile goal for utterances that occur as frequently as these.)

1.	**Ohayoo.**	Ohayoo.
2.	**Oháyoo gozaimàsu.**	Oháyoo gozaimàsu.
3.	**Oháyoo gozaimàsu.**	Ohayoo.
4.	**Koñniti wa.**	Koñniti wa.
5.	**Koñbañ wa.**	Koñbañ wa.
6.	**Oyasumi-nasai.**	Oyasumi-nasai.
7.	**Oyasumi-nasai.**	Sayonara.
8.	**Sayonara.**	Sayonara.
9.	**Sayonara.**	Sayoonara.
10.	**Sayoonara.**	Sayoonara.
11.	**Sayonara.**	Oyasumi-nasai.
12.	**Sitûree.**	Dôozo.
13.	**Sitûree-simasu.**	Dôozo.
14.	**Sitûree-simasu.**	Sayoonara.
15.	**Sitûree.**	Sayonara.
16.	**Sitûree.**	Iie.
17.	**Sitûree-simasita.**	Dôo itasimasite.
18.	**Sitûree-simasita.**	Iie.
19.	**Dôo mo sitûree-simasita.**	Iie, dôo itasimasite.
20.	**Sumímasèñ.**	Iie.
21.	**Dôo mo sumímasèñ.**	Dôo itasimasite.
22.	**Suímasèñ.**	Iie.

23. Suímasèñ desita.   Dôo itasimasite.
24. Suímasèñ desita.   Ie, dôo itasimasite.
25. Dôo mo sumímasèñ desita.   Iie.
26. Sumímasèñ.   Dôozo.
27. Arîgatoo.   Iie.
28. Dôo mo arîgatoo.   Dôo itasimasite.
29. Arîgatoo gozaimasu.   Ie, dôo itasimasite.
30. Dôo mo arîgatoo gozaimasu.   Iie.
31. Arîgatoo gozaimasita.   Dôo itasimasite.
32. Dôo mo arîgatoo gozaimasita.   Iie, dôo itasimasite.
33. Onégai-simàsu.   Dôozo.
34. Onégai-simàsu.   Hâi, dôozo.
35. Dôozo.   Dôo mo.
36. Dôozo.   Arîgatoo gozaimasu.
37. Dôozo.   Sumímasèñ.
38. Moósiwake arimasèñ.   Dôo itasimasite.
39. Moósiwake gozaimasèñ.   Iie, dôo itasimasite.
40. Otukaresama.   Sayonara.
41. Otúkaresama dèsita.   Dôo itasimasite.
42. Suzuki-sañ.   Hâi.
43. Suzuki-sañ, ohayoo.   Oháyoo gozaimàsu.
44. Dôo mo.   Ie.
45. Dôo mo dôo mo.   Dôo itasimasite.
46. Suzuki-sañ, oháyoo gozaimàsu.   Dôo mo dôo mo.
47. Sumímasèñ. Onégai-simàsu.   Hâi, dôozo.
48. Oyasumi-nasai. Sayonara.   Sayonara. Oyasumi-nasai.
49. Sumímasèñ. Sitûree-simasita.   Ie, dôo itasimasite.
50. Sumímasèñ desita. Moósiwake arimasèñ.   Dôo itasimasite.

Lesson 1

INTRODUCTION

In beginning the study of a foreign language, it makes sense to start with short, simple exchanges that occur in normal speech. Observation of the real-life use of languages by native speakers shows that the very simple utterances, of the kind that can be easily mastered by foreigners, tend to rely particularly heavily on context. For example, in the appropriate setting and with the appropriate shared information, "How was it?" would occur at least as frequently in English as "How was the trip you took with your family last week?" Obviously, the first utterance would be easier for a beginning language student to learn. We are going to start out in this text with short, *extremely common* exchanges, but it is crucial that they always be practiced with an appropriate context in mind. Visual aids can be a great help: if I am holding a large, red, English–Japanese dictionary, all I need to say in order to ask the price is "How much is this?" Later on, I will learn how to say, "How much is the large, red, English–Japanese dictionary?", a question which, of course, would be required in certain situations. Obviously, advanced students, because of their larger linguistic repertoire, can handle a greater variety of situations, but for the beginner, we will begin with settings very high in context but low in linguistic requirements. To be sure, context always plays an important part in language use. But in the early lessons of this text, it is crucial that appropriate settings be provided for every exchange. (For this reason, viewing the accompanying video is extremely helpful.) In so doing, realistic and commonly occurring linguistic dialogue will be the result.

SECTION A

Core Conversations (CC)

(*Note*: Every CC in this textbook is presumed to have as one of its participants a non-native speaker of Japanese (N) and a native Japanese (J). The marking follows the role-playing of the accompanying video, but for many conversations, the roles can also be reversed. Remember that the CC that follow are short exchanges that occur as snatches of conversation referring to something in the real world that is unexpressed but contextually understood by both speakers. For possible situations, see the accompanying video. When practicing, *always use appropriate props*.)

1(J)	**Wakárimàsu ka**	(N)	**Êe, wakárimàsu.**
2(N)	**Kyôo simâsu ne**	(J)	**Iya, tiğáimàsu. Asíta simàsu yo.**
3(J)	**Wakárimàsita ka**	(N)	**Êe, wakárimàsita.**
4(J)	**Tukúrimàsita ne**	(N)	**Hâi. Kinóo tukurimàsita.**
5(N)	**Dekímàsita ka**	(J)	**Dekímàsita. Hâi.**
6(J)	**Asíta kimasèñ ne**	(N)	**Iya, kimâsu yo**
7(J)	**Simásèñ ka**	(N)	**Tyôtto . .**
8(J)	**Nomímasèñ ka**	(N)	**Arîğatoo gozaimasu. Itádakimàsu.**
9(J)	**Ikímàsita ne**	(N)	**Iie, ikímasèñ desita.**
10(N)a.	**Sumímasèñ. Wakárimasèñ desita.**	(J)	**Wakárimasèñ desita ka**
b.	**Êe. Dôo mo sumímasèñ.**		

English Equivalents[1]

1(J)	Do you understand?	(N)	Yes, I do (understand).
2(N)	You'll do it today—right?	(J)	No, (it's different). I'll do it tomorrow.
3(J)	Did you understand?	(N)	Yes, I did (understand).
4(J)	You made it—right?	(N)	Yes. I made it yesterday.
5(N)	All done?	(J)	All done. Here you are.
6(J)	You're not coming tomorrow—right?	(N)	No, I *am* coming.
7(J)	Won't you do it (*or* play)?	(N)	I'm afraid not.
8(J)	Won't you have (*lit.* drink) some?	(N)	Thank you. I will (accept).
9(J)	You went—right?	(N)	No, I didn't (go).
10(N)a.	I'm sorry. I didn't understand.	(J)	You didn't (understand)?
b.	That's right. I'm very sorry.		

Breakdowns
(and Supplementary Vocabulary)

1. **wakárimàsu** (SP1)[2]	understand; become understandable
ka (SP2)	/question particle/
êe (SP4)	/affirmation/
2. **kyôo**	today
simâsu	do
ne (SP2)	/confirmatory particle/
iya (SP4)	/negation/
tiğáimàsu	be different; be wrong

1. In general, these are approximate equivalents, representing only one of a number of possibilities. Literal translations are enclosed in parentheses; brackets enclose material required in English which is not expressed in the Japanese.

2. Reference is to the Structural Pattern which follows in this section. It contains relevant explanation for this form and other similar forms in the list.

asítà *or*	
+**asû**[3]	tomorrow
yo (SP2)	/informative particle/
3. **wakárimàsita**	understood; became understandable
4. **tukúrimàsu**	make, construct
tukúrimàsita	made, constructed
hâi (SP4)	/affirmation/
kinôo	yesterday
5. **dekímàsu**	become completed; can do; be possible
dekímàsita	became completed; could do; was possible
hâi	here you are
6. **kimâsu**	come
kimásèñ	not come
kimásèñ neʕ (SP3)	you're not coming—right?
7. **simâsu**	do; play (of games)
simásèñ	not do; not play
tyôtto	a bit; I'm afraid not /i.e., polite refusal/
8. **nomímàsu**	drink
nomímasèñ	not drink
+**tabémàsu**	eat
+**tabémasèñ**	not eat
itádakimàsu	I drink; I eat; I accept /polite/
9. **ikímàsu**	go
ikímàsita	went
i(i)e[4]	/negation/
ikímasèñ desita	didn't go
10. **wakárimasèñ desita**	didn't understand; didn't become understandable

Miscellaneous Notes (MN)

(Numbers correspond to the CC in which the items in question occur.)

The CC of this section are brief exchanges between individuals who maintain a certain amount of distance when communicating with each other. In the accompanying video, the participants are business colleagues or supervisors with their assistants, with one participant in each case to be identified as a non-Japanese. All of the exchanges take place in an office setting, although they are, of course, applicable in other settings.

1. In CC1, (J) checks with (N) on her ability to understand the French material she is looking at.

3. /+/ indicates a supplementary vocabulary item.

4. Parentheses within a Japanese sequence indicate alternate forms which include and exclude the portion within the parentheses. Thus, the alternate forms for this example are **iie** and **ie**. Longer forms are more formal or more emphatic or more careful.

2. In CC2, (N) checks on his colleague's (J's) plans to do some work on the computer. **Tiğáimàsu** is often used as a denial or negation even without an accompanying **i(i)e** or **iya**.

3. In CC3, (J) checks on whether (N) understood a procedure on the computer that he has just demonstrated.

4. In CC4, (J) checks with (N) on his assumption that (N) made up a new computer program.

5. In CC5, (N) checks with the secretary on whether some work has been completed. **Dekímàsu** has a number of different meanings depending on context. In reference to a project—from the preparation of a meal to the construction of a building—it refers to completion. It may also refer to personal ability or capability or possibility. When used of languages, it refers to the ability to handle a language, i.e., proficiency in the language.

6. In CC6, an office supervisor (J) checks on her assumption that a part-time student-worker (N) is not coming tomorrow. **Asû** is a less formal equivalent of **asítà**.

7. In CC7, (N) is invited to join a game of **go** during an office break. **Simâsu** 'do' can refer to all kinds of activity. **Tyôtto**, often with slowed-down articulation, is commonly used as a polite refusal. The literal meaning of the word is 'a bit,' 'a small amount.' Here it implies 'a bit impossible, inconvenient, out of the question, etc.' By saying no more than **tyôtto**, the speaker is less precise and more polite, thereby softening the refusal.

8. In CC8, (J) offers his foreign colleague a cup of coffee. **Itádakimàsu** implies polite, in-group acceptance of something from the out-group, usually the person(s) addressed. Thus, it commonly means 'I (or we) politely accept [something] from you.' It often occurs as a ritual expression immediately before eating or drinking. Its use in direct questions is comparatively rare and should be avoided by the beginning student for the time being, pending additional instruction relating to politeness levels.

9. In CC9, (J) checks on his assumption that his colleague (N) attended an event advertised on a poster they are looking at. **Ikímàsu** refers to motion away from the speaker or locations connected with the speaker. In contrast, **kimâsu** refers to motion toward the speaker. Thus, 'I **ikímàsu** to or toward where you are at the moment, or to your home or office,' but 'others **kimâsu** to or toward me or locations associated with me.'

10. In CC10, (N) apologizes for not having understood a new computer procedure.

Structural Patterns (SP)

1. VERBALS

The vocabulary of any language can be divided into word-classes, such that all members of any one class share certain characteristics that set them apart from members of other classes. For example, in English we associate the verb class with words that behave like 'want'—i.e., that occur in forms like 'wants,' 'wanted,' 'wanting,' etc.

The first class we are going to establish for Japanese is the class to be called VERBALS.[5]

5. A rather unfamiliar term has been deliberately chosen in order to prevent students from mistakenly making assumptions based on knowledge of other languages. For example, if the term 'verb' is used, many students will immediately assume incorrectly that the Japanese category exactly matches the English word class of the same name, and will then rely on translation from English to establish the Japanese class.

DEFINITION: A Japanese VERBAL is a word which has a number of different forms including one form ending in **-màsu** and another in **-màsita**. A sentence which consists of, or ends with, a verbal form (with or without following sentence particles [see SP 2]) is a VERBAL SENTENCE.

In this section, four verbal-related patterns are introduced:

	Affirmative	Negative
Imperfective (= unfinished condition)	**X-màsu** 'X does or will occur'	**X-masèñ** 'X doesn't or won't occur'
Perfective (= finished condition)	**X-màsita** 'X occurred'	**X-masèñ desita** 'X didn't occur'

(X = a verbal stem, i.e., **wakari, iki, nomi,** etc. The above forms are regularly accented as indicated with the rise in pitch occurring on the second mora, unless context results in a loss of accent.)

Now go back to the Core Conversations and identify and analyze all the verbal patterns, paying close attention to their meanings. Note also the following important points:

1. A verbal can occur as a complete sentence by itself: there is no grammatical requirement to express a subject.

2. Unless the context or particular verbal specifically indicates the contrary (which it often does), statements ending in any of the above forms regularly refer to the speaker, and questions to the person addressed. This is reflected in our English equivalents. Literally **Wakárimàsu ka** means something like 'Does understanding occur?'.

3. *Finished* versus *unfinished* is the significant contrast in Japanese, whereas English speakers tend to think in terms of three time distinctions: past, present, and future.

4. The **-mas-** (**-masi-** before consonants) portion of the above forms is a style marker. It signals what will be called DISTAL-STYLE for verbals. This style indicates that the speaker is showing solicitude toward, and maintaining some linguistic distance from, the addressee, i.e., s/he is being less direct and more formal as a sign of deference to the person addressed (and/or the topic of discussion), rather than talking directly, intimately, familiarly, abruptly, or carelessly. This variety of speech is most generally acceptable for foreign adults just beginning their study of the language. Distal-style contrasts with DIRECT-STYLE, introduced later.

This concept of style in Japanese is extremely complex and constitutes one of the most difficult features of the language for the foreigner to master. It requires constant attention, for *there is no neutral style in the Japanese language.* While for a given situation one style may be more appropriate, expected, normal, and unmarked, that same style will be most inappropriate and surprising if used in some other situation. Of course every language reflects stylistic differences (consider English 'How do you do?' versus 'Hi!', which are certainly not interchangeable) but the pervasiveness of the differences in Japanese is overwhelming. Every use of the language requires a stylistic choice. We are starting out with the "safest" style for foreign adult speakers, but other styles will be introduced soon.

Note that in the Core Conversations of this lesson, the speakers all use distal-style in their conversations with each other. The implication is that their relationship—as well as the formality of the situation—dictates the maintenance of indirectness. In contrast, we would not expect to hear this style of speech in casual conversations among Japanese students—especially male students—who are good friends.

5. As structural patterns and their meanings are introduced, the assumption is always that *if* a particular combination having this structure occurs, it will have a comparable meaning. But *not all items occur in all patterns.* Consider an English example:

'It's an interesting book.'	'The book is interesting.'
'It's an expensive trip.'	'The trip is expensive.'
'It's a funny movie.'	'The movie is funny.'
'It's a nice day.'	?

The foreigner who forms 'The day is nice' has uttered a sentence that simply isn't normally used, even though it follows the same structural pattern. Among the vocabulary items in this lesson, **tiḡáimàsu (-màsita)** and **itádakimàsu (-màsita)** are, of course, verbals (in accordance with our definition), but they occur less commonly in our drills because they have more constraints on their usage. **Tiḡáimàsu** is comparatively rare in the negative, and **itádakimàsu** is rare in questions.

Until further notice, new verbals will be identified with **/-màsita/** following the **-màsu** form in the Breakdowns.

2. SENTENCE-PARTICLES: **ka, ne, yo**

DEFINITION: a SENTENCE-PARTICLE is one of a small group of words which occur only at the end of sentences; they qualify the meaning of what has preceded. They regularly follow the preceding word directly without pause.

Ka: a question-marker; occurs at the end of both information questions (i.e., those that ask who, what, when, where, etc.) and yes-no questions; makes a statement into a yes-no question; usually ends in /↗/ (empathetic) or /./ (terminal declarative) intonation.

Ne: a confirmation-seeker; with rising intonation /ʃ/ seeks confirmation of an assumption made by the speaker: 'right?', 'don't you agree?', 'isn't it?', etc.

Yo: a particle of assertion; common in assurances, contradictions, and warnings (to the addressee); indicates that the speaker assumes s/he is providing the addressee with new information or a new suggestion; occurs with both /↗/ and /./ intonations, parallel to their use with **ka**. This particle should be avoided in those situations in which assertion becomes rude. In particular, its use with superiors requires caution. Frequently the closest English equivalent of an occurrence of **yo** turns out to be a particular intonation pattern.

3. NEGATIVE QUESTIONS; INVITATIONS

Negative questions occur in the following types of contexts:

1. to check on or confirm a negative situation already introduced into the context or assumed, on the basis of general context, as correct:

Dekímasèñ.	'I can't do it.'
Dekímasèñ ka↗	'You can't do it?'
Ikímasèñ neʃ	'You're not going to go—right?'

2. to check on the possibility of a negative situation contrary to the speaker's underlying assumptions:

Tukúrimasèñ.	'I'm not going to make [it].'
Dekímasèñ ka	'You can't do it?' (i.e., I thought you could, but . . .)

3. as an invitation:

Kimásèñ ka	'Won't you come?'

4. AFFIRMING AND NEGATING

Hâi, and the more relaxed, conversational **êe**, as introduced in this lesson in response to yes-no questions, indicate agreement. In answer to negative questions the negative of which is already assumed to be correct (negative question type (1) in the preceding note), **hâi/êe** confirms the negation. Compare:

Wakárimàsita ka	'Did you understand?'
Hâi/êe, wakárimàsita.	'Yes, I did.' *and*
Wakárimasèñ desita.	'I didn't understand.'
Wakárimasèñ desita ka	'You didn't understand?'
Hâi/êe, wakárimasèñ desita.	'That's right. I didn't understand.'

Remember that **hâi** is also used when the speaker is handing over something to the addressee: 'here you are' (CC 5).

I(i)e (or **îe**), and the more relaxed, conversational **iya** (or **îya**), indicate lack of agreement in a parallel way. Compare:

Ikímàsu ka	'Are you going?'
I(i)e/iya, ikímasèñ.	'No, I'm not (going).' *and*
Ikímasèñ neʕ	'You're not going—right?'
I(i)e/iya, ikímàsu yo	'No, I *am* going.'

Negatives used in invitations, of course, do not assume the accuracy of a negative situation and therefore do not call for the same kind of answer. Compare:

Tabémasèñ neʕ	'You're not going to eat [it]—right?'
Êe.	'That's right.' (i.e., I'm not going to eat [it].) *and*
Tabémasèñ ka	'Won't you eat [it]?' (invitation)
Êe, arîgatoo gozaimasu.	'Yes, thank you.' (acceptance)

Similarly, in reply to negative questions of type [2] in the preceding note, a **hâi/êe** answer implies agreement with the questioner's underlying assumption of an affirmative, and an **i(i)e/iya** response, the opposite.

Kimásèñ ka	'Aren't you coming?' (i.e., I thought you were.)
Hâi/êe, kimâsu yo *or*	'Yes, I am (coming).'
Iie/iya, kimásèñ yo	'No, I'm not (coming).'

Drills

(Using the accompanying tapes, practice each drill in turn until you can participate accurately and at the appropriate speed without reference to your book. All responses must follow exactly the models provided at the beginning of each drill. Be sure you understand the meaning of everything you are saying. Use visual aids whenever possible: remember that language is always used in a context. Proceed to a following drill only after mastering the one at hand.)

A 1. **Wakárimàsu ka**
'Do you understand?'

   Êe, wakárimàsu.
'Yes, I do (understand).'

2. **Ikímàsu ka**
'Are you going to go?' *or*
'Do you go?'

   Êe, ikímàsu.
'Yes, I am (going to go).' *or*
'Yes, I do (go).'

3. **nomímàsu**; 4. **kimâsu**; 5. **dekímàsu**; 6. **tiğáimàsu**; 7. **simâsu**; 8. **tukúrimàsu**; 9. **tabémàsu**

B 1. **Wakárimàsita ka**
'Did you understand?'

   Êe, wakárimàsita.
'Yes, I did (understand).'

2. **Tabémàsita ka**
'Did you eat [it]?'

   Êe, tabémàsita.
'Yes, I did (eat).'

3. **tukúrimàsita**; 4. **dekímàsita**; 5. **simâsita**; 6. **kimâsita**; 7. **nomímàsita**; 8. **ikímàsita**; 9. **tiğáimàsita**

C 1. **Kyôo simâsu ne**
'You'll do [it] today—right?'

   Tiğáimàsu. Asíta simàsu yo.
'No, I'm going to do [it] tomorrow (I inform you).'

2. **Kyôo ikímàsu ne**
'You're going to go today—right?'

   Tiğáimàsu. Asíta ikimàsu yo.
'No, I'm going to go tomorrow (I inform you.)'

3. **kimâsu**; 4. **tukúrimàsu**; 5. **tabémàsu**; 6. **nomímàsu**; 7. **dekímàsu**

D 1. **Kyôo ikímàsita ne**
'You went today—right?'

   Iya, kinóo ikimàsita yo.
'No, I went yesterday (I inform you).'

2. **Kyôo tukúrimàsita ne**
'You made [it] today—right?'

   Iya, kinóo tukurimàsita yo.
'No, I made [it] yesterday (I inform you).'

3. **simâsita**; 4. **tabémàsita**; 5. **dekímàsita**; 6. **nomímàsita**; 7. **kimâsita**

E 1. **Kinóo ikimàsita ne**
'You went yesterday—right?'

   Iie, asíta ikimàsu yo.
'No, I'm going to go tomorrow (I inform you).'

2. **Kinóo simàsita ne**
'You did [it] yesterday—right?'

   Iie, asíta simàsu yo.
'No, I'm going to do [it] tomorrow (I inform you).'

3. **kimâsita**; 4. **tukúrimàsita**; 5. **tabémàsita**; 6. **nomímàsita**; 7. **dekímàsita**

F 1. **Wakárimàsu ka↙**   **Iie, wakárimasèñ.**
  'Do you understand?'   'No, I don't (understand).'

 2. **Ikímàsu ka↙**   **Iie, ikímasèñ.**
  'Are you going to go? *or*   'No, I'm not (going to go).' *or*
  'Do you go?'   'No, I don't (go).'

 3. **tukúrimàsu**; 4. **dekímàsu**; 5. **kimâsu**; 6. **tabémàsu**; 7. **nomímàsu**; 8. **simâsu**

G 1. **Nomímàsita ka↙**   **Iya, nomímasèñ desita.**
  'Did you drink [it]?'   'No, I didn't (drink).'

 2. **Tukúrimàsita ka↙**   **Iya, tukúrimasèñ desita.**
  'Did you make [it]?'   'No, I didn't (make).'

 3. **ikímàsita**; 4. **kimâsita**; 5. **tabémàsita**; 6. **simâsita**; 7. **wakárimàsita**; 8. **dekímàsita**

H 1. **Ikímasèñ neɂ**   **Êe, ikímasèñ. Sumímasèñ.**
  'You're not going to go—right?' 'That's right, I'm not (going to go). I'm
               sorry.'

 2. **Wakárimasèñ neɂ**   **Êe, wakárimasèñ. Sumímasèñ.**
  'You don't understand—right?' 'That's right. I don't (understand). I'm
               sorry.'

 3. **kimásèñ**; 4. **dekímasèñ**; 5. **simásèñ**; 6. **nomímasèñ**; 7. **tabémasèñ**; 8. **tukúrimasèñ**

I 1. **Kyôo ikímasu ka↙**   **Êe, ikímàsu.**
  'Are you going to go today?' 'Yes, I am (going to go).'

 2. **Kyôo ikímàsita ka↙**   **Êe, ikímàsita.**
  'Did you go today?'   'Yes, I did (go).'

 3. **asíta simàsu**; 4. **kinóo tukurimàsita**; 5. **kyôo simâsu**; 6. **kyôo nomímàsita**; 7. **asíta kimàsu**; 8. **kyôo tabémàsita**

J 1. **Asíta kimàsu ka↙**   **Iya, kimásèñ.**
  'Are you going to come tomorrow?' 'No, I'm not (going to come).'

 2. **Kinóo kimàsita ka↙**   **Iya, kimásèñ desita.**
  'Did you come yesterday?'   'No, I didn't (come).'

 3. **asíta simàsu**; 4. **kinóo tukurimàsita**; 5. **kyôo simâsu**; 6. **kyôo nomímàsita**; 7. **asíta ikimàsu**; 8. **kyôo tabémàsita**

Application Exercises

(The purpose of these exercises is to utilize what you have already learned, and to develop fluency in using it. Don't press your instructor for additional vocabulary—you won't remember it unless it recurs regularly, and for that purpose additional materials would have to be written.)

A. In the following exercises, practice both **ka** and **ne**, affirmative and negative questions, as appropriate.

 1. Using samples of various foreign languages, ask and answer questions relating to comprehension (verbal **wakárimàsu**) and general linguistic ability (verbal **dekímàsu**).

 2. Using maps of various places, together with dates (years, months, days), ask and answer

questions relating to going or having gone to specific places at specific times, as they are pointed out (verbal **ikímàsu**).

3. Using pictures that represent various sports, ask and answer questions about students' general participation, and specific participation yesterday, today, and tomorrow (verbal **simâsu**).

4. Using pictures of various foods and drinks, ask and answer questions relating to eating, drinking, and preparation (verbals **tabémàsu, nomímàsu,** and **tukúrimàsu**).

5. Check on students' attendance yesterday and planned attendance tomorrow (verbal **kimâsu**).

B. Core Conversations: Substitution

Using appropriate props, go through the Core Conversations substituting other familiar verbals in each conversational exchange while retaining the exact original structure of the exchange.

SECTION B

Core Conversations (CC)

1(N)	**Îi desu ka**	(J)	**Îi desu yo**
2(N)	**Îi desu ka**	(J)	**Dôozo.**
3(N)	**Takâi desu ka**	(J)	**Iie, yasûi desu yo**
4(J)	**Totémo omosiròi desu yo.**		
	Simásèñ ka	(N)	**Arîgatoo gozaimasu.**
5(J)	**Omósìròkatta desu ka**	(N)	**Mâa·mâa desu nêe.**
6(N)	**Kaímàsita ka**	(J)	**Êe. Tâkâkatta desu yo.**
7(J)a.	**Dekímàsita ka**	(N)	**Êe, dekímàsita.**
b.	**Yôkatta desu ne!**		
8(J)	**Takâi desu ka**	(N)	**Ie, amári tàkàku nâi desu yo**
9(J)	**Yôku nâi desu nêe.**	(N)	**Êe. Komárimàsita nêe.**
10(N)	**Amári omosìròku nâkatta desu nêe.**	(J)	**Êe, tumáranàkatta desu nêe.**
11(N)	**Yôku dekímàsu nêe.**	(J)	**Iêie, dôo itasimasite.**
12(J)a.	**Asíta ikimàsu yo.**	(N)	**Yôku ikimasu nêe.**
b.	**Êe, mâa.**		

ENGLISH EQUIVALENTS

1(N)	Is it all right?	(J)	Yes, it's fine (I assure you).
2(N)	Do you mind?	(J)	Go right ahead.
3(N)	Is it expensive?	(J)	No, it's cheap (I assure you).
4(J)	It's a lot of fun. Won't you play (*or* do [it])?	(N)	Thank you.
5(J)	Was it interesting?	(N)	So-so.

6(N)   Did you buy [it]?

(J)   Yes. It was expensive (I inform you).

7(J)a. (Has it become) finished?
   b. Great!

(N)   Yes, (it has become) finished.

8(J)   Is it expensive?

(N)   No, it's not very expensive (I assure you).

9(J)   It's not good, is it!

(N)   That's right. We've got a problem, haven't we!

10(N)   It wasn't very interesting, was it!

(J)   That's right. It was boring, wasn't it!

11(N)   You're good at that, aren't you!

(J)   Oh, no! (Don't mention it.)

12(J)a. Say, I'm going [there] tomorrow.
    b. Yes, I guess I do.

(N)   You go there often, don't you!

BREAKDOWNS
(AND SUPPLEMENTARY VOCABULARY)

1. **îi (desu)** (SP1)	is good; is fine; is all right
3. **takâi (desu)**	is expensive; is high
yasûi (desu)	is cheap
+**oókìi (desu)**	is big
+**tiísài (desu)**	is small
+**atárasìi (desu)**	is new, fresh
+**hurûi (desu)**	is old (i.e., not new)
4. **tot(t)emo**	very, extremely
omósiròi (desu)	is interesting; is amusing; is fun
5. **omósìròkatta (desu)** (SP1)	was interesting; was amusing; was fun
mâa·mâa	so-so
nêe (SP3)	/sentence-particle of confirmation, agreement, or deliberation/
6. **kaímàsu /-màsita/**	buy
tâkâkatta (desu)	was expensive; was high
7. **yôkatta (desu)**	was good; was fine; was all right
8. **a(ñ)mari** /+negative/	not much, not very
tâkâku nâi (desu) or	
+**tâkâku arímasèñ** (SP2)	isn't expensive; isn't high
9. **yôku nâi (desu)** or	
+**yôku arímasèñ**	isn't good; isn't all right
komárimàsu /-màsita/	become upset; become a problem
10. **omósìròku nâkatta (desu)** or	
+**omósìròku arímasèñ desita**	wasn't interesting; wasn't amusing; wasn't fun
tumárànai (desu)	is boring; is trifling
tumárànakatta (desu)	was boring; was trifling
11. **yôku dekimasu**	can do well

12. **yôku ikimasu**   go often
    mâa   /expression of qualified agreement/

MISCELLANEOUS NOTES (MN)

Again, all the Core Conversations are exchanges between people who are using distal-style in communicating with each other. In the accompanying video, they are professional colleagues—coworkers and a supervisor with a secretary—and students who do not know each other well.

    1. In CC1, (N) checks with (J) on the quality of some work or the appropriateness of an action. On the accompanying video, (N) asks (J) if it is all right for him to watch a game of **go** in progress.

    2. In CC2, (N) asks for—and receives—permission. On the video, the use of the telephone is involved.

    3. In CC3, the participants discuss the price of an item.
Takâi refers both to expensiveness and inanimate height.

    4. In CC4, (J) invites (N) to join in a game. On the video, the game is **go**, being played during lunch break.
Tottemo is a more emphatic equivalent of **totemo**.

    5. In CC5, (J) checks on (N)'s reaction to a completed event. On the video, he inquires about (N)'s enjoyment of the game of **go** that has just ended. ([N]'s enthusiasm is limited: he lost!)
Mâa·mâa occurs frequently as a non-committal reply to a question.

    6. In CC6, (N) checks on the purchase that (J) just made.

    7. In CC7, the participants are discussing a project that (N) has been working on. On the video, (N) has just completed a jigsaw puzzle.

    8. In CC8, (J)—like (N) in CC3—checks on the cost of a product.
Añmari is a more emphatic equivalent of **amari**.

    9. In CC9, the participants share concern over something that has not gone well.
Komárimàsu implies being put in a position of embarrassment, awkwardness, consternation, conflict, etc. The perfective here implies that the participants have already been placed in that kind of position.

    10. In CC10, the participants agree on their unfavorable reaction to an event they both attended.

    11. In CC11, a compliment concerning ability is politely contradicted by the recipient. On the video, the secretary (J) modestly turns aside the compliment she receives from her supervisor (N) about her skillful use of the computer.
Ieie (or **iêie**) is a more emphatic equivalent of **i(i)e**. Note the polite dismissal of a compliment, using negation and/or **dôo itasimasite**.

    12. In CC12, (J)'s intention to go somewhere (on the video, to a theatrical performance) elicits a comment from (N) about how often (J) goes to such functions.

Structural Patterns (SP)

1. ADJECTIVALS: AFFIRMATIVE IMPERFECTIVE AND PERFECTIVE

Japanese major sentences[6] belong to three types. Verbal sentences have already been introduced. In this section, a second type is introduced: the adjectival sentence, one which

---

    6. We distinguish between major sentences, minor sentences, and fragments. See Introduction II, under these headings.

consists of or ends with an adjectival expression (with or without following sentence particles).

DEFINITION: A Japanese ADJECTIVAL is a word which has a number of forms, including one ending in **-i** and another in **-katta**. The **-i** ending, like the **-u** ending of verbal **-màsu** forms, is the sign of the imperfective; the **-katta** ending, like the **-ta** ending of verbal **-màsita** forms, is the sign of the perfective. These adjectival forms are direct-style, and in casual speech, *may* occur as complete sentences all by themselves. The addition of **desu** serves only to convert them to distal-style, making them parallel to verbal forms containing **-mas-/-masi-**. (For the present, we will be using distal-style exclusively, the only style introduced thus far for verbals.)

Affirmative Adjectivals

	Direct-Style	Distal-Style	Meaning
Imperfective	**X-i**	**X-i desu**	'(it) is or will be X'
Perfective	**X-katta**	**X-katta desu**	'(it) was X'

X = an adjectival root, i.e. **taka-, yasu-, omosiro-,** etc.

Accent: An accented adjectival is typically accented on the mora preceding the **-i** ending (**tumáranai** is an exception); in the **-katta** form, there are alternate accents: on the mora immediately preceding the **-katta** ending (the newer pattern) or on an earlier mora (the traditional pattern). Both accents will be marked, but *of course only one is heard in any given occurrence.* An unaccented adjectival typically acquires an accent (1) on the mora preceding the final **-i** when followed by **desu**, and (2) on the mora preceding the **-katta** ending in all contexts.

Now go back to the Core Conversations and identify and analyze all the affirmative adjectival sentences. Note also the following important points:

1. Our definition of the adjectival is based entirely on form: we are not equating Japanese adjectivals with words which happen to be translated into English as adjectives.

2. The ending of the adjectival is always preceded by another vowel, other than **-e**. This means that adjectivals in their imperfective form all end in **-ai, -ii, -ui,** or **-oi.** This is also the citation form—i.e., the form listed in dictionaries. However, not every word that ends this way is an adjectival. It must have another form ending in **-katta** in order for us to call it an adjectival.

3. **Yôkatta** is derived from **yôi**, which is an older form of the currently preferred **îi**. **Yôi** also does still occur, although usually in particular clichés and/or in formal language. All derived forms of **îi/yôi** are based on the **yo-** root.

Yôkatta (desu) is regularly used in reference to a situation that has turned out to be good, as opposed to **îi desu**, which refers to a continuing static condition that is good, or fine, or agreeable, or okay as is (i.e., 'never mind'), or an as yet unrealized condition.

2. ADJECTIVALS: THE -ku FORM AND THE NEGATIVE

In Section A, we learned that the negative equivalents of verbals ending in **-màsu** and **-màsita** end in **-maseñ** and **-maseñ desita**, respectively. All these forms are distal-style; direct-style verbal patterns will be introduced later.

For the adjectival, we can immediately describe both direct- and distal-style forms (even though direct-style will not be drilled for the time being) because the correspondences are so much simpler.

Direct-Style Adjectivals

	Affirmative	Negative
Imperfective	**X-i** '(it) is or will be X'	**X-ku nâi** '(it) isn't or won't be X'
Perfective	**X-katta** '(it) was X'	**X-ku nâkatta** '(it) wasn't X'

X = an adjectival root, i.e. **taka-, yasu-, omosiro-,** etc.

Accent: If the adjectival is unaccented, the **-ku** form is also unaccented. If the adjectival is accented, the **-ku** form is also accented, either on the same mora as the **-i** form (i.e., the newer pattern) or on a preceding mora (i.e., the more traditional pattern). We will consistently mark both accents since both are occurring variations in the standard language. Some individual speakers alternate between the two patterns, both in the **-ku** form and the **-katta** form. However, in all instances, the accent on the earlier alternative in a given word is the traditional, older, and more conservative, and for some speakers, the only acceptable alternate.

To change the above chart to distal-style, simply add **desu** to each example. While you may *hear* the direct-style being used among Japanese around you, at this level of competence you are advised to *use* only the distal-style.

An alternate for **nâi desu** is **arímasèñ**, and an alternate for **nâkatta desu, arímasèñ desita**. The forms with **arímasèñ**, which follow the patterning of the negatives of verbals, are considered a bit more formal, and in the view of some speakers, are slightly more elegant. Our expanded adjectival chart, then, looks like this:

	Affirmative		Negative	
	Direct	Distal	Direct	Distal
Imperfective	**X-i**	**X-i desu**	**X-ku nâi**	**X-ku nâi desu** *or* **X-ku arímasèñ**
Perfective	**X-katta**	**X-katta desu**	**X-ku nâkatta**	**X-ku nâkatta desu** *or* **X-ku arímasèñ desita**

In examining the chart, several things may strike you on the basis of what you have learned thus far. Isn't the word **nâi**, which has another form ending in -katta and which adds **desu** to form the distal-style equivalent, itself an adjectival? Correct! It is a negative adjectival meaning 'there isn't any. . . .' And don't the negatives **arímasèñ** and **arímasèñ desita** perhaps come from an affirmative verbal **arímàsu**? Also correct! **Arímàsu** refers to inanimate existence ('there is . . .') and will be introduced independently in a later lesson.

In the above chart, it is **nâi, nâkatta,** and **arímasèñ** that are actually negative. When an adjectival precedes and occurs in combination with them, the adjectival itself changes to its corresponding **-ku** form (i.e., the final **-i** is dropped and **-ku** is added). [This is not unlike the English requirement that after 'two', we must change 'apple' to 'apples'; or after 'I am,' 'go' is replaced by 'going', but after 'I have,' it appears as 'gone.'] Note that the **-ku** form is *not* itself negative; it is required by the negative forms that follow. A combination like **tâkâku nâi (desu)** or **tâkâku arímasèñ** means something like 'being expensive—there isn't.'

Our rule can now be extended to cover /adjectival + verbal/ or /adjectival + adjectival/ in more general terms, regardless of whether the combination is affirmative or negative. Compare the following:

Takâi desu.	'It's expensive' but **Tâkâku simâsita** 'I made [it] expensive'; 'I raised the price.'
Yasûi desu.	'It's cheap' but **Yâsûku dekímasèñ ka** 'Can't you make [it] cheap?' 'Can't you lower the price?'
Atárasìi desu.	'It's new' but **Atárasìku tukurimasu.** 'I'm going to make (build, construct, etc.) [it] anew.'

In other words, the adjectival in its **-ku** form (which we will call the STEM) links up with verbals and other adjectivals, affirmative and negative.

Yôku, the **-ku** form of **îi/yôi**, refers to extensive quantity (i.e., 'a good deal'), good quality (i.e., 'well' or 'good'), or frequency ('often'), depending on the context. Study these combinations:

yôku wakarimasu	'understand a good deal or well'
yôku dekimasu	'be very capable'; 'turn out well'; 'do well'
yôku simasu	'do often' (NOT 'well'!)
yôku ikimasu	'go often'

Note the occurrence of **a(ñ)mari** in the negative reply to a **yôku** . . . question:

Yôku kimasu ka	'Do you come here often?'
Iie, a(ń)mari kimasèñ.	'No, I don't come very much.'

3. SENTENCE-PARTICLE: nêe./ne!

Nêe. occurs at the end of sentences (1) as an exclamatory indication of assumed or actual agreement—frequently of admiration or disapproval—between speaker and addressee, implying shared information; or (2) as an indication of subjective reflection by the speaker which is non-abrupt and non-confrontational. Thus:

Amari omósìroku arímasèñ nêe.	'It's not very interesting, is it!'
Êe. Tumárànai desu nêe.	'You're right. It's boring, isn't it!'
Dekímasèñ ka	'Isn't it possible?'; 'Can't you do it?'
Dekímasèñ nêe.	'It isn't possible, is it (as I think about it).'

(The pitch level of the **ne** of **nêe** occurs with considerable variation.)

The avoidance of confrontation is extremely important in Japanese conversation. The frequency of **nêe**—which serves to bond the participants of a conversation in a manner that suggests agreement and compatibility—is striking to the foreigner. Note that **nêe** in many respects contrasts with **yo**: the former stresses shared information, whereas **yo** implies that the speaker is providing new information in an assertive way—to assure or reassure or correct or contradict. While certainly not restricted to such usage, **nêe** in its reflective sense is particularly common with predicates that occur apart from the volition of the speaker. (More will be said about these predicates later.) The comment **Dekímasèñ nêe.** does not convey the speaker's decision not to do something, but rather that it is impossible as viewed objectively; the further implication is that the listener is being drawn in to concur with the comment. Contrastively, **Dekímasèñ yo** is an assertive statement that clearly differentiates the speaker-informer from the listener-informed.

Utterances ending in **nêe.** often refer to persons other than the speaker. Thus:

Yôku dekímàsu nêe.	'You're very capable, aren't you!'
Yôku kimâsu nêe.	'They (known by context) come here often, don't they!'

In Section A, the sentence-particle /neʕ/ was introduced in questions that check on an assumption of shared information. This is obviously a variant of /**nêe.**/. As another alternate, we find occurrences of **ne** without the special rising intonation symbolized by /ʕ/, with a special falling intonation that starts on a high pitch: it resembles the contour of /**nêe.**/ but within a single mora. We will represent this alternate as /**ne!**/. Its meanings are very close to those of /**nêe.**/ but it lacks the exclamatory force of /**nêe.**/.

A problem for the language learner is the fact that even though each variant of this sentence particle conveys a different meaning, in many contexts more than one variant is possible. The result is that different occurrences of an otherwise identical conversation may vary as to whether **nêe.**, **ne!**, or **neʕ** ends a particular sentence. The learner's task is to *know what each alternate signals, and then interpret each occurrence appropriately.*

Drills

(Remember to use appropriate visual aids—if not concretely, at least mentally!)

A 1. **Takâi desu ka**   **Êe, takâi desu yo**
   'Is it expensive?'   'Yes, it is (expensive) (I assure you).'

2. **Omósiròi desu ka**   **Êe, omósiròi desu yo**
   'Is it interesting?'   'Yes, it is (interesting) (I assure you).'

3. **atárasìi**; 4. **oókìi**; 5. **îi**; 6. **hurûi**; 7. **tiísài**; 8. **tumáranai**; 9. **yasûi**

B 1. **Omósìròkatta desu ka**   **Êe, omósìròkatta desu yo**
   'Was it fun?'   'Yes, it was (fun) (I assure you).'

2. **Atáràsìkatta desu ka**   **Êe, atárasìkatta desu yo**
   'Was it fresh?'   'Yes, it was (fresh) (I assure you).'

3. **tumáranakatta**; 4. **yâsûkatta**; 5. **tîísàkatta**; 6. **yôkatta**; 7. **hûrûkatta**; 8. **ôókìkatta**; 9. **tâkâkatta**

C 1. **Îi desu ka**   **Êe, îi desu yo**
   'Is it all right?'   'Yes, it's fine (I assure you).'

2. **Kaímàsita ka**   **Êe, kaímàsita yo**
   'Did you buy [it]?'   'Yes, I did (buy) (I assure you).'

3. **komárimàsu**; 4. **omósìròkatta desu**; 5. **simâsita**; 6. **takâi desu**; 7. **kaímàsu**; 8. **yôkatta desu**

D 1. **Takâi desu neʕ**   **Iie, tâkâku nâi desu yo**
   'It's expensive—right?'   'No, it's not (expensive) (I assure you).'

2. **Omósiròi desu neʕ**   **Iie, omósìròku nâi desu yo**
   'It's interesting—right?'   'No, it's not (interesting) (I assure you).'

3. **oókìi**; 4. **yasûi**; 5. **îi**; 6. **tumáranai**; 7. **tiísài**; 8. **atárasìi**; 9. **hurûi**

● Repeat this drill, replacing **nâi desu** with **arímasèñ** in the responses.

  E 1. **Yôkatta desu ka✓**
      'Was it good?'

Iie, amári yòku nâkatta desu nêe.
'No, (it was) not very (good) (was it—as I think about it)!'

    2. **Tâkâkatta desu ka✓**
      'Was it expensive?'

Iie, amári tàkàku nâkatta desu nêe.
'No, (it was) not very (expensive) (was it—as I think about it)!'

    3. **ôókìkatta**; 4. **atáràsìkatta**; 5. **omósìròkatta**; 6. **tîísàkatta**

● Repeat this drill, replacing **nâkatta desu** with **arímasèñ desita** in the responses.

  F 1. **Tâkâku nâi desu ka✓**
      'Isn't it expensive?' (i.e., I thought it was)

Êe, takâi desu yo✓
'Yes, it is (expensive) (I assure you).'

    2. **Yâsûku arímasèñ desita ka✓**
      'Wasn't it cheap?'

Êe, yâsûkatta desu yo✓
'Yes, it was (cheap) (I assure you).'

    3. **tumárànaku arímasèñ**; 4. **omósìròku nâkatta desu**; 5. **ôókìku nâi desu**; 6. **hûrûku nâkatta desu**; 7. **tîísàku arímasèñ**; 8. **atáràsìku arímasèñ desita**

  G 1. **Îi desu ka✓**
      'Is it good?'

Iie, yôku arímasèñ.
'No, it isn't (good).'

    2. **Kaîmàsita ka✓**
      'Did you buy [it]?'

Iie, kaímasèñ desita.
'No, I didn't (buy).'

    3. **hûrûkatta desu**; 4. **ikímàsu**; 5. **tâkâkatta desu**; 6. **tukúrimàsita**; 7. **omósiròi desu**; 8. **dekímàsu**

  H 1. **Takâi desu ka✓**
      'Is it expensive?'

Iya, tâkâku nâi desu. Yasûi desu yo✓
'No, it isn't (expensive). It's cheap (I assure you).'

    2. **Omósìròkatta desu ka✓**

      'Was it interesting?'

Iya, omósìròku nâkatta desu. Tumárànakatta desu yo✓

'No, it wasn't (interesting). It was boring (I assure you).'

    3. **hurûi**; 4. **yâsûkatta**; 5. **tumárànai**; 6. **tîísàkatta**; 7. **atáràsìkatta**; 8. **oókìi**

  I 1. **Yôku ikímàsu nêe.**
      'You go often, don't you!'

Iêie, amari ikímasèñ yo✓
'No, no, I don't go very much (I correct you).'

    2. **Yôku kaímàsu nêe.**
      'You buy [it] often, don't you!'

Iêie, amari kaímasèñ yo✓
'No, no, I don't buy [it] very much (I correct you).'

    3. **wakárimàsu**; 4. **simâsu**; 5. **nomímàsu**; 6. **tukúrimàsu**; 7. **dekímàsu**; 8. **tabémàsu**; 9. **kimâsu**

  J 1. **Dekímàsita yo✓**
      'It's been completed.'

Dekímàsita ka. Yôkatta desu nêe.
'It's been completed? Isn't that great!'

    2. **Omósìròkatta desu yo✓**

Omósìròkatta desu ka. Yôkatta desu nêe.

'It was fun!'   'It was fun? Isn't that great!'

   3. **kaímàsita**; 4. **wakárimàsita**; 5. **yâsûkatta desu**; 6. **atáràsìkatta desu**; 7. **simâsita**;
     8. **tukúrimàsita**; 9. **ikímàsita**

K 1. **Takâi desu ka**✓   **Êe. Yâsûku dekímasèn ka**✓
    'Is it expensive?'   'Yes. Can't you make it cheap[er]?'

  2. **Tumárànai desu ka**✓   **Êe. Omósìròku dekímasèñ ka**✓
    'Is it dull?'   'Yes. Can't you make it [more] interesting?'

  3. **tiísài**; 4. **oókìi**

Application Exercises

A. In the following exercises, practice both **ka** and **ne** questions and **nêe** exclamations, as appropriate.

   1. Using various books and magazines as visual aids, ask and answer questions relating to buying (verbal **kaímàsu**), cost (adjectivals **takâi** and **yasûi**), and interest (adjectivals **omósiròi** and **tumárànai**). Utilize everything you have learned—sentence particles and words like **tot(t)emo, yôku, a(ñ)mari, mâa**, etc. React to answers with **yôkatta desu nêe**, or **komárimàsu/-màsita nêe**, as appropriate.

   2. Using pictures of various foods and drinks, ask and answer questions about eating, drinking, buying and making, and cost (adjectivals **takâi** and **yasûi**), incorporating items such as **yôku, a(ñ)mari, mâa, komárimàsu/-màsita,** etc., as appropriate.

B. Core Conversations: Substitution

   Using appropriate props, go through the Core Conversations, substituting other familiar appropriate adjectivals and verbals in each exchange while retaining the exact structure of the original.

SECTION C

Eavesdropping[7]

(On the basis of the exchanges on the accompanying audiotape, answer the following questions [in English]. In each case, A refers to the first speaker, and B to the second speaker. As you listen, try to visualize the situation.)

   1. What is the problem with the item under discussion?
   2. Why does B apologize?
 3a. What does A want to know?
  b. How does B react?
   4. When will B go?
   5. Is the item under discussion large, or small?
 6a. What is A's assumption?
  b. Does B agree?
 7a. What assumption is A checking on?
  b. Was A correct?

---

7. This term is not intended to have any unpleasant implications! It is used simply to signal listening in on conversations in which one takes no active part and with which one has no involvement.

8a. What is A's assumption?
  b. Does B agree?
  9. What compliment is A offering B?
10a. What is A checking on?
  b. Why is B holding back?
  c. What is A's judgment?
  11. What description of the item under discussion is offered?
12a. What does A invite B to do?
  b. What is B's response?
13a. What is A going to do?
  b. When will A do it?
  c. What does B question?
14a. What does A invite B to do?
  b. What is B's response?
15a. What activity of B's does A comment on?
  b. What was B's reaction to the item under discussion?
  c. Where do you assume this activity occurred? Why do you think so?

Utilization

What would you say? Provide an appropriate reply (or preceding stimulus) as well, but don't attempt anything you haven't learned. Exploit your strengths but know your limitations!

1. A colleague has just picked up a book written in Chinese. Ask if he understands.
2. You're playing a game. Invite a colleague to play.
3. A colleague has just bought a new dictionary. Ask if it wasn't expensive.
4. You're looking at a theater ad with a colleague. Ask if she goes often.
5. You've just given your assistant instructions. Check on whether he understood.
6. You've just returned after trying to put something into the computer. Apologize and explain that you couldn't do it.
7. You're holding your new dictionary. Tell a colleague that you bought it yesterday; it wasn't very expensive.
8. You've been offered some tea. Accept with thanks.
9. You've been asked if you attended a particular exhibit yesterday. Explain that that's not correct: you are going tomorrow.
10. You've just learned that a colleague knows how to make Chinese food. Ask if he makes it often.
11. Confirm with your colleague your understanding that she is coming tomorrow.
12. You've been working on a project. Inform your supervisor that it's finished, and hand it over.
13. You've been invited to participate in a game. Refuse politely.
14. You are doing a jigsaw puzzle. Tell a colleague that it's a lot of fun and invite her to join you.
15. You are shopping with a colleague and looking at dictionaries. Comment, assuming agreement, on how expensive they are.
16. A colleague has been trying to speak English. Compliment him on his ability.
17. You'd like to speak with a colleague for a moment. Ask if it's all right.
18. You're looking at a dictionary in a bookstore. Confirm that it's new.
19. You're looking at some magazines. Comment, assuming agreement, on how old they are.
20. You and your colleagues have just heard that the work you submitted has to be revised. Express your concern over your predicament.
21. A comment has been made about how often you go to the movies. Agree with reservation.
22. A sweater you have had made is too big. Find out if it can be made small[er].
23. A Japanese visitor has been talking to you at length in Japanese far beyond your level of competence. Apologize and tell her you didn't understand.

24. Your colleagues are discussing beer. Tell them you don't drink it very much.

25. Your colleagues are discussing Japanese food and you've been asked if you have eaten *sushi*. Tell them you ate it yesterday.

26. You've been asked if you had a good time [at a recent party]. Give a noncommittal answer.

Check-up

(Before proceeding to the next lesson, make certain that you can answer these questions about the material that has been introduced in this lesson. Remember that rapid and orderly progress depends on mastery of what has gone before.)

1. What is a verbal? a verbal sentence? Give examples. (A-SP1)[8]

2. What is an adjectival? an adjectival sentence? Give examples. (B-SP1)

3. What is meant by *imperfective* and *perfective*? (A-SP1)

4. What is meant by *direct-style* and *distal-style*? (A-SP1)

5. What signals distal-style for verbals? for adjectivals? (A-SP1, B-SP1)

6. What is the perfective equivalent of: **takâi, kimásèñ, simâsu, oókìi desu, yôku nâi desu, tîìsàku arímasèñ, yâsûku nâi**? (A-SP1), (B-SP1), (B-SP2)

7. What is the difference between **takâi** and **takâi desu**? between **tâkâkatta** and **tâkâkatta desu**? (B-SP1)

8. What is the negative equivalent of verbals ending in **-màsu**? in **-màsita-**? (A-SP1)

9. What is the negative equivalent of adjectivals ending in **-i**? in **-katta-**? (B-SP2)

10. Give two alternate negative equivalents for adjectivals ending in **-i desu**; in **-katta desu**. (B-SP2)

11. What form of an adjectival links up with a following verbal or another adjectival? (B-SP2)

12. Within the combinations **-ku nâi (desu)** and **-ku arímasèñ**, which part is actually negative? (B-SP2)

13. What is a sentence particle? (A-SP2)

14. What is the difference in meaning between a question ending in **ka** and one ending in **ne**? (A-SP2)

15. What is the difference in meaning between a sentence ending in **yo** and one ending in **nêe.**? (A-SP2), (B-SP3)

16. Describe three types of negative questions. How do responses to these three types differ? (A-SP3), (A-SP4)

17. Describe the accent patterns of the verbal and adjectival forms introduced thus far. (A-SP1), (B-SP1), (B-SP2)

8. References are to the relevant Section and Structural Pattern of the current lesson.

Lesson 2

SECTION A

Core Conversations (CC)

1(N) **Nâñ desu ka** (J) **Teḡámi dèsu.**

2(N)a. **Suzuki-sañ.** (J)a. **Nâñ desu ka**

    b. **Odêñwa desu.**   b. **A, dôo mo.**

3(N) **Suzúki-sañ dèsu ka** (J) **Hâi, Suzúki dèsu. Dôozo.**

4(N) **Dôo desu ka Damê desu ka** (J) **Iya, daízyòobu desu yo.**

5(J) **Tanáka-sañ dèsita yo** (N) **Âa, sôo desu ka.**

6(N) **Damê desita nêe.** (J) **Sôo desu nêe.**

7(N) **Nihóñḡo dèsu ka** (J) **Iya, nihóñḡo zya arimasèñ yo. Tyuúḡokuḡo dèsu.**

8(N) **Yamámoto-sañ zya nài desu ka** (J) **A, sôo desu ne!**

9(N)a. **Kîree desu ka** (J) **Sôo desu nêe. Amari kîree zya nâi desu nêe.**

    b. **Âa, sôo desu ka. Zańnèñ desu nêe.**

10(J) **Toókyoo dèsita ka** (N) **Iya, Toókyoo zya arimasèñ desita.**

English Equivalents

1(N) What is it? (J) It's a letter.

2(N)a. Mr/s. Suzuki! (J)a. What is it?

    b. Telephone.   b. Oh, thanks.

3(N) Are you Mr/s. Suzuki? (J) Yes, I am (Suzuki). (Pointing to a chair) Please [sit down].

4(N) How is it? Is it out-of-order? (J) No, it's all right.

5(J) That was Mr/s. Tanaka. (N) Oh, is that right?

6(N) It wasn't any good, was it! (J) That's right, (isn't it)!

7(N) Is that Japanese? (J) No, it isn't (Japanese). It's Chinese.

8(N) Isn't that Mr/s. Yamamoto? (J) Oh, it is, isn't it.

9(N)a. Is she pretty? (J) (Looking at photograph) Hmmm. (She is) not very (pretty), is she!

48

b. Oh really? That's too bad, isn't it!
10(J)   (Asking about a telephone call)
         Was that Tokyo?   (N)   No, it wasn't (Tokyo).

BREAKDOWNS
(AND SUPPLEMENTARY VOCABULARY)

1. **nâñ**   what?
   X dèsu (SP1)   it's X
   teĝami   letter
2. **Suzuki**   (family name)
   -sañ   Mr.; Mrs.; Miss; Ms. /polite/[1]
   deñwa/odêñwa   telephone (call)
   a/âa   oh!
4. **dôo**   what way, how?
   damê   no good
   daízyòobu   all right; safe
5. **Tanaka**   (family name)
   X dèsita (SP1)   it was X
   sôo (SP2)   that way, like that
7. **nihoñĝo**   Japanese language
  +**kokuĝo**   the Japanese mother-tongue of the
                                               Japanese

   tyuuĝokuĝo   Chinese language
  +**eeĝo**   English language
  +**hurañsuĝo**   French language
  +**doituĝo**   German language
  +**supeiñĝo**   Spanish language
  +**rosiaĝo**   Russian language
  +**naniĝo**   what language?
   X zya arímasèñ *or*
   X zya nâi (desu) (SP1)   it's not X
8. **Yamamoto**   (family name)
9. **kîree**   pretty; clean
   zańnèñ   regrettable, too bad, a pity
10. **Tookyoo**   Tokyo
  +**Kyôoto**   Kyoto
   X zya arímasèñ desita *or*
   X zya nâkatta (desu) (SP1)   it wasn't X

1. Hereafter 'Mr/s.' will be used as an abbreviation for these four alternatives.

MISCELLANEOUS NOTES (MN)

As in Lesson 1, the CC of this section are brief exchanges between individuals who maintain a certain amount of distance when communicating with each other.

   1. In CC1, a Japanese graduate student (J) brings some mail to a foreign student (N) who has recently joined the seminar group.
Nâñ desu ka⤸, depending on context, is equivalent to 'What is it?' (i.e., identification of an object) or 'What is it (you want)?' or 'What is it (you said)?'
   2, 3, 5, 8. **-Sañ** is a polite suffix which can be attached to a family name, a given name, or a family name + given name. It may refer to a male or a female, married or unmarried. It is a suffix of respect, and accordingly *is never added to one's own name,* or to the name of a member of one's in-group when speaking to the out-group (cf. CC3[J]).
   2. In CC2, (N) informs his Japanese colleague (J) of a telephone call.
Deñwa may refer to a telephone call or the instrument. **Odêñwa** is a polite alternate that refers to a call having a connection with someone to whom the speaker is being polite.
   3. In CC3, (N) arrives for an interview with Mr. Suzuki, whom she has not previously met.
   4. In CC4, (N) checks on the condition of the computer with his Japanese colleague (J).
Daízyòobu desu rarely occurs in a negative pattern in statements.
   5. In CC5, (J) identifies the person who just passed through the office for his foreign colleague (N). Both **a** and **âa** occur as indications of mild surprise. The longer alternate is more reflective.
   6. In CC6, two colleagues commiserate over a report that has come in.
   7. In CC7, a foreigner (N) checks on the language her colleague is reading. Usually the name of a country + **-ḡo** = the language of that country. **Eeḡo** is the exception to this pattern among the languages included in this lesson. The Japanese study **kokuḡo** in school, but foreigners study **nihoñḡo.**
   8. In CC8, (N) checks with his Japanese colleague (J) on the identity of a familiar-looking figure up ahead on the street. Note the negative question, implying that the speaker basically assumes an affirmative, but is checking on the possibility that the negative may indeed be true (cf. 1A-SP3,[2] question type [2]).
   9. The videotape setting of this conversation is the examination of the formal photograph of a prospective bride for an arranged marriage.
Zañnèñ desu does not normally occur in the negative in statements or as an affirmative question.
   10. In CC10, (J) checks with (N) on a phone call (N) just completed.

Structural Patterns (SP)

1. /NOMINAL + dèsu/

In Lesson 1, verbals (**-màsu/-màsita** words) and adjectivals (**-i/-katta** words) were introduced. We now add a new word-class, the NOMINAL. Using **X** to represent a nominal, the distal-style nominal sentence chart, corresponding to the verbal and adjectival charts of Lesson 1, looks like this:

---

   2. This is the abbreviation for Lesson 1, Section A, Structural Pattern 3. This type of abbreviation will regularly be used. The absence of a lesson reference means that the note occurs in the current lesson section.

	Distal-style	
	Affirmative	Negative
Imperfective	**X dèsu** 'it is and/or will be X (or described in terms of X)'	**X zya**[3] **arímasèñ** *or* **X zya nâi desu** 'it isn't and/or won't be X (or described in terms of X)'
Perfective	**X dèsita** 'it was X (or described in terms of X)'	**X zya arímasèñ desita** *or* **X zya nâkatta desu** 'it wasn't X (or described in terms of X)'

Comparing this chart with the one it most closely resembles—i.e., the adjectival chart—the following important differences should be noted:

1. While **X dèsu** and an adjectival pattern like **takâi desu** *seem* similar, the negative equivalents are very different: **X zya nâi desu** or **X zya arímasèñ** as compared with **tâkâku nâi desu** or **tâkâku arímasèñ**. The same difference shows up in the perfective negative forms.

2. In changing from the affirmative imperfective to perfective, **X dèsu** changes the **dèsu** to a perfective equivalent (to **dèsita**), while **takâi desu** changes **takâi** (to **tâkâkatta**).[4]

3. Both **takâi** and **takâi desu** have the exact same meaning: the only difference is stylistic, i.e., direct-style as opposed to distal-style. However, the difference between the nominal alone and /X + **dèsu**/ is, in most contexts, the difference between 'X' and 'it is or will be X' distal-style.[5]

Words that follow the 'X' pattern will be included in the word-class we call NOMINALS.[6]

Accent: (1) Following an unaccented nominal, **dèsu** and **dèsita** are accented on their first syllable, forming a single accent phrase with the nominal:

    teğámi dèsu

    deńwa dèsita

In the negative equivalent, there are two alternate accent patterns: one (consistently used in this text) results in a single accent phrase with the accent on the negative word:

    teğámi zya arimasèñ (**desita**) *or*

    teğámi zya nài (*or* **nàkatta**) **desu**;

in the alternate pattern, **zya** becomes **zyàa**, acquiring an accent and the resultant patterning:

3. **Zya** is a contraction of **dê wa**, about which more will be said in later lessons. In spoken Japanese, the contracted form is more common (compare *can't* and *don't* in spoken English).

4. Actually, there is a newer, alternate perfective adjectival pattern which parallels the nominal pattern (i.e., **takâi desita**), but this is still a less widely accepted form than **tâkâkatta desu** and will not be used in this text. Should you hear it, you will be able to understand it.

5. The corresponding direct-style equivalents of /nominal + **dèsu**/ and /nominal + **dèsita**/ will be introduced later.

6. This is not a definition of the nominal, in the strict sense, for some words classed as nominals never occur with **dèsu** or any of its forms. However, *provided they do so occur*, they follow the above chart. The nominal class includes all uninflected words (words that never take any endings like **-ku, -katta, -màsita,** etc.) which can occur alone as complete utterances (example: **tottemo**), regardless of whether or not they occur together with **dèsu.**

> teḡámi zyàa arímasèñ (desita)
>
> teḡámi zyàa nâi (*or* nâkatta) desu

with the pitch level of **zyàa** higher than that of the following high pitch.

And (2) following an accented nominal, **dèsu** and **dèsita** lose their accent:

> **damê desu**
>
> **odêñwa desita**

In the negative equivalents, the nominal and the negative word are both accented:

> **odêñwa zya arímasèñ** (desita)
>
> **odêñwa zya nâi** (*or* nâkatta) **desu**

The nominal is statistically the principal word-class in Japanese. Later we will have occasion to divide this enormous class into smaller subclasses, but first let us consider some of the characteristics of the class as a whole.

a. Except for those which have special polite forms (for example, **deñwa/odêñwa**), nominals have only one form. Most of those that designate countable items can refer to singular and plural without distinction. **Teḡami** may refer to 'letter' or 'letters,' depending on context.

b. While most English nouns have nominals as their closest equivalents in Japanese, many Japanese nominals correspond to other classes of English words. For example, **kîree** is a Japanese nominal, but its English equivalent is not a noun. In other words, the items we are calling nominals in Japanese represent a broader class than traditional English nouns, and it will be to our advantage not to try to equate Japanese and English. It is important to avoid the pitfall of analyzing Japanese in terms of English translations.

c. With few exceptions—which will be discussed later—words borrowed into Japanese from foreign languages become nominals in Japanese, regardless of what word-class they belonged to in the foreign language.

A sentence which consists of, or ends with, a /nominal + **dèsu**/ pattern (with or without following sentence-particles) will be called a NOMINAL SENTENCE. This is the third—and final—major sentence type; verbal and adjectival sentences were introduced in Lesson 1. As a cover term for verbal and adjectival and /nominal + **dèsu**/ patterns, wherever they occur within a sentence, we will hereafter use the term PREDICATE. When we learn longer and more complex sentences, we will find that predicates occur within a sentence as well as at the end.

Nominal sentences, like nominals alone and like verbal and adjectival sentences, may refer to animates or inanimates, singular or plural. Depending on context, they may refer to the speaker, the person(s) addressed, or a third party (animate or inanimate). The relationship between **dèsu** and **dèsita** in nominal sentences is just like the difference between **-màsu** and **-màsita** in verbal sentences; it is the difference between imperfective and perfective, between 'unfinished' and 'finished.' In terms of English equivalents, /nominal **X** + **dèsita**/ usually refers to the past, while /**X** + **dèsu**/ covers both the present which is unfinished and also the future. Both forms can refer to a single occurrence or multiple occurrences.

Dèsu and all of its derived forms—i.e., **dèsita** and others to be introduced later—form a separate word-class which is unique. On the basis of the definitions that have been established, **dèsu** cannot be a verbal, or an adjectival, or a nominal. It is purely and simply **dèsu**, a separate category which we will call the COPULA.

Look back now at the nominal sentences in the Core Conversations, and then examine the following additional examples. Each one actually has several possible English equivalents, depending on the context in which it occurs.

Speaking about the capital of Japan: **Toókyoo dèsu.** 'It's Tokyo.'

Speaking about Mr. Suzuki: **Kyôoto desu.** 'He is [from] Kyoto.' *or* 'He's [in] Kyoto.'

Speaking about a text: **Huráñsuǧo zya nài desu ka** 'Isn't it French?'

Speaking about a visitor who just left: **Suzúki-sañ dèsita.** 'It was Mr/s. Suzuki.'

Speaking about an exhibit: **Kîree zya arímasèñ desita.** 'It wasn't pretty.'

Speaking about tomorrow's lecture: **Nihóñǧo dèsu neŗ** 'It will be [in] Japanese, right?'

Speaking about where the person you are addressing has just been: **Kyôoto desu ka**
'Is it Kyoto [that you have returned from]?'

2. Sôo desu

Sôo desu, 'it's like that'; 'it's as you said,' with and without following sentence-particles, occurs very frequently in Japanese. Note carefully the differences among these examples:

Sôo desu. Response to a question.

Sôo desu yo. More emphatic response to a question, emphasizing that the response is informative; with /ー/ intonation offers emphatic reassurance.

Sôo desu nêe. (1) Exclamatory indication of shared knowledge and agreement; or (2) with slowed articulation, indication of deliberation and hesitation and delay in answering a question.

Sôo desu ne! A nonconfrontational reply, indicating actual or assumed agreement.

Sôo desu neŗ Request for confirmation (or denial) of an assumption.

Sôo desu ka. Indication that the speaker has just learned something new; with /ー/ intonation adds indication of surprise and/or doubt or actual questioning.

With these explanations in mind, check back to the Core Conversations, noting the various uses of /**sóo desu** (+ sentence-particle)/. Important signals are transmitted by these different combinations. For example, consider the following:

Damê desu yoー (I assume I'm giving new information)

Sôo desu ka. (New information has, in fact, been received) *or*

Sôo desu nêe. (Actually I am aware of the information)

Kîree desu nêe. (I assume your agreement with my exclamatory comment)

Sôo desu nêe. (Your assumption is correct) *or*

Sôo desu kaー (Actually new information has been received, with interest and/or surprise and/or doubt on my part)

Drills

(Remember visual aids—concrete or imagined!)

A 1. **Teǧámi dèsu kaー**   **Êe, teǧámi dèsu yoー**
   'Is it a letter?'   'Yes, it is (a letter) (I assure you).'

  2. **Sôo desu kaー**   **Êe, sôo desu yoー**
   'Is that so?'   'Yes, it is (so) (I assure you).'

3. **Tookyoo**; 4. **Suzuki-sañ**; 5. **damê**; 6. **daízyòobu**; 7. **kîree**; 8. **eeǧo**; 9. **asítà**

B 1. **Nihóñǧo dèsita neʃ**   **Êe, Nihóñǧo dèsita yo⌣**
    'It was Japanese—right?'   'Yes, it was (Japanese) (I assure you).'

  2. **Kyôoto desita neʃ**   **Êe, Kyôoto desita yo⌣**
    'It was Kyoto—right?'   'Yes, it was (Kyoto) (I assure you).'

  3. **kîree**; 4. **Tanaka-sañ**; 5. **damê**; 6. **deñwa**; 7. **daízyòobu**; 8. **hurañsuǧo**

C 1. **Yamámoto-sañ dèsu ka⌣**   **Êe, Yamámoto-sañ dèsu yo⌣**
    'Is it Mr/s. Yamamoto?'   'Yes, it is (Mr/s. Yamamoto) (I assure you).'

  2. **Ikímàsita ka⌣**   **Êe, ikímàsita yo⌣**
    'Did you go?'   'Yes, I did (go) (I assure you).'

  3. **omósiròi desu**; 4. **kaímàsu**; 5. **doítuǧo dèsu**; 6. **damê desita**; 7. **komárimàsu**;
    8. **tâkâkatta desu**

D 1. **Supéiñǧo dèsu ka⌣**   **Iie, supéiñǧo zya nài desu yo⌣**
    'Is it Spanish?'   'No, it isn't (Spanish) (I inform you).'

  2. **Suzúki-sañ dèsu ka⌣**   **Iie, Suzúki-sañ zya nài desu yo⌣**
    'Is it Mr/s. Suzuki?'   'No, it isn't (Mr/s. Suzuki) (I inform you).'

  3. **damê**; 4. **kîree**; 5. **Tookyoo**; 6. **teǧami**; 7. **deñwa**; 8. **eeǧo**

● Repeat this drill, replacing **nâi desu** with **arímasèñ** in the responses.

E 1. **Deñwa dèsita ka⌣**   **Iie, deñwa zya arimasèñ desita yo⌣**
    'Was it a phone call?'   'No, it wasn't (a phone call) (I inform you).'

  2. **Damê desita ka⌣**   **Iie, damê zya arímasèñ desita yo⌣**
    'Was it broken?'   'No, it wasn't (broken) (I inform you).'

  3. **kîree**; 4. **eeǧo**; 5. **Kyôoto**; 6. **Tanaka-sañ**; 7. **rosiaǧo**; 8. **teǧami**

● Repeat this drill, replacing **arímasèñ desita** with **nâkatta desu** in the responses.

F 1. **Kîree desu ka⌣**   **Iie, kîree zya arímasèñ yo⌣**
    'Is it pretty?'   'No, it isn't (pretty) (I inform you).'

  2. **Kaímàsita ka⌣**   **Iie, kaímasèñ desita yo⌣**
    'Did you buy [it]?'   'No, I didn't (buy) (I inform you).'

  3. **îi desu**; 4. **damê desita**; 5. **simâsu**; 6. **omósìròkatta desu**; 7. **deñwa dèsu**;
    8. **tâkâkatta desu**

G 1. **Kîree desu ne!**   **Sôo desu ne! Kîree desu ne!**
    'It's pretty, isn't it.'   'That's right. It is pretty, isn't it.'

  2. **Komárimàsu ne!**   **Sôo desu ne! Komárimàsu ne!**
    'It's worrisome, isn't it.'   'That's right. It is (worrisome), isn't it.'

  3. **takâi desu**; 4. **damê desu**; 5. **oókìi desu**; 6. **tumárànai desu**; 7. **îi desu**; 8. **tiǧáimàsu**

● In this drill, the exclamatory **nêe** may replace all occurrences of **ne!**

H 1. **Damê desu yo.**   **Âa, sôo desu ka. Damê desu ka.**
    'It's broken (I tell you).'   'Oh, it is? It's broken?'

  2. **Dekímasèñ yo.**   **Âa, sôo desu ka. Dekímasèñ ka.**
    'I can't do it (I tell you).'   'Oh, is that right? You can't do it?'

3. **wakárimasèñ desita**; 4. **hurûi desu**; 5. **daízyòobu desita**; 6. **tyuúgokugo dèsu**; 7. **tâkâku nâi desu**; 8. **komárimàsu**

Application Exercises

(Review again the purpose and recommended procedures for these exercises by looking back at the Application Exercises of Lesson 1, Section A.)

A. In the following exercises, practice /ka‿/ and /neʔ/ questions as well as utterances ending in /ne!/ and /nêe/, as appropriate.

1. Assemble actual objects or pictures of objects representing the nominals introduced in this section. Practice asking and answering appropriate questions in reference to these visual aids: find out what each thing is; whether or not it is X; how it is—whether it is broken or all right; whether or not it's pretty, expensive, new, etc.

2. Assemble written samples of the languages introduced in this lesson and practice identifying them (**Eégo dèsu ka‿**). Have members of the class say something in these foreign languages and then check on what languages were used (**Tyuúgokugo dèsita ka‿**).

3. Make up various comments, exclamations and questions in reference to individual visual aids. Elicit responses that use whatever /**sôo desu** (+ sentence-particle)/ pattern reflects the speaker's reaction.

B. Core Conversations: Substitution

Using appropriate props, go through the Core Conversations, substituting other familiar nominals in each conversational exchange, while retaining the exact original structure as far as possible.

SECTION B

Core Conversations (CC)

1(N)a. **Nâñ desu ka‿**
   b. **Soré dèsu.**

2(N) **Eéwa-zìteñ desu ka‿**

3(N) **Simáséñ ka‿**

4(N) **Âa, señsèe desita ka. Arîgatoo gozaimasu.**

5(J)a. **Sâtoo-sañ zya arímasèñ yo.**
   b. **Wakárimasèñ nêe.**

6(N)a. **Îkura desu ka‿**
   b. **Hoñtoo dèsu ka‿ Yasûi desu nêe.**

7(J)a. **Îkura desita ka‿**
   b. **Takâi desu nêe.**

(J)a. **Dôre desu ka‿**
   b. **Âa, koré dèsu ka. Zîsyo desu yo‿**

(J) **Aré dèsu ka‿ Iie, waée dèsu.**

(J) **Watási dèsu ka‿ Tyôtto . .**

(J) **A, wakárimàsita ka.**

(N) **Sôo desu ka. Zyâa, dâre desu ka‿**

(J)a. **Nihyákù-eñ desu.**

   b. **Sôo desu nêe.**

(N)a. **Yôñseñ-eñ dèsita.**
   b. **Sumímasèñ.**

ENGLISH EQUIVALENTS

1(N)a. What's that?
  b. (It's) that (thing near you).

(J)a. Which one (do you mean)?
  b. Oh, (do you mean) this? It's a dictionary.

2(N) Is that an English–Japanese dictionary?

(J) (Do you mean) that one over there? No, it's Japanese–English.

3(N) Won't you play?

4(N) Oh, was it you (teacher) (who performed some activity)? Thank you.

(J) (Do you mean) me? I'm afraid not.

(J) Oh, you know now (*lit.* it became clear)?

5(J)a. Say, that's not Mr/s. Sato.
  b. It's not clear, (is it)!

(N) Oh? Then who is it?

6(N)a. How much is it?
  b. Really? It's cheap, isn't it!

(J)a. It's ¥200.
  b. It is, isn't it.

7(J)a. How much was it?
  b. How expensive that is!

(N)a. It was ¥4000.
  b. I'm sorry.

BREAKDOWNS
(AND SUPPLEMENTARY VOCABULARY)

1. **dôre** (SP1)   which thing? (usually of three or more)
   sore   that thing (near you *or* just mentioned)
   kore   this thing
   zîsyo   dictionary
   +**hôn**   book
   +**zassi**   magazine
   +**siñbuñ**   newspaper
2. **eéwa-zìteñ**   English–Japanese dictionary
   are   that thing over there
   waee   Japanese–English
3. **watasi** *or*
   +**watakusi** (SP2)   I, me
   +**bôku**   I, me /primarily used by men/
4. **señsèe**   teacher, doctor
   +**gakusee**   student
   +**(o)tomodati**   friend
   +**anâta**   you
5. **Sâtoo**   (family name)
   zyâ(a)   well then, that being the case
   dâre   who?
   +**dônata**   who? /polite/

6. **îkura/oikura** how much?
   nihyákù-eñ (SP3) ¥200
   hoñtoo true; truth
7. **yoñseñ-eñ** ¥4000

Digits

itî	1	**rokû**	6
nî	2	**sitî** *or* **nâna**	7
sañ	3	**hatî**	8
sî *or* **yôñ**	4	**kû** *or* **kyûu**	9
gô	5	(**zyûu**	10)

Hundreds

hyakû	100	**roppyakù**	600
nihyákù	200	**nanâhyaku**	700
sâñbyaku	300	**happyakù**	800
yôñhyaku	400	**kyûuhyaku**	900
gohyákù	500		

nâñbyaku 'how many hundreds?'

Thousands

sêñ/isséñ	1000	**rokúsèñ**	6000
niseñ	2000	**nanásèñ**	7000
sańzèñ	3000	**hassèñ**	8000
yońseñ	4000	**kyuúsèñ**	9000
goseñ	5000		

nańzèñ 'how many thousands?'

Yen

iti-eñ	¥1	**roku-eñ**	¥6
ni-eñ	¥2	**nanâ-eñ**	¥7
sañ-eñ	¥3	**hati-eñ**	¥8
yô-eñ	¥4	**kyûu-eñ**	¥9
gô-eñ	¥5	**zyuu-eñ**	¥10

nâñ-eñ 'how many yen?'

hyaku-eñ	¥100	**señ-eñ**	¥1000
nihyákù-eñ	¥200	**niseñ-eñ**	¥2000
sańbyakù-eñ	¥300 (etc.)	**sañzeñ-eñ**	¥3000 (etc.)
nańbyakù-eñ	'how many hundreds of yen?'	**nañzeñ-eñ**	'how many thousands of yen?'

MISCELLANEOUS NOTES (MN)

Once again, the CC are brief exchanges between individuals who speak to each other with deference and care.

1. In CC1, the foreigner (N) is interested in the package his Japanese colleague (J) has brought into the restaurant.

1, 2. **Zîsyo** is a general term for a dictionary; but in compounds referring to various kinds of bilingual dictionaries, **-zìteñ** regularly occurs.

1, 2, 3. Note the style of the response in these three exchanges. In each case, it begins with a rhetorical verification check in question form, with no expectation of an answer: 'This? It's a dictionary'; 'That? No, it's Japanese–English.' 'Me? I'm afraid not.' This style of response is extremely common in Japanese.

2. In CC2, (N) asks her Japanese colleague to identify a particular dictionary.

3. In CC3, (N) invites the Japanese secretary to play **go.** She refuses politely, indicating some surprise at the invitation. The negative here indicates an invitation, and **tyôtto** a polite refusal.

4. The context of CC4 implies the realization of who previously performed a particular activity. On the accompanying video, the professor (J) had left a book for (N), and (N) has just been informed of this by a fellow student.

Otomodati, the polite alternate of **tomodati,** usually refers to friends of the addressee or of a third person (i.e., the out-group), as an indication of politeness to that person. It is ordinarily not used in reference to friends of the in-group ('my/our friends').

5. In CC5, two colleagues are trying to identify someone who just walked through the office. **Zyâ(a)** relates what follows to the current situation.

Dônata is a more polite equivalent of **dâre,** indicating politeness toward the person(s) to whom it refers.

Note the reflective use of the sentence particle **nêe**: 'It's not clear, is it [as I think about it].'

6. In CC6, a foreign student and his new Japanese acquaintance are looking at books in a bookstore.

Oikura, the polite alternate of **îkura**, indicates politeness toward the person addressed.

The Japanese counting system—including its accentuation—is extremely complex. It will be introduced gradually, in small, manageable chunks. In this lesson, we drill only hundreds and thousands, in combination with the monetary classifier **-eñ** 'yen.'

7. In CC7, (N) has just returned from a shopping errand for her professor (J). She apologizes for the high price she had to pay for the article she purchased.

Structural Patterns (SP)

1. **kore, sore, are, dôre**

> **kore** 'this thing near me'
>
> **sore** 'that thing nearer you,' or 'that thing within sight but slightly removed from speaker and person addressed,' or 'that thing just introduced into the conversation'
>
> **are** 'that thing over there' or 'that thing that you and I/we are both acquainted with' (i.e., an item of shared information)
>
> **dôre** 'which thing?' (usually of a group of at least three)

These words all belong to the nominal class. Like so many members of that class, they may refer to more than one item: 'these,' 'those,' 'which ones?' Insofar as this series is used in reference to people, it usually implies downgrading the in-group in deference to the out-group. This can present special difficulties for the foreigner and is probably best avoided by a beginning student.

2. *PERSONAL REFERENTS*

The first comment that must be made regarding words of personal reference is a warning against their overuse. Their English equivalents, 'I,' 'you,' 'she,' 'they,' etc., occur with much greater frequency. Remember that the English exchange 'Do *you* understand?' 'Yes, *I* do.' has as its most common Japanese equivalent **Wakárimàsu ka** **Êe, wakárimàsu.**, with no overt designation of 'you' or 'I.' This avoidance of designation of person *except in those situations where it has special focus* is a reflection of the Japanese de-emphasis of the individual, and the emphasis on the occurrence itself rather than the individuals involved (unless there is special focus).

But in those special situations which call for the use of personal referents, the speaker is required to choose from a large number of alternates, which differ in such features as politeness, rank, intimacy, and gender.

Consider first three ways of referring to oneself. **Watakusi** 'I' is a polite, formal nominal indicating that 'I' am viewing myself with deference to the addressee. The abbreviated **watasi** is slightly more casual. Both these words are used by men and women, in the appropriate situations. **Bôku**, on the other hand, is traditionally a masculine nominal, a less formal equivalent than **wata(ku)si** for males. However, it is now sometimes used by young girls and by some young women in specific situations not associated with traditional Japanese femininity. It is safe to assume that if the societal roles assumed by men and women become less differentiated, the language will follow the same trend, but **bôku** is still best avoided by foreigners who are female.

A special use of **bôku** is as a term of address (= 'you') for little boys. By the time Japanese children enter school, they have learned that it is only the boys who are expected typically to fill the role of **bôku**.

Parallel to the array of words for the self is a vast number of ways of specifying the addressee—the 'you'—when the situation calls for special focus. Again the criteria for selection relate to the relationship between the speaker and addressee and the amount of deference that is appropriate.

Anâta is a polite 'you' (singular), used in addressing an equal or a subordinate. It is to be carefully avoided in addressing superiors (including teachers) and persons to whom one owes special respect. Like **wata(ku)si** and **bôku**, **anâta** is used much less commonly in Japanese than corresponding words used in English. Surveys and questionnaires may address the anonymous reader as **anâta**, and wives may address their husbands as **anâta**, but its use in general conversation is restricted. Foreign students of Japanese, in particular, should bring to an end their long-standing history of overuse of this word!

A more polite addressee-referent is the person's /family name + **-sañ**/. Thus **Sâtoo-sañ** is equivalent both to 'Mr/s. Sato' (= 's/he') as well as 'you, Mr/s. Sato.' Teachers, doctors (medical and otherwise), lawyers, and persons due special respect are regularly addressed and referred to as **señsèe** or /family name + **-señsèe**/. This reflects the Japanese tendency to utilize roles in their personal reference system, both for address and third-person reference. You will find that kinship terms ('daughter'), professions ('book dealer'), and ranks ('section chief') are among the common designations for the 'you' and the 's/he' of a conversation, indicating again the importance of groups and one's position within them.

Like **-sañ**, **señsèe** is not used in reference to oneself or members of one's in-group when talking to the out-group.

3. COUNTING: DIGITS, HUNDREDS, AND THOUSANDS; -eñ

Japanese use two sets of numerical nominals, one that is native in origin and a second that was originally borrowed from the Chinese. It is this second series, the 'Chinese series,' that is a complete set in the modern language and is used for mathematical computation. We introduce this series in this lesson.

1. Digits: For those numerals listed with alternates, the first of each pair regularly occurs in mathematical counting and counting cadence. In other environments, the second alternates are more common, though not universal: the appropriate form—or, in some cases, forms—must be noted for each new combination.

2. Hundreds are counted in terms of multiples of **hyakû**. By itself, **hyakû** means '100'; when affixed to a numeral from 2 to 9, multiples of 100 are the result. Note the following:

> (1) After **sañ-** '3' and **nañ-** 'how many?', the initial **h** of **hyakû** is changed to **b**.
>
> (2) The combinations /**rokû** + **hyakû**/ and /**hatî** + **hyakû**/ result in changes both to the basic **hyakû** form (to **-pyaku**) and the numerals (from **rokû** to **rop-** and **hatî** to **hap-**).

3. Thousands are counted as multiples of **sêñ**. By itself, as well as in combination with **itî** (in the changed form **is-**), **sêñ** means '1000'; when affixed to a numeral from 2 to 9, multiples of 1000 are the result. Note the following:

> (1) After **sañ-** '3' and **nañ-** 'how many?', the initial **s** of **sêñ** is changed to **z**.
>
> (2) The combinations /**itî** + **sêñ**/ and /**hatî** + **sêñ**/ result in changes to the numerals (from **itî** to **is-** and **hatî** to **has-**).
>
> (3) When a numeral consists of, or begins with, 1000 (as in 1200, 1600, etc.) the **sêñ** alternate is more common. **Iś-sèñ** is the more common alternate when 1000 is not initial in the total numeral (as in 21,000, 111,000, etc., to be introduced later).

4. Classifiers and numbers: The principal use of the basic numerical nominals listed above is in mathematical computation. For counting, Japanese employs a classifier system.

In English, we usually use direct counting: '2 books,' '3 pencils,' '4 friends,' etc. But for some items, we use a classifier system: in contrast with '2 cows' and '2 bulls,' we speak of '4 head of cattle' rather than '4 cattle'; we can have 2 'pieces' or 'slices' or 'loaves' of bread, but ordinarily not '2 breads.' It is this kind of classifier system rather than direct counting that is regularly used in Japanese.

Classifiers combine with numerals to form compound nominals which are used in the counting and/or naming of numbered items. We will adopt the convention of calling these /numeral + classifier/ compounds NUMBERS.

5. -eñ: The classifier **-eñ** is used to count money according to the Japanese monetary unit, the yen. Since the value of the yen in terms of foreign currency changes from day to day, only a check with the international monetary exchange can provide the current figure.

-Eñ combines with the Chinese series of numerals, but '4 yen' is unpredictably **yô-eñ**; '9 yen' is **kyûu-eñ**. **Nanâ-eñ** has currently replaced **siti-eñ** in everyday usage.

Drills

A 1. **Aré dèsu ka⁄**
'Is it that one over there?'

Iya, aré zya nài desu.
'No, it isn't (that one over there).'

2. **Anâta desu ka**↗[7]
   'Is it you?'

   Iya, watá(ku)si zya nài desu *or* **Iya, bôku /M/ zya nâi desu.**
   'No, it isn't (me).'

3. **Seńsèe desu ka**↗
   'Is it the teacher?' *or*
   'Are you a teacher?' *or*
   'Is it you, Doctor/Teacher?'

   Iya, seńsèe zya nâi desu.
   'No, it isn't the teacher.'
   'No, I'm not (a teacher).'
   Iya, watá(ku)si zya nài desu *or* **Iya, bôku /M/ zya nâi desu.**
   'No, it isn't (me).'

4. **Sâtoo-sañ**; 5. **hoñtoo**; 6. **tomodati**; 7. **siñbuñ**; 8. **zîsyo**; 9. **eéwa-zìteñ**; 10. **zassi**; 11. **gakusee**; 12. **hôñ**; 13. **nihyákù-eñ**; 14. **yoñseñ-eñ**

● Repeat this drill, replacing **nâi desu** in the responses with **arímasèñ.**

B 1. **Zîsyo desu ka**↗
   'Is it a dictionary?'

   Koré dèsu ka↗ **Êe, zîsyo desu yo**↗
   '[Do you mean] this? Yes, it is (a dictionary) (I assure you).'

2. **Kaímàsu ka**↗
   'Are you going to buy [it]?'

   Koré dèsu ka↗ **Êe, kaímàsu yo**↗
   '[Do you mean] this? Yes, I am (going to buy) (I assure you).'

3. **atárasìi desu**; 4. **waée-zìteñ desu**; 5. **komárimàsu**; 6. **zaśsi dèsu**; 7. **nomímàsu**; 8. **damê desu**; 9. **omósìròkatta desu**

C 1. **Zîsyo desu ka**↗
   'Is it a dictionary?'

   Aré dèsu ka↗ **Iya, zîsyo zya nâi desu yo**↗
   '[Do you mean] that over there? No, it isn't (a dictionary) (I inform you).'

2. **Dekímàsu ka**↗
   'Can you do [it]?'

   Aré dèsu ka↗ **Iya, dekímasèñ yo**↗
   '[Do you mean] that over there? No, I can't (do) (I inform you).'

3. **supéiñḡo dèsu**; 4. **atárasìi desu**; 5. **teḡámi dèsu**; 6. **simâsita**; 7. **tâkâkatta desu**; 8. **eéwa-zìteñ desu**; 9. **wakárimàsu**

● Repeat this drill, replacing **nâi desu** in the responses with **arímasèñ**, and **nâkatta desu** with **arímasèñ desita.**

D 1. **Takâi desu ka**↗
   'Is it expensive?'

   Soré dèsu ka↗ **Iie, yasûi desu yo**↗
   '[Do you mean] that (near you)? No, it's cheap (I inform you).'

2. **Damê desu ka**↗
   'Is it not working?'

   Soré dèsu ka↗ **Iie, daízyòobu desu yo**↗
   '[Do you mean] that (near you)? No, it's OK (I inform you).'

3. **atárasìi desu**; 4. **tumárànai desu**; 5. **hurûi desu**; 6. **omósiròi desu**

---

7. See SP2 for the persons who can appropriately be addressed in this way.

E 1. **Wakárimàsu ka⟋** **Watá(ku)si** (*or* **bôku** /M/) **dèsu ka⟋ Êe,**
'Do you understand?' **wakárimàsu.**
'[Do you mean] me? Yes, I do (understand).'

2. **Tabémàsita ka⟋** **Watá(ku)si** (*or* **bôku** /M/) **désu ka⟋ Êe,**
'Did you eat [it]?' **tabémàsita.**
'[Do you mean] me? Yes, I did (eat).'

3. **komárimàsita**; 4. **kaímàsu**; 5. **simâsu**; 6. **tukúrimàsita**; 7. **nomímàsu**; 8. **dekímàsita**

F 1. **Kyûu desu ka⟋**[8] **Tiǵáimàsu. Zyûu desu.**
'Is it 9?' 'That's wrong. It's 10.'

2. **Kyûu-eñ desu ka⟋** **Tiǵáimàsu. Zyuú-eñ dèsu.**
'Is it ¥9?' 'That's wrong. It's ¥10.'

3. **itî**; 4. **hatî**; 5. **sañ-eñ**; 6. **nanâ-eñ**; 7. **yôñ**; 8. **ni-eñ**; 9. **rokû**; 10. **sañ**; 11. **sitî**; 12. **hatî-eñ**

G 1. **Hyakú-eñ dèsu.** **Hyakú-eñ dèsu ka. Yasûi desu nêe.**
'It's ¥100.' 'It's ¥100? That's cheap, isn't it!'

2. **Gohyákù-eñ desu.** **Gohyákù-eñ desu ka. Yasûi desu nêe.**
'It's ¥500.' 'It's ¥500? That's cheap, isn't it!'

3. **nihyákù-eñ**; 4. **kyuúhyakù-eñ**; 5. **yoñhyakù-eñ**; 6. **nanáhyakù-eñ**; 7. **roppyakù-eñ**;
8. **happyakù-eñ**; 9. **sañbyakù-eñ**

H 1. **Señ-eñ dèsu.** **Señ-eñ dèsu ka. Takâi desu nêe.**
'It's ¥1000.' 'It's ¥1000? That's expensive, isn't it!'

2. **Goséñ-eñ dèsu.** **Goséñ-eñ dèsu ka. Takâi desu nêe.**
'It's ¥5000.' 'It's ¥5000? That's expensive, isn't it!'

3. **kyuuseñ-eñ**; 4. **niseñ-eñ**; 5. **nanaseñ-eñ**; 6. **yoñseñ-eñ**; 7. **rokuseñ-eñ**; 8. **hasseñ-eñ**; 9. **sañzeñ-eñ**

I 1. **Gohyákù-eñ desu ka⟋** **Iie, tiǵáimàsu. Yoñhyakù-eñ desu yo⟋**
'Is it ¥500?' 'No, that's wrong. It's ¥400 (I inform you).'

2. **Goséñ-eñ dèsu ka⟋** **Iie, tiǵáimàsu. Yoñseñ-eñ dèsu yo⟋**
'Is it ¥5000?' 'No, that's wrong. It's ¥4000 (I inform you).'

3. **nihyákù-eñ**; 4. **nanaseñ-eñ**; 5. **kyuúhyakù-eñ**; 6. **yoñseñ-eñ**; 7. **nanáhyakù-eñ**; 8. **kyuuseñ-eñ**; 9. **yoñhyakù-eñ**; 10. **niseñ-eñ**

J 1. **Yoñhyakù-eñ desu ka⟋** **Iie, gohyákù-eñ desu.**
'Is it ¥400?' 'No, it's ¥500.'

2. **Yoñseñ-eñ dèsu ka⟋** **Iie, goséñ-eñ dèsu.**
'Is it ¥4000?' 'No, it's ¥5000.'

---

8. Situation: The answer to a mathematics problem is being checked.

3. **haṕpyakù-eñ**; 4. **rokuseñ-eñ**; 5. **hyaku-eñ**; 6. **hasseñ-eñ**; 7. **gohyákù-eñ**; 8. **niseñ-eñ**; 9. **roṕpyakù-eñ**; 10. **señ-eñ**

K 1. **Niséñ-eñ dèsita neʕ**   **Ie, nihyákù-eñ desita yo╱**
'It was ¥2000—right?'   'No, it was ¥200 (I inform you).'

2. **Sáñ-byakù-eñ desita neʕ**   **Ie, sańzeñ-eñ dèsita yo╱**
'It was ¥300—right?'   'No, it was ¥3000 (I inform you).'

3. **rokuseñ-eñ**; 4. **kyuúhyakù-eñ**; 5. **yoñseñ-eñ**; 6. **nanaseñ-en**; 7. **haṕpyakù-eñ**; 8. **hyaku-eñ**; 9. **goseñ-eñ**

Application Exercises

A. In the following exercises, again practice /ka╱/ and /neʕ/ questions as well as utterances ending in /ne!/ and /nêe/, as appropriate.

1. Assemble actual objects or pictures of objects representing the nominals introduced in this section and previous sections. Where appropriate, put objects into paper bags (or conceal them in any appropriate way) so that questioning about their identity makes sense. Practice asking and answering questions about the identity and quality of each object, incorporating /**nâñ, dôre, kore, sore, are** + **dèsu ka**/ questions and pointing when appropriate. Examples:

a. **Sińbuñ dèsu ka╱ . . . Koré dèsu ka╱ Êe,** $\left\{\begin{array}{l}\textbf{sińbuñ dèsu} \\ \textbf{sôo desu}\end{array}\right\}$ **(yo).**

b. **Takâi desu ka╱ . . . Soré dèsu ka╱ Iya, yasûi desu (yo).**

c. **Nâñ desu ka╱ . . . Dôre desu ka╱ . . . Aré dèsu. . . . A, aré dèsu ka╱ Hôñ desu (yo).**

2. Using appropriate objects and/or pictures, practice verbal questions, incorporating /**wata(ku)si** (*or* **bôku**) + **desu ka**╱/ in responses. Examples:
In reference to a sport: **Simâsu ka╱ . . . Watási dèsu ka╱ Êe, yôku simâsu yo╱**
In reference to wine: **Nomímàsu ka╱ . . . Bôku desu ka╱ Iya, amári nomimasèñ.**
In reference to a place: **Ikímàsita ka╱ . . . Watákusi dèsu ka╱ Êe, kinóo ikimâsita.**

3. Assemble pictures of people—famous personalities and pictures of Japanese labeled with familiar names (**Suzuki-sañ, Sâtoo-señsee,** etc.). Practice questions relating to identification: **Dâre** (*or* **Dônata**) **desu ka╱**; (name) **dèsu ka╱** (*or* **neʕ**). Also practice identifying members of your group, using similar patterns. Be careful not to use **-sañ** or **-señsèe** in reference to yourself!

4. Assemble appropriate objects and attach yen price tags. Discuss prices, using the following patterns and pointing, as needed:
a. **Îkura desu ka╱ . . . ¥1000 dèsu.**
b. **¥500 desu ka╱ . . . Iie, ¥400 desu (yo).**
c. **Îkura desu ka╱ . . . Dôre desu ka╱ . . . Soré dèsu. . . . Âa, hôñ desu ka╱ ¥500 desu.**

B. Core Conversations: Substitution

Using appropriate props, go through the Core Conversations, substituting other familiar items in each conversational exchange, while retaining the exact original structure as far as possible.

SECTION C

Eavesdropping

(Using the same procedure as in Lesson 1, answer the following questions (in English) on the basis of the recorded material. In each exchange, A refers to the first speaker, and B to the second.)

  1. When is the meeting?
  2. Why does B apologize?
 3a. What is A concerned about?
  b. What is B's condition?
  4. What is the price?
 5a. Who does A think B may be?
  b. Who *is* B?
 6a. Why does A call B?
  b. What does A suspect?
 7a. The price of what is being discussed?
  b. How much does A think it was?
  c. What was the actual price?
  d. What is A's reaction?
  8. Why is A disappointed?
 9a. What is being discussed?
  b. How was it?
  c. What is A's reaction?
10a. Who assumed incorrectly that the visitor was Mr/s. Sato?
  b. Who *was* it?
 11. Who came?
 12. Why does B apologize?
13a. What did B apparently buy?
  b. How was the price?
14a. Who was the visitor?
  b. What is A's assumption? What about B?
15a. What is being discussed?
  b. What language is it written in?

Utilization

(Using the same procedures as in Lesson 1, give appropriate Japanese for the following situations, as well as an appropriate reply [or stimulus].)

  1. There's something lying on the table. Ask what it is.

  2. A colleague has just returned from an art exhibit. Find out if it was pretty.

  3. A lecture you were looking forward to has just been canceled. Express your disappointment, expecting agreement.

  4. At a party, you just caught sight of someone you think you recognize. Ask a colleague if that isn't Dr. Sato.

  5. A colleague has just taken a phone call. Ask if it was Kyoto.

6. A colleague is reading a book in a language unfamiliar to you. Ask if it is Russian.
7. A colleague has just returned from a trip. Ask how it was.
8. You've been asked to identify an object on your desk. Find out which one is meant.
9. You're examining a dictionary in a book store. Ask the price.
10. A colleague was seen talking with a visitor who looked familiar. Check on whether that wasn't Mr. Suzuki.
11. A colleague is about to use the computer. Warn him that it isn't working.
12. You've been asked about something on your desk. After checking that the object close to you is what is to be identified, explain that it is a letter.
13. A colleague is concerned about whether the computer is working. Reassure him that it is fine.
14. A colleague has bought a new dictionary. Ask if it is Japanese–English.
15. You noticed a stranger in the office earlier. Find out who it was.
16. In a bookstore, confirm that the book you are looking at is ¥3000.
17. You've heard that a colleague bought a dictionary for ¥8000. Check on that price and exclaim on how expensive it was.
18. There is a new part-time worker in the office. Find out if she is a student.
19. A meeting has been scheduled and you've been asked if you're going. Check on the fact that *you* are being asked and say that you are not going (i.e., 'Me? I'm not going.').
20. You've just heard something surprising. Ask if it is (really) true.

Check-up

1. To what word-class are words assigned that can occur before **dèsu** in the affirmative and **zya arímasèñ** in the negative? (A-SP1)
2. What is a nominal sentence? (A-SP1)
3. Contrast (1) the perfective equivalents; (2) the negative equivalents; and (3) the negative, perfective equivalents of **damê desu** and **takâi desu.** (A-SP1)
4. What is meant by a *predicate*? (A-SP1)
5. What do we call **dèsu** and all its forms? Why do we not include it in the verbal class? (A-SP1)
6. Contrast the difference between **takâi** and **takâi desu** with the difference between **damê** and **damê desu.** (A-SP1)
7. Describe under what circumstances the following are used: **Sôo desu.; Sôo desu ka.; Sôo desu ka⁁; Sôo desu nêe.** (with regular and slowed articulation); **Sôo desu ne!; Sôo desu neʃ** (A-SP2)
8. To which word-class do **kore, sore, are,** and **dôre** belong? How are the first three distinguished in meaning? (B-SP1)
9. What general warning is given regarding the expression of personal reference in Japanese? what special warnings, in reference to **anâta** and **seńsèe**? (B-SP2)
10. Give two forms of address that are more polite than **anâta.** (B-SP2)
11. Contrast **watakusi, watasi** and **bôku.** To which word-class do they belong? (B-SP2)
12. How are hundreds counted in Japanese? What is special about the equivalents for 100, 300, 600, and 800? (B-SP3)
13. How are thousands counted in Japanese? What is special about the equivalents for 1000, 3000, and 8000? (B-SP3)
14. To what grammatical category does **-eñ** 'yen' belong? How is the term 'number' being defined for Japanese? (B-SP3)
15. Give the Japanese equivalent for ¥4; ¥7, ¥9. (B-SP3)

Lesson 3

SECTION A

Core Conversations (CC)

1(J)a. **Onégai-simàsu.** (N)a. **Anó tèepu desu ka↙**
   b. **Êe.** b. **Hâi, dôozo.**

2(J) **Kaímàsu ka↙** (N) **Konó zìsyo desu ka↙ Êe.**

3(N) **Tukáimàsita ka↙** (J) **Sonó koñpyùutaa desu ka↙ Êe, otótoi tukaimàsita.**

4(J)a. **Kâataa-sañ. Tabémasèñ ka↙** (N)a. **Nâñ desu ka↙**
   b. **Kono kêeki desu yo.** b. **Iya, îi desu yo.**
   c. **Dôozo dôozo.** c. **Sôo desu ka↙ Zya.**

5(N)a. **Kaímàsu ka↙** (J)a. **Êe.**
   b. **Dôno taípuràitaa desu ka↙** b. **Koré dèsu.**
   c. **Nâñ-bañ desu ka↙** c. **Sâñzyuu go-báñ dèsu.**

6(N)a. **Rokúsèñ happyaku nîzyuu nanâ- eñ desu.** (J)a. **Rokúsèñ happyaku zyuúnanà-eñ desita ka↙**

   b. **Iya, rokúsèñ happyaku nîzyuu nanâ-eñ desu.** b. **Âa, dôo mo.**

ENGLISH EQUIVALENTS

1(J)a. May I have [that]? (N)a. [Do you mean] that tape over there?
   b. Yes. b. Here you are.

2(J) Are you going to buy [it]? (N) [Do you mean] this dictionary? Yes.

3(N) Did you use [it]? (J) [Do you mean] that computer? Yes, I used [it] the day before yesterday.

4(J)a. Mr/s. Carter. Won't you have (*lit.* eat) [some]? (N)a. What is it?
   b. [It's] this cake. b. No, that's all right.
   c. Please have some! c. Oh? Well then . . .

5(N)a. Are you going to buy [one]? (J)a. Yes.
   b. Which typewriter is it? b. It's this one.

   c. What number is it?

6(N)a. It's ¥6827.

   b. No, it's ¥6827.

   c. It's #35.

(J)a. Was that [i.e., did you say] ¥6817?

   b. Oh, thanks.

BREAKDOWNS
(AND SUPPLEMENTARY VOCABULARY)

1. **onégai-sìmàsu** I make a request of you (polite)
   têepu (SP1) tape
   anó tèepu (SP2) that tape over there
2. **konó zìsyo** this dictionary
3. **tukáimàsu /-màsita/** use
   końpyùutaa computer
   sonó koñpyùutaa that computer (nearer you)
   otótòi the day before yesterday
4. **kêeki** cake
   konó kèeki this cake
   +**pâi** pie
   +**pûriñ** (custard) pudding
   +**aísukurìimu** ice cream
   +**koóhìi** coffee
   +**otya** tea
5. **taípuràitaa** typewriter
   +**waapuro** word processor
   dôno taípuràitaa which typewriter?
   nâñ-bañ what number?
   sâñzyuu ʹgo-bañ (SP3) #35
6. **nîzyuu nanâ-eñ** ¥27
   +**nîzyuu naná-dòru** $27
   +**nîzyuu naná-sèñto** 27¢

zyûu	10	nîzyuu	20	sâñzyuu	30
zyuúitì	11	nîzyuu itî	21	sâñzyuu itî	31
zyuúnì	12	nîzyuu nî	22	sâñzyuu nî	32
zyûusañ	13	nîzyuu ʹsañ	23	sâñzyuu ʹsañ	33
zyuúsì	14	nîzyuu sî	24	sâñzyuu sî	34
zyûugo	15	nîzyuu gô	25	sâñzyuu gô	35
zyuúrokù	16	nîzyuu rokû	26	sâñzyuu rokû	36
zyuúsitì	17	nîzyuu sitî	27	sâñzyuu sitî	37
zyuúhatì	18	nîzyuu hatî	28	sâñzyuu hatî	38
zyûuku	19	nîzyuu kû	29	sâñzyuu kû	39

yôñzyuu	40	rokúzyùu	60	hatízyùu	80
yôñzyuu itî	41	rokúzyuu itì	61	hatízyuu itì	81
yôñzyuu nî	42	rokúzyuu nì	62	hatízyuu nì	82
yôñzyuu 'sañ	43	rokuzyuu sañ	63	hatízyuu 'sañ	83
yôñzyuu sî	44	rokúzyuu sì	64	hatízyuu sì	84
yôñzyuu gô	45	rokúzyuu gò	65	hatízyuu gò	85
yôñzyuu rokû	46	rokúzyuu rokù	66	hatízyuu rokù	86
yôñzyuu sitî	47	rokúzyuu sitì	67	hatízyuu sitì	87
yôñzyuu hatî	48	rokúzyuu hatì	68	hatízyuu hatì	88
yôñzyuu kû	49	rokúzyuu kù	69	hatízyuu kù	89
gozyûu	50	nanâzyuu	70	kyûuzyuu	90
gozyúu itì	51	nanâzyuu itì	71	kyûuzyuu itî	91
gozyúu nì	52	nanâzyuu nî	72	kyûuzyuu nî	92
gozyuu sañ	53	nanâzyuu 'sañ	73	kyûuzyuu 'sañ	93
gozyúu sì	54	nanâzyuu sî	74	kyûuzyuu sî	94
gozyúu gò	55	nanâzyuu gô	75	kyûuzyuu gô	95
gozyúu rokù	56	nanâzyuu rokû	76	kyûuzyuu rokû	96
gozyúu sitì	57	nanâzyuu sitî	77	kyûuzyuu sitî	97
gozyúu hatì	58	nanâzyuu hatî	78	kyûuzyuu hatî	98
gozyúu kù	59	nanâzyuu kû	79	kyûuzyuu kû	99

Classifier for naming numbers in a series

itî-bañ	#1
nî-bañ	#2
sañ-bañ	#3
yôñ-bañ	(etc.)
go-bañ	
rokû-bañ	
nanâ-bañ	
hatî-bañ	
kyûu-bañ	
zyûu-bañ	
nâñ-bañ	'what number?'

Classifier for counting dollars

itî-doru	one dollar
nî-doru	two dollars
sâñ-doru	three dollars
yôñ-doru	(etc.)
gô-doru	
rokû-doru	
nanâ-doru	
hatî-doru	
kyûu-doru	
zyûu-doru	
nâñ-doru	'how many dollars?'

Classifier for counting cents

iś-señto	one cent
ni-sêñto	two cents
sań-sèñto	three cents
yoń-sèñto	(etc.)
go-sêñto	

rokú-sèñto

naná-sèñto

haś-sèñto

kyuú-sèñto

ziś-sèñto/zyuś-sèñto

nań-sèñto   'how many cents?'

MISCELLANEOUS NOTES (MN)

All the CC in this section are again conversational exchanges between people who maintain a certain distance in their communication. Most of their utterances are major sentences, with predicates in the distal-style.

1. In CC1, (J) needs some tape, but has his hands full at the moment. **Onégai-simàsu** is a polite verbal form which is deferential to the person addressed: 'I (humbly) make a request of you.' It is used only to refer to one's own requests or those of one's in-group.

2. In CC2, (N) is looking at dictionaries in a bookstore.

3. In CC3, (N) and (J) are discussing computer use. Note the new time word, the nominal **otótòi**, occurring immediately before a verbal, indicating the *time when* something has happened. This parallels the use of **kyôo, kinôo,** and **asítà/asû** in Lesson 1. In this pattern, **otótòi, kinôo,** and **asítà** lose their accent.

4. In CC4, (J) offers (N) some refreshments. This conversation is an example of a very common Japanese procedure—the polite initial refusal of a polite offer, followed by acceptance after being further pressed. This phenomenon is of course not limited to Japan, but it seems to occur more routinely there than in many other societies.

Note the use of **îi desu (yo)** as a polite refusal: 'I'm fine as I am'—i.e., without accepting your offer; in other words, 'never mind.' Compare the frequent English use of 'I'm fine' or 'that's all right' as a refusal of an offer.

When substituting **koóhìi** and **otya** in this CC, **tabémasèñ ka** should of course be replaced by **nomímasèñ ka.**

5. In CC5, (N) and (J) are looking at typewriter advertisements.

6. In CC6, (N) reports on the money expended. The yen figure that occurs in this conversation—as well as the amounts in some of the drills that follow—is most likely the total of a financial statement.

Note the alternation between imperfective and perfective. The imperfective represents the continuing amount of the bill. The perfective question refers to the amount that was last cited.

Structural Patterns (SP)

1. LOANWORDS

Têepu is, of course, a word borrowed from English, pronounced according to Japanese phonological patterning. It may designate transparent tape as well as recording tape(s). Such borrowings are extremely common in current Japanese. With few exceptions, they become members of the nominal class in Japanese, and enter into structural patterns accordingly. Frequently they assume special meanings, different from their original English meanings: one must never assume understanding of a Japanese borrowing on the basis of the meaning of its origin.

Borrowings may enter into compounds that represent remarkable mixtures. For example, the **Supeiñ** and **Rosia** of the names for the languages of those countries were borrowed from English; the **Dôitu** of **doitugo** was borrowed from German; and the **-go** of all the language names came originally from Chinese!

The borrowings from English included in this lesson section undoubtedly are words that were borrowed into the culture along with the foreign items they represent. But Japanese has also borrowed many words which duplicate words already in the language. In such cases, the older word may gradually fall into disuse, or the overlapping terms may take on different connotations; but frequently both the old and the new continue as competing forms, representing tradition and innovation.

Remember that a loanword—regardless of its origin—is now Japanese, and both its Japanese pronunciation and its meaning must be mastered.

2. PRE-NOMINALS: **kono, sono, ano, dôno**

We now introduce another set of so-called '**ko-so-a-do** words.' The first set, introduced in Lesson 2B, was the nominal group **kore, sore, are, dôre.** This new group belongs to a different word class, the class called PRE-NOMINALS. As the name implies, its members occur before nominals—as modifiers (i.e., describers) of nominals. The same spatial and referential distinctions apply to all **ko-so-a-do** sets. Compare:

> **kore** 'this thing' *and*
>
> **konó zìsyo** 'this dictionary'
>
> **sore** 'that thing—nearer you'; 'that thing just mentioned' *and*
>
> **sonó koñpyùutaa** 'that computer—nearer you'; 'that computer just mentioned'
>
> **are** 'that thing over there'; 'that thing already familiar' *and*
>
> **anó tèepu** 'that tape over there'; 'that tape already familiar'

All of the above examples can also refer to plural number.

Kono, sono, and **ano** (all of which are unaccented) form a single accent phrase with a following nominal, unless there is a special focus on the nominal (cf. CC4[J]b). Thus:

> **konó kèeki** 'this cake' *but*
>
> **kono kêeki** 'this cáke'

A /pre-nominal + nominal/ sequence occurs in the same patterns as the nominal alone.

3. COUNTING TO 9999; CLASSIFIERS **-bañ, -doru, -señto**

In Lesson 2B, we learned digits, hundreds, and thousands. We now examine the 10–99 numerical combinations, based on **zyûu** '10,' listed with the Breakdowns of this section. Basically, whatever precedes **zyûu** in a compound tells how many tens, and any numerical item after it is to be added. Thus,

> **sâñzyuu** = '30' ('3 tens')
>
> **zyûusañ** = '13' ('10 + 3')
>
> **sâñzyuu ′sañ** = '33' ('3 tens plus 3')

Note also the following:

(1) '1 ten' is simply **zyûu**; compare **hyakû** = '1 hundred.'

(2) Whether the '4,' '7,' or '9' following **zyûu** is **sî** or **yôñ, sitî** or **nâna,** or **kû** or **kyûu** depends on the classifier that follows the combination. For example, when the classifier **-eñ** follows, **yo-** (special!) and **nana-** and **kyuu-** are more common. But in those situations where numerical items occur without a following classifier, **sî, sitî,** and **kû** are more usual.

(3) The accent of a numeral in combination with a classifier may differ from that of the numeral when it occurs alone. The accent of the combination depends on the accent class to which the classifier belongs—and there are many different classes!

When counting involves a combination of thousands, hundreds, tens, and digits, the corresponding items occur in that order without connectives. Study the following examples:

gô '5'

nîzyuu kû '29'

sâñbyaku yôñzyuu itî '341'

hássèñ roppyaku nanâzyuu nî '8672'

happyaku sañ '803'

sáñzèñ rokû '3006'

yoñsèñ hatízyùu '4080'

sêñ hyaku zyuúitì '1111'

The classifier **-bañ** combines with the Chinese series of numerals (cf. the Breakdowns in this section for a listing from 1 to 10) to name members of a numbered series: '#1,' '#2,' '#3,' etc.

The classifiers **-doru** and **-señto** are used to count dollars and cents (cf. the Breakdowns). Note that:

(1) **itî, hatî,** and **zyûu** occur in altered form before **-señto,** i.e., **is-, has-,** and **zis-** or **zyus-;**

(2) Unlike **-señ, -señto** does not itself occur in any altered form (compare **sáñzèñ** '3000' and **sáñ-sèñto** '3¢');

(3) in citing a number consisting of dollars and cents, the two items following each other directly: **zyûu-doru zyuś-sèñto** '$10.10.'

Drills

(Concentrate on pronunciation, fluency, and meaning, always keeping a context in mind! Think about appropriate situations rather than concentrating on English *words* that 'translate'! Always work with tapes! Don't move on to a later drill until you have mastered the one before it!)

A 1. **Sonó tèepu desu ka⤹**   **Êe, konó tèepu desu.**
 '[Do you mean] that tape (near you)?' 'Yes, it's this tape.'

 2. **Sonó koñpyùutaa desu ka⤹** **Êe, konó koñpyùutaa desu.**
 '[Do you mean] that computer (near 'Yes, it's this computer.'
 you)?'

 3. **taípuràitaa**; 4. **otya**; 5. **zîsyo**; 6. **koóhìi**; 7. **siñbuñ**; 8. **hôn**

● Repeat this drill, replacing **sono** with **kono** and vice versa.

B 1. **Dôno têepu desu ka⌐ Koré dèsu**
    ka⌐
    'Which tape do you mean? Is it this
    one?'

    Tiḡáimàsu. Anó tèepu desu yo.
    'No. It's that tape over there!'[1]

  2. **Dôno taípuràitaa desu ka⌐ Koré**
    dèsu ka⌐
    'Which typewriter do you mean? Is it
    this one?'

    Tiḡáimàsu. Anó taipuràitaa desu yo.
    'No. It's that typewriter over there!'

  3. **waapuro**; 4. **kêeki**; 5. **pâi**; 6. **aísukurìimu**; 7. **koóhìi**; 8. **otya**; 9. **siñbuñ**; 10. **zassi**

• Repeat this drill, replacing **ano** in the responses with **kono**, indicating an object near the respondent.

C 1. **Tukáimàsu ka⌐**
    'Do you use it?'

    Sonó koñpyùutaa desu ka⌐ Êe,
    tukáimàsu yo⌐
    'Do you mean that computer? Yes, I do
    (use)!'

  2. **Damê desu ka⌐**
    'It it out of order?'

    Sonó koñpyùutaa desu ka⌐ Êe, damê
    desu yo⌐
    'Do you mean that computer? Yes, it's out
    of order.'

  3. **atárasìi desu**; 4. **îi desu**; 5. **hurûi desu**; 6. **kaímàsu**; 7. **takâi desu**

D 1. **Kinóo tukaimàsita neʃ**
    'You used it yesterday—right?'

    Soré dèsu ka⌐ Iie, otótoi tukaimàsita
    yo⌐
    'Do you mean that? No, I used it the day
    before yesterday.'

  2. **Asíta simàsu neʃ**
    'You're going to do it tomorrow—
    right?'

    Soré dèsu ka⌐ Iie, kyôo simâsu yo⌐
    'Do you mean that? No, I'm going to do it
    today.'

  3. **kyôo tukúrimàsita**; 4. **kinóo kimàsita**; 5. **asû ikímàsu**; 6. **kyôo kaímàsita**

(The following drills are number drills. The ability to handle numbers in a foreign language takes a great deal of practice. As you work on these drills with the tapes, try to retain the Japanese words in your own short-term memory and associate them with numerical symbols without translating them into English words.)

E 1. **Sâñbyaku gozyûu-eñ desu ne!**
    'It's ¥350, isn't it.'

    Sôo desu ne! Sâñbyaku gozyûu-eñ desu
    ne!
    'That's right, isn't it. It's ¥350, isn't it!'

  2. **Nanâzyuu gô-eñ desu ne!**
    'It's ¥75, isn't it!'

    Sôo desu ne! Nanâzyuu gô-eñ desu ne!
    'That's right, isn't it. It's ¥75, isn't it!'

  3. **roppyaku hatízyuu hatì-eñ**; 4. **hyaku yôñzyuu yô-eñ**; 5. **yôñhyaku kyûuzyuu rokû-eñ**; 6. **sañzeñ roppyakù-eñ**; 7. **rokúsèñ nihyaku kyûu-eñ**; 8. **haśseñ gozyúu nanà-eñ**; 9. **goséñ nihyaku rokúzyuu sàñ-eñ**; 10. **séñ happyaku sañzyùu-eñ**

---

1. It is assumed that you are by now sufficiently familiar with the connotation of sentence-particle **yo** to make glosses like 'I inform you,' 'I assure you,' etc., no longer necessary.

F 1. **Nî-bañ desu ka**   Iie, saṅ-bañ dèsu yo
    'Is it #2?'   'No, it's #3.'

  2. **Zyuúsàñ-bañ desu ka**   Iie, zyuúyòñ-bañ desu yo
     'Is it #13?'   'No, it's #14.'

  3. zyuúnanà-bañ; 4. yôñzyuu 'go-bañ; 5. kyûuzyuu kyûu-bañ; 6. sâñbyaku nîzyuu yôñ-bañ; 7. roppyaku hatízyuu itì-bañ; 8. yôñhyaku rokúzyuu rokù-bañ; 9. **sêñ** nihyaku sâñzyuu yôñ-bañ; 10. rokúsêñ gohyaku nanâzyuu hatî-bañ

● Repeat this drill (as a check on the total of a bill) using (1) **-doru** in place of **-bañ**, and (2) **-eñ** in place of **-bañ.**

G 1. **Itî-doru gozyús-sèñto desu ka**   Sôo desu. Itî-doru gozyús-sèñto desu.
    'Is it $1.50?'   'That's right. It's $1.50.'

  2. **Nîzyuu gô-doru, nanâzyuu go-sêñto**   Sôo desu. Nîzyuu gô-doru, nanâzyuu go-
     desu ka   sêñto desu.
     'Is it $25.75?'   'That's right. It's $25.75.'

  3. sâñbyaku hatízyuu nì-doru, yôñzyuu haś-sèñto; 4. nanâhyaku yôñzyuu rokû-doru, sâñzyuu saṅ-sèñto; 5. sêñ roppyaku hatízyuu nanà-doru, zyuś-sèñto; 6. saṅzèñ nanâhyaku gozyûu-doru, gozyús-sèñto

H 1. **Rokúzyùu-doru desu ka**   **Rokúzyuu rokù-doru zya nâi desu ka**
    'Is it $60?'   'Isn't it $66?'

  2. **Sañbyakù-bañ desu ka**   **Sâñbyaku saṅzyùu-bañ zya nâi desu ka**
     'Is it #300?'   'Isn't it #330?'

  3. **Haśseñ-eñ dèsu ka**   **Haśsèñ happyakù-eñ zya nâi desu ka**
     'Is it ¥8000?'   'Isn't it ¥8800?'

  4. hatízyus-sèñto; 5. roppyakù-doru; 6. kyuuseñ-bañ; 7. sañzeñ-eñ

I 1. **Sâñbyaku nîzyuu rokû-bañ desu**   Iie, sâñbyaku rokúzyuu nì-bañ desu yo
    ka   'No, it's #362.'
     'Is it #326?'

  2. **Roppyaku gozyúu itì-eñ desu ka**   Iie, roppyaku zyuúgò-eñ desu yo
     'Is it ¥651?'   'No, it's ¥615.'

  3. hyaku yôñzyuu hatî-bañ; 4. happyaku kyûuzyuu nî-eñ; 5. nanâhyaku sâñzyuu yôñ-bañ; 6. kyûuhyaku nanâzyuu sâñ-doru

J 1. **Nisêñ gohyaku yôñzyuu go-báñ**   Iie, nisêñ yôñhyaku gozyúu go-bañ
    dèsita ka   dèsita yo
     'Was it #2545?'   'No, it was #2455.'

  2. **Kyuúsèñ happyaku nanâzyuu rokû-**   Iie, kyuúsèñ nanâhyaku hatízyuu rokù-
     doru desita ka   doru desita yo
     'Was it $9876?'   'No, it was $9786.'

  3. sêñ sâñbyaku rokúzyuu hatì-eñ; 4. nanásêñ nihyaku zyuúrokù-bañ; 5. yoṅsêñ gohyaku kyûuzyuu rokû-doru; 6. nisêñ nihyaku sâñzyuu hatî-bañ

For additional practice aimed at developing proficiency with numbers, make up drills similar to those above.

Application Exercises

(Refer to the Application Exercises of Lesson 1 for recommended procedures.)

A1. Practice asking and answering questions regarding price in yen and in dollars and cents (not exceeding 9999!), labeling familiar objects appropriately. Use /ka‿/, /neʕ/, and /ne!/ stimuli, and a variety of structural patterns:

    a. Îkura desu ka‿ . . . -eñ (-doru, -señto) desu.

    b. -eñ (-doru, -señto) desu ka‿ . . . ('Yes' and 'no' answers as appropriate)

    c. -eñ (-doru, -señto) desu neʕ . . . ——— zya nâi desu ka‿

2. Expand the exchanges above by beginning each response with a rhetorical verification check on the topic of discussion: Koré (soré, aré) dèsu ka‿ or Konó (sonó, anó) X dèsu ka‿

3. In response to verbal questions, answer including the day (tomorrow, today, yesterday, or the day before yesterday) pointed out on the calendar by a member of the group. Use other visual aids as appropriate. Examples:

    a. (pointing to a movie ad and a calendar date)

       Ikímàsu neʕ . . . Êe, asíta ikimàsu.

    b. (pointing to drills and a calendar date)

       Kinóo simàsita ka‿ . . . Iie, asíta simàsu yo‿

    c. (pointing to a computer and a calendar date)

       Tukáimàsita ka‿ . . . Êe, otótoi tukaimàsita.

4. In response to onéḡai-simàsu accompanied by vague pointing to a group of similar objects, check on which one is meant. Example:

    a. Onéḡai-simàsu. . . .

       Dôno kêeki desu ka‿ . . .

         (pointing specifically) Sonó kèeki desu.

Contrast this with:

    b. Onéḡai-simàsu. . . .

       Dôre desu ka‿ . . .

       Kêeki desu.

after arranging the visual aids and pointing appropriately.

B. Core Conversations: Substitution

  Using appropriate props, review the Core Conversations, substituting other appropriate, familiar items in each conversational exchange while retaining the original structure as far as possible.

SECTION B

Core Conversations (CC)

1(N)a. **Muzúkasii nihoñḡo dèsu nêe.**   (J)   **Sôo desu ka‿**
    b. **Êe. Zeñzeñ wakarimasèñ.**

2(N)a. **Atárasìi zîsyo desu ne!**
   b. **Îkura desita ka╱**
   c. **Hêe╱ Takâi zîsyo desu nêe.**
3(N)a. **Onéḡai-simàsu.**
   b. **Êe, zêñbu desu.**
4(N)a. **Îtu desu ka╱**
   b. **Êe.**
5(N)a. **Kaímàsu ka╱**

   b. **Takâi desu ka╱**
   c. **Yáppàri takâi desu nêe.**
6(N) **Îkura desu ka╱**

(J)a. **Êe. Kinóo kaimàsita.**
   b. **Sáñmañ-eñ dèsita.**

(J) **Sore to soré dèsu neʕ**

(J)a. **Kâiḡi desu ka╱**
   b. **Asítà to asâtte desu.**
(J)a. **Atárasìi no desu ka╱ Kaímasèñ yo╱**
   b. **Êe. Hotôñdo hatímañ-eñ dèsu yo.**

(J) **Oókìi no desu ka╱ Haśsèñ gohyákumàñ desu.**

ENGLISH EQUIVALENTS

1(N)a. What difficult Japanese!
   b. Yes. I don't understand it at all.
2(N)a. That's a new dictionary, isn't it.
   b. How much was it?
   c. Wow! What an expensive dictionary!
3(N)a. I'd like [those].
   b. Yes, I mean all of them.
4(N)a. When is it?
   b. Yes.

5(N)a. Are you going to buy [one]?

   b. Is it expensive?
   c. Then it certainly is expensive, isn't it!
6(N) How much is it?

(J) Oh?

(J)a. Yes. I bought it yesterday.
   b. It was ¥30,000.

(J) You mean that and that—right?

(J)a. Do you mean the conference?
   b. It's tomorrow and the day after (tomorrow).
(J)a. Do you mean a new one? No (*lit.* I'm not going to buy).
   b. Yes. It's almost ¥80,000.

(J) Do you mean the big one? It's 85,000,000.

BREAKDOWNS
(AND SUPPLEMENTARY VOCABULARY)

1. **muzukasii /-katta/**   is difficult
  muzukasii nihoñḡo (SP1)   Japanese that's difficult, difficult Japanese
 + **yasasii /-katta/**   is easy
  zeñzeñ /+ negative/   (not) at all
2. **atárasìi zîsyo**   dictionary that's new, new dictionary
  sáñmàñ (SP2)   30,000 (3 ten thousands)

sañmañ-eñ	¥30,000
hêe✓	(exclamation of surprise)
takâi zîsyo	dictionary that's expensive, expensive dictionary

3. **sore to sore** (SP3) — that and that
   zêñbu — all; the whole thing
4. **îtu** — when?
   kâiḡi — conference, meeting
   asâtte — day after tomorrow
5. **atárasìi no** (SP4) — one(s) that is/are new, new one(s)
   hotôñdo — almost, nearly, all but
   hatimañ-eñ — ¥80,000
   yáppàri — after all [is said and done]
6. **oókìi no** — one(s) that is/are big, big one(s)
   gohyákumàñ — 5,000,000
   haśsèñ gohyákumàñ — 85,000,000

Ten-thousands

itímàñ	10,000	**rokúmàñ**	60,000
nimâñ	20,000	**nanámàñ**	70,000
sańmàñ	30,000	**hatímàñ**	80,000
yońmàñ	40,000	**kyuúmàñ**	90,000
gomâñ	50,000	**zyuúmàñ**	100,000

nańmàñ 'how many ten-thousands?'

MISCELLANEOUS NOTES (MN)

Again, these CC are conversations between people who address each other using careful speech. Their utterances are major sentences, with predicates in the distal-style.

1. In CC1, (N) is struggling with a Japanese text.
Zeñzeñ regularly links up with negative predicates, intensifying the negative meaning: 'not at all.' It also occurs with some affirmative patterns that have a basically negative connotation: **Zeñzeñ damè desu.** 'It's no good at all.'; **Zeñzeñ tiḡaimàsu.** 'It's completely wrong *or* different.' Like **tot(t)emo** and **a(ñ)mari**, **zeñzeñ** qualifies a predicate in terms of manner or degree.

2. In CC2, (N) and (J) discuss the purchase of a dictionary. This is a conversation between colleagues who are discussing an item which would ordinarily have a fixed price. In this kind of situation, it would not be out of the ordinary or rude to inquire about price.
Hêe✓ is an exclamation indicating great surprise.

3. In CC3, (N) talks to a shopkeeper as he makes a purchase.

4. In CC4, coworkers (N) and (J) discuss an upcoming conference.

5. In CC5, coworkers (N) and (J) look over advertisements relating to a possible purchase.
Yáppàri (emphatic form of **yahâri**) indicates that what follows is an occurrence or state that represents a final outcome: 'after all'—it turned out like this; 'in the end'—there was

this development; 'after all is said and done'—this is the way things are. **Yáppàri** and **hotôñdo** 'almost,' like **zeñzeñ, tot(t)emo** and **a(ñ)mari**, link up with predicates and indicate manner or degree.

6. In CC6, coworkers (N) and (J) discuss the price of a condominium, for which they have an advertisement. Note the optional dropping of **-eñ** in citing a high price, parallel to the dropping of 'dollars' in comparable American-English contexts.

Structural Patterns (SP)

1. /ADJECTIVAL + NOMINAL/

In Japanese, a direct-style predicate may occur directly before a nominal as a description of that nominal. Our first examples of this pattern consist of: /adjectival in its **-i** form (= direct-style, imperfective, affirmative) + nominal/. Examples:

muzukasii nihoñḡo	'difficult Japanese' (*lit.* 'is-difficult Japanese')
atárasìi zîsyo	'a new dictionary' (*lit.* 'is-new dictionary')
hurûi siñbuñ	'an old newspaper' (*lit.* 'is-old newspaper')

The above phrases can, of course, represent English plurals.

An /adjectival + nominal/ phrase occurs in the same structural patterns as a nominal alone:

Oókìi hôñ desu.	'It's a big book.'
Yasûi kêeki desita.	'It was cheap cake.'
Omósiròi zassi zya nâi desu.	'It isn't an interesting magazine.'
Sono yasásii hòñ zya nâkatta desu.	'It wasn't that easy book.' (i.e., it wasn't that book which was 'being easy' at that time)

In this last example, the nominal **hôñ** has two preceding descriptive words: **sono** (a pre-nominal) and **yasasii** (an adjectival). A pre-nominal always occurs before the nominal it describes, but it does not necessarily *immediately* precede it. Note the contrast in accent between phrases like **konó hòñ** and **kono takâi hôñ**. Since **kono** describes **hôñ** and not **takâi**, it is not in the same accent phrase as **takâi**.

A combination like **atárasìi zîsyo desu** is still a distal-style nominal predicate (even though its nominal is itself described by a direct-style adjectival predicate); therefore its corresponding negative equivalent is

atárasìi zîsyo zya nâi desu *or*	
atárasìi zîsyo zya arímasèñ	*lit.* 'it is not an is-new dictionary'

However, in response to /adjectival + nominal + **dèsu ka**/ questions, the answer may be a negation of the adjectival quality alone:

Atáràsìku nâi desu. *or*	
Atáràsìku arímasèñ.	'It's not new.'

Thus:

Atárasìi kêeki desu ka⤸	'Is it fresh cake?'
Iie, atárasìi kêeki zya nâi desu. (*or* **arímasèñ.**) *or*	'No, it isn't fresh cake.'

Iie, atáràsìku nâi desu. (*or* **arímasèñ.**)	'No, it isn't fresh.'
Muzúkasii nihoñḡo dèsita ka	'Was it difficult Japanese?'
Iie, muzúkasii nihoñḡo zya nàkatta desu. (*or* **arimasèñ desita.**) *or*	'No, it wasn't difficult Japanese.'
Iie, muzúkasiku nàkatta desu. (*or* **arimasèñ desita.**)	'No, it wasn't difficult.'

2. *COUNTING TEN-THOUSANDS:* -mañ

Japanese numerical expressions of five places or more are grouped by ten-thousands (**-mañ**), in contrast with the English language system, which calculates on the basis of thousands. Thus, in reading the numeral 684237, the English speaker counts off by threes from the right (684,237), and reads in terms of thousands, hundreds, tens, and digits. The same number in Japanese is counted off by fours from the right (68,4237), and reads in terms of ten-thousands, thousands, hundreds, tens, and digits: **rokúzyuu hatimàñ, yoñséñ nihyaku sâñzyuu nâna** '68 ten thousands, 4 thousands, 2 hundreds, 3 tens, seven.'

In order to comprehend large numbers, it is important to remember that the occurrence of **-mañ** signals the fifth place from the right, i.e., four more places in the number. Thus:

yoñmàñ	4 + 4 places = '40,000'
nizyúumàñ	20 + 4 places = '200,000'
sañbyakumàñ	300 + 4 places = '3,000,000'
yoñseñmàñ	4000 + 4 places = '40,000,000'

For succeeding groups of four places in higher numbers, there are additional terms, but in this basic course, we will not drill beyond the ten millions.

3. *PHRASE-PARTICLE* to: sore to sore

In addition to sentence-particles, which occur only at the end of sentences, there are other classes of particles, which occur within sentences and connect what immediately precedes to a later part of the sentence. One such group is the class of PHRASE-PARTICLES, which connect a preceding nominal[2] to a following element. In this section, we introduce the phrase-particle **to** as a connector of the immediately preceding nominal to a following nominal: /nominal A + **to** + nominal B/ = 'B with A,' i.e., 'A and B.' Examples:

kore to sore	'this and that'
watasi to Suzuki-sañ	'Suzuki-san and I'
pâi to aísukurìimu	'pie and ice cream'
konó hòñ to ʼano siñbuñ	'this book and that newspaper'

Just as in English, there is sometimes a standard order for the paired nominals. For example, in English 'X and I' is usual; in Japanese, **watasi to X** is standard. But for most combinations, either order is possible.

An /**A to B**/ combination occurs within the same structural patterns as the second nominal alone.

☠ WARNING: Do not attempt to coordinate verbals or adjectivals by using particle **to**.

2. Other possibilities will be introduced later.

4. NOMINAL no

The nominal **no** 'one,' 'ones,' 'some quantity' replaces a more specific nominal when the context makes the referent clear. It is always preceded by a descriptive expression. Compare:

hurûi taípuràitaa *and*	'an old typewriter'
hurûi no	'an old one';
îi zîsyo *and*	'good dictionaries'
iì no	'good ones';
takâi aísukurìimu *and*	'expensive ice cream'
takâi no	'some that is expensive,' 'expensive "stuff"'

The **kono, sono, ano, dôno** series of pre-nominals may precede an /adjectival + **no**/, but not **no** alone. Examples:

kono yasásìi no	'this easy one'
dôno takâi no	'which expensive one?' *but*
sore	'that one' (NEVER **sono** + **no**!)

Before **no** as before **dèsu**, an unaccented adjectival acquires an accent (a fall in pitch) on the vowel preceding the final **-i.** Compare:

muzukasii nihoñḡo *and*
muzúkasìi desu
muzúkasìi no

Drills

A 1. **Muzúkasii nihoñḡo dèsu nêe.**　　**Sôo desu nêe. Muzúkasìi desu nêe.**
'It's difficult Japanese, isn't it!'　　'That's right, isn't it! It's difficult, isn't it!'

2. **Tumárànai kâiḡi desu nêe.**　　**Sôo desu nêe. Tumárànai desu nêe.**
'It's a dull conference, isn't it!'　　'That's right, isn't it. It's dull, isn't it!'

3. **oókìi taípuràitaa**; 4. **hurûi siñbuñ**; 5. **takâi aísukurìimu**; 6. **yasûi zîsyo**

B 1. **Omósiròi kâiḡi desita nêe.**　　**Êe, omósìròkatta desu nêe.**
'It was an interesting conference, wasn't it!'　　'Yes, it was interesting, wasn't it!'

2. **Muzúkasii eeḡo dèsita nêe.**　　**Êe, muzúkasìkatta desu nêe.**
'It was difficult English, wasn't it!'　　'Yes, it was difficult, wasn't it!'

3. **yasásii hòñ**; 4. **yasûi koóhìi**; 5. **hurûi kêeki**; 6. **tumárànai hôñ**; 7. **takâi zassi**

C 1. **Muzúkasii nihoñḡo zya nài desu ka**　　**Koré dèsu ka** **Muzúkasiku nài desu yo**
'Isn't it difficult Japanese?'　　'Do you mean this? It's not difficult.'

2. **Hurûi zîsyo zya nâi desu ka**　　**Koré dèsu ka** **Hûrûku nâi desu yo**
'Isn't it an old dictionary?'　　'Do you mean this? It's not old.'

3. **omósiròi zassi**; 4. **takâi waapuro**; 5. **îi eéwa-zìteñ**; 6. **atárasìi kêeki**; 7. **tumárànai hôñ**

D 1. **Saṅmaṅ-eṅ dèsu neʔ**　　　　　**Yoṅmaṅ-eṅ zya arimasèṅ ka**
'It's ¥30,000—right?'　　　　　　'Isn't it ¥40,000?'

2. **Zyuúmaṅ-eṅ dèsu neʔ**　　　　**Zyuúitimaṅ-eṅ zya arimasèṅ ka**
'It's ¥100,000—right?'　　　　　'Isn't it ¥110,000?'

3. **rokumaṅ-eṅ**; 4. **hatimaṅ-eṅ**; 5. **kyuumaṅ-eṅ**; 6. **itimaṅ-eṅ**

E 1. **Saṅmàṅ goséṅ-eṅ dèsita neʔ**　　　**Êe, saṅmàṅ goséṅ-eṅ dèsita.**
'It was ¥35,000—right?'　　　　　　'Yes, it was ¥35,000.'

2. **Itímàṅ nisêṅ saṅbyakù-eṅ desita**　　**Êe, itímàṅ nisêṅ saṅbyakù-eṅ desita.**
neʔ
'It was ¥12,300—right?'　　　　　　'Yes, it was ¥12,300.'

3. **yoṅmàṅ rokúsèṅ nanâhyaku gozyûu-eṅ**; 4. **rokúmàṅ haśsèṅ sâṅbyaku yôṅẑyuu**
rokû-eṅ; 5. **nanâzyuu ʹgomaṅ-eṅ**; 6. **hatízyuu nimàṅ, goseṅ-eṅ**; 7. **kyuúzyuumàṅ**
nanásèṅ gohyákù-eṅ; 8. **zyuúnimàṅ rokúsèṅ yôṅhyaku gozyûu-eṅ**; 9. **sâṅzyuu**
yoṅmàṅ, gosêṅ sâṅbyaku rokúzyuu nì-eṅ

F 1. **Kinóo ikimàsita neʔ**　　　　　**Kinôo to kyôo ikimasita.**
'You went yesterday, didn't you?'　'I went yesterday and today.'

2. **Kyôo tukúrimàsu neʔ**　　　　　**Kyôo to asíta tukurimàsu.**
'You're going to make [them] today,　'I'm going to make [them] today and
aren't you?'　　　　　　　　　　tomorrow.'

3. **otótoi tukaimàsita**; 4. **asíta kimàsu**; 5. **kinóo simàsita**; 6. **asíta dekimàsu**

G. (Situation: The questioner is asking about who has just arrived.)

1. **Tanáka-saṅ dèsu ka**　　　　　**Tanaka-saṅ to Suzúki-saṅ dèsu yo**
'Is it Mr/s. Tanaka?'　　　　　　'It's Mr/s. Tanaka and Mr/s. Suzuki!'

2. **Seṅsèe desu ka**　　　　　　**Seṅsèe to Suzúki-saṅ dèsu yo**
'Is it Teacher?'　　　　　　　　'It's Teacher and Mr/s. Suzuki.'

3. **gakusee**; 4. **Yamamoto-saṅ**; 5. **tomodati**; 6. **Sâtoo-saṅ**

H 1. **Atárasìi zîsyo desu neʔ**　　　**Koré dèsu ka Hurûi no zya nâi desu**
'It's a new dictionary, isn't it?'　**ka**
'This one? Isn't it an old one?'

2. **Yasásii hòṅ desu neʔ**　　　　**Koré dèsu ka Muzúkasìi no zya nâi**
'It's an easy book, isn't it?'　　**desu ka**
'This one? Isn't it a difficult one?'

3. **hurûi zassi**; 4. **takâi koóhìi**; 5. **omósiròi hôṅ**; 6. **atárasìi kêeki**; 7. **tumárànai hôṅ**

I 1. **Dekímàsu ka**　　　　　　　**Soré dèsu ka Iya, zeṅzeṅ dekimasèṅ.**
'Can you do it?'　　　　　　　　'Do you mean that? No, I can't do [it] at
all.'

2. **Nomímàsu ka**　　　　　　　**Soré dèsu ka Iya, zeṅzeṅ nomimasèṅ**
'Do you drink this?'　　　　　　'Do you mean that? No, I don't drink [it]
at all.'

3. **wakárimàsu**; 4. **simâsu**; 5. **tabémàsu**; 6. **tukáimàsu**; 7. **tukúrimàsu**; 8. **kaímàsu**

● Repeat this drill, replacing **zeñzeñ** in the responses with (1) **hotôñdo** 'almost (not)' (i.e., it scarcely happens); and (2) with **a(ñ)mari** '(not) very much.'

J (Situation: The responder doesn't hear exactly what the first speaker says, and therefore asks an appropriate question using **dônata, dâre, dôre, nâñ, îtu,** or **îkura**.)

1. **Tanáka-señsèe desu yo⌐**   **Dônata desu ka⌐**
   'It's Dr. Tanaka.'   'Who is it??'

2. **Waée-zìteñ desu yo⌐**   **Nâñ desu ka⌐**
   'It's a Japanese–English dictionary.'   'What is it??'

3. **Aré dèsu yo⌐**   **Dôre desu ka⌐**
   'It's that one over there.'   'Which one is it??'

4. **pûriñ**; 5. **asâtte**; 6. **otya**; 7. **gakusee**; 8. **asítà**; 9. **sañbyakù-eñ**; 10. **kore**; 11. **itimañ-doru**; 12. **tomodati**

Application Exercises

(By now you are familiar with the recommended procedures for this practice. Be sure to exploit everything you know, at the same time patiently postponing trying to say what you cannot yet handle.)

A. Following the procedures of the Application Exercises of Section A of this lesson:

1. For A 1–2, expand the numbers as high as the tens of millions. Real estate ads provide useful visual aids. Check on the current yen-dollar rate, and convert prices from dollars to yen and vice versa.

2. For A3, expand the days to include **asâtte**.

3. For A4, expand the identification questions and responses to include adjectivals and nominal **no**:

Speaker 1: **Onéḡai-simàsu.**   Speaker 2: **Dôre desu ka⌐** *or*
                                                  Dôno X desu ka⌐

    Sono (adjectival) **X** (*or* **no**) **dèsu.**

B. Core Conversations: Substitution

Using appropriate props, review the Core Conversations substituting other appropriate items in each conversational exchange while retaining the exact original structure as far as possible.

SECTION C

Eavesdropping

1. How much did the thing under discussion cost?
2. What is A asking for?
3. Who is being identified?
4a. How much was A's purchase?
b. When was it made?

   c. What is B's reaction?

5a. Who is being discussed?
  b. How is this person performing?

6a. What was A's reaction to the book?
  b. How did B react to it?

7a. What does A ask for?
  b. Why does B apologize?

8a. What is B buying?
  b. What is the total cost?

9a. What does A apparently want to do?
  b. Why has A been hesitating?
  c. What does A learn from B?

10a. What is A's concern?
  b. What is B's assessment?

11a. What did B acquire? When?
  b. What is B's assessment of it?

12a. What is under discussion?
  b. When is it?

13a. What is under discussion?
  b. Whose is it?
  c. When was it acquired?
  d. What does A think of it?

14a. What is A's problem?
  b. What is the apparent reason?
  c. What is B's reaction?

15a. Where is the item under discussion currently located in reference to A and B?
  b. What is A checking on?
  c. What has B recently done to the item?

Utilization

(Follow the recommended procedures. Remember to supply an appropriate answer [or stimulus] for each item.)

1. You've been asked to hand over a book. Find out which book is meant.

2. A colleague is studying French. Ask if it's difficult.

3. You're checking on prices and statement totals: confirm that something is: (1) ¥3500; (2) ¥6700; (3) ¥33,646; (4) ¥838,521; (5) $2,000,000; (6) $7.50.

4. A colleague is asking for a dictionary. Find out if he means the large one.

5. There's an unidentifiable package on the table. Find out if it's (1) cake; (2) tea; (3) ice cream; (4) pudding; (5) coffee; (6) pie; (7) magazines; (8) books; (9) tape

6. You've overheard some discussions about a meeting. Find out when it is.

7. You're making out a schedule for the computer. Ask a colleague if he will be using it the day after tomorrow.

8. You're checking on a colleague's extension number. Confirm that it is #647.

9. You've been offered something to drink. First, turn it down, and then, after being urged, accept.

10. An acquaintance is looking at a dictionary in a bookstore. Warn her that it's not a good dictionary.

11. A colleague is looking for some newspapers. Ask him if he means these old ones that are near you.

12. You're struggling with some Japanese writing. Exclaim (expecting agreement) on what difficult Japanese it is.

13. You've been asked about Japanese. Exclaim (expecting agreement) that it isn't easy.

14. You've been asked about your ability in German. Explain that (1) you don't understand it at all; (2) you don't understand it very well; (3) you scarcely understand it at all.

15. You've just heard something very surprising. Respond appropriately and ask if it's really true.

16. You've been asked to identify a group of people. Explain that they are teachers and students.

17. You've been asked when a certain event took place. Explain that it was yesterday and the day before.

18. People are wondering what is going on in the next room. Ask if it isn't a conference.

19. A colleague seems to be looking for an additional part of a computer printout. Ask if (that) isn't the whole thing.

20. You've just heard the price of the new computer. Exclaim (expecting agreement) that after all is said and done, it is indeed expensive.

Check-up

1. To what Japanese word-class do words borrowed from other languages, almost without exception, belong? (A-SP1)

2. When a word is borrowed from a foreign language into Japanese, in what two areas can one expect changes to occur? (A-SP1)

3. What is meant by **ko-so-a-do** groups? (A-SP2)

4. What is the essential difference between the **kore** group and the **kono** group? (i.e., to what word-class does each group belong?) (A-SP2)

5. How are dollars counted in Japanese? (A-SP3)

6. How are cents counted in Japanese? Read the following: 1¢; 3¢; 8¢; 10¢; $2.50. (A-SP3)

7. How is the classifier **-bañ** used? (A-SP3)

8. What two kinds of modifiers of nominals have been introduced? (A-SP2), (B-SP1)

9. What sentence type does **Takâi zîsyo desu** represent? What is its exact negative equivalent? Is the sentence direct- or distal-style? Is **takâi** (1) affirmative or negative? (2) imperfective or perfective? (3) direct or distal? (B-SP1)

10. What is the major difference between a Japanese number of 10,000 and higher, as compared with English? What is the Japanese equivalent of 10,000? 100,000? 1,000,000? 10,000,000? (B-SP2)

11. What is the difference between a sentence-particle and a phrase-particle? Give an example of each. (B-SP3)

12. What is the meaning of /nominal A + **to** + nominal B/? What warning was given relating to the use of **to**? (B-SP3)

13. What does the nominal **no** mean? How is it used? (B-SP4)

14. In which of the following phrases is it impossible to replace the nominal with **no**? **ii hôñ; ano oókìi zîsyo; kono hurûi pûriñ; dôno siñbuñ; takâi koñpyùutaa; sono eéwa-zìteñ.** (B-SP4)

Lesson 4

SECTION A

Core Conversations (CC)

1(N)a. **Sore, nâñ desu ka⌇**
    b. **Hurosiki?**
2(J)a. **Tênisu simâsu ka⌇**
    b. **Gôruhu wa?**
3(N)a. **Kyôo wa dâre desu ka⌇**
    b. **Tanáka-sañ dèsu ka. Zyâa, asítà wa?**
4(N)a. **Eéwa-zìteñ arímàsu ka⌇**

    b. **A, kono oókìi no desu neʔ**
    c. **Sôo desu ka. . . . Zyâa, koré o kudasài.**
5(N)a. **Tyôtto sumímasèñ. Sono kurôi kâsa, mîsete kudasai.**
    b. **Êe. . . . Tyôtto ôókìku nâi desu ka⌇**

    c. **Sôo desu nêe. . . . Zyâa, koré oneĝai-simàsu.**

(J)a. **Koré dèsu ka⌇ Hurósiki dèsu yo.**
    b. **Êe. Totémo bèñri desu yo⌇**
(N)a. **Ie, tênisu wa simásèñ nêe.**
    b. **Gôruhu wa yôku simâsu yo⌇**
(J)a. **Tanáka-sañ ĝa kimàsu yo⌇**

    b. **Asítà wa Yamámoto-sañ dèsu.**
(J)a. **Eéwa-zìteñ desu ka⌇ Hâi, arímàsu yo⌇ . . . Atárasìi no ĝa arímàsu yo⌇**
    b. **Êe. Nakanaka îi zîsyo desu yo⌇**

    c. **Arîĝatoo gozaimasu.**

(J)a. **A. Âme desu ka⌇**

    b. **Zyâa, kono aôi no wa ikâĝa desu ka⌇**

    c. **Arîĝatoo gozaimasu.**

English Equivalents

1(N)a. What's that?
    b. A furoshiki?
2(J)a. Do you play tennis?

    b. How about golf?
3(N)a. Who is it today?

(J)a. This? It's a furoshiki.
    b. Yes. It's very convenient, you know!
(N)a. No, not tennis. (*lit.* tennis—[I] don't play.)
    b. Golf—I play often.
(J)a. Mr/s. Tanaka is coming.

b. Mr/s. Tanaka? Then how about tomorrow?

4(N)a. Are there [any] English–Japanese dictionaries?

b. Oh, it's this big one—right?

c. Oh? . . . Well, then I'll take (*lit.* give me) this.

5(N)a. Excuse me. Would you let me see (*lit.* please show me) that black umbrella?

b. Yes. . . . Isn't this a little big?

c. Hmmm. . . . Well, I'll take (*lit.* I request) this one.

b. Tomorrow it's Mr/s. Yamamoto.

(J)a. English–Japanese dictionaries? Yes. . . . There's a new one, you know.

b. Yes. That's quite a good dictionary.

c. Thank you.

(J)a. Oh, is it raining?

b. Then how about this blue one?

c. Thank you.

BREAKDOWNS
(AND SUPPLEMENTARY VOCABULARY)

1. **sore, nâñ desu ka** (SP1) — what is that thing?
   hurosiki — (cloth for wrapping)
   bêñri — convenient, handy, easy-to-use
   +**hûbeñ** — inconvenient
2. **tênisu** — tennis
   tênisu simasu (SP1) — play tennis
   tênisu wa simásèñ (SP2) — tennis (at least) [I] don't play
   gôruhu — golf
   +**nâni** — what?
3. **Tanáka-sañ ğa kimàsu** (SP3) — *Mr/s. Tanaka* will/does come
4. **arímàsu /-màsita/** (SP5) — exist (inanimately); have
   nakanaka — quite, considerably
   kudásài (SP6) — please give me/us
   koré o kudasài (SP4) — please give me/us *this one*
5. **kurôi /-katta/** — is black
   aôi /-katta/ — is blue; is green
   +**akai /-katta/** — is red
   +**kiiroi /-katta/** — is yellow
   +**sirôi /-katta/** — is white
   kâsa — umbrella
   misémàsu /-màsita/ — show
   mîsete kudasai (SP6) — please show me/us
   âme — rain
   +**yukî** — snow

tyôtto	a little, a bit
ikâḡa	how? /polite/

MISCELLANEOUS NOTES (MN)

The Core Conversations continue to provide examples of situations that call for the use of distal-style predicates in exchanges that are made up largely of major sentences.

1. In CC1, a foreigner (N) inquires about an object he has never seen before. A furoshiki is a square of material (occasionally plastic) used for wrapping packages and gifts. While it is increasingly being replaced by the shopping bag, it continues as the traditional method of wrapping in Japan.

Note that **bêñri** and **hûbeñ** are nominals: they refer to objects, locations, times of flights, etc.

2. In CC2, business colleagues (J) and (N) discuss participation in sports. Note the use of **nêe** at the end of a response to a question, indicating a reflective, nonconfrontational kind of answer.

Nâñ and **nâni** are alternate forms of the same word. Before **d-** and **n-** in the same accent phrase, the **nâñ** alternate occurs; before **t-** in the same accent phrase, either alternate may occur; elsewhere **nâni** occurs.

3. In CC3, business colleagues (N) and (J) discuss the participants in upcoming meetings.

4. CC4 is a typical shopping situation. (N) is interested in buying an English–Japanese dictionary, and the clerk (J) recommends a good one. Note the clerk's expression of thanks at the time of a sale, to which the customer does not reply.

Nakanaka links up with the adjectival **îi** and describes manner/degree: 'a dictionary that is quite good.' **Nakanaka** often includes the connotation 'more than expected.' In some of its occurrences, it describes a degree approaching that represented by English 'very.'

5. CC5 is another example of a shopping situation. The customer (N) has just come in out of the rain, a fact noted by the salesclerk (J).

Ikâḡa is a more polite equivalent of **dôo**. Both **ikâḡa desu ka** and **dôo desu ka** occur frequently as offers: 'How about——?'

The color words introduced here all have **-i** (imperfective) and **-katta** (perfective) forms and therefore are classified as adjectivals. There are many additional color words describing more precise shades; the adjectivals introduced in this section are the basic terms, which cover a wider range of the spectrum. Thus, broadly speaking, **aôi** may describe both blues and greens (sky, ocean, grass, and green traffic lights, for example), although there are other terms of more limited range. **Aôi** is also the color term used to describe the face of someone who has turned pale.

Structural Patterns (SP)

1. /NOMINAL + PREDICATE/

A predicate, you will remember, is a verbal expression, or an adjectival expression, or a /nominal + **dèsu**/ expression.

In previous lessons, we have encountered /nominal + predicate/ patterns of two kinds:

   (1) The nominal expresses the manner in which, or degree to which, the predicate occurs:

   Amári wakarimasèñ. 'I don't understand very much.'

Hotôñdo damê desu. 'It's almost no good at all.'

Tóttemo muzukasìi desu. 'It's very difficult.'

(2) The nominal expresses the time when the predicate occurs.

Asíta ikimàsu. 'I'm going tomorrow.'

Kinóo tukurimàsita. 'I made it yesterday.'

We now add two additional types of /nominal + predicate/ patterns:

(3) The nominal expresses *who* or *what* (a) performs the activity of the predicate or (b) is described by the condition of the predicate:

Tanáka-sañ kimàsu yo 'Mr/s. Tanaka is coming.'

Konó zìsyo, tiğáimàsu ne! 'This dictionary is different, isn't it!'

Sore, eéwa-zìteñ desu ka 'Is that (thing) an English–Japanese dictionary?'[1]

Kore, îi desu ka 'Is this all right?'

Sono nihoñğo, muzúkasìi desu ka 'Is that Japanese difficult?'

(4) The nominal expresses *who* or *what* is acted upon by an action predicate:

Pâi tabémasèñ ka 'Won't you have some pie?'

Koñpyùutaa tukáimàsita ka 'Did you use the computer?'

Hôñ kaímàsita. 'I bought a book.'

The comma intonation noted above, although very common, is not required.

The sentences in (3) and (4) are perhaps more easily understood if we consider more literal translations:

Sore, eéwa-zìteñ desu ka 'That thing—is it an English–Japanese dictionary?'

Koñpyùutaa tukáimàsita ka 'Computer—did using occur?'

Hôñ kaímàsita. 'Book(s)—buying occurred.'

Unlike (1) and (2) above, which occur in both the spoken and the written language, these new patterns, (3) and (4), belong typically to the spoken language. In the written language, the relationships of (3) and (4) are regularly indicated by particles following the nominals, as described in SP2, SP3, and SP4.[2]

2. PHRASE-PARTICLE **wa**

In addition to sentence-particles, which occur only at the end of sentences, there are PHRASE-PARTICLES, already introduced in connection with **to,** which occur within sentences and which relate the immediately preceding item[3] to something that occurs later in the sentence. The differences among 'I went *to* X/*from* X/*with* X/*by* X, etc.' are all expressed by means of phrase-particles in Japanese.

All particles are pronounced as part of the preceding word: normally there is no pause between a particle and what precedes it.

The particle **wa** following a nominal is a phrase-particle. It links the preceding nominal

1. Compare: **Sono eéwa-zìteñ desu ka** 'Is [it] that English–Japanese dictionary?' in which the pre-nominal **sono** is part of the /nominal + **desu**/ predicate.

2. The fact that certain particles are regularly retained in the written language leads some instructors to prefer to retain them in all classroom drills. It is important to note that the *constant* inclusion of these particles definitely does not reflect normal, unmonitored *conversation.*

3. Phrase-particles may also occur following words other than nominals; but in order to be classed as phrase-particles, they must follow nominals in at least some of their occurrences.

to a predicate occurring later in the sentence. (This contrasts with the phrase-particle **to**, which linked a preceding nominal to a following *nominal* [example: **kore to sore**].) The combination /nominal X + **wa**/ establishes X as a familiar, recognizable item regarding which something is about to be said. What follows applies specifically to X and to no more than X, as far as this particular utterance goes. Thus, **kore wa teḡami desu** explains that this, at least, is a letter: there may be other items which also are letters, but at the moment, the speaker is concerned only with **kore**, and **kore** is described as a **teḡami**.

The phrase-particle **wa** clearly establishes the preceding X as the limit of applicability: the speaker does not insist that X is exhaustive—the only item that in reality applies to this particular predicate—but rather that X is the speaker's only referent of the moment, the only item for which s/he takes current responsibility. For this reason we sometimes cite 'at least' or 'for one' or 'in contrast with others' as an English equivalent for **wa**. There may be other items equally applicable, but 'X at least' applies and is all that is being mentioned in this utterance. Some contexts may *imply* that indeed other items are not included, but this results from the context, not the particle. Consider the following example:

> **Suzuki-sañ wa, gakúsee dèsu.** 'Mr/s. Suzuki *is a student.*'

The speaker is not insisting on an exhaustive connection here between Suzuki and being a student, i.e., that *Suzuki* is necessarily the only one who fills the student category in the given context; the person under discussion is Suzuki, and s/he, *at least*, or s/he, *for one*, is a student. Note also the following parallel examples:

> **Kono nihoñḡo wa, muzúkasìi desu yo** 'This Japanese *is difficult.*'
>
> **Ano gakusee wa, zeñzeñ wakarimasèñ nêe.** 'That student *doesn't understand at all*, does s/he!'
>
> **Ano gakusee wa, tomódati dèsu.** 'That student *is a friend.*'
>
> **Ano tomodati wa, gakúsee dèsu.** 'That friend *is a student.*'

A word of warning: Don't attempt to equate **X wa** in Japanese with the grammatical subject in English. In some instances they do happen to correspond, but **X** may also correspond to an object, or a location, or a point in time, or a number of other grammatical relationships in English, as demonstrated in the examples below.

X wa identifies what item is under discussion; there is focus on what follows. Accordingly, a question word like **dâre** 'who?' **dôre** 'which one?' **nâñ/nâni** 'what?' etc., is *never* directly followed by **wa** under ordinary circumstances, since these items always indicate the unknown and unfamiliar and are usually concerned with exhaustive identification.

Often the element of limited applicability becomes strongly contrastive, corresponding in English to a change in intonation.[4] Example: **Aré wa teḡami dèsu.** 'That one is a letter' (in contrast with some other one, which is something else or unknown). In this kind of pattern, the **wa**-phrase usually has focus-intonation[5] even though there is also strong *meaning* focus on the following predicate.

Additional examples:

> **Tênisu wa simásèñ.** 'Tennis (at least) *I don't play*' (but I probably play other sports).
>
> **Zaśsi wa kaimàsita.** 'The magazine (at least) *I did buy*' (of the things you asked me to buy).

---

4. Compare English: 'This is good.' Intonation: ——➘ ('this' = neutral topic) and: 'This is good.' Intonation: ➚——➚ ('this' = contrasting topic).

5. See Introduction.

Watási wa dekimàsu. 'I (at least) *can do it*' (but I'm not sure about the others in the group).

Kyôo wa ikímàsu. 'Today (at least) *I am going*' (but I may not go every day).

The question now is the difference between members of pairs like:

Ano gakusee, yôku wakárimàsu yo *and*

Ano gakusee wa, yôku wakárimàsu yo

Pâi, tabémàsita. *and*

Pâi wa, tabémàsita.

Asíta tukaimàsu. *and*

Asítà wa, tukáimàsu.

The first example in each pair expresses the 'who,' 'what,' 'when' of the predicate. But the examples that include **wa** emphasize the fact that the speaker is commenting specifically about the **wa** item: in reference to that item, the speaker makes an explicit comment, but the question of whether or not other related items also apply is left open, often with the definite implication of contrast with them. With the particle **wa**, its preceding nominal becomes a member of a set and the other members are outside the range of the utterance.

Consider now the matter of negative answers to yes-no questions.

Tanaka-sañ, kimâsu ka 'Is Mr/s. Tanaka coming?'

  Iie, kimásèñ. 'No, s/he isn't (coming).' *or*

  Iie, Tanáka-sañ wa kimasèñ. 'No, Mr/s. Tanaka (at least) isn't coming' (but others may come).

Pâi, tabémàsu ka 'Are you going to have some pie?'

  Iie, tabémasèñ. 'No, I'm not (going to eat).' *or*

  Iie, pâi wa tabémasèñ. 'No, I'm not going to eat pie (at least)' (but I may eat other things).

Asíta kimàsu ka 'Are you coming tomorrow?'

  Iie, kimásèñ. 'No, I'm not (coming).' *or*

  Iie, asítà wa kimásèñ. 'No, tomorrow (at least) I'm not coming' (but I may come on other days).

Another related use of **wa** is in the combination /nominal X + **wa?**/ occurring as an utterance by itself, i.e., a fragment. This is used when a question, made clear by the context without being specifically stated, is to be applied to X. Thus, **X wa?** = 'What about X?' 'How about X?'—in reference to X, apply the question implied by the situation. This must not be confused with **X desu ka** 'Do you mean X?'

Now re-examine occurrences of **wa** in the Core Conversations and note how the particle is used.

3. PHRASE-PARTICLE ğa

/Nominal X + **ga** + Predicate Y/ = '<u>X</u> does *or* is Y.' It is <u>X</u> that is the doer of an action predicate or affected by a predicate that describes a condition.[6] Examples:

---

6. In many—but by no means all—occurrences, this relationship coincides with what is often termed a grammatical subject.

Tanáka-sañ ḡa simàsu.	'*Tanaka* does (*or* will do) it.'
Koóhìi ḡa îi desu.	'*Coffee* is (*or* will be) good.'
Koré ḡa koñpyùutaa desu.	'*This* is the computer.'

In this pattern, there is focus on X, which (1) often refers to a new item in the conversation—even one which may be unfamiliar to the person addressed—and (2) usually provides exhaustive information within the immediate context. Completely lacking is the notion that X is being compared or contrasted with other items, as in the case of **X wa.**

Compare the following sentences:

1. **Tanáka-sañ ḡa kimàsita.** '[It is] Mr/s. Tanaka [who] came.'
2. **Tanáka-sañ kimâsita.** *or* **Tanáka-sañ kimàsita.** 'Mr/s. Tanaka came.'
3. **Tanáka-sañ wa kimâsita.** *or* **Tanáka-sañ wa kimàsita.** 'Mr/s. Tanaka (at least) came.'

Sentence 1 emphasizes the fact that specifically *Tanaka* was the one who came: there was a 'Tanaka-coming.' Sentence 2 is a more neutral statement that states what Tanaka did (**Tanáka-sañ kimâsita**, with focus on the verbal), or who came (**Tanáka-sañ kimàsita**, with focus on the nominal). Sentence 3 explains what it is that Tanaka *at least* did; Tanaka is the only item for which the speaker is explicitly assuming responsibility, suggesting that there may be others who also came or that other members of a set to which Tanaka belongs perhaps didn't come.

A **wa**-phrase announces a known topic that is to be commented on, and it may reflect a variety of different relationships with the predicate(s) that follow(s), in a loose, disjoined way. A **ḡa**-phrase, on the other hand, has a very precise and close connection with its predicate. In discourse, a **wa**-phrase may extend its meaning over a number of sentences, whereas a **ḡa**-phrase regularly links up only with a predicate in the same sentence.

Consider now the related use—and parallel contrast—between **ḡa**- and **wa**-phrases occurring with negative predicates:

Tanáka-sañ ḡa kimaseñ yo.	'*Mr/s. Tanaka* isn't coming.' (*lit.* 'There will be no Tanaka-coming.') (Tells who isn't coming)
Tanáka-sañ wa kimaseñ yo.	'*Mr/s. Tanaka* (at least) *isn't coming.*' (Tells what Mr/s. Tanaka [at least] will not do.)

In answer to the question **Tanáka-sañ (ḡa) kimàsu ka**, the response **kimáseñ** is a simple, direct negation. However, if Tanaka is mentioned in the response—to be expected particularly if contrast is being emphasized—the particle is **wa**:

Tanáka-sañ ḡa kimàsu ka	'Is *Mr/s. Tanaka* coming?'
Ie, kimásèñ. *or*	'No, s/he isn't (coming).'
Ie, Tanáka-sañ wa kimasèñ.	'No, Mr/s. Tanaka (at least) *is not coming*' (but I'm not making any explicit statement about others who may or may not come).

The frequency of this latter kind of situation must not lead to the mistaken conclusion that one always uses "**ḡa** with the affirmative and **wa** with the negative." This error can only be described as a foreigner's wishful thinking. The actual situation is much more complex.

In replying to an information question that has as its focus a /question word + **ḡa**/, a particularly common reply is /nominal + **desu**/. Examples:

Dôre ḡa damê desu ka	'Which one is broken?'
Koré dèsu.	'(It's) this one.'
Dâre ḡa kimâsu ka	'Who is coming?'
Watási dèsu.	'(It's) me.'
Îtu ḡa îi desu ka	'When will be good?'
Asâtte desu.	'(It's) the day after tomorrow.'
Dâre ḡa simâsita ka	'Who did it?'
Yamámoto-sañ dèsu.	'(It's) Mr/s. Yamamoto.'

Compare now:

Dâre ḡa simâsu ka Tomódati dèsu ka	'Who will do it? Is it your friend?'
Êe, tomódati wa simàsu.	'Yes, my friend (at least) *will do it.*'

in which the introduction of a suggested answer within the second question converts the situation to one involving a yes-or-no answer, and the respondent answers in terms of that topic, without a direct, exhaustive answer to the original question with **ḡa** (which, of course, also occurs, as the direct answer).

Sequences like:

Dôre ḡa damê desu ka	'Which one is broken?'
Koré ḡa damè desu.	'This one is broken.'

although certainly not grammatically impossible, sound rather stiff and unnatural as representatives of actually occurring exchanges, as do the corresponding English equivalents. Note the more realistic format of the Core Conversations and of the Drills that follow.

Check back now to the Core Conversations and study the occurrences of /nominal + **ḡa**/. Note that **ḡa** might be deleted in these examples, but with a reduction of the emphasis and focus conveyed by its inclusion.

4. PHRASE-PARTICLE o

/Nominal X + **o** + activity predicate Y/ = 'activity Y of the predicate operates upon X.'[7] The use of **o** identifies X closely with its predicate and places emphasis and focus on what has been 'acted upon,' usually in an exhaustive sense—as the 'complete story'—within the immediate context. Compare

Tanáka-sañ ḡa tukaimàsita. *and*	'*Mr/s. Tanaka* used (it).'
Tanáka-sañ o tukaimàsita.	'(I) used *Mr/s. Tanaka*' (for a task, for example).

Not all verbals can occur with this kind of **ḡa/o** contrast. Of those you have learned so far, only these apply:

---

7. In many—but by no means all—occurrences, this relationship coincides with what is usually termed a direct object.

$$
\text{X ğa} \quad + \quad \left\{ \begin{array}{l} \textbf{simâsu} \text{ 'do'} \\ \textbf{tukúrimàsu} \text{ 'make'} \\ \textbf{kaímàsu} \text{ 'buy'} \\ \textbf{tukáimàsu} \text{ 'use'} \\ \textbf{nomímàsu} \text{ 'drink'} \\ \textbf{tabémàsu} \text{ 'eat'} \\ \textbf{misémàsu} \text{ 'show'} \\ \textbf{itádakimàsu} \text{ 'I/we eat/drink' (polite)} \\ \textbf{kudásaimàsu} \text{ 'give to me/us' (polite)} \end{array} \right.
$$

Y o +

X is the doer, maker, buyer, etc.; Y is what is done, made, bought, etc.
  Note the following contrasts:

Koré o tukaimàsu.	'I'll use *this one*.' '*This is the one* I'll use.'
Kore tukáimàsu. *or* **Koré tukaimàsu.**	'I'll use this one.'
Kore wa tukáimàsu. *or* **Koré wa tukaimàsu.**	'This one (at least) *I'll use*' (but I'm not commenting on other things that I may or may not use).

The contrasts between **o** and **wa** are exactly parallel to those between **ğa** and **wa** described in the preceding note. DEPENDING ON CONTEXT, a sentence like **Tanáka-san wa tukaimàsu** can mean either 'Mr/s. Tanaka (at least) will use [it]' or 'Mr/s. Tanaka (at least) I'll use.'

  Again, **o/wa** usage with negative predicates is parallel to the **ğa/wa** contrast with negatives. Compare:

Zîsyo o kaímàsu ka⌐	'Are you going to buy *a dictionary*?'
Iie, kaímasèn. *or*	'No, I'm not (going to buy).'
Iie, zîsyo wa kaímasèn.	'No, a dictionary (at least) *I'm not going to buy*' (but I'm not commenting on other things which I may or may not buy).

In replying to information questions whose focus is a /question word + **o**/, a commonly occurring reply is /nominal + **desu**/. Examples:

Nâni o nomímàsita ka⌐	'What did you drink?'
Koóhìi desu.	'(It's) coffee.'
Dôre o tukáimàsu ka⌐	'Which one are you going to use?'
Konó koñpyùutaa desu.	'(It's) this computer.'

This parallels the patterning with **ğa**.

  Return now to the Core Conversations and note the occurrences of phrase-particle **o** in CC4(N)c. If deleted, **kore** would simply lose a bit of its emphasis and focus. On the other hand, the addition of **o** in 2(J)a, 5(N)a, and 5(N)c would give added emphasis and focus.

5. dèsu ~ arímàsu

/Nominal + **dêsu**/ and /nominal + **arímàsu**/ may seem rather similar at first hearing, but these are *very* different constructions with *very* different meanings. The combination /nominal X + **dêsu**/ constitutes a nominal-type predicate, meaning '[something *or* someone] is (*or* will be) equivalent to X or described in terms of X.' **Toókyoo dèsu** can not only define the capital of Japan ('It's Tokyo.') but also answer such diverse questions as 'Where is your home?' 'Where is your mother?' 'Where is he from?' 'Where will you be next year?' 'Where will the conference be held?' etc. Thus we hear combinations like:

Kore wa pâi desu.	'This is *pie*.'
Tomodati wa pâi desu.	'My friend is [having] *pie*.'
Kyôo wa pâi desu.	'Today is *pie*.' (i.e., today's dessert)

In each case, **X wa Y desu** means that 'in regard to X (at least), it's a Y-equivalence-or-connection.'

Consider now the sequence /**pâi arímàsu**/. In this case, we have *not* a predicate alone as in the case of **pâi desu**, but a /nominal + verbal predicate/, meaning 'there is pie' or, by extension, 'I have pie.' Also possible, of course, are **pâi g̃a arímàsu**, which emphasizes 'pie' as the specific thing that is present, and **pâi wa arímàsu** '*there is* pie (at least),' '*I do have* pie (at least).' In contrast, the predicate **pâi desu** is a unit which does not permit this kind of separation by **g̃a** or **wa**.

Compare also the negative equivalents of these two patterns:

Pâi desu ka⌐	'Is it pie?'
Iie, pâi zya nâi desu. *or*	
Iie, pâi zya arímasèñ.	'No, it isn't pie.'
Pâi arímàsu ka⌐	'Is there any pie?'
Iie, nâi desu. *or*	
Iie, arímasèñ. *or*	'No, there isn't.'
Iie, pâi wa nâi desu. *or*	'No, there isn't any pie (at least)'
Iie, pâi wa arímasèñ.	(but there may be other things).

6. REQUESTS; VERBAL GERUNDS

Japanese has a tremendous variety of different patterns for expressing requests. Three such patterns occur in this section. Others will occur later.

1. /Nominal X + **(o)** + **oné g̃ai-simàsu**./ *lit.* 'I request X of you,' 'I ask you for X,' i.e., 'I'd like X,' 'Could I have X.'

Oné g̃ai-simàsu 'I make a request' is a polite verbal referring to the speaker's request; it shows deference to the out-group toward whom the request is directed. It often occurs by itself in making a general request, the nature of which is obvious from the context (for example, in calling a waitress or a porter for service).

2. /Nominal X + **(o)** + **kudásài**./ *lit.* 'Give me X.'

Kudásài is the imperative (command form) of the polite verbal of giving **kudásaimàsu** 'give to me,' or, more precisely, '[out-group] gives to in-group.'[8] When **kudásài** is preceded by /nominal + **(o)**/ or used by itself, it refers only to the actual giving or handing over of an object. **Oné g̃ai-simàsu**, on the other hand, is a general request expression which covers a much broader spectrum of situations. When asking for an object, either expression can be used, but only **oné g̃ai-simàsu** can be used to ask for people (for example, on the telephone). To call a salesperson with **oné g̃ai-simàsu** signals a request for service; **kudásài** in that situation would mean that you actually want something—i.e., to purchase a specific item.

8. Remember that the minimal group is an individual.

3. Gerund + **kudasài**

In addition to the **-màsu, -màsita,** etc. forms already introduced, verbals have another form, ending in **-te** or **-de,** which we will hereafter call the GERUND. Gerunds occur in a number of patterns. One such pattern is a request pattern, consisting of /verbal gerund X + **kudasài**/ 'please X,' 'please X for me,' 'please be kind enough to X' (*lit.* 'please give me X-ing'). **Onégai-simàsu** does not occur in this pattern.

The following request patterns include gerund forms of verbals already introduced. Note that **kudasài** regularly loses its accent following an accented gerund. The accent of the gerund is related to the accent of direct-style forms, to be introduced later.

tabémàsu	**tâbete kudasai**	'please eat'
misémàsu	**mîsete kudasai**	'please show'
tukúrimàsu	**tukûtte kudasai**	'please make'
kaímàsu	**kaŕte kudasài**	'please buy'
tukáimàsu	**tukátte kudasài**	'please use'
ikímàsu	**iŕte kudasài**	'please go'
nomímàsu	**nônde kudasai**	'please drink'
kimâsu	**kitê (or kîte) kudasai**	'please come'
simâsu	**sité kudasài**	'please do'

The gerunds of other verbals that have been introduced, which do NOT regularly occur in request patterns, are:

dekímàsu	**dêkite**
arímàsu	**âtte**
wakárimàsu	**wakâtte**[9]
komárimàsu	**komâtte**
tiğáimàsu	**tiğatte**
itádakimàsu	**itadaite**
kudásaimàsu	**kudásàtte**

These will occur in other gerund patterns, to be introduced later. New verbals will now be introduced in the Breakdowns with their gerunds (i.e., **arímàsu/âtte**). *Be sure to learn the form.*

Drills

A 1. **Are, hurósiki dèsu ka⌇**
   'Is that *a furoshiki*?'

   Aré dèsu ka⌇ Êe, hurósiki dèsu yo⌇
   'That? Yes, it's a furoshiki.'

2. **Hurosiki, aré dèsu ka⌇**
   'Is the furoshiki *that one*?' (i.e., that package over there)

   Hurósiki dèsu ka⌇ Êe, aré dèsu yo⌇
   'The furoshiki? Yes, it's that one.'

3. **asítà/Tanaka-sañ**; 4. **are/teğami**; 5. **anó zìsyo/waee**; 6. **asâtte/kâiği**

B 1. **Suzuki-sañ, simâsu ka⌇**

   Iie, simásèñ.

---

9. May occur in request patterns only when "understanding" refers to an empathetic attitude toward a particular situation (for example, understanding why someone can't grant a favor).

'Is Mr/s. Suzuki *going to do it*?'   'No, s/he isn't (going to do).'

2. **Suzuki-sañ, hurûi desu ka⁀**   **Iie, hûrûku nâi desu.**
'Has Mr/s. Suzuki been here long?'[10]   'No, s/he hasn't (been here long).'

3. **kâigi desu**; 4. **Toókyoo dèsu**; 5. **tukáimàsu**; 6. **gakúsee dèsu**

C 1. **Ikímàsu ka⁀**   **Watási dèsu ka⁀ Iie, tomódati ğa**
'Are you going to go?'   **ikimàsu yo⁀**
          'Me? No, *a friend* is going.'

2. **Tukáimàsita ka⁀**   **Watási dèsu ka⁀ Iie, tomódati ğa**
'Did you use it?'   **tukaimàsita yo⁀**
          'Me? No, *a friend* used it.'

3. **kaímàsu**; 4. **simâsita**; 5. **tukúrimàsu**; 6. **kimâsita**

D 1. **Suzúki-sañ ğa simâsu ka⁀**   **Soré dèsu ka⁀ Iie, Yamámoto-sañ ğa**
'Is *Mr/s. Suzuki* going to do it?'   **simâsu yo⁀**
          'That? No, *Mr/s. Yamamoto* is going to do it.'

2. **Suzúki-sañ ğa tukaimàsita ka⁀**   **Soré dèsu ka⁀ Iie, Yamámoto-sañ ğa**
'Did *Mr/s. Suzuki* use it?'   **tukaimàsita yo⁀**
          'That? No, *Mr/s. Yamamoto* used it.'

3. **tukúrimàsita**; 4. **misémàsu**; 5. **kaímàsita**

E 1. **Dâre ğa simâsu ka⁀ Yamámoto-sañ**   **Êe, Yamámoto-sañ wa simàsu yo⁀**[11]
dèsu ka⁀   'Yes, Mr/s. Yamamoto (at least) *will do it*.'
'Who will do it? Is it Mr/s.
Yamamoto?'

2. **Dâre ğa kimásèñ ka⁀ Yamámoto-sañ**   **Êe, Yamámoto-sañ wa kimasèñ yo⁀**
dèsu ka⁀   'Yes, Mr/s. Yamamoto (at least) *isn't going to*
'Who isn't going to come? Is it Mr/s.   *come*.'
Yamamoto?'

3. **dekímàsu**; 4. **wakárimasèñ**; 5. **tukúrimàsu**; 6. **îi desu**; 7. **gakúsee dèsu**

F 1. **Dôre ğa îi desu ka⁀**   **Koré dèsu. Koré ğa ìi desu yo.**
'*Which one* is good?'   'This one. *This one* is good.'

2. **Dôre ğa hûbeñ desu ka⁀**   **Koré dèsu. Koré ğa hùbeñ desu yo.**
'*Which one* is inconvenient?'   'This one. *This one* is inconvenient.'

3. **yasûi desu**; 4. **omósiròi desu**; 5. **bêñri desu**; 6. **kîree desu**

G (In the responses, use **nâni**, **dâre**, **îtu**, or **dôno X**, as appropriate.)

1. **Sâtoo-sañ wa yôku nâi desu nêe.**   **Zyâa, dâre ğa îi desu ka⁀**
'Mr/s. Sato (for one) *won't be good* (for   'Then who will be good?'
our purposes), will s/he!'

---

10. **Hurûi** used of people refers to long association rather than old age. Compare the use of 'old' in the English combination 'old friend.'
11. In more direct responses, **ğa** would replace **wa** (see p. 91).

2. **Konó kàsa wa yôku nâi desu nêe.**
'This umbrella (at least) *won't be good*, will it!'

   Zyâa, dôno kâsa ğa îi desu ka⌒
'Then which umbrella will be good?'

3. **kyôo**; 4. **têepu**; 5. **Tanaka-sañ**; 6. **asâtte**; 7. **konó koñpyùutaa**

H 1. **Yamámoto-sañ ğa kimàsu neʕ**
'*Mr/s. Yamamoto* is coming—right?'

   Iie, Yamámoto-sañ wa kimásèñ yo⌒
'No, Mr/s. Yamamoto (for one) *is not coming.*'

2. **Yamámoto-sañ ğa dekimasèñ neʕ**
'*Mr/s. Yamamoto* can't do it—right?'

   Iie, Yamámoto-sañ wa dekímàsu yo⌒
'No, Mr/s. Yamamoto (for one) *can.*'

3. **tukúrimàsu**; 4. **kimásèñ**; 5. **atárasìi desu**; 6. **îi desu**; 7. **wakárimasèñ**; 8. **Kyôoto desu**

I 1. **Aôi kâsa wa, ikâğa desu ka⌒**
'How about a blue umbrella?'

   Sono aôi no desu ka⌒ . . . Zyâa, soré kudasài.
'That blue one? . . . (Well then,) let me have that one.'

2. **Akai hurosiki wa, ikâğa desu ka⌒**
'How about a red furoshiki?'

   Sono akâi no desu ka⌒ . . . Zyâa, soré kudasài.
'That red one? . . . (Well then,) let me have that one.'

3. **tiísài taípuràitaa**; 4. **sirôi têepu**; 5. **yasásii hòñ**; 6. **oókìi kêeki**; 7. **atárasìi waéezìteñ**

● Repeat this drill, replacing **kudásài** with **onéğai-simàsu** in the responses.

J 1. **Sonó kàsa onéğai-simàsu.**
'Please let me have that umbrella.'

   Konó kàsa desu ka⌒ Dôozo.
'This umbrella? Here you are.'

2. **Sonó teğami oneğai-simàsu.**
'Please let me have that letter.'

   Konó teğami dèsu ka⌒ Dôozo.
'This letter? Here you are.'

3. **deñwa**; 4. **pûriñ**; 5. **otya**

K 1. **Kaímàsu ka⌒**
'Are you going to buy [some of these]?'

   Êe, koré o kaimàsu.
'Yes, I'm going to buy *this one.*'

2. **Tukáimàsita ka⌒**
'Did you use [some of these]?'

   Êe, koré o tukaimàsita.
'Yes, I used *this one.*'

3. **tabémàsu**; 4. **simâsita**; 5. **tukúrimàsita**; 6. **nomímàsu**

L 1. **Siñbuñ, kaímàsu ka⌒**
'Do you buy newspapers?'

   Iie, siñbuñ wa kaímasèñ nêe.
'No, newspapers (at least) *I don't buy.*'

2. **Gôruhu, simàsu ka⌒**
'Do you play golf?'

   Iie, gôruhu wa simásèñ nêe.
'No, golf (at least) *I don't play.*'

3. **koñpyùutaa, tukáimàsu**; 4. **kêeki, tabémàsu**; 5. **koóhìi, nomímàsu**; 6. **pâi, tukúrimàsu**

M 1. **Kyôo wa ikímasèñ yo**
'Today (at least) *I'm not going to go.*'

Zyâa, asítà wa dôo desu ka Asítà wa ikímàsu ka
'Then how about tomorrow? Tomorrow (at least) *are you going to go?*'

2. **Kyôo wa nihóñĝo zya nài desu yo**
'Today (at least) *it* (the language used) *will not be Japanese.*'

Zyâa, asítà wa dôo desu ka Asítà wa nihóñĝo dèsu ka
'Then how about tomorrow? Tomorrow (at least) *will it be Japanese?*'

3. **yôku nâi desu**; 4. **kâiĝi zya arímasèñ**; 5. **dekímasèñ**; 6. **omósìròku arímasèñ**; 7. **tênisu zya nâi desu**

N 1. **Eéwa-zìteñ arímàsu ka**
'Are there (*or* do you have) any English–Japanese dictionaries?'

Eéwa-zìteñ desu ka Hâi, arímàsu yo
'English–Japanese dictionaries? Yes, there are (*or* we do have).'

2. **Kâsa arímàsu ka**
'Is there (*or* do you have) an umbrella?'

Kâsa desu ka Hâi, arímàsu yo
'An umbrella? Yes, there is (*or* I do have).'

3. **hurosiki**; 4. **otya**; 5. **deñwa**; 6. **siñbuñ**

O 1. **Kâsa arímàsu ka**
'Do you have any umbrellas?'

Êe, îi no ĝa arímàsu yo Konó kàsa desu.
'Yes, we have *some good ones.* They're these umbrellas.'

2. **Hurósiki arimàsu ka**
'Do you have any furoshiki?'

Êe, îi no ĝa arímàsu yo Konó hurosiki dèsu.
'Yes, I have *some nice ones.* They're these furoshiki.'

3. **têepu**; 4. **waapuro**; 5. **zîsyo**; 6. **waée-zìteñ**

P 1a. **Síñbuñ arimàsu ka**

Arímasèñ nêe.

b. **Zyâa, zassi wa?**
'Do you have a paper?'
'Then how about a magazine (at least)?'

Âa, zaśsi wa arimàsu.
'No, I don't (have) . . .'
'Oh, a magazine *I have.*'

2a. **Síñbuñ kaimàsita ka**

Kaímasèñ desita nêe.

b. **Zyâa, zassi wa?**
'Did you buy a paper?'
'Then how about a magazine (at least)?'

Âa, zaśsi wa kaimàsita.
'No, I didn't (buy) . . .'
'Oh, a magazine *I bought.*'

3a. **Asíta dekimàsu ka**

Dekímasèñ nêe.

b. **Zyâa, asâtte wa?**
'Can you do it tomorrow?'

Âa, asâtte wa dekimasu.
'No, I can't . . .'

'Then how about the day after   'Oh, the day after tomorrow *I can.*'
tomorrow (at least)?'

4. **Tanáka-sañ kimàsu/Yamamoto-sañ**; 5. **taípuràitaa tukáimàsita/koñpyùutaa**; 6. **kyôo ikímasu/asú**; 7. **pâi tabémàsu/aísukurìimu**

Q 1. **Têepu o katte kudasài.**   **Wakárimàsita. Zya, watási kaimàsu yo.**[12]
   'Please buy *some tapes.*'   'Very well. (Then) I'll buy them.'

  2. **Koñpyùutaa o tukátte kudasài.**   **Wakárimàsita. Zya, watási tukaimàsu yo.**
   'Please use *the computer.*'   'Very well. (Then) I'll use it.'

  3. **pâi o tukûtte**; 4. **asíta kitè**; 5. **asâtte itte**; 6. **kore o site**; 7. **otyá o nònde**; 8. **kêeki o tâbete**

R 1. **Kurôi desu ka⤹**   **Iya, kûrôku nâi desu yo⤹**
   'Is it black?'   'No, it isn't (black).'

  2. **Bêñri desu ka⤹**   **Iya, bêñri zya nâi desu yo⤹**
   'Is it convenient?'   'No, it isn't convenient.'

  3. **aôi desu**; 4. **kîree desu**; 5. **akâi desu**; 6. **kiíròi desu**; 7. **yasásìi desu**; 8. **yukî desu**; 9. **hûbeñ desu**; 10. **zêñbu desu**; 11. **sirôi desu**; 12. **îi desu**

● Repeat this drill, replacing **nâi desu** with **arímasèñ** in the responses.

S 1. **Muzúkasiku arimasèñ desita neʃ** **Iie, muzúkasìkatta desu yo⤹**
   'It wasn't difficult—right?'   'No, it *was* difficult.'

  2. **Bêñri zya arímasèñ desita neʃ**   **Iie, bêñri desita yo⤹**
   'It wasn't convenient—right?'   'No, it *was* convenient.'

  3. **akáku nàkatta desu**; 4. **hûbeñ zya nâkatta desu**; 5. **zêñbu zya arímasèñ desita**; 6. **âôku arímasèñ desita**; 7. **sîrôku nâkatta desu**

T 1. **Deñwa arimàsu ka⤹**   **Iie, deñwa wa arimasèñ.**
   'Is there a telephone?'   'A telephone—no, there isn't.'

  2. **Deñwa dèsu ka⤹**   **Iie, deñwa zya arimasèñ.**
   'Is it a telephone (call)?'   'No, it isn't a telephone (call).'

  3. **kâiği arímàsu**; 4. **bêñri desu**; 5. **kâsa arímàsu**; 6. **koñpyùutaa arímàsu**; 7. **hûbeñ desu**; 8. **asâtte desu**

U 1. **Asítà wa ikímasèñ yo⤹**   **Zyâa, asâtte itte kudasài neʃ**
   'Tomorrow (at least) I'm not going.'   'Then please go *the day after tomorrow,* would you?'

  2. **Asítà wa tukúrimasèñ yo⤹**   **Zyâa, asâtte tukûtte kudasai neʃ**
   'Tomorrow (at least) I'm not going to 'Then please make [some] *the day after*
   make [any].'   *tomorrow,* would you?'

  3. **kimásèñ**; 4. **simásèñ**; 5. **kaímasèñ**

Application Exercises

A. Display objects or pictures of objects for which you have learned the Japanese term, and practice asking and answering /ka⤹/ and /neʃ/ questions, and making /yo⤹/, /ne!/,

12. The respondent is making clear what s/he will do. Males may replace **watasi** with **bôku.**

and /**nêe.**/ statements with appropriate responses, covering the following categories. Make your exchanges realistic: for example, if appropriate, put some objects in paper bags—or wrap them in furoshiki—to make identification questions likely.

1. Identification: **Sore (wa), nâñ desu ka**✓; /nominal/ **(wa), dôre desu ka**✓; **Dôre ḡa** /nominal/ **dèsu ka**✓; **Sono** /adjectival/ **no (wa), nâñ desu ka**✓; **Dôre ḡa** /adjectival/ **no desu ka**✓; **Kore (wa),** /nominal/ **dèsu ka**✓; **Sono** /nominal/ **(wa), îkura desu ka**✓; **Dôre** /or **dôno** + nominal/ **ḡa** /nominal of price/ **dèsu ka**✓

2. Existence: display objects and remove them, in turn. Ask:

    Nâni ḡa arímàsu ka✓

    Nâni ḡa arímàsita ka✓

3. Activities: have each member of the group 'use' one object (or picture of an object) and then return it to the instructor. Pointing to an object, ask:

    Dâre ḡa tukáimàsita ka✓

    /name-**sañ**/ **ḡa tukáimàsita ne**ʕ

Pointing to a group member:

    Nâni (o) tukáimàsita ka✓

    /nominal/ **(o) tukáimàsita ne**ʕ

4. Requests: request objects using the patterns /nominal **(o) + kudásài**/ and /nominal **(o) + oneḡai-simàsu**/. Request activities—i.e., showing, doing, buying, using, going, and coming—using the pattern /verbal gerund + **kudasài**/.

B. Core Conversations: Substitution

Practice the Core Conversations, making appropriate substitutions—other nominals, verbals, adjectivals, and pre-nominals—but retaining the basic framework exactly. In particular, use CC4 and 5 to practice various shopping situations.

SECTION B

Core Conversations (CC)

1(N)a. **Konó nòoto, gô-satu oneḡai-simasu.**

    (J)a. **Gô-satu desu ne**ʕ

   b. **Sore kara, oókìi huutoo wa arímàsu ka**✓

    b. **Hâi. Arímàsu yo**✓

   c. **A. Wakárimàsita. Kore, sâñ-mai kudasai.**

    c. **Arîḡatoo gozaimasu.**

2(J)a. **Irássyaimàse.**

    (N)a. **Koñna boorupeñ, arímàsu ka**✓

   b. **Syôosyoo omati-kudasai**✓ ... **Tyoódo onazi zya nài desu kedo, ikâḡa desu ka.**

    b. **Sôo desu nêe. ... Mâa, kore, nî-hoñ kudasai.**

3(N)a. **Kore, îkura desu ka**✓

    (J)a. **Îp-poñ nihyákù-eñ desu.**

   b. **Zyâa, akâi no nî-hoñ to, aôi no sâñ-boñ oneḡai-simasu.**

    b. **Hâi.**

c. **A. |Anoo| Kurôi no mo, nî-hoñ kudasai.**

d. **Hâi.**

4(J)a. **Kamî arímàsu ka⌐**

b. **Oókìi no oneḡai-simasu.**

c. **Kasíkomarimàsita.**

d. **Maído arìḡatoo gozaimasu. . . . Hâi, oturi, roṕpyakù-eñ. Matá dòozo.**

(N)a. **Dôñna no desu ka⌐**

b. **Hâi.**

ENGLISH EQUIVALENTS

1(N)a. Let me have five of these notebooks.

b. Next, how about large envelopes—do you have any?

c. Oh, I see. Give me three of these.

2(J)a. (Welcome.)

b. Just a moment, please. . . . It's not exactly the same, but how about this?

3(N)a. How much are these?

b. Then let me have two red ones and three blue ones.

c. Oh—uh—give me two black ones, too.

d. Here you are [handing over the money].

4(J)a. Do you have any paper?

b. I'd like some that's big.

(J)a. That's five—right?

b. Yes, we do. [Pointing them out]

c. Thank you.

(N)a. Do you have this kind of ballpoint pen?

b. Hmm. . . . I guess I'll take two of these.

(J)a. They're ¥200 each.

b. All right.

c. Certainly.

d. Thank you. . . . Here you are, ¥600 change. Please [come] again.

(N)a. What kind (of thing)?

b. Here you are.

BREAKDOWNS
(AND SUPPLEMENTARY VOCABULARY)

1. **nôoto**	notebook
gô-satu (SP1, SP2)	five bound volumes
sore kara	after that, next
huutoo	envelope
sâñ-mai (SP1)	three thin, flat objects
2. **boorupeñ**	ballpoint pen
koñna boorupeñ (SP3)	this kind of ballpoint pen
+**pêñ**	pen
+**eñpitu**	pencil

syôosyoo	a little
omáti-kudasài	please wait
tyoodo	exactly
onazi	same
/predicate + **kedo**/ *or*	
+/predicate + **ğa**/ (SP4)	/predicate/; (but)
nî-hoñ (SP1)	two long, cylindrical objects
3. **îp-poñ**	one long, cylindrical object
sâñ-boñ	three long, cylindrical objects
|**anoo**| (SP5)	uh
kurôi no mo (SP6)	black one(s) too
maido	every time
oturi	change (from a money transaction)
mata	again
4. **kamî**	paper
+**biñseñ**	stationery
dôñna no	what kind of one(s)?
+**soñna no**	that kind of one(s)
+**añna no**	that kind of one(s)

-satu: *Classifier for counting bound volumes*	**-mai:** *Classifier for counting thin, flat objects*	**-hoñ:** *Classifier for counting long, cylindrical objects*
iś-satù	**itî-mai**	**îp-poñ**
nî-satu	**nî-mai**	**nî-hoñ**
sâñ-satu	**sâñ-mai**	**sâñ-boñ**
yôñ-satu	**yôñ-mai**	**yôñ-hoñ**
go-sátù	**go-mai**	**go-hoñ**
rokú-satù	**rokû-mai**	**rôp-poñ**
nanâ-satu/sitî-satu	**nanâ-mai/sitî-mai**	**nanâ-hoñ/sitî-hoñ**
haś-satù	**hatî-mai**	**hâp-poñ/hatî-hoñ**
kyûu-satu	**kyûu-mai**	**kyûu-hoñ**
zyuś-satù/ziś-satù	**zyûu-mai**	**zyûp-poñ/zîp-poñ**
nâñ-satu 'how many volumes?'	**nâñ-mai** 'how many thin, flat objects?'	**nâñ-boñ** 'how many long, cylindrical objects?'

MISCELLANEOUS NOTES (MN)

1. CC1 is, of course, a shopping situation. Both customer and clerk use a careful style of speech with predicates in the distal-style.
Nôoto is an abbreviated—and much more commonly used—version of **noótobùkku**, a borrowing from English. This kind of abbreviation is extremely common.
Sore kara is a frequently occurring connective. Compare also **kore kara** 'after this.'

Note the use of **huutoo wa** in a contrastive sense—i.e., **huutoo** in contrast with **nôoto**.

2. CC2 is also a shopping situation, reflecting the same general style of speech as CC1. **Irássyaimàse**, and the more direct equivalent **irássyài**, are both imperative (command) forms of a polite verbal about which more will be said later. At this point, only these forms, meaning literally 'come!' will be introduced. Communication between customer and sales clerk regularly begins with one of these forms as the clerk's initial utterance.

Syôosyoo omati-kudasai is a polite, stylized request form that asks the addressee to wait. The pattern will be analyzed later; at this point, it should be learned as a unit.

Tyoodo is a nominal: here it links up with a predicate (**onázi zya nài desu**) to describe manner: 'it isn't the same exactly.' Compare: **tyoódo ìi desu** 'it's just right'; **tyoódo señ-eñ dèsu** 'it's exactly ¥1000.'

Onazi is a nominal: **onázi dèsu/dèsita, onázi zya nài desu/nàkatta desu** or **onázi zya arimasèñ/arimasèñ desita.**

Sôo desu nêe, pronounced in this context with marked slowing down, indicates deliberation. **Mâa** indicates some reservation and reluctance on the speaker's part.

3. CC3 is another shopping situation and another example of the same overall style of speech as CC1 and CC2.

Kasíkomarimàsita is a regular perfective, distal-style verbal form, signaled by **-màsita**. It implies that the speaker has received a request or order from a superior and will carry it out.

Maído arìgatoo gozaimasu (*lit.* thank you every time) is another ritual expression, commonly used by shopkeepers as an expression of gratitude for customers' continuing business.

Oturi is change returned after overpayment; it does *not* mean 'change' in the sense of 'small change' or 'change as opposed to bills.' In (J)d, the clerk announces the amount of the customer's change (**oturi**) that is being returned: it comes to ¥600 (**roppyakù-eñ**). **Oturi, roppyakù-eñ** is a fragment.

Matá dòozo 'again, please' is a fragment that invites the addressee (customer or visitor) to come again.

4. In CC4, (J) is asking (N), an office colleague, for something—in this case, some large sheets of paper. The style is careful, with distal-style predicates. The nominal **no** substitutes not only for countable nominals but also mass nominals. Thus, if books are the subject of conversation, **takâi no** refers to 'expensive one(s)'; but in the case of ice cream, pudding, paper, stationery, etc., **takâi no** refers to 'some that is expensive.'

Structural Patterns (SP)

1. *CLASSIFIERS:* -satu, -mai, -hoñ

In 2B-SP3, the Japanese system of counting, requiring the use of classifiers, was described. Even in counting unit objects, classification is involved: the nominal occurs in its usual, unchanging form, and the numeral is compounded with a classifier that designates the classification to which the object belongs. Thus, in counting notebooks, **nôoto** designates the specific object, and /numeral + **-satu** (the classifier for bound volumes such as books, magazines, dictionaries, and albums)/ indicates the number. The classifier **-mai** is used in counting units of thin, flat objects such as sheets, blankets, furoshiki, mats, etc.; and **-hoñ** counts units of (roughly) long, cylindrical objects, including pens, pencils, umbrellas, arms, legs, flowers, trees, bottles, tapes, etc.

In forming the number compounds consisting of /Chinese series numeral + classifier/, note the similarities between **-mai** and **-mañ** '10,000,' between **-hoñ** and **hyakû** '100,' and between **-satu** and **-señ** '1000' and **-señto** 'cent': the significant feature is the initial consonant. Study the complete lists above, at the end of the Breakdowns of this section.

2. EXTENT

A nominal (linked to a predicate) which asks or answers the question 'how much?', 'how many?', 'how long?', or 'how far?' occurs without a following phrase-particle. Thus: **Zyûu-eñ kudasai.** 'Please give me ¥10.' This construction is not to be confused with: **Soré (o) kudasài.** 'Please give me that.' which offers the alternate of including a particle, and involves a 'what' or 'who(m)' relationship rather than quantity.

In expressing a quantity of a specific item X which is in a **ga** or **o** or **wa** or no-particle relationship with the predicate, X occurs followed by its regular phrase-particle—which may of course be the no-particle option—and the extent expression occurs without a following particle.

> **Eñpitu o nî-hoñ kudasai.** 'Please give me two pencils.' (*lit.* 'Please give me pencils to the extent of two cylindrical objects.')
>
> **Zîsyo ga sâñ-satu arimasu.** 'There are (*or* I have) three dictionaries.' (*lit.* 'There are dictionaries to the extent of three bound volumes.')
>
> **Hurosiki nî-mai onegai-simasu.** 'I'd like two furoshiki.' (*lit.* 'I request furoshiki to the extent of two thin, flat objects.')

Note also these important points:

(1) If the identity of the quantified item is understood from the context, it does not require specific mention. **Îp-poñ** is a request for one pen if the addressee is holding pens.

(2) A quantity expression may be followed by an appropriate particle when it does not occur as an extent construction. For example, it may be followed by **wa**, once again implying the limit of applicability: **Îp-poñ wa arímàsu.** '*There is* one (at least).'

(3) When two quantified nominals /N/ in a **ga** or **o** pattern are joined (i.e., N2 with N1), the order is: /N1 + particle + number + **to**, + N2 + particle + number/. Again, in appropriate contexts, the particle may be no particle (cf. CC3[N]b).

Consider now the following examples:

(1) **Tyoódo ìi desu.** 'It's just fine.'

(2) **Kinóo kimàsita.** 'I came yesterday.'

(3) **Zyuú-eñ kudasài.** 'Please give me ¥10.'

In all three cases, a nominal links up directly with a predicate without an intervening particle[13] (no [**ga**] or [**o**] alternate is possible). Note the relationships: in (1), the nominal describes manner/degree; in (2), the 'time when' of the predicate; in (3), the extent of the predicate.

3. THE koñna SERIES

We now add a third **ko-so-a-do** series, the **koñna** group:

> /**koñna, soñna, añna, dôñna** + nominal X/ = 'this (that, etc.) kind of X'

---

13. In other words, we are NOT talking about /nominal + **dèsu**/, where the nominal is itself part of the nominal predicate.

Again, only the question alternate, **dôñna**, is accented.[14] Remember that in addition to spatial relationships, **so-** words can refer to items just mentioned, and **a-** words to items already familiar to the person addressed.

In *some* contexts—and with certain marked voice qualifiers and/or facial expressions—the **koñna** series can have negative connotations (e.g., **añna señsèe** 'that kind of [problematic] teacher').

4. CLAUSE-PARTICLES: kedo AND ğa

A CLAUSE-PARTICLE is one which is nonfinal in major sentences, and follows predicates only. **Kedo** and **ğa** (different from phrase-particle **ğa**) are clause-particles.

In /predicate X + **kedo** (*or* **ğa**), + predicate Y/, predicate X provides preliminary, relevant information for predicate Y; frequently—though by no means always—predicate X offers a contrast with Y, giving rise to the usual association of **kedo** and **ğa** with 'but' and 'however' in English. These are clearly the most common English equivalents of **kedo/ğa**, but there are many examples where English requires two independent sentences as the equivalent of a complex Japanese sentence that includes **kedo** or **ğa**. Compare:

> **Watási wa gakusee dèsu kedo** (*or* **ğa**), **tomodati wa gakúsee zya nài desu.**

'I'm a student, but my friend isn't (a student).' *and*

> **Watasi wa gakúsee dèsu kedo** (*or* **ğa**), **kore wa îkura desu ka**⌇

'I'm a student. How much is this?' (i.e., asking the price when special student rates are offered).

Note the following additional points:

1. The predicate preceding **kedo** and **ğa** may be imperfective or perfective, but *never* a gerund.

2. **Kedo** is particularly common in conversation; **ğa** seems a bit stiffer.

3. The longer—and slightly more formal and/or emphatic—alternates of **kedo** are **keredo, kedomo,** and **keredomo.**

4. Frequently, sentences in conversation end with /predicate + **kedo** or **ğa**/. Such sentences are included in the category called MINOR SENTENCES. /Sentence-final predicate + **kedo** or **ğa**/ indicates that more is implied without being actually stated. Often this is a device to present material politely: 'I make this statement but'—this is not the only possibility; *or* what do *you* think? *or* I hope you don't object; *or* what happens now? Such sentences are polite for the very reason that they sound inconclusive and nonconfrontational. Compare:

> **Ikímàsu ka**⌇ 'Are you going?'

> **Êe, ikímàsu yo**⌇ 'Yes, I'm going (I assure you).' *or* (significantly gentler): **Êe, ikímàsu kedo/ğa . . .** 'Yes, I'm going but—' (is there a problem? do you object? is there something I should know? etc.)

These **kedo/ğa** minor sentences leave the dialogue open and enable the speaker deliberately to allow for comments from others. In contrast, the sentence-particle **yo** implies that the final word on the topic has been given.

5. Frequently a /nominal + **desu**/ clause ending in **kedo/ğa** serves to introduce the topic of discussion:

14. But before nominal **no** the unaccented items of the series acquire a final syllable accent: **koñnà no** 'this kind of one.'

Anó nòoto desu kedo, îkura desu ka↗ 'It's that notebook over there [that I'm talking about]; how much is it?'

Eéwa-zìteñ desu ḡa, arímasèñ ka↗ 'It's English–Japanese dictionaries [that I'm talking about]; do(n't) you have any?'

5. HESITATION NOISES

Normal speech is regularly interrupted by fillers, which we can call 'hesitation noises.' They occur in a variety of circumstances, for example, when the speaker pauses to think, or as an indication of reluctance to express what follows. Every language has its own distinctive hesitation noises, to be mastered by foreigners just as one masters vocabulary items in general.

The most common hesitation noise in English is one that we represent in writing as 'uh.' To use this when speaking Japanese is to color our Japanese with a strikingly foreign and unnatural quality, no matter how accurate our control of the language is otherwise. It is therefore extremely important to observe how native Japanese speakers hesitate, and to imitate this feature of the language no less carefully than any other.

Anoo in CC3 is one of the most common Japanese hesitation noises. Items in this group will be enclosed within vertical bars | |. Note that |**anoo**| is pronounced with level pitch.

|**Anoo**| Can you become accustomed to using it |**anoo**| when you are speaking Japanese???

6. PHRASE-PARTICLE mo

The phrase-particle **mo** 'also,' 'even' patterns like **wa**[15] but with a very different meaning: X **wa** indicates that the following predicate is to be applied at least to X, but nothing more; X **mo** indicates that it applies to X 'in addition.' Compare:

(1) **Nihóñḡo ḡa ìi desu.** '*Japanese* will be good.' (Japanese is it!)

Nihóñḡo wa ìi desu. 'Japanese (at least) *will be good.*' (Other things will or will not be good, but I'm explicitly commenting only on Japanese.)

Nihóñḡo mo ìi desu. 'Japanese, too, *will be good.*' (Something else is good; Japanese is an addition.)

(2) **Zaśsi o kaimàsita.** 'I bought a *magazine.*'

Zaśsi wa kaimàsita. 'A magazine (at least) *I bought.*'

Zaśsi mo kaimàsita. 'I *bought* a magazine, too.'

(3) **Kyôo ikimasu.** 'I'm going *today.*'

Kyôo wa ikimasu. 'Today (at least) *I'm going.*'

Kyôo mo ikimasu. 'Today, too, *I'm going.*'

(4) **Kyôo wa ikímasèñ.** 'Today (at least) *I'm not going.*'

Asítà wa? 'How about tomorrow?' (as compared with today, are you going or not?)

Asítà mo? 'Tomorrow, too?' (are you not going?)

Additional examples:

Watási mo ikimàsita. '*I* went, *too*' (in addition to someone else who went).

---

15. Not included here is a discussion of /extent expression + **mo**/, which requires special explanation and will be introduced later.

Tênisu mo simásèñ. 'I don't play tennis, either' (in addition to something else I don't play).

Kyôo mo âme desu nêe. 'It's rain(ing) *today, too*' (in addition to another time it rained).

The particle **mo** directly follows an item that is additional. Thus in expressing the fact that '*Tanaka* bought a computer, *too*,' we find **Tanaka-sañ mo**; but if 'Tanaka bought *a computer, too*,' the Japanese equivalent will include **koñpyùutaa mo**.

In some contexts the nominal preceding **mo** and the following predicate may both be additional:

Pâi o tukúrimàsita. Sore kara, aísukurìimu mo kaímàsita. 'I made a pie. And I bought ice cream, too.'

Drills

A 1. **Konó nòoto wa?**   **Nî-satu kudasai.**
  'How about these notebooks?'   'Please give me two.'

 2. **Konó pèñ wa?**   **Nî-hoñ kudasai.**
  'How about these pens?'   'Please give me two.'

 3. **hurosiki**; 4. **hôñ**; 5. **eñpitu**; 6. **zîsyo**; 7. **kamî**; 8. **waée-zìteñ**; 9. **huutoo**
● Repeat this drill using other numerals in the responses.

B 1. **Kono pêñ to eñpitu wa?** |Anoo| **Pêñ o îp-poñ to, eñpitu o sâñ-boñ**
  'How about these pens and pencils?'   **oneğai-simasu.**
            'Uh—I'd like one pen and three pencils.'

 2. **Kono hôñ to zassi wa?** |Anoo| **Hôñ o iś-satù to, zassi o sâñ-satu**
  'How about these books and   **oneğai-simasu.**
  magazines?'   'Uh—I'd like one book and three
            magazines.'

 3. **eéwa-zìteñ/waée-zìteñ**; 4. **nôoto/kamî**; 5. **eñpitu/kamî**
● Repeat this drill using other numerals in the responses.

C 1. **Pêñ ikâğa desu ka⁄**   **Êe. Końna pèñ o sâñ-boñ kudasai.**
  'How about pens?'   'Yes, give me three of this kind (of pen).'

 2. **Nôoto ikâğa desu ka⁄**   **Êe. Końna nòoto o sâñ-satu kudasai.**
  'How about notebooks?'   'Yes, give me three of this kind (of
            notebook).'

 3. **zîsyo**; 4. **zassi**; 5. **hurosiki**; 6. **eñpitu**; 7. **huutoo**; 8. **hôñ**
● Repeat this drill using other numerals in the responses.

D 1. **Sońna kamì wa îkura desu ka⁄**   **Itî-mai hyakú gozyùu-eñ desu.**
  'How much is that kind of paper?'   'It's ¥150 for one sheet.'

 2. **Sońna boorupeñ wa îkura desu ka⁄**   **Îp-poñ hyakú gozyùu-eñ desu.**
  'How much is that kind of pen?'   'It's ¥150 for one.'

 3. **zassi**; 4. **eñpitu**; 5. **nôoto**; 6. **hurosiki**; 7. **huutoo**

E 1. **Pêñ arímàsu ka⁄**   **Dôñna pêñ desu ka⁄**

'Do you have any pens?'   'What kind of pens (do you mean)?'

2. **Kamî arímàsu ka⤸**   **Dôñna kamî desu ka⤸**

'Do you have any paper?'   'What kind of paper (do you mean)?'

3. **kâsa**; 4. **zassi**; 5. **nôoto**; 6. **zîsyo**; 7. **biñseñ**

F 1. **Eñpitu kudasài.**   **Sumímasèñ ğa, eñpitu wa nâi desu nêe.**

'Please give me a pencil.'   'I'm sorry, but *I don't have* a pencil . . .'

2. **Biñseñ kudasài.**   **Sumímasèñ ğa, biñseñ wa nâi desu nêe.**

'Please give me some stationery.'   'I'm sorry, but *I don't have* any stationery . . .'

3. **boorupeñ**; 4. **kamî**; 5. **kâsa**; 6. **siñbuñ**

- Repeat this drill, replacing **ğa** with **kedo** in the response.

G 1. **Oókìi nôoto arímàsu ka⤸**   **Sumímasèñ ğa, oókìi no wa arímasèñ.**

'Do you have any large notebooks?'   'I'm sorry, but *we don't have* any large ones.'

2. **Aôi kâsa arímàsu ka⤸**   **Sumímasèñ ğa, aôi no wa arímasèñ.**

'Do you have any blue umbrellas?'   'I'm sorry, but *we don't have* any blue ones.'

3. **akái pèñ**; 4. **kiiroi hurosiki**; 5. **atárasìi zassi**; 6. **sirôi kamî**

- Repeat this drill, replacing **ğa** with **kedo** in the responses.

H 1. **Kurôi kâsa arímàsu ka⤸**   **Kâsa wa arímàsu kedo, kurôi no wa arímasèñ.**

'Do you have a black umbrella?'   'I do have an umbrella, but a black one I don't have.'

2. **Oókìi huutoo arímàsu ka⤸**   **Huútoo wa arimàsu kedo, oókìi no wa arímasèñ.**

'Do you have any large envelopes?'   'I do have envelopes, but large ones I don't have.'

3. **atárasìi zassi**; 4. **yasásii hòñ**; 5. **tiísài eéwa-zìteñ**; 6. **akai hurosiki**

- Repeat this drill, replacing **kedo** with **ğa** in the responses.

I 1. **Zassi to siñbuñ, kaímàsu ne⤹**   A. **Siñbuñ wa kaimàsu ğa . .**

'You're going to buy a magazine and a paper—right?'   'Oh. I'm going to buy a paper (at least), but . . .'

2. **Tanaka-sañ to Sâtoo-sañ, kimâsita ne⤹**   A. **Sâtoo-sañ wa kimâsita ğa . .**

'Mr/s. Tanaka and Mr/s. Sato came— right?'   'Oh. Mr/s. Sato (at least) came, but . . .'

3. **asítà/asâtte/ikímàsu**; 4. **kêeki/pâi/tukúrimàsu**; 5. **taípuràitaa/waapuro/arímàsu**; 6. **hurañsuğo/supeiñğo/tukáimàsu**

- Repeat this drill, replacing **ğa** with **kedo** in the responses.

J 1. **Ano kêeki to pâi, takâi desu ka⤸**   **Kêeki wa takâi desu kedo, pâi wa tâkâku nâi desu yo⤸**

'Are those cakes and pies expensive?'

'The cakes are expensive but the pies aren't (expensive).'

2. **Kyôo to asita, ikímàsu ka⌐**   **Kyôo wa ikímàsu kedo, asítà wa**
'Are you going today and tomorrow?'   **ikímasèñ yo⌐**
'Today I'm going but tomorrow I'm not (going).'

3. **Sâtoo-sañ/Suzuki-sañ/kimâsu**; 4. **eeḡo/hurañsuḡo/muzúkasìi desu**; 5. **taípuràitaa/ koñpyùutaa/tukáimàsu**; 6. **ano pâi/aísukirìimu/tabémàsu**; 7. **koñna otya/koóhìi/ nomímàsu**; 8. **hôñ/zassi/atárasìi desu**

• Repeat this drill, replacing **kedo** with **ḡa** in the responses.

K 1. **Yamámoto-sañ wa kimàsu ḡa,**   **Suzúki-sañ mo kimàsu yo⌐**
     Suzuki-sañ wa?   'Mr/s. Suzuki is coming, too.'
     'Mr/s. Yamamoto (at least) is coming, but what about Mr/s. Suzuki?'

2. **Taípuràitaa wa arímasèñ ḡa,**   **Koñpyùutaa mo arímasèñ yo⌐**
     koñpyùutaa wa?   'There isn't a computer, either.'
     'There's no typewriter (at least this much is lacking), but what about a computer?'

3. **kono hurosiki/takâi desu/ano hurosiki**; 4. **konó zìsyo/itímàñ goseñ-eñ/anó zìsyo**; 5. **kore/hûbeñ desu/are**; 6. **konó hòñ/omósìròku nâi desu/anó hòñ**

L 1. **Watási wa ikimàsu ḡa, Suzuki-sañ**[16]   **Watasi mo ikímàsu yo⌐**
     wa?   'I'm going, too.'
     'I'm going. How about you, Mr/s. Suzuki?'

2. **Watási wa dekimasèñ ḡa, Suzuki-sañ**   **Watasi mo dekímasèñ yo⌐**
     wa?   'I can't do it, either.'
     'I can't do it. How about you, Mr/s. Suzuki?'

3. **simâsu**; 4. **onázi dèsu**; 5. **itádakimàsu**; 6. **nihóñḡo dèsu**; 7. **gakúsee dèsu**; 8. **komárimàsu**

Application Exercises

A. Collect samples of pens, pencils, paper, notebooks, books, magazines, dictionaries, furoshiki, etc., of various colors, sizes, and newness. Use the following situations as the basis for conversational practice.
1. Request specific numbers of objects.
2. Ask (1) how many and (2) what kinds there are of specific objects.

16. Mr/s. Suzuki is being addressed politely.

3. In answer to a request for a particular object, find out what kind is wanted.

4. Find out the unit price of various objects.

5. Check on whether pairs of different objects are new, expensive, interesting, etc. Include examples which require a contrastive answer that uses **kedo** (or **ḡa**).

6. After requesting one object, ask for another in addition.

7. Request different numbers of two different objects, using a single, complex sentence.

(Are you using Japanese hesitation noises???)

B. Core Conversations: Substitution

Return to the Core Conversations and practice them again, making appropriate substitutions wherever possible. Your vocabulary is now sufficient to carry out a number of different shopping situations. After each new version, ask and answer questions about what happened, using perfective forms.

SECTION C

Eavesdropping

(Answer the following questions, in English, on the basis of the accompanying recorded material. In each exchange, A refers to the first speaker, and B to the second.)

1a. What is A asking about?
  b. What is B's proficiency?
2a. What is A asking about?
  b. What does B have?
3. What is regrettable?
4a. What does A invite B to do?
  b. On what basis does B refuse?
5. How do the things under discussion compare?
6a. What is the subject of discussion?
  b. What does B urge A to do? Why?
7. What has B agreed to do?
8. What three items is A shopping for?
9a. What does A request first?
  b. What does A settle for?
10. What is B reassuring A about?
11a. What is B apparently required to write with?
  b. What is the initial problem?
12a. What is being purchased?
  b. What is the unit cost of the item?
  c. How many are purchased?
13a. What is the topic of discussion?
  b. Why is A upset?
14a. What is B buying? What colors?
  b. What is the unit price for each color?
  c. How many of each color does B buy?
  d. How much does B give the clerk?
15a. What is A buying?
  b. What color is the item A looks at first? Second?

c. What color item does the clerk suggest?

d. What color does A decide on in the end?

Utilization

(Be sure to include a stimulus and/or response for each elicited item.)

1. Ask Ms. Tanaka if she plays golf. How about tennis?
2. Ask a visitor to wait a moment.
3. Warn Mr. Suzuki that it's raining. Find out if he has an umbrella.
4. Inform a colleague that Ms. Yamamoto has come.
5. At the reception desk, ask for Mr. Sato.
6. At the bookstore, find out if they have Japanese–English dictionaries.
7. Ask a salesclerk to show you that red furoshiki. Then ask to see that yellow one, too.
8. Find out if that large dictionary over there is an English–Japanese dictionary.
9. Find out who Ms. Tanaka is.
10. A colleague is holding a wrapped package. Find out what it is.
11. Tell a colleague that you have a new Japanese–English dictionary.
12. Tell a new acquaintance that you don't play tennis, but you play golf a good deal.
13. Inform a colleague that this new typewriter is very inconvenient.
14. Comment (expecting agreement) on how convenient this new computer is.
15. An order for supplies is being drawn up. Ask a colleague to buy 300 envelopes.
16. At the coffee shop, ask your colleague what he is going to drink.
17. Ask the salesclerk for three sheets of yellow paper and two sheets of blue paper.
18. You've been asked about your use of typewriters and computers. Explain that you do use a computer a good deal, but you barely use the typewriter at all.
19. Find out the price of this kind of stationery, and then check if the stationery over there is the same.
20. Ask for: one small envelope; two sheets of white paper; three red pencils; one small notebook.
21. Find out what kind (of one) the new computer is.
22. You've just made a purchase. Find out what happened to your change (*lit.* 'How about the change?')
23. Find out if these typewriters are exactly the same.
24. You are discussing upcoming conferences. Find out if there will be one tomorrow, too.
25. How does a salesclerk welcome customers? express thanks for continuing business? invite customers to come again?

Check-up

1. Describe the difference in meaning:

     Tomódati kimàsita.

     Tomódati ğa kimàsita.

     Tomódati wa kimàsita. (A-SP1), (A-SP2), (A-SP3)

2. Describe the difference in meaning:

     Siñbuñ kaimàsita.

     Siñbuñ o kaimàsita.

     Siñbuñ wa kaimàsita. (A-SP1), (A-SP2), (A-SP4)

3. Generally speaking, what phrase-particle never occurs immediately following an interrogative (**nâni, dâre, îtu,** etc.)? (A-SP2)

4. Describe the difference in meaning:

Hurósiki dèsu ka⤸

Hurosiki wa? (A-SP2)

5. Describe the difference in meaning:

   Tomódati ga tukaimàsita.

   Tomódati o tukaimàsita. (A-SP3), (A-SP4)

6. Describe the difference in meaning:

   Koóhìi desu.

   Koóhìi arimasu.

   What is the negative equivalent of each? (A-SP5)

7. What is meant by the 'gerund' form of the verbal? Give three examples. (A-SP6)

8. What is one use of the verbal gerund? (A-SP6)

9. Give two ways of asking for a thing and one way of asking for a person. (A-SP6)

10. State two differences between **kudásài** and **onégai-simàsu**. (A-SP6)

11. Name three verbals which do not occur in request forms. (A-SP6)

12. How are the following objects counted in Japanese? Books; pens; furoshiki; pencils; envelopes; paper; umbrellas; dictionaries; magazines. (B-SP1)

13. What is meant by an 'extent' pattern in Japanese? How is extent indicated? (B-SP2)

14. In what three patterns introduced thus far does a nominal without a following particle link up with a predicate (*not* in a [ga] or [o] context)? Give an example of each. (B-SP2)

15. What is the difference in meaning between **konó hòn** and **końna hòn**? (B-SP3)

16. What is meant by a clause-particle? (B-SP4)

17. What is the difference between /nominal + ga/ and /predicate + ga/? (A-SP3), (B-SP4)

18. What does **kedo** or **ga** at the end of a sentence mean? (B-SP4)

19. What tendency must be avoided when hesitating? Name one common Japanese hesitation noise. (B-SP5)

20. Explain the difference in meaning:

    Kâigi ga arímàsu neʕ

    Kâigi wa arímàsu neʕ

    Kâigi mo arímàsu neʕ (B-SP6)

21. Explain the difference between:

    Tanáka-sañ mo kaimàsita. *and*

    Sińbuñ mo kaimàsita. (B-SP6)

Lesson 5

SECTION A

Core Conversations (CC)

1(N)a. **Môtto yasûi no g̃a irímàsu nêe.**

    (J)   **Sôo desu nêe. Koré wa dòo desu ka⤳ Tyôtto tiísài desu kedo . .**

    b. **Iya, îi desu yo.** [calling to clerk] **Koré kudasaài.**

2(N)a. **Końnà no wa, koré dakè desu ka⤳**

    (J)a. **Ie, takúsañ gozaimàsu kedo . .**

    b. **Zyâa, itû-tu kudasai.**

    b. **Itû-tu desu neʕ**

    c. **Sore kara, kono aôi no mo, miĺ-tu oneg̃ai-simàsu.**

    c. **Aôi no wa, soré dakè desu nêe.**

    d. **Zyâa, kore o moó mit-tu kudasài.**

    d. **Kasíkomarimàsita. Hoká ni nàni ka?**

    e. **Soré dakè desu.**

3(N)a. **Kabañ wa, kono tiísài no dakê desu ka⤳**

    (J)   **Ie, oókìi no mo, sukôsi wa gozáimàsu yo⤳ . . . Koré dèsu kedo . .**

    b. **Âa, tyoódo ìi desu nêe. Koré kudasài.**

ENGLISH EQUIVALENTS

1(N)a. We need a cheaper one, don't we! [i.e., cheaper than the one we're looking at]

    (J)   That's right (isn't it). [picking up another kind] How about this one? It's a little small, but . . . [what do you think?]

b. No, that's fine. [calling to clerk]
Give us this one.

2(N)a. Is this all [you have] of ones like
this?

     (J)a. No, we have a lot, but . . . [how
many do you need?]

b. Then let me have five.

     b. That's five, right?

c. Then I'd like three of these blue
ones, too.

     c. That's all we have of the blue
ones . . .

d. In that case, give me three more
of these.

e. That's all.

     d. Certainly. Anything else?

3(N)a. Are these small ones the only bags
[you have]?

     (J) No, we do have (at least) a few large
ones. . . . They're these, but . . . (will
they do?)

b. Oh, [this] is just fine. Let me have
this one.

BREAKDOWNS
(AND SUPPLEMENTARY VOCABULARY)

1. **môtto**	additional, more
môtto yasûi no	one that is cheaper, cheaper one(s)
irímàsu /itte/ (SP1)	need, want; be required, be wanted
2. **koré dakè** (SP2)	just this/these
takúsàñ	many, much
gozáimàsu⁺ **/-màsite/** (SP3)	exist (inanimately); have /polite/
itû-tu (SP4)	five units (inanimate)
miꜜt-tù	three units (inanimate)
soré dakè	just that/those
moó miꜜt-tù (SP5)	three more units
hoka ni	besides, additionally
nâni ka	something
3. **kabañ**	bag, briefcase, satchel
+**suútukèesu**	suitcase
+**haꜛñdobàggu**	handbag
+**syoꜛppiñḡubàggu**	shopping bag
tiísài no dakê	just a small one/small ones
sukôsi	a small amount; a few

-tu: *Classifier for counting units of inanimate objects*

hitô-tu	1 unit	**miꜛt-tù**	3 units
hutá-tù	2 units	**yoꜛt-tù**	4 units

itû-tu	5 units	yat́-tù	8 units
mut́-tù	6 units	kokôno-tu	9 units
nanâ-tu	7 units	tôo	10 units

îku-tu 'how many units?'

MISCELLANEOUS NOTES (MN)

1. CC1 is a shopping situation in which two colleagues talk over their requirements before they make their decision on what to buy. On the accompanying video, they are buying a filing folder at a stationery store. The style is careful, with distal-style final predicates.

(N)a. **Môtto** links up directly with a predicate (here **yasûi**) and describes an additional amount or degree: **Môtto tâbete kudasai.** 'Eat more!' **Môtto oókìi zîsyo ḡa arímàsu ka✓** 'Are there any bigger dictionaries?' etc.

(J) **Kore wa**: the **wa** here is contrastive.
Tyôtto, which links up directly with a predicate, indicates a small amount as an extent pattern: **Tyôtto wakárimàsita.** 'I understood a little'; **Tyôtto hûbeñ desu.** 'It's a bit inconvenient'; etc. **Tyôtto** also occurs as a 'belittler'—similar to the unstressed 'just' in English expressions like 'Could I just ask you something?'—suggesting a lack of serious importance, often for the sake of politeness: **Tyôtto oneḡai-simasu.**; **Tyôtto sumímasèñ.**; etc. Compare also the use of **tyôtto** as a refusal (2B-CC3), suggesting that there is just 'a bit' of a problem preventing agreement or acceptance.

(N)b. **Koré kudasaài**: Since there is no particular stress on the actual selection when (N) calls to the clerk in this CC, the sequence is more apt to occur without particle **o** following **kore.** Note the lengthening of the second /a/ vowel as the customer calls out to the clerk who is at the other end of the store.

2. CC2 is also a shopping situation, but here the participants are a customer and a clerk. The customer uses the same careful style of speech, with **dèsu/-màsu** predicates (i.e., distal-style) and **kudásài** request forms. The clerk is speaking not only in a careful style; he is being polite as well, as evidenced by the use of **gozáimàsu** (cf. SP3, following) and **kasíkomarimàsita.**

Note the occurrences of **wa** signaling shifting, contrasting limited applicability. Note also the extent expressions—both numbers and **takúsàñ** 'a large quantity'—linked directly to predicates without particles.

(N)b, c, d. Contrast **sore kara** 'then' = 'after that' with **zyâ(a)** 'then' = 'in that case.'

(J)c. **Nêe** here is an example of its use in a reflective, nonconfrontational sense, which is gentle, nonaggressive, and even apologetic.

(J)d. **Hoká ni nàni ka?** is a fragment to be learned as a unit at this point; it will be analyzed later. Note that the **ka** of **nâni ka** 'something' is *not* the sentence-particle **ka.**

3. CC3 is another shopping situation with a customer and clerk as participants. As in CC2, the clerk's use of **gozáimàsu** is evidence of politeness. Both participants use a careful speech style, with distal-style predicates.

(J) **Sukôsi wa gozáimàsu** 'a few (at least) we do have.'
Sukôsi and **tyôtto** partially overlap in their usage: in some situations either may be used—but in such cases, **tyôtto** is a bit more casual and informal. However, **sukôsi** does *not* share **tyôtto**'s use as a 'belittler' nor as a polite refusal.

(N)b. Since (N) has been shown only one kind of bag, there is no emphasis on selection; hence **koré kudasài** without particle **o** is more likely.

The supplementary nominals are obviously words borrowed from English, but are none-theless now integral items in the Japanese vocabulary. The widespread carrying of bags and containers of varying shapes and sizes is a striking feature of the society.

Structural Patterns (SP)

1. DOUBLE-ḡa PREDICATES

Compare the following two pairs:

    (1)a. **Watási ḡa tukaimàsita.** '*I* used it.'

      b. **Koré o tukaimàsita.** 'I used *this*.' *and*

    (2)a. **Watási ḡa irimàsu.** '*I* need it.'

      b. **Koré ḡa irimàsu.** 'I need *this*.'

Tukáimàsu (1) belongs to a group of predicates[1] we will hereafter call OPERATIONAL PREDICATES; and verbals which can occur as such predicates, OPERATIONAL VERBALS. All predicates which may occur in combination with a /nominal + o/ phrase are in this category, although this is *not* a requirement for inclusion in the class. Such predicates regularly relate to an occurrence which can be brought about on purpose, by human decision or will. Examples of operational verbals already introduced include: **simâsu, tukúrimàsu, nomí-màsu, tabémàsu, itádakimàsu, ikímàsu,** and **kimâsu.** Additional examples (including other types of operational predicates) will be introduced later. The nominal in a /nominal + ḡa + operational/ sequence will be referred to as the OPERATOR; this is the person or thing that performs the operation or activity. The nominal in a /nominal + o + operational/ sequence, the 'acted upon', will be called the OPERAND.[2] In examples (1)a and b above, **watasi** is the operator, **kore** the operand, and **tukáimàsita** an operational verbal.

In contrast, in the **irimàsu** (2) examples above, both the 'needer' and the 'needed' are followed by ḡa.[3] **Irímàsu** belongs to a group of predicates we will call AFFECTIVE PREDICATES, and verbals which can occur as such predicates, AFFECTIVE VERBALS. These relate to con-ditions or occurrences which come about apart from human decision, will, or volition, such as understanding, needing, and being able. They never occur with /nominal + o/ phrases, but may occur with two types of /nominal + ḡa/ phrases, as in (2) above. Any predicate which can link up with two ḡa-phrases is affective, although this is not a requirement for inclusion in the class. Both of the nominals followed by ḡa will be called AFFECTS. When both occur in the same sequence, as in:

    Ano gakusee ḡa eéḡo ḡa wakarimàsu. '*That student* understands *English*,' i.e., '*That is the student* who is *English*-comprehending,'

the order of the two affects is fixed: affects of the first type will be called PRIMARY AFFECTS and those of the second type, SECONDARY AFFECTS. Thus, **ano gakusee** is a primary affect, **eeḡo** a secondary affect, and **wakárimàsu** an affective verbal.

---

  1. Recall that a predicate is a verbal expression, or an adjectival expression, or a /nominal + **dèsu**/ expression.

  2. Often—*but by no means always*—the 'operator' coincides with the subject in traditional terminology, the 'op-erand' with the direct object, and the 'operational predicate' with a transitive verb. But given the significant number of exceptions, it is better not to think in these traditional terms.

  3. Of course, with a change of focus, these ḡa-phrases, as well as the ḡa- and o-phrases in (1), may be replaced by **wa**-phrases or **mo**-phrases.

In addition to **irímàsu** and **wakárimàsu, dekímàsu** 'be possible', 'can do' is also a double-**ğa**, affective verbal. Additional affective verbals and other types of affective predicates will be introduced later.

The affective verbal **arímàsu** is also double-**ğa** in the sense that it may occur with two /nominal + **ğa**/ phrases, but its occurrences with only one affect are more common in the secondary affect relationship:

> **Ano gakusee ğa koñpyùutaa ğa arimasu.** '*That student* has *a computer.*'

> **Koñpyùutaa ğa arimasu.** 'There is (*or* I have) *a computer.*'

Possible, but less common, is /person + **ğa** + **arimasu**/ alone, with the meaning 'person has [it],' comparable to **anó gakusee ğa irimàsu (wakarimàsu, dekimàsu)**, '*That student* needs (understands, can do) [it],' all of which occur in a broader range of contexts.

Double-**ğa** predicates may occur in the following combinations with differences of focus:

> **X ğa Y ğa** + predicate

> **X wa Y ğa** + predicate

> **Y wa X ğa** + predicate

> **X wa Y wa** + predicate

> **Y wa X wa** + predicate

Examples:

> **Sâtoo-sañ ğa eéğo ğa dekimàsu.** 'It's *Mr/s. Sato* who is *English*-capable.'

> **Sâtoo-sañ wa eéğo ğa dekimàsu.** 'Mr/s. Sato (for one) is capable in *English.*'

> **Eéğo wa Sâtoo-sañ ğa dekimasu.** 'In English (at least), it's *Mr/s. Sato* who is capable.'

> **Sâtoo-sañ wa eéğo wa dekimàsu ğa . .** 'Mr/s. Sato (for one) *is capable* in English (at least), but . . .' (I'm not commenting on other languages).

> **Eéğo wa Sâtoo-sañ wa dekímàsu ğa . .** 'Concerning English—Mr/s. Sato (at least) *is capable,* but . . .' (I'm not commenting on other people).

Note that: (1) when the 'who' and 'what' are both expressed with particle **ğa**,[4] the 'who' precedes; (2) when a **wa**-phrase and a **ğa**-phrase both occur, the **wa**-phrase usually precedes; (3) when two **wa**-phrases occur, at least the second one is regularly contrastive; (4) **X** and **Y** may also occur without following **wa** and **ğa**, with the usual variation in focus.

The volitional/nonvolitional distinction reflected by operational/affective predicates is an important one in Japanese, and it exerts an influence on many patterns of the language. For example, in certain contexts—particularly in reference to oneself—the assertive sentence-particle **yo** is more apt to occur with operational predicates, but reflective **nêe** is particularly common with affective predicates (over which the individual has no control).

2. dakê

/Nominal **X** + **dakê**/ = 'to the extent of X,' 'just X'

The combination functions like a nominal of extent, and as such frequently links up directly with a following predicate to indicate the extent to which the predicate applies. In this pattern, **dakê** usually loses its accent. Thus:

> **Koré dake kaimàsita.** 'I bought just this.'

---

4. This type of sequence is most apt to occur within patterns indicating cause, condition, provision, etc., to be introduced in later lessons.

Tomódati dake kimàsita. 'Just a friend came.'

Kyôo dake dekimasu. 'I can do it just today.'

Koré dake wakarimasèñ. 'This much is incomprehensible.'

The nominal predicate **X dakê desu** describes a 'just X,' 'X-extent,' or 'X-limitation' situation. This occurs commonly in the pattern: /nominal **Y** + **(wa)** + **X dakê desu**/ = 'Y is described in terms of an X-limitation,' i.e., Y is the general category and X is its limitation. Note now how varied the English equivalents for this construction can be:

Kabañ wa koré dakè desu ka 'Are *these* the only bags?'

Zîsyo wa oókìi no dakê desu ka 'Do you have only *big* dictionaries?'

Oókìi no wa zîsyo dakê desu ka 'Are all the big ones *dictionaries*?'

Oókìi no wa takâi no dakê desu ka 'Are the big ones just *expensive* ones?'; 'Do you have only *expensive* big ones?'

Now ignore the English and examine the Japanese questions again, this time as /general category + **wa** + limitation + **dakê desu ka**/, i.e., 'Speaking of bags—is it just these?' 'Speaking of dictionaries—are they limited to big ones?' etc. Here again is a clear demonstration of the necessity to avoid trying to speak Japanese as a direct translation of English!

3. gozáimàsu +

Gozáimàsu is the polite equivalent of **arímàsu.** Both of these verbal forms are distal-style, as evidenced by **-mas-,** but in addition, **gozáimàsu** has a polite stem, which indicates deference and respect toward the person addressed (represented by /+/). In general, forms of **arímàsu** can be replaced by corresponding forms of **gozáimàsu,** but the reverse is not always true.[5] The polite equivalent of both **arímasèñ** and **nâi desu** is **gozáimasèñ,** and of both **arímasèñ desita** and **nâkatta desu, gozáimasèñ desita.**

Except for its use in ritual expressions (**arîgatoo gozaimasu, ohǎyoo gozaimàsu,** etc.), **gozáimàsu** occurs only in very polite, careful speech, including the language of service personnel. It is also heard frequently in public announcements. Note that in the Breakdowns, even the gerund for this verbal was cited in distal-style (**gozáimàsite**), the only gerund form for this verbal that occurs in modern Japanese.

The speaker's relationship to the person addressed determines the appropriateness of **gozáimàsu:** a Japanese secretary might use it in speaking to the company president, but the president would definitely not use it in addressing the secretary; a waiter might use it in addressing a customer, but the reverse would be unusual. It would not ordinarily occur in conversation among close friends nor in the language of young people or children. Beginning language students will find it to be a verbal they hear more often than use—except of course in ritual expressions used by everyone.

4. THE JAPANESE SERIES OF NUMERALS AND CLASSIFIERS: -tu

In addition to the previously introduced Chinese series of numerals, Japanese has a second series which is native to the Japanese language. We will hereafter refer to these numerals as the Japanese series.

Except for a few special forms, the Japanese series remains in the present-day language only through 10. Its principal occurrence is in combination with the classifier **-tu,** used to

5. For example, it is impossible to substitute **arímàsu** in **ohǎyoo gozaimàsu.**

count units of inanimate objects (cf. the list at the end of the Breakdowns). For some objects, this is the only way of counting; for others, the speaker has a choice of using this classifier or a more specialized one. It is this classifier that one uses if the specialized one is not known—provided the object being counted is inanimate and occurs in single units. Given the frequency of its occurrence, it is important to master the **hitô-tu** series thoroughly.

Note that the /t/ in **-tu** numbers is doubled (i.e. lengthened) when the numeral has only one syllable: **mit́-tù, yot́-tù, mut́-tù,** and **yat́-tù.** Note also the irregular **tôo** 'ten units.'

As a continuation of the **-tu** series beyond 10, the Chinese series is used, without **-tu.** Thus, while **itî** alone means only the mathematical entity 'one,' and **hitô-tu** refers to '1 unit,' **zyuúitì,** depending on context, means either the numeral '11' or '11 units.' Compare:

Nî-eñ arimasu.	'I have ¥2.'
Hutá-tu[6] arimàsu.	'I have 2 (units of a known category).'
Zyuúnì-eñ arimasu.	'I have ¥12.'
Zyuúni arimàsu.	'I have 12 (units of a known category).'

The Japanese series also occurs with other classifiers besides **-tu,** some of which will be introduced later.

5. / **moo** *+ QUANTITY/*

/**Moo** + a number or indefinite quantity expression/ = 'the named quantity in addition.' In this pattern there is no pause following **moo**: the entire sequence forms one unit and a single accent phrase. Examples:

moó hitò-tu	'one more unit'
moo hyaku-eñ	'¥100 more'
moó nì-hoñ	'two more long, cylindrical objects'
moó sukòsi *or*	
moó tyòtto	'a little more,' 'a few more'

Compare:

Moó sukòsi yasûi no (o) kudásài. 'Please give me one that's a little cheaper.' (i.e., is cheap to the extent of a little more)

Môtto yasûi no (o) kudásài. 'Please give me one that's cheaper.' (i.e., is cheap to a greater extent)

Yasûi no mo kudásài. 'Please give me a cheap one, too.'

☠ WARNING: **Moo** and **mo** are two entirely different words!

Drills

A 1. **Dôre ḡa irímàsu ka◞ Koré dèsu ka◞**
'Which one do you need? Is it this one?'

    Ie, aré ḡa irimàsu kedo . .
'No, I need that one, but . . .' (I hope it's not a problem).

2. **Dôre o kaímàsu ka◞ Koré dèsu ka◞**

    Ie, aré o kaimàsu kedo . .

---

6. Note that **nî** is absolutely impossible here.

'Which one are you going to buy? Is it this one?'

'No, I'm going to buy that one, but . . .' (I hope it's not a problem).

3. **wakárimasèñ**; 4. **tukáimàsita**; 5. **tabémàsu**; 6. **dekímàsu**

B 1. **Sâtoo-sañ ḡa irímasèñ neʃ**
'Mr/s. Sato doesn't need it—right?'

Iie. Watási dèsu yo. Watási ḡa irimasèñ.
'No, it's me. I don't need it.'

2. **Sâtoo-sañ ḡa ikímàsu neʃ**
'Mr/s. Sato is going—right?'

Iie. Watási dèsu yo. Watási ḡa ikímàsu.
'No. It's me. I'm going.'

3. **wakárimasèñ**; 4. **simâsita**; 5. **tukáimàsu**; 6. **dekímasèñ**

C 1. **Nihóñḡo mo dekímàsu ka**
'Can you [speak] Japanese, too?'

Nihóñḡo dèsu ka Sukôsi wa dekímàsu ḡa . .
'Japanese? I can [speak] it a little (at least) but . . .' (I wouldn't say more than that).

2. **Tanáka-sañ mo wakarimàsu ka**
'Does Mr/s. Tanaka understand, too?'

Tanáka-sañ dèsu ka Sukôsi wa wakárimàsu ḡa . .
'Mr/s. Tanaka? S/he understands a little (at least), but . . .' (I wouldn't say more than that).

3. **tyuuḡokuḡo/wakárimàsu**; 4. **ano gakusee/dekímàsu**; 5. **doituḡo/wakárimàsu**; 6. **tomodati/dekímàsu**

D 1. **Kore wa, Suzúki-sañ ḡa irimasu neʃ**
'This one Mr/s. Suzuki needs—right?'

Soré dèsu ka Iêie, Sâtoo-sañ ḡa irímasu yo
'That one? No, no, Mr/s. Sato needs [it].'

2. **Kore wa, Suzúki-sañ ḡa kaimàsu neʃ**
'This one Mr/s. Suzuki is going to buy—right?'

Soré dèsu ka Iêie, Sâtoo-sañ ḡa kaímàsu yo
'That one? No, no, Mr/s. Sato is going to buy [it].'

3. **dekímàsu**; 4. **simâsita**; 5. **wakárimàsu**; 6. **tukúrimàsita**

E 1. **Suzuki-sañ wa, koré ḡa irimàsu neʃ**
'Mr/s. Suzuki needs these—right?'

Suzúki-sañ dèsu ka Iêie, aré ḡa irimàsu yo.
'Mr/s. Suzuki? No, no, s/he needs those over there.'

2. **Suzuki-sañ wa, koré o kaimàsu neʃ**
'Mr/s. Suzuki is going to buy these—right?'

Suzúki-sañ dèsu ka Iêie, aré o kaimàsu yo.
'Mr/s. Suzuki? No, no, s/he's going to buy those over there.'

3. **tukáimàsu**; 4. **wakárimàsu**; 5. **simâsu**; 6. **dekímàsu**

F 1. **Kabañ wa, koré dakè desu ka**
'Is this the only bag?'

Kabáñ dèsu ka Iie, kabañ wa, takúsañ arimàsu kedo . .
'Bag? No, there are lots of bags, but . . .' (what exactly did you want?)

2. **Oókìi no wa, koré dakè desu ka**   **Oókìi no desu ka** **Iie, oókìi no wa,**
'Is this the only big one?'   **takúsañ arimàsu kedo . .**
                                         'Big one? No, *there are lots* of big ones,
                                         but . . .' (what exactly did you want?)

3. **kâsa**; 4. **yasásìi no**; 5. **biñseñ**; 6. **suútukèesu**; 7. **yasûi no**; 8. **nôoto**

G 1. **Tiísài kabañ wa, môtto arímàsu ka**   **Ie, tiísài no wa soré dakè desu ga . .**
'Are there any more small bags?'   'No, that's all, for small ones, but . . .'
                                         (would any other kind do?)

2. **Kurôi kâsa wa, môtto arímàsu ka**   **Ie, kurôi no wa, soré dakè desu ga . .**
'Are there any more black umbrellas?'   'No, that's all, for black ones, but . . .'
                                         (would any other kind do?)

3. **yasûi huutoo**; 4. **aôi hurosiki**; 5. **atárasìi zîsyo**; 6. **sirôi kamî**

H 1. **Kabañ wa, kono tiísài no dakê desu**   **Iie. Oókìi no mo takúsañ arimàsu yo**
ka   'No, there are lots of big ones, too.'
'Are these small ones the only bags?'

2. **Kâsa wa, kono oókìi no dakê desu**   **Iie. Tiísài no mo takúsañ arimàsu yo**
ka   'No, there are lots of small ones, too.'
'Are these big ones the only
umbrellas?'

3. **zîsyo/hurûi**; 4. **pêñ/takâi**; 5. **zassi/tumárànai**

I 1. **Kaímàsu ka**   **Êe, koré dake kaimàsu.**
'Are you going to buy [some]?'   'Yes, I'm going to buy just this.'

2. **Simâsu ka**   **Êe, koré dake simàsu.**
'Are you going to do [some]?'   'Yes, I'm going to do just this.'

3. **irímàsu**; 4. **dekímàsu**; 5. **nomímàsu**; 6. **arímàsu**

J 1. **Soré wa arimàsu.**   **A, gozáimàsu ka.**
'That we do have.'   'Oh, do you have it?' /polite/

2. **Soré wa tàkàku arímasèñ.**   **A, tâkàku gozáimasèñ ka.**
'That is not expensive.'   'Oh, it's not expensive?' /polite/

3. **arímàsita**; 4. **muzúkasiku nài desu**; 5. **arímasèñ**; 6. **atárasìku nâkatta desu**;
7. **arímasèñ desita**

● In drill J, the responder is being more polite than the original speaker. Repeat the drill (1) making the original speaker more polite than the responder, and (2) making both speakers use the polite style.

K 1. **Kore wa, hutátu arimàsu ga . .**   **Hitô-tu dake kudasai.**
'There are two of these, but . . .' (how   'Give me just one.'
many do you want?)

2. **Kore wa, itû-tu arímàsu ga . .**   **Yoť-tu dake kudasài.**
'There are five of these, but . . .' (how   'Give me just four.'
many do you want?)

3. **yát-tù**; 4. **mít-tù**; 5. **tôo**; 6. **yót-tù**; 7. **nanâ-tu**; 8. **zyuúitì**; 9. **mut-tù**; 10. **kokôno-tu**; 11. **zyuúnì**

L 1. **Kâsa wa?**   **Îp-poñ wa arímàsu kedo . .**
      'How about umbrellas?'   'There is one (at least), but . . .' (will that do?)

   2. **Zassi wa?**   **Iś-satù wa arímàsu kedo . .**
      'How about magazines?'   'There is one (at least), but . . .' (will that do?)

   3. **eñpitu**; 4. **syóppiñḡubàggu**; 5. **zîsyo**; 6. **taípuràitaa**; 7. **hurosiki**

● Repeat this drill, substituting other numerals in the responses.

M1. **Soré oneḡai-simàsu.**   **Îku-tu desu ka**
      'Let me have those.'   'How many (do you mean)?'

   2. **Kamî oneḡai-simasu.**   **Nâñ-mai desu ka**
      'Let me have some paper.'   'How many sheets (do you mean)?'

   3. **eñpitu**; 4. **nôoto**; 5. **huutoo**; 6. **kêeki**; 7. **peñ**

N 1. **Kabañ môtto arímàsu ka**   **Êe, moó huta-tu arímàsu kedo . .**
      'Are there any more bags?'   'Yes, there are two more, but . . .' (will that do?)

   2. **Boorupeñ môtto arímàsu ka**   **Êe, moó nì-hoñ arímàsu kedo . .**
      'Are there any more ballpoint pens?'   'Yes, there are two more, but . . .' (will that do?)

   3. **eéwa-zìteñ**; 4. **syóppiñḡubàggu**; 5. **kâsa**; 6. **suútukèesu**; 7. **kamî**; 8. **huutoo**

● Repeat this drill, substituting other numerals in the responses.

O 1. **Tyôtto tîísàku nâi desu ka**   **Sôo desu ne! Môtto oókìi no wa nâi desu**
      'Isn't it a bit small?'   **ka**
      'It is, isn't it. Isn't there a larger one (in contrast)?'

   2. **Tyôtto tâkâku nâi desu ka**   **Sôo desu ne! Môtto yasûi no wa nâi desu**
      'Isn't it a bit expensive?'   **ka**
      'It is, isn't it. Isn't there a cheaper one (in contrast)?'

   3. **tumárànaku**; 4. **hûrûku**; 5. **ôókìku**

● Repeat this drill, replacing **môtto** 'more' with **moó sukòsi** 'a little more' in the responses.

Application Exercises

A1. Again, with the help of objects and pictures of objects that represent vocabulary that has been introduced, practice asking and answering questions and making requests, using the following patterns:

   a. /Nominal/ **(wa) îku-tu arímàsu ka**

b. /Nominal/ (o) /number/ **kudásài . . . A. Moo** /number/ **onéĝai-simàsu.**

c. /Nominal X/ (o) /number/ **kudásài. Sore kara,** /nominal Y/ **mo** /number/ **kudásài.**

d. /Nominal X/ (wa) /nominal Y/ **dakê desu ka**⤸[7] **. . . Iie,** /nominal Z/ **mo arímàsu.**

e. /Nominal/ (wa) **môtto arímàsu ka**⤸ **. . . Iie,** /number/ **dakê desu.**

f. $\left\{ \begin{array}{l} \textbf{Môtto} \\ \textbf{Moó sukòsi} \end{array} \right\}$ /adjectival/ **no ĝa irímàsu ĝa, arímàsu ka**⤸

2. Check on who needs certain items and what items individual members of the group need.

3. Check on who understands (**wakárimàsu**) and can handle (**dekímàsu**) various languages, and what languages individual members of the group know.

B. Core Conversations: Substitution

Practice the Core Conversations, making appropriate substitutions in vocabulary without changing the basic framework. Be sure to retain the original Japanese patterns that you have heard on the tapes. Gestures must also be appropriate. And remember: Customers and clerks are rarely seated during the kinds of shopping situations exemplified in these Core Conversations!

SECTION B

Core Conversations (CC)

1(N)a. **Kore wa, miñna kinóo no siñbuñ dèsu ne!**

b. **Kyôo no wa?**

(J)a. **Hâi.**

b. **Kyôo no desu ka**⤸ **Sûĝu kimâsu yo.**

2(J)a. **Mimâsita ka**⤸—**Tanaka-sañ no atárasìi kuruma.**

b. **Dôitu no supóotukàa desu yo.**

c. **Aré dèsu yo. Ano gurêe no kurúma dèsu.**

(N)a. **Dôñna no desu ka**⤸

b. **Hee**⤸ **Sôo desu ka. Îi desu nêe.**

c. **Âa, kîree na kurúma dèsu ne!**

3(N)a. **Kore to kore, mít-tu-zùtu oneĝai-simasu. . . . Sore kara, sore mo itû-tu-hodo kudasai.**

b. **Sirôi no o oneĝai-simasu.**

(J) **Dôñna irô ĝa yorósìi desu ka**⤸

4(N)a. **Koóhìi ikâĝa desu ka**⤸

(J)a. **A. Arîĝatoo gozaimasu. Itádakimàsu.**

---

7. Expand this pattern by using adjectival modifiers. Example: **Oókìi zîsyo wa takâi no dakê desu ka**⤸

b. **Osatoo wa?**

5(N) **Kore mo sore mo, onázi zassi dèsu ka⤴**

b. **Dôo mo. . . . Oísìi desu nêe. . . . Gotísoosama dèsita.**

(J) **Ie, tiǧáimàsu yo⤸**

ENGLISH EQUIVALENTS

1(N)a. These are all yesterday's papers, aren't they.
  b. What about today's?

(J)a. Yes.
  b. Today's? They'll be here (*lit.* come) very soon.

2(J)a. Did you see it—Mr/s. Tanaka's new car?
  b. It's a German sportscar.
  c. That's it! It's that gray car over there.

(N)a. What kind (of one) is it?
  b. Wow! Really? That's great, isn't it!

  c. Oh, what a beautiful car!

3(N)a. I'd like three each of these and these. . . . And then give me (about) five of those, too.
  b. Let me have white ones.

(J) What color would you like?

4(N)a. How about some coffee?
  b. How about sugar?

(J)a. Oh, thank you. I'll have some.
  b. Thanks. . . . It tastes good, doesn't it! . . . It was delicious.

5(N) Are both this one and that one the same magazine?

(J) No, they're different.

BREAKDOWNS
(AND SUPPLEMENTARY VOCABULARY)

1. **mińnà**	all (everything or everybody)
kinoo no siñbuñ (SP1)	yesterday's paper(s)
kyôo no (SP1)	today's one(s)
sûǧu	soon, right away, promptly; readily
2. **mimâsu** /**mîte**/	look at, see
kuruma	car
Mimâsita ka⤸—kuruma. (SP2)	Did you see it?—the car.
Tanaka-sañ no kuruma	Mr/s. Tanaka's car
supóotukàa	sportscar
Dôitu	Germany
Dôitu no supóotukàa	German sportscar
+**zitêñsya**	bicycle
gurêe *or*	
+**haiiro**	gray
gurêe no kuruma	gray car

+ **gurîiñ** *or*	
+ **mîdori**	green
+ **tyairo**	brown
kîree na kuruma (SP1)	beautiful car
3. **mít-tu-zùtu**	three units each
itû-tu-hodo (SP3)	about five units
irô	color
dôñna irô	what (kind of) color?
+ **naniiro**	what color?
yorosii /-katta/	is good, is fine; never mind
4. **satôo/osatoo**	sugar
+ **mîruku**	milk
+ **kootya**	(black) tea
+ **(o)sake**	saké
+ **bîiru**	beer
+ **wâiñ**	wine
oisii /-katta/	is delicious, is good tasting
gotisoosama	a feast, a treat
5. **kore mo sore mo** (SP4)	both this one and that one
onazi zassi (SP1)	same magazine

Country Names

Nihôn/Nippòñ	Japan
Tyûuğoku	China
Taíwàñ	Taiwan
Kâñkoku	South Korea
Oósutorària	Australia
Îñdo	India
Amerika *or*	
Beekoku	U.S.A.
Kânada	Canada
Iğirisu *or*	
Eekoku	England
Hurañsu	France
Dôitu	Germany
Itaria	Italy
Supêiñ	Spain
Sôreñ *or*	
Sobíèto	U.S.S.R.

Miscellaneous Notes (MN)

1. CC1 is a brief exchange in a seminar room, between (N) and (J), acquaintances who maintain some distance, as evidenced by the style of speech.

(N)a. **Miǹnà** occurs here as an indicator of extent: these are today's papers 'to the extent of all of them.' In addressing a group of people, the less emphatic **mina** is compounded with **-saǹ : minâsaǹ** 'you all.'

(J)b. The nominal **sûg̊u** indicates time in a nonspecific sense ('very soon,' 'soon,' 'immediately,' 'any minute now') and manner ('readily,' 'without difficulty'). Compare **sûg̊u dekimasu** 'I can do it right away, readily'; **sûg̊u wakarimasita** 'I understood immediately, without difficulty.'

2. CC2 is a brief conversation between two colleagues who come upon Mr/s. Tanaka's car as they walk down the street. Their speech style is careful, with distal-style predicates.

(J)a. The verbal **mimâsu** (gerund: **mîte**) is an operational verbal which occurs with /nominal + **o**/ operands: **X g̊a Y o mimâsu** 'X looks at Y.' It corresponds to English 'see' only in those contexts where 'see' is equivalent to 'look at' or 'view'—*not* when 'see' is equivalent to 'meet up with.' Thus: **Anó gakusee (o) mìte kudasai.** 'Look at that student'; **Soré (o) mimàsita.** 'I saw (= looked at) that'; **Tanáka-saǹ (o) mimàsita** 'I saw (= looked at) Mr/s. Tanaka' (perhaps a doctor's utterance; *not* used in the sense 'I met with,' 'I had contact with').

(J)c. Unlike the previously introduced more basic color words, which were all adjectivals, these new color words, indicating shades, are nominals. Within this group, borrowings from English are becoming increasingly common.

3. CC3 is an excerpt from a shopping situation, in which (N) is the customer and (J) the clerk. The speech style is careful, with distal-style predicates.

(N)a. **-Zùtu** enters into compounds with quantity expressions to form a distributive: depending on context, **X-zùtu** means 'X of each' or 'X for each,' or 'X at a time.' The compound is regularly accented on the first mora of **-zùtu**.

(J). Note the use of **dôǹna irô** in asking for the identification of a color. **Yorosii** is an adjectival, similar to **îi** in underlying meaning but more formal and much more limited in the contexts in which it occurs. Unlike **îi,** it rarely occurs in the negative.

(N)b. Note the inclusion of particle **o** when the speaker is clearly indicating a selection.

4. CC4 is a 'coffee-break conversation.' The office visitor is being served something to drink (usually tea or coffee in such cases), a regular procedure in Japan. The polite **itádakimàsu** 'I will eat/drink/accept' is said at the time of acceptance of the offer and/or just before beginning to eat/drink. Silence while enjoying the break and the refreshment is not uncommon: patterns of talking and the social rules for silence are very different in Japan and America. The speech style is careful, with distal-style predicates. The conversation also contains a number of polite forms.

(J)b. 'Good' food and drink is **oisii** in Japanese, not **îi**. **Gotísoosama dèsita,** *lit.* 'it was a feast,' is a ritualistic expression that implies thanks for food or drink. It is regularly said by the guest/recipient at the conclusion or any eating or drinking event, elaborate or simple. **Tya** is the generic term for tea, particularly as an agricultural product. **Otya** (with the polite **o**-prefix) usually refers to Japanese-style green (or brown) tea as a beverage; **kootya** is 'black tea,' the variety more commonly drunk outside of Japan.

Bîiru and (o)sake have long been popular alcoholic drinks in Japan, but wine, along with hard liquor, is gaining in popularity. Drinking in Japan is a common activity; however, driving after drinking is assiduously avoided.

5. CC5 is a single exchange that might occur in any number of settings. The participants are using a careful style, with distal-style predicates.

COUNTRY NAMES

Nihôñ and **Nippòñ** are alternate forms of the same name. This kind of **-h/-pp-** alternation has already been encountered, in counting hundreds, for example. **Amerika** and **Iğirisu,** borrowings from English, are currently more common than the earlier names. The Japanese country names that are borrowings from foreign languages are nonetheless Japanese words and should be pronounced as such. (Compare the English pronunciation of 'France' in an English context. It is quite different from the native French pronunciation which occurs in French language contexts.)

Structural Patterns (SP)

1. NOMINAL MODIFIERS OF NOMINALS

a. /Nominal X + **no** + nominal Y/ = 'an X-kind of Y.' 'X-kind' can indicate possessor, location, price, derivation, etc.; in other words, an /**X no Y**/ is a Y described *in some way* by X. Examples:

Amerika no deñwa	'American telephones,' 'the telephones in America'
nihóñğo no hòñ	'Japanese-language books'
Tanáka-sañ no taipuràitaa	'Mr/s. Tanaka's typewriter'
kabáñ no irò	'the color of the bag'
dâre no kabañ	'whose bag?'
gurêe no kuruma	'a gray car'
niséñ-eñ no hòñ	'a ¥2000 book'
asíta no kàiği	'tomorrow's conference,' 'the conference tomorrow'

One nominal may have more than one modifier. Thus:

watakusi no hurûi taípuràitaa	'my old typewriter'
Tanaka-sañ no atárasìi kuruma	'Mr/s. Tanaka's new car'
tomodati no Amérika no koñpyùutaa	'my friend's American computer'
ano gurêe no kuruma	'that gray car'

In such cases the second modifier regularly begins a new accent phrase.

The modifying nominal may also be modified. Thus:

ano oókìi kabañ no irô	'the color of that big bag'
tomodati no kuruma no irô	'the color of my friend's car'

The above kinds of phrases may occur in all the same types of patterns as the final nominal alone. The important point to note is that in /**X no Y**/, the X describes the Y. Compare:

Kinóo no siñbuñ (o) kaimàsita. 'I bought yesterday's paper.'

Kinoo siñbuñ (o) kaimàsita. 'I bought a paper yesterday.' *Also*

Kono ni-sátù no hôñ (o) kaímàsita. 'I bought these two books.' (explains which books were bought) *and*

Konó hòñ (o) ni-sátu kaimàsita. 'I bought two of these books.' (explains to what extent there was buying)

This **no**—which for the time being will be called a 'connective' but will be analyzed and discussed in greater detail in a later lesson—must be kept distinct from the previously introduced nominal **no** 'one,' 'ones.' Observe what happens when these two **no** come together:

Hurûi kabañ desu.	>	**Hurûi no desu.**		
'It's an old bag.'		'It's an old one.'		
Gurêe no kuruma desu.	>	*__Gurêe no + no desu.__[8]	>	**Gurêe no desu.**
'It's a gray car.'		'It's a gray one.'		
Watási no hòñ desu.	>	*__Watasi no + no desu.__	>	**Watási nò desu.**
'It's my book.'		'It's my one.' ('It's mine.')		

In other words, /connective **no** + nominal **no**/ is contracted into a single **no** which is at once the connective and the nominal. This **no** (unlike either of the components alone) is accented if the preceding word is unaccented.[9]

In describing a nominal as an item that is near the speaker—**kore**—we might form a phrase like *__kore no hon__ 'the book which is described as this thing.' But /**kore** + **no**/ contracts into **kono**; such contractions give rise to the already familiar pre-nominal series **kono, sono, ano, dôno.**

b. /Nominal X + **na** + nominal Y/ = 'an X-kind of Y.' Within the major nominal word-class is a subclass distinguished by the fact that while most nominals are followed by **no** when describing a following nominal (as in [a] above), the members of this subclass are followed by **na**. They will hereafter be referred to as NA-NOMINALS. All **na**-nominals refer to qualities, but not all nominals of quality are necessarily **na**-nominals. From now on, all newly introduced **na**-nominals will be identified by the designation /**na**/ in the Breakdowns. The **na**-form itself will be analyzed in a later lesson.

Remember that **na**-nominals *are* nominals, occurring in the usual /nominal + **dêsita**/ and /nominal + **zya arímasèñ**/, etc. patterns. It is the /nominal X + **na** + nominal Y/ pattern that makes them a special subclass.

Na-nominals introduced thus far are: **kîree, bêñri, hûbeñ, zañnèñ, damê, daízyoobu.**[10]

When **na**-nominals modify the nominal **no**, the combination /**na** + **no**/ results: no contraction occurs. Thus: **kîree na no** 'a pretty one.'

c. /Nominal + nominal/ Nominals which can link up with nominals directly, without **no** or **na**, all belong to special subcategories. One group we have already met is the class of compound numbers, like **itímàñ ni-sêñ gohyaku sâñzyuu gô-eñ** '¥12,535.' Another group consists of 'changelings'—words which started out in another word-class and later moved over to the nominal class. An example of this group is **onazi**. We find **onázi dèsu, onázi dèsita, onázi zya arimasèñ** (or **nài desu**)—clearly indicating membership in the nominal

---

8. An asterisk before a Japanese sequence means that this particular sequence does NOT occur.

9. But note that /nominal **no** + connective **no**/—the reverse order—does NOT contract: compare **atárasìi kabañ no irô** 'the color of the new bag' and **atárasìi no no irô** 'the color of the new one.'

10. While **daízyòobu** is a **na**-nominal, its actual occurrences in the pre-nominal position which requires the **na**-form are comparatively rare.

class. But where we would expect **onazi** linked to a following nominal with **no** or **na**, we find instead the surprising **onazi zassi** 'same magazine.' This is a remnant of its original membership in the adjectival class[11] before it moved over to the nominal class, its regular affiliation today.

A third group of /nominal + nominal/ patterns is the phrases consisting of /**moo** + quantity nominal X/, meaning 'X in addition' (example: **móo sukòsi** 'a little more'). Here the **moo** indicates the manner in which the following quantity is to be interpreted. Again, only a special subclass of nominals is involved.

2. INVERTED SENTENCES

The major sentences introduced prior to this section all ended with a predicate—verbal, adjectival, or /nominal + **desu**/—with or without following sentence-particles. But very often in conversation, we encounter what amounts to an inverted sentence: it's as if what should have been the beginning of the sentence occurs at the end. For example: in CC2, the major sentence **Tanaka-sañ no atárasìi kuruma mimâsita ka** occurs as **Mimâsita ka—Tanaka-sañ no atárasìi kuruma.** Note that what is normally sentence-*final* intonation occurs *within* an inverted sentence.

Inverted sentences are often the result of afterthoughts or amplifications. After beginning a sentence, the speaker may decide s/he should have given more details initially, and a correction of the oversight is made by inserting them at the end of the Japanese sentence. In other cases, the speaker may add on to the major thrust of the message, which is stated initially, further details which are felt to be useful in clarifying the intent. In general, inverted sentences are more frequent in relaxed, informal conversation.

3. -hodo

Following quantity expressions, **-hodo** indicates approximation; it implies that the stated quantity is the upper limit, i.e., 'about as much as ———.' The corresponding question word is **dore-hodo** 'about how much?'

In Japanese, nonspecificity is closely associated with politeness. In particular, when **-hodo** is used with small numbers, it tends to have this implication. Whereas 'about two things' sounds rather strange in English, **hutá-tù-hodo** is not at all unusual in Japanese.

4. kore mo sore mo

/Nominal X + **mo** + nominal Y + **mo**/ = 'both X and Y,' 'X *and* Y.' The pattern indicates a parallel linkage of two nominals with a predicate: often the two nominals together represent an entirety within the given context ('children *and* adults,' 'friends *and* enemies,' 'big ones *and* small ones,' etc.); sometimes they represent a marked, notable combination on the given occasion ('drink beer *and* wine,' 'eat pie *and* cake,' etc.). Examples:

Pâi mo kêeki mo oísìi desu. 'The pie *and* cake are good.'

Taípuràitaa mo koñpyùutaa mo tukaimasu. 'I'm going to use the typewriter *and* the computer.'

Kyôo mo asítà mo kimasu. 'I'm coming today *and* tomorrow.'

Compare now the **X to Y** and **X mo Y mo** patterns:

Hôñ to zaśsi (o) kaimàsita.   'I bought a book and a magazine.'

11. This affiliation continues to be reflected in written Japanese in the **-ku** form **onaziku** 'similarly.'

Hôñ mo zaśsi mo kaimàsita.	'I bought both a book and a magazine'; 'I bought a book *and* a magazine.'

In addition to the meaning difference, there is a pattern difference: /**X to Y**/ fills the same slot within a sentence as **Y** alone—a nominal: it occurs immediately before **dèsu**, or before phrase-particles like **ḡa, o, wa,** and **mo**; /**X mo Y mo**/, on the other hand, patterns like **Y mo** alone and therefore regularly links up directly with a predicate (verbal, adjectival, or /nominal + **desu**/).

Drills

A 1. **Dâre no kurúma dèsu ka⌐**
  'Whose car is it?'

  Sôo desu nêe. . . . Seńsèe no kuruma zya nâi desu ka⌐
  'Let's see . . . Isn't it the teacher's car?'

2. **Dâre no kabáñ dèsu ka⌐**
  'Whose bag is it?'

  Sôo desu nêe. . . . Seńsèe no kabañ zya nâi desu ka⌐
  'Let's see . . . Isn't it the teacher's bag?'

3. **kâsa**; 4. **eeḡo**; 5. **teḡami**; 6. **kootya**

B 1. **Kyôo no siñbuñ dèsu ka⌐**
  'Is it today's paper?'

  Iie, kinóo no siñbuñ dèsu yo⌐
  'No, it's yesterday's paper.'

2. **Kinóo no kàiḡi desita ka⌐**
  'Was it yesterday's conference?'

  Iie, otótòi no kâiḡi desita yo⌐
  'No, it was the conference the day before yesterday.'

3. **asâtte no kâiḡi desu**; 4. **kinóo no deñwa dèsita**; 5. **asíta no kàiḡi desu**; 6. **kinóo no siñbuñ dèsu**

C 1. **Ano kuruma wa?**
  'What about that car?'

  Anó kuruma dèsu ka⌐ Watási nò desu kedo . .
  'That car? It's mine (= my one) but . . .' (why do you ask?)

2. **Ano kabañ wa?**
  'What about that bag?'

  Anó kabañ dèsu ka⌐ Watási nò desu kedo . .
  'That bag? It's mine but . . .' (why do you ask?)

3. **huutoo**; 4. **biñseñ**; 5. **oturi**; 6. **kamî**

D 1. **Seńsèe no kurúma dèsu ka⌐**
  'Is that the teacher's car?'

  Êe, seńsèe no desu yo⌐
  'Yes, it's the teacher's (one).'

2. **Kinóo no siñbuñ dèsu ka⌐**
  'Is that yesterday's paper?'

  Êe, kinóo nò desu yo⌐
  'Yes, it's yesterday's (one).'

3. **tomodati no kabañ**; 4. **Huráñsu no supootukàa**; 5. **Nihoñ no biñseñ**; 6. **Amerika no zassi**

● Repeat the preceding drill, changing the responses to the negative by replacing **êe** with **iie** and **dèsu** with **zya nâi desu**.

E. In this drill, move the descriptive word from its position before **dèsu** to a new position immediately before the nominal, making any changes that are required.

1. **Seńsèe no kuruma, kîree desu ne!**   **Êe, kîree na kurúma dèsu ne!**
   'The doctor's car is pretty, isn't it.'   'Yes, it's a pretty car, isn't it.'

2. **Tanáka-sañ no supootukàa, gurîiñ**   **Êe, gurîiñ no supóotukàa desu ne!**
   desu ne!   'Yes, it's a green sportscar, isn't it.'
   'Mr/s. Tanaka's sportscar is green,
   isn't it.'

3. **Suzuki-sañ no kabañ/atárasìi desu;** 4. **Nihóñ no bìiru/oísìi desu;** 5. **koṅna tèepu/ bêñri desu;** 6. **anó gakusee no zìsyo/onázi dèsu;** 7. **kono atárasìi koṅpyùutaa/hû-beñ desu**

F 1. **Oísii kootya dèsu ka⌐**   **Sôo desu yo⌐ Oísìi no desu.**
   'Is it good tea?'   'Right. It's (some that's) delicious.'

2. **Kîree na zaśsi dèsu ka⌐**   **Sôo desu yo⌐ Kîree na no desu.**
   'Is it a pretty magazine?'   'Right. It's a pretty one.'

3. **Gurêe no kurúma dèsu ka⌐**   **Sôo desu yo⌐ Gurêe no desu.**
   'Is it a gray car?'   'Right. It's a gray one.'

4. **bêñri na koṅpyùutaa;** 5. **tomódati no ziteñsya;** 6. **muzúkasii hòñ;** 7. **nimáñ-eñ no zìsyo;** 8. **mîdori no hurosiki;** 9. **damê na têepu;** 10. **gurîiñ no kâsa;** 11. **hurûi zi-teñsya**

G 1. **Nihoñ no kuruma arímàsu ka⌐**   **Êe, arímàsu yo⌐—takusañ.**
   'Are there any Japanese cars?'   'Yes, there are—lots.'

2. **Nihóñġo no hòñ kaímàsita ka⌐**   **Êe, kaímàsita yo⌐—takusañ.**
   'Did you buy any Japanese books?'   'Yes, I did (buy)—lots.'

3. **kêeki tabémàsita;** 4. **bîiru nomímàsita;** 5. **osatoo irímàsu;** 6. **kamî tukáimàsu;** 7. **pûriñ tukúrimàsita**

H 1. **Koṅna zassi, ikâġa desu ka⌐**   **Sôo desu nêe. Zyâa, iś-satu-zùtu kudásài.**
   'How about magazines like these?'   'Let me see. Well, give me one of each.'

2. **Koṅna hurosiki, ikâġa desu ka⌐**   **Sôo desu nêe. Zyâa, ití-mai-zùtu kudásài.**
   'How about furoshiki like these?'   'Let me see. Well, give me one of each.'

3. **eñpitu;** 4. **kêeki;** 5. **pêñ;** 6. **kamî;** 7. **nôoto;** 8. **huutoo**

I 1. **Kamî irímàsu ka⌐**   **Sôo desu ne! Nî-mai-hodo onéġai-**
   'Do you need any paper?'   **simàsu.**
             'That's right. Let me have (about) two
             sheets.'

2. **Nôoto irímàsu ka⌐**   **Sôo desu ne! Nî-satu-hodo onéġai-**
   'Do you need any notebooks?'   **simàsu.**
             'That's right. Let me have (about) two.'

3. **huutoo;** 4. **eñpitu;** 5. **hurosiki;** 6. **boorupeñ**

J 1. **Sâtoo-sañ ğa mimàsu ka‿**
'Is *Mr/s. Sato* going to look at it?'

 Êe, Sâtoo-sañ mo watási mo mimàsu yo‿
'Yes, both Mr/s. Sato and I will look at it.'

 2. **Sâtoo-sañ ğa osáke dèsu ka‿**
'Is *Mr/s. Sato* [having] sake?'

 Êe, Sâtoo-sañ mo watási mo osake dèsu yo‿
'Yes, both Mr/s. Sato and I are [having] sake.'

 3. **komárimàsu;** 4. **gakúsee dèsu;** 5. **tukáimàsu;** 6. **irímàsu**

K 1. **Koré o mimàsu ka‿**
'Are you going to look at *this one*?'

 Êe, kore mo aré mo mimàsu yo‿
'Yes, I'm going to look at both this one and that one.'

 2. **Koré ğa muzukasìi desu ka‿**
'Is *this one* difficult?'

 Êe, kore mo aré mo muzukasìi desu yo‿
'Yes, both this one and that one are difficult.'

 3. **hûbeñ desu;** 4. **irímàsu;** 5. **damê desu;** 6. **tukáimàsu;** 7. **îi desu;** 8. **kaímàsu**

L 1. **Końna irò wa, damê desu yo.**
'This (kind of) color (at least) *is no good.*'

 Zyâa, dôñna irô ğa yorósìi desu ka‿
'Then what (kind of) color would be good?'

 2. **Kêeki no hôñ wa, damê desu yo.**
'A book on cake (at least) *won't do.*'

 Zyâa, nâñ no hôñ ğa yorósìi desu ka‿
'Then what book (*lit.* a book of what) would be good?'

 3. **kyôo;** 4. **watasi;** 5. **osake;** 6. **konó zìsyo;** 7. **eeğo**

M 1. **Oísìi desu ka‿**
'Is it tasty?'

 Ie, oísiku nài desu yo.
'No, it isn't (tasty).'

 2. **Wâiñ desu ka‿**
'Is it wine?'

 Ie, wâiñ zya nâi desu yo.
'No, it isn't (wine).'

 3. **mińnà desu;** 4. **haíiro dèsu;** 5. **îi desu;** 6. **sûğu desu;** 7. **mîdori desu;** 8. **zêñbu desu;**
 9. **kîree desu;** 10. **aôi desu;** 11. **tyaíro dèsu;** 12. **siрôi desu**

Application Exercises

A1. Using various items (books, pens, pencils, paper, etc.) belonging to members of the group, check on ownership, condition, appearance, price, etc., using a variety of patterns such as:

 a. **Sono** /object/ **(wa), dâre no desu ka‿**
 b. **Sono** /description + object/ **(wa), dâre no desu ka‿**

 c. /————-sañ/ **no** /object/ **(wa),** $\begin{cases} \textbf{îkura} \\ \textbf{atárasìi} \\ \textbf{dôñna irô} \end{cases}$ **desu ka‿**

          naníiro dèsu ka‿

    d. /Object/ **mo** /object/ **mo,** ———-**sañ nò desu ka**⤸

    e. /Description/ **no (wa),** /object/ **dakê desu ka**⤸

    f. /Object/ **(wa),** /description/ **no dakê desu ka**⤸

Be sure to include colors and prices in your descriptions.

    2. Act out shopping situations, requesting approximate quantities (using **-hodo**), distributive quantities (using **-zùtu**), additional quantities (using **moo**), and additional items (using **mo**).

    3. Using pictures of various kinds of automobiles, identify them as to country of origin, describing them also as to color, newness, cost, etc.

B. Core Conversations: Substitution

Practice the Core Conversations, making substitutions in vocabulary, but retaining the basic framework exactly. Be sure to use appropriate props, gestures, and intonation patterns. If the situation calls for it, stand up! Using the videotape as your guide, bow when appropriate.

SECTION C

Eavesdropping

(Answer the following questions, in English, on the basis of the accompanying recorded material. In each exchange, A refers to the first speaker, and B to the second.)

 1a. What are A and B looking at?
  b. What kind is it?
  c. Who was mistaken about identifying it?
  d. What was the mistake?
 2a. What is A concerned about?
  b. What does A request?
 3. What does B want?
 4. Who came?
 5a. What does A want?
  b. What is B's first assumption as to the number requested?
  c. What is the correct number?
  d. What is B's name?
 6a. What is being discussed?
  b. How is it described?
  c. What does B request?
  d. How does A respond?
 7a. What is a probable setting for this conversation?
  b. What specifically is being discussed?
  c. What is B's request?
 8a. What is A looking for?
  b. What color is it?
  c. Why is A upset?
 9. What is B buying? How many? What color?
10a. What is B going to do?
  b. What invitation does B extend to A?
  c. What is A's concern?

   d. What is B's reaction?

11a. What has A just done?

   b. What is B urging?

   c. How does A react?

12a. What were A's two mistaken impressions?

   b. Why does A thank B?

   c. What is A apparently going to buy?

13a. Where does this conversation probably take place?

   b. What does A hope there are more of?

   c. How many more are there?

14a. What are A and B discussing?

   b. What kind is it?

   c. Which member of the conversation is probably not Japanese? What is the evidence?

15a. What does A request, initially?

   b. What is the problem?

   c. What possible problem is raised in connection with the suggested substitute?

   d. What color is the substitute?

   e. How many are there?

   f. How many does A buy?

Utilization

(Remember to include a stimulus and/or response for each elicited item.)

1. Find out if all those magazines over there are Chinese-language ones.

2. A colleague is looking for Mr. Sato. Tell her that he's coming very soon.

3. You've located magazines in a number of foreign languages at the bookstore. Inquire about French-language ones.

4. Tell a colleague to look at the new sportscar over there.

5. Find out what kind (of one) the teacher's new car is.

6. Comment on what an inconvenient computer this is.

7. Ask the shopkeeper for three each of these red and these black ballpoint pens.

8. Ask the shopkeeper for (about) five of those large envelopes. Then ask for two sheets of the large paper, too.

9. Comment on how delicious green tea is.

10. As a host(ess): offer coffee; offer milk and sugar; urge a guest to eat/drink more.

11. As a guest: begin eating/drinking; comment on how delicious the food/drink is; after being urged to have more, accept just a little; conclude your eating/drinking.

12. Find out what kind (of one) that gray car is.

13. A suggestion has been made to order wine. Check on what kind of wine would be good.

14. Ask your colleague if what is near you and what is near him are the same wine.

15. Ask your supervisor (politely!) if he has today's paper.

16. Warn a colleague that although the cake is good, the pie isn't good at all.

17. Find out if both this green tea and the brown (kind) are Japanese tea.

18. You're having coffee with a friend. Ask for a little more sugar.

19. The clerk has just shown you a bag. Explain that you need a larger one.

20. The instructor has asked who needs a Japanese–English dictionary. Tell her that you do.

21. Ask the clerk if these are the only small shopping bags.

22. Ask the clerk if the brown ones are the only large furoshiki.

23. You've been examining a suitcase that is very expensive. Ask the clerk if she (also) has a cheaper suitcase of the same color.

24. You are discussing your office situation. Explain that there are lots of typewriters but just one computer.

25. Find out the owner of this black car.

Check-up

1. What do we call verbals like **kaímàsu, tukúrimàsu, tukáimàsu**, etc., which may occur with /nominal + **o**/ phrases? What do we call the person (or thing) performing the operation? the 'acted upon?' With what particles are these marked? (A-SP1)

2. How do verbals like **wakárimàsu, dekímàsu,** and **irímàsu** differ in meaning from those described in (1) above? What do we call this type? What does the designation 'double-**ga** predicates' refer to? What is the difference between a primary and secondary affect? What is special about **arímàsu** as an affective verbal? (A-SP1)

3. What does **dakê** mean? In /**X wa Y dakê desu**/ sentences, which nominal represents the general category under discussion? Which represents the limitation? (A-SP2)

4. What is the polite equivalent of **arímàsu**? Toward whom does it indicate politeness? In general, can forms of **arímàsu** be made polite by replacing them with the corresponding form of this polite verbal? Is the reverse also true? (A-SP3)

5. What is the classifier **-tu** used to count? Which set of numerals does it compound with? How high does this series extend? How are higher numbers handled, in a continuation of this series? When is the /t/ of **-tu** numbers doubled (i.e., lengthened)? (A-SP4)

6. When does **moo** indicate additional quantity? Contrast **moo, môtto,** and **mo**. (A-SP5)

7. What is the most common pattern for making one nominal describe another? (B-SP1)

8. Discuss the difference in the following patterns: **kîree na kuruma** 'pretty car,' **gurêe no kuruma** 'gray car,' and **kurôi kuruma** 'black car.' (B-SP1)

9. What is the difference between the **no** of **tomodati no kuruma** and of **kurôi no**? (B-SP1)

10. When the nominal **hôñ** 'book' is replaced by **no** 'one' in the following, what sequences result?

       Kurôi hôñ desu > ?

       Watási no hôñ desu > ?

       Kîree na hôñ desu > ?   (B-SP1)

11. What is unusual about the phrase **onazi zassi**? (B-SP1)

12. What is meant by an 'inverted sentence?' Under what circumstances do such sentences frequently occur? (B-SP2)

13. What is the meaning of **-hodo** following a quantity expression? What connotation does it often have? (B-SP3)

14. What is the difference in meaning between /**X to Y**/ and /**X mo Y mo**/? How does their structural patterning differ? Compare **Koóhìi to otyá (o) kaimàsita.** and **Koóhìi mo otyá mo nomimàsita.** (B-SP4)

15. What three types of distribution does **-zùtu** indicate? With what kind of expressions does it compound? (B-MN3)

Lesson 6

SECTION A

Core Conversations

1(N)a. **Tyôtto ukáğaimàsu ğa . .**
   b. **Uénò-eki, kotíra no hòo desu ka⌄**

   c. **A, wakárimàsita. Dôo mo arîğatoo gozaimasita.**

2(N) **Sumímasèñ. Paáku-bìru wa, dôtira desu ka⌄**

3(N)a. **Sumímasèñ. Deñwa wa, dôtira desu ka⌄**

   b. **Êe.**
   c. **A, wakárimàsita wakárimàsita.**

4(J) **Mâe ni koósyuudèñwa arímàsu neˀ**

(J)a. **Hâi.**

   b. **Sôo desu. Moó sukòsi sakí ni arimàsu.**

(J) **Paáku-bìru desu ka⌄ Sâa. Tyôtto wakárimasèñ nêe. Konó heñ nì wa arímasèñ nêe.**

(J)a. **|Anoo| Mukoo ni baíteñ ğa arimàsu ne!**
   b. **Ano baiteñ to dêğuti no aída dèsu.**

(N) **Êe. Mâe ni mo usíro nì mo arímàsu yo⌄**

ENGLISH EQUIVALENTS

1(N)a. May I ask you a question?
   b. Is Ueno Station in this direction?

   c. Oh, I see. Thank you very much.
2(N) Excuse me. Where(abouts) is the Park Building?

(J)a. Certainly.
   b. That's right. It's a little farther ahead.

(J) The Park Building? Hmmm. I'm afraid I don't know. It's not around here (at least).

135

3(N)a. Excuse me. Where(abouts) is the telephone?

   b. Yes.

   c. Oh, I see, I see.

4(J)   There's a public phone in front, isn't there?

(J)a. Uh, over there there's a stand (isn't there).

   b. It's between that stand and the exit.

(N)   Yes. There's one in front *and* in back.

BREAKDOWNS
(AND SUPPLEMENTARY VOCABULARY)

1. **ukáḡaimàsu** ↓ /ukaḡatte/	(I) inquire, (I) ask /polite/
êki	station
Uénò-eki (SP1)	Ueno Station
+**Toókyòo-eki**	Tokyo Station
kotira (SP2)	this side, this way, hereabouts, here; this alternative (of two)
+**sotira** *or*	
+**atira**¹	that side, that way, thereabouts, there; that alternative (of two)
hôo	direction, way, side; alternative
kotíra no hòo	this direction; this alternative
saki (SP3)	ahead
moó sukòsi saki (SP4)	a little farther ahead
sakí ni arimàsu (SP5)	it's located ahead
2. **bîru**	office building
Paáku-bìru	the Park Building
dôtira	which side? which way? whereabouts? where? which alternative?
sâa	hmmm!
heñ	area, vicinity
konó heñ ni arimàsu	it's located in this area
konó heñ nì wa (SP6)	in this area (at least)
+**miti**	street, road
3. **mukoo**	over there; beyond
mukóo ni arimàsu	it's located over there
baiteñ	concession stand, kiosk
+**misê/omise**	store, shop
dêḡuti	exit
+**iriḡuti**	entrance

1. The usual difference found between **so-** and **a-** words applies here.

aida	interval, space between
baiteñ to dêḡuti no aida	between the concession stand and the exit
4. **mâe**	front; in front
mâe ni arimasu	it's located in front
koósyuudèñwa	public telephone
+**koobañ**	police box
+**tôire** *or*	
+**teârai/otéàrai**	toilet
usíro	back; in back, behind
usíro ni arimàsu	it's located in back
mâe ni mo usíro nì mo	both in front and in back

MISCELLANEOUS NOTES

The CCs of this lesson are all connected with location and asking and giving directions, control of which is an essential skill in Japan. The unnamed streets and the many buildings without numbers present a constant challenge. This phenomenon can perhaps be regarded as an extension of the in-group/out-group structuring of Japanese society. Members of an in-group are familiar with the location of things with which they have some connection, but traditionally there has been no reason to establish a system that made the location of everything—including one's home—immediately obvious to the entire population.

Detailed directions are regularly given in terms of landmarks, distances, named intersections, and stations on public transportation lines. Addresses, which are based on areas and blocks and on lots numbered according to the order in which they were originally registered, are principally for postal use—in a mail system that is impressively efficient.

In CC1, 2, and 3, the participants are strangers, in each case a foreigner asking directions of a Japanese stranger. In general, foreigners are probably less reluctant to approach Japanese strangers in this way. Japanese seem more apt to turn to a policeman or a shopkeeper for directions. However, if foreigners do seek help from a Japanese, they often receive unusually solicitous help, sometimes extending to being accompanied to their final destination. This is particularly true outside of the large cities.

Given the fact that CC1, 2, and 3 are conversations between strangers, it is not surprising that their speech style reflects distance. All final predicates are in the distal-style.

1(N)a. **Ukáḡaimàsu**↓ 'I inquire,' like **itádakimàsu**↓ and **onéḡai-simàsu**↓, is a polite verbal that refers deferentially to the activity of the speaker (or the speaker's in-group) vis-à-vis the out-group: 'I/we (deferentially) inquire of you.' The use of **tyótto** politely minimizes the importance of the inquiry. This minor sentence ending in **ḡa** or **kedo** (*lit.* 'I'm just going to ask you [something] but' [is it all right?]) is a frequently used introduction to a request for information.

(N)c. **Wakárimàsita** 'understanding occurr*ed*'—i.e., as a result of the explanation.

2(N) **Bîru,** an abbreviation of the loanword **bîrud(e)iñḡu,** regularly refers to Western-style, commercial buildings.

(J) **Sâa** indicates here that the speaker is pondering his answer. The use of **nêe** in two successive sentences emphasizes his deliberation, with a connotation of sharing rather than confrontation. **Tyôtto wakárimasèñ.:** *lit.* 'it's a bit unclear.'

4. CC4 is an exchange between two colleagues who use a speech style that reflects distance. The final predicates are distal-style.

(J) Public phones are color-coded in Japan. The red phones are for local calls only, blue for limited long distance as well, yellow covering long distance throughout Japan, and green all long-distance including overseas calls. Calls on green phones can be paid with a prepaid 'telephone card', eliminating the need for coins.

Koobañ are usually small, one- or two-room buildings, located in every neighborhood of Japanese cities, where policemen are constantly on duty.

Tôire, an abbreviation of the loanword **tôiretto**, is now a word in common usage. In Japanese this is a polite word. **Teârai**, and the more polite **otéàrai** (used more commonly by women), is a native Japanese equivalent; literally meaning 'the hand-washing [place],' it represents a polite avoidance of using a specific term for an 'unmentionable.' This same function is served by the use of a foreign word (i.e., **tôire**). After all, foreign words lack the emotional content of one's native language.

Structural Patterns

1. PHRASES AND COMPOUNDS

Toókyoo no èki is a /nominal X + **no** + nominal Y/ phrase in which **Tookyoo** modifies (= describes) **êki**: 'station(s) in Tokyo,' 'Tokyo station(s),' 'stations of Tokyo,' 'Tokyo's stations,' etc.

Toókyòo-eki, on the other hand, is a single, compound nominal which names one particular station, Tokyo Station. Thus, while **Toókyòo-eki** is among the group described as **Toókyoo no èki,** only one particular **Toókyoo no èki** is **Toókyòo-eki.** The accent pattern of a compound is not predictable on the basis of the accentuation of its component parts (cf. **Tookyoo** + **êki** > **Toókyòo-eki**).

> **Toókyoo no èki wa Toókyòo-eki dakê desu ka**⤸ 'Is Tokyo Station the only station in Tokyo?'

> **Iêie, takúsañ arimàsu yo**⤸ 'No, no. There are many.'

Compound nominals consisting of a /proper name + category name/ are very common types of names for specific members of the category. Examples: **Uénò-eki, Kyoótò-eki, Paáku-bìru.**

2. THE **kotira** SERIES

The **kotira, sotira, atira, dôtira** series, another nominal **ko-so-a-do** group, refers to:
(1) one alternative of two
(2) one side of two
(3) direction
(4) general location

In the last meaning, members of this series serve to indicate location in terms that are slightly less precise, for the sake of politeness. Thus:

kotira   'this alternative (of two)'; 'this side'; 'I' (i.e., this side of the conversation) /polite/;[2] 'this direction'; 'here(abouts)'

2. This use is particularly common on the telephone.

sotira	'that alternative (of two)'; 'the side near you'; 'you' (i.e., your side of the conversation /polite/;[2] 'that direction'; 'there(abouts)'
atira	'that alternative over there (of two)'; 'that side over there'; 'that direction (over there)'; 'over there'; 'that place (known to us)'; 'there(abouts)'
dôtira	'which one of two?' 'which side?' 'which direction?' 'where(abouts)?'

While each member of this set may, by itself, refer to an alternative or a direction or side, combinations with the nominal **hôo** 'alternative,' 'side,' 'direction,' are also very common. Example: **kotíra no hòo** 'this alternative,' 'this side,' 'this direction.'

3. PLACE WORDS

Words like **saki, mâe, usiro, mukoo,** and **aida** are nominals which designate location.[3]
Saki refers to an area up ahead, on the same road or path or route. It is regularly preceded by a modifier.
Mâe may refer either to the front part of something or the area in front of something, depending on context.
Usiro, parallel to **mâe**, refers to the back part of a thing or the area in back.
Mukoo refers to an area on the far side, or beyond, a designated point relative to the location of the speaker. It may also refer to 'over there' in the sense of 'abroad,' 'out of the country.'
Aida refers to the space between two entities or two groups of entities.
　Remembering that /**X no Y**/ is a kind of **Y**, consider the following phrases:

êki no mukoo	'beyond the station'
mukóo no èki	'the station beyond'
bîru no mâe	'(in) front of the building'
mâe no bîru	'the building in front'
êki no mâe no bîru	'the building in front of the station'
Tanaka-sañ no usiro	'in back of Mr/s. Tanaka'
ano mise no aida	'between those stores'
dêġuti to 'baiteñ no aida	'between the exit and the concession stand'
watasi to 'tomodati no aida	'between my friend and me'
baiteñ to 'deñwa no aida no tôire	'the toilet between the concession stand and the telephone'
dêġuti no mukoo no baiteñ no usiro	'(in) back of the concession stand beyond the exit'

Observing the usual functioning of the particles in question, we note:

　Mukóo ġa èki desu ka⤻ 'Is *over there* the station?' (I'm looking for the station) *and*
　Mukoo wa êki desu ka⤻ 'Is over there *the station*?' (I'm trying to determine what is over there)

　In 5B-SP1, we learned that /connective **no** + nominal **no**/ is contracted into a single **no**. Thus:

---

3. Except for **usiro** and **mukoo**, these words may also refer to location in time as well as space. This usage will be treated later.

Mukóo no[4] èki desu. 'It's the station beyond.' >

***Mukoo no[4] no[5] dèsu.** > **Mukóo nò[6] desu.** 'It's the one beyond.'

However, /nominal **no** or contracted **no** + connective **no**/ does *not* contract. Thus:

Ano sirôi bîru no mukóo dèsu. 'It's beyond that white building.' >

Ano sirôi no[5] no[4] mukóo dèsu. 'It's beyond that white one.' *and*

Mukóo no èki no mâe desu. 'It's in front of the station over there.' >

***Mukoo no[4] no[5] no[4] mâe desu** > **Mukóo nò[6] no[4] mâe desu.** 'It's in front of the one over there.'

4. moó sukòsi saki

When one nominal describes another nominal, the regular pattern is /**X no Y**/, as in **mukóo no èki** 'the station beyond.'

However, we have already learned that there are subclasses of nominals (the **na**-nominals and extent nominals, for example) that have special characteristics. Another subclass is a class of nominals whose meaning reflects possible division by degree. For example, we can speak of something that is 'farther ahead,' or 'farthest front,' or 'top-most,' but not *'farther book,' or *'most station,' etc. These 'degree-able' nominals we will hereafter refer to as RELATIONALS. They occur not only in regular nominal patterns, but also may be directly preceded by quantity expressions without an intervening particle. Compare:

êki no saki 'up ahead of the station' *but*

sukôsi saki 'a little ahead'

môtto saki 'farther ahead'

mit́-tù saki 'three ahead' (depending on context, may refer to traffic lights, intersections, etc.)

Quantity expressions can also be expanded to /**moo** + quantity/ 'quantity in addition' within such patterns. Thus: **moó sukòsi saki** 'a little farther ahead.'

5. PATTERNS OF LOCATION; PHRASE-PARTICLE ni

/Place-nominal **X** + **ni** + **arímàsu**/ = '[something] is located (inactively) in X.' In this pattern, **X ni** tells where something is located. **Ni** is a phrase-particle. Examples:

Toókyoo ni arimàsu. 'It's in Tokyo.'

Usíro ni arimàsita. 'It was in back.'

Êki ni arímàsu ka⤳ 'Is it in the station?'

Konó zìsyo ni arímàsu neʃ 'It's in this dictionary—right?'

Paáku-bìru, dôtira ni arímàsu ka⤳ 'Where (i.e., in what place) is the Park Building?'

Note that here, *as always*, it is important to identify the basic function of the particle, not a particular English equivalent. The Japanese equivalents of 'it's *in* the desk, *on* the desk, *under* the desk, *near* the desk, *next to* the desk, etc.' may all contain particle **ni** indicating location, in contrast with a great variety of English patterns. *Think in terms of functions and relationships—not English words!*

---

4. Connective.
5. Nominal.
6. Contraction of /connective **no** + nominal **no**/.

Another pattern of location in Japanese is /place-nominal X + **dèsu**/, but location is only one possible meaning of this combination. Remember that /**X dèsu**/ ranges in meaning from '[something or somebody] equals [is exactly equivalent to] X' to 'is in some way described by X.' It is the latter meaning that applies when /**X dèsu**/ is identified as a pattern of location. Thus, while **Toókyoo ni arimàsu** refers *only* to the location of something in Tokyo, **Toókyoo dèsu** = 'It's Tokyo' (identification), *or* 'It's in Tokyo,' *or* 'S/he's in Tokyo,' *or* 'S/he's a Tokyoite,' etc. Which meaning fits depends on the context.

In question-and-answer sequences, it is possible to find /place nominal **ni arímàsu**/ answers to **dèsu**-questions and vice versa, as well as structurally parallel answers.

6. MULTIPLE PARTICLES

We have already learned that /**X wa**/ indicates that X is the limit to which the predicate is being applied in the given context, implying that there *may* also be other items that in reality do apply (i.e., 'X at least,' 'X for one') or that X is being contrasted with other items, while /**X mo**/ indicates that X *additionally* applies to the predicate ('X too,' 'X also,' 'even X').

In this section we find that the X of /**X wa**/ and /**X mo**/ may also consist of a /nominal + particle/, resulting in multiple particles. The particle in such cases is regularly a particle other than **ḡa** or **o**. The usual meaning of **wa** and **mo** is now applied to the entire preceding combination. Compare:

Konó èki ni arimasu. 'There's [one] in this station.'

Konó èki ni wa arímàsu ḡa . . 'There is [one] in this station (at least), but . . .' (I'm not commenting on other stations).

Konó èki ni mo arimasu. 'There's [one] in this station, too.'

Following an unaccented nominal, **ni** is accented before **wa** and **mo** (cf. CC4[N]).

Be careful to distinguish between:

Deñwa wa kotíra nì mo arimasu. 'Telephones are *here, too*.' (in addition to other places) *and*

Deñwa mo kotíra ni arimàsu. '*Telephones* are here, *too*.' (in addition to other things).

7. WORD ORDER

Examination of major sentences[7] reveals the following facts about word order in Japanese:

1. Sentences end in a predicate (a verbal expression, adjectival expression, or /nominal + **dèsu**/ expression) with or without following sentence-particles.

2. A modifier of a nominal always precedes the nominal.

3. Phrases ending in **wa** usually occur at the beginning of the sentence.

4. The relation between a nominal and the predicate it links up with is indicated by a following phrase-particle (or lack of particle), resulting in relatively free order for the nominal phrases. Both: **Tomodati ḡa siñbuñ o kaimàsita.** and **Siñbuñ o tomódati ḡa kaimàsita.** refer to the same activity. Also, **Hôñ o takúsañ kaimàsita.** and **Takusañ, hôñ o kaímàsita.** describe the same occurrence.

5. For a given combination, there is a normal, common, unmarked order which differs only in emphasis and focus from the same items sequenced differently. In *unmarked* sequencing,

a. a **ḡa**-phrase precedes an **o**-phrase, both occurring close to the predicate;

7. Not under consideration here are inverted sentences, minor sentences, or fragments.

   b. **wa**-phrases occur initially;
   c. time-related phrases occur before place-related phrases;
   d. extent expressions follow the measured nominal.

Example: **Tomodati wa 'kinoo zîsyo o nî-satu kaímàsita.** 'A friend bought two dictionaries yesterday.'

Focus is indicated by accent patterns[8] and/or particles. It can also be reinforced by shifting the order of phrases while maintaining the same particles. Examples:

   Tomódati ǧa kinoo ikimàsita. (focus on **tomodati ǧa**)

   Takúsañ zassi o kaimàsita. (focus on **takusañ**)

   Soré o kinoo kaimàsita. (focus on **sore**)

Note the following location patterns, which show a contrast in particles as well as in order and focus:

   Êki wa môtto sakí ni arimàsu.   'The station is farther *ahead*.'

   Êki ǧa môtto sakí ni arimàsu.   '*A/The station* is farther ahead.'

   Môtto saki ni êki ǧa arimasu.   'Farther ahead there's *a/the station*.'

   Môtto saki ni êki wa arímàsu ǧa . .   'Farther ahead there *is* a station (at least), but . . .' (I'm not commenting on other things).

   Môtto sakí nì wa êki wa arímàsu ǧa . .   'Farther ahead (at least) there *is* a station (at least) but . . .' (I'm not commenting on what things are in other places).

   Môtto saki ni êki wa arímasèñ ka⤹   'Is(n't) there a station (for one thing) farther ahead?' (asking directions: the speaker hopes there *is* a station but [politely] implies the possibility of a negative).

Drills

A 1. **Êki, dôtira desu ka⤹ Môtto sakí dèsu ka⤹**
      'Where's the station? Is it farther ahead?'

   Êki desu ka⤹ Êe, môtto sakí dèsu yo⤹
   'The station? Yes, it's farther ahead.'

   2. **Tôire, dôtira desu ka⤹ Kotíra dèsu ka⤹**
      'Where's the rest room? Is it this way?'

   Tôire desu ka⤹ Êe, kotíra dèsu yo⤹
   'The rest room? Yes, it's this way.'

   3. **koobañ/mâe**; 4. **baiteñ/mukoo**; 5. **iriǧuti/atira**; 6. **koósyuudèñwa/usiro**

B 1. **Mukoo wa, êki desu ka⤹**
      'Is [the place] over there *a station*?'

   Êe, êki desu yo⤹ Êki ǧa mukóo dèsu.
   'Yes, it's a station. *A station* is over there.'

   2. **Mâe wa, deñwa dèsu ka⤹**
      'Are [the things] in front *telephones*?'

   Êe, deñwa dèsu yo⤹ Deñwa ǧa màe desu.
   'Yes, they're telephones. *Telephones* are in front.'

---

8. See Introduction.

3. usiro/baiteñ; 4. aida/omise; 5. mukoo/Toókyòo-eki

C 1. **Tyôtto ukáḡaimàsu kedo, Uénò-eki**   **Uénò-eki desu ka✓ Sâa. Tyôtto**
    wa, kotíra no hòo desu ka✓   **wakárimasèñ nêe.**
    'Excuse me. Is Ueno Station *this way*?'   'Ueno Station? Hmm. I'm afraid I don't
                                            know.'

   2. **Tyôtto ukáḡaimàsu kedo, dêḡuti wa,**   **Dêḡuti desu ka✓ Sâa. Tyôtto**
      kotíra no hòo desu ka✓   **wakárimasèñ nêe.**
      'Excuse me. Is the exit *this way*?'   'The exit? Hmm. I'm afraid I don't know.'

   3. **Paáku-bìru**; 4. **baiteñ**; 5. **tôire**; 6. **koósyuudèñwa**; 7. **otéàrai**

D 1. **Paáku-bìru wa, konó heñ ni**   **Paáku-bìru desu ka✓ Iya, konó hen nì**
    arimàsu ka✓   **wa arímasèñ nêe.**
    'Is the Park Building *around here*?'   'The Park Building? No, I'm afraid *it's not*
                                           around here (at least).'

   2. **Iriḡuti wa, mukóo dèsu ka✓**   **Iríḡuti dèsu ka✓ Iya, mukóo nì wa**
      'Is the entrance over there?'   **arímasèñ nêe.**
                                         'The entrance? No, I'm afraid *it's not* over
                                         there (at least).'

   3. **tôire/mâe desu**; 4. **dêḡuti/usíro dèsu**; 5. **koósyuudèñwa/konó saki dèsu**

E 1. **Sore wa, konó bìru ni arímàsu ka✓**   **Êe. Konó bìru ni mo anó bìru ni mo**
    'Are they (the topic of discussion) in   **arímàsu yo✓**
    this building?'   'Yes. They're in this building *and* in that
                                          building.'

   2. **Sore wa, konó zìsyo ni arímàsu ka✓**   **Êe. Konó zìsyo ni mo anó zìsyo ni mo**
      'Are they in this dictionary?'   **arímàsu yo✓**
                                            'Yes. They're in this dictionary *and* in that
                                            dictionary.'

   3. **êki**; 4. **siñbuñ**; 5. **miti**; 6. **heñ**; 7. **hôñ**; 8. **misê**

F 1. **Mâe desu ka✓**   **Mâe zya nâi desu nêe.**
    'Is it the front?' *or* 'Is it in front?'   'It's *not* the front.' *or* 'It's *not* in front.'

   2. **Mâe ni arímàsu ka✓**   **Mâe ni wa arímasèñ nêe.**
      'Is it in front?'   'It's *not* in front (at least).'

   3. **usíro dèsu**; 4. **mukóo dèsu**; 5. **aída ni arimàsu**; 6. **konó saki dèsu**; 7. **usíro ni arimàsu**

G 1. **Koósyuudèñwa wa, ano mise no**   **Koósyuudèñwa desu ka✓ Êe, mâe desu**
    mâe desu ka✓   **ne!**
    'Is the public phone in front of that   'The public phone? Yes, it's in front.'
    store?'

   2. **Êki wa, ano mise no mukóo dèsu**   **Êki desu ka✓ Êe, mukóo dèsu ne!**
      ka✓   'The station? Yes, it's beyond.'

'Is the station beyond those stores?'

3. **Paáku-bìru/saki**; 4. **tôire/mâe**; 5. **deñwa/usiro**

H 1. **Mukoo ni koósyuudèñwa ḡa**　　　**Sôo desu ne! Koósyuudèñwa ḡa arímàsu**
   arímàsu kedo . .　　　**ne!**
   'Over there there's a *public phone,*　'That's right. There's *a public phone,* isn't
   but . . .' (weren't you looking for one?)　there.'

   2. **Mukoo ni baíteñ ḡa arimàsu kedo . .**　**Sôo desu ne! Baíteñ ḡa arimàsu ne!**
   'Over there there's a *concession stand,*　'That's right. There's *a concession stand,* isn't
   but . . .' (weren't you looking for one?)　there.'

   3. **koobañ**; 4. **tôire**; 5. **êki**; 6. **otéàrai**

I 1. **Kono heñ ni deñwa arimasèñ ka⤾**　**Deñwa dèsu ka⤾ Arímàsu yo⤾ Kotíra no**
   'Is(n't) there a telephone around　　　**hòo desu.**
   here?'　　　　　　　　　　　　　'A telephone? Yes, there is. It's this way.'

   2. **Konó bìru ni tôire arímasèñ ka⤾**　**Tôire desu ka⤾ Arímàsu yo⤾ Kotíra no**
   'Is(n't) there a restroom in this　　　**hòo desu.**
   building?'　　　　　　　　　　　'A restroom? Yes, there is. It's this way.'

   3. **konó èki/baiteñ**; 4. **konó èki/otêarai**; 5. **kono heñ/koobañ**; 6. **kono heñ/êki**; 7. **kono**
   baiteñ/mîruku

J 1. **Konó bìru no ʼbaiteñ wa?**　　　**Konó bìru ni wa ʼbaiteñ wa arímasèñ**
   'What about the concession stand in　**nêe.**
   this building?'　　　　　　　　　'In this building (at least), I'm afraid there
   　　　　　　　　　　　　　　　is no concession stand (at least).'

   2. **Kono heñ no ʼkoobañ wa?**　　　**Konó heñ nì wa ʼkoobañ wa arímasèñ**
   'What about the police box in this　　**nêe.**
   area?'　　　　　　　　　　　　　'In this area (at least), I'm afraid there is
   　　　　　　　　　　　　　　　no police box (at least).'

   3. **bîru/koósyuudèñwa**; 4. **êki/tôire**; 5. **misê/deñwa**; 6. **baiteñ/mîruku**

K 1. **Mâe no baíteñ dèsu neʃ**　　　**Êe, mâe no desu.**
   'You mean the stand in front—right?'　'Yes, it's the one in front.'

   2. **Usíro no dèḡuti desu neʃ**　　　**Êe, usíro nò desu.**
   'You mean the rear exit—right?'　　'Yes, it's the one in the rear.'

   3. **mukóo no tòire**; 4. **atira no koobañ**; 5. **konó heñ no èki**; 6. **konó miti no misè**

L 1. **Anó èki no mâe no deñwa dèsu neʃ**　**Êe, êki no mâe no desu.**
   'You mean the phone in front of that　'Yes, it's the one in front of the station.'
   station—right?'

   2. **Anó koobañ no usiro no misè desu**　**Êe, koobañ no usíro nò desu.**
   neʃ　　　　　　　　　　　　　'Yes, it's the one in back of the police box.'
   'You mean the shop in back of that
   police box—right?'

3. **baiteñ/mukoo/tôire**; 4. **bîru/saki/misê**; 5. **êki/misê/kêeki**

M 1. **Ano sirôi bîru no mâe desu ka**   **Êe, sirôi no no mâe desu.**

   'Is it in front of that white building?'   'Yes, it's in front of the white one.'

2. **Ano gurêe no kuruma no usíro**   **Êe, gurêe no no usíro dèsu.**

   dèsu ka   'Yes, it's in back of the gray one.'

   'Is it in back of that gray car?'

3. **atárasìi koñpyùutaa/mukoo**; 4. **oókìi bîru/saki**; 5. **guríiñ no supóotukàa/usiro**

N 1. **Iríguti no mukoo dèsu ka**   **Êe. Iríguti to baíteñ no aida dèsu.**

   'Is it beyond the entrance?'   'Yes. It's between the entrance and the

                                    stand.'

2. **Deñwa no mukoo dèsu ka**   **Êe, Deñwa to baíteñ no aida dèsu.**

   'Is it beyond the telephones?'   'Yes, it's between the telephones and the

                                      stand.'

3. **tôire**; 4. **dêguti**; 5. **teârai**; 6. **koósyuudèñwa**

O 1. **Dôtira no hôo ga takâi desu ka**   **Kotíra no hòo ga takâi desu nêe.**

   'Which one (of two) is [more]   *'This one* is [more] expensive.'

   expensive?'

2. **Dôtira no hôo ga muzúkasìi desu**   **Kotíra no hòo ga muzúkasìi desu nêe.**

   ka   *'This one* is [more] difficult.'

   'Which one (of two) is [more]

   difficult?'

3. **oisii**; 4. **îi**; 5. **atárasìi**; 6. **yasasii**

Application Exercises

A1. Spread out closed paper bags and boxes containing pens, pencils, newspapers, books, magazines, etc. In order to answer questions, students must actually check the contents. Make position changes during the course of the drill. Ask (and answer) questions such as these:

    a. **Sotira ni X ga arímàsu ka**; **Sotira (wa) X desu ka**

    b. **Sotira ni X ga arímàsu ga, Y wa?**; **Sotira (wa) X dèsu ga, Y wa?**

    c. **Sotira ni nâni ga arímàsu ka**; **Sotira (wa) nâñ desu ka**

    d. **Kotira ni X ga arímàsu kedo, sotíra nì mo arímàsu ka**

    e. **X (wa) dôtira ni arímàsu ka**; **X (wa) dôtira desu ka**

2. Using models[9] of stations, office buildings, telephones, stands, and rest rooms, locate them appropriately and ask (and answer) questions of the following kind:

    a. **/Place/ ni X ga arímàsu ka**; **/place/ (wa) X desu ka**

  9. A simple kind of model consists of a small container (a styrofoam bowl, a berry box, etc.) or a block of wood with an appropriate picture affixed to the top.

b. **X (wa) dôtira** $\begin{cases} \textbf{desu} \\ \textbf{ni arímàsu} \end{cases}$ **ka✔**

c. **X (wa) Y no** /place/ $\begin{cases} \textbf{dèsu} \\ \textbf{ni arímàsu} \end{cases}$ **ka✔**

d. **X (wa) nâñ no** /place/ $\begin{cases} \textbf{dèsu} \\ \textbf{ni arímàsu} \end{cases}$ **ka✔**

e. **X (wa) nâñ to nâñ no aída** $\begin{cases} \textbf{dèsu} \\ \textbf{ni arímàsu} \end{cases}$ **ka✔**

f. **X (wa)** /place/ $\begin{cases} \textbf{dèsu} \\ \textbf{ni arímàsu} \end{cases}$ **ḡa, Y wa?**

g. /Place A/ **ni X ḡa arímàsu ḡa,** /place B/ **ni wa?**

/Place A/ **wa X desu ḡa,** /place B/ **wa?**

3. Using the same visual aids as in (2), practice asking directions and providing answers, utilizing such expressions as **tyôtto ukáḡaimàsu ḡa; sâa; tyôtto wakárimasèñ nêe; moó sukòsi; |anoo|; sôo desu nêe; wakárimàsita**, as well as echo questions in your exchanges. Be sure that your intonations are Japanese and not a transfer of English intonations that reflect thinking in English.

4. Set out pairs of objects differing in price, quality, newness, degree of interest, difficulty, etc. Ask (and answer) the following questions:

a. **Dôtira ḡa** $\begin{cases} \textbf{takâi} \\ \textbf{îi} \\ \textbf{atárasìi} \\ \textbf{omósiròi} \\ \textbf{muzúkasìi} \\ \textbf{oísìi} \end{cases}$ **desu ka✔**

b. **Konó hòo ḡa** /quality/ **dèsu ka✔**

c. /Thing/ **no hôo ḡa** /quality/ **dèsu ka✔**

d. **Kono** /thing/ **no hôo ḡa** /quality/ **dèsu ka✔**

B. Core Conversations: Substitution

Review the Core Conversations, making appropriate substitutions in the location words and the items being located. As usual, retain the basic patterns and the overall construct of the conversations. Pay special attention to your intonation, timing, and gestures.

SECTION B

Core Conversations

1(N)a. **Amérika-taisìkañ wa Toránomoñ dèsu neʃ**

    (J)a. **Êe, sôo desu ḡa . .**

  b. **Toranomoñ no dôko desyoo ka.**

      b. **Oókura-hòteru no sûḡu sôba desu.**

2(N)a. **Sumímasèñ.**

    (J)a. **Hâi.**

b. **Kokó no tosyòkañ wa dôko desyoo ka.**

b. **Tosyôkañ desu ka✓ Ano sirôi oókìi tatêmono no tonári dèsu kedo . .**

c. **Hidáridònari desu ka✓**

c. **Ie, miǧídònari desu.**

d. **A, wakárimàsita. Dôo mo 'osewasama.**

3(N)a. **Are wa ryokáñ desyòo ka nêe.**

(J)a. **Sâa, döo desyoo ka nêe. . . . Yappàri ryokáñ dèsu ne!**

b. **Takâi desyoo nêe.**

b. **Sôo desyoo nêe.**

4(N) **Amérika-ryoozìkañ dôko desyoo ka.**

(J) **Dôko desyoo ka nêe.**

5(N) **Sumímasèñ. Asoko wa yuúbìñkyoku desyo?**

(J) **Hidári no hòo desu ka✓ Sôo desu yo✓**

ENGLISH EQUIVALENTS

1(N)a. The American Embassy is in Toranomon—right?

(J)a. Yes, that's right, but . . . (do you know where?)

b. Where in Toranomon would it be?

b. It's right near the Hotel Okura.

2(N)a. Excuse me.

(J)a. Yes?

b. Where would the library here be?

b. The library? It's next to that big, white building, but . . . (do you see it?)

c. Is it (next door) on the left?

c. No, it's (next door) on the right.

d. Oh, I see. Thanks for your help.

3(N)a. I wonder if that's an inn.

(J)a. Hmm, I wonder. . . . It *is* an inn, isn't it.

b. It must be expensive!

b. It must be!

4(N) Where would the American consulate be?

(J) Where *would* it be!

5(N) Excuse me. That place over there is a post office—right?

(J) Do you mean on the left? Yes, it is.

BREAKDOWNS
(AND SUPPLEMENTARY VOCABULARY)

1. **taísìkañ**   embassy
   Amérika-taisìkañ   American Embassy
   Toranomoñ   (a section of Tokyo)
   dôko (SP1)   what place? where?

Toranomoñ no dôko	where in Toranomon? what part of Toranomon?
desyòo (SP2)	/tentative of **dèsu**/
hôteru	hotel
Oókura-hòteru	Hotel Okura
sôba	nearby
sûĝu sôba	immediate vicinity
+ **mukooĝawa**	opposite side, the other side
2. **koko**	this place, here
tosyôkañ	library
kokó no tosyòkañ	the library here, the library in this place
tatêmono	building
(o)tonari	next door, adjoining place
hidari	left
hidáridònari	next door on the left
miĝi	right
miĝídònari	next door on the right
osewasama	(thank you for) your helpful assistance
3. **ryokañ**	Japanese-style inn
X desyòo ka nêe (SP3)	I wonder if it's X!
4. **ryoózìkañ**	consulate
Amérika-ryoozìkañ	American Consulate
5. **asoko**	that place (over there), there
+ **soko**	that place, there
yuúbìñkyoku	post office
hidári no hòo	the left side, the left direction
+ **gekizyoo**	theater
+ **eéĝàkañ**	movie theater
+ **kooeñ**	park
+ **byooiñ**	hospital
+ **terâ/otera**	Buddhist temple
+ **zìñzya**	Shinto shrine
+ **kyookai**	church

MISCELLANEOUS NOTES

The CC in this section all relate to the giving of directions and locating and identifying particular buildings. The participants generally use a careful, deferential style of speech, with final predicates in the distal-style.

1. In CC1, a foreigner (N) asks a Japanese colleague (J) about the location of the American Embassy.

Sûḡu sôba 'immediate vicinity' is another example of a /nominal + nominal/ sequence without intervening connective. **Sûḡu** occurs in this kind of pattern in combination with a number of place nominals: **sûḡu mâe** 'right in front'; **sûḡu usiro** 'right in back'; **sugu soko** 'right there'; **sûḡu mukoo** 'immediately beyond.'

2. In CC2, a foreigner (N) asks a Japanese stranger (J) about the location of a library on a campus.

(J)b. **Tatêmono,** a general word for 'building,' occurs here with three modifiers: **ano, sirôi,** and **oókìi.** Note the order of color before size, in contrast with English.

(N)c, (J)c. The compound nominals **miḡídònari** and **hidáridònari** have the nominal **tonari** as their second part, in a slightly altered form. This kind of change will be discussed in detail later. **Tonari** may refer to a building, a room, or even a person: the crucial feature is adjoining location.

(N)d. **Osewasama** is a polite, ritualistic fragment based on the nominal **sewâ** 'help,' 'care,' 'assistance.' With an added **dèsita,** it becomes a distal-style major sentence of increased formality.,

3. In CC3, two acquaintances puzzle over the identification of a building.

(N)a. **Ryokañ,** the Japanese-style inn, is markedly different from the Western-style **hôteru** in both the style of rooms and of service.

(J)a. **Yáppàri** indicates that the building is indeed an inn after all—i.e., when sufficient evidence has become available.

4. In CC4, two colleagues try to locate the American Consulate on a map.

5. In CC5, a foreigner (N) checks the identification of a building with a stranger (J). The **-kañ** of **eéḡàkañ**—and of **tosyôkañ, ryokañ, taísìkañ,** and **ryoózìkañ**—is a word-partial (i.e., never a word by itself) which refers to public buildings.

Structural Patterns

1. THE **koko** *SERIES*

In this section, another nominal **ko-so-a-do** series is introduced, this group referring to specific place.

koko	'this place (near the speaker)'; 'here'
soko	'that place (nearer the person addressed)' *or* 'that place just introduced in the conversation'; 'there'
asoko	'that place over there (removed from speaker and addressee) *or* 'that place known to speaker and addressee'; 'there'; 'over there'
dôko	'what place?' 'where?'

In those contexts in which the **kotira** series refers to location (rather than direction or alternatives), it is a less precise, and accordingly softer and slightly more polite, equivalent of the **koko** series.

Remember that a place word + **dèsu** refers either to equivalence or to location or other kind of connection, depending on context. Thus:

(1) **Koko (wa) dôko desu ka**   'What place is this (place)?' 'Where am I?'

(2) **Koko (wa) Kyôoto desu.**   'This place is *Kyoto*.'

(3) **Tanaka-sañ (wa) asóko dèsu.**   'Mr/s. Tanaka is *over there*.'

(4) **Soko (wa) kokó dèsu yo.** 'That place (just introduced in this conversation) is *this place*.'

Note the following contrast:

/**dôko no X**/ = a kind of X, 'the X of what place?' 'the X (which is) where?'

/**X no dôko**/ = a kind of **dôko**, 'what place in X?' 'where in X?' 'what part of X?' (*lit.* 'what place of X?')

Thus:

Dôko no tosyôkañ ğa îi desu ka. 'What library (*lit.* the library of what place) is good?'

Kokó no tosyòkañ desu. '(It's) the library here.'

Anó hòñ wa tosyôkañ no dôko ni arímàsu ka. 'Where in the library (*lit.* in what place of the library) is that book?'

Tosyôkañ no kokó dèsu. 'It's in this part (*lit.* this place) of the library.'

2. **desyòo**

Compare: **Sôo desu.** 'That's right.'

  Sôo desyoo. 'That's probably right.'

Desyòo is the TENTATIVE equivalent of **dèsu** (both are distal-style), indicating probability, lack of certainty, imprecision, and/or indirectness. The last meaning is particularly common in questioning. Like **dèsu**, it occurs after nominals and adjectivals and follows similar accent patterning. Additional analysis and patterns will be introduced later. Examples:

(1) **Damê desyoo.**
  'It's probably no good.'

(2) **Takâi desyoo.**
  'It's probably expensive.'

(3) **Tâkâkatta desyoo.**
  'It probably was expensive.'

(4) **Oísiku nài desyoo.**
  'It probably isn't tasty.'

(5) **Yôku nâkatta desyoo.**
  'It probably wasn't good.'

(6) **Kîree zya nâi desyoo.**
  'It probably isn't pretty.'

(7) **Zêñbu zya nâkatta desyoo.**
  'It probably wasn't the whole thing.'

(8) **Oókìi no desyoo.**
  'It's probably a big one.'

(9) **Kîree na no desyoo.**
  'It's probably a pretty one.'

(10) **Gurêe no desyoo.**
  'It's probably a gray one.'

(11) **Señ-eñ nò desyoo.**
  'It's probably a ¥1000 one.'

With question (rising) intonation /?/, unaccented **desyoo** (or, commonly, **desyo**) seeks confirmation from the person addressed. /**Desyo(o)?**/ and /**dèsu neʔ**/ questions are very similar in meaning except that the /**desyo(o)?**/ alternative is a more tentative question, somewhat similar to English 'wouldn't you say that . . . ?' Thus:

(1) **Takâi desyoo?** 'Wouldn't you say it's expensive?' 'It's expensive, don't you think?'

  Êe, sôo desu ne! 'Yes, that's right, isn't it.' *or*

  Êe, sôo desu yo. 'Yes, that's right, I assure you.' *or*

Mâa, takâi desyoo nêe. 'I guess it probably is expensive, isn't it!'

(2) **Takâi desu ne**⌐ 'It's expensive—right?'

    Êe, sôo desu ne! 'Yes, that's right, isn't it.' *or*

    Êe, sôo desu yo⌐ 'Yes, that's right, I assure you.' *or*

    Mâa, takâi desyoo nêe. 'I guess it probably is expensive, isn't it.'

The third reply to both (1) and (2) is not a precise, direct answer to the question, but rather a shift to lack of certainty.

In *ka*-questions, again **desyòo** implies an indirectness that is more polite. The suggestion is that the person addressed should not feel required to have the precise answer. (Compare English questions like 'What would that be?' 'What do you suppose that is?' 'What could that be?' etc., with the direct 'What's that?'). **Desyòo ka** questions commonly end in period /./ intonation.

3. /**ka + nê(e)**/

Ka-questions are frequently followed by sentence particle /**ne!**/ or /**nêe.**/ suggesting deliberative reflection concerning the question and/or a shared reaction to it. In response to a statement ending in **yo**—an assertion—such questions may express considerable doubt. Examples:

(1) **Dêĝuti (wa) dôko desyoo ka nêe.** 'I wonder where the exit is—don't you wonder, too!'

(2) **Damê desu yo**⌐ 'That's no good.'

    Sôo desu ka nêe. 'Oh, really? Hmm. I wonder.'

Frequently /**ka nêe.**/ questions occur in response to *questions* when both parties share a lack of information. If the stimulus question is an information question (i.e., a who-what-when-where question), the response echoes the question word; but in reply to a yes-no question, the response uses **dôo.** Particularly common is the occurrence of **desyôo** in such exchanges. Examples:

Nâñ desyoo ka. 'What do you suppose it is?'

    Nâñ desyoo ka nêe. 'What is it, indeed!'

Dâre desyoo ka. 'Who would that be?'

    Dâre desyoo ka nêe. 'Who *would* it be?'

Oísìi desyoo ka. 'Do you suppose it tastes good?'

    Dôo desyoo ka nêe. 'I wonder!' (*lit.* 'How would it be?'—I agree.)

Drills

A 1. **Sonó taisìkañ wa Toókyoo dèsu yo**⌐   **Tookyoo no dôko desu ka**⌐
    'That embassy is in Tokyo.'   'Where in Tokyo is it?'

  2. **Sono byooiñ wa Toránomoñ dèsu yo**⌐   **Toranomoñ no dôko desu ka**⌐
    'That hospital is in Toranomon.'   'Where in Toranomon is it?'

3. **kooeñ/Kyôoto**; 4. **otera/kono heñ**; 5. **gekizyoo/Hurañsu**; 6. **tatêmono/Iğirisu**; 7. **zîñzya/mukoo**; 8. **kyookai/Amerika**

B 1. **Are wa Uéno-kòoeñ ni arímàsu ğa . .**
   'That's in Ueno Park, but . . .' (do you know where?)

   Uéno-kòoeñ no donó heñ dèsu ka⌐
   'What part of Ueno Park (is it)?'

2. **Ano baiteñ wa Toókyòo-eki ni arímàsu ğa . .**
   'That stand is in Tokyo Station, but . . .' (do you know where?)

   Toókyòo-eki no donó heñ dèsu ka⌐
   'What part of Tokyo Station (is it)?'

3. **soñna koñpyùutaa/Paáku-bìru**; 4. **koñna taipuràitaa/Amérika-taisìkañ**; 5. **anó tatèmono/Kyôoto**

C 1. **Asítà wa tosyôkañ desu.**
   'Tomorrow will be the library' (i.e., the place where I'll be, for example).

   Dôko no tosyôkañ desu ka⌐
   'What library (lit. the library of what place) will it be?'

2. **Asítà wa byoóiñ dèsu.**
   'Tomorrow will be the hospital.'

   Dôko no byoóiñ dèsu ka⌐
   'What hospital will it be?'

3. **taísìkañ**; 4. **gekizyoo**; 5. **ryoózìkañ**; 6. **eéğàkañ**

D 1. **Asoko wa ryokáñ desyòo ka.**
   'Would that place be an inn?'

   Sâa. Dôo desyoo ka nêe. . . . Yáppàri ryokáñ dèsu ne!
   'Hmm. I wonder. . . . It *is* an inn, isn't it.'

2. **Asoko wa ryoózìkañ desyoo ka.**
   'Would that place be a consulate?'

   Sâa. Dôo desyoo ka nêe. . . . Yáppàri ryoózìkan desu ne!
   'Hmm. I wonder. . . . It *is* a consulate, isn't it.'

3. **êki**; 4. **tosyôkañ**; 5. **otéàrai**; 6. **byooiñ**; 7. **kyookai**; 8. **zîñzya**

E 1. **Oísìi desu ka⌐**
   'Does it taste good?'

   Êe, oísìi desyoo nêe.
   'Yes, it probably is tasty, isn't it!'

2. **Ryokáñ dèsu ka⌐**
   'Is it an inn?'

   Êe, ryokáñ desyòo nêe.
   'Yes, it probably is (an inn), isn't it!'

3. **muzúkasìkatta desu**; 4. **kîree desu**; 5. **daízyòobu desu**; 6. **yorósìi desu**; 7. **Yamámoto-sañ dèsu**; 8. **gakúsee dèsu**; 9. **koré dakè desu**; 10. **hitótu-zùtu desu**; 11. **tâkâkatta desu**

F 1. **Asoko wa koóeñ dèsu neˤ**
   'That place is a park—right?'

   Iya, koóeñ zya nài desyoo?
   'No, it's not a park, is it?'

2. **Asoko wa takâi desu neˤ**
   'That place is expensive—right?'

   Iya, tâkâku nâi desyoo?
   'No, it's not expensive, is it?'

3. **otéra dèsu**; 4. **oísìi desu**; 5. **hûbeñ desu**; 6. **kâiği desu**; 7. **kyoókai dèsu**; 8. **omósiròi desu**; 9. **kîree desu**; 10. **zîñzya desu**; 11. **omósìròkatta desu**; 12. **yâsûkatta desu**

G 1. **Ano kooeñ, dôko desyoo ka.** **Dôko desyoo ka nêe.**
'Where would that park be?' 'Where *would* it be!'

2. **Anó tatèmono, byoóiñ desyòo ka.** **Dôo desyoo ka nêe.**
'Would that building be a hospital?' 'I wonder!'

3. **kabañ/îkura**; 4. **señsèe/dônata**; 5. **kâiḡi/asítà**; 6. **gakusee/dâre**; 7. **hôñ/nihoñḡo**;
8. **yuúbiñkyoku/dôtira**; 9. **bîru/nâñ**; 10. **kuruma/dâre no**; 11. **zîñzya/atíra no hòo**

H 1. **Uénò-eki wa kotíra no hòo desu neʕ** **Sáa, kotíra no hòo desu ka nêe. Tyôtto**
'Ueno Station is this way—right?' **wakárimasèñ nêe.**
'Hmm, is it this way? I wonder. I'm afraid
I don't know.'

2. **Toókyoo-hòteru wa mukóoḡawa** **Sâa, mukóoḡawa dèsu ka nêe. Tyôtto**
dèsu neʕ **wakárimasèñ nêe.**
'The Hotel Tokyo is on the other 'Hmm, is it on the other side? I wonder.
side—right?' I'm afraid I don't know.'

3. **Toránomoñ-byòoiñ/otéra no sòba**; 4. **Kanáda-taisìkañ/atíra no hòo**; 5. **Uéno-
kòoeñ/kono heñ**

I 1. **Asoko wa takâi desu yo↙** **Kokó mo takài desyoo?**
'That place is expensive.' '*This* place is expensive, too, isn't it?'

2. **Anó tatèmono wa hurûi desu yo↙** **Konó tatèmono mo hurûi desyoo?**
'That building is old.' '*This* building is old, too, isn't it?'

3. **asoko/oísìi desu**; 4. **ano tyuuḡokuḡo/muzúkasìi desu**; 5. **asoko/yasûi desu**; 6. **anó
hòteru/damê desu**; 7. **asoko/kîree desu**

J 1. **Asoko ni ryokáñ ḡa arimàsu ka↙** **Ryokáñ dèsu ka↙ Asóko nì wa nâi**
'Are there any inns in that place?' **desyoo.**
'Inns? In that place (at least) there
probably aren't any.'

2. **Anó tosyòkañ ni eéḡo no hòñ ḡa** **Eéḡo no hòñ desu ka↙ Anó tosyòkañ ni**
arímàsu ka↙ **wa nâi desyoo.**
'Are there any English-language 'English-language books? In that library (at
books in that library?' least) there probably aren't any.'

3. **asoko/zîñzya**; 4. **anó hòteru no sôba/kooeñ**; 5. **koko/oókìi hôteru**; 6. **kono heñ ni/
koósyuudèñwa**; 7. **mukooḡawa/kyookai**; 8. **kotíra no hòo/tôire**; 9. **tonári no bìru/
baiteñ**

K 1. **Miḡi ni eéḡàkañ ḡa arímàsu neʕ** **Miḡí nì mo hidári nì mo arímàsu yo↙**
'On the right there's a movie 'On the right *and* on the left there are
theater—right?' [theaters].'

2. **Mâe ni deñwa ga arimàsu neʕ** **Mâe ni mo usíro nì mo arímàsu yo↙**
'In front there's a telephone—right?' 'In front *and* in back there are [phones].'

3. **hidari/misê**; 4. **usiro/baiteñ**; 5. **miḡídònari/koósyuudèñwa**; 6. **hidáridònari/oókìi
tatêmono**

L 1. **Koǹna tosyòkañ wa kokó dakè desu**   **Iêie, takúsañ arimàsu yo⌇—koǹna**
   ka⌇   **tosyòkañ wa.**

   'Is this place the only library like   'No, no, there are many—libraries like
   this?'   this.'

   2. **Koǹna ryokañ wa kokó dakè desu**   **Iêie, takúsañ arimàsu yo⌇—koǹna**
   ka⌇   **ryokañ wa.**

   'Is this place the only inn like this?'   'No, no, there are many—inns like this.'

   3. **gekizyoo**; 4. **tatêmono**; 5. **misê**; 6. **byooiñ**; 7. **miti**; 8. **otera**

Application Exercises

A. Repeat Application Exercises A1, 2, and 3 of Section A, expanding them with the new
place words and building names introduced in this section; the use of **desyòo** in questions
and in answers; the use of the **koko** series; and /**ka nê(e)**/ questions.

B. Core Conversations: Substitution
   In practicing the Core Conversations with substitutions, include items that relate to your
own locale. Develop conversations that might occur between a Japanese visiting your area
and a Japanese-speaking resident.

SECTION C

Eavesdropping

(Answer the following on the basis of the accompanying tape. A = first speaker; B = second speaker.)
   1a. What is A trying to identify?
    b. What does B tell A?
    2. Where did B stay in Kyoto?
   3a. Where does this conversation occur?
    b. What does B express concern about?
   4a. What two buildings are under discussion?
    b. What possible location of them does A check on?
    c. Where are they actually located?
   5a. What is A's mistaken concern?
    b. What does A learn from B?
   6a. What is A looking for? located where?
    b. What does A learn from B?
    7. Who are B's neighbors?
   8a. What is A looking for?
    b. Where does A think it is?
    c. What does B suggest about what is in that location?
    d. What is A's reaction?
   9a. What are A and B looking for?
    b. Why are they upset?
    c. What is thought of as a possible solution?
    d. Why does it prove unnecessary to pursue it?

10a. What is A looking for?
  b. Where does A think it might be?
  c. Where is it actually? Give three descriptions of its location.
11a. What is A looking for?
  b. What is A's mistaken assumption about its location?
  c. What is the actual location? Give two descriptions.
  d. What does B reassure A about?
12a. What is A looking for?
  b. How does B begin to provide directions?
  c. What happens before B finishes?
13a. What is A's mistaken assumption?
  b. Describe the size and location of the item under discussion.
  c. What invitation does B offer?
  d. What is A's response?
14a. What is A looking for?
  b. Where is it? Give three descriptions of it.
15a. What is A inquiring about?
  b. Where is it?
  c. What does B suggest in answer to A's question?
  d. What is A's response?
  e. That being the case, what is B's response to A's original question?

Utilization

(In producing the Japanese equivalents for what follows, utilize everything you have learned. Precede questions with apologies; use echo questions; express appreciation for information; hesitate appropriately. In other words, speak *Japanese,* not translated English. Be sure to expand this exercise by providing accompanying questions and/or answers as appropriate.)

1. Approach a stranger and ask directions to the Hotel Okura.
2. Check on whether Tokyo Station is in this direction.
3. You've been asked directions to the French Consulate. Explain that it's (1) a little farther ahead; (2) beyond the station; (3) next door to the embassy.
4. You've been asked directions to the restroom. After pointing out the public phones over there, explain that it's between those phones and the exit.
5. You've been asked if there are any telephones around here. Explain that there are some both to the left and to the right of the stand.
6. Find out where the entrance to that park is.
7. Approach a stranger and find out if there is around here (1) a police box; (2) a restroom; (3) a telephone; (4) a hotel; (5) a post office.
8. Find out if the German Embassy is on this street.
9. You've been asked directions to the Toranomon Hospital. Explain, apologetically, that it's not clear to you where it is. Add that at least it's not in this area.
10. Inform a colleague that up ahead there's (1) a phone; (2) a police box; (3) a shrine; (4) a temple; (5) a stand.
11. Exclaim on how many hotels *and* inns there are in Japan.
12. Inquire about the identity of the building (1) between the station and the post office; (2) across from the park; (3) beyond the hospital; (4) in front of the embassy; (5) next door to the church; (6) next to the library on the right.
13. You've been told that the Hotel Okura is in Tokyo. Find out where in Tokyo it is.
14. You've learned that something is wrong with the computer. Find out what part ('what place') of the computer is broken.

15. Your colleague has been telling you how beautiful a particular park is. Find out what park ('the park where') she means.

16. You've been told that Mr/s. Yamamoto is coming here tomorrow. Find out which Yamamoto ('of what place') it is.

17. You've been asked to identify a stranger. Explain that you're not sure, but he's probably a student.

18. Confirm your assumption that both the embassy and the consulate are the same building.

19. Confirm your assumption that this wine is delicious.

20. Exclaim (expecting agreement) on how expensive that new hotel must be.

21. You've been asked where the newspaper is. Indicate that you have the same question.

22. You've been asked if that (place) is a church. Indicate that you have the same question.

23. Express wonder as to what that large, white building is.

24. You've just been informed of something new, but indicate that you still maintain some question in your mind.

25. You've been asked whether a particular Japanese computer is new. Reply (1) that it is (and you are sure); (2) that it probably is; (3) that it must be (and you assume the questioner would be inclined to agree); (4) that it probably isn't; (5) that it isn't (and you're sure).

26. X has just commented that Kyoto hotels must be expensive (assuming your agreement). (1) Agree (you aren't sure, either); (2) agree (you are positive); (3) indicate that you are wondering about it.

27. Find out if Ueno Park is the only park in Tokyo.

Check-up

1. What is the difference, in structure and meaning, between /**Toókyoo no èki**/ and /**Toókyòo-eki**/? (A-SP1)

2. What are the members of the **kotira** series? (A-SP2) the **koko** series? (B-SP1) To what word-class do they belong?

3. How does the **kotira** series differ in meaning from the **koko** series? (A-SP2), (B-SP1)

4. What is the difference in meaning between **bîru no mâe** and **mâe no bîru**? (A-SP3)

5. What happens to the combination /connective **no** + nominal **no**/? to the reverse combination /nominal **no** + connective **no**/? to /contracted **no** + connective **no**/? Give an example of each. (A-SP3)

6. What are relational nominals? What special pattern do they enter into? (A-SP4)

7. Contrast the patterns of /**hôteru no mâe**/, /**sukôsi mâe**/, and /**móo sukòsi mâe**/. (A-SP4)

8. What two patterns can be used to describe the location of things? What is the difference in usage between these two patterns? (A-SP5)

9. Name two phrase-particles that may occur immediately following another phrase-particle. Give examples. Name two phrase-particles which are NOT ordinarily followed by these two particles. (A-SP6)

10. Explain the difference in meaning between:
    Deñwa mo mìğí ni arimàsu. *and*
    Deñwa wa mìğí nì mo arimasu. (A-SP6)

11. How does Japanese distinguish between:
    The telephone is *in back* and
    In back there's *a telephone*? (A-SP7)

12. What is the difference in meaning between **dôko no hôñ** and **hôñ no dôko**? (B-SP1)

13. **Soko** may refer to location close to the person addressed, and **asoko,** to a location removed from both speaker and person addressed. What are other common meanings of **soko** and **asoko**? (B-SP1)

14. What is the basic difference between sentences ending in /**dèsu.**/ and those ending in /**desyòo.**/; between /**desyòo.**/ and /**desyo(o)?**/? What do we call the **desyòo** form? (B-SP2)
15. What does the combination /**ka nê(e)**/ indicate? (B-SP3)
16. Describe a pattern that covers a *question* response to another question. (B-SP3)

Lesson 7

SECTION A

Core Conversations

1(N)a. **Tyôtto giṅkoo màde itte kimàsu.**
   b. **Itte kimàsu. . . . Tadaima.**

(J)a. **Itte (i)rassyài.**
   b. **Okáeri-nasài.**

2(N)a. **Hôñya e itte kimàsu kedo, nâni ka arímàsu ka⌇**

   b. **Ée, îi desu kedo, zyâa, sonó hòñ no ʹnamae o osíete kudasài. A, sumímasèñ kedo, kâite kudásaimasèñ ka⌇**

(J)a. **Zyâa, hôñ o is-satu katte kìte kudásaimasèñ ka.**

   b. **Hâi. . . . Zyâa, warûi desu kedo, onéḡai-simàsu.**

3(N)a. **Nakámura-sañ irassyaimàsu ka⌇**
   b. **Zyâa, Nîsida-sañ wa?**

(J)a. **Îma tyôtto orímasèñ ḡa . .**
   b. **Nîsida desu ka⌇ Nîsida wa sań-ḡai ni orimàsu ḡa . .**

   c. **A, sôo desu ka. Dôo mo.**

4(N)a. **Kyôo wa dôko de tabémàsita ka⌇**
   b. **Oísìi desu ka⌇—asoko.**

(J)a. **Tikâ no atárasìi ʹkissateñ de.**
   b. **Êe. Nakámura-sañ mo imàsita yo⌇**

ENGLISH EQUIVALENTS

1(N)a. I'm going to the bank. (*lit.* I'll come just having gone as far as the bank.)
   b. 'Bye. (*lit.* I'll come having gone.) . . . [N leaves and returns] I'm back. (*lit.* [I've] just now [returned].)

(J)a. 'Bye. (*lit.* Come, having gone!)

   b. Hi! (*lit.* Return!)

2(N)a. I'm going to the bookstore. Is there anything [you need]? (*lit.* I'll come having gone to the bookstore; is there anything?)

(J)a. Then would you be kind enough to buy (*lit.* come having bought) a book for me?

158

b. Yes, that'll be fine, but then tell me the name of the book. Oh, I'm sorry [to bother you] but would you be kind enough to write it?

3(N)a. Is Mr/s. Nakamura in?

b. Then how about Mr/s. Nishida?

c. Oh, thanks.

4(N)a. Today where did you eat?

b. Is it good—that place?

b. Certainly. I really shouldn't bother you but would you do this for me? (*lit.* It's bad [of me] but I make [this] request.)

(J)a. S/he isn't here now, but . . . (would anyone else do?)

b. [Mr/s.] Nishida? [Mr/s.] Nishida is on the third floor, but . . . (is there anything I can do?)

(J)a. At the new coffee shop in the basement.

b. Yes. You know, Mr/s. Nakamura was there, too.

BREAKDOWNS
(AND SUPPLEMENTARY VOCABULARY)

1. **giñkoo** — bank
   giñkoo màde (SP1) — as far as the bank
   itte kimàsu (SP2) — go and (then) come (*lit.* come having gone)
   +**maírimàsu** ↓ /**mâitte**/ — I/we (in-group members) come /polite/
   tadâima — just now
   Tadaima. — Hello. I'm back!
   kaérimàsu /**kâette**/ — return (home)
   okáeri-nasài — return! welcome back! /imperative/
2. **hôñya** — bookstore; book dealer
   +**hanâya** — flower shop; florist
   +**depâato** — department store
   +**buñbooğuya** — stationery store; stationery dealer
   +**gakkoo** — school
   +**daiğaku** — university, college
   +**daíğakùiñ** — graduate school
   +**kookoo** — high school
   hôñya e (SP1) *or*
   hôñya ni (SP1) — to the bookstore
   katte kimàsu — buy and (then) come (*lit.* come having bought)
   katte kìte kudásaimasèñ ka (SP3) — would(n't) you be kind enough to buy and (then) come?
   (o)namae — name

osíemàsu /osiete/	teach; give instruction or information
kakímàsu /kâite/	write; draw
kâite kudásaimasèñ ka	would(n't) you be kind enough to write/ draw for me?
warûi /-katta/	is bad; is wrong

3. **Nakamura** — (family name)

irássyaimàsu ↑ /irássyàtte/ (SP5)	be in a place (animate); come /polite/
imâsu /ite/ (SP4)	be in a place (animate)
îma	now
orímàsu ↓ /ôtte/	I am (*or* in-group members are) in a place /polite/
Nîsida	(family name)
+ ik-kai	first floor; one floor
sañ-ḡai	third floor; three floors

4. **dôko de** / + action predicate/ (SP1) — in/at what place?

tikâ	underground
kissateñ/kíssàteñ	coffee shop, tearoom
+ mazûi /-katta/	tastes bad

-kai: *Classifier for counting and naming floors*

ik-kai	one floor; first floor	rok-kai
ni-kai	two floors; second floor	nana-kai/siti-kai
sañ-ḡai	three floors; third floor	hak-kai/hati-kai
yoñ-kai		kyuu-kai
go-kai		zyuk-kai/zik-kai

nañ-ḡai 'what floor?' 'how many floors?'

MISCELLANEOUS NOTES

1,2. CC1 and CC2 are typical conversations between two colleagues of roughly the same rank, who interact on a fairly formal basis, hence the frequency of distal-style. In the accompanying video, these conversations are between Mr. Yamada and Ms. Miller, who work at adjoining desks in a small foreign trading firm. Mr. Yamada has been with the company longer.

1. The goodbyes and hellos of CC1 are those regularly used in leaving and returning to one's own home or office, situations in which **sayonara** is *not* used. (The goodbyes are analyzed in SP2 following.)

(J)a. **Irássyài(màse)** was previously introduced as a shopkeeper's welcome to a customer. It is an imperative (= command) form of a polite verbal, discussed in SP5 following. The **-màse** form, a distal-style imperative, is not included in this CC since it is too formal for this setting.

(J)b. The verbal **kaérimàsu** refers to returning to a home base—i.e., one's own home, one's own office, one's homeland. Thus, Japanese who are abroad **kaérimàsu** to Japan, but when foreigners return there, they **matá ikimàsu** or **matá kimàsu.**

Okáeri-nasài is an imperative pattern based on this verbal; again, there is a distal-style equivalent ending in **-màse**, which is too formal for the setting of this CC.

2(N)a. Note: **hôñ** 'book(s)' and **hôñya** 'bookstore'; **hanâ** 'flower(s)' and **hanâya** 'flower shop'; **buñbòoḡu** 'stationery,' 'writing materials' and **buñbooḡuya** 'stationery store.' The addition of **-sañ** to these shop terms transforms them into polite terms, commonly used in addressing the respective shopkeepers.

Nâni ka, to be analyzed in a later lesson, occurred earlier in **Hoká ni nàni ka?** 'Anything else?'

Note that the /**. . . kedo**/ sequence is in no sense contrastive here: as usual, it provides information useful in interpreting the remainder of the sentence appropriately.

(J)a. (J) specifies that he is requesting just one book to be bought as a favor to him.

(N)b. **Sonó hòñ** refers to the book just introduced into the conversation.

Onamae is a polite reference to someone else's name—never one's own. **Onamae wa?** (*without* a following **nâñ desu ka**) is an informal but polite way to ask a person for his/her name.

Note the contrast between **misémàsu**, which covers the act of showing in the sense of letting someone see, and **osíemàsu**, which covers teaching, providing information, and showing in the sense of showing someone how to do something.

(J)b. **Warûi** is an adjectival which covers a wide range of 'badness,' from being evil, wrong, out-of-sorts, spoiled, etc., to its use here, which is a form of apology. It is commonly used in accepting a gift: **Warûi desu nêe** is somewhat similar to English 'You shouldn't have done it!' 'I really shouldn't accept this!'

3. CC3 is a typical exchange between a visitor from outside looking for people who belong to the same in-group as the person addressed. The in-group/out-group connotations are discussed in SP5, following.

(N)a. Note that, in this situation, there is regularly *no phrase-particle* following the nominal.

(J)a. **Îma** is a time nominal: **îma desu** 'it's now'; **îma zya nâi desu** 'it isn't now'; **îma simasu** 'I'm going to do it now'; **îma no Nihôñ** 'the Japan of the present.'

(J)b. Note the use of **wa** indicating that Nishida is being discussed in contrast to Nakamura.

-kai/-ḡai is a classifier which counts *and* names floors. Context (and/or phrase-particles) distinguishes the two meanings: **Ni-kái arimàsu** 'There are two floors' (= extent pattern, no particle); **Ni-kái ni arimàsu.** 'It's on the second floor' or less commonly 'They're on two floors' (= pattern of inanimate location, phrase-particle **ni**).

4. CC4 is an office conversation. Final predicates are in the distal-style, but the fragment (J)a and the inverted sentence (N)b suggest some informality, matching the topic (cf. SP5 following).

(N)a. **Kyôo wa** 'today, in contrast with other days'

(J)a. **Tikâ**, a nominal, also occurs with **-kai** numbers (**tikâ ik-kai, tikâ ni-kai, tikâ san-gai**, etc.), referring to underground floors, common in large Japanese department stores and office buildings.

Kissateñ are well-frequented establishments which serve tea, coffee, and other light refreshments. They are extremely popular among the Japanese. In Tokyo alone they number in the thousands.

(N)b. Note that the taste adjectivals **oisii** and **mazûi** are used in reference to eating places as well as food and drink.

Structural Patterns

1. PHRASE-PARTICLES: /PLACE + **màde** *OR* **e** ~ **ni** + **ikímàsu**/,
/PLACE + **de** + **tabémàsu**/

a. **màde**: /place nominal X + **màde** + predicate Y/ = 'Y applies as far as X,' i.e., 'up to and including X but not beyond.' **Màde** marks the final limit of application. The place-nominal preceding **màde** may be not only a geographical location but also such varied places as a part of a machine or a point in a book or a segment of a tape.

Màde is accented unless the preceding nominal is accented. Examples:

Koóeñ màde ikímàsita. 'I went as far as the park.'

Kokó màde simâsita. 'I did it up to and including this place'; 'I went this far' (for example, in a lesson).

Dôko made ikímàsu ka 'How far are you going?'

b. **e/ni**: /place nominal X + **e** *or* **ni** + predicate of motion Y/ = 'motion Y moves to *or* into *or* onto X.' Particles **ni** and **e** are often interchangeable in this pattern, but **e** also involves the direction of the motion, while **ni** concentrates on the final location. In fragments where a motion predicate is implied but not obvious from the context, only **e** is possible. Examples:

Toókyoo e/ni ikimàsita. 'I went to Tokyo.'

Dôko e/ni ikímàsu ka 'Where (to what place) are you going?'

Asita 'mata kotíra e/ni kimàsu ka 'Are you coming here (to this place) again tomorrow?'

Konó kamì ni kakímàsita. 'I wrote it on(to) this paper.'

Îma dôtira e? 'Where are you going?' (*lit.* 'Now toward where[abouts])?'[1]

The phrase-particles **e** and **ni** are NOT interchangeable before predicates of static, inactive location:

Giñkoo ni arimàsu. 'It's in the bank.' (**e** is impossible.)

Konó hòteru ni baíteñ (g̃a) arimàsu ka 'Is there a stand in this hotel?' (**e** is impossible.)

The phrase-particle **ni** is a particle of location, but it is only in combination with a specific predicate that one can determine whether the location is a continuing one, an original one that changes, or the final one. In **giñkoo ni arimàsu**, reference is to a continuing location without any activity. However, with predicates of motion, /place + **ni**/ refers to the final location. Thus, in **giñkoo ni ikimàsu, giñkoo** refers to the location *after* the going takes place—when I go *to the bank*, I am *in* the bank only *after* I get there. It is therefore not surprising that the fragment **Dôtira ni?** without a specific predicate clearly understood from the immediate linguistic context would be meaningless.

c. **de**: /place nominal X + **de** + predicate of activity Y/ = 'activity Y takes place in/at place X.' /Place + **de**/ identifies the *location* of the activity. Examples:

---

1. The question **Dôtira e?** is often used informally among Japanese as a casual greeting, comparable to the English 'How are you?' which expects no detailed, factual answer. In such situations, there is no expectation of a reply that includes one's actual destination; a frequent answer is **Tyôtto sokó màde.** 'Just as far as there,' even though **soko** is undefined.

Toókyoo de kaimàsu. 'I'll buy it in Tokyo.'

Nihôñ de konó hòñ o kakímàsita. 'I wrote this book in Japan.'

Compare:

Kokó ni arimàsu. 'It is (statically) located here.' *and*

Kokó ni kakimàsu. 'I'll write it (onto) here' (my name onto this paper, for example).
and

Kokó de kakimàsu. 'I'll write it here' (the activity of writing will take place in this location).

Phrases ending in the above particles may also occur followed by **wa** or **mo**:

Kyôoto made wa ikímàsu ǧa . . 'I am going as far as Kyoto (at least) but . . .' (I probably won't go farther).

Huráñsu e ikimàsita ka⤸ 'Did you go to France?'

Iie, Huráñsu è wa ikímasèñ desita. 'No, I didn't go to France (but I may have gone elsewhere).'

Amérika dè mo Nihôñ de mo nihôñgo o osiemàsita. 'I taught Japanese both in America and in Japan.'

Note that **e** and **ni** are accented following an unaccented nominal and preceding **wa** and **mo**.

2. VERBAL GERUND + kimâsu

Until this section, the gerund (**-te**) form of the verbal has occurred only within request patterns. However, the request itself was actually expressed by the verbal of giving, **kudásài,** that accompanied it; the gerund indicated what kind of activity was to be performed for ('given to') the speaker.

The gerund is a form which (1) links up with a predicate; and (2) implies a realized state or activity.[2] In requests, it is a realized state or activity that is asked for.

Consider now the combination **itte kimâsu**: the combination states that someone 'is going to come here (*or* repeatedly comes here) *having gone somewhere.*' Comparable situations are usually described in English in terms of two coordinate activities linked by 'and,' e.g., 'go and come.' In Japanese, the gerund construction is subordinate to the following predicate, and the two form a closely linked pair.

☠ WARNING: Note that under no circumstances can the phrase-particle **to** be used to join verbal X and verbal Y to mean 'do X and do Y.'

The /verbal gerund + **kimâsu**/ pattern, in the examples in the CC of this section, describe an activity to be performed elsewhere or a movement to another place, followed by a coming [back] to the present location. This overlaps in many instances with English errand patterns, but note the difference: in English we usually express the going and the doing but omit explicit mention of the returning; in Japanese, the going is omitted, but the doing and coming are expressed. Thus, English 'go and buy' becomes Japanese 'buy and come,' or, more literally, 'having bought, come.'

---

2. By 'realized' is meant 'at least begun'; it may or may not be finished. Compare English 'I will do' and 'I'm going to do' as unrealized, and 'I am doing' and 'I did' as realized.

3. POLITE REQUESTS: **kudásaimasèñ ka**

In the /**-te** + **kudásài**/ request pattern, the polite verbal **kudásaimàsu** occurs in its imperative (= command) form: **itte kudasài** 'please go' (*lit.* 'give me going'). In form, this combination is direct and abrupt, but the politeness of the verbal itself and the fact that the request is made in terms of something that is to be given to the speaker make the combination relatively polite.

However, the request can be made less direct and significantly softer by replacing the imperative **kudásài** with a corresponding distal-style negative question: **itte kudasaimasèñ ka** 'would you be kind enough to go?' (*lit.* 'won't you give me going?'). The use of the negative here is undoubtedly related to its use in invitations.

In addition to requesting activities (with verbal gerunds), things (expressed as nominals) can also be requested in parallel constructions: **Soré (o) kudasài** and **Soré (o) kudasaimasèñ ka**.

4. ANIMATE LOCATION: **imâsu**

The verbal **arímàsu**, indicating an inanimate, inactive kind of existence, has already been introduced. In this section, we meet the verbal that stands in contrast to this: **imâsu**, gerund /**ite**/, represents an animate kind of existence. Among its many uses, it indicates the animate existence or location (without action) of humans and animals. Examples:

> **Gakúsee ğa imàsu ka⁻** 'Are there students [here]?'
>
> **Dâre ğa imâsita ka⁻** 'Who was [there]?'
>
> **Asítà mo imâsu ka⁻** 'Will you be [here] tomorrow, too?'
>
> **Moó sukòsi ité kudasài.** 'Please stay (*lit.* be [here]) a little longer.'
>
> **Tanaka-sañ wa, Kyôoto ni imâsu kedo; kuruma wa, Toókyoo ni arimàsu.** 'Mr/s. Tanaka is in Kyoto, but the car is in Tokyo.'

Like **arímàsu, imâsu** occurs with /place nominal + **ni**/ phrases, indicating location without activity.

5. POLITENESS: IN-GROUP/OUT-GROUP

The Core Conversation predicates thus far have been distal-style predicates: the participants have been colleagues who maintain a certain distance—who do not speak to each other as close friends or intimates.

But even within this style—as well as within direct-style—Japanese differentiates between plain and polite forms. Whereas distal-style reflects the degree of closeness and the level of formality the speaker feels toward the addressee, the second axis—which relates to politeness—is determined by the relative positions of the person to whom the predicate refers, the addressee, and the speaker.[3]

Playing a crucial role in this is the distinction between in-group and out-group. Any individual Japanese belongs to a number of societal groups—the family, the school group, the work group, clubs, sports teams, etc.—and of primary importance in determining the kind of language to be used on any occasion is the identification of these groups in the setting of the moment. The groups are constantly shifting, depending on the participants and the speaker's viewpoint. Group affiliation is so basic that it is probably valid to consider an individual who, at the moment, is operating in isolation, as a "minimal in-group."

---

3. Of course, the person referred to may *be* the addressee or the speaker.

How does this work? Let's consider Ms. Yamamoto, who works under Mr. Nishida, a top executive in a Japanese company. Within the in-group of the company, she of course refers to Mr. Nishida in polite language—whether speaking directly to him, or about him in conversing with her own peers. But when a member of an out-group—e.g., another company—visits and asks for **Nîsida-sañ**, who is a member of her (= Yamamoto's) in-group, even though Mr. Nishida outranks her within the organization, she refers to him as **Nîsida** in speaking to the outsider. The polite **-sañ** is the kind of form that cannot be used of in-group members (including self, the smallest in-group) when talking to the out-group (cf. CC3[J]b).

We will now distinguish three major kinds of politeness in Japanese predicates:

1. Honorific politeness (symbol / ↑ /) marks forms which exalt the person to whom they refer. These items are never used in reference to the in-group of the moment; oneself is, of course, always in-group.

2. Humble politeness (symbol / ↓ /) marks forms which humble the person to whom they refer. These items are regularly used in reference to the in-group of the moment; again, the self is regularly in-group.

3. Neutral politeness (symbol / + /) indicates politeness toward the addressee regardless of the referent of the item. For example, **gozáimàsu** is a polite alternative of **arímàsu** without any particular in-group/out-group considerations. This type of politeness is similar to the use of distal-style predicates in that it involves only speaker/addressee. Significantly, the verbal **gozáimàsu** occurs only in the distal-style.

The following chart identifies the polite verbals that have been introduced thus far according to the kind of politeness they reflect, along with their plain equivalents insofar as they, too, are already familiar.

Distal-Style Verbals

	Plain	Polite		
		Polite/ ↑ /	Polite/ ↓ /	Polite/ + /
'be in a place' (animate)	**imâsu**	**irássyaimàsu**	**orímàsu**	
'come'	**kimâsu**	**irássyaimàsu**	**maírimàsu**	
'eat'	**tabémàsu**		**itádakimàsu**	
'drink'	**nomímàsu**		**itádakimàsu**	
'receive'			**itádakimàsu**	
'be in a place' (inanimate)	**arímàsu**			**gozáimàsu**
'request'			**onéḡai-simàsu**	
'give to the in-group'		**kudásaimàsu**		

This chart will require extensive expansion as we move into more complex material, but even in this simple form, it demonstrates the basic principles.
Remember:

(1) All these verbals—even the plain forms—are distal-style and therefore demonstrate a degree of formality and distance from the addressee.
(2) The plain forms do not reflect any special politeness.
(3) The honorific-polite / ↑ / forms are used only in polite reference to out-group members: depending on group make-up, these may be the person(s) addressed or third persons, but never the speaker.[4]
(4) The humble-polite / ↓ / forms are used only in reference to in-group members when speaking politely to the out-group; the most common in-group is the speaker, politely addressing the out-group (often the addressee).
(5) **Gozáimàsu** is polite / + / to the addressee, but neither exalts nor humbles its referent.

In CC3, the out-group visitor inquires politely for Mr/s. Nakamura, using **irássyaimàsu.** The use of the verbal **orímàsu** in reference to Nakamura in the reply indicates that the speaker belongs to Mr/s. Nakamura's in-group. Either speaker—or both—had the option of using **imâsu,** the plain alternate. Whether or not to use polite style depends on many factors: relative rank and position, age, gender, setting, topic, and individual personality. For the Japanese, high rank and age are particularly associated with polite address, and women, in general, use polite language more commonly than men.

Drills

A 1. **Ikímàsita neʕ**
'You went—right?'

Êe, kokó màde ikímàsita kedo, îi desu kaↄ
'Yes, I went this far (pointing to a place on the map). Is that all right?'

2. **Simâsita neʕ**
'You did it—right?'

Êe, kokó màde simâsita kedo, îi desu kaↄ
'Yes, I did it up to this point (pointing to a place in the lesson). Is that all right?'

3. **mimâsita**; 4. **dekímàsita**; 5. **kakímàsita**; 6. **osíemàsita**

B 1. **Giñkoo wa Toránomoñ dèsu kaↄ**
'Is the bank (the one you went to) in Toranomon?'

Ie, konó heñ no giñkoo e ikimàsita.
'No, I went to a bank around here.'

2. **Hôñya wa Toókyòo-eki no sôba desu kaↄ**
'Is the bookstore (the one you went to) near Tokyo Station?'

Ie, konó heñ no hòñya e ikímàsita.
'No, I went to a bookstore around here.'

3. **depâato/Ueno**; 4. **kissateñ/Oókura-hòteru no sôba**; 5. **tosyôkañ/daiğaku no tonari**; 6. **eéğàkañ/Ueno**

● Repeat this drill, replacing **e** with **ni** in the responses.

C 1. **Anó teğami kakimàsita kaↄ**   **Êe, gaḱkoo de kakimàsita.**

4. Remember that the makeup of in-groups and out-groups is constantly shifting. One's colleagues within a large in-group can become the out-group of a conversation involving only members of that group.

'Did you write that letter?'   'Yes, I wrote it at school.'

2. **Kóñpyùutaa tukáimàsita ka**✓   **Êe, gakkoo de tukaimàsita.**
'Did you use the computer?'   'Yes, I used it at school.'

3. **tyuúğokuğo osiemàsita;** 4. **Nîsida-sañ no kuruma mimâsita;** 5. **tênisu simâsita;**
6. **anó zassi kaimàsita**

D 1. **Tikâ no kissateñ de tabemàsita ka**✓   **Ie, sokó dè wa tabémasèñ desita.**
'Did you eat in the coffee shop in the   'No, I didn't eat there (in contrast with
basement?'   where I *did* eat).'

2. **Konó depàato e kimâsu ka**✓   **Ie, kokó è wa kimásèñ.**
'Will you come to this department   'No, I won't come here (in contrast with
store?'   where I *will* come.)'

3. **Kyôoto made ikímàsita;** 4. **konó gakkoo ni kimàsu;** 5. **Toókyoo de kakimàsita;**
6. **taísìkañ de mimâsita;** 7. **Uéno-kòoeñ e ikímàsita;** 8. **Amérika no daiğaku ni
arimàsu;** 9. **byoóiñ màde ikímàsita**

E 1. **Kóñpyùutaa arímàsu ka**✓   **Êe, sañ-ğai ni arimàsu.**
'Are there any computers?'   'Yes, they're on the third floor.'

2. **Kóñpyùutaa tukáimàsu ka**✓   **Êe, sañ-ğai de tukaimàsu.**
'Do you use the computers?'   'Yes, I use them on the third floor.'

3. **Nakámura-sañ imàsu;** 4. **eéğo osiemàsu;** 5. **baíteñ arimàsu;** 6. **kore dekímàsu;**
7. **gakúsee imàsu**

F 1. **Kore kara hôñya desu ka**✓   **Êe, tyôtto hôñya e ìtte kimàsu kedo ..**
'After this, is it the bookstore [you're   'Yes, I'm going (*lit.* I'll come [back] having
going to]?'   gone) to the bookstore just for a bit,
    but . . .' (did you want something?)

2. **Kore kara giñkoo dèsu ka**✓   **Êe, tyôtto giñkoo e itte kimàsu kedo ..**
'After this, is it the bank [you're   'Yes, I'm going to the bank just for a bit,
going to]?'   but . . .' (did you want something?)

3. **hanâya;** 4. **depâato;** 5. **buñbooğuya;** 6. **yuúbìñkyoku;** 7. **tosyôkañ**

G 1. **Anó teğami kakimàsita ka**✓   **Koré kara kàite kimasu.**
'Did you write that letter?'   'I'm going to go and write it now.' (After
    this I'll write it and come [back].)

2. **Koóhìi nomímàsita ka**✓   **Koré kara nòñde kimasu.**
'Did you have (*lit.* drink) some   'I'm going to go and have some now.'
coffee?'   (After this I'll drink it and come [back].)

3. **kóñpyùutaa tukáimàsita;** 4. **atárasìi taípuràitaa mimâsita;** 5. **eéwa-zìteñ
kaímàsita;** 6. **aísukurìimu tabémàsita**

H 1. **Asíta kimàsu ne**ʔ   **Êe. Anâta[5] mo kitê kudásaimasèñ ka**✓
'You're coming tomorrow, aren't you?'   'Yes. Won't you please come, too?'

---

5. Substitute /name + **-sañ**/ or **séñsèe**, if appropriate, for politeness and respect.

2. **Gakkoo e itte kimàsu neˤ**   **Êe. Anâta mo iʧte kìte kudásaimasèñ ka⤸**
   'You're going to the school (and   'Yes. Won't you please go (and come back),
   coming back), aren't you?'   too?'

3. **hanâ kaímàsu**; 4. **asítà mo imâsu**; 5. **koñpyùutaa tukáimàsu**; 6. **atárasìi taípuràitaa
   mîte kimasu**; 7. **teǵami kakimàsu**; 8. **gíñkoo màde iʧte kimàsu**

I 1. **Gakusee wa?**   **Gakúsee dèsu ka⤸ Imâsu kedo . .**
   'How about the students?'   'The students? They're here, but . . .' (why
         do you ask?)

  2. **Kuruma wa?**   **Kurúma dèsu ka⤸ Arímàsu kedo . .**
   'How about a car?'   'A car? There is one, but . . .' or 'I have
         one, but . . .' (why do you ask?)

  3. **koóhìi**; 4. **Nakamura-sañ**; 5. **boorupeñ**; 6. **syoppíñgubàggu**; 7. **Yamamoto-sañ**;
   8. **hôñya-sañ**; 9. **oókìi no**

J 1. **Asita 'mata konó gìñkoo ni kimàsu.**   **Asítà wa señsèe mo konó gìñkoo ni
   'I'm coming to this bank again   irassyaimàsu yo⤸**
   tomorrow.'   'Tomorrow (at least) the teacher will also
         come to this bank.'

  2. **Asita 'mata anó hòteru ni imasu.**   **Asítà wa señsèe mo anó hòteru ni
   'I'll be in that hotel again tomorrow.'   irássyaimàsu yo⤸**
         'Tomorrow (at least) the teacher will also
         be in that hotel.'

  3. **konó kissateñ e kimàsu**; 4. **anó daiǵaku ni imàsu**; 5. **konó yuubìñkyoku ni kimasu**

K. In this drill, the cue questions are in plain distal-style. The responses are humble-polite
/ ↓ /, indicating that the responder is being more polite than the questioner. What kind of
situation gives rise to this?

  1. **Asita kokó ni imàsu ka⤸**   **Hâi, orímàsu.**
   'Will you be here tomorrow?'   'Yes, I will (be here).'

  2. **Konó kèeki o tabémàsu ka⤸**   **Hâi, itádakimàsu.**
   'Are you going to eat this cake?'   'Yes, I am (going to eat).'

  3. **konó kissateñ e kimàsu**; 4. **wâiñ o nomimasu**; 5. **asâtte konó bìru ni imasu**; 6. **asita
   kokó màde kimasu**

L 1. **Señsèe no onámae dèsu ka⤸**   **Hâi, señsèe no desu.**
   'Is it the doctor's name?'   'Yes, it's the doctor's (one).'

  2. **Kîree na hanâ desu ka⤸**   **Hâi, kîree na no desu.**
   'Are they pretty flowers?'   'Yes, they're pretty ones.'

  3. **ano buñbooǵuya no biñseñ**; 4. **tikâ no kissateñ**; 5. **ik-kai no baiteñ**; 6. **tonári no
   hanàya**; 7. **Nîsida-sañ no osake**; 8. **hûbeñ na gakkoo**; 9. **haiiro no kuruma**;
   10. **bêñri na koñpyùutaa**; 11. **sañmañ-eñ no zìsyo**

M1. **Warûi desu ka⤸**   **Wârûku nâi desyoo?**

'Is it bad?'   'It's not bad, is it?'

2. Îma desu ka⌄   Îma zya nâi desyoo?

'Is it now?'   'It's not now, is it?'

3. mazûi desu; 4. sań-g̃ai dèsu; 5. tikâ desu; 6. kîree desu; 7. tonári dèsu; 8. zéñbu desu; 9. yasásìi desu; 10. hutátu-zùtu desu; 11. oísìi desu; 12. mîdori desu

N 1. **Konó kèeki mazûi desu ne!**   **Sôo desu ne! Mazûi kêeki desu ne!**

'This cake tastes awful, doesn't it.'   'Doesn't it! It's awful cake, isn't it!'

2. **Anó depàato hûbeñ desu ne!**   **Sôo desu ne! Hûbeñ na depâato desu ne!**

'That department store is inconvenient, isn't it.'   'Isn't it! It's an inconvenient department store, isn't it!'

3. **kono namae muzúkasìi desu; 4. ano hana kîree desu; 5. kono kissateñ bêñri desu; 6. kono osake oísìi desu; 7. anó kàig̃i asítà desu; 8. kono siñbuñ kyôo desu**

Application Exercises

A1. Expand your model town with models of the new types of buildings and shops introduced in this section, and practice the following kinds of conversation. Be sure to include the rituals—**Sumímasèñ; tyôtto ukág̃aimàsu g̃a . . ; dôo mo (arîg̃atoo [gozáimàsita]); osewasama;** and hesitation noises and echo questions—whenever appropriate.

a. Move **Nakamura-sañ, Nîsida-sañ, Tanaka-sañ**, etc. in and out of various buildings. Ask the following questions after each move:

(1) /——— -sañ/ (wa) dôko e/ni/made ikímàsita ka⌄

(2) /——— -sañ/ (wa) îma dôko ni imâsu ka⌄

(3) /——— -sañ/ (wa) dôko ni imâsita ka⌄

b. Using new vocabulary, review patterns introduced earlier with new vocabulary by asking and answering questions related to identification of the buildings, relative location of the buildings to each other, existence or nonexistence of a particular kind of building in a particular location. Be sure to point, as necessary. Sample questions:

(1) **Kore ~ koko ~ kotira (wa) nâñ desu ka⌄**

(2) **Kore ~ koko ~ kotira (wa) /gakkoo/ dèsu ka⌄**

(3) **Kono heñ ni /giñkoo/ (g̃a) arimàsu ka⌄**

(4) **/Daig̃aku/ (wa) dôko ni arímàsu ka ~ dôko desu ka⌄**

(5) **/Kissateñ/ no màe ni nâni g̃a arímàsu ka⌄**

(6) **/Kooeñ/ ni dâre g̃a imâsu ka⌄**

(7) **/Sâtoo-sañ/ (wa) dôko ni imâsu ka ~ dôko desu ka⌄**

(8) **/Hôñya/ (wa) /giñkoo/ no tonari dèsu ka ~ tonári ni arimàsu ka⌄**

(9) **/Hôñya/ g̃a /giñkoo/ no tonari dèsu ka ~ tonari ni arimàsu ka⌄**

(10) **/Hanâya no 'tonari (wa) /hôñya/ desu ka⌄**

(11) **/Hanâya/ no tonári g̃a /hòñya/ desu ka⌄**

(12) **/Hanâya/ no 'tonari (wa) nâñ desu ka⌄**

(13) **Dôko g̃a /hôñya/ desu ka⌄**

(14) /Giñkoo/ to /yuúbìñkyoku/ no aída no bìru (wa) nâñ desu ka⌐

In your questions, practice using **desyòo** as well as **dèsu**; and vary your answers by using **X desyo(o)?** and **X zya nâi desu ka⌐** as alternates for **X desu**. Remember that active *control* of language depends on active *use*.

2. Practice asking members of your group (1) whether they have particular objects (typewriters, computers, cars, dictionaries, newspapers, etc.); and (2) where they bought them. Use this exercise to drill and internalize the vocabulary *that has already been introduced*.

3. Have each member of the group announce that s/he is going on an errand to a particular place. On the basis of that place, have another group member politely request that s/he buy something. Example:

> **Kore kara, depâato e iƭte kimàsu/mairimàsu.**
>
> **Zyâa, warûi desu kedo, kurôi 'boorupeñ (o) sâñ-boñ-hodo kaƭte kìte kudásai-masèñ ka⌐**
>
> **Sâñ-boñ desu neʃ Hâi, îi desu yo⌐ Iƭte kimàsu/mairimàsu.**
>
> **Iƭte (i)rassyâi (màse).**

These exchanges can be expanded to cover the return (i.e., **Tadaima. . . . Okáeri-nasài[màse]**), monetary settlement, and thanks.

B. Core Conversations: Substitution

Review the Core Conversations, making appropriate substitutions. Act out the exchanges, moving around and gesturing as appropriate.

SECTION B

Core Conversations

1(N)a. **Nisîzaka-señsee no otaku wa,
Mêziro no dôtira desyoo ka.**

    (J)   **|Eeto| Tyôtto muzúkasìi desu nêe.
Tîzu o kakímasyòo.**

   b. **Zyâa, konó kami no urà ni
onéǧai-simàsu.**

2(N) **Nâñ de ikímasyòo ka. Tâkusii ǧa
îi desyoo ka.**

    (J)   **Iya, arûite ikimasyoo.**

3(N)a. **Tyôtto, okíki-sitài ñ desu
kedo . .**

    (J)a. **Hâi.**

   b. **|Anoo] Pâruko wa koƭti no hòo
desyoo ka.**

      b. **Hai?**

   c. **|Anoo| Pâruko e ikítài ñ desu
kedo . .**

      c. **A, zyâa, kore o maƭsùǧu itte, tuǧî
no koosateñ de 'hidari e maǧatte,
sûǧu desu yo.**

4(N)a. **Sumímaseñ kedo, tuğî no siñğoo no tyôtto temae de yuútàañ-site, sokó de tomete kudasài.**
   b. **Êe.**

(J)a. **Yuútàañ desu ka⤸**
   b. **Dekímàsu ka nêe. Abúnài ñ desu kedo nêe.**

ENGLISH EQUIVALENTS

1(N)a. Where in Mejiro would Dr. Nishizaka's home be?

(J) Uh, it's a little difficult (to explain). Why don't I draw a map.

   b. Then would you put it (*lit.* I request [it]) on the back of this paper?

2(N) How (i.e. by what) should we go? Would a cab be good?

(J) No, let's walk.

3(N)a. Say, I'd like to ask you something but . . . (is it all right?)

(J)a. Go right ahead.
   b. What did you say?

   b. Would Parco be in this direction?
   c. Uh, I'd like to go to Parco but . . . (I'm not sure how to go.)

   c. Oh, well then, go straight along this [street], turn left at the next intersection, and it's right there.

4(N)a. Excuse me, but would you make a U-turn just this side of the next light, and stop (the cab) there?
   b. Yes.

(J)a. A U-turn?
   b. I wonder if I can. It's (that it's) dangerous but . . . [it may be possible], I guess.

BREAKDOWNS
(AND SUPPLEMENTARY VOCABULARY)

1. **Nisîzaka-señsee**   Dr. *or* Professor *or* Teacher Nishizaka
   +**uti**   house, home; household; in-group
   +**iê**   house, home; household
   +**outi** *or*
      otaku   house, home; household; out-group
                                          /polite/
   Mêziro   (section of Tokyo)
   +**Giñza**   (section of Tokyo)
   |**eeto**| uh /hesitation noise/
   tîzu   map

kakímasyòo (SP1)	let's write, let's draw; I guess I'll write (*or* draw)
urâ	reverse side
+omótè	front side
2. nâñ de (SP2)	by means of what?
ikímasyòo	let's go; I guess I'll go
ikímasyòo ka	shall I/we go?
tâkusii	taxi
+bâsu	bus
+deñsya/dêñsya	electric train
+tikatetu	subway
arúkimàsu /arûite/	walk
arûite ikimasu	go by walking, go on foot (*lit.* get there having walked)
arûite ikimasyoo	let's go on foot; I guess I'll go on foot
+siñkàñseñ	bullet train
+kisyâ	railroad train
+hikôoki	airplane
3. kikímàsu /kiite/	ask
okíki-simàsu ↓ (SP3)	I/we ask you /polite/
okíki-sitài /-katta/ ↓ (SP4)	I/we want to ask you /polite/
okíki-sitài ↓ ñ desu (SP4)	it's that I/we'd like to ask you /polite/
+omâwarisañ ni kikimasu	ask a policeman
Pâruko	Parco (name of department store)
+sûupaa	supermarket
+yaoya	fruit and vegetable store
+kuukoo	airport
kot̀tì	/informal alternate of **kotira**/
ikitai /-katta/	want to go
ikítài ñ desu	it's that I'd like to go
koré o ikimàsu (SP2)	go along this (e.g., street)
maśsùg̃u	straight
maśsùg̃u itte, (SP5)	having gone straight; going straight and . . .
tug̃î	next
koosateñ	intersection
+kâdo	street corner
mag̃árimàsu /mag̃atte/	make a turn
hidari e mag̃atte,	having turned to the left; turning to the left and . . .

4. **siṅ̈goo**	traffic light
+**tukiatari**	end of the street, corridor, etc.
temae	this side (of)
tyôtto temae	a little this side (of)
yuútàaṅ-simasu	make a U-turn
yuútàaṅ-site,	having made a U-turn; making a U-turn and . . .
tomémàsu /tomete/	stop (something); bring to a halt
abunai /-katta/	is dangerous
abúnài ṅ desu	it's that it's dangerous

-dai: *Classifier for counting vehicles and machines*

itî-dai	**rokû-dai**
nî-dai	**nanâ-dai/ sitî-dai**
sâṅ-dai	**hatî-dai**
yôṅ-dai	**kyûu-dai**
go-dai	**zyûu-dai**

nâṅ-dai 'how many vehicles/machines?'

-keṅ: *Classifier for counting buildings and shops*

îk-keṅ	**rôk-keṅ**
nî-keṅ	**nanâ-keṅ/ sitî-keṅ**
sâṅ-g̈eṅ	**hâk-keṅ/ hatî-keṅ**
yôṅ-keṅ	**kyûu-keṅ**
gô-keṅ	**zyûk-keṅ/ zîk-keṅ**

nâṅ-g̈eṅ 'how many buildings/shops?'

MISCELLANEOUS NOTES

1. In CC1, a foreigner (N) asks a Japanese associate (J) directions to Professor Nishizaka's home. On the accompanying video, the participants are Ms. Brown and Mr. Kato, who study in the same seminar room. Their speech reflects distance and a continuing lack of familiarity: they use distal-style predicates exclusively.

In traveling around Japan, the foreigner is struck by the fact that streets tend to be extremely irregular and few of them have names; it is areas that are regularly named or numbered. When going to a station, a well-known hotel, building, temple or shrine, etc., the name alone will be sufficient. But in other situations—for example, in going to a private home, a company office, a small restaurant, etc.—the usual procedure is to obtain a detailed map that clearly shows your destination. In taking a taxi, one starts out by indicating the general area and then giving precise directions.

(N)a. **Seńsèe,** like **-saṅ,** can be added to a proper name (never one's own!). It is used in reference to professors, teachers, doctors, lawyers, etc., and also as a term of respect to one's superior, but not in self-identification except when talking to children or young people. **Uti** is regularly used in reference to the speaker's own home or in-group; in reference to others' homes or in-groups, **otaku** and **outi** are polite and **uti** is plain. Many items which are assigned individual ownership in English ('my wife,' 'my children,' 'my school,' 'your company,' etc.) are viewed more commonly in terms of a household or in-group in Japanese. Accordingly, /**otaku no** + nominal/ and /**uti no** + nominal/ are very common phrases, and frequently the equivalent of 'your' and 'my' in English.

Mêziro no dôko 'where in Mejiro? Compare: **dôko no Mêziro** 'the Mejiro (which is) where?'

(J) **Eeto,** like **anoo,** is a common hesitation noise.

(N)b. **Urâ** and **omótè** refer to the back and front of things which specifically have such a distinction: buildings, cloth, coins (cf. English 'heads' and 'tails'), books, etc. **Urâ ni** here describes the place *onto which* writing is requested.

2. In CC2, two colleagues discuss how they will get to their destination. On the accompanying videotape, the foreigner, Mr. Carter (N), defers to his superior in the company, Mr. Yoshida (J), to make the decision. The speech style reflects distance.

Siñkàñseñ refers to the new, high-speed, trunk-line trains that run between the major cities of Japan.

(J) **Arúkimàsu** refers to the act of walking. While the verbal may be used alone with destinations, usually in such situations it occurs in the gerund form followed by the appropriate motion verbal: **arûite ikimasu** 'walk [there]'; **arûite kimasu** 'walk here'; **arûite kaerimasu** 'walk home.'

3. In CC3, a foreigner (N) approaches a Japanese stranger (J) on the street to ask directions.

(N)a. With **kikímàsu,** /nominal + o/ indicates the thing asked, and /person nominal + ni/, the person to whom the question is put.

(N)b. **Sûupaa** is a shortening of **suúpaamàaketto.**

Kottì, sottì, attì, and **dôtti** occur as slightly less formal equivalents of the **kotira** series.

(J)b. **Hai?** with question intonation occurs frequently as an indication that whatever was just said was not understood. Another commonly occurring alternate is **E(e)?** In response, usually a rewording of what was originally said is offered.

(J)c. **Kore** refers here to the street on which the conversation takes place. **Tuǵî** is, of course, a nominal. Compare: **tuǵî no êki** 'the next station' and **Toókyòo-eki no tuǵî** 'next after Tokyo Station.'

4. CC4 takes place in a taxicab. The passenger gives the driver specific directions.

(N)a. **Tukiatari** refers to the end of a street or corridor, either a dead end or a T-intersection.

Temae 'this side of' is the opposite of **mukoo** 'beyond.' **X no temae** and **X no mukoo** designate locations relative to the speaker. **Tyôtto temae** is parallel in structure to **môtto saki**: these are relationals preceded by extent expressions.

Yuútàañ, a borrowing from English, now refers not only to a U-turn as a driving term, but also to the return portion of an excursion, especially one lasting several days. On January 5, Tokyo Station is packed with 'U-turn travelers' returning to Tokyo after the New Year's holidays.

Tomémàsu always implies a preceding /nominal + (o)/; if clear from the context, it is not expressed. Here, **tâkusii (o)** is understood.

(J)b. **Abunai,** the direct-style adjectival, occurs by itself or with sentence-particle **yo,** as a warning: 'Look out!' Even here, the Japanese avoid a confrontational imperative, noting the existing condition instead: 'it's dangerous.' Note the driver's use of **nêe** as he deliberates over the possibility of a U-turn. The sentence-particle **nê(e)** occurs at the end of minor as well as major sentences.

Structural Patterns

1. VERBALS: **-masyòo**

When the **-màsu** form of a verbal is replaced by **-masyòo**, the resulting form is the distal-style CONSULTATIVE. Suggestions involving the speaker alone and the speaker plus person(s) addressed occur in this form. The difference in reference is determined by context. /Consultative + **ka**/ questions frequently end in period /./ intonation. Examples:

Ikímasyòo.	'I guess I'll go'; 'Why don't I go.' *or* 'Let's go.'
Kaímasyòo.	'I guess I'll buy [it]'; 'Why don't I buy [it].' *or* 'Let's buy [it].'
Koré (o) tukaimasyòo neʃ	'Let's use this one, shall we?' *or* 'Why don't I use this one, huh!'
Matá kimasyòo ka.	'Shall I/we come here again?'

Note that consultative verbals are regularly operational rather than affective; they refer to activities that can be brought about by human decision or will. After all, it is impossible to *suggest* that we understand, or need, or be able.

In an affirmative reply to a consultative question referring to the speaker + person(s) addressed, the consultative is repeated, or **soó simasyòo** 'let's do it that way' is used as a replacement form. Example:

Tyôtto koóhìi (o) nomímasyòo ka.	'Shall we have some coffee?'
Êe, nomímasyòo. *or*	'Yes, let's have [some].'
Êe, soó simasyòo.	'Yes, let's do that.'

This consultative form is used much more commonly in Japanese than its English equivalent. Frequently it is the sociolinguistic equivalent of an English imperative or direct instruction, thus demonstrating the Japanese preference for consensus, cooperative action, and avoidance of confrontation. Instead of telling people what they are to do, such situations are often presented as suggestions for joint action. An example is the Japanese version of the English advertising slogan, 'Drink Coca-Cola!': **Kôoku o nomímasyòo** 'Let's drink Coke,' the Japanese-language equivalent suggests. 'Cigarettes can be dangerous to your health' appears in Japan with the Japanese equivalent of: 'For the sake of [our] health, let's try not to smoke too much.' and 'Drive carefully!' turns up as 'Let's move gently.'

In reply to a consultative question referring to the speaker only, the affirmative answer is a request form. Thus:

Ikímasyòo ka.	'Shall I go?'
Êe, onégai-simàsu. *or*	'Yes, please (*lit.* I request it).'
Êe, iĺte kudasài(masèñ ka). *or*	'Yes, (would you) please go.'
Êe, soó site kudasài(masèñ ka).	'Yes, (would you) please do that.'

In polite style, only the humble-polite /↓/ occurs in the consultative, since the speaker is always included. When it refers to the speaker plus person(s) addressed, the implication is usually close, concerted action plus politeness. Thus:

Koóhìi (o) itádakimasyòo.	'I guess I'll have some coffee.' *or* 'Let's have some coffee.'

2. PHRASE-PARTICLES: /tâkusii de ikimasu/; /koré o ikimàsu/

a. /Nominal X + **de** + predicate Y/ = 'predicate Y occurs *by means of X.*' Compare now:

Kokó de simàsita.	'I did [it] here.' (A-SP1)
Koré de simàsita.	'I did [it] with this' (i.e., by means of this).

The two patterns are distinguished by the type of nominal preceding **de**: in the locational pattern, the nominal is a place nominal; in the means pattern, the nominal is inanimate and non-place. Examples:

Ziteñsya de kimâsita.	'I came by bicycle.'
Koñpyùutaa de tukúrimasyòo.	'Let's do (*lit.* make) [it] by computer.'
Eñpitu de kàite kudasai.	'Please write in pencil.'

This phrase-particle **de**, like the locational particle, may be followed by **wa** or **mo**, and is then accented if the preceding nominal is unaccented.

Eñpitu dè wa kakímasèñ desita.	'I didn't write [it] in pencil' (but with something else).
Eégo dè mo nihóñgo dè mo osiemasu.	'I teach both in English and in Japanese.'

b. /Place nominal X + **(o)** + operational predicate Y of motion/ = 'motion Y occurs *through the area* X.' This /nominal + **(o)**/ phrase is simply a subtype of *operand,* discussed in 5A-SP1. Here, the range of the activity is an area, and the operational predicate describes motion that occurs within or through that area. Examples:

Konó miti (o) arukimasyòo.	'Let's walk along this street.'
Koré (o) itte kudasài.	'Go along this one' (e.g., this street).
Tuğî no kâdo (o) mağárimasyòo ka.	'Shall I turn the next corner?' (*lit.* 'Shall I make a turn *through* the next corner area?')

With the last example, compare:

Tuğî no kâdo de mağárimasyòo ka.	'Shall I make a turn *at* the next corner?'

While these are two different patterns in both Japanese and English, the actual meanings of these particular utterances are very similar.

As is usual for phrase-particle **o** patterns, the **o** does not normally occur when the preceding noun shifts to a **wa** or **mo** relationship:

Ano miti wa kinóo arukimàsita.	'That road (at least) I walked along yesterday.'
Tuğî no kâdo mo mağárimasyòo ka.	'Shall I turn the next corner, too?'

3. HUMBLE-POLITE VERBALS: okíki-simàsu

In Section A of this lesson (cf. SP5), we discussed polite-style, including the humble-polite /↓/, which regularly refers to the speaker's in-group (including the speaker alone). Examples like **itádakimàsu, maírimàsu,** and **orímàsu** represent cases where the humble-polite verbals have totally different roots from their plain-style equivalents.

But most humble-polite examples are actually derived from their plain equivalents. The formation works like this:

A plain verbal in the **-màsu** form minus **-màsu** = a plain STEM; /**o-** + stem + **-simàsu**/ = the humble-polite equivalent. Examples:

Plain Verbal	Stem	Humble-Polite	Meaning
kikímàsu	**kiki**	**okíki-simàsu** ↓	'ask'
kakímàsu	**kaki**	**okáki-simàsu** ↓	'write'
osíemàsu	**osie**	**oósie-simàsu** ↓	'teach,' 'show how,' 'inform'
misémàsu	**mise**	**omíse-simàsu** ↓	'show'

Note the literal meaning of the humble forms: 'I do (**simâsu**) asking, writing, teaching, showing, that involves you or someone to whom I'm showing deference (**o-**).'

An already familiar example of this pattern is **onégai-simàsu,** derived from the verbal **negáimàsu** 'request.' In this case, the basic verbal is itself humble / ↓ /, but the derived form is more polite in a humble sense.

Not all verbals occur in the /**o-stem-simàsu**/ pattern, which regularly implies a definite involvement of the referent, representing activities that are performed by the speaker *for* that person.

4. ADJECTIVALS IN **-tai**; *INTRODUCTION TO THE EXTENDED PREDICATE*

/Verbal stem X + **-tai** = an ADJECTIVAL meaning 'want to X.' The stem is the **-màsu** form minus **-màsu** (cf. SP3, above). Examples: **ikitai** 'want to go'; **tabétài** 'want to eat'; **sitai** 'want to do.'

Note these regular derived adjectival forms, based on the verbal **ikímàsu** 'go' (stem **iki**):

	Direct-style	Distal-style
Affirmative		
Imperfective: 'I want to go'	**ikitai**	**ikítài desu**
Perfective: 'I wanted to go'	**ikítàkatta**	**ikítàkatta desu**
Negative		
Imperfective: 'I don't want to go'	**ikítaku nài**	**ikítaku nài desu** *or* **ikítaku arimasèñ**
Perfective: 'I didn't want to go'	**ikítaku nàkatta**	**ikítaku nàkatta desu** *or* **ikítaku arimasèñ desita**

There are four special features to note in regard to the **-tai** form:

1. Only operational verbals have regularly occurring derivative **-tai** forms. Accordingly, there are no regularly occurring **-tai** forms for affective verbals like **wakárimàsu, arímàsu, irímàsu, dekímàsu,** which are affective verbals.

2. A nominal that occurs followed by particle **o** before an operational verbal may occur with **ḡa** before the **-tai** derivative. Example:

Hôn o kaimasu. *but*	'I'm going to buy a book.'
Hôñ o kaítài desu. *or*	
Hôñ ḡa kaítài desu.	'I want to buy a book.'

Clearly a form like **kaitai** has both a verbal quality (in **kai-**) and an adjectival quality (in **-tai**). The alternative with **o** reflects a connection with the verbal part of the predicate, while the **ḡa** alternate reflects the adjectival nature of the final **-tai** portion. We might look on the **o**-alternative as indicating that what I want to do is buy-a-book; but the **ḡa**-alternative focuses on the book as a thing there-is-a-desire-to-buy. Thus, the choice of **o** puts focus on an activity, whereas choosing **ḡa** emphasizes the nominal of the **ḡa** phrase. In some contexts there may be a decided preference for one over the other.

3. The **-tai** form occurs very commonly in the combination /**-tài ñ desu**/, an important pattern about which more will continue to be said in future lessons. The pattern will be called the EXTENDED PREDICATE. It consists of /imperfective or perfective predicate (usually direct-style) + nominal **ñ** + **desu**/.[6] At this first stage, we will use only adjectival predicates before **ñ,** including **-tai** adjectivals.

Consider now:

> **tabétài desu** *and* **tabétài ñ desu**
>
> **oísìi desu** *and* **oísìi ñ desu**

The first member of each pair is the familiar distal-style adjectival pattern: 'I want to eat' and 'it's delicious.' The second members are actually /nominal + **desu**/ predicates, with the nominal **ñ** preceded by a describing adjectival (structured just like **oókìi hôñ desu** 'it's a big book,' **oísii kèeki desu** 'it's a delicious cake,' and **oísìi no desu** 'it's a delicious one.') The **ñ** here, the usual form in conversation, is a contraction of **no** (which occurs commonly in written Japanese) and means something like 'case,' 'matter,' 'involvement.' Though clearly related to the nominal **no** 'one(s)' that was introduced previously, its overall patterning requires that it be treated separately.

What, then, do combinations like **tabétài ñ desu** and **oísìi ñ desu** really mean? The pattern relates what precedes **ñ** to something in the real world which is known or assumed to be known by the person addressed, as well as being known by the speaker. The pattern often serves as an explanation. Examples:

(a) Looking at a new dictionary, I might remark **Takâi desu nêe.**, as a comment on the dictionary. But if my colleague were surprised to learn that I was not going to buy it, I might say, **Takâi ñ desu yo.**, i.e., 'It's that it's expensive' (that explains my not buying it).

(b) Trying to read a Japanese newspaper, I might remark **Muzúkasìi desu nêe.**, as a comment on the text. But if my colleague noted that I had decided to give up on the newspaper and switch to something easier, I might say, **Muzúkasìi ñ desu yo.**, i.e., 'It's that it's difficult' (that explains my giving it up).

(c) In CC4, the taxi driver comments **abúnài ñ desu** 'it's that it's dangerous' (that explains my concern about making a U-turn).

(d) Approaching a policeman, I might remark **Oókura-hòteru e ikítài ñ desu kedo . .** 'It's that I want to go to the Hotel Okura' (that explains my talking to you). Here, the extended predicate pattern sets the stage for what is about to be said.

The **-tai** form occurs very commonly within an extended predicate pattern (**-tai ñ desu**), since this kind of open assertion of what one wants to do is apt to be expressed in Japanese as an explanation—for an activity, statement, question, suggestion, or request.

Note the perfective and negative extended predicate patterns, in which the adjectival is transformed:

---

6. Other variants will be introduced in Lesson 9.

	Distal-Style	
	Affirmative	Negative
Imperfective	**ikítài ñ desu** 'it's that I want to go'	**ikítaku nài ñ desu** 'it's that I don't want to go'
Perfective	**ikítàkatta ñ desu** 'it's that I wanted to go'	**ikítaku nàkatta ñ desu** 'it's that I didn't want to go'

4. In statements, the **-tai** form regularly refers to something the speaker wants to do him/herself.[7] Insofar as it occurs in questions, it usually refers to the addressee, but this usage does NOT represent the invitational implications of most English questions like 'Do you want to ———?' 'Would you like to ———?' You will remember that such invitations are expressed in Japanese by the negative imperfective of verbals. Compare:

Asítà mo kimásèñ ka⌇ *and*	'Won't you (i.e. wouldn't you like to) come again tomorrow?' /invitation/
Asítà mo kitâi ñ desu ka⌇	'Is it the case that you want to come again tomorrow?' /non-invitation/

Accent: Some **-tai** forms are accented (on the **-ta-**) and some unaccented;[8] but before **ñ** and before **desu,** all adjectivals are accented. Derived accented forms in **-ku** and **-katta,** and others to be introduced later, continue to be accented on the **-ta-**.

5. VERBAL GERUNDS: /**-te,**/

The verbal gerund (the **-te** form), + **kudásài(masèñ ka)** in request patterns and + **kimâsu** in errand patterns, has been introduced previously. Parallel to the latter type is the combination **arûite ikimasu** (CC2). In all these combinations, there is no break between the gerund and what follows.

In all gerund patterns, the underlying meaning of the gerund is the same: it links up with a following predicate with the implication of actualization of the gerund action or state. This will not necessarily mean completion in all its uses—but at least a start. Thus:

Siñbuñ (o) katte kimàsu.	'I'll come (i.e. arrive here) having bought a paper.'
English:	'I'll buy a paper and come'; *or* (usually) 'I'll go and buy a paper.'
Êki e arûite ikimasu.	'I'll go to (i.e. arrive at) the station, having walked.'
English:	'I'll walk to the station.'
Koóhìi (o) nôñde kaerimasyoo.	'Let's go home having drunk coffee.'
English:	'Let's have coffee and go home'; *or* (usually) 'Let's have some coffee before we go home.'

7. An exception is when it is stated that the speaker is indirectly reporting something s/he heard, thinks, suspects, etc. about someone else's wishes.
8. This depends on the accent of the underlying verbal (cf. Lesson 9).

Katte kudasài.   'Please buy [it]' i.e., 'Please grant me *actualized* buying.'

In all these examples, there is a very close relationship between the gerund and what follows: it often describes an accompanying condition of the following predicate, or the means by which it is accomplished.

We now introduce the gerund *with comma intonation,* i.e. slightly slowed down articulation with or without a following pause, and followed by a new accent phrase.

When the gerund ends in comma intonation, there is often a notion of increased separation between the gerund and what follows, *even though the basic notion of actualization is still present.* In other words, the following predicate may occur distinct from the gerund but assuming its actualization.[9]

When we speak of the 'following predicate,' we in no sense suggest that it must be *immediately* following: in most examples, there will be intervening phrases which also link up with the 'following predicate.' One phrase which often occurs—optionally—immediately following the gerund is **sore kara** 'after that,' 'and then'; its inclusion is restricted to events which are sequential, and emphasizes that fact.

In English, we describe *coordinate* actions or states: 'X and (then) Y'; in Japanese, we use a *subordinate* approach: 'having actualized X, (then) Y.'

NOTE: Regardless of whether the final predicate is perfective, imperfective, consultative, tentative, imperative, or a **-tai** form, the gerund occurs without change. Thus:

Koosateñ de 'miǧi ni maǧatte, sûǧu
- (a) **tomémàsu.**
- (b) **tomémàsita.**
- (c) **tomémasyòo.**
- (d) **tométe kudasài.**
- (e) **tométài ñ desu ǧa . .**

Literal Translation

(a) 'I'll stop right away, having turned right at the intersection.'

(b) 'I stopped right away, having turned right at the intersection.'

(c) 'Let's stop right away, having turned right at the intersection.'

(d) 'Please stop right away, having turned right at the intersection.'

(e) 'It's that I want to stop right away, having turned right at the intersection, but . . .'

English Equivalent

'I'll turn right at the intersection and (then) stop right away.'

'I turned right at the intersection and (then) stopped right away.'

'Let's turn right at the intersection and (then) stop right away.'

'Please turn right at the intersection and (then) stop right away.'

'I want to turn right at the intersection and (then) stop right away, but . . .'

This pattern also permits sequences of more than one gerund: /————**te,** ————**te,** (. . .) + final predicate/.

---

9. Compare: **katte kudasài** 'please (grant me) buy(ing),' and **katte, kudásài.** 'Having bought it, give it to me' ('Buy it and [then] give it to me').

But even with comma intonation, the gerund may designate a condition which directly affects—even results in—the following predicate. Only context determines the relationship. With the immediately preceding set of examples, compare:

Koosateñ de 'miḡi ni maḡatte, sûḡu desu.   'It will be right there, having turned to the right at the intersection,' i.e., 'Turn right at the intersection and it will be right there.'

In this example, the **sûḡu desu** condition *depends upon* what precedes. Compare now:

(a) **Kyôoto e siñkàñseñ de itte, hikôoki de kaérimàsita.**

'I went to Kyoto by bullet train and returned by plane.'

(b) **Kyôoto e siñkàñseñ de ikímàsita kedo, hikôoki de kaérimàsita.**

'I went to Kyoto by bullet train but returned by plane.'

In (a), I am describing the condition I was in ('having gone to Kyoto by bullet train') when I returned. In (b), I am presenting some background information before announcing that I returned by plane. Given the real-life contrast between the two, the English equivalent has 'but.' But now consider this pair:

(c) **Siñkàñseñ de itte, omósìròkatta desu yo⤸**

'Having gone by bullet train, it was fun'; 'It was fun to have gone by bullet train'; 'I went by bullet train, and it was fun.'

(d) **Siñkàñseñ de ikímàsita kedo, omósìròkatta desu yo⤸**

'I went by bullet train; it was fun.'

In (c), there is a direct connection in the speaker's mind between the travel by bullet train and the enjoyment experienced. In (d), the speaker is describing his/her enjoyment but first provides information that will enable listeners to interpret the following comment appropriately: in effect 'you should know that I went by bullet train; I enjoyed it.' However, *if* the speaker ordinarily dislikes travel by bullet train, (d) can again be interpreted as a contrastive sentence, similar to (b) above: 'I went by bullet train, but it was fun.'

Drills

A 1. **Îma kaérimasyòo ka.**   **Sôo desu ne! Îma kaérimasyòo.**
'Shall we go home now?'   'Right! Let's go home now.'

2. **Zêñbu simásyòo ka.**   **Sôo desu ne! Zêñbu simásyòo.**
'Shall we do the whole thing?'   'Right! Let's do the whole thing.'

3. **asíta ikimasyòo**; 4. **matá kimasyòo**; 5. **môtto tabémasyòo**; 6. **moó sukòsi nomímasyòo**

B 1. **Tîzu kakímàsita ka⤸**   **Iie. Kakímasyòo ka⤸**
'Did you draw a map?'   'No. Shall I draw (one)?'

2. **Onamae osíemàsita ka⤸**   **Iie. Osíemasyòo ka⤸**
'Did you tell [them] your name?'   'No. Shall I tell [them]?'

3. **ano uti mimâsita**; 4. **anó zìsyo misémàsita**; 5. **taípuràitaa tukáimàsita**; 6. **tîzu kaímàsita**

C 1. **Tîzu kakímasyòo ka⌐**
'Shall I draw a map?'

Êe, kâite kudásaimasèñ ka⌐
'Yes, would you be kind enough to draw [one]?'

2. **Mata asita kimásyòo ka⌐**
'Shall I come again tomorrow?'

Êe, kitê kudásaimasèñ ka⌐
'Yes, would you be kind enough to come?'

3. **asítà made imásyòo**; 4. **anó hòñ no namae osíemasyòo**; 5. **tîzu misémasyòo**; 6. **osake kaímasyòo**; 7. **ano teḡami mimásyòo**; 8. **kêeki tukúrimasyòo**

● Repeat this drill, replacing **kudásaimasèñ ka⌐** in the responses with **kudasài.**

D 1. **Tâkusii de ikímasyòo ka.**
'Shall we go by taxi?'

Êe, tâkusii ḡa îi desyoo ne! Tâkusii de ikímasyòo.
'Yes, *a taxi* would be good, wouldn't it! Let's go by taxi.'

2. **Pêñ de kakímasyòo ka.**
'Shall we write with a pen?'

Êe, pêñ ḡa îi desyoo ne! Pêñ de kakí-masyòo.
'Yes, *a pen* would be good, wouldn't it! Let's write with a pen.'

3. **bâsu de kaérimasyòo**; 4. **kurúma de kimasyòo**; 5. **nihóñḡo de kakimasyòo**; 6. **mîruku de tukúrimasyòo**; 7. **hikôoki de ikímasyòo**; 8. **siñkàñseñ de kaérimas-yòo**; 9. **tikátetu de kimasyòo**; 10. **anó miti de kaerimasyòo**

E 1. **Arûite ikímàsu ka⌐**
'Are you going to walk there?'

Sôo desu nêe. . . . Watási wa arùite ikimasyoo.
'Hmm. . . . I guess I (at least) will walk.'

2. **Deñsya de kimàsu ka⌐**
'Are you coming by electric train?'

Sôo desu nêe. . . . Watási wa deñsya de kimasyòo.
'Hmm. . . . I guess I (at least) will come by electric train.'

3. **urâ ni kakímàsu**; 4. **kokó de tukurimàsu**; 5. **arûite kaérimàsu**; 6. **eéḡo de osie-màsu**; 7. **kotíra de mimàsu**

F 1. **Dôozo, kiíte kudasài.**
'Please go ahead and ask.'

Arîḡatoo gozaimasu. Zyâa, tyôtto okíki-simàsu.
'Thank you. (Then) I will (ask a bit).'

2. **Dôozo, nôñde kudasai.**
'Please go ahead and drink.'

Arîḡatoo gozaimasu. Zyâa, tyôtto itádakimàsu.
'Thank you. I will (drink a bit).'

3. **mîsete**; 4. **kitê**; 5. **tâbete**; 6. **ite**; 7. **kâite**

G 1. **Zitêñsya de ikímàsu ka⌐**
'Are you going by bicycle?'

Ikítài ñ desu ḡa . .
'The fact is I'd like to (go), but . . .' (I'm not sure I can).

2. **Gôruhu simâsu ka.**
'Are you going to play golf?'

Sitâi ñ desu ḡa . .
'The fact is I'd like to (play), but . . .' (I'm not sure I can).

3. **koósateñ de maḡarimàsu;** 4. **omâwarisañ ni kikímàsu;** 5. **otáku ni kaerimàsu;** 6. **omótè ni kakímàsu;** 7. **Pâruko de kaímàsu;** 8. **nihóñḡo osiemàsu;** 9. **końpyùutaa tukáimàsu**

H 1. **Dôre o kaímasyòo ka.**
'Which one shall we buy?'

Soñnà no ḡa kaítàkatta ñ desu kedo . .
'The fact is I wanted to buy one like that but . . .' (what do *you* think?)

2. **Dôre o mimásyòo ka.**
'Which one shall we look at?'

Soñnà no ḡa mitâkatta ñ desu kedo . .
'The fact is I wanted to look at one like that but . . .' (what do *you* think?)

3. **tukáimasyòo;** 4. **tabémasyòo;** 5. **nomímasyòo**

I 1. **Kuúkoo ni ikimàsu ka**
'Are you going to the airport?'

Êe. Ikítaku nài ñ desu kedo . .
'Yes. The fact is I don't want to go, but . . .' (I must).

2. **Huráñsuḡo osiemàsu ka**
'Are you going to teach French?'

Êe. Osíetaku nài ñ desu kedo . .
'Yes. The fact is I don't want to teach it, but . . .' (I must).

3. **teḡámi kakimàsu;** 4. **waápuro tukaimàsu;** 5. **asita matá kimàsu;** 6. **oúti e kaerimàsu**

● Repeat this drill, replacing **-màsu** in the questions with **-màsita,** and **nài** in the responses with **nâkatta,** where appropriate.

J 1. **Omósìròku nâi ñ desu ka**
'Do you mean that it's not interesting?' (i.e., is that the explanation?)

Êe, tumárànai ñ desu nêe.
'That's right. (It's that) it's boring!'

2. **Oísiku nài ñ desu ka**
'Do you mean that it's not tasty?'

Êe, mazûi ñ desu nêe.
'That's right. (It's that) it tastes awful!'

3. **atáràsìku nâi;** 4. **yôku nâi;** 5. **yâsûku nâi;** 6. **yasásiku nài**

K 1. **Dôno miti o ikímàsu ka**
'Which road are you taking (*lit.* going)?'

|Eeto| **Anó miti dèsu yo. Anó miti o ikimàsu.**
'Uh. It's that road. I'm going along that road.'

2. **Dôno kâdo o maḡárimàsita ka**
'What corner did you turn?'

|Eeto| **Anó kàdo desu yo. Anó kàdo o maḡárimàsita.**
'Uh. It's that corner. I turned that corner.'

3. **miti/arúkimàsita;** 4. **miti/kimâsu**

Before doing drills L through O, be sure to read SP5 carefully.

L 1. **Kuúkoo e ikimàsu ka**⤸   **Êe. Tyôtto iƭte kimàsu kedo . .**
  'Are you going to the airport?'   'Yes. I'm just going to go and come [back], but . . .' (is that all right?)

  2. **Omâwarisañ ni kikímàsu ka**⤸   **Êe. Tyôtto kiíte kimàsu kedo . .**
  'Are you going to ask the policeman?'   'Yes. I'm just going to go and ask [him] (*lit.* come having asked), but . . .' (is that all right?)

  3. **otáku ni kaerimàsu;** 4. **tîzu kaimàsu;** 5. **mití kikimàsu**

M 1. **Arúkimàsu ka**⤸   **Êe, arûite ikimasu.**
  'Are you going to walk?'   'Yes, I'll go [there] on foot' (*lit.* get there having walked).

  2. **Koóhìi nomímàsu ka**⤸   **Êe, nôñde ikimasu.**
  'Are you going to have coffee?'   'Yes, I'll have [some] before I go' (*lit.* go having drunk).

  3. **tîzu mimâsu;** 4. **mití kikimàsu;** 5. **anó siñḡoo no kàdo maḡárimàsu;** 6. **kurúma tomemàsu;** 7. **kêeki tabémàsu**

N 1. **Tukíatari màde ikímàsu ka**⤸   **Êe, tukíatari màde itte, sûḡu desu yo**⤸
  'Do you go to the end (of the street)?'   'Yes, you go to the end, and it's right there.'

  2. **Sûupaa no kâdo maḡárimàsu ka**⤸   **Êe, sûupaa no kâdo maḡatte, sûḡu desu**
  'Do you turn the corner where the   **yo**⤸
  supermarket is?'   'Yes, you turn the supermarket corner, and it's right there.'

  3. **koósateñ no temae de maḡarimàsu;** 4. **tikátetu no èki no mâe de yuútàañ-simasu;**
  5. **tuḡî no siñḡoo de miḡí ni maḡárimàsu;** 6. **anó hòteru no urâ ni ikímàsu**

O 1. **Kyôo tênisu simâsu ka**⤸   **Êe. Tyôtto site, sore kara utí e**
  'Are you going to play tennis today?'   **kaerimàsu.**
          'Yes, I'll play for a bit and then go home.'

  2. **Kyôo atárasìi kuruma mimâsu ka**⤸   **Êe. Tyôtto mîte, sore kara utí e**
  'Are you going to look at new cars   **kaerimàsu.**
  today?'   'Yes, I'll look for a bit, and then go home.'

  3. **sûupaa e ikímàsu;** 4. **konó koñpyùutaa tukáimàsu;** 5. **teḡámi kakimàsu**

● Repeat this drill, replacing the **-màsu** form in the question and the response with (1) **-màsita;** and (2) **-masyòo.**

P 1. **Kurúma arimàsu ka**⤸   **Êe, nî-dai arimasu.**
  'Is there a car?' *or* 'Do you have a   'Yes, there are two.' *or* 'Yes, I have two.'
  car?'

  2. **Hanâya arímàsu ka**⤸   **Êe, nî-keñ arimasu.**
  'Is there a flower shop?'   'Yes, there are two.'

3. **tîzu**; 4. **tâkusii**; 5. **kissateñ**; 6. **bâsu**; 7. **koñpyùutaa**; 8. **omise**; 9. **uti**; 10. **zîsyo**; 11. **hanâ**; 12. **hurosiki**; 13. **kabañ**

● Repeat this drill, using other numerals.

Q 1. **Abúnài desu ka**⌃
'Is it dangerous?'

Iie, abúnaku nài desu.
'No, it isn't (dangerous).'

2. **Maśsùg̊u desu ka**⌃
'Is it straight? *or* 'Do you go straight?'

Iie, maśsùg̊u zya nâi desu.
'No, it isn't straight.' *or* 'You don't go straight.'

3. **tug̊î desu**; 4. **tukíatari dèsu**; 5. **warûi desu**; 6. **kâdo desu**; 7. **omótè desu**; 8. **mazûi desu**.

● Repeat this drill in the perfective.

R 1. **Siñg̊oo no mukóo dèsu ka**⌃
'Is it beyond the traffic light?'

Ie, temáe dèsu.
'No, it's this side.'

2. **Hôteru no urâ desu ka**⌃
'Is it the rear of the hotel?'

Ie, omótè desu.
'No, it's the front.'

3. **otaku no mâe**; 4. **tosyôkañ no miğídònari**; 5. **kissateñ no 'temae**; 6. **sono kami no omótè**; 7. **buñbooğuya no 'usiro**; 8. **kabañ no 'hidari**

Application Exercises

A1. Practice making suggestions for joint activities—for example, playing tennis, buying a dictionary, going to the new department store, etc.—and pursue the conversation with other members of the group. Include reactions to the suggestions and follow-up questions and answers. Utilize to the fullest possible extent everything you have learned.

2. Using a fully expanded model town, practice asking a stranger directions to a particular location. Be sure to indicate not only where you are going, but where you are starting out from. In formulating the answers, use the newly introduced complex sentence pattern of CC3 and CC4 of this section.

3. Again using the model town, act out taxi rides, using plans of the following kind:

Instruction #1	*Instruction #2*	*Instruction #3*	*Fare*
a. Go toward Mejiro.	Turn left at the next corner;	stop in front of the bank.	¥1100
b. Go toward Toranomon.	Go to the end of the street;	stop a little this side of the hospital.	¥760
c. Go toward Tokyo Station.	Make a U-turn beyond the next light;	go a little beyond that big, white building and stop.	¥430

Take advantage of the fare segment to review numbers and practice the payment patterns introduced in earlier lessons.

B. Core Conversations: Substitution

Return to the Core Conversations and practice them with appropriate vocabulary substitutions. Be sure that your substitutions are indeed appropriate: don't produce utterances so original that the Japanese have never thought of them!

SECTION C

Eavesdropping

(Answer the following on the basis of the accompanying tape. A = the first speaker; B = the second speaker.)

1a. Whose whereabouts is A asking about?
 b. Where is that person?
2. What are A and B concerned about?
3a. Where might this conversation be taking place?
 b. Identify A and B.
 c. What is the destination?
4a. Where is Nishida?
 b. Describe the relationships among A, B, and Nishida.
5a. What is A's suggestion?
 b. What is B's decision?
 c. What timely occurrence is mentioned?
6a. Where is this conversation probably taking place?
 b. Who has just arrived?
 c. What does B report? Give details.
7a. How did A and B come here?
 b. Who speaks more politely?
 c. Who is Nishizaka?
8a. Where is B going?
 b. How is B going to each of these places?
9a. Where might this conversation be taking place?
 b. What suggestion does B oppose?
 c. What is B's substitute request?
10a. Where might this conversation be taking place?
 b. What does A want B to do? Where?
11a. What does A want to know?
 b. What is A told?
 c. Why does B apologize?
 d. What does B offer to do?
12a. What does A want to buy?
 b. Where is A thinking of buying it?
 c. What possible objection does B raise?
 d. What is B's alternate suggestion?
 e. What is A's reaction?
13a. What are A and B looking for?
 b. Where are A and B at the moment?
 c. What is the problem?
 d. What solution does A offer?
 e. What is B's reaction?

14a. Where is A going?
   b. What does A ask B?
   c. What does B want? What color? How many?
15a. What is A looking for?
   b. What does B ask? Why?
   c. How does A plan to go?
   d. Where is A told to turn? In what direction? How many times?
   e. Where is the place A is looking for in relation to what landmark?

Utilization

(Don't forget to provide appropriate stimulus questions and/or replies for each of the following. Use hesitation noises, echo questions, and sentence particles to make your Japanese natural.)

1. Tell a colleague that you're going
   a. to the airport (1) by bus; (2) by electric train;
   b. to Kyoto (1) by plane; (2) by bullet train;
   c. to the station (1) by bicycle; (2) on foot.
2. Stop a stranger and ask (politely):
   a. if there is a stationery store this side of the department store;
   b. if there is a coffee shop in the basement of this building;
   c. if there is a bank up ahead;
   d. if the store right beyond that supermarket is a flower shop;
   e. if the next station is Ueno Station.
3. Tell the taxi driver:
   a. to go in the direction of Mejiro;
   b. to turn right at the next intersection;
   c. to stop at the front of that hospital;
   d. to turn left at the end of this street;
   e. to stop here.
4. Tell a stranger that you want to go to the Okura Hotel but you don't know the way (*lit.* '*the road* isn't comprehended'). Ask if he'll give you instructions.
5. You've been asked directions to your university. Explain that you go straight along this street as far as the traffic light, turn right at that corner, and the entrance is right there.
6. In explaining where Mr. Yamamoto's house is, say that it's about six buildings ahead.
7. You've been asked about a recent trip. Explain that you did go to England but you didn't go as far as Germany.
8. You and your colleague are lost. Suggest that you ask a policeman the way.
9. Ask a new acquaintance (politely) where his home is.
10. Tell a colleague that you walked here but you're going to return home by subway.
11. Ask if you can make a U-turn here.
12. Comment that you don't use trains very much in America.
13. A car is coming. Shout a warning to someone about to cross the street.
14. Suggest going to the station by taxi.
15. You've been asked your name. Warn that it's a difficult name, and then ask (politely) if you should write it.
16. You don't have any paper with you for a map you've been asked to draw. Tell your colleague that you guess you'll draw it on the back of this envelope.
17. Ask a visitor (politely) if she would be kind enough to write her name on this paper, with a pen.
18. Ask at the reception desk if Dr. Nakamura is in.
19. Tell an out-group member (politely) that your colleague Tanaka is on the third floor.

20. Tell a colleague that you're going to go and have some coffee (i.e., drink coffee and come [back]).

21. Ask the secretary if she would go and buy some cake.

22. Apologetically ask a colleague if she would go and buy today's paper for you (she is going out anyway).

23. Tell a colleague that you want to buy a map of Tokyo. Ask what kind of store would be good.

24. Your colleague has just informed you that he isn't going to the theater. Check on whether it's that he doesn't want to go.

25. You've been told this dictionary is no good. Check on whether its being old is the explanation.

26. Comment that there are two beautiful new sportscars in front of the house next door. Express wonder as to whose they are.

Check-up

1. What phrase-particles indicate /place to which/? Is there any difference between them? (A-SP1)

2. How are 'go to X' and 'go as far as X' distinguished in Japanese? (A-SP1)

3. Explain the differences among: **kokó ni arimàsu; kokó ni imàsu;** and **kokó de simàsu.** (A-SP1), (A-SP4)

4. What are the literal meanings of the combinations /**tâbete kimasu**/ and /**tâbete ikimasu**/? With what rather different English patterns do they often overlap? (A-SP2), (B-SP5)

5. How can /**-te kudasài**/ request forms be made more indirect, softer, and more polite? (A-SP3)

6. What is the difference between polite-style and distal-style? (A-SP5)

7. What is the relationship between politeness and in-group/out-group considerations in Japanese? (A-SP5)

8. What is meant by honorific politeness and humble politeness? Give examples of each. What symbols are we using to distinguish these two concepts? (A-SP5)

9. What two different kinds of humble-polite verbals have been introduced? How does one form humble-polite verbals that follow a regular pattern? (B-SP3)

10. What is neutral politeness? What symbol are we using? Give an example. (A-SP5)

11. How are suggestions expressed in Japanese? (B-SP1)

12. What is the difference in meaning between questions ending in **-màsu ka** and those ending in **-masyòo ka**? (B-SP1)

13. Contrast the phrase-particles in (a) and (b); and in (b) and (c): (a) **koré de simàsu;** (b) **kokó de simàsu;** and (c) **kokó o magarimàsu.** (B-SP2)

14. What do derivatives of verbals ending in **-tai** mean? To what form of the verbal is **-tai** affixed? To what word-class do **-tai** forms belong? Why are they assigned to that class? To whom do **-tai** forms regularly refer? (B-SP4)

15. In the /**-tài ñ desu**/ combination, what is the meaning of **ñ**? To what word class does **ñ** belong? (B-SP4)

16. Give a negative equivalent of **ikítài desu; ikítàkatta desu; ikítài ñ desu; ikítàkatta ñ desu.** (B-SP4)

17. Describe the difference between **mazûi desu ka** and **mazûi ñ desu ka** in terms of a typical situation in which each might occur. (B-SP4)

18. How can the two sentences: **Bâsu de ikímàsita.**
Arûite kaérimàsita.
be combined into a single sentence? Give two alternate possibilities and explain the difference in meaning. (B-SP5)

19. Given the sentence **Siñgoo màde itte, migí e magarimàsu.** What changes would be made to convert the sentence (a) to the perfective? (b) to a suggestion? (c) to a request? (B-SP5)

Lesson 8

SECTION A

Core Conversations

1(N)a. **Kyôo wa tuítatì desu ne!**
    b. **Suíyòobi zya nâi ñ desu ka⌇**
    c. **A, sôo desita nêe! Damê desu nêe—watasi.**

2(N)a. **Îma nâñ-zi desu ka⌇**

    b. **Zyâa, âto ití-zikañ-g̀urai desu ne⌇**

3(N)a. **Kore kara Nâg̃oya e?**

    b. **Kaérì wa?**

4(J)a. **Zyûg̃yoo wa, ití-nitì nań-zikañ-g̀urai desu ka⌇**

    b. **Doyôobi wa?**
    c. **Âa, soré wa rakù de îi desu nêe.**

(J)a. **Iie, sâñzyuu ití-nitì desu yo⌇**
    b. **Kayôobi desyoo?**

(J)a. **Sumímasèñ. Tokée nài ñ desu. . . . A, tyôtto mâtte kudasai. . . . Itî-zi gô-huñ desu.**

    b. **Êe.**
(J)a. **Ñ. Nâg̃oya de 'mik-ka tomatte, sore kara Kyôoto.**
    b. **Zyuúyok-ka-g̀oro.**

(N)a. **|Eeto| Gês·sûi·kîñ wa yo-zîkañ de, kâa·môku wa ni-zîkañ dakê desu.**
    b. **Do·niti wa yasúmì desu.**

ENGLISH EQUIVALENTS

1(N)a. Today's the first, isn't it.

    b. You mean it's not Wednesday?
    c. Oh, that's right! I'm hopeless—I [am].
2(N)a. What time is it (now)?

(J)a. No, it's the thirty-first (I assure you).
    b. Surely it's Tuesday, isn't it?

(J)a. I'm sorry. I don't have a watch. . . . Oh, wait a second. (Looking at a wall clock) It's five after one.

b. Then it's about one hour to go, isn't it?

3(N)a. After this (to) Nagoya?

   b. When will you be back? (*lit.* [How about] your return?)

4(J)a. About how many hours a day are your classes?

   b. What about Saturday?

   c. Oh, that's nice and easy, isn't it!

b. Yes.

(J)a. Yeah. I'll stop at Nagoya for three days, and then Kyoto.

   b. About the fourteenth.

(N)a. Uh, Mon-Wed-Fri it's four hours, and Tues-Thurs it's just two hours.

   b. Sat-Sun are days off.

BREAKDOWNS
(AND SUPPLEMENTARY VOCABULARY)

1. **tuítatì**[1] (SP1)	first of the month
sânzyuuití-nitì	thirty-first of the month; thirty-one days
suíyòo(bi)[1]	Wednesday
kayôo(bi)	Tuesday
sôo desita (SP2)	that was it! /recall/
2. **nâñ-zi**	what time?
tokee	clock, watch
matímàsu /**mâtte**/	wait
-zi[1] (SP1)	/classifier for naming o'clocks/
-huñ[1] (SP1)	/classifier for naming and counting minutes/
itî-zi gô-huñ (SP1)	1:05
+ **itî-zi go-hûñ-suĝi**	five minutes after one
+ **itî-zi go-hûñ-mae**	five minutes to one
âto	later; remaining
-zikañ[1] (SP1)	/classifier for counting hours/
ití-zikañ-ĝùrai (SP3)	about one hour
âto ití-zìkañ	one hour left
3. **kore kara**	from this point, next after this
Nâĝoya	(city in Japan)
ñ (SP4)	yeah
mik-ka	third of the month; three days
tomárimàsu /**tomatte**/	come to a halt; stop over
kaérì/okaeri	a return
zyûuyok-ka	fourteenth of the month; fourteen days
zyuúyok-ka-ĝòro	about the fourteenth of the month

1. See complete list, below.

4. **zyûḡyoo** — school time, class time
  ití-nitì — one day
  nań-zikań-ḡùrai — about how many hours?
  gês·sûi·kîñ — Mon-Wed-Fri
  yozîkañ de (SP5) — being four hours
  kâa·môku — Tues-Thurs
  doyôo(bi) — Saturday
  dôo·nîti/do·niti — Sat-Sun
  yasúmì/oyasumi — vacation; holiday; time off
  rakû /na/ — easy, comfortable, relaxed

-huñ: *Classifier for counting minutes and naming the minute of the hour*

îp-puñ	**rôp-puñ**
nî-huñ	**nanâ-huñ/sitî-huñ**
sâñ-puñ	**hâp-puñ/hatî-huñ**
yôñ-puñ	**kyûu-huñ**
gô-huñ	**zyûp-puñ/zîp-puñ**

  nâñ-puñ 'how many minutes/ what minute?'

-zikañ: *Classifier for counting hours*

ití-zìkañ	**rokú-zìkañ**
ni-zîkañ	**naná-zìkañ/sití-zìkañ**
sań-zìkañ	**hatí-zìkañ**
yo-zîkañ	**ku-zîkañ**
go-zîkañ	**zyuú-zìkañ**

  nań-zìkañ 'how many hours?'

-zi: *Classifier for naming the o'clocks*

itî-zi	**rokû-zi**
nî-zi	**sitî-zi/nanâ-zi**[2]
sâñ-zi	**hatî-zi**
yô-zi	**kû-zi**
gô-zi	**zyûu-zi**

  nâñ-zi 'what time?'

Days of the week

getúyòo(bi)	'Monday'
kayôo(bi)	'Tuesday'
suíyòo(bi)	'Wednesday'
mokúyòo(bi)	'Thursday'
kińyòo(bi)	'Friday'
doyôo(bi)	'Saturday'
nitíyòo(bi)	'Sunday'
nańyòo(bi)	'what day of the week?'

-ka/-niti: *Classifier for counting days and naming dates*

tuítatì	'the first day of the month'		
ití-nitì	'one day'		
hutu-ka	'the second'	*or*	'2 days'
mik-ka	'the third'	*or*	'3 days'
yok-ka	'the fourth'	*or*	'4 days'
itu-ka	'the fifth'	*or*	'5 days'
mui-ka	'the sixth'	*or*	'6 days'
nano-ka	'the seventh'	*or*	'7 days'

2. This alternate is commonly used in public announcements.

yoo-ka	'the eighth'	*or*	'8 days'
kokóno-kà	'the ninth'	*or*	'9 days'
too-ka	'the tenth'	*or*	'10 days'
zyuúiti-nitì	'the eleventh'	*or*	'11 days'
zyuúni-nitì	'the twelfth'	*or*	'12 days'
zyûusañ-niti	'the thirteenth'	*or*	'13 days'
zyûuyok-ka	'the fourteenth'	*or*	'14 days'
zyûugo-niti	'the fifteenth '	*or*	'15 days'
zyuúroku-nitì	'the sixteenth'	*or*	'16 days'
zyuúsiti-nitì	'the seventeenth'	*or*	'17 days'
zyuúhati-nitì	'the eighteenth'	*or*	'18 days'
zyûuku-niti	'the nineteenth'	*or*	'19 days'
hatu-ka	'the twentieth'	*or*	'20 days'
nîzyuu ití-nitì	'the twenty-first'	*or*	'21 days'
nîzyuu ni-nítì	'the twenty-second'	*or*	'22 days'
nîzyuu sâñ-niti	'the twenty-third'	*or*	'23 days'
nîzyuu 'yok-ka	the twenty-fourth'	*or*	'24 days'
nîzyuu gô-niti	'the twenty-fifth'	*or*	'25 days'
nîzyuu rokú-nitì	'the twenty-sixth'	*or*	'26 days'
nîzyuu sití-nitì	'the twenty-seventh'	*or*	'27 days'
nîzyuu hatí-nitì	'the twenty-eighth'	*or*	'28 days'
nîzyuu kû-niti	'the twenty-ninth'	*or*	'29 days'
sañzyùu-niti	'the thirtieth'	*or*	'30 days'
sâñzyuu ití-nitì	'the thirty-first'	*or*	'31 days'
nâñ-niti	'what date?'	*or*	'how many days?'

Supplementary City Names

Sapporo	Sapporo	**Sañhurañsìsuko**	San Francisco
Yokohama	Yokohama	**Rôñdoñ**	London
Oosaka	Osaka	**Beruriñ**	Berlin
Kôobe	Kobe	**Pâri**	Paris
Hukûoka	Fukuoka	**Mosukuwa**	Moscow
		Pêkiñ	Peking
Nyuúyòoku	New York	**Hôñkoñ**	Hong Kong
Wasîñtoñ	Washington	**Sôoru**	Seoul
Sîkaǧo	Chicago		

MISCELLANEOUS NOTES

1. A foreigner (N) straightens out her confusion over today's date with a Japanese colleague. The speech style is deferential, with distal-style final predicates. Note the use of the

extended predicate in (N)b, with a negative nominal predicate preceding **ñ**: 'does that (the fact that it's the thirty-first) mean that it's not Wednesday?'

The days of the week all have alternate forms with and without final **-bi**. The longer form may be a bit more formal, but otherwise there is really no significant difference between the two alternates.

Note the inverted sentence: the emphatic message is **damê desu** with the later amplification that 'I'm talking about myself.'

2. In CC2, two colleagues are waiting together for something that has been previously scheduled. For example, it might be the start of a conference, the arrival of a third person, their departure on a trip, etc. The speech style is deferential, with distal-style final predicates. Note that the Japanese apologizes for not having a watch. Given the time-consciousness of urban Japanese, one would interpret this situation in terms of the absence of a watch on this particular occasion rather than the speaker's not owning one.

Îma occurs much more commonly when asking the time in Japanese than 'now' occurs in English. Note the use of the extended predicate in (J)a. 'It's that I don't have a watch' (that explains why I am not able to tell you the time).

Matímàsu, previously encountered in its stem form within **omáti-kudasài** (a more polite form than **mâtte kudasai**), is an operational verbal of action. Note: **tomódati (o) matimàsita** 'I waited for a friend'; **kokó de matimasyòo** 'let's wait here.'

Âto is a nominal which basically refers to a rear position, or later point, or remainder. Here it links up with a nominal predicate, specifying the period of time—'it's about one hour'— that remains before the scheduled event occurs. Compare /**moo** + quantity/, which indicates an amount in addition (5A-SP5).

3. CC3 is an exchange between two people who are on more familiar terms than has previously occurred in the Core Conversations (cf. SP4 following). In the accompanying video, this CC marks the beginning of the use of a more relaxed communication style between Sue Brown, a foreign student (N), and her fellow student, Kato (J), as they associate with each other more and become closer friends. Here, they discuss (J)'s travel plans.

(N)a. Notice again the contrast between **sore kara** 'after that' (i.e., a point just designated) and **kore kara** 'after this.'

(J)a. **Mik-ka** may refer to a point in time ('the third of the month') or a period of time ('three days'). Sometimes the difference in meaning is determined by context, but its occurrence here without a following particle before a predicate establishes it as an extent ('how long') pattern.

Compare **tomémàsu** 'bring to a halt' and **tomárimàsu** 'come to a halt.' While both are operational verbals, only **tomémàsu** occurs with particle **o** phrases, indicating what is stopped. By extension, these verbals are also used in reference to stopping over at a place: **tomémàsu** 'put [someone] up,' 'offer lodging,' but **tomárimàsu** '[someone] stops over.' They may also refer to the parking of vehicles. Note also: /place X + **de**/ and /place X + **ni**/ reflecting the difference between location of the occurrence of stopping and goal or static location. Examples: **Tikâ ni tomémasyòo.** 'Let's park [it] in the basement.' **Usíro de tomete kudasài.** 'Please stop [it] in back.'

(N)b. **Kaérì** is a nominal derived from a verbal. Except for accent, it coincides with the verbal stem. We will find that nominals derived from verbals are regularly the stem (= **-màsu** form minus **-màsu**), although there may be a difference in accent.

4. CC4 is a discussion of school hours, but the distal-style final predicates used by both participants suggest that they are not close friends engaged in casual conversation. On the

accompanying video, this CC has as its participants the foreign student-boarder (N) and his Japanese landlady (J).

(J)a. **Zyûĝyoo** refers to the actual occurrence of instruction.

With **ití-nitì naṅ-zìkañ desu ka,** compare **îp-poñ nihyákù-eñ desu** (4B-CC3).

(N)a, b. In listing a combination of days of the week, abbreviations are frequently used. The short form for each day consists of the **-yòo(bi)** form minus **-yòo(bi)**.[3] Note that in these abbreviations **gêtu-** becomes **gêk-** before a following **k-** and **gês-** before **s-**; and one-mora items (i.e., **ka-** and **do-**) add a mora by lengthening their vowels (except that **do** may retain a short alternate when it occurs at the beginning of a sequence: **do·niti** or **dôo·nîti**).

(N)b. **Yasúmì,** like **kaérì,** is a nominal derived from a verbal—i.e., the stem form. In this case, the verbal is **yasúmimàsu** /yasûñde/ 'rest'; 'take time off.' Compare **Oyásumi-nasài** 'Good night.'

(J)c. The comment about the relaxed (**rakû**) schedule derives from the fact that most Japanese schools have classes half-day on Saturday.

Structural Patterns

1. TIME CLASSIFIERS: -ka/-niti, -zikañ, -zi, -huñ

a. **-ka/-niti:** Study carefully the items in the **-ka/-niti** series listed above. This is the most difficult number series to master, because it vacillates between the Japanese and Chinese numeral series, and because there are so many irregular forms. The Japanese themselves master as complex a series as this only because it is used so commonly. This should suggest that mastery is also important for the foreigner. Points to note:

(1) Except for **tuítatì** and **ití-nitì,** all members of the series can refer either to a point in time (which day of the month) or a period of time (how many days). In other words, this classifier both names and counts; only grammatical structure and/or context distinguishes the two meanings. However, the addition of **-kañ** forms alternates which can refer only to periods of time. Examples: **hutu-kakañ** '2 days'; **zyuuiti-nitikañ** '11 days.'

(2) Note the irregular items: **mui-ka; nano-ka; yoo-ka; hatu-ka.** Note also that adjustments to the numerals result in forms of at least two mora preceding **-ka.** Compare **mik-ka** and **miś-tù** '3 units.'

(3) Even beyond **too-ka,** when the series has shifted to the Chinese Series of numerals and a different form of the classifier itself, all items ending in 'four' revert to **yok-ka** (Japanese Series), combined with **zyûu,** and **nîzyuu,** etc. from the Chinese Series.

(4) In naming days of the month, the series obviously does not extend beyond 31, but it extends indefinitely for counting days.

b. **-zi** and **-zikañ:** For naming hours and counting hours, there are separate classifiers distinguished by the presence or absence of **-kañ,** which implies duration. Thus, **-zi** names the o'clocks and **-zikañ** counts hours, both combining with the Chinese numerals. **Zikañ** also occurs as an independent word, referring to 'time' in general (example: **Zikáñ ĝa arimasèñ.** 'There's no time'; 'I don't have time'). Points to note:

(1) In both series, 4 is irregular, with **yo-** occurring instead of the more usual **yoñ** or **si-** (cf. **yô-eñ** '¥4').

---

3. The abbreviations regularly have first-mora accent.

(2) **Sitî-zi** until recently was the only regularly occurring equivalent for '7 o'clock.' But the **nana-** alternate is becoming popular, particularly in public announcements, where **iti-** and **siti-** are frequently confused.

(3) Timetables often use a 24-hour clock, starting with **rêe-zi** 'zero o'clock.'

c. **-huñ**: Like **-ka/-niti**, **-huñ** is a classifier that both names and counts; in any given context it either names a particular minute of the hour or counts the number of minutes. The alternate **-huñkañ** is sometimes used for the durational meaning only. Points to note:

(1) In combining with the numerals of the Chinese Series, the numerals and **-huñ** undergo most of the same kinds of changes as occur with other classifiers beginning with **h-** (cf. **-hoñ**).

(2) Whereas most classifiers beginning with **h-** occur with initial **b-** following **ñ** (cf. **sâñ-boñ** and **nâñ-boñ**), **-huñ** changes to **-puñ** (**sâñ-puñ, nâñ-puñ**).

(3) Most irregular is the item **yôñ-puñ**. Examination of other classifiers beginning with **h-** reveals that only **-huñ** has a changed form following **yoñ-** (compare **yôñ-hoñ**).

(4) In telling time, two systems are used:

(a) /o'clock/ + /minute of the hour/

6:15	**rokû-zi zyuúgò-huñ**
8:55	**hatî-zi gozyúu gò-huñ**

(b) /o'clock/ + either /minute before the hour + **-mae**/[4] or /minute after the hour + **-suḡì**/

5 of 9	**kû-zi go-hûñ-mae**[5]
quarter after 6	**rokû-zi zyuúgo-hùñ-suḡi**[5]

Note also: /o'clock + **-màe**/ = 'before the o'clock' (example: **kuzí-màe**[5] 'before 9'); /o'clock + **-suḡì**/ = 'after the o'clock' (example: **kuzí-suḡì**[5] 'after 9'). **Mâe** as an independent nominal refers to past time, i.e., 'before,' in general.

All time words are nominals and enter into the usual nominal patterns.

2. THE PERFECTIVE IN RECALL

The use of the perfective in Japanese regularly refers to an action or condition viewed as completed. In situations involving currently continuing—or future—actions or conditions, its use may refer to the speaker's previous knowledge, which is now being recalled. In English, we frequently use the past tense in such situations: looking across the room at someone I had met previously, I might ask a friend, 'What *was* his name?' certainly not referring to a name no longer in use.

In CC1, the use of **sôo desita ne!** implies that 'it was like that' before I lost track, but now I have recalled that it is indeed Tuesday.

Consider a further example: Imagine that I have just received information contrary to what I believed to be true, but either because I'm still not sure, or because the situation dictates against my strongly contradicting what has just been said, I might use the perfective in an extended predicate pattern, suggesting that I am reminded of a contrary impression:

Asítà wa Sâtoo-señsee desu ne! 'Tomorrow will be Professor Sato, won't it.'

---

4. With the growing popularity of digital watches, this pattern is becoming less common.
5. Note the accent shift.

>   **Nîsida-señsee zya nâkatta ñ desu ka⤸**   'Wasn't it (*lit.* is it the case that it wasn't
>   [to be]) Professor Nishida?'

Consider also:

>   **Amérika-taisìkañ, dôko desu ka⤸**   'Where's the American Embassy?'

>   **|Eeto| Toránomoñ dèsita ne!**   'Uh, it was Toranomon, wasn't it.' (i.e., as I recall it)

Similarly, **arímàsita** occurs when one finds what one has been looking for: 'it was here [and now I've found it].'

3. APPROXIMATION: -ḡòro AND -ḡùrai

-Ḡòro 'about' forms a compound with a preceding time expression that indicates a point in time (NOT a duration of time). Thus:

ni-zí-ḡòro	'about 2 o'clock'
yô-zi sáñzyup-puñ-ḡòro	'about 4:30'
tuítati-ḡòro	'about the first of the month'
doyóobi-ḡòro	'about Saturday'
ima-ḡoro	'nowadays' (*lit.* 'about now')

These are all answers to the question **itu-ḡoro** 'about when?'

-Ḡùrai 'about' forms a compound with a preceding extent expression. Thus:

ití-niti-ḡùrai	'about one day'
yo-zíkañ-ḡùrai	'about four hours'
go-húñ-ḡùrai	'about five minutes'
sukósi-ḡùrai	'(about) a little'
go-mái-ḡùrai	'about five sheets'
toó-ḡùrai	'about ten (units)'
itímañ-eñ-ḡùrai	'about ¥10,000'

The corresponding general question words are **dono-ḡurai** and **dore-ḡurai** 'about how much?' both of which occur commonly.[6] Note also: **kono-ḡoro** 'these days,' 'recently,' and **kono-ḡurai** 'about this much.' Except for some special combinations which are unaccented, **-ḡòro** and **ḡùrai** compounds are regularly accented on **-ḡo-** and **-ḡu-** respectively.

The previously introduced **-hodo** following quantity expressions (5B-SP3) is similar in meaning to **-ḡùrai,** except that **-hodo** includes a connotation of 'about to the extent of,' 'about as much as.'

Note the result of compounding **-ḡòro/-ḡùrai** contrastively with items of the **-huñ** and the **-ka/-niti** series:

>   **zíp-puñ-ḡòro** 'about ten after the hour' / **zíp-puñ-ḡùrai** 'about ten minutes'

>   **mík-ka-ḡòro** 'about the third of the month' / **mík-ka-ḡùrai** 'about three days'

Now we introduce a complication. While **-ḡòro** as an indication of an approximate point in time has long been the accepted form—and still continues to be the only form in use by some speakers—the **-ḡùrai** alternate is taking over **-ḡòro** territory in the speech of more and more Japanese. Traditionally, **-ḡùrai** indicated only approximate *quantity,* but it is rapidly becoming a general term for approximation, particularly when the combination is not

---

6. Alternate forms are **dono-kurai** and **dore-kurai.**

ambiguous (for example, **saṅ-zi-g̀ùrai**). At this juncture, to distinguish between **-g̀òro** and **-g̀ùrai** is always safe; but the foreigner should not be surprised to hear **-g̀ùrai** in a formerly '-g̀òro only' context.

It is important to note that the occurrence of **-g̀ùrai** and **-g̀òro** in general is much more common in Japanese than 'about' is in English. Vagueness and lack of precision are frequent as a sign of politeness in Japanese. In particular, it is often considered rude to appear to pin down too precisely the time of action of others.

4. CASUAL-STYLE

CC3 provides our first example of a conversation in casual-style. Previously, all CC have been examples of more careful speech, with final predicates in distal-style.

The participants of CC3 are two students, a Japanese and a foreigner, who have become more informal in speaking with each other. Previously, at a time when they had first met, they used more deferential conversation, with distal-style final predicates. This kind of style shift is more common among students and young people who are peers. While CC3 does not include any actual direct-style inflected forms, it reflects a casual style in every sentence.

(N)a: The use of a fragment lacking a predicate is more casual than a corresponding major sentence in the distal-style, which might here include some form of **ikímàsu**. The question status of the utterance depends entirely on question intonation.

(J)a: **Ṅ** is a casual equivalent of **êe,** used commonly, though by no means exclusively, by males. At the other end of the scale is the very formal affirmative, **hâa.** The **Nâg̀oya . . . Kyôoto** sentence is an example of the dropping of sentence-final **dèsu** following a nominal, which frequently occurs in direct-style speech. In distal-style, we would expect **sore kara, Kyôoto desu.**

(N)b: **Kaérì wa?** is a fragment—a casual equivalent of **Kaérì wa dôo** (or **îtu**) **desu ka.** Again, the question status of the utterance depends on question intonation.

(J)b: This utterance, like (J)a, is an example of the direct-style dropping of the **dèsu** of a sentence-final nominal predicate.

Hereafter, we will use the terms CASUAL and CAREFUL to refer to speech styles. Casual speech is marked by the frequent use of fragments without predicates, particular vocabulary items (like **ṅ** 'yeah'), many contractions, and direct-style inflected forms. Careful speech has fewer fragments without predicates and more major sentences, particular formal vocabulary items, fewer contractions, and more distal-style inflected forms (i.e., **-màsu/dèsu** forms) at least in sentence-final predicates. Note that *both casual- and careful-style can be polite or plain.* More will be said about this later. Clearly, casual and careful styles are not absolutes: they represent a range from maximally casual to maximally careful, with countless degrees in between. We label a particular conversation on the basis of the majority of all the signals given.

5. THE COPULA GERUND: **de:** /rakû de îi desu/

Verbal gerunds are forms ending in **-te** or, for some verbals, **-de**. Uses have been discussed in 4A-SP6, 7A-SP2, SP3, and 7B-SP5. Given the patterning of Japanese, if verbals have gerunds we would predict that *probably* adjectival and nominal predicates also have corresponding gerund forms.

In this section we introduce the gerund form for the nominal predicate: /nominal + copula gerund **de**/.[7]

7. Do not attempt to substitute adjectivals for nominals in this pattern.

The uses of this combination that we are immediately concerned with are those parallel to the uses of verbal gerunds introduced in 7A-SP2 and 7B-SP5.[8]

Basically, the combination /nominal X + **de**/ = 'X being realized': in other words, we are once again involved in the notion of actualization. Compare:

> **Konó misè (wa) îi desu ne!** 'This shop is nice, isn't it.'
>
> **Konó misè de îi desu ne!** 'Given that it *is* this shop, it will be fine, won't it' (for our purposes, the selection of this shop will do).

Note how different these two sentences are: the first is a comment on the quality of the shop; the second comments on the choice of the shop—i.e., which shop *it is* to be, for whatever purpose, whether as a place to buy an item, a place to photograph, rent, buy, hide—whatever.

Consider now CC4(J)c. Here N's schedule is described as **îi desu.** Why? **Rakû de** 'being easy, comfortable, unpressured,' i.e., 'being easy, it's nice.' As a general pattern, /nominal X + **de** + **îi desu**/ = 'being X, it's nice, fine, OK'; 'for it to be X is nice, fine, good.' In those cases in which the nominal X describes a quality, a close English equivalent for the combination with **îi desu** is 'is nice and X': **rakû de îi desu** 'it's nice and easy'; **bêñri de îi desu** 'it's nice and convenient'; **kîree de îi desu** 'it's nice and pretty/clean.'

But if a nominal predicate in the gerund can occur before **îi desu,** what about verbal and adjectival gerunds? We will postpone the latter because the form itself has not yet been introduced; but the combination with verbals can certainly be handled immediately. Compare:

> **Hôñ de îi desu ka⌇** 'Is it all right for it to be a book?' 'Will a book be all right?' (as a gift, for example). (Note that there is *no* mention here of a good book!)
>
> **Tukátte ìi desu ka⌇** 'Is it all right to use [this]?' i.e., 'Will having used [this] be all right?'
>
> **Eñpitu de kàite îi desu yo⌇** 'It's all right to write in pencil,' i.e., 'Having written in pencil will be all right.'

We can now move to an opposite situation:

> **Hûbeñ de komárimàsu nêe.** 'Being inconvenient, it's a nuisance, isn't it!' 'It's a nuisance that it's inconvenient, isn't it!'
>
> **Muzukasii nihoñḡo de komárimàsu yo⌇** 'I'm upset at its being difficult Japanese.'

In many of the above examples, there is an implication that the condition or action of the gerund is directly responsible for what transpires in the following predicate. When something is 'inconvenient and a nuisance,' the assumption is that it is a nuisance *because* it is inconvenient. But this implication does not always accompany the gerund, as we have seen in examples of the usage of verbal gerunds in previous lessons. Compare now:

> /Nâḡoya ni miḱ-ka tomarimàsu./ + /Sore kara, Kyôoto e ikimasu./ = **Nâḡoya ni ′miḱ-ka tomatte, sore kara, Kyôoto e ikimasu.** 'I'll stop in Nagoya for three days, and then I'll go to Kyoto.' (*lit.* 'Having stopped. . . , then I'll go. . .') *and*
>
> /Gês·sûi·kîñ wa yo-zîkañ desu./ + /Kâa·môku wa ni-zîkañ dakê desu./ = **Gês·sûi·kîñ wa yo-zîkañ de, kâa·môku wa ni-zîkan dakê desu.** 'Mon-Wed-Fri are

---

8. /Nominal + **de**/ does not occur in request patterns.

four hours, and Tues-Thurs are just two hours.' (*lit.* 'Mon-Wed-Fri being four hours, Tues-Thurs are just two hours.')

Obviously, there is no cause-and-result connection within these examples, but rather two consecutive statements described in Japanese terms of a subordinate predicate followed by a principal, final predicate. The pattern *allows* for situations that have a cause-and-result connection, but it is not a requirement of the pattern. In sentences of this type, **de**, like verbal gerunds, usually has *comma* intonation (cf. 7B-SP5), but the same intonation may also occur in sentences in which the gerund implies a causal connection.

Drills

A 1. **Kyôo wa, tuítatì desu ne** ⌐   **Iie, hutú-ka dèsu yo.**
    'Today is the first, isn't it?'   'No, it's the second.'

  2. **Kyôo wa, yoḱ-ka dèsu ne** ⌐   **Iie, itú-ka dèsu yo.**
    'Today is the fourth, isn't it?'   'No, it's the fifth.'

  3. **kokóno-kà**; 4. **mik-ka**; 5. **zyuúsàñ-niti**; 6. **yoo-ka**; 7. **hutu-ka**; 8. **zyûuku-niti**; 9. **itu-ka**; 10. **hatu-ka**; 11. **too-ka**; 12. **nîzyuu 'yok-ka**; 13. **nano-ka**; 14. **mui-ka**

• Repeat this drill, substituting responses that include a date that is one day *earlier* than the date in the stimulus questions.

B 1. **Kâigi wa, suíyòobi desu ne!**   **E? Mokúyòobi desyo(o)?**
    'The conference is Wednesday, isn't it.'   'What? Surely it's Thursday, isn't it?'

  2. **Kâigi wa, getúyòobi desu ne!**   **E? Kayôobi desyo(o)?**
    'The conference is Monday, isn't it.'   'What? Surely it's Tuesday, isn't it?'

  3. **nitíyòobi**; 4. **kińyòobi**; 5. **kayôobi**; 6. **mokúyòobi**; 7. **doyôobi**

• Repeat this drill, substituting responses that include a day that is one day *earlier* than the day in the stimulus questions, and using /-**yòobi** minus -**bi**/ alternates.

C 1. **Siñkàñseñ wa, itî-zi desu ka**↗   **Iie, tyoodo nî-zi desu yo**↘
    'Is the bullet train one o'clock?'   'No, it's exactly two o'clock.'

  2. **Siñkàñseñ wa, sâñ-zi desu ka**↗   **Iie, tyoodo yô-zi desu yo**↘
    'Is the bullet train three o'clock?'   'No, it's exactly four o'clock.'

  3. **hatî-zi**; 4. **rokû-zi**; 5. **zyûu-zi**; 6. **sitî-zi**

D 1. **Bâsu wa, nî-zi yôñ-puñ desu.**   **Yoń-pùñ-suḡi desu ne**⌐ **Wakárimàsita.**
    'The bus is 2:04.'   'That's 4 minutes after—right? Fine.'

  2. **Bâsu wa, kû-zi hâp-puñ desu.**   **Hap-pùñ-suḡi desu ne**⌐ **Wakárimàsita.**
    'The bus is 9:08.'   'That's 8 minutes after—right? Fine.'

  3. **yô-zi sâñ-puñ**; 4. **sitî-zi zyûp-puñ**; 5. **itî-zi nî-huñ**

E 1. **Îma itî-zi gô-huñ desu ne**⌐   **Konó tokee dè wa, itî-zi zyûp-puñ desu**
    'It's 1:05 now—right?'   **kedo . .**
                       'By this clock it's 1:10, but . . .' (I don't
                       know which is correct).

2. **Îma sân-zi zyûp-puñ desu neˆ**
'It's 3:10 now—right?'

Konó tokee dè wa, sân-zi zyûugo-huñ desu kedo . .
'By this clock it's 3:15, but . . .'

3. **sitî-zi zyûugo-huñ**; 4. **kû-zi noñzyùp-puñ**; 5. **gô-zi sañzyùp-puñ**; 6. **zyuúitì-zi nizyûp-puñ**

F 1. **Âto nañ-zikañ-ḡùrai desu ka**
'About how many hours are left?'
(until a particular time)

Âto go-zíkañ-ḡùrai desu ne!
'It's about five hours to go.'

2. **Âto nañ-ḡeñ-ḡùrai desu ka**
'About how many buildings are left?
(in connection with a particular task)

Âto go-kéñ-ḡùrai desu ne!
'It's about five buildings to go.'

3. **nâñ-niti**; 4. **nâñ-puñ**; 5. **nâñ-dai**; 6. **îku-tu**; 7. **nâñ-satu**; 8. **nâñ-boñ**; 9. **nâñ-mai**

G 1. **Okaeri wa, doyôobi desu ka**
'Will you return on Saturday?'

Mâa, doyóobi-ḡòro⁹ desyoo ne!
'I suppose it will be about Saturday.'

2. **Zyûḡyoo wa, go-zíkañ desu ka**
'Will instruction be five hours?'

Mâa, go-zíkañ-ḡùrai desyoo ne!
'I suppose it will be about five hours.'

3. **hikôoki/sitî-zi**; 4. **oyasumi/tuítatì**; 5. **kâiḡi/ni-zîkañ**; 6. **deñsya/itî-zi sañzyùp-puñ**; 7. **Nâḡoya/ití-niti**

H 1. **Señsèe no okaeri wa, asâtte desu yo**
'The teacher will be back the day after tomorrow.'

A, sôo desita ne! Asâtte desita ne!
'Oh, that was it! It was the day after tomorrow, wasn't it.'

2. **Tuḡî no yasúmì wa, sañzyùu-niti desu yo**
'Our next day off is the thirtieth.'

A, sôo desita ne! Sañzyùu-niti desita ne!
'Oh, that was it! It was the thirtieth, wasn't it.'

3. **kâiḡi/doyôobi**; 4. **kaérì/siñkàñseñ**; 5. **tuḡî/Nâḡoya**; 6. **Amérika-ryoozìkañ/nî-zi**; 7. **Kâataa-sañ/eeḡo**; 8. **zyûḡyoo/rokú-zìkañ**

I 1. **Rakû na bâsu desu nêe.**
'Isn't it a comfortable bus!'

Sôo desu nêe. Rakû de îi desu nêe.
'It is, isn't it! It's nice and comfortable, isn't it!'

2. **Hûbeñ na tatêmono desu nêe.**
'Isn't it an inconvenient building!'

Sôo desu nêe. Hûbeñ de komárimàsu nêe.
'It is, isn't it! It's inconvenient and a bother, isn't it!'

3. **kîree na hanâ**; 4. **damê na têepu**; 5. **bêñri na utî**

J 1. **Tokée wa dòo desyoo ka.**
'How about a watch?' (as a possible gift for a friend)

Sâa, tokee de îi desyoo ka.
'Hmm. Do you suppose (being) a watch would be all right?'

2. **Zitêñsya wa dôo desyoo ka.**

Sâa, zitêñsya de îi desyoo ka.

9. Also possible: **-ḡùrai**.

'How about a bicycle?'   'Hmm. Do you suppose (being) a bicycle would be all right?'

3. **eéwa-zìteñ**; 4. **hanâ**; 5. **biñseñ**; 6. **wâiñ**

K 1. **Kono ryokañ ni tomárimàsu ka**   **Tomatte îi desyoo?**
'Are you going to stop at this inn?'   'It's all right to stop, isn't it?'

2. **Tomodati ni misémàsu ka**   **Mîsete îi desyoo?**
'Arc you going to show [it] to a friend?'   'It's all right to show [it], isn't it?'

3. **tonari no deñwa tukáimàsu**; 4. **îma kaérimàsu**; 5. **tuḡî no kâdo maḡárimàsu**; 6. **omâwari-sañ ni kikímàsu**

L 1. **Kono tokee wa, gomáñ-eñ dèsu ka**   **Kotira no tokee wa gomañ-eñ de, âto wa yoñ-mañ-eñ dèsu.**
'Are these watches ¥50,000?'   'This watch is ¥50,000, and the rest are ¥40,000.'

2. **Konó zitèñsya wa, yoñmañ-eñ dèsu ka**   **Kotíra no zitèñsya wa yoñmañ-eñ de, âto wa sañmañ-eñ dèsu.**
'Are these bicycles ¥40,000?'   'This bicycle is ¥40,000, and the rest are ¥30,000.'

3. **tîzu/roppyakù-eñ**; 4. **kabañ/sañzeñ-eñ**; 5. **hanâ/nihyákù-eñ**; 6. **wâiñ/niseñ-eñ**

M 1. **Asita, yasumi?**   **Ñ, yasumi.**
'Off tomorrow?'   'Yeah, [I'm] off.'

2. **Kore kara, Nâḡoya made?**   **Ñ, Nâḡoya made.**
'Next [are you going] as far as Nagoya?'   'Yeah, as far as Nagoya.'

3. **îma/yô-zi**; 4. **asita/zyûḡyoo**; 5. **êki made/tâkusii de**; 6. **asita/Kyôoto e**

● Repeat this drill, substituting distal-style (a) in the questions only; (b) in the responses only; and (c) in both questions and responses, assuming appropriate role changes.

N 1. **Zyûḡyoo wa, getúyòo to kayôo desu ka**   **Êe, gêk·kâa desu ne!**
'Is instruction Monday and Tuesday?'   'Yes, it's Mon-Tues.'

2. **Yasúmì wa, doyôo to nitíyòo desu ka**   **Êe, dô·nîti desu ne!**
'Are your days off Saturday and Sunday?'   'Yes, they're Sat-Sun.'

3. **kâiḡi/suíyòobi to kiñyòobi**; 4. **hikôoki/kayôobi to mokúyòobi to doyôobi**; 5. **daiḡaku/getúyòobi to suíyòobi to mokúyòobi**

Application Exercises

A1. Using a model clock, move the hands to indicate various times, and ask and answer questions about what time it is. Include **tyoodo** and **-ḡòro** (~ **-ḡùrai**) when appropriate.

2. Using a calendar for the current month, ask and answer questions relating to what day of the week particular dates are.

3. After setting specific times for the next conference, the next day off, the next bus, etc., ask and answer questions relating to the amount of time remaining until the event, using **âto**.

4. Distribute cards to each member of the group, describing a trip: include first destination; length of stay; second destination; approximate date of return. Practice informal conversations relating to these trips.

5. Ask and answer questions about the number of hours of instruction on different days of the week.

6. Using the **X wa Y desu ka⁀** pattern, ask questions that require a negative answer. Reply using the **Z zya nâkatta ñ desu ka⁀** pattern. Example:

> **Koósyuudèñwa wa îk-kai desu neʔ**
>
> 'The public phone is on the first floor—right?'
>
> **Tikâ zya nâkatta ñ desu ka⁀**
>
> 'Wasn't it in the basement?'

B. Core Conversations: Substitution

Practice variations on the Core Conversations, paying special attention to timing. Keep in mind who is talking with whom in each exchange, clearly establishing differences that account for careful- versus casual-style.

SECTION B

Core Conversations

1(N)a. **Tosyôsitu wa nâñ-zi made desu ka⁀**

        (J)a. **Yo-zí-hàñ made desu kedo, îma irássyaimàsu ka⁀**

b. **Ie, kyôo wa 'yamete, asíta no gòḡo mairimasu.**

        b. **Zyâa, kotira wa gôḡo kara desu ka⁀**

c. **Ie, mâiniti zyûu-zi ni wa mairimasu.**

2(N)a. **Kokó kara Siñzyuku màde donó-ḡurai kakarimàsu ka⁀**

        (J)a. **Tâkusii de desu ka⁀**

b. **Iya, dêñsya de.**

        b. **Sôo desu nêe. Sañzip-puñ-ḡùrai zya arímasèñ ka⁀**

3(N)a. **Kotósi no zyuu-ḡatù kara iḱ-kaḡetu-ḡùrai Yoóròppa e itte kimasu.**

        (J)a. **Hoñtoo dèsu ka⁀ Îi desu nêe. Oyásumi dèsu ka⁀**

b. **Yasumi? Tóńde mo nài. Sigóto dèsu yo.**

c. **Êe. Mâa neʕ**

4(N)a. **Zûibuñ hurûi hôñ desu nêe.**

b. **Taisyoo zyûu-neñ? Sore wa 'seereki nâñ-neñ desyoo.**

(J)a. **Dê mo, tanósìmi desyoo?**

(J)a. **Sôo desu nêe. . . . Âa, Taisyoo zyûu-neñ desu yo‿**

b. **Sêñ kyûuhyaku nîzyuu itî-neñ desu neʕ**

ENGLISH EQUIVALENTS

1(N)a. How late is the library open? (*lit.* Until what time is the library?)

b. No, for today I'll give up the idea, and I'll go tomorrow afternoon.

c. No, every day at 10:00 I come here.

2(N)a. About how long does it take from here to Shinjuku?

b. No, by (electric) train.

3(N)a. I'm going (*lit.* I'll come [back] having gone) to Europe for about a month, starting this October.

b. Vacation? Heavens no! It will be work.

c. Yes, I guess so.

4(N)a. This is an awfully old book, isn't it!

b. Taisho 10? What year would that be in the Western calendar?

(J)a. (It's) until 4:30; are you going now?

b. Then will you be here starting in the afternoon? (*lit.* Will this place be from the afternoon?)

(J)a. Do you mean by cab?

b. Hmm. Isn't it about 30 minutes?

(J)a. Really? Isn't that great! Will it be a vacation?

b. Even so, you're looking forward to it, aren't you?

(J)a. It is, isn't it! . . . Oh, it's Taisho 10.

b. That's 1921, isn't it?

BREAKDOWNS
(AND SUPPLEMENTARY VOCABULARY)

1. **tosyôsitu**	library (a room)
nâñ-zi made (SP1)	until what time?
nâñ-zi made desu ka (SP2)	until what time is it?
yo-zí-hàñ	4:30
yo-zí-hàñ made	until 4:30
irássyaimàsu ↑ **/irássyàtte/** (SP3)	go; come; be (animate) /polite/
yamémàsu /yamete/	give up [something]; quit

gôḡo	afternoon; P.M.
+ **gôzeñ**	A.M.
+ **âsa**	morning
+ **yôru** *or*	
+ **bañ**	evening, night
maírimàsu ↓ /**mâitte**/ (SP3)	go; come /polite/
gôḡo kara (SP1)	from the afternoon, starting in the afternoon
mâiniti	every day
+ **mâiasa**	every morning
+ **mâibañ**	every night
+ **maisyuu**	every week
+ **maituki/maiḡetu**	every month
+ **maitosi/maineñ**	every year
+ **taitee**	usually
zyûu-zi ni (SP1)	at 10 o'clock
2. **Siñzyuku**	(section of Tokyo)
kokó kara Siñzyuku màde (SP1)	from here to Shinjuku
kakárimàsu /**kakâtte**/	be required, take (of time or money)
+ **hûne**	boat, ship
3. **kotosi**	this year
-ḡatu[10] (SP4)	/classifier for naming the months/
kotósi no zyuu-ḡatù kara	from this October, starting this October
-kaḡetu[10] (SP4)	/classifier for counting months/
+ **-syuukañ**[10] (SP4)	/classifier for counting weeks/
Yoóròppa	Europe
toñde mo nài	heavens no! don't be silly! that's ridiculous!
siḡoto/osîḡoto	work
dê mo	even so, however, but
tanósìmi *or* **tanosimi** *or*	
tanósimì	pleasure, fun, joy
4. **zûibuñ**	awfully, exceedingly
Taisyoo	Taisho Era (1912–1926)
+ **Mêezi**	Meiji Era (1868–1912)
+ **Syoowa**	Showa Era (1926–1989)
+ **Heesee**	Heisei Era (1989–)
-neñ[10]	/classifier for naming and counting years/
seereki	Western calendar
nâñ-neñ	what year? how many years?
nâñ-neñ desyoo. (SP5)	what year (*or* how many years) would it be?
+ **gâñ-neñ**	the year 1 (of an era)

10. See complete list, below.

-syuukañ: *Classifier for counting weeks*

iś-syùukañ	**rokú-syùukañ**
ni-syûukañ	**naná-syùukañ**
sań-syùukañ	**haś-syùukañ**
yoń-syùukañ	**kyuú-syùukañ**
go-syûukañ	**zyuś-syùukañ/ziś-syùukañ**
nań-syùukañ	'how many weeks?'

-ḡatu: *Classifier for naming months*

itî-ḡatù	'January'
ni-ḡátù	'February'
sân-ḡatu	'March'
si-ḡátù	'April'
gô-ḡatu	'May'
rokú-ḡatù	'June'
sitî-ḡatù	'July'
hatî-ḡatù	'August'
kû-ḡatu	'September'
zyuú-ḡatù	'October'
zyuúiti-ḡatù	'November'
zyuúni-ḡatù	December'
nân-ḡatu	'what month?'

-kaḡetu: *Classifier for counting months*

iḱ-kàḡetu	**roḱ-kàḡetu**
ni-kâḡetu	**naná-kàḡetu/sití-kàḡetu**
sań-kàḡetu	**haḱ-kàḡetu/hatí-kàḡetu**
yoń-kàḡetu	**kyuú-kàḡetu**
go-kâḡetu	**zyuḱ-kàḡetu/ziḱ-kàḡetu**
nań-kàḡetu	'how many months?'

-neñ: *Classifier for naming and counting[11] years*

gân-neñ	'first year of an era'	**go-neñ**
itî-neñ	'one year'	**rokû-neñ**
nî-neñ	'the year 2'; 'two years'	**nanâ-neñ/sitî-neñ** **hatî-neñ**
sañ-neñ		**kyûu-neñ/ku-neñ**
yo-neñ		**zyûu-neñ**
nân-neñ	'what year?' 'how many years?'	

MISCELLANEOUS NOTES

1. CC1 is an example of polite careful-style speech, used more commonly, but by no means exclusively, by women. Note the numerous contrastive uses of **wa**. On the accompanying videotape, Sue Brown (N) is talking with her supervisor (J), a woman.

Tosyôsitu is a library room, distinguished from **tosyôkañ**, a library building.

/**Hañ-** + classifier/ = half of one unit; /number + **-hàñ**/ = number + one-half. Thus: **hañ-zìkañ** 'a half-hour'; **yo-zíkañ-hàñ** '4½ hours'

. . . yamete . . . maírimàsu 'having given up [the idea] . . . I'll go. . .'; 'I'll give up [the idea] . . . and go . . .'

Gôḡo is used both as a general term for afternoon as well as for 'P.M.', the opposite of **gôzeñ** 'A.M.' **Âsa** is a more conversational, less technical term for 'morning.'

Yôru and **bañ** both cover the same period of the day and in many contexts are inter-

---

11. An alternate classifier for the durational meaning *only* (i.e., how many years?) is **-neñkañ**.

changeable. However, there are some special combinations requiring one or the other that will have to be learned individually.

Maitosi/mainen: both **-tosi** and **-nen** are roots meaning 'year,' the former a native Japanese root and the latter borrowed from Chinese. These two words are virtually interchangeable, but in general when there is a choice of this kind, the Chinese borrowing tends to be more formal, or stiffer, or—in some instances—more learned. Only **tosî** may occur as an independent word.

Maituki/maigetu: See the preceding note. Here, **-tuki** is the native root and **-getu** the root of Chinese origin. Only **tukî** may occur as an independent word, meaning 'month' or 'moon.'

2. CC2 is a typical conversation in essentially plain careful-style. It includes one fragment with sentence-final **dèsu** omitted ([N]b). On the accompanying video, Mr. Carter (N) questions his colleague, Mr. Suzuki (J), on a subject related to transportation.

(N)a. **Kakárimàsu** is an affective verbal which never links up with /nominal + o/ phrases. Depending on context, it commonly refers to either the time or the money requirement for a particular task; if expressed, *what* is required is followed by (**ga**); *how much* is required constitutes an extent expression (no following particle).

(J)b. The negative question provides information with a connotation of lack of absolute certainty.

3. CC3 is essentially a careful-style conversation with distal-style final predicates, but casual-style features in (N)b and (N)c. The occurrence of **Yasumi?** is not a particularly significant style marker here, since it simply echoes a word that was just uttered. However, **tonde mo nài** is clearly a direct-style adjectival sentence, and (N)c is a fragment. This kind of stylistic mixture is common, resulting in the continuum from very careful to very casual, referred to previously, assignment to which depends on the nature of the stylistic mix. On the video, Mr. Carter (N) is telling his colleague, Mr. Suzuki (J), about a forthcoming trip.

(N)a. **Kotosi**: undoubtedly a contraction of **konó tosì**. Compare also **maitosi** 'every year.'

(N)b. **Tonde mo nài**: This sentence, occurring here in direct-style, is a reply that suggests dismissal of what has just been said as wrong, absurd, ridiculous, unthinkable. Distal-style plain and polite alternates would end in **nâi desu** or **arímasèn** and **gozáimasèn**. In some contexts, this sentence would be extremely rude, and in others, very polite: it depends entirely on what has just been said.

Sigoto, a nominal, occurs with the verbal **simâsu: sigóto (o) simàsu** 'do work.' **Osîgoto** is a polite alternate referring to the work of others (i.e., the out-group).

(J)b. **Dê mo** is a common sentence beginning which provides contrast with what immediately preceded. This is an abbreviation for **soré dè mo** 'even if it is that'; this will be analyzed later.

Tanósìmi 'pleasure,' often implying expectation, is another example of a nominal derived from a verbal (in its stem form). In this case, the verbal is **tanósimimàsu /tanósìnde/** 'take pleasure in.'

4. CC4 is a careful-style conversation, with final predicates in distal-style. On the accompanying video, the participants are a foreign student (N) and his Japanese professor (J), discussing a very old book on the professor's desk. The introductory utterance in (N)b, consisting of /nominal?/, is actually an echo of an item in (J)a for which (N) requires explanation. In such circumstances, /nominal?/ is the normal pattern and not really significant in signaling style.

(N)a. **Zûibun** is a nominal which, like **to(t)temo** and **a(n)mari**, links up directly with predicates and describes manner/degree. **Zûibun hurûi desu** 'it's extremely old'; **zûibun**

kakarimasu 'it takes an awful lot'; **zûibuñ hûbeñ desu** 'it's awfully inconvenient.' It occurs commonly—though *not* exclusively—with words that have negative connotations.

(J)a. **Mêezi, Taisyoo, Syoowa, Heesee:** The native system of designating years in Japan is based on which year within an emperor's reign a year falls: the first year of a reign (until the following January first) is **gâñ-neñ**; from then on, the remaining years of the reign are numbered with the Chinese series of numerals + the classifier **-neñ**. But increasingly, the Western calendar (**seereki**) has come into use, with years numbered as in the West + **-neñ**.

Structural Patterns (SP)

1. PHRASE-PARTICLES: **nâñ-zi** *made*; **koko** *kara*; **zyûu-zi** *ni*

a. **màde**: In 7A, /location X + **màde**/ = 'as far as X' was introduced. We now extend the use of **màde** to include its occurrence following time expressions (nominals) to indicate 'time until which': /time X + **màde**/ = 'until X,' 'up to *and including* X.' As usual, **màde** loses its accent following an accented word. Examples:

Asâtte made imasu.	'I'll be here until the day after tomorrow.'
Nî-zi made matímàsita.	'I waited until 2 o'clock.'
Go-zíkañ-ḡùrai made dekimasu.	'I can do it for up to about five hours.'
Kayôobi made wa mâiniti kimâsita.	'Until Tuesday I came here every day.'

b. **kara**: The particle **kara**, previously encountered only in the combinations **sore kara** and **kore kara,** in general marks what precedes as the starting point of an activity or state: /Location X + **kara**/ = 'from location X,' 'starting from location X.' 'Location' includes places, points in a sequence, people, etc. /Time X + **kara**/ = 'starting at time X and continuing,' 'from time X on.' Examples:

Iḡírisu kara kimàsita.	'I came [here] from England.'
Amérika kara ikimàsita.	'I went [there] from the U.S.'
Watási kara simàsu ka↗	'Are you going to do it, starting with me?'
Kono teḡami (wa) señsèe kara kimasita.	'This letter came from the teacher.'
Doyôobi kara imâsita.	'I was here from Saturday on.'
Sâñ-zi kara simasyoo.	'Let's do it starting at 3.'

Sequences of /X **kara** Y **mâde**/ 'from X to Y' are extremely common:

âsa kara bań màde	'from morning until night'
yasásii hòñ kara muzúkasìi no made	'from easy books to hard ones'
Tookyoo kara Kyôoto made	'from Tokyo to Kyoto'
tikâ kara yôñ-kai made	'from the basement to the fourth floor'

c. **ni**: A time expression that indicates the time when a predicate happens or applies occurs either without a following particle (cf. **kyôo simasu**) or followed by particle **ni**,[12] depending on the individual time expression. In general, (1) time words like **kyôo, asítà,** and **îma,** whose meanings are relative to the time of use, and (2) generic time words like

---

12. In this case, locational particle **ni** indicates location in time as opposed to space.

âsa, bañ, gôḡo, mâiniti, etc., and (3) time expressions ending in -ḡòro are more apt to occur without ni in this pattern. Most other expressions take ni.[13] Examples:

Yô-zí ni kimâsita.	'I came at 4 o'clock.'
Doyôobi ni mimâsita.	'I saw [it] on Saturday.'
Sití-zi-ḡòro kimâsita.	'I came at about 7 o'clock.'
Îma ikimasu.	'I'll go now.'
Kyôo kaímàsita.	'I bought [it] today.'
Mâiniti tukaimasu.	'I use [it] every day.'

Japanese tends to be more specific than English in distinguishing between 'time *at* which' and 'time *starting from* which.' For example, the Japanese equivalent of English 'the program starts *at 8*' would certainly include hatî-zi kara.

Remember that not all occurrences of time words are tied to a predicate in a 'time of occurrence' relationship. Some time expressions indicate when something started or ended; others occur as the item being discussed or as the description of a following nominal. Thus:

Suíyòo made imâsita.	'I stayed until Wednesday.'
Suíyòo kara tukaimasu.	'I'll use [it] from Wednesday on.'
Suíyòo ḡa îi desu.	'*Wednesday* will be good.'
Suíyòo no zyûḡyoo desita.	'It was Wednesday's class.'

Note that phrases ending in any one of the particles màde, kara, and ni link up with predicates in all the examples cited. Note also that these phrases may be followed by wa or mo, with the usual shift in meaning. Examples:

Asítà made wa imâsu kedo . .	'I'll be here until tomorrow (at least) but . . .' (not necessarily after that).
Kiñyòo kara wa imásèñ ḡa . .	'After Friday I won't be here but . . .' (I'll probably be here before that).
Asítà mo zyuú-ḡatu tuitatì ni mo imâsu ka⟋	'Will you be here both tomorrow and on October first?'

Following an unaccented nominal, ni and kara are accented before wa and mo (kokó nì wa, Toókyoo karà mo, etc.).

2. /NOMINAL + PHRASE-PARTICLE + dèsu/

We will now extend our definition of the nominal predicate to include both /nominal + desu/ and /nominal + phrase-particle + desu/. The new pattern occurs with two distinct kinds of usage.

1. yo-zí-hàñ made desu *lit.* 'it is until 4:30'; gôḡo kara desu *lit.* 'it is from the afternoon.' /Nominal + mâde desu/ = 'it is until X,' 'it extends as far/long as X,' i.e., 'it continues until X,' 'it lasts until X,' 'it ends at X,' 'it goes as far as X.' /Nominal + kara desu/ = 'it is from X,' 'it extends from X,' 'it starts at X.' As a type of nominal predicate, this variety also uses a zya nâi desu or zya arímasèñ negative:

---

13. This includes 'time when' expressions with -ḡùrai, the newer usage now gaining acceptance. Compare mik-ka tukaimàsita 'I used it for 3 days'; mik-ka ni tukaimàsita 'I used it on the 3rd'; mik-ka-ḡòro tukáimàsita 'I used it on about the 3rd'; mik-ka-ḡùrai tukáimàsita 'I used it for about 3 days'; and (new) mik-ka-ḡùrai ni tukáimàsita 'I used it on about the 3rd'.

Kono teḡami (wa) seńsèe kara zya nâi desu.
    'This letter is not from the teacher.'

Very few phrase-particles occur in this pattern; actually **mâde** and **kara** are the major examples.[14]

2. **Tâkusii de desu ka⌄**: Unlike the examples in (a) above, this utterance has an important limitation as to where it can occur: it never occurs as the first item of a conversation. In this type of usage, **dèsu** is being used as a replacement for the specific predicate of the previous utterance. It is only in this kind of utterance that we ever find particles like **ḡa, o, mo, de**, etc. immediately preceding **dèsu**. Examples:

Tabémàsita yo⌄ 'I ate it.'

Nâni o desu ka⌄ 'What is it (that you ate)?'

Dekímasèń nêe. 'I can't do it!'

Nâni ḡa desu ka⌄ 'What is it (that you can't do)?'

Komárimàsita. 'I've become upset.'

Watási mò desu yo⌄ 'It's I, too (who have become upset).'

3. *POLITE-STYLE:* **irássyaimàsu** ↑ ~ **maírimàsu** ↓ 'go'

The honorific-polite / ↑ / verbal **irássyaimàsu** denotes not only motion toward this place ('come'), and animate existence without motion ('be in a place,' 'stay'), but also motion away from here ('go'). Thus, *in terms of English equivalents,* we must now define the verbal as 'come,' 'go,' 'be,' or 'stay.' Only accompanying particles and/or context distinguish among these senses. However, we should really not think of the word as having four meanings but rather that, in its politeness, it is associated with lack of precision, and that this single honorific verbal covers a large territory of meaning for which English is lacking a single equivalent.

In the humble-polite / ↓ /, **maírimàsu** covers both motion toward and motion away from here, but not static location.

We can chart the usage of these verbals as follows:

	Distal-Style		
Plain		Polite	
	Humble-Polite		Honorific-Polite
ikímàsu			
kimâsu }	**maírimàsu**	}	**irássyaimàsu**
imâsu	**orímàsu**		

4. *CLASSIFIERS:* **-syuukań; -ḡatu; -kaḡetu; -neń(kań)**

Study the lists at the end of the Breakdowns above, and note the following points:

1. **-Syuukań** is a classifier that counts duration in weeks (cf. **-zikań**, which counts duration in hours). The special forms of **itî, hatî,** and **zyûu** that occur before this classifier parallel those that regularly occur before classifiers beginning with /s/ (cf. **-satu, -seńto**). When approximate, this classifier compounds with **-ḡùrai**, but never with **-ḡòro**.

---

14. Remember that in /nominal + **nò** + **desu**/ sequences, the **no** is a contraction of /particle **no** + nominal **no**/, not a particle alone.

2. **-Ḡatu** is a naming classifier for the months of the year. Note the **sî** alternate for '4,' **sitî** for '7,' and **kû** for '9.' This is a 'time when' classifier, occurring with **-ḡòro** in approximation.

3. **-Kaḡetu** is a classifier that counts duration in months. In this case, the durational **-kañ** that occurs in **-zikañ** and **-syuukañ** is replaced by **ka-** at the beginning of the classifier. The special forms of **itî, rokû, hatî,** and **zyûu** that occur before this classifier parallel those that regularly occur before classifiers beginning with /k/ (cf. **-kai, -keñ**). However, there is no change in the classifier itself following **sañ-** and **nañ-**. When approximate, **-kaḡetu** regularly compounds with **-ḡùrai**, but never with **ḡòro**.

4. **-Neñ** is a classifier that both names and counts the years beyond 'one,' (for which **gâñ-neñ** *names* ['the year 1'] and **itî-neñ** *counts* ['one year']). The less common alternate classifier **-neñkañ**,[15] like **-zikañ, -syuukañ,** and **-kaḡetu**, only counts units of duration and therefore occurs with **-ḡùrai** but never with **-ḡòro** in approximation. Compare: **zyuú-neñ-ḡòro** 'about the year 10,' and **zyuú-neñ-ḡùrai** 'about ten years.'

In dates that include more than one time designation (i.e., year and month, or month and date, etc.), the regular order runs from large unit to small, with no intervening phrase particles.

Example: **Sêñ kyûuhyaku gozyúu sitì-neñ ′siti-ḡatu nîzyuu sití-nitì** 'July 27, 1957.'

But compare: **Hatíḡatù no hutú-ka dèsu ka** 'Do you mean the second *of August*?'

Remember that while quantity expressions are never followed by **-ḡòro**, 'time when' expressions are often followed by **-ḡùrai** in the present-day speech of many Japanese, although normally only in contexts which are not ambiguous. Thus **-ḡùrai** can alternate with **-ḡòro**, but not **-ḡòro** with **-ḡùrai**.

5. *QUESTIONS WITHOUT* **ka: Nâñ-neñ desyoo.**

Previously introduced question types include:
    (1) questions ending in sentence-particles **ka** and **neſ** (1A-SP2)
    (2) questions ending in **desyoo?** (6B-SP2)
    (3) fragments ending in /ʔ/ (8A-SP4)

In this section, a new type occurs;:
    /interrogative + **desyòo.**/

This kind of question, ending in **desyòo** or **-masyòo** with period /./ intonation, depends entirely on the interrogative (= question word—**nâni, dâre, dôko,** etc.) for its status as a question. It alternates freely with the same sequence + **ka**, but is slightly more casual. Compare:

    Dônata desyoo. *or*
    Dônata desyoo ka. 'Who would that be?' *but*
    Tanáka-sañ desyòo. 'That's probably Mr/s. Tanaka.'
    Tanáka-sañ desyòo ka. 'Would that be Mr/s. Tanaka?'
    Tanaka-sañ desyoo? 'I assume that's Mr/s. Tanaka, isn't it?'

Also:
    Nâñ-zi ni ikimasyoo. *or*
    Nâñ-zi ni ikimasyoo ka. 'What time shall I/we go?' *but*

---

15. Less common alternates for **-neñkañ** are **-kaneñ** and **kaneñkañ**.

Sân-zi ni ikimasyoo. 'Let's go/I guess I'll go at 3 o'clock.'
Sân-zi ni ikímasyòo ka. 'Shall I/we go at 3 o'clock?'

These questions without **ka** can be followed by **nê(e)** in the same way as questions with **ka**.

Drills

A 1. **Tosyôsitu wa, nâñ-zi made desu ka⌐**
'How late is the library open?' (*lit.*
'Until what time is the library?')

     Tosyôsitu desu ka. Sâa, nâñ-zi made desyoo ka nêe.
'The library? Hmm, how late *would* it be!'

  2. **Taísìkañ wa, nâñ-zi kara desu ka⌐**
'What time does the embassy open?'
(*lit.* 'From what time is the embassy?')

     Taísìkañ desu ka. Sâa, nâñ-zi kara desyoo ka nêe.
'The embassy? Hmm, (from) what time *would* it be?'

  3. **tikatetu/nâñ-zi made**; 4. **konó siñkàñseñ/dôko made**; 5. **kono deñsya/dôno êki made**; 6. **kono heñ no gakkoo/îtu kara**; 7. **Nîsida-señsee/nañyòobi kara**

B 1. **Yô-zi kara simâsu yo⌐**
'I'll do it from 4 [on].'

     |Anoo| **Yô-zi kara nañ-zi-ḡòro made desu ka⌐**
'Uh—from 4 until about what time (will it be)?'

  2. **Hatí-zi-hàñ kara matímàsita yo⌐**
'I waited from 8:30 [on].'

     |Anoo| **Hatí-zi-hàñ kara nañ-zi-ḡòro made desu ka⌐**
'Uh—from 8:30 until about what time (is it) [that you waited]?'

  3. **too-ka/tukáimàsita**; 4. **getúyòobi/tomárimàsu**; 5. **nano-ka/imâsu**

C 1. **Mâiniti ni-zí-ḡòro kimasu ka⌐**
'Do you come every day at about 2?'

     Êe, mâiniti nî-zi kara sâñ-zi made imasu.
'Yes, I'm here every day from 2 to 3.'

  2. **Mâiasa ku-zí-ḡòro kimâsu ka⌐**
'Do you come every day at about 9?'

     Êe, mâiasa kû-zi kara zyûu-zi made imasu.
'Yes, I'm here every day from 9 to 10.'

  3. **maisyuu/doyôobi**; 4. **maituki/tuítatì**; 5. **maitosi/sití-ḡatù**; 6. **maituki/hatu-ka**; 7. **maitosi/si-ḡátù**

D 1. **Ikímàsu ne!—Nâḡoya e.**
'You're going, aren't you—to Nagoya.'

     Êe, getúyòobi ni ikimasu.
'Yes, I'm going on Monday.'

  2. **Simâsita ne!—gôruhu o.**
'You played, didn't you—golf.'

     Êe, getúyòobi ni simasita.
'Yes, I played on Monday.'

  3. **kimâsu/matâ**; 4. **tomárimàsu/Kyôoto de**; 5. **imâsita/tosyôsitu ni**; 6. **mimâsita/ano atárasìi koñpyùutaa o**; 7. **yamémàsita/daiḡaku o**

E 1. **Yoóròppa wa, kotósi dèsita neʃ**
'Europe was [to be] this year, wasn't it?'

     Êe. Kotósi ikimàsu.
'Yes, I'm going this year.'

  2. **Giñkoo wa, nî-zi desita neʃ**

     Êe. Nî-zi ni ikímàsu.

'The bank was [to be] 2 o'clock, wasn't it?' 'Yes, I'm going at 2.'

3. **tosyôsitu/âsa**; 4. **kuukoo/asítà**; 5. **yuúbìñkyoku/doyôobi**; 6. **señsèe no otaku/yôru**; 7. **Kyôoto/kû-ḡatu**; 8. **taísìkañ/tuítatì**; 9. **gakkoo/gês·sûi·kîñ**; 10. **daiḡaku/mâiniti**; 11. **ryoózìkañ/zyuúiti-zi-ḡòro**; 12. **tosyôkañ/ku-zí-hañ-gùrai**[16]

F. The responses of this drill are all in the humble-polite style, regardless of whether the questions are polite- or plain-style. This reflects the relationship between the responder and the questioner.

1. **Tosyôsitu e irássyaimàsu ka⌐** **Êe, maírimàsu.**
   'Are you going to the library?' 'Yes, I am (going).'

2. **Bañ màde imâsu ka⌐** **Êe, orímàsu.**
   'Will you stay here until the evening?' 'Yes, I will (stay).'

3. **koko e irássyaimàsu**; 4. **kono teḡami o misémàsu**; 5. **onamae o kakímàsita**; 6. **wâiñ o nomímàsita**; 7. **kêeki o tabémàsu**; 8. **Nâḡoya made irássyaimàsita**

G 1. **Tokée o kaimàsita yo⌐** **Tokee o? Dôko de desu ka⌐**
   'I bought a watch.' 'A watch? At what place (is it) [that you bought it]?

2. **Señsèe o zûibuñ matímàsita yo⌐** **Señsèe o? Dôko de desu ka⌐**
   'I waited for the teacher for a long 'The teacher? At what place (is it) [that you time.' waited]?'

3. **mití o kikimàsita**; 4. **tênisu o simâsita**; 5. **Dôitu no bîiru o nomímàsita**

H 1. **Kore kara mâiniti simâsu yo⌐** **Nâni o desu ka⌐**
   'I'm going to do it every day from 'What (is it) [that you are going to do]?' now on.'

2. **Môtto irímàsu yo⌐** **Nâni ḡa desu ka⌐**
   'I need more.' 'What (is it) [that you need]?'

3. **Zyâa, tukúrimasyòo neʃ**; 4. **Kokó nì wa takúsañ arimàsu nêe.**; 5. **Tanósìmi desu nêe.**; 6. **Sâtoo-sañ ḡa yôku wakárimàsu nêe.**; 7. **Asoko de kaímàsita yo⌐**; 8. **Omâwarisañ ni kikímàsita yo⌐**; 9. **Zañnèñ desu nêe.**

I 1. **Kokó kara Siñzyuku màde, donó- ḡurai̇ kakarimàsu ka⌐** **Kokó kara Sinzyuku màde desu ka⌐ Zûibuñ kakárimàsu yo⌐**
   'About how long does it take from 'From here to Shinjuku? It takes a long here to Shinjuku?' time!'

2. **Tosyôkañ kara kokó màde donó- ḡurai kakarimàsu ka⌐** **Tosyôkañ kara kokó màde desu ka⌐ Zûibuñ kakárimàsu yo⌐**
   'About how long does it take from the 'From the library to here? It takes a long library to here?' time.'

---

16. Some speakers will use only **-ḡòro** here.

3. **koko/señsèe no otaku**; 4. **kuukoo/koko**; 5. **koko/ryoózìkañ**; 6. **Uéno-kòoeñ/koko**

J 1. **Kore kara nañ-syuukañ-g̃ùrai**
Yoóròppa ni imâsu ka⤸
'About how many weeks will you be
in Europe after this?'

Yôku wakárimasèñ g̃a, âto yoñ-syuukañ-
g̃ùrai zya nâi desyoo ka.
'I'm not sure, but I wonder if it isn't about
four weeks to go.'

2. **Kore kara nañ-niti-g̃ùrai konó**
ryokañ ni tomarimàsu ka⤸
'About how many days will you stay in
this inn after this?'

Yôku wakárimasèñ g̃a, âto yok-ka-g̃ùrai
zya nâi desyoo ka.
'I'm not sure, but I wonder if it isn't about
four days to go.'

3. **nañ-neñ-g̃ùrai/eég̃o osiemàsu**; 4. **nañ-zikañ-g̃ùrai/konó hòñ mimâsu**

K 1. **Kotósi no kùg̃atu kara, sañ-kàg̃etu-**
hodo Kyôoto e itte kimasu.
'I'm going to Kyoto for about three
months starting this September (and
coming [back]).'

Zyâa, okaeri wa, zyuúni-g̃atu-g̃òro desu
ne!
'Then you'll be back about December,
won't you.'

2. **Kyôo kara, hutu-ka-hodo Nâg̃oya e**
itte kimasu.
'I'm going to Nagoya for about two
days (from) today (and coming
[back]).'

Zyâa, okaeri wa, asátte-g̃òro desu ne!
'Then you'll be back (about) the day after
tomorrow, won't you.'

3. **si-g̃átu zyùugo-niti/sañ-syùukañ/Yoóròppa**; 4. **itî-zi/sañ-zìkañ/tosyôkañ**; 5. **too-ka**
kara/too-ka/Kânada; 6. **getúyòobi/yok-ka/tomódati no utì**

L 1. **Ano sig̃oto wa, îtu kara desyoo.**
'That work would be starting when?'

Sâa. Îtu kara desyoo nêe.
'Hmm. Starting when—I wonder!'

2. **Yoóròppa wa, nâñ-neñ made**
desyoo.
'Europe would be (i.e., you would be
in Europe) until what year?'

Sâa. Nâñ-neñ made desyoo nêe.
'Hmm. Until what year—I wonder!'

3. **tug̃î no kâig̃i/nañyòobi**; 4. **okaeri/nâñ-g̃atu**; 5. **zyûg̃yoo/nâñ-zi made**

M 1. **Syoówa gàñ-neñ wa, sêñ kyûuhyaku**
nîzyuu rokû-neñ desu neʕ
'Showa 1 is 1926—right?'

Syoówa gàñ-neñ desu ka⤸ |Eeto| Sôo
desu ne! Sêñ kyûuhyaku nîzyuu rokû-
neñ desu ne!
'Showa 1? Uh, that's right. It's 1926, isn't
it.'

2. **Syoówa zyùu-neñ wa, sêñ**
kyûuhyaku sâñzyuu go-néñ dèsu
neʕ
'Showa 10 is 1935—right?'

Syoówa zyùu-neñ desu ka⤸ |Eeto| Sôo
desu ne! Sêñ kyûuhyaku sâñzyuu go-néñ
dèsu ne!
'Showa 10? Uh, that's right. It's 1935, isn't
it.'

3. **Taísyoo gàn-neñ/sêñ kyûuhyaku zyuúnì-neñ**; 4. **Mêezi gân-neñ/sêñ happyaku rokúzyuu hatì-neñ**; 5. **Syoowa 'gozyuu ku-neñ/sêñ kyûuhyaku hatîzyuu 'yo-neñ**; 6. **Mêezi 'go-neñ/sêñ happyaku nanâzyuu nî-neñ**; 7. **Taisyoo hatî-neñ/sêñ kyûuhyaku zyûuku-neñ**

N 1. **Kotíra è wa, bań màde kimásèñ yo⁀**
'I'm not coming here (at least) until the evening.'

Dê mo, kimâsu neʔ
'But you are coming—right?'

2. **Asóko è wa, asíta no àsa made kaérimasèñ yo⁀**
'I'm not returning there (at least) until tomorrow morning.'

Dê mo, kaérimàsu neʔ
'But you are returning—right?'

3. **ano teğami/yôru/kakímasèñ**; 4. **giñkoo e/asû/ikímasèñ**; 5. **końpyùutaa/asâtte/tukáimasèñ**; 6. **ano siğoto/asítà/simásèñ**

Application Exercises

A. With the addition of the time words, your repertoire of conversational possibilities has increased geometrically, and practice on the many possibilities open to you is of the greatest importance. But at the same time, much remains that you cannot handle yet. Exploit what you can say and wait patiently for the rest to be introduced gradually.

1. Using a calendar, ask and answer questions pertaining to dates: check (a) what day of the week particular dates fall on; (b) the dates of a particular day of the week following another date (example: **tuítatì no tuğî no doyôobi** 'the next Saturday after the first').

2. Distribute cards describing trips: date and time of departure, destination, means of transportation; date and time of return, means of transportation. Practice asking and answering questions about the trips, *using Japanese conversational style* that includes **desyòo**, sentence-particles, perfective of recall, inverted sentences, fragments, etc. In other words, avoid making your conversations sound like a police interrogation! Assign specific identities to the conversation participants (professor, university president, company executive, colleague in the same company/different company, etc. [no close friends until Lesson 9!]), and conduct follow-up conversations in the third person (e.g., 'where did Professor Yamamoto go?'), using appropriate politeness levels.

3. Have each member of the group make up questions to be answered by other group members on the basis of fact. These may relate to the participants' daily schedules (hour of arrival and departure, class schedule, location of home, means of transportation, etc.) or to local schedules (bank, post office, library, department store and supermarket hours, etc.).

4. Ask and answer questions relating to how long it takes from place X to place Y by means of transportation Z (or by walking).

5. Have each member of the group prepare 'time problems' to be presented—and answered—orally in class. (Examples: 'I go to school every day at 9:00 and stay for six hours. What time do I go home?' 'I went to Kyoto on Monday and stayed for five days. When did I return?')

B. Core Conversations: Substitution

In practicing the CC with appropriate substitutions, follow each new version with questioning relating to the new contents.

SECTION C

Eavesdropping

(Answer the following on the basis of the accompanying tape. A = the first speaker, B = the second speaker, in each conversation.)
  1a. What is A asking about?
   b. What does A learn?
  2a. What is A concerned about?
   b. What place does B suggest?
   c. What is A's reaction?
  3a. What is A asking regarding Kyoto?
   b. What does B tell A?
   c. What is A's reaction?
  4a. When does B usually return home?
   b. What are the exceptions?
   c. Comment on the style of this conversation.
  5a. When does B have class? Give the days and hours.
   b. What is the subject of instruction?
  6a. What does A want to buy?
   b. What is A's question?
   c. What information does B provide?
  7a. What place is the topic of conversation?
   b. Where is it?
   c. How do A and B regard the location?
  8a. Who is being discussed?
   b. Where does this person go and how often? What about this year?
   c. How do A and B feel about this?
   d. Comment on the relationship between A and B, and the person under discussion.
  9a. Where is B going?
   b. What are B's plans for the day?
   c. Suggest where this conversation might be taking place, and explain the basis for your answer.
 10a. Who is being discussed?
   b. Where was this person? when? for how long?
 11a. How does B react to A's question, and why?
   b. Where is B going to stay? What is A's reservation?
   c. How does B feel?
 12a. What time is it?
   b. What does A suggest?
 13a. What does A want?
   b. Why is B able to agree to the request?
 14a. What is B's work schedule?
   b. What does B do on Sunday?
   c. How does B get there?
   d. How long does it take?

e. What polite-style verbal form occurs in this conversation? What does it indicate?

15a. What is being discusssed?

　b. What about this object is of particular interest? Give details.

16a. When does A want B to come again? Give the day and date of the original request.

　b. Why is the date changed?

　c. Give the time, day, and date to which it is changed.

17a. Where is B going? to do what?

　b. How is B going?

　c. How will B get around after arriving there?

　d. When will B return?

18a. What place is A inquiring about?

　b. How long does it take to get there? by what means of transportation?

　c. Why is A surprised?

19a. What is B doing today?

　b. Why is A surprised?

　c. What is the explanation?

　d. What is today's date?

　e. What date did A think it was?

20a. Where is B going? when? for how long?

　b. What is different about this year's itinerary?

　c. How often does B make such trips?

　d. How does B feel about them?

Utilization

(Remember to provide a stimulus and/or response for each item. Practice until you can deliver the Japanese convincingly, at normal speed and with appropriate intonation.)

　1. Ask a colleague how late the bank is open.

　2. Find out when the shops around here open in the morning.

　3. Ask a classmate (in casual-style) if his classes usually start in the afternoon.

　4. You've been asked what time Mr. Sato is coming here tomorrow. Explain that you're not sure, but he will be here at 9:30, at least.

　5. Find out if there is a library in this building.

　6. Ask a new acquaintance (politely) if she goes to Europe every year.

　7. You've been asked by your superior if you're going to Shinjuku tomorrow. Explain that you've given up on tomorrow and will go on Saturday.

　8. Confess to a colleague enrolled in a language school with you that you'd like to quit this kind of school.

　9. Suggest that you give up this computer and use the one over there.

　10. Tell a colleague that the next boat is [at] 10:38 A.M.

　11. Ask a colleague when (from what time until what time) she'll be here tomorrow.

　12. You've been askcd when you will return here. Answer: (a) at about 3:30; (b) on Sunday; (c) in April; (d) on July 1st; (e) on September 14th; (f) on December 20th; (g) tomorrow afternoon.

　13. Find out how long it takes: (a) from here to Tokyo Station by cab; (b) from Tokyo to Nagoya by bullet train; (c) from Shinjuku to Ueno by electric train; (d) from Tokyo to Kyoto by plane.

　14. You've just been asked by an acquaintance how long it takes for you to get home. Ask if she means by subway.

　15. A colleague has announced he can't do something. Check on what it is [he can't do].

　16. Tell an acquaintance that you are going (and coming [back]): (a) to Kyoto for a week this September; (b) to England for about 10 days in July; (c) to Europe for 6 months, starting this April.

17. You've been asked about a recent trip. Explain that you stopped in England for ten days, and then went to France and Germany for one week.

18. Comment that this is an awfully expensive dictionary. Find out if there aren't any cheaper ones.

19. An acquaintance is complaining about this library. Suggest that it is convenient, however.

20. Check on whether Showa 50 is 1975.

21. Find out in about what year Mr. Suzuki went to Germany and how many years he was there.

22. A friend is leaving for Nagoya tomorrow. Ask (casual-style) if it's a vacation.

23. You've been asked the price of a particular book. As you try to recall, suggest a $10.00 price.

24. Describe your class hours last year as Mon-Wed-Fri 9:00–1:00; Tues-Thurs 1:30–4:30; and Sat-Sun off. This year they're different.

25. Comment that your university is (a) nice and convenient; (b) a problem because of its inconvenience.

26. The secretary is waiting for your colleague. Tell her it's all right to wait here.

27. You've been asked about a book you are looking at. Comment that it's Japanese (language) and very difficult.

28. You and a friend are waiting for a performance to begin. Inquire (casually) how many minutes remain [i.e., until it starts].

29. You've been asked the time. Explain that you don't have a watch.

30. In response to a comment by a colleague: (a) agree wholeheartedly; (b) agree as to its probable validity; (c) raise some doubt as to your agreement; (d) react with surprise; (e) put it down as ridiculous; (f) express relief that things turned out that way; (g) express enthusiasm, admiration, etc. for the situation described.

Check-up

1. What is the difference between a 'counting classifier' and a 'naming classifier?' Give three examples of each. Give three examples of classifiers that fit both categories. (A-SP1), (B-SP4)

2. Describe two ways of telling time in Japanese. (A-SP1)

3. When might **Tanáka-saň dèsita ka** occur in answer to a question as to someone's name? (A-SP2)

4. How is approximation expressed in Japanese? How are 'time at which' and duration of time distinguished? (A-SP3)

5. What do we mean by 'casual-style?' When is it used? With what style does it contrast? (A-SP4)

6. What is the gerund of a nominal predicate? How is it used? Give examples (A-SP5)

7. What is the difference in meaning between **koré ğa/wa ìi desu** and **koré de ìi desu**? (A-SP5)

8. What do the Japanese equivalents of 'It will be all right to make a U-turn' and 'I made a U-turn and then stopped the car' have in common? (A-SP5)

9. What is the difference in meaning between **sâň-zi kara simâsita** and **sâň-zi made simâsita**? between **sâň-zi kara simâsita** and **sâň-zi ni simâsita**? (B-SP1)

10. Describe the two ways to indicate the time at which something occurs, depending on the time expression. (B-SP1)

11. Where may **dèsu** occur besides immediately following an adjectival or nominal? Are such occurrences categorized as adjectival predicates, or nominal predicates? Why? (B-SP2)

12. Under what circumstances may **dèsu** directly follow phrase-particles **ğa, o, mo** and **de**? (B-SP2)

13. For what plain verbals is **irássyaimàsu** the honorific-polite equivalent? How does **maírimàsu** relate to **irássyaimàsu**? (B-SP3)

14. What classifier is used to count months? weeks? years? to name months? years? Give the Japanese equivalent of: 6 months; 8 weeks; 1 year; 4 years; April; July; September. (B-SP4)

1
P₂₀₃

p. 210

15. What is the difference between **-neñ** and **-neñkañ**? (B-SP4)
16. What are the dates of the Meiji era? Taisho? Showa? How is the first year of an era designated? (B-SP4)
17. Give an example of a question type that does not end in **ka, ne,** or /?/. (B-SP5)

nanner deshoo

Lesson 9

SECTION A

Core Conversations

1′(J)	Îi?	(N)	Ñ. Îi yo⌐
1″(J)	Îi?	(N)	Îi wa yo⌐
2′(J)	Hoñtoo?	(N)	Hoñtoo dà yo.
2″(J)	Hoñtoo?	(N)	Hoñtoo yo⌐
3′(J)	Dekîru?	(N)	Kore? Ñ. Dekîru yo⌐
3″(J)	Dekîru?	(N)	Kore? Ñ. Dekîru wa yo.
4(J)a.	Kore wakâru?	(N)a.	Ññ⌐ Dâre kara no teḡami?
b.	Kimura-kuñ.	b.	Âa, naruhodo.
5(J)a.	Raisyuu matá irassyàru?	(N)a.	Maírimàsu kedo . .
b.	Watakusi, tyôtto osóku nàru kedo . .		
c.	Êe, zyûu-zi made ni wa.	b.	Dê mo, irássyàru desyoo?
6(J)a.	Kyôo ′Tanaka-sañ ′asuko ni iru?	(N)a.	Irû desyoo.
b.	Isóḡasìi?	b.	Betu ni isóḡasìku nâi desyoo. Yobímasyòo ka.
c.	Ñ.		

ENGLISH EQUIVALENTS

1(J)	Is it OK?	(N)	Yeah, it's fine.
2(J)	Is that true?	(N)	It's true.
3(J)	Do you know how to play? (*lit.* Can you do it?)	(N)	This? Yeah, I can play.
4(J)a.	Do you understand this?	(N)a.	Uh-uh. Who's the letter from? (*lit.* A letter from whom?)
b.	Kimura.	b.	Oh! I should've known!
5(J)a.	Are you going again next week?	(N)a.	Yes, I am, but . . . (is there any problem)?
b.	I'm going to be a little late, but . . . (I hope that's all right).	b.	But you *are* going, aren't you?

    c. Yes, by 10 o'clock (at least).
6(J)a. Is Mr/s. Tanaka over there
        today?
    b. Is s/he busy?

    c. Yeah.

(N)a. I assume s/he is.
    b. Probably not especially (busy). Shall
        I call him/her?

BREAKDOWNS
(AND SUPPLEMENTARY VOCABULARY)

1. **wa** (SP3)   /assertive sentence-particle/
2. **hońtoo dà** (SP2)   /direct-style equivalent of **hońtoo dèsu**/
3. **dekîru** (SP1)   /direct-style equivalent of **dekímàsu**/
4. **wakâru**   /direct-style equivalent of **wakárimàsu**/
    ń̂ń (SP3)   /casual-style negation/
    dâre kara no teğami (SP4)   letter from whom?
    Kimura-kuñ   Mr. Kimura
  + **kimi**   you /familiar/
    naruhodo   to be sure! of course! indeed! that makes
                                                sense

5. **raisyuu**   next week
  + **râiğetu**   next month
  + **raineñ**   next year
  + **koñsyuu**   this week
  + **koñğetu**   this month
  + **kêsa**   this morning
  + **kôñbañ**   this evening, tonight
    irássyàru ↑   /direct-style equivalent of **irássyaimàsu**/
    osoi /-katta/   is late; is slow
    narímàsu /nâtte/   become
    nâru   /direct-style equivalent of **narímàsu**/
    osóku nàru (SP5)   become late; become slow
  + **hayâi** /-katta/   is early; is fast
    irássyàru ↑ **desyoo** (SP6)   probably go *or* probably come *or* probably
                                                be (animate) /polite/
    zyûu-zi made ni (SP7)   by 10:00
6. **asuko**   /alternate of **asoko**/
    iru   /direct-style equivalent of **imâsu**/
    irû desyoo   probably be (animate)
    isóğasìi /-katta/   is busy
    betu ni /+ negative/   not especially
    yobímàsu /yoñde/   summon, call

Miscellaneous Notes

1,2,3: CC1–3, each given in two versions—the second of which is feminine or gentle—provide our first examples of casual-style conversations that include direct-style final predicates of the three predicate types (cf. SP1 and SP2, following). They are typical of informal conversations among close friends. In the accompanying video, some of the participants who started out using careful-style (with distal-style final predicates) in earlier lessons are now shifting to casual-style (with direct-style final predicates) in some contexts, as they become more relaxed and informal.

4. CC4 is a casual-style conversation between two friends. Note the lack of distal-style. They are puzzling over a letter from Kimura, a mutual friend, who is apparently known for his illegible handwriting.

(N)a. **Ǹñ** is a very informal negation, comparable to English 'uh-uh.'
. . . teḡami? is a direct-style equivalent of **. . . teḡámi dèsu ka** (cf. SP2).

(J)b. **-Kuñ**, like **-sañ**, is added to names—family names, given names, or a sequence of both—but never to the speaker's own name. However, unlike **-sañ**, it is used only in reference to one's peers or subordinates, and much more commonly, though not exclusively, in reference to males. Note that Japanese adults are more apt to use **-kuñ** affixed to a last name than to use first names in addressing and referring to their close male associates. While Japanese adapt to the preference of many Westerners for the use of first names while abroad and/or when interacting with Westerners, within their own society they have a marked preference for the use of last names.

(N)b. **Naruhodo** is an extremely common word. As a reply, it implies that the speaker acknowledges what has just been said as something s/he has failed to realize, but now sees makes sense. It is not unusual for one participant in a segment of conversation to utter only a string of **naruhodo** at intervals, indicating a reaction of ready acceptance of statements that seem completely reasonable.

5. CC5 is a conversation in which the foreigner (N) uses polite distal-style and the Japanese (J) polite casual-style, indicating a difference in rank. In the video, Sue Brown (a student) is chatting with Mr. Carter's wife, who is Japanese. Polite casual-style occurs more commonly in women's speech, indicating warmth and a relaxed attitude within the framework of politeness.

(J)a. In addition to the special time expressions which are compound nominals, there are time expressions which are phrases: **asíta no àsa, asita no bañ, asâtte no gôḡo**, etc.

(N)a. **Maírimàsu kedo . .** is a humble-polite ↓ minor sentence. Note the use of a distal-style verbal preceding **kedo**, in contrast with (J)b, following.

(J)b. This is a minor sentence with a direct-style predicate (**nâru**) preceding **kedo** (cf. SP1). **Watakusi** sets the speaker apart from the twosome. Besides its regular **-ku** form, **osoi** has a derivative nominal: **osókù** 'late (time).'

(N)b. While **irássyàru** is itself direct-style, the combination with **desyoo** is distal-style (cf. SP6).

(J)c. We have here a fragment without an expressed predicate; the implied predicate is derived from the preceding utterance.

6. CC6, when compared with CC5, offers striking similarities and contrasts. Again, (J) is using casual-style, with direct-style final predicates, while (N) is using distal-style, suggesting a difference in rank. However, in contrast with CC5, the style is plain, not polite. Our sample video scene brings together two male bank employees, a Japanese supervisor (J)

and his foreign subordinate (N). The subordinate shows his respect by maintaining his distance through the use of distal-style. Ms. Tanaka, the topic of discussion, is a female consultant who does part-time work for the bank; she is referred to as **Tanaka-sañ**, but her position does not call for the use of polite verbals.

(J)a. **Asuko** is a more casual, conversational equivalent of **asoko**.

(N)a. **Irû desyoo**: while **iru** is itself direct-style, the combination with **desyoo** is distal-style (cf. **irássyàru desyoo** in CC5, and SP6).

(J)b. **Isógasìi** may refer to people (**Tanáka-sañ ğa isogasìi**) or a task (**siğóto ğa isoğasìi**) or a place (**kokó ğa isoğasìi**), but *not* a telephone line or an area that is busy in the sense of crowded. **Oísoğasìi** is a polite equivalent, used in reference to the out-group.

(N)b. /**Betu ni** + negative predicate X/ implies that something is 'not particularly X' or 'not especially X.' It frequently occurs by itself as a fragment, in which case it implies the appropriate negative predicate: **Muzúkasìi desu ka‿ . . . Betu ni.** 'Is it difficult?' . . . 'Not particularly.'

Structural Patterns

1. VERBALS: DIRECT-STYLE, IMPERFECTIVE, AFFIRMATIVE

If you were to look up words like 'eat,' 'drink,' 'go,' and 'come' in an English–Japanese dictionary, you would find—probably to your surprise—entries without a **-màsu** form. Actually, they would be the direct-style equivalents, which are regularly used as citation (dictionary) forms. (Compare the direct-style forms **takâi, oókìi, abunai**, etc. which are used as citation forms for the adjectival.) We will now analyze the direct-style of the verbal and show how the distal-style is derived from it.

Japanese verbals can be divided into four subclasses: vowel verbals, consonant verbals, special polite verbals (only five in this group) and irregular (only two).

Vowel verbals have roots ending in a vowel (either **i** or **e**). To form the direct-style imperfective, they add **-ru**. Examples:

    dekî-ru 'it is (*or* will be) possible'; '[I] can (*or* will be able to) do'

    tabê-ru '[I] eat *or* will eat'

Consonant verbals have roots ending in a consonant. To form the direct-style imperfective, they add **-u.** Examples:

    nôm-u '[I] drink *or* will drink'

    yob-u '[I] call *or* will call'

Special polite verbals are five verbals that have roots ending in **-ar** and share several special characteristics. To form the direct-style imperfective, they add **-u.** Examples:

    irássyàr-u ↑ '[you] go *or* will go, *or* come *or* will come, *or* are *or* will be (located)'

    kudásàr-u ↑ '[you] give *or* will give to me (*or* us)'

The two *irregular verbals* are vowel verbals with several different roots; the root for the direct-style imperfective ends in **-u**, and the ending is **-ru**:

    kû-ru '[I] come *or* will come'

    su-ru '[I] do *or* will do'

Note the following important points. Work through these slowly and carefully: they will affect your future work in Japanese!

a. Every citation form of a verbal ends in **-u**, but not every word ending in **-u** is a verbal (cf. **asû** 'tomorrow,' **otaku** 'home,' **rakû** 'comfortable,' etc.). Remember the definition of a verbal (cf. 1A-SP1).

b. If the citation form of a verbal ends in /consonant other than **-r** + **u**/, it *must* be a consonant verbal (example: **kâk-u** '[I] write *or* will write').

c. If a verbal citation form ends in **-ru**, check the preceding vowel:

(1) All **-oru** verbals are consonant verbals, i.e., **-or** + **u** (example: **ôr-u** '[I] am *or* will be [located]');

(2) Except for **kûru** and **suru**, all **-uru** verbals are consonant verbals, i.e., **-ur** + **u** (example: **tukûr-u** '[I] make *or* will make');

(3) Except for the five polite verbals in the third category above (which will be identified), all **-aru** verbals are consonant verbals, i.e., **-ar** + **u** (example: **wakâr-u** '[I] understand *or* will understand');

(4) All **-iru** and **-eru** verbals require that additional information be provided in order to determine whether they are vowel verbals (**-i** + **ru** and **-e** + **ru**) or consonant verbals (**-ir** + **u** and **-er** + **u**). The distinction is crucial in predicting all derivative forms. Examples:

    i-ru '[I] am *or* will be (located),' a vowel verbal, and

    misê-ru '[I] show *or* will show,' a vowel verbal, *but*

    ir-u '[I] need *or* will need'; '[it] is *or* will be required,' a consonant verbal, and

    kâer-u '[I] return *or* will return,' a consonant verbal

d. All verbals which end in two vowels in their citation form are consonant verbals: the consonant in this case is **-w-**, which has been lost in modern Japanese everywhere except before **a**. In other words, we will find this **-w-** present when we encounter verbal derivatives that involve /**w** + **a**/, but before the **-u** ending of the imperfective, the **-w-** has been lost. Example: *kaw-u > **kau** '[I] buy *or* will buy.'

e. The citation form of verbs in English is regularly either the infinitive ('to go') or the infinitive without 'to' ('go'). For example, we might ask, "How do you say '(to) buy' in Japanese?" Accordingly, in our lists of breakdowns, we regularly give forms like 'buy,' 'go,' 'turn,' etc. as the English equivalent for Japanese verbals. While this is perfectly justifiable as an agreed-upon procedure, it is important for the student to be aware of the fact that a citation form like **iku** is actually the direct-style imperfective, and may occur by itself as a complete sentence. In fact, **Iku? ... Iku.** is a conversation! ('Are you going? ... I am (going).')

Before moving on, it will be useful to make certain that we can identify verbals as to their subclass, given only the form that dictionaries provide. The following is a list of verbals you have never before encountered. Try your hand at identifying each as to whether it (a) must be a vowel verbal, *or* (b) must be a consonant verbal, *or* (c) is indeterminate without further information. (Do not be concerned about the special polite **-aru** category, since the five verbals in that group will be identified for you as they occur.) Following each verbal is the reference to relevant guidance provided above; check the accuracy of your answers by referring to those sections.

tûku (b)	**dêru** (c-4)	**okureru** (c-4)
hanâsu (b)	**kayou** (d)	**kâtu** (b)
aǧaru (c-3)	**yômu** (b)	**hâiru** (c-4)
hakobu (b)	**siru** (c-4)	**sinu** (b)

tutómèru (c-4)	**môosu** (b)	**miêru** (c-4)
modôru (c-1)	**okuru** (c-2)	**suu** (d)

We now face the question of how to move from the direct-style citation form of the verbal to the corresponding distal-style **-màsu** form. Actually, **-màsu** is itself an imperfective consonant verbal consisting of /root **-mas** + imperfective ending **-u**/. The special features of verbal **-màsu** include (1) the fact that it never occurs at the beginning of a word, and (2) that its only meaning is 'distal-style.'

   -Màsu, then, forms a compound verbal as it is added to another verbal.
Question: To what form of the initial verbal does **-màs-u** attach?
Answer: The stem.
Question: What is a verbal stem?
Answer: (1) For vowel verbals, stem and root are the same.
         (2) For consonant verbals, stem = root + **i**.[1]
         (3) For special polite verbals, root in **-ar** > stem in **-ai**.
         (4) For irregular verbals, root **ku** 'come' > stem **ki**; root **su** 'do' > stem **si**.

Note that the stem has already been introduced in two other patterns. It is (1) the form to which **-tai** is added (7B-SP4), and (2) the form which occurs in the humble-polite pattern (i.e., /**o** + stem + **suru**/ [7B-SP3]). Also, when a nominal is derived from a verbal, it is regularly the stem (cf. **kaérì** from **kâeru**; **yasúmì** from **yasûmu**), although the accent may be different.

   The following is a list of all the verbals that have been introduced thus far, including the citation (dictionary) form, root, stem, and **-màs-u** form.

Citation Form (Imperfective, direct-style)	Root	Stem	-màs-u Compound (Imperfective, distal-style)	English Equivalent
Vowel Verbals				
i-ru	**i**		**imâs-u**	be (animate)
dekî-ru	**dêki**		**dekímàs-u**	be possible; can do; become finished
mî-ru	**mî**		**mimâs-u**	look at
misê-ru	**mîse**		**misémàs-u**	show
osie-ru	**osie**		**osíemàs-u**	teach
tabê-ru	**tâbe**		**tabémàs-u**	eat
tome-ru	**tome**		**tomémàs-u**	bring to a halt
yame-ru	**yame**		**yamémàs-u**	quit
Consonant Verbals				
-b- **yob-u**	**yob**	**yobi**	**yobímàs-u**	call
-k- **arûk-u**	**arûk**	**arûki**	**arúkimàs-u**	walk
ik-u	**ik**	**iki**	**ikímàs-u**	go
itadak-u ↓	**itadak**	**itadaki**	**itádakimàs-u**	eat; drink; accept
kâk-u	**kâk**	**kâki**	**kakímàs-u**	write

1. Just as the **w** of **w**-root verbals is lost before **u**, it is also lost before **i**. See (d) above.

	kik-u	kik	kiki	kikímàs-u	ask
-m-	nôm-u	nôm	nômi	nomímàs-u	drink
-r-	âr-u	âr	âri	arímàs-u	be (inanimate)
	kakâr-u	kakâr	kakâri	kakárimàs-u	be required
	komâr-u	komâr	komâri	komárimàs-u	be(come) upset
	maḡar-u	maḡar	maḡari	maḡárimàs-u	(something) turns
	nâr-u	nâr	nâri	narímàs-u	become˙
	tomar-u	tomar	tomari	tomárimàs-u	come to a halt
	wakâr-u	wakâr	wakâri	wakárimàs-u	understand; be comprehensible
	kâer-u	kâer	kâeri	kaérimàs-u	return
	ir-u	ir	iri	irímàs-u	need; be required
	mâir-u ↓	mâir	mâiri	maírimàs-u	go; come
	ôr-u ↓	ôr	ôri	orímàs-u	be (animate)
	tukûr-u	tukûr	tukûri	tukúrimàs-u	make
-t-	mât-u	mât	mâti	matímàs-u	wait
-w-	ka-u	kaw²	kai	kaímàs-u	buy
	neḡa-u ↓	neḡaw²	neḡai	neḡáimàs-u	request
	tiḡa-u	tiḡaw²	tiḡai	tiḡáimàs-u	differ
	tuka-u	tukaw²	tukai	tukáimàs-u	use
	ukaḡa-u ↓	ukaḡaw²	ukaḡai	ukáḡaimàs-u	inquire

Special Polite Verbals

	gozâr-u +	gozâr	gozâi	gozáimàs-u	be (inanimate)
	kudásàr-u ↑	kudásàr	kudásài	kudásaimàs-u	give to me
	irássyàr-u ↑	irássyàr	irássyài	irássyaimàs-u	go; come; be (animate)

Irregular Verbals

	kû-ru	kû/kî/kô	kî	kimâs-u	come
	su-ru	su/si	si	simâs-u	do

Accent: Note that some verbals are accented and others unaccented. A verbal whose citation form has an accent also has an accent on the stem: in the case of vowel verbals the accent is one mora earlier (provided the accent isn't already on the initial mora), and for consonant verbals it is on the same mora as in the citation form. Thus: **tabêru/tâbe** but **wakâru/wakâri**. All **-màsu** forms are accented on the **-ma-** mora, although in some contexts the accent may be lost.

Hereafter, new verbals will be listed in their citation form in the Breakdowns, with **-ru** as a designation for vowel verbals, **-u** for consonant verbals, and **-aru** for special polite verbals.

The uses of direct-style verbals introduced thus far include:

(1) as sentence-final predicates (with or without following sentence particles). With question intonation, they become questions (cf. SP3, following).

2. The **w** is retained only before endings that begin with **a** (to be introduced later).

(2) before clause-particles **kedo** and **ḡa** (cf. SP3, following).

(3) before **desyòo** to form a distal-style tentative predicate (cf. SP6, following)

These uses apply to adjectival predicates as well.[3] For nominal predicates, see SP2, SP3, and SP6, following.

2. **dà**

The imperfective direct-style copula is **dà**. It occurs immediately following a nominal or phrase-particle, but never following an adjectival. Thus:

sôo da	direct-style equivalent of **sôo desu**
sâñ-zi made da	direct-style equivalent of **sân-zi made desu**

Dà is unaccented following an accented word or phrase.

Examining the three direct-style predicate types, we now find:

tiḡau	'it's different'
oókìi	'it's big'
onázi dà	'it's the same'

Verbals become distal-style through compounding with **-mas-**, as described in the preceding note. Adjectival and nominal predicates, however, add the distal-style marker **dèsu**. But when **dèsu** is added to a nominal predicate, **dà**—an extremely unstable form which is dropped in a number of contexts—is lost. (More will be said about **dà** in SP3 and SP6.) Thus:

tiḡau + distal **-màs-** > **tiḡáimasu.**[4]

takâi + distal **dèsu** > **takâi desu.**

onázi dà + distal **dèsu** > (*onázi dà desu) > **onázi dèsu.**

Note also that direct-style verbals and adjectivals form questions simply by adding question intonation; but in the parallel pattern for the nominal predicates, **dà** is again lost:

dekîru + /?/ > **dekîru?**	'is it possible?'
îi + /?/ > **îi?**	'is it all right?' *but*
hoñtoo dà + /?/ > **hoñtoo?**	'[is it] true?'

Dà may also be dropped in sentence-final position, or before most sentence-particles. In other words, the direct-style equivalent of **Sôo desu.** may be **Sôo da.** or **Sôo.**; of **Sôo desu ne!**, either **Sôo da ne!** or **Sôo ne!**; but of **sôo desu kedo**, *only* **sôo da kedo** (since **kedo** is not a sentence-particle).

3. *MORE ON STYLE: CAREFUL AND CASUAL; DISTAL AND DIRECT; POLITE AND PLAIN; GENTLE AND BLUNT; MASCULINE AND FEMININE*

As oral proficiency in Japanese increases, we are faced with added complications relating to style. In particular, we must examine a number of different scales, each representing a continuum between two extremes with multiple divisions.

Careful and Casual. The continuum which ranges from the most careful to the most casual involves an overall style of language. In particular, the following features are involved:

---

3. The /direct-style adjectival + nominal/ pattern (e.g., **oókìi hôñ**) will be expanded to include all predicate types later.

4. One occasionally hears combinations like **ikímàsu desu**, but such combinations are considered nonstandard.

Careful	*Casual*
Predominant use of distal-style predicates in sentence-final position, and elsewhere where optional	Predominant use of direct-style predicates
Fewer fragments	More fragments
Fewer contracted forms	More contracted forms
Longer, more complex sentences	Shorter, simpler sentences
Less use of sentence-particles, particularly those marked as colloquial, assertive, confirmatory, brusque, coarse, etc.	More frequent use of such particles

We describe language as being more careful or more casual on the basis of a measure of all the above-mentioned features. Remember that how one addresses a partner in a conversation is determined by the speaker's relation to the addressee: the relationship is *not necessarily reciprocal*. Thus A's position and/or age and/or gender may permit casualness in communicating with B, whereas B may be required to maintain careful-style because of his/her position vis-à-vis A.

Distal and Direct. Whether or not a particular predicate is distal-style or direct-style is precise and easily determined. However, in examining a language sample to determine where it fits on the careful-casual continuum, it is necessary to distinguish different patterns in which predicates occur. For example: **Konó hòn wa takâi desu.** is a significant distal-style occurrence, since the speaker did not choose the equally possible direct-style **takâi** (without **dèsu**). However, in **kore wa takâi hôn desu, takâi hôn** is not significant in assigning the conversation—or even the sentence—to one style or another, since an adjectival describing a following nominal is regularly in the direct-style.[5]

The clause-particles **kedo** and **ḡa**, although very similar in meaning, present contrast in stylistic usage. The predicate preceding **ḡa** usually matches the final predicate of the sentence in terms of distal- or direct-style (and /direct-style + **ḡa**/ is comparatively rare in the spoken language, particularly in female speech). On the other hand, provided the final predicate is distal-style,[6] either direct- or distal-style may precede **kedo**, and therefore, the choice that is made may be significant in the interpretation of overall style.

Polite and Plain. Like distal- and direct-style predicates, polite and plain predicates are easy to identify; but they must be kept distinct from the distal-direct difference. Study the following diagramming that covers 'motion away from the speaker.'

		Direct	Distal
Plain		**iku**	**ikímàsu**
Polite	Honorific ↑	**irássyàru**	**irássyaimàsu**
	Humble ↓	**mâiru**	**maírimàsu**

The polite/plain distinction is in a different category from distal/direct and therefore will be specially designated. If a conversation is markedly polite (i.e., contains a significant

---

5. Distal-style adjectivals are possible before only a few special nominals, and their occurrence is marked as evidence of extremely careful style.

6. With a final predicate in direct-style, the predicate preceding **kedo** is also direct-style.

number of polite forms), we will identify it as polite-careful or polite-casual; otherwise we will not comment on this feature.

Among the categories in the diagram above, the direct-style humble-polite is comparatively rare, particularly as a sentence-final predicate.

The direct-style, neutral-polite **gozâru** + is a basic form often included in lists of verbals and verbal charts for completeness, but this particular form does not occur in normal speech; this verbal occurs only in the distal-style (**gozáimàsu**).

Politeness may also be indicated by the use of the polite prefixes **o-** and **go-**, added to some nominals and adjectivals, and of certain vocabulary items (for example, **ikâḡa** is polite, whereas **dôo** is plain).

Blunt and Gentle; Masculine and Feminine. Here we have another continuum, which ranges from language which is markedly blunt, virile, tough, and aggressive through a neutral point to style which is markedly gentle, empathetic, and soft. The extremes are those few patterns used almost exclusively by one sex or the other.

One of the myths relating to Japanese is that there are *many* structures and features used exclusively by one sex. While this may have been more valid in the past, today most Japanese tend to use a greater range of styles, differentiated by situation. There are occasions when men use a softer, more empathetic style of the kind traditionally identified as 'feminine' (particularly when speaking with women and children), and occasions when women elect to speak in a rougher, more blunt, 'masculine' style. Regarding the masculine-feminine continuum, the following points are important:

1. Actually the chief difference between *male* and *female* Japanese is pitch and intonation rather than structures. There are, of course, items that are exclusively male or female, but in most cases, it is more accurate to speak of utterances as being more *blunt* or *gentle*.

2. In general, women are more apt to use polite-style and/or distal-style than men; therefore, frequency rather than the actual patterns used is significant. In other words, concentrated polite language and/or concentrated distal-style are more feminine.

3. The use of honorific-polite, direct-style forms in sentence-final predicates is more typical of feminine language. Example: **Irássyàru?** 'Are you going?'

4. The sentence-particle **wa** (not to be confused with the phrase-particle **wa**, which follows only nominals or other phrase-particles), pronounced with /⤴/ intonation in sentence-final position,[7] or followed by sentence-particles **yo** or **nê(e)**, is one example of truly *feminine* speech. **Wa** is a particle of mild assertiveness; it never follows tentative, consultative, or imperative forms. It may follow only imperfectives or perfectives, direct-style[8] or distal-style.

5. The occurrence of direct-style verbals and adjectivals before **yo** and **nê(e)** is only slightly blunt within casual-style. With direct-style nominal predicates, there is a greater distinction between blunt- and gentle-style: **X dà yo** and **X da nê(e)** are markedly blunt; **X yo** and **X nê(e)**, with **dà** dropped, are more gentle.

1. **dâre kara no teḡami** '*A LETTER FROM WHOM?*'

In 8B-SP2, the nominal predicate was extended to include /nominal + phrase-particle + **dèsu**/. In parallel fashion, we now extend /nominal X + **no** + nominal Y/, described in 5B-SP1, to include /nominal X + phrase-particle + **no** + nominal Y/ = 'Y described by the phrase /X + phrase-particle/.' Examples:

---

7. With /./ intonation, however, **wa** is commonly used by men.
8. Including **dà**, in spite of the fact that **dà** is often claimed to be a male form!

sâñ-zi kara no zyûḡyoo 'class that starts at 3 o'clock' (*lit.* 'class from 3 o'clock')

Toókyoo màde no bâsu 'the bus [that goes] as far as Tokyo'

The important point to note is that, whereas phrases like **sâñ-zi kara** and **Toókyoo màde** either occur before **dèsu** or link up with a predicate, the addition of the connective **no** makes them link up with a nominal. Compare:

Sâñ-zi kara desu. 'It's from 3 o'clock on.'

Sâñ-zi kara zyûḡyoo (o) mimasu. 'I'm going to watch class from 3 o'clock on' (regardless of when the class starts).

Sâñ-zi kara no zyûḡyoo (o) mimasu. 'I'm going to watch the class that starts at 3 o'clock' (regardless of when I'm going to watch it).

Before **no, kara** is accented on its final mora, following an unaccented nominal: **tomódati karà no teḡami.**

5. *ADJECTIVAL* + **nâru: osóku nàru** *'BECOME LATE'*

In 1B-SP2, we encountered the **-ku** form of the adjectival linking up with verbals and adjectivals, including the combinations **-ku nâi (desu)** and **-ku arímasèñ** (the negative adjectival patterns). Examples:

Abúnaku nài desu. 'It's not dangerous.'

Sîrôku simâsita. 'I made [it] white.'

Yôku wakárimàsita. 'I understood well.'

Hâyâku kimâsita. 'I came early.'

A particularly common combination, introduced in this section, is /adjectival **-ku** form X + verbal **nâru**/ = 'become X,' 'get to be X.' Examples:

Yâsûku narímàsita. 'It became cheap.'

Muzúkasiku narimasèñ yo. 'It won't become difficult.'

Yôku narímasèñ desita. 'It didn't improve' (*lit.* 'It didn't become good').

In this pattern, the **-ku** form and **nâru** are never interrupted by other phrases.

Combinations that include some form of **osóku nàru** occur frequently in apologies for lateness. For example: **Osóku nàtte, sumímasèñ.** 'I'm sorry to be late.'

The **-tai** derivatives of verbals, which are themselves adjectivals (cf. 7B-SP4), also occur before **nâru: Yoóròppa e ikítaku narimàsita.** 'I've come to want to go (*lit.* I became wanting to go) to Europe.' The **-ku nâru** sequence contrasts with the **-i** form of the adjectival in that it implies a change. Compare:

Kotosi wa yasûi desu. . . . Raíneñ mo yasùi desyoo. 'It's cheap this year.' . . . 'It will probably be cheap next year, too.' *and*

Kotosi wa yasûi desu kedo, raineñ wa tâkâku narímàsu yo⤸ 'This year it's cheap, but next year it will be(come) expensive.'

The verbals **suru** and **nâru** complement each other in describing 'causing to be' (= **suru**) as compared with 'getting to be' (= **nâru**). In other words, if I 'make my English easy' (= **eeḡo o 'yasasiku suru**), then 'my English becomes easy' (= **eeḡo ḡa yasásiku nàru**). Note the contrast in particles reflecting the usual contrast observed with operational verbals: **eeḡo o** = 'English' as the operand, i.e., the operated upon; **eeḡo ḡa** = 'English' as the operator, i.e., the thing which becomes.

6. *TENTATIVE PREDICATES IN* **desyòo**

Desyòo is the TENTATIVE equivalent of **dèsu**, indicating probability and lack of definiteness (cf. 6B-SP2). Like **dèsu**, it is distal-style.

/Direct-style predicate X + **desyòo**/ = probable occurrence of X, and is distal-style. The combination is considered a complex distal-style predicate. Following an accented verbal, **desyòo** is unaccented; but in the case of an unaccented verbal, either the verbal acquires an accent on its final syllable or **desyòo** is accented: **kûru + desyòo > kûru desyoo; iku + desyòo > ikû desyoo** or **ikú desyòo**. Examining this pattern in relation to the three predicate types, we find the following kinds of examples:

(1) **tukau** '[someone] uses *or* will use' > **tukáù desyoo** '[someone] probably uses *or* will use'

(2) **takâi** '[it] is *or* will be expensive' > **takâi desyoo** '[it] probably is *or* will be expensive'

(3) **yasúmì da** '[it] is *or* will be vacation' > (***yasúmì da desyoo**) > **yasúmì desyoo** '[it] probably is *or* will be vacation'

Once again the unstable **dà** is lost.

We have previously encountered examples like **takâi desyoo** and **yasúmì desyoo**, but the verbal examples are new: their introduction awaited the introduction of the direct-style verbal in this section. Note these points:

1. Patterns of types (2) and (3) have occurred earlier (6B-SP2), but we are noting now for the first time that /nominal + **desyòo**/ implies a 'dropped **dà**,' a frequently occurring phenomenon.

2. These **desyòo** forms rarely refer directly to the speaker. There are other patterns in the language that indicate lack of certainty in reference to self. They will be introduced in upcoming lessons.

3. Previous comments referring to **desyòo.** versus **desyo(o)?** apply equally to /verbals + **desyòo**/. **Wakâru desyo(o)?** 'You understand, don't you?'

4. Distal-style verbals ending in **-màsu** may also occur before **desyòo**, resulting in **-màsu desyoo** sequences. They are more markedly careful-style. However, distal-style adjectival and nominal predicates ending in **dèsu** do *not* occur before **desyòo**.

5. **Desyo(o)?** may occur independently when attempting to elicit agreement in regard to something that has just been said: 'Isn't that right?'

7. **zyûu-zi made ni** *'BY 10 O'CLOCK'*

The phrase-particle **ni** following a time expression indicates the *time when* something occurs; and /a time expression X + **màde**/ denotes a period of time extending up to and including X. If we combine these two concepts, we are talking about a point of time within the period that extends until X, i.e., what in English is expressed as 'by X.' That is to say, if I am coming here 'by 4 o'clock,' I will arrive *at* some time (**ni**) within the period that extends *until* (**màde**) 4, and when 4 o'clock arrives, I'll be here.

While **X màde** and **X ni** may occur with both verbals of action and inaction, the /**X màde ni**/ combinations regularly occur with action verbals only. Thus:

Doyôobi made imasu. 'I'll be here until Saturday.'

Doyôobi made kimasu. 'I'll come until Saturday' (repeated activity).

Doyôobi ni imasu. 'I'll be here on Saturday.'

Doyôobi ni kimasu. 'I'll come on Saturday.'
Doyôobi made ni kimasu. 'I'll come by Saturday.' 'I'll be here by Saturday.'
Phrase-particle **wa** may occur following /**X mâde ni**/, with the usual shift in focus.[9] Example:
Tyôtto osóku kimàsu kedo, sâñ-zi made ni wa kimâsu. 'I'm coming a little late, but by 3 o'clock (at least) I'll be here.'

Drills

Answer appropriately, according to gender: only women should use the **wa + yo** combination. /F/ = female.

A 1. **Oísìi?**   **Oísìi yo**
    'Is it tasty?' **Oisii wa yo** /F/
                   'It is (tasty).'

   2. **Sôo?**   **Sôo da yo**[10]
    'Really?'   **Sôo yo**
               'That's right.'

   3. **isógasìi**; 4. **kôñbañ (da)**;[11] 5. **osoi**; 6. **muzukasii**; 7. **raísyuu (dà)**; 8. **hayâi**; 9. **asóko (dà)**; 10. **abunai**

● Repeat this drill, reflecting differences of position by (a) converting the questions to distal-style (using **dèsu ka**) and (b) converting the responses to distal-style patterns (adjectival or nominal + **dèsu yo**).

B 1. **Dekîru?**   **Ñ. Dekîru yo Kimi wa?**
    'Can you do it?' **Ñ. Dekîru wa yo Anâta wa?** /F/
                     'Yeah. I can. How about you?'

   2. **Yobu?**   **Ñ. Yobu yo Kimi wa?**
    'Are you going to call [him/her]?' **Ñ. Yobû wa yo Anâta wa?** /F/
                                        'Yeah. I am (going to call). How about you?'

   3. **yameru**; 4. **mâtu**; 5. **tomaru**; 6. **wakâru**; 7. **kiku**; 8. **âru**; 9. **suru**; 10. **kâeru**; 11. **nômu**; 12. **tabêru**; 13. **iku**; 14. **komâru**; 15. **kâku**

● Repeat this drill, reflecting differences of position by (a) converting the questions to distal-style (/**-màsu ka**/ patterns) and (b) converting the responses to distal-style (/**-màsu yo**/ patterns).

C 1. **Sâtoo-sañ, imâsu neʕ**   **Irû desyoo.**
    'Mr/s. Sato is in—right?'   'S/he probably is.'

   2. **Sâtoo-sañ, kimâsu neʕ**   **Kûru desyoo.**
    'Mr/s. Sato is coming—right?' 'S/he probably is (coming).'

---

9. Less common is **mo** following **màde ni**, implying an 'emphatic additional,' i.e., 'even': **Asû made ni mo dekîru desyoo.** 'It will probably be(come) completed even by tomorrow.'
10. The response alternate with **dà** is blunt, without **dà**—gentle.
11. **Dà** in parentheses in a drill substitution item will indicate that it must be dropped when substituted within the given pattern. In this drill only, deletion occurs just in the gentle-style responses.

3. **yamémàsu**; 4. **tomárimàsu**; 5. **kaérimàsu**; 6. **tukáimàsu**; 7. **irímàsu**; 8. **kakímàsu**; 9. **dekímàsu**; 10. **kaímàsu**; 11. **ikímàsu**; 12. **simâsu**; 13. **tukúrimàsu**; 14. **mimâsu**; 15. **osíemàsu**; 16. **matímàsu**

D 1. **Sâtoo-señsee, kyôo irássyaimàsu ka⌐**
'Is Dr. Sato going today?'[12]

Êe, kyôo mo asítà mo irássyàru desyoo?
'Yes, s/he's going today *and* tomorrow, isn't s/he?'

2. **Sâtoo-señsee, koñsyuu irássyaimàsu ka⌐**
'Is Dr. Sato going this week?'[12]

Êe, koñsyuu mo raisyuu mo irássyàru desyoo?
'Yes, s/he's going this week *and* next week, isn't s/he?'

3. **kôñbañ**; 4. **koñğetu**; 5. **kotosi**; 6. **kyôo no gôğo**

E 1. **Sono teğami wa, tomódati karà desu ka⌐**
'Is that letter from a friend?'

Sôo desu. Tomódati karà no teğámi dèsu kedo . .
'That's right. It's a letter from a friend, but . . .' (why do you ask?)

2. **Sonó zyùğyoo wa, râiğetu made desu ka⌐**
'Does that class go on until next month?'

Sôo desu. Râiğetu made no zyûğyoo desu kedo . .
'That's right. It's a class [that continues] until next month, but . . .' (why do you ask?)

3. **deñwa/Nîsida-kuñ kara**; 4. **gakkoo/Mêezi kara**; 5. **deñsya/Uéno màde**; 6. **hanâ/ tomodati kara**; 7. **kâiği/raísyuu màde**; 8. **giñkoo/Taisyoo kara**

F 1. **Sono teğami, dâre kara desu ka⌐**
'Who is that letter from?'

Dâre kara no teğámi desyòo ka nêe.
'Who from, indeed!' (*lit.* 'It's a letter from whom, indeed!')

2. **Sonó bàsu, dôko made ikímàsu ka⌐**
'How far is that bus going?'

Dôko made no bâsu desyoo ka nêe.
'How far, indeed!' (*lit.* 'It's a bus as far as where, indeed!')

3. **zyûğyoo/nâñ-zi kara simâsu**; 4. **kâiği/dôko de simâsu**; 5. **gakusee/dôko kara kimâsita**; 6. **hanâ/dâre kara desu**

G 1. **Koko no siğoto wa, isóğasìi desu nêe.**
'The work here is [keeping us] busy, isn't it!'

Êe. Zûibuñ isóğasìku narímàsita nêe.
'Yes, it's become very busy, hasn't it!'

2. **Asoko no miti wa, abúnài desu nêe.**
'The road over there is dangerous, isn't it!'

Êe. Zûibuñ abúnaku narimàsita nêe.
'Yes, it's become very dangerous, hasn't it!'

3. **ano kissateñ/mazûi**; 4. **konó zyùğyoo no eeğo/muzukasii**; 5. **kotosi no atárasìi kuruma/takâi**; 6. **anó zyùğyoo/tumárànai**

12. Or 'coming' or 'staying' or 'is present here (or there)'.

H 1. **Muzúkasìi desu ka⬐**
'Is it difficult?'

Êe. Yasásìkatta ñ desu ğa, tyôtto muzúkasiku narimàsita nêe.
'Yes. The fact is that it was easy, but it's become a bit difficult.'

2. **Oókìi desu ka⬐**
'Is it big?'

Êe. Tîisàkatta ñ desu ğa, tyôtto ôókìku narímàsita nêe.
'Yes. The fact is that it was small, but it's become a bit big.'

3. **takâi**; 4. **yasasii**; 5. **oisii**; 6. **warûi**; 7. **mazûi**; 8. **yasûi**; 9. **tiísài**

I 1. **Osîğoto wa, isóğasìi desu ka⬐**
'Is your work [keeping you] busy?'

Êe. Mâe wa, amari isóğasìku nâkatta kedo; kono-ğoro isóğasìku narímàsita nêe.
'Yes. It wasn't too busy before, but these days it is' (*lit.* has become busy).

2. **Zyûğyoo wa, omósiròi desu ka⬐**
'Is the class interesting?'

Êe. Mâe wa, amari omósiròku nâkatta kedo; kono-ğoro omósiròku narímàsita nêe.
'Yes. It wasn't too interesting before, but these days it is' (*lit.* has become interesting).

3. **Nihóñ no aisukurìimu/oisii**; 4. **soñna kuruma/hayâi**; 5. **koñna koñpyùutaa/yasûi**; 6. **ano ryokañ/îi**

J 1. **Anâta wa yamémasèñ neʃ**
'You (at least) are not going to quit—right?'

Ie, watasi mo yamétaku narimàsita nêe.
'No, I've come to want to quit, too.'

2. **Anâta wa kaérimasèñ neʃ**
'You (at least) are not going back home—right?'

Ie, watasi mo kaéritàku narímàsita nêe.
'No, I've come to want to go back, too.'

3. **ikímasèñ**; 4. **kimásèñ**; 5. **koko de siğóto simasèñ**

K 1. **Koñğetu ikù desyoo?**
'You're going this month, aren't you?'

Iya, koñğetu wa ikimasèñ kedo, râiğetu made ni wa ikítài desu nêe.
'No, this month I'm not going, but I want to go by next month (at least).'

2. **Kêsa yobû desyoo?**
'You're going to call [him] this morning, aren't you?'

Iya, kêsa wa yobímasèñ kedo, asíta no àsa made ni wa yobítài desu nêe.
'No, this morning I'm not going to call [him], but I want to call [him] by tomorrow morning (at least).'

3. **koñsyuu mìru**; 4. **kotósi tukùru**; 5. **koñğetu kau**; 6. **kôñbañ kâku**

L 1. **Ikû desyoo?**

Êe, ikímàsu yo⬐—raísyuu màde ni wa.

'You're going, aren't you?' 'Yes, I am (going)—by next week (at least).'

2. **Matá kùru desyoo?** **Êe, kimâsu yo—raísyuu màde ni wa.**

'You're coming again, aren't you?' 'Yes, I am (coming)—by next week (at least).

3. **dekîru**; 4. **kâeru**; 5. **suru**; 6. **yameru**; 7. **yobu**; 8. **kiku**

M1. **Yobímasyòo ka** **Êe, yońde kudasaimasèñ ka**
'Shall I call [her]?' 'Yes, would you (call)?'

2. **Kakímasyòo ka** **Êe, kâite kudásaimasèñ ka**
'Shall I write?' 'Yes, would you (write)?'

3. **kimásyòo**; 4. **kikímasyòo**; 5. **kaérimasyòo**; 6. **kaímasyòo**; 7. **matímasyòo**

Application Exercises

A1. Practice asking and answering questions about future activities and locations of *other members* of your group or any persons known by the group, using **desyòo** patterns to indicate probability. Include newly acquired time expressions (**kôñbañ, raisyuu,** etc.). (Remember: **desyòo** is rarely used in reference to the speaker.)

2. Ask and answer questions relating to daily schedules, incorporating ——— **màde,** ——— **màde ni,** ——— **kara,** ——— **ni,** and extent patterns. Cover hour of arrival here, length of time in class, days in class, departure for home, etc.

3. Collect (or draw) pairs of pictures of the same kind of object that differ only in size, price, difficulty, color,[13] etc., and place two contrasting pictures on one sheet of paper, one labeled 'previously' and the other 'now.' Practice the patterns of Drills H and I of this section as you view the pictures.

4. Using appropriate objects or pictures, ask and answer questions using the pattern /X **kara~made no Y**/, i.e., **Dâre kara no teḡámi dèsu ka; Dôko made no bâsu desu ka; Nâñ-zi made no kâiḡi desu ka**

5. Using topics of the kind described in Application Exercises 8B-A3, practice relay drills: the instructor asks group member A about group member B, who gives A the information requested; A then relays the information back to the instructor as a probability. In this kind of drill, the instructor and A interact in distal-style but A and B use direct-style (i.e., Instructor [distal] > A [direct] > B [direct] > A [distal] > Instructor). Example:

Instructor to A: **B-sañ wa, kôñbañ kimâsu ka** 'Is Mr/s. B coming here tonight?'

A to B: **Kôñbañ kûru?** 'Are you coming tonight?'

B to A: **Ñ, kûru (wa) yo** 'Yeah, I am (coming).'

A to instructor: **Êe, B-sañ wa, kôñbañ kûru desyoo.** 'Yes, Mr/s. B is probably coming tonight.'

☠ WARNING: Your present level of proficiency requires that B-to-A direct-style responses use *only* the *affirmative imperfective*. The corresponding negative and perfective forms will be introduced in upcoming lessons.

---

13. Use only colors that are represented by adjectivals in Japanese.

B. Core Conversations: Substitution

Practice the Core Conversations, making appropriate substitutions. In particular, practice adjusting style (careful/casual, distal/direct, blunt/gentle) on the basis of the participants. Assign roles to members of the group that provide a variety of conversation partners.

SECTION B

Core Conversations

1(N) **Kimura-sañ ni deńwa kàketa?** (J) **Ñ. Kâketa kedo, rûsu datta.**

2(N)a. **Osóku nàtte, sumímasèñ.** (J)a. **Nâni ka âtta ñ desu ka⤸**

   b. **Hatî-zi ni utí o dèta ñ desu kedo; zîko de dêñsya ğa okúretà ñ desu.** b. **Zya, taíheñ dàtta desyoo.**

   c. **Êe. Sumímasèñ.**

3(N)a. **Toókyòo-eki made iʼtte kudasài.** (J)a. **Nihoñğo ozyóozu dèsu nêe. Nihôñ wa nağâi ñ desu ka⤸**

   b. **Iie. Asítà de, tyoodo rokú-syùukañ ni nâru ñ desu kedo . .** b. **Hêe⤸ Rokú-syùukañ? Rokú-syùukañ de, sońna ni zyoozù ni nâru ñ desu ka⤸**

   c. **Ie, mukôo de tyôtto beńkyoo-site kita ñ desu.** c. **Yaṕpàri nêe.**

4(N)a. **Kyôo wa, Mîyazi-sañ miémasèñ desita nêe. Gobyóoki nà ñ desyoo ka.** (J) **Ie, syuʼtyoo nà ñ desu yo.**

   b. **A, sôo desu ka.**

5(J)a. **Kâeru no?** (N)a. **Ñ. Osaki ni.**

   b. **Tyôtto hayâi ñ zya nai?** b. **Ñ. Yoózi ğa àru no.**

   c. **Zya, mata.**

ENGLISH EQUIVALENTS

1(N) Did you telephone Mr/s. Kimura? (J) Yeah. I called but s/he was out.

2(N)a. I'm sorry to be late. (J)a. Did something happen? (*lit.* Is it that there was something?)

   b. (The fact is that) I left home at 8:00, but (it's that) the train was delayed because of an accident. b. Then it must have been awful.

   c. Yes. I'm sorry.

3(N)a. Please go to Tokyo Station. (J)a. How good your Japanese is! Have you been in Japan long? (*lit.* Is it the case that Japan is long [for you]?)

b. No. (The fact is that) it will be exactly six weeks (being) tomorrow, but (that doesn't explain everything).

c. No, I studied a little abroad before coming. (*lit.* It's that I came having studied a bit over there.)

4(N)a. Today Mr/s. Miyaji didn't show up, did s/he. Would it be that s/he's sick?

b. Oh.

5(J)a. (Is it that) you're going home? [14]

b. Isn't it a little early?

c. See you! (*lit.* Well then, again.)

b. What? Six weeks! You mean you get to be that good in six weeks?

c. Oh, that explains it!

(J) No, (it's that) s/he's away on a business trip.

(N)a. Yeah. So long. (*lit.* [I'm leaving] ahead of you.)

b. Yeah. (It's that) I have something to attend to.

BREAKDOWNS
(AND SUPPLEMENTARY VOCABULARY)

1. **Kimura-sañ ni**	to Mr/s. Kimura
kakêru /-ru; kâkete/	suspend (something)
deñwa (o) kakèru *or*	
deñwa (o) suru *or*	
deñwa-suru	make a telephone call
kâketa (SP1)	/direct-style equivalent of **kakémàsita**/
rûsu	absence from home
rûsu datta (SP2)	/direct-style equivalent of **rûsu desita**/
2. **âtta**	/direct-style equivalent of **arímàsita**/
nâni ka âtta ñ da (SP3)	it's that there was something
dêru /-ru; dête/	go out, come out, leave
utí (o) dèru	leave home
dêta	/direct-style equivalent of **demâsita**/
dêta ñ da	it's that [I] left
zîko	accident
+**kâzi**	a fire
+**zisiñ**	earthquake
okureru /-ru; okurete/	become late or delayed
zîko de okureru	become late because of an accident
okureta	/direct-style equivalent of **okúremàsita**/

14. The form of this question suggests that (N) is making preparations to leave.

okúretà ñ da	it's that [it] became late or delayed
taiheñ /na/	terrible, dreadful, serious
taíheñ dàtta	/direct-style equivalent of **taíheñ dèsita**/
taíheñ dàtta desyoo	it was probably terrible
3. **zyoózù/ozyoozu /na/**	skillful, skilled
+ **hetâ /na/**	unskillful, poor at
naĝâi /-katta/	is long
+ **mizíkài /-katta/**	is short
naĝâi ñ da	it's that it's long
rokú-syùukañ ni nâru (SP4)	become six weeks, get to be six weeks
nâru ñ da	it's that [it] becomes
soñna ni (SP5)	to that extent; like that
zyoózù ni nâru	become skillful, become skilled
beñkyoo-suru (SP6)	study
kitâ	/direct-style equivalent of **kimâsita**/
kitâ ñ da	it's that [I] came
4. **Mîyazi**	(family name)
miêru /-ru; mîete/	appear, show up
(go)byooki	sick; sickness
(go)byoóki nà ñ da (SP3)	it's that [s/he] is sick
syuttyoo	business trip
syuĺtyoo nà ñ da	it's that it's a business trip
5. **kâeru no** (SP3)	a matter of going home
osaki ni	ahead /polite/
hayâi ñ da	it's that it's early *or* fast
hayâi ñ zya nai? (SP3)	isn't it the case that it's early *or* fast?
yoozi	things to do, business
yoózi ĝa àru no	a matter of there being things to do

MISCELLANEOUS NOTES

1. CC1 is a simple exchange between two individuals whose relationship permits the use of casual-style. It is unmarked for gender, although the participants on the accompanying video are both women.

Kimura-sañ ni: /person nominal X + **ni**/ linked to action verbal **kakêru** = 'to X,' similar to other 'goal' uses of **ni**.

Kakêru, a vowel verbal, is an operational verbal which may occur with /nominal + (o)/ phrases. Its basic meaning of 'suspend' or 'hang' extends from *hanging* pictures to *splashing* water, *sprinkling* sugar, *applying* brakes, and *telephoning* (suspending a conversation over wires).

2. CC2 is a typical conversation in the careful-style, marked by distal-style predicates

throughout. On the accompanying video, the participants are a foreign bank employee (N) and the office secretary (J).

Nâni ka 'something' occurred previously in **Hoká ni nàni ka?** and **Nâni ka arímàsu ka⟋** It will be analyzed in a later lesson.

Dêru 'emerge'; 'go out'; 'come out'; 'leave,' a vowel-verbal, is an operational verbal which occurs with /place nominal + (o)/ phrases indicating the place left (examples: **gaḱkoo (o) dèru** 'leave school' *or* 'graduate from school,' **kokó (o) dèru** 'leave here'). It also occurs in combination with **ni** phrases of goal, frequent in indicating attendance at an event: **zyûḡyoo ni dêru** 'go (out) to class,' **gakkoo ni dèru** 'go (out) to school,' **kâiḡi ni dèru** 'attend a conference'; but note also **deńwa ni dèru** 'answer the telephone'; and **kono miti wa Nâḡoya ni dêru** 'this road leads (*lit.* goes out) to Nagoya.' With **kara** phrases, there is special emphasis on the point of origin: **Toókyoo kara dèru** 'leave from Tokyo.' This verbal also covers the departure of trains and the publication ('coming out') of books.

Zîko, kâzi, zisiñ: Compare **koko ni kurúma ḡa arimàsita** 'there was a car here' and **koko de zîko ḡa arímàsita** 'there was an accident here.' The combination of /nominal implying activity + âru/ is also regarded as an expression of activity and requires a /place nominal + de/ phrase to express the location of the activity.

Okureru, a vowel-verbal, is an affective verbal: **tomodati ḡa okureru** 'my friend will be(come) delayed'; **siḡoto ḡa okureru** 'the work falls behind schedule.' **Okureru**, unlike **osoi**, regularly implies lateness or delay in meeting a fixed time. Note also: **kâiḡi *ni* okureru** 'be(come) late *for* a conference'; **zîp-puñ okureru** 'be(come) ten minutes late'; **okúrete dèru** 'leave late' (behind schedule).

Zîko de okureru 'become late, being [connected with]—i.e., because of—an accident.' In this pattern, **de** follows a nominal that indicates the reason or cause. Note also: **zîko ḡa âtte, okureru** 'become late, there having been an accident.'

Taiheñ is a **na**-nominal: **taíheñ na kàzi** 'a terrible fire'; **taiheñ na siḡoto** 'demanding work.' It also occurs linked to a predicate without a following particle as an indication of degree/manner—in this case, 'very,' 'extremely,' 'awfully,' without negative connotations: **taiheñ tiḡau** 'be very different'; **taíheñ omosiròi** 'is a lot of fun.'

3. CC3 is a dialogue that frequently occurs in taxicabs when foreigners speak Japanese. As it becomes less surprising for Japanese to hear their language spoken by foreigners, this kind of conversation is becoming less typical, but it will undoubtedly continue for a considerable length of time at least in the rural areas, even if not in Tokyo.

Zyoózù da is an affective, double-**ḡa** predicate: both the person who is skilled and the area of skill are followed by **ḡa/wa**; and **zyoózù** is a **na**-nominal: **eéḡo ḡa/wa zyoozù da** 'his/her English is good'; **tomódati ḡa zyoozù da** 'my friend is good at [it]'; **zyoózù na eeḡo** 'good English'; **zyoózù na tomodati** 'a skillful friend.'

The reference to skill in CC3 is polite encouragement for the foreigner trying to handle Japanese: with no follow-up comment, it usually means little more than that. However, with amplification, it can be taken as a genuine compliment. One common form that genuine compliments take is reference to long residence in Japan, reflecting the commonly held—though often mistaken—assumption that this is the only road to any significant level of proficiency.

Naḡâi, and its opposite **mizíkài**, refer both to space and time: **naḡâi miti** 'a long road'; **nâḡâku kakâru** 'take long'; **mizîkàku suru** 'shorten' (*lit.* 'make short').

Asítà de: when it *actually is* tomorrow, it will be exactly six weeks. Similarly, **rokú-syùukañ de**: when it *actually is* six weeks, one gets to be proficient (cf. 8A-SP5).

Mukoo, besides referring to space 'beyond' a particular point (**êki no mukoo** 'beyond the station'), may also refer to space 'over there' in the sense of 'abroad.'

4. CC4 is a typical office dialogue between two colleagues using careful-style with distal-style predicates. On the accompanying video, Mr. Yamada and Ms. Miller are the participants.

5. CC5 is a casual-style conversation. The video setting is a graduate seminar room, with two students the participants. All utterances either are fragments or end with direct-style predicates. In the speech of the foreigner, the occurrence of **âru no** in statement-final position without a following **da** is more typical of gentle-style. On the accompanying video, (N) is a woman.

Osaki is a polite equivalent of **saki** 'up ahead' (6A), used here in a time sense. **Osaki ni** occurs commonly in two types of situations: (1) as an apology by the speaker for his/her own going/leaving ahead of the person(s) addressed (the usage here); and (2) as an invitation to the addressee to go ahead of the speaker; in this usage, the utterance usually includes **dôozo**.

Zyâa, mata is a commonly occurring, informal 'so long!' 'see you!'

Structural Patterns

1. VERBALS: DIRECT-STYLE, PERFECTIVE, AFFIRMATIVE

In Section A (SP1), we learned the citation (dictionary) form of verbals, which turned out to be the direct-style imperfective affirmative. Example: **tabê-ru** '[I] do eat *or* will eat.' We now add the perfective equivalent. The pattern for the perfective is /verbal root + perfective ending **-ta**/. For vowel-verbals, whose roots end in **i** or **e**, this pattern presents no phonological problems. Examples: **mî-ta** '[I] looked at'; **tâbe-ta** '[I] ate.' However, when we add **-ta** to consonant-verbal roots (which always end in consonants), except for verbals like **mât-ta**, the consonant combinations that result are combinations that do not occur in Japanese. Adjustments are made on the basis of the particular consonant at the end of the root: THE SAME ADJUSTMENT IS MADE FOR ALL ROOTS ENDING WITH THAT CONSONANT. This means that as long as we know the perfective of one sample verbal for each consonant, we can handle the forms of all verbals in the language from now on! Actually, we know a great many of these adjustments already, because THE PERFECTIVE IS IDENTICAL WITH THE GERUND EXCEPT FOR THE FINAL VOWEL.

The consonants which may occur at the end of a consonant verbal root are: **t, r, w, s, k, g, m, b, n**. Of these, we have already encountered examples of all except **g** and **n**. Samples of these will occur in later lessons. By selecting a sample for each consonant and memorizing that sample, we have a model for general usage.

	Imperfective	*Perfective*			*Gerund*
t	mât-u			mât-ta	mât-te
r	wakâr-u	*wakâr-ta	>	wakât-ta	wakât-te
w	ka(w)-u	*kaw-ta	>	kat-ta	kat-te
s	-màs-u	*-mâs-ta	>	-màsi-ta	-màsi-te
k	kâk-u	*kâk-ta	>	kâi-ta	kâi-te
m	nôm-u	*nôm-ta	>	nôñ-da	nôñ-de
b	yob-u	*yob-ta	>	yoñ-da	yoñ-de

Note the following points:

(1) **-màs-u** serves as a general model for /s/ verbals, but it occurs only as the distal-style marker in distal-style compounds: /verbal stem + **-màs-u**/ (cf. A-SP1). The gerund of **-màs-u**, **-màsi-te**, has occurred thus far only in **dôo itasimasite**; it will be discussed further in later lessons.

(2) Given the imperfective, the perfective can always be predicted, but the reverse is not true. For example, **katta** might be the perfective of **kau** or **karu** or **katu**; actually, all three verbals exist (although with different accent).

(3) Some perfectives and gerunds end in **-da** and **-de** instead of the more usual **-ta** and **-te**.

(4) One otherwise regular consonant verbal has irregular perfective and gerund forms: **iku** 'go' > **itta, itte**. All other /k/ verbals follow the pattern of **kâku** above, i.e., **kâku** > **kâita**, **kiku** > **kiita**, **arûku** > **arûita**, etc.

The perfectives of the special polite verbals in **-àru** follow the same pattern as **wakâr-u** above, except that there are alternate forms for some of the five verbals.

irássyàr-u: (*irássyàr-ta) > **irássyàt-ta** *or*   **irássyàt-te** *or*
                               irâsi-ta   **irâsi-te**

kudásàr-u: (*kudásàr-ta) > **kudásàt-ta** *or*   **kudásàt-te** *or*
                               kudásùt-ta   **kudásùt-te**

While we can derive corresponding forms for **gozâru** (i.e., **gozâtta** and **gozâtte**), in actual fact **gozâru** occurs only in distal-style **-màsu** compounds.

The two irregular verbals form their perfectives and gerunds on the basis of the **ki** and **si** alternates of their roots: **ki-tâ, si-ta**.

The following chart is a summary of the perfective and gerund models covered thus far:

	Imperfective	*Perfective*	*Gerund*
Vowel Verbals			
e	**tabêru**	**tâbeta**	**tâbete**
i	**mîru**	**mîta**	**mîte**
Consonant Verbals			
t	**mâtu**	**mâtta**	**mâtte**
r	**wakâru**	**wakâtta**	**wakâtte**
w	**kau**	**katta**	**katte**
s	**-màsu**	**-màsita**	**-màsite**
k	**kâku** *but*	**kâita**	**kâite**
	iku	**itta**	**itte**
m	**nômu**	**nôñda**	**nôñde**
b	**yobu**	**yoñda**	**yoñde**
Special Polite Verbals			
	irássyàru	**irássyàtta** *or*	**irássyàtte**
		irâsita	**irâsite**
	kudásàru	**kudásàtta** *or*	**kudásàtte**
		kudásùtta	**kudásùtte**
	(*gozâru)	(*gozâtta)	(*gozâtte)

Irregular Verbals

kûru	kitâ	kitê
suru	sita	site

Accent: The accentuation of the perfective is parallel to that of the stem and of the gerund. As usual, a whispered syllable may cause an accent shift.

The uses of the direct-style verbal perfective parallel exactly the uses of the direct-style imperfective (cf. A-SP1, SP6). In some cases the form occurs as a direct-style predicate; but when it combines with **desyòo**, the combination is identified as a distal-style perfective tentative. Examples:

Wakâtta desyoo. '[S/he] probably understood.'

Káttà desyo(o)? 'I assume you bought it, didn't you?'

The verbal gerund and its uses introduced thus far were discussed in 4A-SP6, 7A-SP2, SP3, 7B-SP5, and 8A-SP5.

Before proceeding to the next note, test your ability to produce direct-style perfectives and gerunds by working with the following unfamiliar verbals. You can check your results by consulting the vocabulary list at the end of the book. *All items are consonant verbals.*

Dictionary entry	How would you say
hâiru 'enter'	Please come in.
yamu 'cease'	It probably stopped (raining).
hanâsu 'talk'	[He] probably talked.
narabu 'line up'	Please line up.
naku 'cry'	[She] probably cried.
warau 'laugh'	[She] probably laughed.
osu 'push'	Please push.
hiku 'pull'	Please pull.
môtu 'take hold'	Please take hold of [this].
noru 'board'	[He] probably boarded.

Question: Which, if any, of the above verbals would you not have recognized as necessarily being a consonant verbal by its form?

Hereafter, all new verbals will be listed in the Breakdowns in their citation form with identification of their subclass (**-ru** = vowel verbal; **-u** = consonant verbal; **-aru** = special polite verbal) and their direct-style perfective, following the already established procedure for adjectivals. Example: **kakêru /-ru; kâketa/.**

2. dàtta

The perfective of direct-style **dà** is **dàtta**, accented unless the preceding word or phrase is accented. Like **dà**, **dàtta** occurs only following nominals or phrase-particles, never following an adjectival. Thus:

Zîko datta. 'It was an accident.'

Sâñ-zi kara datta. 'It was from 3 o'clock on.'

Examining the three direct-style perfective predicate types, we find:

kat-ta '[I] bought it' (verbal root + **-ta**)

oísì-katta '[it] was delicious' (adjectival root + **-katta**)

damê datta '[it] was no good' (nominal + **dàtta**)

Perfective verbals become distal-style by forming a compound of /verbal stem + **-màs-** + verbal ending **-ta**/, resulting in a form ending in **-màsita**.

Perfective adjectivals add **dèsu** to form the distal-style **oísìkatta desu**. (An alternate, newer form in **-i desita** has already been discussed [cf. 1B-SP1].)

The distal-style perfective of nominal predicates is derived from the distal-style imperfective: **dèsu** > **dèsita**.

Using the examples cited above, the derivation of the perfective distal-style can be shown thus:

kau + distal **-màs** > **kaímàsu** + perfective **-ta-** > **kaímàsita**

oisii + perfective **-katta** > **oísìkatta** + distal **dèsu** > **oísìkatta desu**

damê da + distal **dèsu** > (*damê da desu) + deletion of **dà** > **damê desu** + perfective **-ta** > **damê desita**

The distal-style perfective tentative, on the other hand, results from the addition of **desyòo** to all three direct-style predicate types:

kattà desyoo '[s/he] probably bought it'

oísìkatta desyoo '[it] was probably delicious'

damê datta desyoo '[it] was probably no good'

For some adult foreign-language students, detailed explanations like the one just given are not only helpful but essential. For others, anything that even remotely suggests grammar is so frightening that they resist before they even try to understand. Each student must devise his/her own best method of learning, but the goal for everyone is accurate control of the foreign language. Usually that goal is achieved most efficiently if the student is familiar with the system that underlies every language. But for everyone—even those students who thoroughly enjoy analysis as analysis—the actual practice of the patterns requires much more time and effort in order to be able to *use* the language with facility. Remember that systematic foreign-language learning involves *fact* and *act,* in a ratio of '1 : beyond measure.'

3. THE EXTENDED PREDICATE

In 7B-SP4, we encountered the adjectival *extended predicate* pattern:

abúnài ñ desu 'it's that it's dangerous'

ikítài ñ desu 'it's that I want to go'

The pattern was explained as one that relates what the speaker is saying to something in the real world that is assumed to be known by the person addressed as well. This notion of shared information—together with its implications—is very important. When used appropriately, the extended predicate can create a feeling of closeness, empathy, understanding, and warmth; but in some contexts, it is totally inappropriate to create such impressions. The speaker must always be concerned as to (1) whether there is in fact shared information; and (2) whether it is proper to acknowledge it openly.

Consider this example: You are at the airport meeting a Japanese dignitary who is arriving after a fourteen-hour flight. To make some comment about the fact that he must be tired would of course be appropriate. But what would the implication be if you used an extended predicate and asked a question meaning 'Is it that you are tired?'—i.e., that you look the way you do—droopy, dragging, worn out. This would be an occasion to stay away from the extended predicate.

However, to avoid the construction at all times is not only *not* a safe and easy way out; in some contexts, it is absolutely wrong. In other words, when the context itself openly creates shared information, the extended predicate must be used.

Returning to the two examples cited above, we note that the /**n̄ desu**/ is preceded by *direct-style* adjectivals. We should immediately suspect that the pattern can be extended to include direct-style verbal and nominal predicates, as well.

The Core Conversations of this lesson provide a number of examples:[15]

	CC2	CC3
Verbals	**âtta n̄ desu**	**nâru n̄ desu**
	dêta n̄ desu	**kitâ n̄ desu**
	okúretà n̄ desu	

Accent: An unaccented verbal acquires an accent on its final syllable preceding **n̄**.

Nominal predicates: For the nominal predicate within the extended predicate, we find that once again the **dà** form shows its instability: in this case, it does not disappear, but rather assumes the special form **nà**, accented following an unaccented word or phrase. Previously we encountered this form only following a **na**-nominal and preceding another nominal (examples: **kîree na uti** 'a pretty house,' **hûben na tosyôkan̄** 'an inconvenient library'). In the extended predicate, /nominal predicate X **dà** + **n̄ desu**/ > /X **nâ n̄ desu**/, regardless of whether **X** is a **na**-nominal or not. Thus:

Kîree na n̄ desu. 'It's that [she]'s pretty.'[16]

Señsèe na n̄ desu. 'It's that [s/he]'s a doctor.'

And again, **dàtta** is stable and unchanging.

Kâzi datta n̄ desu. 'It's that it was a fire.'

The negative equivalents for adjectival and nominal predicates[17] are both adjectival patterns that include **nâi** or **nâkatta**:

Oísiku nài n̄ desu. 'It's that it's not tasty.'

Rakû zya nâi n̄ desu. 'It's that it's not comfortable.'

Zisín zya nàkatta n̄ desu. 'It's that it wasn't an earthquake.'

In 7B-SP4 we learned that tentative equivalents of distal-style extended predicates are formed by changing final **desu** to **desyoo**:

Okúretà n̄ desyoo. 'It's probably that [s/he] was delayed.'

Byoóki dàtta n̄ desyoo. 'It's probably that [s/he] was sick.'

The extended predicate also has a direct-style equivalent, which involves the substitution of **dà** for final **dèsu**:

âru n̄ desu > âru n̄ da

However, this form is more typical of blunt-style speech, except when followed by the

15. For the meanings, check back to the English Equivalents of the Core Conversations.

16. In these glosses, 'it' refers to the related circumstances or item of shared information with which the following is being connected.

17. Note that verbal negative extended predicates have not been covered, because direct-style verbal negatives have not yet been introduced.

feminine sentence-particle /**wa**⤹/. It is particularly marked as blunt when it occurs in final position in a sentence or pre-final before **yo**. *In that position,* gentle-style speech is marked by the dropping of the unstable **dà** and the replacement of **ñ** by its uncontracted equivalent **no**. Thus:

> **ikû ñ da (yo).** /blunt/
>
> **ikû no (yo).** /gentle/

These forms are marked as typically 'blunt' or 'gentle,' but not as strictly 'masculine' or 'feminine.' The **no** alternative with question intonation occurs commonly in direct-style extended predicate questions (cf. CC5).

Direct-style	Distal-style
Kâeru no?	**Kâeru ñ desu ka**⤹

While this direct-style pattern is classified as 'gentle' (i.e., empathetic, soft, and more typical of female speech), it is also used by men, particularly when talking familiarly to women and children.

Compare now the following pair:

> a. **Yôku nâi no?**
>
> b. **Îi ñ zya nai?**

In (a), the negation applies to the initial adjectival of the extended predicate pattern: 'Is it the case that it's not good?' 'Do you mean it's not good?' In (b), it is the **ñ da** ending of the extended predicate that has been negated, with a loss of accent on **nâi**: 'Isn't it the case that it's good?' (i.e., I think it is good: am I wrong?) While the (a) type of negation occurs in all kinds of patterns, the (b) type occurs typically in questions (which may, of course, be distal-style, as well).

It is important to distinguish the various kinds of question-final **no** that have been introduced. There are some ambiguous patterns, but most occurrences can be identified by the word-classes involved. Compare:

Direct-style	*Distal-style*	
(1) **Señsèe?**	**Señsèe desu ka**⤹	'Is s/he a teacher?'
(2) **Señsèe no?**	**Señsèe no desu ka**⤹	'Is it the teacher's (one)?'
(3) **Señsèe na no?**	**Señsèe na ñ desu ka**⤹	'Is it that s/he's a teacher?'
(4) **Señsèe no na no?**	**Señsèe no na ñ desu ka**⤹	'Is it that it's the teacher's (one)?'
(5) **Hurûi?**	**Hurûi desu ka**⤹	'Is it old?'
(6) **Hurûi no?**	**Hurûi no desu ka**⤹	'Is it an old one?'
(7) **Hurûi no?**	**Hurûi ñ desu ka**⤹	'Is it that it's old?'
(8) **Hurûi no na no?**	**Hurûi no na ñ desu ka**⤹	'Is it that it's an old one?'

Basically, the extended predicate entails the adding on to a predicate of either /**ñ** + some form of **dà** or **dèsu**/, or **no** (sentence-final); and before this **ñ/no**, **dà** becomes **nà**. In (2) above, **no** = the contraction of connective **no** + nominal **no** 'one,' filling both functions; the first **no** of (4) is the same; in (6), **no** = nominal 'one,' and the first **no** of (8) is the same; all other **no** are the **no/ñ** of the extended predicate. In (6) and (7), there is ambiguity in the two direct-style patterns: these can be distinguished only by context. It must also be pointed out that in rapid speech, *all* **no** before **dà/dèsu** are subject to contraction to **ñ**, whereas in written Japanese, **ñ** is apt to be regularly replaced by **no**, creating some additional cases of ambiguity, but making it all the more important to understand the underlying patterns and word-classes involved.

*4. /NOMINAL + **ni** + **nâru**/: **zyoózù ni nâru** 'BECOME SKILLED/SKILLFUL'*

/Nominal X + **ni** + **nâru**/ = 'become X'
This use of **ni** is obviously related to the 'goal' function already seen in patterns like **Tookyoo ni iku** 'go to Tokyo' and **Kimura-sañ ni deńwa (o) kakèru** 'telephone (to) Mr/s. Kimura.' In other words, this is another example of **ni** identifying the preceding nominal as the final location or state. Points to note:

    1. /**X ni nâru**/ 'become X' is never interrupted by other phrases.

    2. /**X ni nâru**/ contrasts with /**X-ku nâru**/ only on the basis of the word-class to which the goal expression X belongs: **damê ni nâru** 'become no good' (**damê** = nominal); **yôku nâru** 'become good' (**yôku** < **îi/yôi** = adjectival)

*5. **soñna ni** 'TO THAT EXTENT'*

The /**koñna, soñna, añna, dôñna**/ series was originally discussed in 4B-SP3. Until now, it has occurred only immediately preceding a nominal: **koñna uti** 'this kind of home.' The **koñna** series can also occur before the particle **ni**; the phrase links up with a predicate: /**koñna ni** + predicate X/ = 'X to this degree,' 'X like this.' Examples:

    Koñna ni hetà na ñ desu ka⁻ 'Is it that [they]'re *this* incapable?'

    Soñna ni omosiròi ñ desu ka⁻ 'Is it that [it]'s *that* amusing?'

    Añna ni hùbeñ na ñ desu ka⁻ 'Is it that [it]'s *that* inconvenient?'

    Dôñna ni wakâru ñ desu ka⁻ 'To what degree is it [he] understands?'

The **koñna** and **kono** series are different in many respects, as demonstrated by the following chart.

	Koñna-*Series*	**Kono**-*Series*
Pronunciation	3 mora; final vowel *a*	2 mora; final vowel *o*
Meaning	'this/that kind'	'this/that'
Word-class	Nominal—special subclass*	Pre-nominal
Structural Patterns	(1) Pre-nominal† (2) + **ni**	Pre-nominal only

*Cf. 6A-SP4. Given the patterns in which the **koñna** series occurs, its members must be classified as a special subclass of nominals. Their special feature is their occurrence immediately before nominals, without an intervening particle.
†**Koñna**-nominals also sometimes occur immediately preceding **dèsu**.

*6. VERBAL COMPOUNDS IN -suru: **beñkyoo-suru** 'STUDY'*

Words borrowed into Japanese from foreign languages have traditionally joined the Japanese nominal class. In forming a verbal from such nominals, the regular procedure has been to combine them with **suru** 'do' to form a compound verbal, inflected like **suru** alone. To cite a recent example, English 'knock' > Japanese **nokku** (a nominal) > **nokku-suru** (a verbal).

In an earlier period, the Japanese acquired countless such verbals based on Chinese roots. A high proportion of such items in a Japanese language sample is an indication of a more learned level of language. (Compare English characterized by vocabulary based on borrowed Latin and Greek roots as opposed to native Germanic roots: 'comprehend' as compared with 'understand,' 'proximity' or 'propinquity' as compared with 'nearness.')

Beñkyoo 'study' is a nominal based on borrowed Chinese roots. The derivative compound verbal is **beñkyoo-suru,** an operational verbal which occurs with /nominal + (o)/ phrases indicating the thing studied. Note also: **syuttyoo-suru** 'go away on business'; and **zyuḡyoo-suru** 'teach classes,' 'give lessons.'

In addition to such compounds, there are also /nominal + (o) + **suru**/ phrases, many of which are based on nominals of native Japanese origin, and some of borrowed origin. In fact, some phrases exist side by side with a corresponding compound. Compare:

(1) **Nihóñḡo (o) beñkyoo-simàsita.**   'I studied Japanese.'

(2) **Nihóñḡo no beñkyoo (o) simàsita.**   'I made a study of Japanese.'

In some contexts it is impossible to decide whether an occurrence of /nominal + **suru**/ represents /nominal-**suru**/ or /nominal (o) **suru**/ with the **o** deleted. If there is no clear evidence requiring analysis as '**o**-deletion' (as there is in [2] above), we will assume a **suru**-compound.

Drills

A 1. **Deñwa kâketa?**
'Did you telephone?'

  Ñ. Kâketa yoↄ
  Ñ. Kâketa wa yoↄ /F/
  'Yeah. I telephoned.'

2. **Nîsida-kuñ 'yoñda?**
'Did you call Nishida?'

  Ñ. Yoñda yoↄ
  Ñ. Yoñdà wa yoↄ /F/
  'Yeah. I called him.'

3. **siḡoto 'yameta**; 4. **Kyôoto de 'tomatta**; 5. **tîzu kâita**; 6. **ano kuruma mîta**; 7. **otya âtta**; 8. **Sâtoo-kuñ 'ita**; 9. **deñwa ni dêta**

B 1. **Isóḡasìi?**
'Are you busy?'

  Ñ. Kinôo mo isóḡasìkatta kedo . .
  'Yeah. I was busy yesterday, too, but . . .'
  (why do you ask?)

2. **Rûsu?**
'Is [he] out?'

  Ñ. Kinôo mo rûsu datta kedo . .
  'Yeah. [He] was out yesterday, too, but . . .'
  (why do you ask?)

3. **hayâi**; 4. **yasúmì (da)**; 5. **byoóiñ (dà)**; 6. **mazûi**; 7. **muzukasii**; 8. **kâiḡi (da)**

C 1. **Nakamura-kuñ wa kimásèñ desita neↃ**
'Nakamura didn't come—right?'

  Kitâ desyoo?
  'He came, didn't he?'

2. **Yamamoto-sañ wa rûsu zya arímasèñ desita neↃ**
'Mr/s. Yamamoto wasn't out—right?'

  Rûsu datta desyoo?
  'S/he was out, wasn't s/he?'

3. **tomodati/deñwa-simásèñ desita**; 4. **gakusee/kaérimasèñ desita**; 5. **hôñya-sañ/ komárimasèñ desita**; 6. **ano ryokañ/rakû zya arímasèñ desita**; 7. **ano miti/abúnaku arimasèñ desita**

D 1. **Kêsa hâyaku utí o demàsita yo**   **Nań-zi-ġòro dêta ń desu ka**
    'I left home early this morning.'   'About what time is it you left?'

   2. **Kôñbañ seńsèe no otaku ni deńwa o kakemàsu yo**   **Nań-zi-ġòro kakêru ń desu ka**
    'I'll call the doctor's home this evening.'   'About what time is it you'll call?'

   3. **Nîsida-kuñ wa kinóo kaerimàsita;** 4. **ano gakusee wa asíta no àsa kimàsu;** 5. **asâtte anó kuruma o mimàsu;** 6. **kinóo no àsa anó kàdo de zîko ġa arímàsita;** 7. **asíta no àsa kuúkoo e ikimàsu**

E 1. **Oísii osake o nomimàsita yo**   **Dôko de nôñda ń desu ka**
    'I drank some delicious wine.'   'Where is it you drank it?'

   2. **Atárasìi tokee o kaímàsu yo**   **Dôko de kaû ń desu ka**
    'I'm going to buy a new watch.'   'Where is it you're going to buy it?'

   3. **anó ryokañ màde no miti o kikímàsita;** 4. **rosíaġo o osiemàsu;** 5. **Oósutorària no wâiñ o kaímàsita;** 6. **gôġo kara tênisu o simâsu;** 7. **Mêezi no zîsyo o mimâsita;** 8. **oókìi kâzi ġa arímàsita**

F 1. **Anó señsèe wa Nakámura-señsèe desu yo**   **Âa, Nakámura-señsèe na ń desu ka.**
    'That doctor is Dr. Nakamura.'   'Oh, you mean that's Dr. Nakamura.'

   2. **Anó kàiġi wa doyôobi desita yo**   **Âa, doyôobi datta ń desu ka.**
    'That conference was Saturday.'   'Oh, you mean it was Saturday.'

   3. **ano gakusee/Tanáka-kuñ dèsu;** 4. **kimi/raísyuu dèsu;** 5. **anó hòñ/Taísyoo dèsu;** 6. **yasúmì/râiġetu made desu;** 7. **ano zisiñ/Nâġoya desita;** 8. **anó koñpyùutaa/daíġaku nò desu;** 9. **anó zyùġyoo/kyuú-syùukañ desita**

G 1. **Tuġî no yasumi, mizíkài desyoo?**   **A, mizíkài ń desu ka**
    'The next vacation is short, isn't it?'   'Oh, you mean it's short?'

   2. **Otótoi no kàiġi, nâġâkatta desyoo?**   **A, nâġâkatta ń desu ka**
    'The conference the day before yesterday was long, wasn't it?'   'Oh, you mean it was long?'

   3. **ano ryokañ/rakû zya nâi;** 4. **ano miti/abunai;** 5. **Kimura-kuñ/rûsu zya nâkatta;** 6. **okaeri/osoi**

H 1. **Îma kâeru yo**   **A, kâeru no?**
    'I'm going home now.'   'Oh, (is it that) you're going home?'

   2. **Byoóki dà yo.**   **A, byoóki nà no?**
    'I'm sick.'   'Oh, (is it that) you're sick?'

   3. **kôñbañ mo miêru;** 4. **deńwa ni dèta;** 5. **kâiġi naġâi;** 6. **rûsu datta;** 7. **yoózi àru;** 8. **taíheñ dà;** 9. **zisíñ dàtta;** 10. **ano miti abúnàkatta;** 11. **Kimura-kuñ syuťtyoo dà;** 12. **mizîkàku nâi**

I 1. **Kotosi no yasumi, naġâi?**   **Mizíkài ń zya nai?**

'Is this year's vacation long?' | 'Isn't it the case that it's short?'

2. **Ano deñsya, hayâi?** | **Osôi ñ zya nai?**
'Is that train fast?' | 'Isn't it the case that it's slow?'

3. **sonó hòñ/omósiròi**; 4. **seńsèe no kuruma/atárasìi**; 5. **koñna siḡoto/muzukasìi**;
6. **tugî no kâiḡi/naḡâi**

J 1. **Zîko ḡa âtta ñ desu ka⌒** | **Êe. Zîko de ití-zikañ-hodo okuretà ñ**
'(Is it that) there was an accident?' | **desu yo⌒**
| 'Yes. (The fact is) I was about one hour
| late because of the accident.'

2. **Zisíñ ḡa àtta ñ desu ka⌒** | **Êe. Zisiñ de ití-zikañ-hodo okuretà ñ**
'(Is it that) there was an earthquake?' | **desu yo⌒**
| 'Yes. (The fact is that) I was about one
| hour late because of the earthquake.'

3. **kâiḡi**; 4. **kâzi**; 5. **zyûḡyoo**; 6. **siḡoto**; 7. **yoozi**; 8. **deñwa**

K 1. **Taiheñ desyoo?** | **Êe. Taíheñ ni narimàsita ne!**
'It's awful, isn't it?' | 'Yes. It's become awful, hasn't it.'

2. **Rok̆-kàḡetu desyoo?** | **Êe. Rok̆-kàḡetu ni narímàsita ne!**
'It's six months, isn't it?' | 'Yes. It's come to six months, hasn't it.'

3. **hûbeñ**; 4. **kîree**; 5. **rakû**; 6. **onazi**; 7. **tosyôsitu**; 8. **bêñri**; 9. **mîdori**; 10. **yukî**

L 1. **Koósyuudèñwa wa, mâe desu neʃ** | **Êe. Kyôneñ made wa usíro dàtta kedo;**
'The public phone is in front, isn't it?' | **mâe ni narímàsita ne!**
| "Yes. Until last year it was in back, but
| [now] it's in front' (*lit.* became in front,
| didn't it).

2. **Końna zitèñsya wa, takâi desu neʃ** | **Êe. Kyôneñ made wa yâsûkatta kedo;**
'This kind of bicycle is expensive, isn't | **tâkâku narímàsita ne!**
it?' | 'Yes. Until last year it was cheap, but [now]
| it's expensive' (*lit.* became expensive, didn't
| it).

3. **Kâataa-sañ no nihoñḡo/ozyoozu**; 4. **baiteñ/urâ**; 5. **konó daiḡaku no yasumì/**
mizíkài; 6. **eéḡo no zyùḡyoo/omósiròi**; 7. **konó hòteru/bêñri**; 8. **tikâ no kissateñ/**
oisii

M 1. **Yo-néñ-màe kara konó ryoozìkañ** | **Êe. Kotosi de yonéñ ni nàru ñ desu nêe.**
desu ka⌒ | 'Yes. (It's that) it comes to four years
'Have you been in this consulate for | (being) this year, doesn't it!'
the last four years?' (*lit.* Is it this
consulate from four years ago?)

2. **Haś-syuukañ-màe kara konó siḡoto** | **Êe. Koñsyuu de haś-syùukañ ni nâru ñ**
dèsu ka⌒ | **desu nêe.**

'Have you been [doing] this work for the last eight weeks?'

'Yes. (It's that) it comes to eight weeks (being) this week, doesn't it!'

3. **rok̀-kàǧetu/nihoñǧo no beñkyoo**; 4. **too-ka/byooiñ**; 5. **kokóno-kà/syuttyoo**

N 1. **Nâǧoya made zûibuñ kakárimàsu yo‿ Yozíkañ-ǧùrai desu ka nêe.**
'It takes a long time to Nagoya. I wonder if it's about four hours!'

    A. Soǹna ni kakàru ñ desu ka.
'Oh. You mean it takes that long (*lit.* to that extent)?'

2. **Êki de zûibuñ matímàsita yo‿ Nizíkan-hodo dèsita ka nêe.**
'I waited a long time at the station. I wonder if it was about as much as two hours.'

    A. Soǹna ni màtta ñ desu ka.
'Oh. You mean you waited that long?'

3. **nâǧaku beñkyoo-simàsita/roku-neñ-hodo**; 4. **zûibuñ tiǧáimàsu/itimañ-eñ-hodo**;
5. **zûibuñ hûbeñ desu/kokó karà wa ití-zikañ-ǧùrai**

O 1. **Dâre ǧa eéǧo ǧa zyoozù desyoo ka.**
'Who do you suppose is good in English?'

    Tanáka-sañ dèsu. Tanáka-sañ ǧa zyoozù desu yo‿
'It's Mr/s. Tanaka. *Mr/s. Tanaka* is good.'

2. **Dâre ǧa huráñsuǧo ǧa wakàru desyoo ka.**
'Who do you suppose understands French?'

    Tanáka-sañ dèsu. Tanáka-sañ ǧa wakarimàsu yo‿
'It's Mr/s. Tanaka. *Mr/s. Tanaka* understands.'

3. **zîsyo/iru**; 4. **doituǧo/dekîru**; 5. **rosiaǧo/hetâ (da)**; 6. **eéǧo/damê (da)**; 7. **nihoñǧo/kîree (da)**; 8. **siǧoto/hayâi**

P 1. **Yamamoto-sañ wa, eéǧo ǧa wakarimàsu ne˞**
'Mr/s. Yamamoto understands *English*, doesn't s/he?'

    Eéǧo wa wakarimasèñ kedo, huráñsuǧo ǧa wakàru ñ desu yo‿
'English—no, (but) it's French s/he understands.'

2. **Yamamoto-sañ wa, eéǧo ǧa zyoozù desu ne˞**
'Mr/s. Yamamoto is good *in English*, isn't s/he?'

    Eéǧo wa zyoozù zya arímasèñ kedo, huráñsuǧo ǧa zyoozù na ñ desu yo‿
'English—no; (but) it's French s/he's good at.'

3. **dekímàsu**; 4. **hetâ desu**; 5. **damê desu**; 6. **kîree desu**

Q 1. **Eeǧo wa, Yamámoto-sañ ǧa wakarimàsu ne˞**
'It's Mr/s. Yamamoto who understands English—right?'

    Yamámoto-sañ wa wakarimasèñ kedo, Tanáka-sañ ǧa wakàru ñ desu yo‿
'Mr/s. Yamamoto—no; (but) it's Mr/s. Tanaka who understands.'

2. **Eeǧo wa, Yamámoto-sañ ǧa zyoozù desu ne˞**

    Yamámoto-sañ wa zyoozù zya arímasèñ kedo, Tanáka-sañ ǧa zyoozù na ñ desu yo‿

'It's Mr/s. Yamamoto who's good in
English—right?'

'Mr/s. Yamamoto—no, (but) it's Mr/s.
Tanaka who's good.'

3. **dekímàsu**; 4. **hetâ desu**; 5. **îi desu**

Application Exercises

A1. Practice complimenting various members of the group on their proficiency in foreign languages they have studied. Proceed with the conversations, finding out where and when they studied, for how long, etc. Be sure to use the extended predicate wherever appropriate, as well as expressions like **soñna ni, yáppàri, zyoózù, naḡâi, naruhodo, totemo**.

2. Make up sample weekly schedules for Mr/s. Tanaka and Dr. Miyaji. Ask specific questions about where one of them was on a particular day at a particular time. Answer in terms of the *probable* location, determined on the basis of the schedule. Be sure to include in the schedule only places that you can express in Japanese.

3. Repeat Application Exercise A3 of Section A of this lesson, adding items from the nominal class, to incorporate /**X ni nâru**/ patterns. For example, all the color nominals (**gurîiñ, gurêe,** etc.) can now be used.

4. Repeat Application Exercise A5 of Section A, incorporating questions about completed activities in order to practice the direct-style perfective. Include practice on the extended predicate in both the casual- and careful-style portions of the exchanges.

B. Core Conversations: Substitution

Practice the Core Conversations, making substitutions not only in the situations themselves but also in the conversation's participants, to the extent appropriate. Use a clear, unambiguous method to make roles obvious throughout the conversation. Extensive practice is needed in order to develop a constant awareness of the close connection between how one talks to various participants.

SECTION C

Eavesdropping

(Answer the following on the basis of the accompanying audiotape. A = the first speaker, B = the second speaker, in each conversation.)
1a. Who is being discussed?
  b. What is A's concern?
  c. What is the actual situation?
2a. What did A do yesterday?
  b. What was the problem?
  c. What explanation does B offer?
3a. Under what circumstances might this conversation occur?
  b. Describe what happens.
4a. Who is being discussed?
  b. What is A's comment about that person?
  c. What possible explanation does B offer?
  5. How does B describe the intersection under discussion? Why?

6a. Where is B apparently going to go?

 b. What is A's concern?

 c. How does B reassure A?

 7. How are this month's work and next month's distinguished?

8a. What does A ask B to do? Why?

 b. Why can't B comply?

 c. Contrast the speech styles of A and B.

9a. When will there be no conference?

 b. Why is B busy?

10a. Where is the conference being held this year?

 b. Where will it be held in the future?

 c. What participants of this year's conference are identified?

11a. What does A offer to do?

 b. How does B react to the offer?

 c. Where does A think Suzuki is?

 d. Where is Suzuki, actually?

 e. Comment on the relative ranks of A and B.

12a. Where is B going?

 b. How long will B be gone?

 c. What time will B return?

13a. What is being discussed?

 b. What is the situation at B's school?

 c. What is A's reaction?

14a. Where did B go yesterday? Why?

 b. Why does A say **yappàri**?

15a. Who answered the phone yesterday?

 b. Where did the call come from?

 c. What language was used?

 d. What comment does B make about that language?

16a. Who is busy? Until when?

 b. How long does the work take?

17a. What does A ask B about?

 b. What is described as 'too bad'?

 c. What advice and encouragement does A offer?

18a. How did B come here?

 b. Who was late?

 c. What was the reason? Give details.

 d. Describe and account for A's change in attitude.

19a. What happened yesterday? Where?

 b. How serious was it?

20a. What is B going to do? Starting when? Why?

 b. What is B's worry?

 c. What encouragement does A offer?

 d. What is B's reaction?

Utilization

(Remember: Provide an appropriate stimulus and/or response in addition to the utterance specifically described below. Unless there is indication to the contrary, use distal-style throughout.)

 1. You've been asked about a colleague. State (with a request for confirmation)[18] that he will

18. Use the **desyoo?** pattern.

(probably): show up soon; stop in Kyoto; ask the doctor; be here tomorrow, too; go home late; need a dictionary.

2. You've been asked about a colleague. State (with a request for confirmation)[18] that he (probably): telephoned the doctor; drew a map to his home; studied French in France; got sick; bought a new car; went home early; asked at the police box; became awfully upset; understood everything.

3. You've been asked to comment on a situation. State (with a request for confirmation)[18] that (probably) it's too bad; it was no good; it was dangerous; it's inconvenient; it tasted awful; it's pretty; it's true; it was comfortable; it's a pleasure; it was awful.

4. You've been asked when a colleague is returning from Kyoto. Explain that you're not sure, but he probably will be back by about 10:30 tomorrow morning.

5. You've just heard that there was an earthquake and your colleague was in the subway. Express sympathy by commenting that it must have been awful.

6. You've been asked if you can do this work right away. Explain that this month it's impossible, but next month it will probably be possible.

7. Find out when the next bullet train for Kyoto leaves.

8. Find out where the letter from Dr. Tanaka is.

9. Exclaim (expecting agreement) on how expensive cars have become.

10. Comment (expecting agreement) that the vacations here have become short.

11. Compliment Mr. Tanaka on how good his English has become.

12. You've been asked about the English competence of two Japanese employees in the office. Comment that Ms. Miyaji is very good but Ms. Nishida is poor.

13. You've been asked about driving from Tokyo to Kyoto. Warn that it takes long by car (at least).

14. Ask someone you've just met if she's been in Tokyo long.

15. A colleague has just commented on Mr. Suzuki's absence yesterday. Offer as an explanation: (it's) that he was sick; (it's) that he was away on business; (it's) that he had matters to attend to.

16. You've learned that your colleague telephoned Mr. Nakamura but he was out. Ask what time (it was that) he called.

17. Compliment a colleague on her French. Find out where (it is) she studied.

18. Apologize for being late. Explain that (it's that) there was an earthquake and the subway was delayed for half an hour.

19. The telephone is ringing. Ask a colleague if she'd be kind enough to answer. Explain that (it's that) your Japanese is poor.

20. You've just heard how long Mr. Yamamoto has been in Europe. Express your surprise by asking if (it's a fact that) it's that long.

21. A colleague has been transferred to Europe. Find out if that means he'll be there both this year and next year.

22. Tell a colleague that there was an accident at this intersection again this morning.

23. You've been asked if you're busy. Answer that you aren't, particularly.

24. (Among close friends):[19] State that: you're going home early today; you'll be away on business starting tomorrow; you were 30 minutes late because of an accident.

25. (Among close friends):[19] You've been asked to identify someone at the other end of the room. Explain that it's Dr. Miyaji, and he's the new Japanese language teacher.

26. (Among close friends):[19] A friend has just commented on some delicious wine. Ask where (it is) he bought it.

27. (Among close male friends): Attract Tanaka's attention by calling his name. Tell him you'll be on vacation next week. What about him?

28. (Among close friends): [19] Ask Ms. Yamamoto if she's busy tonight.

29. You're going home before your colleagues. What would you say?

19. Use blunt or gentle style, as appropriate.

30. You and your teacher have arrived at a doorway at the same moment. What would you do and say?

31. You've just heard something completely reasonable to your way of thinking; in fact, you might have expected this in view of what you know. What would you say?

Check-up

1. What is the difference between **wakâru** and **wakárimàsu**? (A-SP1)

2. The form *wakâru* consists of /root **wakar-** + ending **-u**/. What is **wakárimàsu** made up of? (A-SP1)

3. We speak of four verbal classes in Japanese: vowel verbals, consonant verbals, special polite verbals, and irregular verbals. Describe each class. (A-SP1)

4. Given only the citation (dictionary) form of a verbal, is it always possible to derive its other forms? If not, under what circumstances is it impossible? (A-SP1)

5. Given the citation form of a verbal, how is the perfective formed? (Include all four verbal classes.) (B-SP1)

6. What is the difference between **wakâtta** and **wakárimàsita**? How are the two forms analyzed? (cf. 2, above) (B-SP1)

7. Given only the perfective or gerund of a verbal, is it always possible to know what the citation form (i.e., the imperfective form) is? Explain. (B-SP1)

8. How is the gerund of a verbal formed, given the perfective, or vice versa? (B-SP1)

9. What is **dà** and what may it follow? What is its perfective equivalent? (A-SP2), (B-SP2)

10. Given: **Wakâru.**

       Abunai.

       Kîree da.

These are representative of the three predicate types, and are all imperfective, direct-style, and affirmative. Convert them to (a) distal-style; (b) perfective; (c) distal-style perfective; (d) distal-style tentative (= probable); (e) distal-style perfective tentative. (A-SP1), (A-SP2), (A-SP6), (B-SP1), (B-SP2)

11. How is casual-style distinguished from careful-style? (A-SP3)

12. Give examples of markedly feminine patterns; of blunt and gentle patterns. (A-SP3)

13. Phrases like **sâñ-zi kara** and **Toókyoo màde** link up directly with predicates. What happens when such phrases describe nominals? (A-SP4)

14. In English, 'it became long' and 'it became pretty' are identical as to the structural pattern they illustrate. Compare the Japanese equivalents. What accounts for the difference? (A-SP5), (B-SP4)

15. Compare the meanings of the following:

       Yô-zi made imasu.

       Yô-zi ni imasu.

       Yô-zi made ni kimasu. (A-SP7)

16. What is meant by the extended predicate?

    Given: **Wakâru.**

       Abunai.

       Kîree da.

Convert these predicates to (a) distal-style extended predicates; (b) distal-style tentative (= probable) extended predicates; (c) distal-style perfective extended predicates; (d) distal-style perfective tentative extended predicates. What form does the extended predicate take at the end of sentences in blunt and in gentle direct-style? (B-SP3)

17. By contrasting the circumstances under which **Îma kaérimàsu ka** versus **Îma kâeru ñ desu ka** might occur, describe the basic usage of the extended predicate. (B-SP3)

18. How does the **kono**-series differ from the **koñna**-series in meaning? in structural patterns? What does /**koñna + ni**/ mean? (B-SP5)

19. To what Japanese word-class do loanwords from other languages regularly belong? How do such loanwords join the Japanese verbal class? Give examples. (B-SP6)

20. **Beñkyoo-suru** is a compound word, and **beñkyoo (o) suru** a phrase. What difference emerges when they are preceded by a nominal such as **nihoñḡo**? (B-SP6)

Lesson 10

SECTION A

Core Conversations

1(N)a. **Anô ko wa, dôko no ko desyoo**
nêe.

    (J)a. **Uti no Tâkasi de gozaimasu.**

  b. **Otaku no Tâkasi-tyañ de**
(i)rassyaimasu ka. Ôókìku onári
ni narimàsita nêe. Oíkutu de
(i)rassyaimàsu ka⌣

    b. **Sêñǧetu itû-tu ni narimasita.**

  c. **Kawáìi desu nêe.**

2(N)a. **Itóo-sañ irassyaimàsu ka⌣**

    (J)a. **Hâi, orímàsu ǧa . .**

  b. **Oríeñtaru-bòoeki no Debóra-**
Mìraa desu ǧa . .

    b. **Oyákusoku de gozaimàsu ka⌣**

  c. **Hâi. |Anoo| Nî-zi no yakúsoku**
dàtta ñ desu kedo, tyôtto
hayáme ni mairimàsita.

    c. **Syôosyoo omáti-kudasài.**

3(J)a. **Ano gaiziñ, dâre?**

    (N)a. **Otoko no hito?**

  b. **Oñna no hitò da kedo . .**

    b. **Âa, kânozyo neʕ Arúbàito no**
gakúsee nà ñ da kedo . .

  c. **Âa, naruhodo.**

4(N)a. **Kyôo no zêmi ni dêru?**

    (J)a. **Ññ⌣ Dênai. Komâru?**

  b. **Ññ⌣ Betú ni kamawànai kedo,**
otótòi mo dênakatta wa nêe.

    b. **Ññ⌣ Otótòi wa dêta yo.**

  c. **Âa, sôo ka.**

ENGLISH EQUIVALENTS

1(N)a. Whose child (*lit.* the child of what
place) do you suppose that (child)
is?

    (J)a. That's our Takashi.

  b. That's your Takashi? How he's
grown! (*lit.* He's become big,
hasn't he!) How old is he?

    (J)b. He turned five last month.

c. Isn't he cute!

2(N)a. Is Mr/s. Ito in?

    b. I'm Deborah Miller from Oriental Trade, but . . . (may I see him/her?)

    c. Yes. Uh, the fact is it was a 2 o'clock appointment, but I came a bit early.

3(J)a. Who's that foreigner?

    b. I mean the woman, but . . . (do you see the person I mean?)

    c. Oh, that's who she is!

4(N)a. Are you going to today's seminar?

    b. No, it doesn't especially matter, but you didn't attend the day before yesterday either, did you!

    c. Oh, you did, didn't you!

(J)a. Yes, s/he is, but [you are . . . ?]

    b. Do you have (*lit.* Is it) an appointment?

    c. Please wait a moment.

(N)a. The man?

    b. Oh, her? (What it is is) she's a student working part-time.

(J)a. No, I'm not (going). Will it cause problems?

    b. That's not right. The day before yesterday I did attend.

BREAKDOWNS
(AND SUPPLEMENTARY VOCABULARY)

1. **ko** *or*	
+**kodomo**	child, young person
+**okosān** (SP1)	child /polite/
+**âkatyañ**	baby
Tâkasi	(male given name)
Tâkasi-tyañ	Master Takashi /politc/
+**musuko**	son
+**musukosañ** *or*	
+**bôttyañ**	son /polite/
+**musúmè**	daughter
+**musumesañ** *or*	
+**ozyôosañ**	daughter /polite/
X de gozaimàsu+ (SP2)	is X; is described in terms of X /neutral-polite/
X de (i)rassyaimàsu ↑ (SP2)	is X; is described in terms of X /animate; honorific-polite/
onári ni nàru ↑ (SP3)	become /honorific-polite/
îkutu/oikutu *or*	
+**nâñ-sai** (SP1)	how old? (of people)
sêñgetu (SP4)	last month
+**señsyuu**	last week

kawáìi /-katta/	is cute
2. booeki	foreign trade
Oríeñtaru-bòoeki	'Oriental Tradé' (company name)
Debóra-Mìraa	Deborah Miller
(o)yakusoku	appointment; promise
hayame ni	in good time, early
3. gaiziñ *or*	
+gaíkokùziñ	foreigner
hitô	person
+katâ	person /polite/
otókò	male
otóko no hitò	man
oñnà	female
oñna no hitò	woman
+tosíyòri	old person
+wakâi /-katta/	is young
+wakâi hito	young person
+otona	adult
kânozyo	she
kânozyo neʔ (SP5)	she—you know?
+kâre	he
+anô hito *or*	he; she
+anó katà	he; she /polite/
arúbàito	part-time work, usually performed by students
4. zêmi	seminar
dênai /-katta/ (SP6)	/direct-style equivalent of **demásèñ**/
kamâu /-u; kamâtta/	mind, care, concern oneself about
kamáwànai /-katta/	/direct-style equivalent of **kamáimasèñ**/
+yuúbè	last night
Dênakatta wa nêe.	[You] didn't attend, did you! /direct-style; feminine/
Sôo ka.	/direct-style equivalent of **Sôo desu ka.**/

-sai: *Classifier for counting years of human age*

îs-sai	rokû-sai
nî-sai	nanâ-sai/sitî-sai
sâñ-sai	hâs-sai
yôñ-sai	kyûu-sai
gô-sai	zîs-sai/zyûs-sai
	nâñ-sai 'how old?'

-tu: *Classifier for counting years of human age*

hitô-tu, hutá-tù, etc. (cf. list,
   5A, Breakdowns
hâtati

Miscellaneous Notes

1. CC1 is an extremely polite conversation, in careful-style. Predicates are all distal-style, and there are no fragments. Although markedly feminine patterns are lacking, the politeness level is such that CC1 can be identified as occurring much more frequently as a conversation between women. On the accompanying video, the participants are professional women who work for different organizations and are acquaintances but not close friends; they have met accidentally and are chatting in a hotel lobby.

(N)a. **Anô ko . . . desyoo nêe**: The **dôko** question (without **ka**) is followed by **nêe**, implying that the speaker assumes the addressee may also be wondering. Note the unusual accenting of **anô ko**, suggesting that the item might be considered a compound word: **anôko**.

dôko no ko; uti no Tâkasi: Note the identification of a child in terms of place or group rather than individual person. Contrast English 'whose child?' and 'my son,' etc.

(J)a, (N)b. **Uti no** and **otaku no** reflect a contrast between in-group and out-group.

(N)c. **kawâii**: Be particularly careful, in pronouncing this word, to use a Japanese /a/ in the first as well as the second mora, and to make the /i/ vowel long. Unfortunately, a careless American-style mispronunciation of this word can result in telling a proud Japanese mother that her offspring is 'frightening!'

2. CC2 is a typical 'reception-desk conversation' between an outside visitor and a receptionist. Both use careful, polite style, affected by group affiliation: the visitor uses **irássyaimàsu** in reference to Ito, but Ito's colleague uses **orímàsu** in reference to her own in-group member, even if a superior, when talking to the out-group.

(N)b. **Oríeñtaru-bòoeki**: It is not unusual for companies, particularly those that have ties with the West, to adopt names that are a combination of new borrowings and native words. (Among so-called 'native words' are many that are based on roots originally borrowed from Chinese. **Booeki** is in that category.) Note also: **booeki-suru** 'conduct foreign trade.'

(J)b. **(O)yakusoku**: Note also **yakusoku-suru** 'promise' (verb).

(N)c. /**Hayame ni** + predicate of activity/ implies activity that is early in reference to a fixed time—an appointment, an opening, etc.

3. CC3 is a markedly casual-style conversation, containing minor sentences and fragments and direct-style predicates. The conversation takes place between close friends. On the video, the participants are two students, a man (J) and a woman (N).

(J)a. **Gaiziñ** is the commonly used term for a foreigner—specifically a Caucasian. Other foreigners—Chinese, Koreans, etc.—are more apt to be referred to in terms of their particular nationality. **Gaiziñ** is used much more commonly in Japanese than 'foreigner' is in English. In some contexts, though definitely not all, it has an exclusionary connotation which is interpreted as pejorative. The more formal term is **gaíkokùziñ,** which is much less commonly heard in conversational Japancse and has less tendency to be restricted to Westerners.

(J)b. **Tosíyòri**, a single nominal, refers to an elderly person; its opposite, **wakâi hito**, is a phrase. Note the resulting phrasal pattern contrasts: **tosíyòri no señsèe** but **wakâi señsèe**. The former, depending on context, can mean either 'the elderly teacher' or 'the elderly person's teacher' (cf. 5B-SP1). More will be said about this contrast later.

(N)b. **Arúbàito** is a borrowing from German *Arbeit* 'work.' In Japanese, it refers specifically to part-time work or moonlighting, usually performed primarily in order to earn money.

4. CC4 is also a casual-style conversation. While there are no minor sentences or fragments, all predicates are direct-style, and the sentences tend to be short. The occurrence of sentence-final **wa nêe** indicates that (N) is a woman; and blunt **dêta yo**, particularly in reply to a **wa nêe** utterance, suggests that (J) is a man. On the video, the two students of CC3 are again the participants.

(N)a. **Zêmi** is a shortening of a borrowing of the German word for seminar. The initial **z** makes the origin clear. Many Japanese borrowings relating to education and medicine have a German origin.

(N)b. **kamâu**: This verbal occurs most commonly in its negative derivatives, meaning 'it makes no difference,' 'it doesn't matter.' In direct-style, this negative is often comparable to English 'I don't care.' It is frequently used, as here, as an opposite of **komâru**.

(J)b. **otótòi wa**: Note the strongly limiting and contrastive use of **wa**: 'the day before yesterday, at least.'

Sôo ka is a direct-style equivalent of **sôo desu ka**. Whereas /nominal + ?/ is a generalized pattern involving the dropping of **dâ** and is parallel to /verbal + ?/ and /adjectival + ?/ (cf. **Wakâru? Tâkâkatta? Hoñtoo?**), the linking of sentence-particle **ka** to direct-style predicates in similar fashion is more restricted; insofar as it does occur, it is blunt-style and more typical of male speech. **Sôo ka** is one of the combinations which does occur—and extremely commonly. With /./ intonation, this is an example of a blunt type of utterance which is also used commonly by females.

Structural Patterns

1. NOTES ON PEOPLE; COUNTING AGES

In this lesson, we increase significantly the vocabulary that relates to people, and we find, not surprisingly, that for much of it, there is once again involvement of in-group/out-group distinctions and questions of hierarchy (i.e., who outranks whom).

Tâkasi is our first occurrence of a Japanese given name, used here in reference to a child. Unlike American society, Japanese is definitely *not* a society that uses given names casually. While women use, and are addressed by, given names more commonly than men, even use by them is limited and implies a close relationship. Within a family, usually only those who are younger than the speaker are addressed by their given names (more on this in later lessons). The use of given names is increasing, but it is still rare for a wife to address or refer to her husband by his first name, except in the case of young people in informal settings.

Many Japanese adopt foreign customs when dealing with foreigners, using given names freely both in address and reference. However, this should not be interpreted as a Japanese custom.

In a Japanese full name, the family name precedes the given name: **Nakamura Tâkasi**. However, when abroad, Japanese, unlike other Asians, usually switch to Western-style order. In English-language publications, some use the native order and others the inverted Western-style order. This can be extremely confusing if the reader doesn't recognize which name is which.

Note that Western-style names retain their usual order in Japan (cf. CC2).

While many given names cannot be immediately identified as masculine or feminine, there are some special characteristics that are helpful in distinguishing gender:

(1) 3-mora names whose final mora is **-o** are masculine. Examples: **Haruo, Yukio, Akio, Yosio, Takeo, Kazuo**

(2) 3-mora names whose final mora is **-ko**, **-e**, or **-yo** are feminine. Examples: **Hâruko, Yûkiko, Âkiko, Yôsiko, Kâzuko, Yôoko, Sâtiko, Kazue, Yosie, Kazuyo**

(3) 4-mora names are masculine. Examples: **Yosîhiko, Masâkazu, Masânori, Tomôaki**

The only neutral personal referents among the new vocabulary are **âkatyañ, gaiziñ, gaíkokùziñ, tosíyòri,** and **otona**. All the others require comments relating to in-group/out-group. **Okosañ, ko,** and **kodomo** all mean 'child,' both as the opposite of 'adult' and as 'offspring.' **Okosañ**, a polite term, refers only to the child(ren) of the out-group. **Ko** and **kodomo** are equivalent in meaning, but **kodomo** is a term of general usage, whereas the abbreviated **ko** occurs only in special combinations and is always preceded by a modifier: **anô ko, otókò no ko, uti no ko,** etc.

-tyañ is the familiar, diminutive equivalent of **-sañ**, regularly affixed to the given name of children and to that of young adults as a term of intimacy. Like **-sañ**, it is never used in reference to oneself, or to a member of the in-group when talking to the out-group.

Musukosañ and **bôttyañ** are polite terms for 'son,' used only in reference to the out-group. **Bôttyañ** usually refers to sons who are children or young, unmarried adults; in such cases, it is more polite than **musukosañ**, which is the only usual term for adult, married sons. In addition, **bôttyañ** may be used to refer to a male child or young, male adult without any notion of son relationship. A 'typical **bôttyañ**' is a young man who has been brought up in the bosom of the family and has led a sheltered, protected life.

Musumesañ and **ozyôosañ** 'daughter' are parallel in usage to **musukosañ** and **bôttyañ**, respectively.

Hitô is the most generalized word referring to 'person.' However, it is not ordinarily used specifically in reference to oneself. And in reference to others, it is a neutral term, lacking the politeness of **katâ**. Combinations of **hitô** with the **kono**-series (i.e., **konô hito, sonô hito**, etc.; note the special accent) are common third person referents ('he' and 'she'). In these combinations, the referent is singular.

Kâre and **kânozyo** are third person singular referents ('he' and 'she') which, like **anâta**, should be used with special care. Their usual use is in reference to peers or subordinates whose position requires no special respect. In recent years, the use of these words has been increasing, but they continue to be avoided when reference requires respect. **Kânozyo** is also sometimes used as a term of address, i.e., as 'you' in addressing young women, and as a term of reference for a girlfriend.

Years of human age are counted either with /Chinese series numerals + classifier **-sai**/ or with the **hitô-tu, hutá-tù** series. (For listings, see the Breakdowns above.) With **-sai**,

(1) the usual changes in the numerals 1, 8, and 10 that occur before classifiers beginning with **s-** also occur;

(2) the classifier itself does not change following **sañ-** and **nañ-**; and

(3) while '7 years old' is **nanâ-sai** or **sitî-sai**, '9 years old' is only **kyûu-sai**.

With **hitô-tu**:

As usual, this series extends only through ten. Beyond ten, numerals of the Chinese series are used, without a classifier; but '20 years of age' has the irregular form **hâtati**; and '14,' '24,' etc. regularly end in **sî**.

2. POLITE EQUIVALENTS OF dà

The copula **dà**, constituting (with its various forms) a separate word-class, forms a predicate in combination with a preceding nominal (**kânozyo da**) or a phrase ending with a phrase-particle (**kânozyo kara da**).

When a nominal predicate refers to a human, **dà** has an honorific-polite equivalent, **de (i)rassyàru**, which is inflected like **irássyàru** alone, except that the initial **i** is frequently dropped following the **de**. The combination may be unaccented following an accented nominal. Examples:

Anó katà (wa), dônata de (i)rassyaimasu ka⤻ 'Who is that person?'

Nîsida-sañ de (i)rassyaru desyoo? 'You are Mr/s. Nishida, aren't you?'

When the nominal predicate (a) does *not* refer to a human, or (b) refers to the in-group—which, of course, may be the self alone—the neutral polite(+) equivalent of **dà** is **de gozàru**, which actually *occurs only in the distal-style*. The tentative of **de gozaimàsu** is **de gozaimasyòo**. Again, the combination may lose its accent following an accented nominal or phrase. Examples:

Watasi, Oríeñtaru-bòoeki no Tanáka de gozaimàsu. 'I am Tanaka, from Oriental Trade.'

Tuǧî no kâiǧi wa, asítà de gozaimasu. 'The next conference is tomorrow.'

Kono ryokañ wa, bêñri de gozaimasyoo? 'This inn is convenient, isn't it?'

The **de** in these combinations is the gerund of **dà**. In their negative equivalents, particle **wa** is added: **X de wa irássyaimasèñ; X de wa gozáimasèñ.** If X is unaccented, **de** is accented (**dè**).

Actually, the **zya** that was introduced in the **X zya arímasèñ/nâi (desu)** pattern is a contraction of **dè wa**. The uncontracted **dè wa** occurs regularly in written style, whether direct- or distal-style, plain or polite. In the spoken language, the contracted equivalent **zya** is more common in plain-style, particularly when followed by **nâi (desu)**; but in polite-style, the uncontracted **dè wa** is preferred. It must be noted, however, that the opposite is also possible in both styles.

☠ WARNING: The polite equivalents described in this note do *not* occur following adjectivals. Their occurrence parallels **dà**, not **dèsu**.

3. HONORIFIC-POLITE VERBALS: /o- + STEM + ni + nâru/ ↑

Polite verbals like **irássyàru** ↑, **gozâru** + , and **itadaku** ↓ , which have totally different roots from their plain partners, are very limited in number. Most verbals that occur in polite-style have honorific and humble equivalents that are actually based on the plain verbal. In 7B-SP3, we learned the humble pattern /o- + stem + -suru/. Examples: **oyobi-suru** ↓ (humble-polite of **yobu**), **omati-suru** ↓ (humble-polite of **mâtu**), etc. These forms refer to the in-group, usually in the sense of performing an action in behalf of the out-group.

Our new pattern is honorific-polite ↑, used in deferential reference to the out-group: /o- + stem + **ni** + **nâru**/. Examples: **odé ni nàru** ↑ (from **dêru**); **okáeri ni nàru** ↑ (from **kâeru**); **owákari ni nàru** ↑ (from **wakâru**). Note the consistent accent pattern.

Just as some verbals have humble equivalents which are not formed according to the regular patterns, irregular honorific equivalents also occur. For example, this new pattern does not apply to **suru** and **mîru**.

Iku, kûru, and **iru** constitute a special case. On the one hand, they have an unpredictable honorific equivalent, **irássyàru**↑. But they also have an alternate honorific, based on this new pattern but irregularly formed: **oíde ni nàru**↑.[1] Both **irássyàru** and **oíde ni nàru** are honorific-polite equivalents of **iku, kûru,** and **iru**. They are interchangeable, but **irássyàru** currently appears to be in wider use.

It has already been pointed out that when a nominal is derived from a verbal, it is in the stem form (cf. nominals **kaérì, yasúmì, tanósìmi,** etc.). A form like **omati-suru** 'I wait for you,' in which the stem has polite prefix **o-**, means literally '[I] do waiting connected with you.' In contrast, **omáti ni nàru** '[you] wait' describes 'a becoming or development into (i.e., **nâru**) waiting connected with you,' an example of indirection reflecting politeness.

4. NOMINALS OF RELATIVE TIME

The chart on the next page summarizes time expressions whose meaning in the real world is relative to the time of usage (i.e., **kyôo** means 'August second' only if uttered on August second). Remember that these expressions link up directly with predicates without a following particle, when indicating the time *when* of an occurrence. (Examples: **kyôo iku, kinóo mìta, asâtte suru,** etc.) Forms not previously introduced are marked with a /+/. The chart is not intended to be complete: there are many alternate forms, reflecting differences in style. The items included are all common in the spoken language, and those that are new are items not difficult to add to your current repertoire.

5. **Kânozyo neʕ**

In CC3, the particle **ne** occurs in an example of a new, derivative **ne** pattern. In spoken Japanese, a sentence is frequently broken up into shorter spans, with **ne** (i.e., **neʕ** or **ne!** or even **nêe**.) added to the nonfinal one(s). Thus:

> **Anô hito, gaíziñ dèsu yo⤳ > Anô hito neʕ Gaíziñ dèsu yo⤳**

> **Kinoo yoózi ğa àtte, okúrete kità ñ da yo. > Kinoo ne! Yoózi ğa àtte ne! Okúrete kità ñ da yo.**[2]

The use of this **ne** conveys a strong concern on the part of the speaker for the continuing attention and understanding of the person addressed. Japanese conversation places heavy emphasis on the participation of the addressee(s) as well as the speaker,[3] and the use of **ne** is one way to involve the hearer(s). Each occurrence of **ne** requires, if not a verbalized **êe, hâi, sôo, ñ,** etc., at least a firm nod. The appropriate rhythm of **ne** and the acknowledgment by the hearer is a crucial feature of 'comfortable conversation.' It is extremely important for foreigners to learn how to become skilled 'nodding (but not dozing!) listeners.' This feature of Japanese actually has a name: **aizuti** refers to regular signals by a hearer that s/he is listening and involved in the conversation.

Sometimes there is a special focus on the item followed by **ne**, as in the case of a com-

1. Do not confuse this **oide** with **ode** (polite stem of **dêru**).
2. Note that when the **ne** are dropped, the fragments can be combined into a unified, meaningful utterance. Some foreigners of limited Japanese proficiency mistakenly think that a rapid string of /nominal + **ne**/ sequences, with an occasional /verbal + **ne**/ thrown in, can remove the necessity for bothering with particles or structural patterns. Unfortunately, this practice results in something that has been aptly named 'abominable fluency.' It is usually incomprehensible to most native speakers. If thoroughly internalized, this approach leads to a terminal, incurable condition that precludes the development of language proficiency.
3. Consider how frequently **nê(e)**, even at the end of major sentences, serves the same purpose. Speaker and hearer(s) form a mutually involved group.

Time Expressions

Category	−2 (= last before last)	−1 (= last)	Present	+1 (= next)	+2 (= next after next)	every-
Day: +hî	otótòi	kinôo	kyôo	asítà / asû	asâtte	máiniti
Morning: àsa	otótoi no àsa	kinôo no àsa	kêsa	asíta no àsa	asâtte no àsa	+máiasa
Night: bañ	ototoi no bañ	yuúbè	kôñbañ	asita no bañ	asâtte no bañ	+máibañ
yôru	otótoi no yòru		+kôñya	asita no yòru	asâtte no yòru	+maiyo
Week: +syuu	+señséñsyuu	señsyuu	koñsyuu	raisyuu	+saraisyuu	maisyuu
Month: +tukí	+señséñǧetu	séñǧetu	koñǧetu	ráiǧetu	+saraiǧetu	maituki
						+maiǧetu
Year: +tosî	+otótosi	kyôneñ	kotosi	raineñ	+saraineñ	maitosi
						maineñ

paratively short utterance like the example of CC3: 'Oh, her, you know? She's . . .' But often **ne** seems almost like a filler, as the speaker acknowledges the presence of the addressee and plots the ongoing discourse, and the addressee processes what s/he is hearing.

6. VERBALS: DIRECT-STYLE NEGATIVE DERIVATIVES

We have already learned both the direct-style and distal-style negative equivalents of adjectival and nominal predicates. (See chart, next page.)

We will now add the direct-style negative derivatives of verbals. These negatives are all adjectivals based on the *verbal root*. (The verbal root, you will remember, is the citation form minus **-ru** for vowel verbals and minus **-u** for consonant and special polite verbals.) To the root, we add **-na-i** for vowel verbals and **-ana-i** for consonant and special polite verbals:

Citation Form (= affirmative imperfective)	Root	Negative Imperfective
Vowel Verbals		
mîru 'look at'	**mi**	**mî-na-i**
tabê-ru 'eat'	**tabe**	**tabê-na-i**
Consonant Verbals		
nâr-u 'become'	**nar**	**nar-âna-i**
mât-u 'wait'	**mat**	**mat-âna-i**
ka(w)-u 'buy'	**kaw**	**kaw-ana-i**
Special Polite Verbals		
irássyàr-u ↑ 'go,' 'come,' 'be'	**irassyar**	**irássyar-àna-i**
kudásàr-u ↑ 'give me'	**kudasar**	**kudásar-àna-i**
Irregular Verbals		
suru 'do'	**su/si/se**	**si-na-i**
kû-ru 'come'	**ku/ki/ko**	**kô-na-i**

Accent: The **-(a)na-i** negative of an unaccented verbal is also basically unaccented, but follows the same patterns as other unaccented adjectivals. Compare:

	akai	akâkatta	akaku	akâi desu	akâi no
(iku)	ikanai	ikánàkatta	ikanaku	ikánài desu	ikánài no

The **-katta** form acquires an accent on the syllable immediately preceding the ending. The **-(a)na-i** form acquires an accent on the **-na-** syllable in certain contexts, such as before **dèsu, desyòo,** and nominal **no.**

The **-(a)na-i** negative of an accented verbal is accented on the syllable immediately preceding the **-na-** in all forms. Thus:

(tabêru)	tabênai	tabênaku	tabênakatta	tabênai desu	tabênai no
(nômu)	nomânai	nomânaku	nomânakatta	nomânai desu	nomânai no

Note the following points:

(a) It was previously pointed out that verbals ending in /vowel + **u**/ in their citation form, like **kau** above, are actually **w**-consonant verbals, but that the **w** is lost everywhere in modern Japanese except before **a**. In the direct-style negative, we have our first example of the retention of the **w**, before **-ana-i**.

Adjectival and Nominal Predicates
Imperfective and Perfective, Affirmative and Negative

		Imperfective		Perfective	
		Affirmative	*Negative*	*Affirmative*	*Negative*
Adjectival 'be expensive'	Direct	(tákà)i	(tákà)ku nái	(tákà)katta	(tákà)ku nákatta
	Distal	(tákà)i desu	(tákà)ku {nái desu / arímasèñ}	(tákà)katta desu	(tákà)ku {nákatta desu / arímasèñ desita}
Nominal 'be out'	Direct	(rûsu) da	(rûsu) zya nái	(rûsu) datta	(rûsu) zya nákatta
	Distal	(rûsu) desu	(rûsu) zya {nái desu / arímasèñ}	(rûsu) desita	(rûsu) zya {nákatta desu / arímasèñ desita}

(b) The two irregular verbals have alternate roots that occur unpredictably. **Sinai** and **kônai** are our first examples of nonparallel derivatives for these two verbals.

(c) The verbal **âru**, otherwise a regular consonant verbal, has an irregular negative, with which we are already very familiar. Instead of the expected ***ar-âna-i**, the actual negative is simply **nâ-i**.

(d) Like **nâi**, all the direct-style negatives are, of course, adjectivals. This immediately tells us that the perfective is formed by dropping final **-i** and adding **-katta**, and that the addition of **desu** to imperfectives and perfectives converts them to distal-style.

But what about forms like **tabémasèñ** and **wakárimasèñ desita**, which are also distal-style and negative?[4] Actually the language has competing forms. Consider the following derivation sequences:

(1) **wakâr(u)** /+ distal-style/ > **wakárimàs(u)** /+ negation/ > **wakárimasèñ**

(2) **wakâr(u)** /+ negation/ > **wakáràna(i)** /+ distal-style/ > **wakárànai desu,** *and also*

(3) **wakâr(u)** /+ distal-style/ > **wakárimàs(u)** /+ negation/ > **wakárimasèñ** /+ perfective/ > **wakárimasèñ desita**

(4) **wakâr(u)** /+ negation/ > **wakáràna(i)** /+ perfective/ > **wakárànakatta** /+ distal-style/ > **wakárànakatta desu**

In both (1) and (2), the final forms are distal-style, negative, and imperfective, and in both (3) and (4) they are distal-style, negative, and perfective; but the derivation occurs in a different order. We can say that (1) is the negative of a distal-style but (2) is the distal-style of a negative. Similarly, (3) is the perfective of a negative of a distal-style, whereas (4) is the distal-style of a perfective of a negative. It is certainly not necessary for you to remember how this derivation proceeds; but it *is* necessary for you to know and understand the resulting competing forms. They are all in common, everyday usage, but the **-mas-** forms tend to be considered by some to be a bit more elegant and 'proper.'

The following list includes the direct-style negative for all verbals introduced thus far:

Vowel Verbals

iru/inai 'be (animate)'	**dekîru/dekînai**	**mîru/mînai**	**dêru/dênai**
kakêru/kakênai	**miêru/miênai**	**misêru/misênai**	**okureru/okurenai**
osieru/osienai	**tabêru/tabênai**	**tomeru/tomenai**	**yameru/yamenai**

Consonant Verbals

yobu/yobanai	**arûku/arúkànai**	**iku/ikanai**	**itadaku/itadakanai**
kâku/kakânai	**kau/kawanai**	**kiku/kikanai**	**nômu/nomânai**
âru/nâi	**kakâru/kakárànai**	**komâru/komárànai**	**maḡaru/maḡaranai**
nâru/narânai	**tomaru/tomaranai**	**wakâru/wakárànai**	**kâeru/kaérànai**
iru/iranai 'need'	**mâiru/maírànai**[a]	**ôru/orânai**	**mâtu/matânai**
kamâu/kamáwànai	**neḡâu/neḡáwànai**	**tiḡau/tiḡawanai**	**tukau/tukawanai**
ukaḡau/ukaḡawanai			

---

4. The **ñ** at the end of the **-masèñ** forms originated as a contraction of **nai**.

Special Polite Verbals

| (*gozâru)/(*gozárànai[b]) | kudásàru/ | irássyàru/ |
| | kudásarànai | irássyarànai |

Irregular Verbals

suru/sinai   **kûru/kônai**

[a]Extremely rare form.
[b]Not in actual use.

Direct-style negatives occur in the same patterns as the affirmatives from which they are derived. When forming a predicate together with a following distal-style **desyòo**, the combination is considered a distal-style predicate. Examples:

Eñpitu âru? . . . Nâi. 'Got a pencil?' . . . 'No, (I don't have).'

Zêmi ni dêru? . . . Dênai (wa) yo⤸ 'Are you attending the seminar?' . . . 'No, I'm not (attending).'

Wakâtta? . . . Wakárànakatta (wa) nêe. 'Did you understand?' . . . 'No, I didn't (understand, did I—as I think it over).'

Ikímàsu ka⤸ . . . Kyôo wa ikánài kedo, asítà wa ikímàsu yo⤸ 'Are you going?' . . . 'Today I'm not going, but tomorrow I am (going).'

Señsèe mo irássyaimàsu ka⤸ . . . Iie, irássyarànai desyoo. 'Is the doctor coming, too?' . . . 'No, he probably isn't (coming).'

Ano gaiziñ imâsita ka⤸ . . . Iie, inâkatta desyoo? 'Was that foreigner there?' . . . 'No, he wasn't, was he?'

In the usual negating of an extended predicate, it is the predicate preceding the **ñ/no** that is negated:

Dekînai ñ desu ka⤸ 'Is it that you can't do it?' (for example, to explain why you're not doing it).

Yobánàkatta no? 'Didn't you call [him]?' (for example, to explain why he hasn't appeared).

But compare:

Dekîru ñ zya nai? 'Isn't it (the case) that you can do it?' (i.e., I thought you could).

Dekînai ñ zya nai? 'Isn't it (the case) that you can't do it?' (i.e., I thought you couldn't).

As a direct contradiction of a negative, it is possible to negate the negative, following the usual pattern! Thus: **Dekînai nêe. . . . Dekînaku nâi yo.** 'You can't do it, can you!' . . . 'I *can so!*' (*lit.* 'I'm not not able'). This usage is colloquial, and more common in casual-style. However, there are other uses of the **-ku** form of negatives of more general use. In 9A-SP5, we observed the difference between **takâi** 'it is expensive' and **tâkâku nâru** 'it becomes expensive.' Since negatives are also adjectivals, it is not surprising to find that they, too, may link up with **nâru**, in their **-ku** forms, of course. Examples:

Wakárànaku narimasita. 'I don't understand any more.' (*lit.* 'I became not understanding.')

Dekînaku nâru desyoo. 'S/he'll probably become unable to do it.'

Ano koosateñ (wa), abunaku nakú narimàsita nêe. 'That corner isn't dangerous any more, is it!' (*lit.* 'It became not-dangerous.')

Beñkyoo-sitaku nakú narimàsita yo⌐ 'I've reached the point where I don't want to study.' (*lit.* 'I became not wanting to study.')

The last example develops in this way:

suru /+ **-tai**/ > **sitai** /+ negation/ > **sitáku nài** /+ **nâru**/ > **sitaku nakú nàru**
/+ distal-style/ > **sitaku nakú narimàsu** /+ perfective/ > **sitaku nakú narimàsita**

Drills

A 1. **Anô ko wa, mií-tù desita ka⌐**
'Was that child 3?'

Îku-tu desita ka nêe. Yoí-tù zya nâkatta desu ka⌐
'How old was s/he! Wasn't s/he 4?'

2. **Yamamoto-kuñ wa, nîzyuu kyûu-sai desita ka⌐**
'Was Yamamoto 29?'

Nâñ-sai desita ka nêe. Sáñzyùs-sai zya nâkatta desu ka⌐
'How old was he! Wasn't he 30?'

3. **Tâkasi-tyañ/nanâ-sai**; 4. **ano gaiziñ/zyûuku**; 5. **anô hito/nîzyuu sâñ-sai**; 6. **kâre/ hâtati**; 7. **kânozyo/zyuúkyùu-sai**

B 1. **Otaku no Tâkasi-tyañ de (i)rassyaimasu ka⌐**
'Is that your Takashi?'

Êe, uti no Tâkasi de gozaimasu.
'Yes, it's our Takashi.'

2. **Otáku no ozyòosañ de (i)rassyaimasu ka⌐**
'Is that your daughter?'

Êe, utí no musumè de gozaimasu.
'Yes, it's our daughter.'

3. **musukosañ**; 4. **musumesañ**; 5. **bôttyañ**; 6. **okosañ**

● Repeat this drill, varying the politeness levels: (1) replace **de irassyaimàsu** in the questions with **dèsu**; (2) replace **de gozaimàsu** in the responses with **dèsu**; (3) use **dèsu** in both questions and responses. When making these changes, keep in mind the changes in the participants/relationships that are implied.

C 1. **Suzúki-sañ de (i)rassyaimàsu ka⌐**
'Are you Mr/s. Suzuki?'

Hâi, Suzúki de gozaimàsu kedo . .
'Yes, I'm Suzuki, but . . .' (why do you ask?)

2. **Itóo-señsèe no bôttyan de (i)rassyaimasu ka⌐**
'Are you Dr. Ito's son?'

Hâi, Itóo no musuko de gozaimàsu kedo . .
'Yes, I'm the Ito son, but . . .' (why do you ask?)

3. **Nakamura Tâkasi-sañ**; 4. **Debóra-Kàataa-sañ**; 5. **Nîsida-señsee**; 6. **Yamámoto-sañ no ozyòosañ**

D 1. **Anó taipuràitaa de kakímasu yo⌐**
'I'm going to write with that typewriter.'

A. Señsèe mo anó taipuràitaa de okáki ni narimàsu yo⌐
'Oh. The teacher is going to write with that typewriter, too.'

2. **Anó misè de kaímàsita yo**‍
   'I bought [something] in that store.'

    A. Señsèe mo anó misè de okái ni narimàsita yo‍
    'Oh. The teacher bought [something] in that store, too.'

3. **omâwarisañ ni kikímàsita;** 4. **taiheñ isógàsìku narimasita;** 5. **zûibuñ matímàsita;** 6. **tyuugokugo ga sukôsi wakarimasu;** 7. **añna wàiñ wa 'amari nomímaseñ**

E 1. **Oyóbi-simasyòo ka.**
    'Shall I call [him]?'

    A. Oyóbi ni nàtte kudasaimaseñ ka‍
    'Oh, would you (call)?'

2. **Omáti-simasyòo ka.**
    'Shall I wait?'

    A. Omáti ni nàtte kudasaimaseñ ka‍
    'Oh, would you (wait)?'

3. **okíki-simasyòo;** 4. **okáki-simasyòo;** 5. **otúkuri-simasyòo;** 6. **okáke-simasyòo**

F 1. **Itoo-sañ ni okíki ni narimàsu ne**ʃ
    'You're going to ask Mr/s. Ito—right?'

    Hâi. Okíki-simàsu.
    'Yes. I'll ask.'

2. **Nâgoya e oíde ni narimàsu ne**ʃ
    'You're going to Nagoya—right?'

    Hâi. Maírimàsu.
    'Yes. I am (going).'

3. **tîzu o okáki ni narimàsu;** 4. **koñnà no o otúkuri ni narimàsu;** 5. **koóhìi o onómi ni narimàsu;** 6. **koko e oíde ni narimàsu;** 7. **môtto omáti ni narimàsu**

● Repeat this drill, alternating politeness levels, replacing (1) the polite forms in the questions with plain equivalents, and (2) the polite forms in the responses with plain equivalents, keeping in mind the participants implied.

G 1. **Anó kàiḡi wa, râiḡetu de gozaimasu ka**‍
    'Is that conference next month?'

    Anó kàiḡi desu ka‍ **Señḡetu de gozaimasita kedo . .**
    'That conference? It was last month, but . . .' (weren't you informed?)

2. **Anó zèmi wa, asíta no bañ de gozaimàsu ka**‍
    'Is that seminar tomorrow night?'

    Anó zèmi desu ka‍ **Yuúbè de gozaimasita kedo . .**
    'That seminar? It was last night, but . . .' (weren't you informed?)

3. **siḡoto/raineñ;** 4. **yasúmì/raisyuu;** 5. **eéḡo no zyùḡyoo/asítà**

● Repeat this drill, replacing **de gozaimàsu/-màsita** with **dèsu/dèsita** according to the procedures described following Drill F, above.

H 1. **Ozyôosañ, dôo?**
    'How's your daughter?'

    A. Musúmè neʃ **Byóoki nà ñ da yo.[5]**
    Byóoki nà no yo.
    'Oh, my daughter—you know?—the fact is she's sick.'

2. **Tâkasi-tyañ, dôo?**
    'How's Takashi?'

    A. Tâkasi neʃ **Byóoki nà ñ da yo.[5]**
    Byóoki nà no yo.

5. The first alternate is blunt, the second gentle.

'Oh, Takashi—you know?—the fact is he's sick.'

   3. **bôttyañ**; 4. **musumesañ**; 5. **okosañ**; 6. **musukosañ**

I 1. **Iku?**   **N̂ñ** **Ikanai.**
    'Are you going?'   'Uh-uh. I'm not (going).'

   2. **Kûru?**   **N̂ñ** **Kônai.**
    'Are you coming?'   'Uh-uh. I'm not (coming).'

   3. **suru**; 4. **dêru**; 5. **kâeru**; 6. **mâtu**; 7. **yobu**; 8. **tomodati iru**; 9. **eñpitu iru**; 10. **âru**

● Repeat this drill in distal-style, using the **-(a)nài desu** alternates in the responses.

J 1. **Nâñ-niti kara syuttyoo-surù ñ desu**   A. **Syuttyoo-sinài ñ desu yo.**
    ka   'Oh, the fact is I'm not going away.'
    'Starting what date (is it) you'll be
    away on business?'

   2. **Dôko de señsèe o mâtu ñ desu ka**   A. **Matânai ñ desu yo.**
    'Where is it you are going to wait for   'Oh, the fact is I'm not going to wait.'
    the doctor?'

   3. **asita nâñ-zi ni kûru**; 4. **dono-ḡurai kono ryokañ ni tomaru**

K 1. **Dêta?**   **N̂ñ** **Dênakatta.**
    'Did you attend?'   'Uh-uh. I didn't (attend).'

   2. **Tukatta?**   **N̂ñ** **Tukáwanàkatta.**
    'Did you use [it]?'   'Uh-uh. I didn't (use).'

   3. **yoñda**; 4. **yameta**; 5. **âtta**; 6. **mâtta**; 7. **tometa**; 8. **kâita**; 9. **katta**; 10. **kiita**; 11. **kâketa**;
    12. **kâetta**

● Repeat this drill in distal-style, using the **-(a)nakatta desu** alternates in the responses.

L 1. **Anô hito wa, raisyuu kimâsu ka**   **Kônai desyoo ne!**
    'Is s/he coming next week?'   'S/he probably isn't (coming, is s/he).'

   2. **Anô hito wa, kêsa miémàsita ka**   **Miênakatta desyoo ne!**
    'Did s/he appear this morning?'   'S/he probably didn't (appear, did s/he).'

   3. **deñwa o kakemàsita**; 4. **zêmi ni demâsu**; 5. **kâiḡi ni okúremàsita**; 6. **eéḡo ḡa**
    dekimàsu; 7. **rosíaḡo ḡa wakarimàsu**; 8. **Toókyoo ni kaerimàsita**; 9. **kurúma ḡa**
    arimàsu; 10. **waápuro o kaimàsu**

M 1. **Señsèe mo irássyaimàsu ne**   **Señsèe wa, irássyarànai desyoo?**
    'The teacher is coming, too—right?'   'The teacher (at least) isn't coming—isn't
                                           that the case?'

   2. **Señsèe mo omíe ni narimàsita ne**   **Señsèe wa, omíe ni narànakatta desyoo?**
    'The teacher put in an appearance,   'The teacher (at least) did not put in an
    too—right?'   appearance—isn't that the case?'

   3. **kudásaimàsu**; 4. **otúkai ni narimàsita**; 5. **okómari ni narimàsita**; 6. **odéki ni**
    narimàsu

N 1. **Suru?** **Sinai.**
　　'Are you going to do [it]?' 'I'm not (going to do).'

　 2. **Wakâi?** **Wâkâku nâi.**
　　'Is s/he young?' 'S/he isn't (young).'

　 3. **Gaiziñ?** **Gaíziñ zya nài.**
　　'Is s/he a foreigner?' 'S/he isn't (a foreigner).'

　 4. **kânozyo (da)**; 5. **ikitai**; 6. **arúbàito (da)**; 7. **dêru**; 8. **mîeta**; 9. **yobu**; 10. **sitâkatta**; 11. **yameru**; 12. **mâtu**; 13. **oísìkatta**; 14. **hûbeñ datta**; 15. **kiita**; 16. **Uénò-eki made (da)**; 17. **kamî 'iru**; 18. **kawáìi**; 19. **kûru**; 20. **kâita**; 21. **kâetta**; 22. **kitâ**; 23. **katta**; 24. **kâketa**; 25. **nômu**; 26. **tabêru**; 27. **gaíziñ dàtta**; 28. **kodómo nò (da)**; 29. **raíneñ karà (da)**; 30. **sêñḡetu datta**

O 1. **Otóko no katà mo oñna no katà mo kûru?** **Otóko no katà wa kûru kedo, oñna no katà wa kônai.**
　　'Will men *and* women come?' 'Men will come but women will not (come).'

　 2. **Konó kèeki mo anó pài mo oísìi?** **Konó kèeki wa oísìi kedo, anó pài wa oísiku nài.**
　　'Are this cake *and* that pie tasty?' 'This cake is tasty but that pie is not (tasty).'

　 3. **Itoo-sañ mo bôttyan mo rûsu?** **Itóo-sañ wa rùsu da kedo, bôttyañ wa rûsu zya nâi.**
　　'Are Mr/s. Ito *and* his/her son out?' 'Mr/s. Ito is out, but his/her son is not (out).'

　 4. **kâre/kânozyo/dekîru**; 5. **koñsyuu/raisyuu/isógasìi**; 6. **tosíyòri/wakâi hito/iru**; 7. **kêsa/yuúbè/tukatta**; 8. **Iḡirisu/Itaria/nâḡâkatta**; 9. **zisiñ/kâzi/âtta**; 10. **señsèe/gakusee/gaiziñ (da)**; 11. **getúyòo/kayôo/yasúmì datta**; 12. **otókò no ko/oñnà no ko/kûru**; 13. **otona/kodomo/iku**

P 1. **Kâre, demásèñ ka⤸** **Dênaku narimasita nêe.**
　　'Doesn't he attend?' 'He doesn't attend any more.' (*lit.* 'He became non-attending, didn't he.')

　 2. **Kâre, kimásèñ ka⤸** **Kônaku narimasita nêe.**
　　'Doesn't he come?' 'He doesn't come any more.' (*lit.* 'He became non-coming, didn't he.')

　 3. **tukáimasèñ**; 4. **wakárimasèñ**; 5. **dekímasèñ**; 6. **beñkyoo-simasèñ**; 7. **tukúrimasèñ**; 8. **ikímasèñ**; 9. **nomímasèñ**

Q 1. **Hurañsuḡo beñkyoo-sinài ñ desu ka⤸** **Êe. Kono-ḡoro 'beñkyoo-sitaku nakú narimàsita nêe.**
　　'Do you mean you don't study French?' 'Yes. I've come to not want to study [it] recently.'

　 2. **Señsèe ni narânai ñ desu ka⤸** **Êe. Kono-ḡoro narítàku nakú narimàsita nêe.**
　　'Do you mean you aren't going to

become a teacher?' 'Yes. I've come to not want to become [one] recently.'

3. **arúbàito 'yamenai**; 4. **Amerika e kaéranai**; 5. **Yoóròppa e 'ikanai**; 6. **asoko mînai**

R 1. **Komâru?** **Komâru nêe.**
'Does it upset you?' **Komâru wa nêe.** /F/
'It does (upset), doesn't it!'

2. **Oñna no hito?** **Oñna no hitò da nêe.**
'Is it a woman?' **Oñna no hitò da wa nêe.** /F/
'It is (a woman), isn't it!'

3. **kawáìi**; 4. **tiḡau**; 5. **kâre (da)**; 6. **detâi**; 7. **wakâtta**; 8. **oísìkatta**; 9. **kônakatta**; 10. **hoñtoo (dà)**; 11. **taíheñ (dà)**; 12. **mâtu**; 13. **otóna (dà)**

S 1. **Tosíyòri ḡa komâru no?**
'Is it that the elderly get upset?'

Tosíyòri ḡa komâru { **ñ da nêe.**[5]
{ **no nêe.**

'(It is that) the elderly do get upset (don't they)!'

2. **Tosíyòri na no?**
'Is it that it's an elderly person?'

Tosíyòri na { **ñ da nêe.**[5]
{ **no nêe.**

'(It is that) it is an elderly person, (isn't it)!'

3. **wakâi**; 4. **wakâi katâ na**; 5. **gaíziñ mo mìeta**; 6. **kurôi no na**; 7. **âtta**; 8. **señsèe ḡa irâsita**; 9. **señsèe no na**; 10. **raíneñ màde na**; 11. **oñna no katà datta**

Application Exercises

A1. Make up a limited family tree covering the relationships introduced thus far. (Allow room for additional family relationships to be added later.) Assign each person a name, sex, and age. Practice asking and answering questions relating to the information on the chart: inquire about (a) the names and the ages of the particular individuals and of their relatives; (b) the relationship between two designated people; (3) the identification of people of specific ages (i.e., 'who is the 34-year-old man?'). Include yes/no questions as well as information questions. Practice using a variety of styles—casual and careful, plain and polite—as you assume different roles and relationships vis-à-vis the person addressed.

2. Ask and answer questions that include the vocabulary of the chart in SP4 of this section, using a calendar when necessary. Find out such information as what day of the week the fourteenth of last month was, what year of Showa the year before last was, what someone did last night, whether someone studies every night, etc. Again, assume different roles and use an appropriate variety of styles.

3. Repeat Application Exercises A6 and B4 of Lesson 9, incorporating negative answers. Example:

Instructor to A: **B-sañ (wa) asíta kimàsu ka**⤹
A to B: **Asíta kùru?**

_____

5. The first alternate is blunt, the second gentle.

B to A: (**Asítà wa) kônai (wa) yo**⌐

A to instructor: (**Asítà wa) kimásèñ.**

B. Core Conversations: Substitution

Practice the Core Conversations, making substitutions not only in the situations themselves but also in the conversation participants to the extent appropriate. Use a clear, unambiguous method to make roles obvious throughout the conversation practice.

SECTION B

Core Conversations

1(N)a. **Kitamura-sañ wa keḱkoñ-site (i)màsu ne!**

      (J)a. **Êe. Kyôneñ Amérika de kekkoñ-sità ñ desu.**

  b. **Amerika de?**

      b. **Êe. Ôkusañ síttè (i)ru ñ desu kedo, niḱkèeziñ na ñ desu yo.**

  c. **Âa, sôo desu ka. Sirímasèñ desita.**

2(J)a. **Hayasi-kuñ kitê (i)ru ne!**

      (N) **Hâi. Zútto màe ni irâsite, îma ukétuke no tokorò de okyákusàma o mâtte (i)rassyaimasu ğa . .**

  b. **A, sôo ka.**

3(J)a. **Kimura-sañ îma nâni sitê (i)ru?**

      (N)a. **Têepu kiítè (i)ru—tonari no kyoositu de.**

  b. **Kûbota-sañ mo?**

      b. **Iya, Kûbota-sañ wa kaíğìsitu de señsèe to hanâsite (i)ru wa yo**⌐

  c. **Zyâa, Matuda-sañ wa?**

      c. **Kyôo wa kônai wa yo**⌐

4(N)a. **Nâni mîte (i)ru no?**

      (J)a. **Atárasìi kyoókàsyo.**

  b. **Kaítà no?**

      b. **Ññ**⌐ **Tomódati kara karità no.**

ENGLISH EQUIVALENTS

1(N)a. Mr. Kitamura is married, isn't he.

      (J)a. Yes. (The fact is) he got married in the U.S. last year.

  b. In the U.S.?

      b. Yes. (The fact is) I know his wife; she's of Japanese descent.

  c. Oh, really. I didn't know.

2(J)a. Hayashi is here (*lit.* has come), isn't he.

      (N)a. Yes. He came a long while ago, and he's waiting for a visitor at the reception desk (*lit.* the receptionist's place) [just] now, but . . . (did you want to see him?)

b. Oh.

3(J)a. What's Mr/s. Kimura doing now?

    b. Mr/s. Kubota, too?

    c. Then what about Mr/s. Matsuda?

4(N)a. What are you looking at?

    b. Did you buy it?

(N)a. S/he's listening to tapes—in the classroom next door.

    b. No, Mr/s. Kubota is talking with a professor in the conference room.

    c. S/he's not coming today.

(J)a. A new textbook.

    b. Uh-uh. I borrowed it from a friend.

BREAKDOWNS
(AND SUPPLEMENTARY VOCABULARY)

1. **Kitamura** — (family name)
   kekkoñ-suru — get married
   keḱkoñ-sitè (i)ru (SP1) — be married
   + **rikoñ-suru** — get divorced
   ôkusañ — wife (of an out-group member) /polite/
   + **tûma** — my wife; wife
   + **kânai** — my wife
   + **gosyûziñ** — husband (of an out-group member) /polite/
   + **otto** — my husband; husband
   + **syûziñ** — my husband
   siru/-u; sitta/ (SP2) — find out, get to know
   sit́tè (i)ru — know
   + **zôñzite (i)ru** ↓ — know /humble-polite/
   + **gozôñzi da** ↑ — know /honorific-polite/
   niḱkèeziñ — person of Japanese ancestry
   + **nihóñzìñ** or
   + **nippoñzìñ** — Japanese person

2. **Hayasi** — (family name)
   kitê (i)ru — have come; be coming (habitually)
   mâe — time before, past time
   zút́to màe — way before, long ago
   uketuke — receptionist
   tokórò — place, location
   + **kyaku** or
   + **okyakusañ** /polite/ or
   okyákusàma /polite/ — guest; visitor; customer
   mâtte (i)ru — be waiting

3. **sitê (i)ru** — be doing
   kiku /-u; kiita/ — listen, hear
   kiítè (i)ru — be listening; be hearing

kyoositu	classroom
Kûbota	(family name)
kaíĝìsitu	conference room
hanâsu /-u; hanâsita/	talk, speak
señsèe to hanâsu (SP3)	talk with a señsèe
hanâsite (i)ru	be talking
Matuda	(family name)
4. mîte (i)ru	be looking at
kyoókàsyo	textbook
kariru /-ru; karita/	borrow; rent (from someone)
tomodati kara kariru *or*	
tomodati ni kariru (SP4)	borrow from a friend
+kasu /-u; kasita/	lend; rent (to someone)

Nationalities

Amérikàziñ *or* Beékokùziñ	Kañkokùziñ
Doítùziñ	Oósutorariàziñ
Huráñsùziñ	Soréñzìñ
Iĝírisùziñ *or* Eékokùziñ	Supéiñzìñ
Iñdòziñ	Tyuúĝokùziñ
Itáriàziñ	nâniziñ 'what nationality?'
+îs-see '1st generation' ⎫	Used in reference to Japanese who have
+nî-see '2nd generation' ⎬	settled abroad; the **îs-see** are the original
+sâñ-see '3rd generation' ⎭	émigrés, the **nî-see** the second generation,
	etc.

MISCELLANEOUS NOTES

1. CC1 is a typical careful-style conversation between two adults whose relationship dictates the maintenance of some distance. On the videotape, two business colleagues (Carter and Suzuki) are talking together over coffee at a **kissateñ**. Except for a single fragment ([N]b) all utterances are major sentences, and predicates are distal-style.

Note (J)'s use of extended predicates: Kitamura's being married now is explained in terms of his having married last year in the U.S. The marriage in the U.S. is related to the fact that the wife is a Japanese-American, and knowledge of this information is explained by the fact that (J) knows her.

(N)'s check on Kitamura's marital status—a personal matter—is handled by checking with (J), a third party. This technique is certainly not peculiar to Japan, but it is particularly common among the Japanese.

(J)b. **Ôkusāñ, gosyûziñ**, etc.: Just as the vocabulary for sons and daughters reflects in-group/out-group distinctions, the vocabulary for spouses is similarly differentiated. The generic terms for husband and wife are **otto** and **tûma**; these terms can also be used for one's own spouse. **Syûziñ** and **kânai** are more polite terms specifically for one's own husband and wife (i.e., polite in a humble sense). However, in referring to the spouse of an out-group member—'your or her/his husband/wife'—polite-honorific terms must be used: **gosyûziñ** and **ôkusañ**. These terms may also be used in address. And when it is necessary to distinguish between Mr. and Mrs., a /name + **-sañ** + **no**/ precedes the spouse term: **Kitamura-sañ no gosyûziñ** 'Mr. Kitamura'; **Suzúki-sañ no òkusañ** 'Mrs. Suzuki.'

☠ WARNING: Be sure that your pronunciation of **ôkusañ** is differentiated from that of **okosañ** 'child.'

2. CC2 is a conversation between two persons of very different rank. On the videotape, (J) is Mr. Yoshida, the division chief, and (N) is Mr. Carter, his subordinate. Mr. Hayashi, the topic of discussion, is subordinate or equal to (J) (hence **Hayasi-kuñ**) but superior to (N) (hence [N]'s use of **irâsite . . . irássyaimàsu** in reference to him). (J) uses plain casual-style, evidenced by direct-style predicates in the plain form. In contrast, (N) uses careful polite-style, with honorific-polite and distal-style forms. His use of **ḡa** at the end of his utterance is polite in that it opens the way for (J) to make a request if he wishes to.

(N) **Mâe** has occurred previously (1) as a place word (**êki no mâe** 'front of the station'); and (2) compounded with time words that indicate a point in time (**nî-zi go-hûñ-mae** '5 to 2'; **ni-zí-màe** 'before 2'). **Mâe** also occurs with the general meaning of 'time before': **mâe ni kitâ** '[I] came before'; **mâe wa sôo datta kedo** 'before it was like that, but.' **Mâe**, both as place word and time word, can be differentiated as to degree or extent: **môtto mâe** 'earlier'; **zûibuñ mâe** 'awfully long ago'; **sukôsi mae** 'a little while ago'; **zyûu-neñ mâe** '10 years ago.' **Zutto màe** 'before by a great degree,' 'way before' is in this category. Note the difference in accent between **zíp-pùñ-mae** '10 to the hour' and **zîp-puñ mâe** or **zíp-puñ màe** '10 minutes ago.'

tokórò: The phrase /**X no tokórò**/ refers to the place where X is located, either in general or at a given moment. **Ukétuke no tokorò** is the location of the receptionist of a business or government office or any public building. **Tanáka-sañ no tokorò** might refer to Tanaka's regular location—home or office—or where Tanaka is located at the moment.

okyákusàma: The suffix **-sama** is a more polite alternate of **-sañ**. It occurs in polite speech in such words as **ôkusama, ozyôosama**, and **okosama**. However, it does not always alternate with **-sañ** and its use is not limited to animate nominals: for example, you have already encountered **-sama** in **gotisoosama**. A parallel **ñ/ma** alternation occurs in the case of some **-tyañ** forms: for example, **bôttyama** is a more polite alternate of **bôttyañ**.

3. CC3 is a casual-style conversation between two close friends; predicates are direct-style; two utterances are fragments; and one utterance is an inverted sentence. (N) is definitely female, as evidenced by her use of **wa yo** as a sentence ending. On the videotape, the participants are students, with (J) a male. His utterances are not marked for gender, but the fact that he is male suggests that the three individuals he identifies by /family name + **-sañ**/ are either definitely female or else superiors or only casual acquaintances. Close male friends would regularly be identified as /family name + **-kuñ**/ by another male.

(N)a. **kiku**: The meaning of this operational verbal covers the domain of hearing and listening as well as asking. The operator (i.e., asker/listener/hearer) may be followed by particle **ḡa** (or **wa**) and the operand (i.e., the thing asked, listened to, or heard) by particle **o** (or **wa**). See also SP4 following.

kyoositu: **Situ** 'room' occurs in many compounds, but never as an independent word. Compare also **tosyôsitu** and **kaíḡìsitu**.

4. CC4 is another casual-style conversation, marked by fragments and direct-style predicates. The participants on the videotape are the same as in CC3.

Note the extended predicates, (N)a 'You are looking at something, but what is it you are looking at?' (N)b 'Is your having the textbook to be explained in terms of your having bought it?' (J)b 'It's that I borrowed it.'

(J)b. **Kariru** covers the temporary use of someone else's possession(s), whether or not payment is being made, thus extending over the domains of both 'borrow' and 'rent' in English. Similarly, **kasu** covers the letting out of one's own possessions for use by others, whether or not payment is received, extending over the domains of English 'lend' and 'rent (out).'

Structural Patterns

1. VERBAL GERUND + (i)ru

In earlier lessons we concentrated on perfective and imperfective verbal forms, along with the derivative gerund which linked up with another predicate. Using the verbal **tukáimàsu** as an example, we covered:

tukau/tukáimàsu '[I] will use,' '[I] do use'

tukatta/tukáimàsita '[I] used'

tukátte kudasài 'please use' (*lit.* 'give me using')

tukátte kùru/kimàsu '[I]'ll go and use' (*lit.* 'I'll come having used')

tukatte îi (desu) 'it will be all right to use (*lit.* 'having used will be all right')

tukatte, sore kara, kâetta/kaérimàsita '[I] used [it], and then returned home'

The most obvious missing item in the above list is something that refers to the present moment: how does one express a present activity or state? But we *have* learned a verbal that refers to a present animate condition: **iru/imâsu**. We have also learned that the gerund links up with other predicates and implies 'actualization'—i.e., that something has been realized, whether or not it is finished. With these two notions in mind, we form the combination:

tukátte imàsu[6] '[I] am using'

Very literally, the combination means '[I] continue to be in a state that results from using that already started.'

Let us now examine some actual occurrences of this new combination:

Tîzu (o) kâite imasu. 'I'm drawing a map.'

Sińbuñ (o) mìte imasu. 'I'm looking at the paper.'

Kêeki (o) tukûtte imasu. 'I'm making a cake.'

Deńwa (o) kakete imàsu. 'I'm telephoning.'

With the above examples, compare:

Nâni (o) simâsu ka↗ 'What do you do?' *or* 'What are you going to do?'

Tîzu (o) kakimasu. 'I draw maps.' *or* 'I'm going to draw a map.'

The **-te imàsu** combinations above may also refer to a future situation which has not yet begun: in such cases, they indicate an activity or state extending over a period of time after the start of which something else will or might occur. For example, if I learn that you will

---

6. All examples in the distal-style can, of course, also occur in the direct-style.

telephone me tonight (**deńwa o kakemàsu**), I might reply, **mâtte imasu** 'I'll be waiting,' i.e., 'I will be in a state described as already (actualized) waiting.' Similarly, a friend will come (**kimâsu**) to my house tomorrow, when I 'will already be studying' (**beńkyoo-site imàsu**).

Now consider the activities involved in the **-te imàsu** examples above. They are all actions that are processes involving repeated, continuing activity. In contrast with this, consider Japanese verbals, of which there are many which regularly refer to a simple change of state from X to Y, i.e., the realization of a new state.[7] Examples in this category are **kekkoń-suru** 'get married'; **rikoń-suru** 'get divorced'; **yameru** 'quit'; **nâru** 'become'; **tomaru** 'come to a halt'; **tomeru** 'bring to a halt'; **wakâru** 'become comprehensible'; and motion verbals like **iku** 'go,' i.e., 'get to a place'; **kûru** 'come,' i.e., 'get here'; **kâeru** 'arrive home'; and **dêru** 'emerge.'

The gerund of one of these verbals /+ **iru** (or a distal and/or polite equivalent)/ usually refers *not* to a present activity or process but rather to a continuation of a present state (**iru**) resulting from an already completed occurrence. Thus:

> **kekkoń-site imàsu** '[I] am married' (i.e., I am in a state that results from having become married)
>
> **rikóń-site imàsu** '[I] am divorced'
>
> **ifte imàsu** '[I] have gone' (*not* 'I am at this moment on my way')
>
> **kitê imasu** '[I] have come,' '[I] am here'
>
> **kâette imasu** '[I] have returned,' '[I] am back'
>
> **dête imasu** '[I] have left,' '[I] am out' (for example, in reference to school)

These combinations may also refer to a future state. Consider a situation in which I say that by the time I arrive (**ikímàsu**) in Japan, a particular friend will already be out of school, i.e., will have graduated (**dête imasu**).

Given the appropriate contexts, these two categories of verbals may become difficult to distinguish. Thus it is also possible for **mîte imasu** to indicate that 'I have seen [something]'—not reflecting a continuing activity but the state that results from seeing; it may also refer to a repeated, continuing activity: for example, whenever he comes (**kimâsu**), I'm already looking at reports (**mîte imasu**); and **ifte imàsu** may refer to my repeated arrival at a destination (*not* one, single occasion of going), as in the case of my attending school.

The important feature of meaning of the **-te iru** pattern is the *effect* the occurrence represented by the **-te** form has on the referent. Compare these examples: If asked where Mr. Tanaka is at this moment, I might answer, **Kâńkoku ni ifte imàsu**. 'He has gone to Korea.' But the same statement might be used as an explanation of why he seems to know details relating to Korea: he has at some time gone there and continues to be affected by that fact, even though he is not there now. Usually **końpyùutaa o tukátte imàsu** refers to present (or future) activity over a period of time. But in the appropriate context, it might refer to the fact that someone *has used* a computer and is therefore affected even after the usage ends.

---

7. Note that Japanese and English verbs do not match up well in the area of process versus change of state. In English, we can say that 'John is coming,' meaning he is on his way. In Japanese, he is either *going to* **kûru** or he already **kitâ**; the Japanese verbal refers to an instantaneous change of state from unrealized to realized. Another example: Observing a car that is slowing down, I may say in English, 'That car is stopping.' In Japanese, it is either 'going to stop' (**tomaru**) or it 'stopped' (**tomatta**).

The **-te iru** pattern is also extremely common in the negative. Consider these examples: In reply to a question as to whether I am now using a computer, I can reply

Tukátte imasèñ 'I'm not using [it].'

The same answer might occur in answer to a question as to whether I will be using the computer tomorrow when the maintenance crew is due: 'I will not be using it.' But a particularly common use of this same sentence is in reply to a question as to whether or not I have used a computer: in that case, too, 'I am not in a state that results from computer usage,' i.e., 'I haven't used it.' Compare also: **itte imasèñ** '[I] haven't gone'; **kitê imásèñ** '[s/he] hasn't come'; **yaméte imasèñ** '[I] haven't quit.' The poor match between Japanese and English is particularly obvious in this /verbal gerund + **iru**/ pattern: depending upon context, a combination like **tukûtte imásèñ** may be the equivalent of English 'I'm not making [it],' or 'I won't be making [it],' or 'I haven't made [it].'

The perfective of **iru** may also occur following the gerund, with a predictable shift in meaning: **tâbete imasita** 'I was eating' or 'I had eaten (by a particular point in the past)'; **kâette imasita** 'I was back,' 'I had returned (by a particular point in the past).'

Obviously context plays an important part in the exact interpretation of these examples. But the important point to be stressed again is that this pattern emphasizes a continuing effect of an activity. Frequently, even in a negative answer to a **-màsita ka** question which asks about a *specific* past experience, a **-te imásèñ** form occurs, pointing up a lasting effect. Compare:

Señsyuu soré o kikimàsita ka 'Did you hear that last week?'

Iie, kikímasèñ desita. 'No, I didn't.' *or*

Iie, kiíte imasèñ. 'No. I am not in a state that results from having heard it.'

The latter is considered a more 'caring' answer if the questioner is believed to have hoped for an affirmative answer.

Affecting the **-te iru** pattern in general are the following:

a. **Iru** is regularly described as a verbal that refers to *animate* existence, but the **-te iru** combination occurs with inanimate referents as well, thereby transferring to inanimates the notion of animated activity or state. Thus: **Anó hòñ wa dête imasu.** 'That book has come out'; **Mâe ni 'kuruma ga sâñ-dai tomátte imàsu.** 'There are three cars parked in front'; **Teḡámi ga kitè imasu.** 'A letter has come.'

b. The pattern, predictably, has various polite alternates. Either the gerund and/or **iru** may be made polite.

Kekkoñ-site irassyaimàsu ↑ ka 'Are you married?' /honorific-polite/

Tomódati o màtte orimasu ↓. 'I'm waiting for a friend.' /humble-polite/

Kore (o) otúkai ni nàtte ↑ irassyaimasu ↑ ka 'Are you using this?' /honorific-polite/

Omáti-site ↓ orimàsu ↓.[8] 'I'll be waiting for you.' /a humble-polite ritual expression/

When the referent is inanimate, the polite alternate of **-te iru** is **-te ôru**, occurring in such cases as a neutral-polite form. Thus: **Tikatetu ḡa tomátte orimàsu.**+ 'The subway is stopped.'

c. The **-te iru** sequence is a unit pattern, pronounced without intervening pause. In normal, relaxed speech, **-te ôru** > **-t(e) ôru**, and the initial **i** of both **iru** and **irássyàru** is

---

8. This is a common polite reply to someone who has just indicated that s/he will be arriving/visiting/calling, etc. at some future time.

regularly dropped.[9] This has become so widespread that one occasionally comes upon items such as **tâbeteru** (= **tâbete [i]ru**) and **ittemàsu** (= **itte [i]màsu**). Since the Japanese receive no guidance in regard to word division from their own writing system (they leave no spaces within sentences), their representation of Japanese by means of romanization is apt to show great variation in this area. Our own word division is based on linguistic analysis and attempts to be consistent in observing certain underlying principles of the Japanese language. But regardless of what system one chooses for personal use, it is necessary to be able to read many different systems as well as totally arbitrary and inconsistent representations. After all, romanization is a *foreign* system for expediting the acquisition of the spoken language by *foreigners*; not surprisingly, it is of only minimal interest or concern to most Japanese.

2. siru; zoṅzìru ↓

The verbal **siru**, a consonant verbal (**sir-u**), is an operational verbal meaning 'acquire knowledge,' 'find out,' 'learn.' It occurs most commonly in the **-te (i)ru** pattern: **sittè (i)ru** '[I] know,' i.e., '[I] have found out.' The usual negative equivalent is **siranai**, indicating '[I] don't find out,' '[I] don't get to know.'

Since this is viewed as a personally determined activity, the area acted upon (the operand) may occur with particle **o**. Contrast this to the use of particle **ḡa** with the affective double-**ḡa** verbal **wakâru**; 'become clear,' 'become comprehensible.'

    Tanáka-sañ o sitte (i)màsu ka 'Do you know Mr/s. Tanaka?'

    Mití ḡa wakarimàsu ka 'Is the road clear [to you]?

Further evidence for the operational status of **siru** is the fact that we can say **siritai** 'I want to find out/know.' **Wakâru**, in contrast, does not ordinarily occur in the **-tai** form.

    Wakâru, like **siru**, usually refers to a state, rather than an activity, in its **-te iru** form. Compare:

    Wakárimàsu. 'I (repeatedly, in general) understand.'

    Wakárimàsita. 'I understood' (often: 'I understood what you just said'; *or* 'I see!'— now that you explained.)

    Wakâtte (i)masu. 'I have understood' ('I am in a state of already having become comprehending')

In contexts having to do with comprehension, **wakâru** is clearly the appropriate verbal. However, in many contexts related to 'knowing,' there is question as to whether one uses **wakâru** or **siru**. In general, **wakâru** has to do with recognition and 'being apparent' and 'being able to tell,' whereas **siru** relates to knowledge and acquisition of fact. *In some situations,* **wakárimaseñ** occurs as a less aggressive reply to a **sitte (i)màsu ka** question, when the speaker might be expected to know the answer:

    (To a taxi driver) **Paáku-bìru (o) sitte imàsu ka** 'Do you know the Park Building?'

      Wakárimaseñ nêe. 'I'm afraid it's not clear to me.'

Sirímaseñ in this context would sound as if the driver were doing nothing about his ignorance.

---

9. An unaccented gerund acquires a final-mora accent before contracted **-te** or **-ta** (from **ite/ita**): **tukatte** + **ta** > **tukáttè ta**. The accent of sequences that include **(i)-** is regularly marked according to the contracted alternate.

Another common negative reply is **sirímasèñ nêe**, which is deliberative and noncon-frontational.

Sirímasèñ desita 'I didn't know' (until you told me) is a common response to a new piece of information (cf. CC1[N]c).

The polite equivalents of **siťtè (i)ru** are **siťte (i)rassyàru** ↑ and **siťt(e) òru** ↓, which may also occur, of course, in distal-style.

There are additional polite equivalents of **siru**, based on a humble verbal **zoñzìru** ↓ (an operational vowel verbal). Thus:

zôñzite ↓ **(i)masu** is a humble-polite equivalent of **siťte (i)màsu**;

zôñzite ↓ **orimasu** ↓ is a more humble-polite equivalent of **siťte orimàsu** ↓;

zoñzimasèñ ↓ is a humble-polite equivalent of **sirímasèñ**.

Unlike most humble verbals, **zoñzìru** has a polite-honorific derivative, made up of /go- + stem zôñzi + dà/. Thus: **Gozôñzi** ↑ **desu ka** 'Do you know?' This alternates with **Siťte (i)rassyaimàsu** ↑ **ka**, also a polite-honorific. Both **gozôñzi** ↑ **zya nâi** and **gozôñzi** ↑ **nâi** occur in negative equivalents, although these are structurally different.

3. /NOMINAL + to + PREDICATE/: señsèe to hanâsu 'TALK WITH A TEACHER'

Before the current lesson, the phrase-particle **to** occurred only as a connector of nominals: /**X to Y**/ = 'Y with X,' i.e., 'X and Y.' Examples:

Kore to soré dèsu. 'It's this one and that one.'

Koóhìi to otyá (ḡa) arimàsu. 'There's coffee and tea.'

Otera to zîñzya (o) mimâsita. 'I saw temples and shrines.'

But the particle **to** can also link a nominal to a predicate: /nominal X + **to** + predicate Y/ describes the occurrence of Y 'in accompaniment with X': X to **hanâsu** 'talk with X.' The important feature to note is the notion of accompaniment, *not* the English equivalent 'with,' for as usual there is not an exact match between Japanese and English: **to** is definitely not the Japanese equivalent of every 'with' that occurs in English, and the reverse is equally mismatched. Thus we find examples of the following kinds:

nihóñzìñ to kekkoñ-suru 'marry a Japanese'

kore to tiḡau 'be different from this'

koré to onazi dà 'be the same as this' *but*

eñpitu de kàku 'write with a pencil'

mîruku de tukûru 'make [something] with milk'

têepu de beñkyoo-suru 'study with tapes'

Compare now the following two examples:

    (a) **Kâre to, kânozyo ḡa kekkoñ-suru** *'she* is going to marry him'

    (b) **Kâre to kânozyo ḡa kekkoñ-suru** 'he and she are getting married' (not necessarily to each other)

In (a), **kâre to** links up with the predicate, the verbal **kekkoñ-suru**; in (b), **kâre to** links up with the following nominal **kânozyo**. The phrasing and intonation of the two sentences distinguish them.

Particle **to** may, of course, be followed by **wa** or **mo**, with the usual modifications in meaning, and with the acquisition of an accent if the preceding nominal is unaccented.

Señsèe to wa hanásimàsita kedo . . 'I did talk with the professor (at least) but . . .' (I'm not commenting on talking with anyone else).

Koré tò mo tiḡau. 'It's different from this one, too.'

4. MORE ON PHRASE-PARTICLES **kara** *AND* **ni:** /**tomodati kara** *(OR* **ni**) **kariru**/

We have already pointed out that fundamentally the phrase-particle **ni** is a particle of location, but that depending on the predicate with which it links up, it may indicate original, or continuing, or ultimate location. It is therefore of great importance always to study **ni** together with the different kinds of predicates that may follow. Consider, for example:

(a) **Toókyoo ni ikimàsu.** 'I'm going to Tokyo.'

(b) **Toókyoo ni imàsu.** 'I'm in Tokyo.'

In (a), the /place + **ni**/ phrase describes the ultimate location—the location when the activity of **ikímàsu** is completed. In (b), conversely, a continuing location co-occurs with **imâsu**.

In this lesson, we find yet another kind of relationship involving an /**X** + **ni**/ phrase. When followed by **kariru,** the **ni** phrase describes an original location prior to the activity of the predicate. Thus, if I describe a book in terms of **tomódati ni karimàsita,** I am stating that the book was located with my friend *before* borrowing took place, i.e., I borrowed it 'from a friend.' Another verbal that functions in the same way is **itadaku** when it refers to receiving rather than eating or drinking: **señsèe ni itádakimàsita.** 'I received it from the doctor.' In such uses, **ni** alternates with **kara,** while with predicates of motion, **ni** and **kara** have almost opposite meanings! Study these examples:[10]

ni	kara
Similar usage	
tomodati ni kariru	**tomodati kara kariru** 'borrow from a friend'
señsèe ni itadaku	**señsèe kara itadaku** 'receive from a doctor'
tomodati ni kiku	**tomodati kara kiku** 'hear from a friend'
Contrastive usage	
asuko ni iku 'go to that place'	**asuko kara iku** 'go from that place'
asúko ni dèru 'go out to that place'	**asúko kara dèru** 'go out from that place'
Toókyoo ni kùru 'come to Tokyo'	**Toókyoo kara kùru** 'come from Tokyo'
Toókyoo ni kàeru 'return to Tokyo'	**Toókyoo kara kàeru** 'return from Tokyo'
Tookyoo ni ′deñwa (o) suru 'make a phone call to Tokyo'	**Tookyoo kara ′deñwa (o) suru** 'make a phone call from Tokyo'

The following **ni** phrases do not occur with **kara** either with a similar or with a different meaning:

tomódati ni misèru 'show to a friend'

tomodati ni kasu 'lend to a friend'

---

10. These examples are actually direct-style sentences, but are cited—and translated—as phrases.

tomódati ni kàku   'write to a friend'
tomodati ni osieru   'teach (to) a friend'
tomodati ni kiku   'ask a friend'

Drills

A 1. **Kitamura-sañ wa, tyôtto mâe ni**   **Êe. Tyôtto mâe kara mîete (i)masu nêe.**
   miémàsita neˤ
   'Mr/s. Kitamura came a little while   'Yes. S/he's been here (since) a little while
   ago—right?'   (ago).'

 2. **Kitamura-sañ wa, sêñḡetu anó hòñ**   **Êe. Sêñḡetu kara karíte (i)màsu nêe.**
   o karímàsita neˤ
   'Mr/s. Kitamura borrowed that book   'Yes. S/he's had it on loan since last month.'
   last month—right?'

 3. **señsyuu kaerimàsita**; 4. **otótoi kimàsita**; 5. **sêñḡetu yamémàsita**; 6. **yuúbe**
   ikimàsita

B 1. **Eeḡo, beńkyoo-site (i)màsu ka**   **Îma desu ka Beńkyoo-site (i)masêñ.**
   'Are you studying English?'   'Now? [No,] I'm not (studying).'

 2. **Konó zìsyo, tukátte (i)màsu ka**   **Îma desu ka Tukátte (i)masêñ.**
   'Are you using this dictionary?'   'Now? [No,] I'm not (using).'

 3. **kono zassi/mîte**; 4. **señsèe/mâtte**; 5. **teḡami/kâite**; 6. **eeḡo/osiete**

C 1. **Kinoo beńkyoo-simàsita ka**   **Êe. Kinôo wa âsa kara báñ màde**
   'Did you study yesterday?'   **beńkyoo-site (i)màsita yo**[11]
                                            'Yes. Yesterday I was studying from
                                            morning till night.'

 2. **Kinoo koñpyùutaa o tukáimàsita**   **Êe. Kinôo wa âsa kara bañ màde tukátte**
   ka   **(i)màsita yo**
   'Did you use the computer yesterday?'   'Yes. Yesterday I was using it from
                                                morning till night.'

 3. **arúbàito o simâsita**; 4. **kêeki o tukúrimàsita**; 5. **teḡámi o kakimàsita**; 6. **deńwa o**
   kakemàsita

D 1. **Anó hòñ demâsita ka**   **Iie, dête (i)másêñ.**
   'Did that book come out?'   'No, it hasn't come out.'

 2. **Anó hòñ mimâsita ka**   **Iie, mîte (i)másêñ.**
   'Did you see that book?'   'No, I haven't seen it.'

 3. **ano kodomo yobímàsita**; 4. **kânozyo kimâsita**; 5. **Kitamura-sañ miémàsita**;
   6. **deńwa simàsita**; 7. **końna koñpyùutaa tukáimàsita**

---

11. **Beńkyoo-simàsita** is also possible here, but the **-te (i)màsita** pattern emphasizes the fact that the activity *was going on* over a period of time (during which other events may have occurred).

E 1. **Watasi wa, kono-ḡoro, amari huráñsuḡo o beñkyoo-sit(e) orimasèñ yo.**
'Me—I haven't been studying French much lately.'

    Âa, Matúda-señsèe mo, amari beñkyoo-site (i)rassyaimasèñ nêe.
'Oh, Dr. Matsuda hasn't been studying much either, has s/he!'

2. **Watasi wa, kono-ḡoro, amari teḡámi o kàit(e) orímasèñ yo.**
'Me—I haven't been writing letters much lately.'

    Âa, Matúda-señsèe mo, amari kâite (i)rássyaimasèñ nêe.
'Oh, Dr. Matsuda hasn't been writing much either, has s/he!'

3. **koñpyùutaa o tukatte**; 4. **gôruhu o site**; 5. **gakúsee to hanàsite**; 6. **zêmi ni dête**; 7. **tosyôkañ e itte**; 8. **kotíra e kitè**

F 1. **Sore, otúkuri ni nàtte (i)rassyaru ñ desu ka⤹**
'(Is it that) you're making that?'

    Êe, tukûtt(e) orimasu.[12]
'Yes, I am (making).'

2. **Sore, otúkai ni nàtte (i)rassyaru ñ desu ka⤹**
'(Is it that) you're using that?'

    Êe, tukátt(e) orimàsu.
'Yes, I am (using).'

3. **omati**; 4. **okaki**; 5. **okiki**; 6. **okari**; 7. **okasi**

G 1. **Nâḡoya o sitte (i)màsu ka⤹**
'Do you know Nagoya?'

    Nâḡoya desu ka⤹ Sirímasèñ nêe.
'Nagoya? [No,] I don't (know).'

2. **Anó nikkèeziñ o sitte (i)màsu ka⤹**
'Do you know that person of Japanese ancestry?'

    Anó nikkèeziñ desu ka⤹ Sirímasèñ nêe.
'That person of Japanese ancestry? [No,] I don't (know).'

3. **Hayasi Tâkasi-sañ**; 4. **ano gaiziñ**; 5. **anó oñna no señsèe**; 6. **kono heñ no otera**

● Repeat this drill, replacing **sitte (i)màsu** with **gozôñzi desu** in the questions, and replacing **sirímasèñ** with **zoñzimasèñ** in the responses.

H 1. **Nikkèeziñ to kekkoñ-site (i)màsu neʔ**
'S/he's married to a person of Japanese ancestry—right?'

    Âa, sôo desu ka. Nikkèeziñ to kekkoñ-sitè (i)ru ñ desu ka.
'Oh, really? (Is it the case that) s/he's married to a person of Japanese ancestry?'

2. **Anó kyookàsyo to tiḡáimàsu neʔ**
'It's different from that textbook—right?'

    Âa, sôo desu ka. Anó kyookàsyo to tiḡáu ñ desu ka.
'Oh, really? (Is it the case that) it's different from that textbook?'

3. **okyakusañ/hanásimàsita**; 4. **kotira no kyoositu/onázi dèsu**; 5. **kânozyo/ikímàsita**

I 1. **Konó kyookàsyo wa karíte (i)màsu.**
    Dâre ni karítè (i)ru ñ desu ka⤹

12. Note that the responses in this drill can be made even more humble-polite by replacing the plain gerunds with corresponding humble-polite gerunds (**otukuri-site, otukai-site, omati-site,** etc.). However, such usage usually carries an implication of 'doing for (you).'

'This textbook—I'm borrowing.' 'From whom is it that you are borrowing it?' (*or* 'Who from?')

2. **Ano teḡami wa kakímàsita.** **Dâre ni kâita ñ desu ka‿**
'That letter—I wrote.' 'To whom is it that you wrote it?' (*or* 'Who to?')

3. **ano uti/kasíte (i)màsu;** 4. **utí màde no tîzu/misémàsita;** 5. **sore/hanásimàsita;**
6. **sore/kikímàsita;** 7. **eḡo/osíete (i)màsu**

J 1. **Konó kàsa wa karíte (i)màsu.** **Dâre kara karítè (i)ru ñ desu ka‿**
'This umbrella—I've borrowed.' 'From whom is it that you've borrowed it?' (*or* 'Who from?')

2. **Teḡámi ḡa kimàsita.** **Dâre kara kitâ ñ desu ka‿**
'A letter has arrived.' 'From whom is it that it came?' (*or* 'Who from?')

3. **sore wa yuúbe kikimàsita;** 4. **kore wa kokó de kaimàsita**

K 1. **Kore wa, kânai ḡa tukúrimàsita.** **Ee? Ôkusan ḡa? Sôo desu ka.**
'This one my wife made.' 'Huh? Your wife? Really?'

2. **Kore wa tûma ḡa kaímàsita.** **Ee? Ôkusañ ḡa? Sôo desu ka.**
'This one my wife bought.' 'Huh? Your wife? Really?'

3. **musuko/karíte (i)màsu;** 4. **musúmè/kakímàsita;** 5. **kodomo/tukátte (i)màsu**

L 1. **Kaíḡìsitu de okyákusañ ḡa màtte** **A. Kaíḡìsitu de desu ka‿ Wakárimàsita.**
(i)masu yo‿ 'Oh, in the conference room? OK.'
'There's a visitor waiting in the
conference room.'

2. **Ukétuke no torokò de Amérika no** **A. Ukétuke no tokorò de desu ka‿**
hitò ḡa mâtte (i)masu yo‿ **Wakárimàsita.**
'There's an American (person) 'Oh, at the reception desk? OK.'
waiting at the reception desk.'

3. **kyoositu/gaiziñ;** 4. **baíteñ no màe/Tanáka-sañ no òkusañ;** 5. **omóte no dèḡuti/**
gosyûziñ

M 1. **Nî-see no hito mo, sâñ-see no hito** **Sâñ-see no hito wa· miênakatta kedo ..**
mo, miémàsita ka‿ 'Sansei (at least) did not come, but . . .'
'Did both nisei and sansei come?' (perhaps others did).

2. **Niḱkèeziñ mo, îs-see no hito mo,** **Îs-see no hito wa hanásànakatta kedo ..**
hanásimàsita ka‿ 'The issei (at least) did not talk, but . . .'
'Did both the nikkeijin and the issei (perhaps others did).
talk?'

3. **huráñsùziñ/doítùziñ/demâsita;** 4. **otona/kodomo/okúremàsita;** 5. **tyuúḡokùziñ/**
kañkokùziñ/kimàsita; 6. **iñdòziñ/rosíàziñ/wakárimàsita**

N 1. **A. Anô hito wa nihóñḡo ḡa** **Anô hito desu ka‿ Nihóñziñ na ñ desu**
dekimàsu nêe. **yo‿**

'Oh! S/he can speak Japanese, can't s/he!'

'Her/him? (It's that) s/he's Japanese!'

2. **A. Kânozyo wa, doítuğo ğa dekimàsu nêe.**

'Oh! She can speak German, can't she!'

Kânozyo desu ka⁀ Doítùziñ na ñ desu yo⁀

'Her? (It's that) she's German!'

3. **kâre/tyuuğokuğo**; 4. **anó otoko no hitò/itariağo**; 5. **anó oñna no hitò/supeiñğo**; 6. **anô ko/rosiağo.**[13]

Application Exercises

A1. Extend the family tree you are developing to include a number of husbands and wives. Follow the procedures outlined in Application Exercise A1 of 10A. Use this opportunity both to use the new kinship vocabulary and to review the old.

2. Using pictures of famous people from around the world, ask and answer questions relating to nationality, approximate age, marital status, and name of spouse.

3. Distribute cards to members of your group, establishing an imaginary identity: name, nationality, special features (for example, nikkeijin, sansei, etc.), age, marital status, education (for example, graduate of Tokyo University). Conduct direct interviews (politely!) and also third person question-and-answer practice (in both careful/polite and casual/plain style).

4. Instruct members of your group to carry out particular tasks, and while they are actually performing them, have other group members ask them what it is they are doing. Examples: 'Write your name on this paper'; 'Look at the magazines over there'; 'Draw a map to your house'; 'Ask a friend the way (= **miti**) to his/her house'; 'Teach a friend some French'; 'Show a friend your Japanese textbook'; 'Drink coffee'; 'Eat this'; 'Call a cab.'

5. Make a list of dates of particular events (examples: Mr. Ito's arrival in the U.S., Ms. Matsuda's return to Japan, Mr. Miyaji's arrival here, Ms. Nakamura's quitting Oriental Trade, Mr. Tanaka's marriage, Mr. Yamamoto's divorce). Practice asking and answering questions, using all the patterns available for conveying that one bit of information. (Assume that the results of that event are still in effect.)

Examples:

Nâñ(-neñ) mâe ni ikímàsita ka⁀   'How many (years) ago did s/he go?'

Nâñ(-neñ) ni ikímàsita ka⁀   'In what (year) did s/he go?'

Îma made nâñ(-neñ) itte (i)màsu ka⁀   'How many (years) has s/he been gone, up until now?'

Nâñ(-neñ) kara itte (i)màsu ka⁀   'Since what year has s/he been gone?'

Náñ(-neñ) màe kara itte (i)màsu ka⁀   'Since how many years ago has s/he been gone?

B. Core Conversations: Substitution

Practice the Core Conversations, making substitutions that do not alter the basic patterns

---

13. **Rosíàziñ**, often used conversationally, can of course be replaced by the more technically correct **Soréñziñ**.

of the conversations. Again, change the participants so as to affect the language style that is appropriate. However, be sure that the subject matter is appropriate to the participants!

C. Core Conversations: Review

At this juncture, having completed the first ten lessons of the text, run through all the Core Conversations of Lessons 1–10, preferably by viewing the videotape, but if that is impossible, by listening to the audiotapes. Do the conversations still sound thoroughly familiar? Are they surprisingly easy to follow, compared to the time when you first encountered them? Arc you ENCOURAGED by your progress?

If you are not able to respond with a definite *yes* to these questions, it would be advisable to review further before moving ahead.

SECTION C

Eavesdropping

Answer the following on the basis of the accompanying audiotape. (A = the first speaker, and B = the second speaker, in each conversation)
1a. What does A want to know?
 b. What time does B specify?
2a. Who is being commented on?
 b. How old does B judge that person to be?
3a. What is A concerned about?
 b. What is its location, as described by B?
4a. What does A request?
 b. How does B respond?
5a. Who has just returned home?
 b. What has that person been doing? Since when?
 c. Whom does B admire? Why?
6a. Who is being discussed?
 b. How old is that person?
 c. Why is A surprised?
7a. Who is it that A is looking for?
 b. Where is that person?
 c. What is that person doing?
 d. Compare the ranks of A and B.
8a. Who is B?
 b. Who is waiting for B? Where?
 c. Who does B think that person is? Why?
9a. Who came here last week?
 b. Why was there no difficulty?
10a. What does A admire?
 b. How does A think B acquired this?
 c. How did B actually acquire it?
11a. What information mentioned by A does B already know?
 b. How did B learn it?
 c. What travel does it involve?
 d. What reason is mentioned for B's being particularly interested?
12a. Who is A?

b. Where is A going tomorrow, and why?
c. How does B feel about this kind of activity?
d. How does A feel about himself?
e. What is B's reaction?
13. What does A want from B? Why? Give details.
14a. Who is it that A is looking for?
b. Where is that person?
c. Describe that person: age, sex, nationality, education.
15a. What does A describe as a pleasure?
b. Who is Takashi?
c. When did Takashi marry?
d. Describe his bride. Give details.
16a. What does A believe about B's husband? Why?
b. What is the actual situation?
c. What does B modestly claim?
17a. What does A describe as having been interesting?
b. Who was there besides A?
c. Why doesn't B know any details?
18a. What does A recall about B?
b. Until when did that continue?
c. What is B doing now?
19a. Why is B surprised?
b. What has A done in connection with the matter under discussion? What was the result?
20a. What kind of work is B doing?
b. What are the ages and nationalities of the individuals involved?
c. What difficulty connected with the work does B mention?

Utilization

(Given your current proficiency, you can now use the following as the basis for short conversations similar to the Core Conversations. In some cases, even lengthy conversations are possible. Utilize everything you have learned, including hesitation noises and **aizuti**.)

1. Ask a stranger who has just walked into the office if she is Ms. Miyaji. Be polite!
2. Introduce yourself (politely) as /name/ from Oriental Trade.
3. Ask a visitor (politely) to write his name here.
4. Tell a colleague that Dr. Yamamoto is probably not coming today.
5. Ask a close friend who that foreigner over there is.
6. Approach a receptionist and find out if Mr. Kato is in. Tell her you have a 10:30 appointment, but you came a little early.
7. Exclaim on how cute little Takashi is. Find out how old he is.
8. A colleague is about to leave for home. Ask him if that means he is not going to attend the seminar that starts at 4:00.
9. Mr. Ito is accompanied by a child. Find out if it is his daughter; son; child.
10. Ask about the identity of that child over there.
11. Ask a colleague what kind of part-time work Japanese students do.
12. You've heard the price of admission at a particular theater. Ask if both adults and children are the same.
13. Ask if both men and women attend Dr. Ito's seminar.
14. There will be a three-day conference beginning the month after next. Ask your boss (politely!) if he will attend.

15. Tell a colleague that both old people and young people are attending the Saturday English classes.

16. Find out if the Nakamura baby's name is Takashi.

17. Find out who that person over there is. Ask your question politely.

18. A young stranger is making tea for office personnel. Ask a close friend who that is.

19. You've been asked a close friend's age. Answer that he'll be twenty in April.

20. Starting the week after next, class will begin at 8:30. You've been asked if that bothers you. Answer that it doesn't especially matter, but find out what time it ends.

21. Tell a colleague that Mr. Miller's wife is of Japanese descent, but she doesn't understand Japanese at all.

22. Tell a close friend, who has been asking about another friend, Kubota (male), that he got married in the U.S. last month and came back to Japan immediately with his wife.

23. A colleague is looking for Ms. Matsuda, a mutual friend. Explain that a little while ago she was talking with a foreigner at the reception desk, but you, too, wonder where she is now.

24. Ask a close friend what (it is) he's doing.

25. In answer to the preceding question, answer that you are (a) waiting for a cab; (b) listening to Japanese tapes; (c) making a cake; (d) drinking coffee.

26. You are discussing Mr. Kitamura's history with a colleague. Tell her that in 1983, he probably wasn't [already] married.

27. You've been asked about various past experiences. Explain that you have not (a) been (= gone) to Europe (in contrast with other places); (b) talked with your teacher in Japanese (in contrast with other languages); (c) seen the new textbook (in contrast with the old ones).

28. Ask your teacher (politely) if she knows (a) Takashi Hayashi; (b) Kyoto.

29. Tell a colleague that at that school (at least) they probably are not teaching Chinese.

30. Tell your supervisor, in answer to his question about Dr. Miller, that you do know her but you don't know her husband. Speak politely.

31. Ask a colleague if he would be kind enough to lend you ¥500.

32. Comment (expecting agreement) that the new textbook is very different from the old one.

33. A colleague was surprised to hear that Mr. Kubota is an American. Explain that (it's that) he's nisei.

34. A stranger is looking for the English class. Tell her that they are using the classroom near the reception desk.

35. A close friend is looking for Ms. Kitamura. Tell him that she's talking with a foreign visitor in the conference room.

36. Inquire where (it is) in this hotel that one rents typewriters.

37. Your colleague is surprised that you are driving to Kyoto. Explain that (it's that) you borrowed a car from a friend.

38. You've just heard that the new part-time worker is seventeen. Check on the fact that he is that young.

39. You've just learned something new. Express surprise and tell your friend that you didn't know that.

40. A business associate has announced that he is coming to see you tomorrow. Tell him that you'll be waiting.

Check-up

1. What is the difference in usage between items in groups like (a) **musuko** and **musukosañ/bôttyañ**; (b) **musúmè** and **musumesañ/ozyôosañ**; (c) **ko/kodomo** and **okosañ**? (A-SP1)

2. Contrast **kâre/kânozyo, sonô hito**, and **sonó katà**. (A-SP1)

3. What two series are used to count human age? Give two equivalents for 'twenty years old.' (A-SP1)

4. What is the honorific-polite equivalent of **nihóñzìñ desu**? the neutral-polite equivalent? What are the negative equivalents of the two polite forms? (A-SP2)

5. Describe a derivative honorific-polite pattern of verbals which do not have special polite equivalents. What is the alternate for **irássyàru** within this pattern? (A-SP3)

6. What is the difference in meaning between time words beginning **señ-** and those beginning **señseñ-**? between those beginning **rai-** and those beginning **sarai-**? (A-SP4)

7. What are **aizuti**? Describe their use and the implications. (A-SP5)

8. Negative verbal derivatives ending in **-maseñ** are distal-style. How are the direct-style equivalents formed? Why are they classed as adjectivals? (A-SP6)

9. Describe an alternate distal-style negative for (a) **-maseñ** forms; (b) **-maseñ desita** forms. (A-SP6)

10. What form of direct-style negative occurs before the verbal **nâru**? Give examples. (A-SP6)

11. What is the difference in meaning between **simâsu** and **sité (i)màsu**? between **kimâsu** and **kitê (i)masu**? (B-SP1)

12. Give the Japanese equivalents of the following: 'I'm studying'; 'I'll be waiting' (when you arrive); 'I'm married'; 'I've quit'; 'I haven't gone to Japan'; 'I wasn't listening'; 'I've returned'; 'My watch had stopped' (i.e., when I looked at it); 'I'm not teaching' (B-SP1)

13. What is the basic meaning of **siru**? Explain the form and meaning of **sitte (i)màsu**. What is its usual negative equivalent? (B-SP2)

14. Describe the differences between **wakárimàsu** and **sitte (i)màsu**. (B-SP2)

15. Give honorific-polite and humble-polite equivalents (two of each) for **sitte (i)màsu**. (B-SP2)

16. Particle **to** may link nominals or link a nominal with a predicate. Give an example of each. (B-SP3)

17. What is the underlying meaning of particle **ni**? How is its meaning modified, depending on the predicate with which it is linked? Give examples. (B-SP4)

18. In the combination **tomodati ni kariru**, what particle may alternate with **ni**? (B-SP4)

Lesson 11

SECTION A

Core Conversations

1(N)a. **Yuube 'Hasimoto-sañ no onîisañ ni aímàsita yo**

    (J)a. **Sôo desu ka. Yasásii hitò desyoo?**

b. **Êe. Sore ni, eeḡo ḡa suḡôku zyoózù de, biḱkùri-simasita.**

    b. **Âa, mukôo ni nâḡâku itâ kara.**

c. **Dê mo, zyoózù desu nêe.**

2(N)a. **Aĺtàkàku nâtta kara, otaku to utí no kàzoku de, issyo ni nâni ka simásèñ ka**

    (J) **Âa, îi âidea desu nêe. Zyâa, kânai to 'soodañ-site, mata âto de deńwa-simàsu kara . .**

b. **Onéḡai-simàsu. Hatî-zi ni wa kâette (i)ru to omóimàsu kara . .**

3(J)a. **Oyasumi wa dôo suñ no?**

    (N)a. **Hoḱkàidoo e ikítai to omòtte (i)ru ñ desu kedo . .**

b. **Hoḱkàidoo? Hitô-ri de ikû no?**

    b. **Ie. |Anoo| Yamanaka-kuñ to 'Yamanaka-kuñ no imootosañ to, sań-nìñ de.**

c. **Âa, zyâa, omósiròi daroo ne!**

4(N) **Kâre wa dôo site îtu mo osókù made kaísya ni irù ñ desyoo nêe.**

    (J) **Raśsyu-àwaa ḡa iyâ da kara desyoo.**

English Equivalents

1(N)a. Say, I met Mr/s. Hashimoto's (older) brother last night.

    (J)a. Oh. He's pleasant, isn't he?

b. Yes. What's more, I was amazed at how proficient his English is.

    b. Oh, [that's] because he was abroad for a long time.

   c. Even so, he is good, isn't he!

2(N)a. Since it's gotten warm, wouldn't you [like to] do something together, (being) your family and ours?

                            (J) Oh, that's a good idea! (In that case) I'll talk it over with my wife, and then I'll telephone you (again) later so . . . (that's how we can arrange it).

   b. Would you do that? At 8 o'clock I'll be back home I think, so . . . (call after that).

3(J)a. What are you going to do about your vacation?

                          (N)a. I've been thinking that I'd like to go to Hokkaido, but . . . (I'm not certain).

   b. Hokkaido? Are you going alone?

                           b. No. Uh, with (Mr.) Yamanaka and his (younger) sister, (being) three of us.

   c. Oh, then it should be fun!

4(N) Why do you suppose it is that he is always in the office until late?

                         (J) It's probably because he hates the rush hour.

BREAKDOWNS
(AND SUPPLEMENTARY VOCABULARY)

1. **Hasimoto**	(family name)
(o)nîisañ (SP1)	older brother (of an out-group member or as a term of address) /polite/
+**âni**	older brother; my older brother
+**(o)nêesañ**	older sister (of an out-group member or as a term of address) /polite/
+**ane**	older sister; my older sister
âu /-u; **âtta**/	meet, see (a person)
X ni âu	meet person X, see person X
yasásii hitò	a person who is gentle, kind, nice
+**muzúkasii hitò**	a person who is hard to get on with, hard to please
sore ni	onto that, on top of that, in addition
suĝôi /-**katta**/	is awful, wonderful, weird, terrific
suĝôku zyoózù da	is awfully skilled/skillful
biḱkùri-suru	become surprised

mukôo ni itâ kara (SP2)	because [he] was abroad; [he] was abroad so . . .
2. at(á)takài /-katta/	is warm
+ suzúsìi /-katta/	is cool
+ atûi /-katta/	is hot
+ samûi /-katta/	is cold (of atmospheric temperature only)
at(á)tàkàku nâtta kara	because it became warm; it became warm so . . .
kâzoku	family; my family
+ gokâzoku	family of the out-group /polite/
issyo	togetherness
issyo ni suru (SP3)	do together
âidea	idea
(go)soodañ-suru	consult, talk over
âto de	later on
deñwa-simàsu kara	because [I] will telephone; [I] will telephone so . . .
omôu /-u; omôtta/ (SP4)	think
kâette (i)ru to omôu	think that [I] will have returned, i.e., will [already] be back
kâette (i)ru to omóimàsu kara	because [I] think [I] will be back; [I] think [I] will be back so . . .
3. dôo suru?	how will [you] act? what will [you] do?
dôo suñ no?	/assimilated equivalent of **dôo surû no?**/
Hokkàidoo	Hokkaido (northernmost main island of Japan)
+ Hôñsyuu	Honshu (main island of Japan)
+ Kyûusyuu	Kyūshū (main island of Japan)
+ Sikôku	Shikoku (main island of Japan)
ikítai to omòtte (i)ru	[I]'ve been thinking [I]'d like to go
hitô-ri	one person; alone; single
hitô-ri de iku	go alone (*lit.* being one person)
Yamanaka	(family name)
imóotò/imootosañ[1]	younger sister
+ otóotò/otootosañ[1]	younger brother
+ (go)kyôodai[1]	brothers and sisters, siblings
sań-nìñ	3 people
sań-nìñ de	being 3 people

1. The longer form is a polite form used in reference to the out-group.

omósiròi daroo (SP5)	/direct-style equivalent of **omósiròi desyoo**/
4. **dôo site**	how come? how? why?
+ **nâze**	why?
îtu mo	always
osókù made	until late
kaisya	a company, a firm
+ **zimûsyo**	office
raśsyu-àwaa	rush hour
iyâ /**na**/	unpleasant, disagreeable
iyâ da kara da	it's because it is unpleasant

-ri/-niñ: *Classifier for counting human beings*

hitô-ri	**rokû-niñ**
hutá-rì	**nanâ-niñ/sitî-niñ**
sań-nìñ	**hatî-niñ**
yo-nîñ	**ku-nîñ**
go-nîñ	**zyûu-niñ**

nâñ-niñ 'how many people?'

MISCELLANEOUS NOTES

As we move on into more advanced Japanese, it becomes apparent that matching up the Japanese conversations with close English equivalents that sound natural is becoming increasingly difficult. Again, it is important to point out that natural Japanese is not a translation of natural English, and vice versa.

1. CC1 is a careful-style conversation between two colleagues who continue to maintain distance in their relationship. On the videotape, the participants are Deborah Miller and Mr. Yamada, employees of the Oriental Trading Company, who work at adjoining desks.

(N)a. **Âu,** an operational, **w**-root consonant verbal (negative **aw-âna-i**), may be used either in reference to meeting a person for the first time, or when simply making contact with a person already known. (Contrast **hitô [o] mîru** 'look at a person.') It is not surprising that native speakers of Japanese have great difficulty controlling 'see" and 'meet' in English. The person met is followed by **ni** or **to**: **tomódati ni àtta** 'I met a friend,' 'I saw (and made contact with) a friend'; **tomódati to àtta** 'I met with a friend.' When **to** is used, the emphasis is on a mutual meeting of associates.

(N)b. The meaning of **suğôi** might best be explained as what a very small Japanese child once said at his first encounter with a full-grown giraffe in the zoo! When it links up with another predicate, in the **-ku** form, it describes manner, i.e., the 'how' of the following predicate (cf. [SP3], following). In the colloquial speech of young adults, **suğôi** occurs as an uninflected nominal of manner: **suğôi kîree desu.** Compare English 'She's awful pretty.' (The standard language equivalent would, of course, be **Sûğôku kîree desu.**)

Zyoózù de, biḱkùri-simasita: 'being proficient, I became surprised.' For this use of the gerund, see 8A-SP5. **Eeḡo ḡa** preceding **zyoózù de** shows an exhaustive² and close link between those two segments, indicating that **eeḡo** is specifically *not* linked with **bikkùri-simasita**. Compare: **Tomodati *wa* zyoózù de yôku eéḡo o tukaimàsu.** 'My friend, being proficient, uses English often,' in which **tomodati wa** links up with both parts of the sentence (cf. SP2, following).

(J)b. **Nâḡàku iru** 'be [somewhere] long' is another example of an adjectival in its **-ku** form linking up with a predicate and describing how (cf. SP3, following).

2. Again, in CC2 two business associates who maintain some distance in their relationship conduct a conversation in careful-style. On the accompanying videotape, Mr. Carter suggests a joint family outing to Mr. Suzuki, both employees of the Continental Bank, who occupy adjoining desks.

(N)a. **Attakài** is a common spoken alternate of **atátakài**. The implication is 'nice and warm,' and this is the adjectival that describes typical spring weather and unusually pleasant weather in the winter. **Suzúsìi** 'nice and cool' is the description of typical fall weather and unusually pleasant summer weather. **Atûi** and **samûi** refer to the more extreme typical weather of summer and winter, and the unusual extremes of other seasons. **Atûi** 'is hot' is a general term for hot temperature, and may be applied to anything that fits that description. **Samûi**, on the other hand, refers only to atmospheric temperature. Accordingly, today may be **atûi** or **samûi**, but coffee can *never* be **samûi**.

Otaku to uti refers to 'your household and my household.' As a description of **kâzoku**, the linking **no** is required. Since **uti** is the closer describing word, **kâzoku** rather than **gokâzoku** occurs. The invitation to do something together is extended in terms of its 'being your and our family' who will constitute the participants.

The call that (J) will make will occur 'having consulted with my wife.' **Mata** refers loosely here to talking over the idea again rather than specifically making another phone call. In Japanese society, where such heavy emphasis is placed on consulting and reaching consensus among all parties involved before proceeding with any project—from a family picnic to changing the design of an automobile—it is not surprising that **soodañ-suru** (**gosoodañ-suru** for polite reference to consultation with the out-group) is a very frequently encountered word. To an unacculturated Westerner, the process can require a period of time which causes surprise, bafflement, or even exasperation.

Âto de 'being a subsequent point' (cf. 8A, CC2).

(N)b. Compare **kâeru to omôu** 'I think I'll return' and **kâette (i)ru to omôu** 'I think I'll (already) have returned.' **Hatî-zi ni wa** implies that at least at 8:00 (N) will be back (but maybe not before).

3. CC3 is a conversation between a ranking (J) and his subordinate (N). (J) uses casual-style: the questions ending in **no?** are typical of an empathetic, gentle direct-style. The final-predicate **daròo**, also direct-style, is more typical of blunt speech. (N)'s two utterances are both minor sentences, but the occurrence of a distal-style predicate before **kedo** reflects speech that is more careful than (J)'s. On the videotape, a professor (J) is speaking informally in his office with Sue Brown (N), one of his students. Note the three extended predicates: (J)a, 'How is it you will handle your vacation?' (N)a, 'It's explained in terms of my thinking I'd like to go to Hokkaido', and (J)b, 'Does that mean you are going alone?'

(J)a. **Dôo suru** 'how will you handle——?' 'what will you do about——?' 'how will

2. 'Exhaustive' indicates that **eeḡo** is closely linked to its predicate as the only item involved, with no implied comparison with anything else.

you act?' contrasts with **nâni o suru** 'what will you do?' Note also: **dôo sita** 'what happened?' 'how did [you] handle———?' **Suñ no** is a more relaxed, informal equivalent of **surû no**.

(J)b. Since Hokkaido is rather far from Tokyo, (J) exhibits some surprise until he knows that (N) is not going alone. Compare: **hitô-ri iku** 'one person is going'; **hitô-ri de iku** 'go, being one person,' i.e., 'go alone'; **hutá-rì de iku** 'go as a twosome'; **kâzoku de suru** 'do as a family' (cf. CC2, above). **Hitô-ri** also occurs as 'single' (unmarried).

(N)b. (N) is going to Hokkaido *not* **hitô-ri de** 'being one person,' but rather **sañ-nìñ de** 'being 3 people'; this results from the fact that she is going 'with X and Y.'

4. Two colleagues, using careful-style, are discussing a mutual associate's habit of staying late in the office. On the accompanying videotape, Mr. Yamada and Deborah Miller discuss the question as they eat together at a restaurant after work. (N)'s question ending in **nêe** implies that (J) is expected to agree with the posing of the question.

(N) **Dôo site,** in origin the gerund derivative of **dôo suru**, links up with a predicate and asks: '(acting) how?' 'how come?' 'why?' Examples: **Dôo site soré o tukùru ñ desu ka** 'How is it you make that?' **Dôo site wakárimàsita ka** 'How come you understood?' **Dôo site yamérù ñ desu ka** 'Why is it you're quitting?' However, it has now acquired a kind of unit status: it may occur directly before **dèsu** (unlike the normal verbal gerund) as if a nominal (**Dôo site desu ka** 'Why is it?'). **Nâze** 'why?' occurs as a slightly more blunt equivalent of **dôo site** in those contexts in which it asks for a reason.

Îtu mo 'always' (i.e., 'all the "whens"') is comparable in pattern to **dôo mo** 'in every way' (i.e., 'all the "hows"'). More will be said about this pattern in a later lesson.

Osókù 'late time' is a nominal derived from an adjectival, based on the **-ku** form of the adjectival. Additional parallel examples will be introduced in later lessons.

Kaisya is a private company or corporation, but in many contexts in which English would locate someone in 'his/her office', the Japanese locates the individual **kaisya ni. Zimûsyo** refers specifically to an office, i.e., a place where business activities are conducted; it is *not* a doctor's office or a professor's office.

(J) **Iyâ** is a /**na**/ nominal; with **dà** it constitutes a double-**ga** affective predicate. **Dâre ga iyâ desu ka** 'Who doesn't like it?' or 'Who is disliked?'; **Nâni ga iyâ desu ka** 'What don't you like?' This is our first example of a double-**ga** predicate whose primary *and* secondary affects may both be animate: **Watasi ga anó señsèe ga iyâ desu.** '*I* dislike that teacher.'

Structural Patterns

1. MORE ON THE FAMILY; COUNTING PEOPLE

We now add brothers and sisters to the emerging Japanese family. The cover term is **kyôodai** (**gokyôodai** in polite reference to the out-group), which covers all of one's siblings. However, if we differentiate by sex, we must also differentiate by relative age. One way to designate brothers as opposed to sisters in general is with phrases such as **otóko no kyòodai** and **oñna no kyòodai**, but these combinations occur only rarely.

Whether one's brother(s) and sister(s) are older or younger is extremely important in recognition of hierarchy. Usually I call only younger family members by their given names; all older members are generally addressed with the *polite* terms that designate the relationship. This means that if I talk *about* my siblings to the out-group, I use the generic terms **âni, ane, otóotò**, and **imóotò**. But when I *address* them or talk *about* them within the family,

I use **(o)nîisañ**[3] and **(o)nêesañ**[3] for my older siblings, and given names for the younger. When I talk to out-group members about *their* siblings, I of course use the polite terms: **(o)nîisañ, (o)nêesañ, otootosañ,** and **imootosañ.** Also, **(o)nîisañ** and **(o)nêesañ** are regularly used to address children who are strangers.

When **-sama** replaces **-sañ** in the above polite items, the result is terms of even greater respect. And in some families, polite alternates ending in **-tyañ** and **-tyama** are also used; while polite, they are also more intimate.

The generic term for family is **kâzoku,** also used in reference to one's own family. To refer politely to the family of an out-group member, **gokâzoku** is used.

The classifier for counting people occurs in two different forms (**ri** and **niñ**), each of which uses a different numeral series. (See the complete list above, following the Breakdowns.) Note particularly the combination for 'four': **yo-niñ.** Note also the distinction in meaning between phrases like: **sono hutá-rì no kodomo** 'those two children'[4] and **sono hutá-tù no kodomo** 'that/those two-year-old child(ren),' and between: **sono zyûugo-niñ no gakusee** 'those fifteen students' and **sono zyûugo no gakusee** 'that/those fifteen-year-old student(s).'

2. /PREDICATE X + kara/: 'BECAUSE X'

In earlier lessons, **kara** was introduced following nominals that indicated a point of origin: **kyôo kara** 'from today'; **Tookyoo kara** 'from Tokyo'; **tomodati kara** 'from a friend'; **kore kara** 'from this point,' 'next.'

We now introduce **kara** following a predicate in the imperfective or perfective or tentative; this predicate is now a point of origin in the sense that it indicates the *cause* or *origin* of what follows.

/Predicate X + **kara** + predicate Y/ = 'because X, Y'; 'X, so Y'; 'X, therefore Y' (i.e., 'from the occurrence of X comes the occurrence of Y'). Examples:

Kinóo ittà kara, kyôo wa 'ikanai. 'I went yesterday, so I'm not going today.'

Yasásìi kara, yôku wakâru. 'I understand it very well because it's easy.'

Byoóki dà kara, uti ni iru. 'I'm sick, so I'm at home.'

Dôo site and **nâze** questions that ask for a reason require **kara** in the answer much more strictly than 'because' is required in similar situations in English.

The predicate before **kara** follows the pattern of the predicate before **kedo**: if the final predicate is direct-style, only the direct-style occurs before **kara**; but if the final predicate is distal-style, or a polite request, either distal- or direct-style may occur before **kara,** the former indicating more careful style. Before **kara,** an unaccented predicate acquires an accent—a verbal on its final syllable and an adjectival on the vowel preceding final **-i.** Examples:

Zutto màe kara nihóñḡo beñkyoo-sitè (i)ru /-site (i)màsu kara, yôku wakâru desyoo. '[S/he] has been studying Japanese (since) a long while (ago), so [s/he] probably understands very well.'

Takâi (desu) kara, kaímasèñ. 'I'm not going to buy it, because it's expensive.'

Yukî datta/desita kara, utí kara demasèñ desita. 'It was snow[ing], so I didn't go out of the house.'

---

3. Alternates with and without /o-/ occur. Women tend to prefer the alternate that includes /o-/.
4. Compare **sonó huta-rì no kodomo** 'child(ren) of those two people.'

Asóko dà/dèsu kara, koko de yuútàañ-site kudasai. 'That's the place, so please make a U-turn here.'

Tâkâkatta kara, kawánàkatta. 'It was expensive, so I didn't buy it.'

Damê da kara, komâtte (i)ru. 'I'm upset because it doesn't work.'

☠ Three warnings are in order:

1. The sequence *before* **kara** is the reason or cause, and what follows, the result. Be careful not to reverse the order.

2. The direct-style equivalent of distal-style adjectivals ending in **desu** is an adjectival alone. Be careful *not* to use **da** immediately following adjectivals.

3. On the other hand, nominal predicates must include some form of **dà** or **dèsu** before **kara** in order to constitute a causal pattern. Without it, a different pattern results. Compare:

nihóñzìñ da/desu kara 'because [I] am Japanese'

nihóñzìñ kara 'from a Japanese'

Compare now the following pair:

Tomodati ğa osóku kità kara, deñwa simàsita.

Tomodati wa osóku kità kara, deñwa simàsita.

In the first example, **tomodati**, followed by **ğa**, is closely and exhaustively linked with the following predicate and has no direct connection with the final predicate. In contrast, **tomodati wa** in the second example announces the general referent for the entire sentence. Thus, translating:

'Since my friend arrived late, I telephoned.' *but*
'Since my friend arrived late, s/he (the friend) telephoned.'

This same phenomenon occurs with a number of other patterns, notably the gerund patterns described in 8A-SP5. As an example, note CC1(N)b of this section and the related discussion in the MN.

It was pointed out in 8A-SP5 that, in some contexts, the gerund may describe the reason for what follows in a sentence:

Byooki de kônakatta. 'Being sick, I didn't come.'

Structurally, however, the message here is simply: 'given the actualization of the gerund, I didn't come.' As was explained in Lesson 8, in many examples of this pattern, there is no causal connection: it depends totally on context. However, the **kara** pattern described here specifically identifies an occurrence or situation *from which* a result develops: it is always causal.

Causal patterns ending in **kara** frequently occur as minor sentences, when the conclusion is obvious from the context (cf. CC1[J]b, 2[J], 2[N]b). In such cases, either distal-style or direct-style may occur, depending on the overall careful- or casual-style of the discourse.

Just as /nominal X + **kara**/ may occur directly before **dèsu** constituting a nominal-like predicate, /predicate X + **kara**/ occurs in parallel fashion:

Dôo site ikánài ñ desu ka⌐ ... Byóóki dà kara desu.

'Why is it you're not going?' ... 'It's because I'm sick.'

Kâre, doítuğo ğa zyoozù desu nêe. ... Dôitu ni nâğâku itâ kara desyoo.

'Isn't he good in German!' ... 'It's probably because he was in Germany for a long time.'

3. PATTERNS OF MANNER

The manner in which a predicate occurs—the 'how'—may be expressed by another predicate or by a nominal. Consider the following predicate examples:

Okúrete kimàsita. 'I came late' (behind schedule). Manner is expressed by a verbal in the gerund form.

Suğôku zyoózù desu. 'S/he's amazingly skilled.' Manner is expressed by an adjectival in the **-ku** form.

Hitô-ri de ikimasu. 'I'm going alone' (*lit.* 'being one person'). Manner is expressed by a nominal predicate in the gerund form.

Nominal patterns of manner may include (a) a nominal alone, or (b) a nominal followed by particle **ni** (locating the activity within a certain domain: compare English 'perform *in* haste'), or (c) a nominal either with or without following **ni**. Thus:

Tyoódo ìi desu. 'It's exactly right.'

Hoǹtoo ni omosiròi desu. 'It's really interesting.'

Hoká ni nàni ka? 'Anything in addition?'

Betú ni kamaimasèñ. 'It doesn't especially matter.'

Maśsùğu (ni) iťte kudasài. 'Go straight.'

Sûğu (ni) wakárimàsita. 'I understood right away.'

Issyo, introduced in this section, belongs to the group of nominals which take particle **ni** when occurring in a manner construction:

Iśsyo dèsu. '[We]'re together.'

Iśsyo zya nài desu. '[We]'re not together.' *but*

Iśsyo ni ikimasyòo. 'Let's go together.'

Issyo also belongs to a small subgroup of nominals with which a preceding /nominal X + **to**/ phrase can be linked as a subordinate rather than a coordinate:

Tomódati to issyo ni kimàsita. 'I came together with my friend.'

Compare:

Ane wa âni to issyo ni kaérimàsita. 'My (older) sister went home together with my (older) brother.' *and*

Ane to âni wa iśsyo ni kaerimàsita. 'My sister and my brother (i.e., brother with sister) went home together.'

The meaning of these two sentences is very similar, although there is a definite contrast in structure. Insofar as there is any difference in meaning, the first example implies that **âni** is the principal and **ane** the accompaniment; in the second example, the two participants are on a more equal footing.

As a group, /**na**/ nominals are regularly followed by particle **ni** when they describe the manner in which a predicate occurs:

kîree ni kâku 'write beautifully'

zyoózù ni hanâsu 'speak skillfully'

iyâ ni samûi 'is disagreeably cold'

4. omôu; X to omôu

Omôu is an operational, **w**-consonant verbal (negative **omów-àna-i**) that refers to having thoughts and opinions. It occurs most commonly preceded by particle **to**, which in turn follows a sequence expressing the thought:

/**X to omôu**/ = '[I] think X.'

In this pattern, X has the same form as an independent sentence, but is regularly in the direct-style. This **to** is identified as a quotative particle; it directly follows the quoted thought. A basically unaccented word or phrase preceding **to** occurs with alternate accent patterns: it either continues to be unaccented, or acquires the same accent patterning that precedes **kedo**. Examples:

Omósiròi to omoimasu. 'I think it's fun.'

Asíta iku to omoimàsu kedo . . 'I think I'll go tomorrow, but . . .' (I'm not making a definite statement).

Iyâ da to omôtte, yamémàsita. 'Thinking that it was unpleasant, I gave it up.'

Oísii to omòtte, takúsañ tabemàsita. 'Thinking it was tasty, I ate a great deal.'

Note that the form in which the 'thought' is quoted depends on the original form of the thought:

Señsèe ğa irássyàru to omôtta ñ desu kedo . . '(It's that) I thought the doctor would come, but . . .' (s/he may not).

If **irássyàru** is changed to **irássyàtta**, the English equivalent, in turn, would be changed to 'the doctor had come.' The implication is that the original thought was: **Señsèe ğa irássyàtta** 'The doctor came.' (See also CC2[N]b.)

Thinking that is regarded as an occurrence repeated over a period of time is indicated by **omôtte (i)ru** '[I]'m thinking' or '[I]'ve been thinking.' 'Wondering' can be expressed as 'thinking a question':

Ane mo iśsyo ni ikanài ka to omôtte, deñwa (o) simàsita. 'Wondering if my (older) sister wouldn't go with me, too, I telephoned.'

Nâni ğa îi ka to omôtte (i)ru ñ desu kedo nêe. 'I'm wondering (or I've been wondering) what will be good, but (I'm not sure).'

Negation within the quotation and negation of the verbal **omôu** are possible:

(1) **Sâmûku nâi to omoimasu.**

(2) **Samûi to wa omóimasèñ.**

(3) **Kônai to wa omóimasèñ.**

Sentence (1) is a definite statement of belief, i.e., that it isn't cold. Sentence (2), in contrast, states that the speaker does *not* have a conviction that it is *cold* (at least), implying that that is as far as s/he will go in this statement; it may even be a bit on the cool side—but not *cold*. Sentence (3) is a negative statement to the effect that the speaker does *not* believe that someone is *not coming* (at least), although there may be some implied qualification (determined by context) about the coming, such as coming late, or coming unprepared, or coming reluctantly, etc.

Given the Japanese preference for not making unqualified, dogmatic statements, it is accurate to assume that the /**X to omôu**/ pattern occurs VERY frequently. Even in a statement of personal wants and desires, it is common to append **to omôu** to a **-tai** form (cf. CC3[N]a).

The combination implies that the speaker does in fact entertain the thought that s/he wants to do whatever is stated in the **-tai** form, very different in connotation from the direct English translation: 'I think I want to————.' Imagine your reaction to an English-language invitation beginning, 'I think I'd like to invite you!' A more accurate English rendition of the Japanese pattern would be: 'My thought is that I want to————.' (In terms of equivalents, English would more often occur without any reference to thinking.)

Omôu may also be preceded by **dôo** and **sôo**, occurring as expressions of manner:

Dôo omoimasu ka⌐ 'What (*lit.* how) do you think?'

Soó omoimàsu. 'I think so.'

5. *THE DIRECT-STYLE TENTATIVE COPULA:* **daròo**

Daròo is the direct-style equivalent of **desyòo**, i.e., a tentative form. Examples:

Sôo daroo. 'It's probably so.'

Abúnài daroo nêe. 'It's probably dangerous, isn't it!'

Sûgu kûru daroo. 'S/he'll probably come soon.'

Dekînai ñ daro(o)? 'It's probably that s/he can't do it, don't you think?'

All of the preceding examples, in which **daròo** is part of the final predicate, are typical of blunt speech. However, within a sentence, the form is not marked as blunt or gentle:

Samûi daroo kedo, Hoḱkàidoo e ikítai to omoimàsu. 'It will probably be cold, but (my thought is) I'd like to go to Hokkaido.'

Samûi daroo kara, Hoḱkàidoo e ikítaku nài to omoimasu. 'It's probably cold, so (my thought is) I don't want to go to Hokkaido.'

Señsèe ḡa asíta irassyàru daroo to omoimasu. 'I think the doctor will probably come tomorrow.'

Desyòo, you will remember, does not ordinarily refer to oneself. The same is true of **daròo**. The accentuation of **daròo** patterns follows that of **desyòo** patterns (see 6B-SP2).

Drills

A 1. **Onîisañ irássyaimàsu ka⌐**
'Is your (older) brother in?'

Âni desu ka⌐ Tyôtto orímasèñ kedo . .
'My (older) brother? He's not in (for a bit) but . . .' (can I help you?)

2. **Imootosañ irássyaimàsu ka⌐**
'Is your (younger) sister in?'

Imóotò desu ka⌐ Tyôtto orímasèñ kedo . .
'My (younger) sister? She's not in (for a bit) but . . .' (can I help you?)

3. **musukosañ**; 4. **onêesañ**; 5. **musumesañ**; 6. **gosyûziñ**; 7. **bôttyañ**; 8. **ozyôosañ**; 9. **otootosañ**

B 1. **Ane ḡa 'siḡoto o yamémàsu yo⌐**
'My (older) sister is quitting work.'

Onêesañ ḡa? Hee⌐ Îtu oyáme ni nàru ñ desu ka⌐
'Your (older) sister? Not really! When is it she's quitting?'

2. **Syûziñ ğa Yoóròppa e ikímàsu yo⤷**   **Gosyûziñ ğa? Hee⤷ Îtu irássyàru ñ desu**
   'My husband is going to Europe.'   **ka⤷**
                                       'Your husband? Not really! When is it he's
                                       going?'

3. **kodomo/kotira e kaérimàsu**; 4. **otóotò/koko e kimâsu**; 5. **imóotò/Nihôñ o demâsu**;
   6. **âni/uti o kaímàsu**

C 1. **Okósañ imàsu ka⤷**   **Kodómo dèsu ka⤷ Hutá-rì imâsu yo⤷**
   'Do you have (*lit.* are there) any   'Children? I have two.'
   children?'

2. **Tâkusii arímàsu ka⤷**   **Tâkusii desu ka⤷ Nî-dai arímàsu yo⤷**
   'Are there any cabs?'   'Cabs? There are two.'

3. **nîsee no hito**; 4. **kyoókàsyo**; 5. **kâsa**; 6. **hôñya**; 7. **arúbàito no gakusee**; 8. **gaiziñ**;
   9. **taípuràitaa**; 10. **nikkèeziñ**; 11. **tîzu**; 12. **kabañ**

• Repeat this drill, replying in each case with the appropriate number representing '3.'

D 1. **Hasimoto-sañ wa 'koñsyuu kimásèñ**   **Sôo desu ka. Dôo site⁵ kônai ñ desu ka⤷**
   yo⤷
   'Mr/s. Hashimoto isn't coming this   'Oh? Why is it s/he isn't coming?'
   week.'

2. **Hasimoto-sañ wa 'yuube miémasèñ**   **Sôo desu ka. Dôo site miênakatta ñ desu**
   desita yo⤷   **ka⤷**
   'Mr/s. Hashimoto didn't appear last   'Oh? Why is it s/he didn't appear?'
   night.'

3. **siğoto o yamémàsu**; 4. **koñpyùutaa wa tukáimasèñ**; 5. **señsèe to soódañ-site
   (i)màsu**; 6. **anó gakusee tò wa hanásimasèñ desita**

E 1. **Koñna rassyu-àwaa wa mâiniti desu**   **Êe. Mâiniti da kara komâtte (i)ru ñ desu**
   ka⤷   **yo.**
   'Are rush hours like this every day?'   'Yes. They're every day, so it's really
                                       bothersome.'

2. **Koko wa âtûku narimasu ka⤷**   **Êe. Âtûku nâru kara komâtte (i)ru ñ**
   'Does this place get hot?'   **desu yo.**
                                       'Yes. It gets hot, so I'm bothered [by it].'

3. **kono eeğo/muzúkasìi desu**; 4. **anó zimùsyo/hûbeñ desu**; 5. **âsa/samûi desu**;
   6. **ano gakusee no ceğo/hetâ desu**; 7. **ano arúbàito no gakusee/yamémàsu**;
   8. **sonó kyookàsyo/damê desu**; 9. **okosañ/kâette (i)másèñ**; 10. **kore/tiğáimàsu**

F 1. **Kyôo wa atûi desu nêe.**   **Êe. Koñna ni àtùku nâtta kara, miñna**
   'Isn't it hot today!'   **bikkùri-site (i)ru ñ desu.**
                                       'That's right. Everyone is surprised,
                                       because it got this hot.'

---

5. **Nâze** is also possible here.

2. **Yamanaka-sañ wa dekímaséñ nêe.**
'Mr/s. Yamanaka can't do [it], can s/he!'

Êe. Koṅna ni dekìnaku nâtta kara, miṅna bikkùri-site (i)ru ñ desu.
'That's right. Everyone is surprised because s/he became so incapable.'

3. **Kûbota-sañ wa iyâ desu nêe.**
'Mr/s. Kubota is unpleasant, isn't s/he!'

Êe. Koṅna ni iyà ni nâtta kara, miṅna bikkùri-site (i)ru ñ desu.
'That's right. Everyone is surprised, because s/he became so unpleasant.'

4. **kêsa/suzúsìi desu**; 5. **Yamanaka-sañ/wakárimaséñ**; 6. **seṅsèe/muzúkasìi desu**; 7. **kôñbañ/atátakài**; 8. **Kitamura-sañ/zyoózù desu**; 9. **Hayasi-sañ no ozyôosañ/ kîree desu**

G. The exchanges of this drill would all take place outside of the particular country that is mentioned.

1. **Anô hito wa 'nihoṅgo ga ozyóozu dèsu nêe.**
'Isn't s/he good in Japanese!'

Nihôñ ni nâĝaku itâ kara desyoo.
'It's probably because s/he was in Japan for a long time.'

2. **Anô hito wa 'doitugo ga ozyóozu dèsu nêe.**
'Isn't s/he good in German!'

Dôitu ni nâĝaku itâ kara desyoo.
'It's probably because s/he was in Germany for a long time.'

3. **tyuuĝokugo**; 4. **huraṅsugo**; 5. **itariaĝo**

H 1. **Seṅsèe to soódañ-simasèñ ka⤸**
'Wouldn't you [like to] talk it over with the doctor?'

A. Îi âidea desu nêe. Iśsyo ni soodañ-simasyòo.
'Oh, that's a great idea. Let's discuss it together.'

2. **Kyôo no zêmi ni demásèñ ka⤸**
'Wouldn't you [like to] attend today's seminar?'

A. Îi âidea desu nêe. Iśsyo ni demasyòo.
'Oh, that's a great idea. Let's go together.'

3. **atárasìi 'kuruma o mimásèñ**; 4. **koóhìi o nomímasèñ**; 5. **gôruhu o simásèñ**; 6. **ano atárasìi 'kissateñ e ikímasèñ**; 7. **seṅsèe to aímasèñ**

I 1. **Hitô-ri de zêmi ni dêru ñ desu ka⤸**
'(Is it that) you'll attend the seminar alone?'

Ie, tomódati to issyo ni demàsu.
'No, I'll attend together with a friend.'

2. **Hitô-ri de 'kotira e kûru ñ desu ka⤸**
'(Is is that) you'll come here alone?'

Ie, tomódati to issyo ni kimàsu.
'No, I'll come together with a friend.'

3. **tosyôkañ e iku**; 4. **kono siĝoto o suru**; 5. **seṅsèe to âu**; 6. **Nihôñ e kâeru**; 7. **omâwarisañ to hanâsu**; 8. **seṅsèe to soodañ-suru**

J 1. **Kâre, zyoózù desu nêe.**
'Isn't he proficient!'

Êe. Suĝôku zyoózù de, bikkùri-simasita.
'Yes. I was amazed at how extremely proficient he is.'

2. **Anó hikòoki, rakû desu nêe.**   **Êe. Suḡôku rakû de, biḱkùri-simasita.**
'Isn't that plane comfortable!'   'Yes. I was amazed at how extremely comfortable it is.'

3. **ano gakkoo/hûbeñ**; 4. **ano gakusee/hetâ**; 5. **kono eeḡo/damê**; 6. **kânozyo no eeḡo/kîree**

K 1. **Asítà mo kaísya ni imàsu neʔ**   **Êe. Irû to omoimasu.**
'You'll be at the company tomorrow   'Yes. I think I'll be [there].'
too, right?'

2. **Tanáka-sañ no òkusañ o sitte (i)màsu neʔ**   **Êe. Sittè (i)ru to omoimasu.**
'You know Mrs. Tanaka, right?'   'Yes. I think I know her.'

3. **sore wa zêñbu wakárimàsita**; 4. **raineñ konó utì o kásimàsu**; 5. **asâtte mo arúbàito no gakusee o yobímàsu**; 6. **koñna siḡoto wa muzúkasìi desu**; 7. **koñna tokorò wa hûbeñ desu**; 8. **señsyuu no kàiḡi wa omósìròkatta desu**; 9. **kâre no mâe no siḡoto wa boóeki dèsita**

L 1. **Señsèe to oái-surù⁶ ñ desu ka⤽**   **Oai-sitai to omôtte (i)ru ñ desu kedo . .**
'(Is it that) you're going to meet with   'I've been thinking that I'd like to meet
the professor?'   [with him/her], but . . .' (I don't know
whether I can).

2. **Kore kara têepu o kikû ñ desu ka⤽**   **Kikitai to omôtte (i)ru ñ desu kedo . .**
'(Is it that) you're going to listen to   'I've been thinking that I'd like to listen,
tapes next?'   but . . .' (I don't know whether I can).

3. **arúbàito no gakusee to hanâsu**; 4. **kuruma o kariru**; 5. **zêmi o 'yameru**; 6. **señsèe ni nâru**; 7. **raíneñ màde 'kotira ni iru**; 8. **supóotukàa o 'kau**

● Repeat this drill, replacing **omôtte (i)ru** of the responses with **omôu.**

M 1. **Itoo-sañ no âkatyañ wa, sañ-kàḡetu desita neʔ**   **Ni-kâḡetu zya nai ka to omóimàsu kedo . .**
'Mr/s. Ito's baby was three months   'I wonder if s/he isn't two months old,
old—right?'   but . . .' (I'm not sure).

2. **Konó bìru no tikâ ni, hôñya ḡa nî-keñ arimasita neʔ**   **Îk-keñ zya nai ka to omóimàsu kedo . .**
'There were two bookstores in the   'I wonder if it isn't one (shop), but . . .' (I'm
basement of this building—right?'   not sure).

3. **tonári no bìru wa, yoñ-kai dèsita**; 4. **Kûbota-sañ no bôttyañ wa, mi-ttù desita**; 5. **tuḡî no zêmi wa, muí-ka dèsita**; 6. **anó zimùsyo ni, arúbàito no gakusee ḡa sañ-niñ imàsita**

6. Note the use of the humble-polite in a question, indicating that the speaker and addressee are in the same in-group vis-à-vis the professor who outranks them.

N 1. **Suğôi desu nêe.**
   'Isn't it terrific!'

   Watási mo suğòi to omôtte (i)ta ñ desu yo⤸
   'I, too, was thinking that it was terrific.'

2. **Iyâ desu nêe.**
   'Isn't it disagreeable!'

   Watási mo iyà da to omôtte (i)ta ñ desu yo⤸
   'I, too, was thinking, it was disagreeable.'

3. **rakû desu;** 4. **kîree desu;** 5. **kawáìi desu;** 6. **hûbeñ desu;** 7. **zańnèñ desu;** 8. **mazûi desu;** 9. **wakâi desu**

O 1. **Onîisañ wa, mata âto de kimâsu neʔ**
   'Your (older) brother is coming again later—right?'

   Kûru daroo to omóimàsu kedo . .
   'I think he'll probably come, but . . .' (I'm not sure).

2. **Tanáka-sañ no gokàzoku wa, Toókyoo dèsu neʔ**
   'Mr/s. Tanaka's family is [in] Tokyo—right?'

   Toókyoo daròo to omóimàsu kedo . .
   'I think they're probably [in] Tokyo, but . . .' (I'm not sure).

3. **okyakusañ/osókù made imasu;** 4. **Hayasi-sañ/keḱkoñ-site (i)màsu;** 5. **Matuda-sañ/ano kaisya o yamémàsita;** 6. **îma no Hoḱkàidoo/samûi desu;** 7. **kânozyo/kaíğìsitu de mâtte (i)masu;** 8. **kâre/komárimàsita;** 9. **anô hito/byoóki dèsita;** 10. **Ta-naka-sañ no otootosañ/hitô-ri desita;** 11. **ano ryokañ/yasûi desu;** 12. **Yamamoto-sañ/uti o karíte (i)màsu;** 13. **kâre rûsu desu**

P 1. **Sore wa, dôo site desyoo ka.**
   'Why would that be?'

   Dôo site desyoo nêe.
   'Why, indeed!'

2. **Kore wa, kyoókàsyo desyoo ka.**
   'Would this be a textbook?'

   Dôo desyoo nêe.
   'I wonder!'

3. **koko/dôko;** 4. **kâiği/nańyòobi;** 5. **kaérì/nâñ-ğatu;** 6. **asoko/kyoositu**

• Repeat this drill in blunt-style, replacing **desyòo** with **daròo**.

Q 1. **Hitô-ri de Hoḱkàidoo e ikû ñ desu ka⤸**
   '(Is it that) you're going to Hokkaido alone?'

   Iie. Âni to 'ane to, sań-nìñ de ikû n desu yo⤸
   'No. (It's that) I'm going with my (older) brother and (older) sister—the three of us.'

2. **Hitô-ri de 'kotira e kûru ñ desu ka⤸**
   '(Is it that) you're coming here alone?'

   Iie. Âni to 'ane to, sań-nìñ de kûru ñ desu yo⤸
   'No. (It's that) I am coming with my (older) brother and (older) sister—the three of us.'

3. **kono siğoto o suru;** 4. **ano uti o kariru;** 5. **Nihôñ e kâeru;** 6. **koré o tukùtta**

Application Exercises

A1. Enlarge your imaginary family tree to include a number of brothers and sisters, as-signing names and ages to each. In addition, add spouses and children for some of these siblings, also identified as to name and age. Following the outline in Lesson 10A, Application Exercises, practice asking and answering questions about this family.

2. Have each group member prepare five complex statements which include a /predicate + **kara**/ sequence. Example: **Kinoo 'tomodati ni aítài to omôtte, tomodati no uti ni deńwa o kàketa kedo, rûsu datta kara, utí e kàette beńkyoo-simàsita.** After each such example is presented to the group, have the author ask detailed content questions, to be answered by the other group members.

3. Have group members ask each other questions which elicit answers that include / sentence + **to** + **omôu**/. In responding, use hesitation noises, echo questions, **mâa, sâa, yáppàri,** etc. as appropriate.

B. Core Conversations: Substitution

Follow the usual procedure, making vocabulary substitutions, as appropriate, within the Core Conversations. As the situations of the CC become more clearly defined, it will be necessary to keep those situations in mind when making substitutions, in order to avoid producing a dialogue which may be linguistically correct, but culturally inappropriate— even unthinkable. Always bear in mind who your conversation partner is. Under ordinary circumstances, it will not be another **gaiziñ**!

SECTION B

Core Conversations

1(J)a. **Hisásiburi dèsu nêe.**
  b. **Okâwari arímaseñ ka**

  c. **Êe, arîgatoo gozaimasu.**
2(N)a. **Watanabe-sañ. Utí no kànai desu.** (Addressing wife) **Kotira, moñbùsyoo no 'Watanabe-sañ.**

  (J')a. **Kâataa de gozaimasu. Îtu mo syûziñ ğa osêwa ni nâtt(e) orimasu.**

  b. **Iêie. Beńkyoo-sit(e) orimàsu kara, sukôsi wa dekímàsu ğa . .**

  (N)b. **Mâa, gaíkokuğo dèsu kara nêe.**

(N)a. **Hoñtoo ni.**
  b. **Êe, okağesama de. Otáku no minàsañ mo?**

(J)a. **Ôkusama de (i)rassyaimasu ka**
     Watánabe dèsu. Hazímemàsite.

  b. **Kotíra kòso. Gosyuziñsama wa, nihoñğo ğa ozyóozu de (i)rassyaimàsu nêe.**

  c. (Addressing husband) **Muzúkasiku nài desu ka**

3(N)   **Tyôtto gosyóokai-simàsu.
Kotira, mońbùsyoo no
'Watanabe-sañ. Kotira wa
'Toodai no Ôono-señsee.**

(J)   **Watánabe de gozaimàsu.
Hazímemàsite.**

(J')   **Ôono de gozaimasu. Dôozo
yorosiku.**

ENGLISH EQUIVALENTS

1(J)a.   It's been a long time, hasn't it!
b.   How is everything? (*lit.* There isn't any change?)

(N)a.   [It] really [has].

b.   Fine (*lit.* yes), thank you. Everyone at your place, too?

c.   Yes, thank you.
2(N)a.   Mr/s. Watanabe. My wife. (Addressing wife) This is Mr/s. Watanabe, from the Ministry of Education.

(J')a.   (I'm Carter.) My husband is always obliged to you for your help.

(J)a.   (Are you) Mrs. [Carter]? (I'm Watanabe.) How do you do?

b.   No, no. He's studying so he can handle it a little (at least), but . . . (he isn't really proficient).

b.   *I'm* obliged to *him*. Your husband is very proficient in Japanese, isn't he!

(N)b.   Well, it's a foreign language, so (it's not surprising that it's difficult), don't you agree.

c.   (Addressing Mr. Carter) It's not difficult?.

3(N)a.   I['d like to] make some introductions. This [is] Mr/s. Watanabe, from the Ministry of Education. This [is] Professor Ono, of Tokyo University.
(J')   (I'm Ono.) Glad to meet you.

(J)   (I'm Watanabe.) How do you do?

BREAKDOWNS
(AND SUPPLEMENTARY VOCABULARY)

1.   **hisasiburi** (SP1)   after a long interval
+ **sibâraku**   a while
+ **gobúsata-simàsita**   I've neglected to be in touch
kawari/okâwari   a change
okaḡesama de   thanks for asking; thanks to you
minâsañ   everyone /polite/
2.   **mońbùsyoo**   Ministry of Education

+ **gaímùsyoo**	Foreign Ministry
+ **oókuràsyoo**	Finance Ministry
+ **hazîmete**	the first time
Hazímemàsite.	How do you do.
sewâ/osêwa	care, assistance
osêwa ni naru	become obliged for assistance
kotíra kòso	this very side
gaikokuğo	foreign language
3. **(go)syookai-suru**	introduce
Toókyoo-dàiğaku/Toodai	Tokyo University
+ **Kyoóto-dàiğaku/Kyoodai**	Kyoto University
+ **Hoḱkaidoo-dàiğaku/Hokudai**	Hokkaido University
+ **Kyuúsyuu-dàiğaku/Kyuudai**	Kyushu University
Dôozo yorosiku.	Please [treat me] favorably.

SUPPLEMENTARY FAMILY TERMS (cf. SP2)

Honorific-Polite	*Generic*	*English Equivalent*
goryôosiñ	**ryôosiñ**	both parents
oyagosañ	**oyâ**	parent
otôosañ	**titî; titioya**	father
okâasañ	**hâha; hahaoya**	mother
ozîisañ	**sôhu**	grandfather
obâasañ	**sôbo**	grandmother
ozisañ	**ozi**	uncle
obasañ	**oba**	aunt
oitokosañ	**itôko**	cousin

MISCELLANEOUS NOTES

1,2,3. The three CCs of this section are formal, ritualistic exchanges, which are analyzed in detail in SP1, following. All are careful-style, and include a number of polite utterances.

1(J)a. The nominals **hisasiburi** and **sibâraku** are used ritualistically upon renewed contact after some time. **Hisasiburi** includes a nuance of non-contact; **sibâraku** refers only to an indefinite time period.

(N)a. **Hoñto(o) ni** is a manner expression which occurs frequently as an indication of agreement and support.

(J)b. **Kawari** is a nominal derived from a verbal (**kawaru** '[something] changes') in its stem form, the usual derivative form. The polite **okâwari** implies 'change in reference to the out-group.' Another meaning is 'second helping.' The ritualistic **Okâwari arímasèñ ka⤴** regularly occurs without an intervening phrase-particle.

(N)b. **Okağesama de** indicates the speaker's appreciation for interest ('thanks for asking') and/or for assistance ('thanks to you'). It always accompanies or implies favorable or pleasant information.

Minâsañ is the polite equivalent of **mińnà**, referring only to the out-group.

2(N)a. The **moñbùsyoo** is the Japanese Ministry of Education, which controls the education system throughout Japan. The **gaímùsyoo** and **oókuràsyoo** are also government ministries, the former responsible for foreign affairs, including all foreign embassies, and the latter for Japan's finance.

(J)a. **Hazîmete** 'the first time' is a nominal which, unlike most nominal derivatives of verbals, started out as the gerund of a verbal, in this case, the vowel-verbal **hazimeru** 'begin [something].' This new nominal differs from the regular gerund in its accent: nominal, **hazîmete**; gerund, **hazimete**. **Hazímemàsite**, in origin, is an equivalent distal-style gerund which now occurs both as a verbal and a special nominal. In its latter usage, it indicates a first meeting, similar to 'How do you do' or 'Glad to meet you.'

(J')a. **Osêwa** previously occurred in the ritual expression **osewasama**, which expressed thanks for assistance (6B). **Osêwa ni naru** is used in reference to the recipient of assistance: 'become obliged [to you] for [your] assistance.' The /**-te (i)ru**/ sequence describes a realized condition with continuing effect: '[he] has become obliged'; with **îtu mo** the condition is always being realized.

(J)b. **Kòso** is an emphatic phrase-particle: /**X kòso**/ indicates that it is indeed X which is relevant, and nothing else. Here, **kotíra kòso** contradicts the notion that Carter is obliged to Watanabe: the obligation, Watanabe claims politely, is located **kotira**, i.e., on this side—with Watanabe.

Gaikokuğo is the language of a **gaikoku** 'foreign country.'

3(N) The polite **gosyookai-suru** is used when introducing the out-group. Compare: **syoókai-site kudasài** 'please introduce me/us.'

Toodai is an abbreviation which follows a frequently occurring pattern. Compare: **Kyoodai** (= Kyoto University), **Hokudai** (= Hokkaido University), **Kyuudai** (= Kyushu University).

(J') **Yorosiku** is the **-ku** form of the adjectival **yorosii** 'is good,' 'is fine.' The **-ku** form in sentence-final position implies a request: 'May [things] go well'; 'May our acquaintance be pleasant.' **Yorosiku**, with or without following **onégai-simàsu**, also occurs as a general request for consideration, assistance, and helpful service for oneself or a member of one's in-group. And **Ôkusañ ni yorosiku.** extends regards and good wishes to the wife of an acquaintance.

Structural Patterns

1. RITUAL; INTRODUCTIONS

There are certain social situations which call for the use of fixed, stylized utterances and exchanges. In English, when greeted with 'Hi! How are you?' we rarely reply with a detailed account of our physical condition. The usual response is, 'Fine, thanks. How are *you?*' Some variation is permitted: 'thank you' instead of 'thanks,' or omission of the entire first sentence, or simply 'Hi!' But basically this is an English ritualized exchange which occurs countless times in daily life. 'How do you do' is another example, in this case a particularly confusing question if subjected to a literal analysis of its meaning. But it is the expected utterance to be used when introduced, whatever its linguistic history or source.

Japanese is particularly rich in ritualized utterances. For the foreigner attempting to learn the language, this can be an advantage and a disadvantage. It means that if we carefully memorize exchanges that are regularly used in specified situations, we are guaranteed to 'say the right thing.' But it also means that if we *don't* memorize—if we resist 'clichés' and depend on an original creation of our own making—our chances of saying what is appropriate, or even what is comprehensible to the native speaker, are very slim. Imagine the confusion we would cause by using **sayonara** instead of **iŧte kimàsu** as we left a Japanese home where we were staying, to go to the office one morning. And imagine the bafflement that would result if we tried to participate in an introduction without knowing the exact ritual! Obviously foreigners are excused for many of their errors, but the more one *depends* on such forgiveness, the more one impedes natural, comfortable communication. And the greatest danger is that an error regarded as minor and unimportant by the foreigner may be interpreted by the native speaker not as linguistic ignorance but rather as a totally different message—including, on occasion, a social insult.

To sum up: As we move ahead in Japanese, we must always be concerned with the question of how the *Japanese* handle a given situation linguistically, and in the area of ritual, rote memorization is the only safe, efficient course.

Now let's examine the Core Conversations of this lesson.

1. CC1, as a unit, should be memorized verbatim, for use as a conversation opener between acquaintances whose relationship requires some formality but not an extreme level of politeness. This is not to imply that this is the *only* ritualized exchange for this kind of situation, but it is a particularly common one.

Possible variations, altering only the style, include:

Hisásiburi dèsu (nêe). > **Hisasiburi (nêe).** /direct/; > **Hisásiburi de gozaimàsu (nêe).** /polite/ Also possible is **Ohisasiburi.**

Hoñto(o) ni: adding one of the preceding to change from a fragment to a major sentence = more careful.

Okâwari arímasèñ ka > **Okâwari gozáimasèñ ka** /polite/

(N)b. usually occurs in this form.

Arîgatoo gozaimasu. > **Arîgatoo.** /direct/; > **Dôo mo.** /casual fragment/

2 and 3. CC2 and CC3 are typical introduction-ritual exchanges. The principal possible variations involve alternates of the copula, i.e., whether to use /nominal/ or /nominal + **dèsu**/ or /nominal + **de gozaimàsu** or **de (i)rassyaimàsu**/. Even in a very polite conversation, unrelieved use of the polite copula alternates is considered stylistically awkward. But the choice made for each occurrence carries a message to the listener(s). The following are points to note carefully:

a. In performing an introduction, it is common, but not required, to announce what is about to occur: **Tyôtto gosyóokai-simàsu.**

b. According to strict rules of etiquette, the lower-ranking member of those being introduced is presented to the higher-ranking person first. Of course, out-group members automatically outrank in-group members in this particular hierarchy.

c. A wife assumes the rank of her husband in social exchanges that focus on the husband, and vice versa when the wife is the focus.

d. When the parties being introduced are identified with **kotira** (or **kore** as an alternate for an in-group member), the second occurrence is followed by particle **wa**, indicating the contrast (cf. 3[N]a).

e. Although names are incorporated into the introduction itself, the person introduced regularly repeats his/her own name, with **dèsu** or **de gozaimàsu**. (Contrast the reaction in English if you were to *repeat* your own name. It would probably imply that the introducer had mispronounced it!)

f. Even in introductions, given names are usually omitted. However, of critical importance is the organization or location with which the individual is connected. Here, again, *group affiliation* is of prime importance in the identification of an individual.

g. Either **Hazímemàsite.** or **Dôozo yorosiku.**—or both—may be said by a person being introduced.

h. If there has been any previous connection—direct or indirect—with the person to whom one is being introduced, either through family or outside affiliation, Mrs. Carter's utterance (2[J']a) regarding **osêwa** becomes a ritual.

i. When foreigners who speak Japanese (even minimally!) are participants in an introduction, a complimentary comment on language proficiency is extremely common. It is more polite to turn aside complimentary statements than to appear to accept them as fact. Even Mr. Carter's high level of proficiency is modestly described as **sukôsi wa dekímàsu g̃a** 'he can handle it a little (at least), but . . .' (he isn't really proficient).

Almost inevitable in conversations about language in Japan (and there is *much* greater interest in and talk about language in Japan than in most societies) is a reference by Japanese to the difficulty of their language. In CC2, Mr. Carter politely suggests that foreign languages in general are difficult to master. He softens his comment, which might otherwise appear to be an aggressive contradiction, by using **mâa** and **nêe** and by using wording which does not disallow that Japanese *is* difficult.

In general, considerable significance is attached to formal introductions in Japan: they are not regarded lightly. One's connections and affiliations are of crucial importance in the society, and one way to develop a network is through introductions, but 'introducers' assume responsibility when bringing people together. Given a situation in which individuals, only some of whom know each other, happen to come in temporary contact, it is more than possible that no introductions will take place if there is no obvious reason for the individuals involved to establish a connection. (Contrast the American who may introduce even his dog to a guest!)

This discussion of introductions should remind the student of the Japanese language that every utterance in the language is sending out important messages that go far beyond the question of what a particular vocabulary item means in English.

2. THE EXTENDED FAMILY

The additional family terms listed at the end of the Breakdowns again have alternate forms. The basis for deciding which alternate to use in a given context is the same as that described previously: the polite terms are used for family members of the out-group,[7] and for one's own family members who are older, in address and in reference within the family; but in talking *about* one's own family members to the out-group, the generic terms are used. One exception is that young people often use the polite terms even in referring to their own grandparents, undoubtedly reflecting recognition of the considerable difference in age. Note that older relatives often refer to themselves with the appropriate polite term when addressing children and young people. Thus, a mother calls herself **okâasañ** when talking to her children.

The acquisition of the two sets of terms is a gradual process for native speakers. Japanese children learn many of the polite forms first, as terms of address. The use of family terms

---

7. Note how this procedure makes even unmodified nominals unambiguous: if I talk to an out-group member about **okâasañ**, obviously I mean that person's mother.

as designations for various categories of people without any familial connection, already mentioned in previous lessons, is common in Japan. Thus: **obasañ** 'woman,' **ozisañ** 'man,' **obâasañ** 'old woman,' **ozîisañ** 'old man.'

Drills

A 1. **Kore, uti no kânai desu.**
'This is my wife.'

A, ôkusama de (i)rassyaimasu ka. Hazímemàsite.
'Oh, are you Mrs. ——? How do you do?'

2. **Kore, uti no titî desu.**
'This is my father.'

A, otôosama de (i)rassyaimasu ka. Hazímemàsite.
'Oh, are you ——'s father? How do you do?'

3. **sôhu**; 4. **tûma**; 5. **hâha**; 6. **sôbo**; 7. **ozi**; 8. **ryôosiñ**; 9. **oba**; 10. **musuko**; 11. **âni**; 12. **musúmè**; 13. **otóotò**; 14. **ane**; 15. **imóotò**

B 1. **Watanabe-sañ no gosyûziñ mo kimâsu neʃ**
'Mr. Watanabe is coming too—right?'

Gosyûziñ mo ôkusañ mo kimâsu yoↄ
'Mr. *and* Mrs. are coming.'

2. **Watanabe-sañ no 'ozisañ mo ikímàsu neʃ**
'The Watanabe uncle is going too—right?'

Ozisañ mo 'obasañ mo ikímàsu yoↄ
'The uncle *and* aunt are going.'

3. **onîisañ/miémàsu**; 4. **ozîisañ/gozôñzi desu**; 5. **musukosañ/keќkoñ-site (i)màsu**; 6. **otôosañ/niќkèeziñ desu**; 7. **otootosañ/imâsu**

C 1. **Dôo site 'Itoo-sañ no ôkusañ ǧa kûru to omôu ñ desu kaↄ**
'Why is it you think Mrs. Ito is coming?'

Gosyûziñ ǧa 'asoko de mâtte (i)ru kara . .
'Because her husband is waiting over there.'

2. **Dôo site 'Itoo-sañ no okâasañ ǧa kûru to omôu ñ desu kaↄ**
'Why is it you think Mr/s. Ito's mother is coming?'

Otôosañ ǧa 'asoko de mâtte (i)ru kara . .
'Because his/her father is waiting over there.'

3. **onêesañ**; 4. **obâasañ**; 5. **ozyôosañ**; 6. **obasañ**; 7. **imootosañ**

D 1. **Mîyazi-sañ wa, bôttyañ ǧa imâsu neʃ**
'Mr/s. Miyaji has a son—right?'

Okósañ wa irù ñ da kedo, ozyôosañ zya nai ka to omóimàsu nêe.
'S/he does have a child, but I wonder if it isn't a daughter.'

2. **Mîyazi-sañ wa, onîisañ ǧa imâsu neʃ**
'Mr/s. Miyaji has an older brother—right?'

Gokyôodai wa irû ñ da kedo, onêesañ zya nai ka to omóimàsu nêe.
'S/he does have a sibling, but I wonder if it isn't an older sister.'

3. **imootosañ**; 4. **musumesañ**; 5. **onêesañ**; 6. **ozyôosañ**; 7. **musukosañ**; 8. **otootosañ**

E 1. **Kore, hâha ḡa kakímàsita kedo . .**
'*My mother* wrote this, but . . .'
(perhaps you know).

Okâasañ ḡa okáki ni nàtta ñ desu ka.
Sirímasèñ desita.
'*Your mother* wrote it? I didn't know.'

2. **Kôñya, titî ḡa kimâsu kedo . .**
'*My father* is coming tonight, but . . .'
(perhaps you know).

Otôosañ ḡa irássyàru ñ desu ka.
Sirímasèñ desita.
'*Your father* is coming? I didn't know.'

3. **kore/kânai/tukáimàsu**; 4. **anó utì/âni/karímàsu**; 5. **yuube/ane/hanásimàsita**;
6. **sore/kodomo/kikímàsita**

● Repeat this drill, replacing **sirímasèñ desita** with **zoñzimasèñ desita** in the responses.

F 1. **Anó katà wa, Yamanaka-sañ no ôkusañ desu ka⤹**
'Is that (person) Mrs. Yamanaka?'

Êe, ôkusañ desu kedo, gozôñzi nâi desu ka⤹ Gosyóokai-simasyòo ka.
'Yes, it is (Mrs.); don't you know her? Shall I introduce you?'

2. **Anó katà wa, Yamanaka-sañ no gosyûziñ desu ka⤹**
'Is that (person) Mr. Yamanaka?

Êe, gosyûziñ desu kedo, gozôñzi nâi desu ka⤹ Gosyóokai-simasyòo ka.
'Yes, it is (Mr.); don't you know him? Shall I introduce you?'

3. **bôttyañ**; 4. **ozîisañ**; 5. **obasañ**; 6. **onîisañ**

G 1. **Kiíte (i)rassyarànai to omóimàsu kedo, ane ḡa kekkoñ-surù ñ desu yo⤹**
'I imagine you haven't heard, but my (older) sister is getting married.'

Onêesañ ga? Hoñtoo dèsu ka. Sirímasèñ desita.
'Your (older) sister? Really? I didn't know.'

2. **Kiíte (i)rassyarànai to omóimàsu kedo, imootosañ ni oái-sità ñ desu yo⤹**
'I imagine you haven't heard, but I met your (younger) sister.'

Imóotò ni? Hoñtoo dèsu ka. Sirímasèñ desita.
'My (younger) sister? Really? I didn't know.'

3. **musúmè ḡa daíḡaku o dèta**; 4. **gosyûziñ ḡa mâtte (i)rassyaru**; 5. **otóotò ḡa ´rikoñ-sita**

● Repeat this drill, replacing **sirímasèñ desita** with **zoñzimasèñ desita** in the responses.

H 1. **Ano kata, okâasañ de (i)rassyaimasu ka⤹**
'Is that (person) your mother?'

Êe, uti no hâha de gozaimasu.
'Yes, that's my (*lit*. the household's) mother.'

2. **Ano kata, gosyûziñ de (i)rassyaimasu ka⤹**
'Is that (person) your husband?'

Êe, uti no syûziñ de gozaimasu.
'Yes, that's my (*lit*. the household's) husband.'

3. **ozîisañ**; 4. **obasañ**; 5. **ozisañ**; 6. **obâasañ**; 7. **otôosañ**

I 1. **Îma hazîmete nihóñḡo o beñkyoo-site (i)rù ñ desu neˢ**
'You're studying Japanese for the first time now—right?'

Iie, hazîmete zya nâi desu. Mâe ni mo beñkyoo-simàsita kara . .
'No, it's not the first time. (Because) I studied before [this], too.'

2. **Kyôo hazîmete konó kaisya no hitò to soódañ-site (i)rù ñ desu neˢ**
'You're consulting with someone from this company for the first time today—right?'

Iie, hazîmete zya nâi desu. Mâe ni mo soódañ-simàsita kara . .
'No, it's not the first time. (Because) I consulted before [this], too.'

3. **kotosi/koñna samûi tokórò ni iru**; 4. **koñsyuu/kono kyoositu o tukatte (i)ru**; 5. **koñḡetu/Toókyoo no utì o karite (i)ru**; 6. **kôñbañ/Hasimoto-sañ no otaku e iku**

J 1. **Dekímàsu neˢ**
'You can do it—right?'

Mâa, sukôsi wa dekímàsu ḡa . .
'Well, I can do a little (at least), but . . .' (I won't claim any more).

2. **Wakárimàsita neˢ**
'You understood—right?'

Mâa, sukôsi wa wakárimàsita ḡa . .
'Well, I understood a little (at least), but . . .' (I won't claim any more).

3. **siíte (i)màsu**; 4. **kikímàsita**; 5. **matímàsu**; 6. **kaímàsu**

K 1. **Kîree desu nêe—anó ozyòosañ.**
'Isn't she pretty—that young lady.'

Sôo desu nêe. Kîree na ozyôosañ desu nêe.
'Isn't she! She's a pretty young lady, isn't she!'

2. **Kawáìi desu nêe—anó bòttyañ.**
'Isn't he cute—that little boy.'

Sôo desu nêe. Kawáìi bôttyañ desu nêe.
'Isn't he! He's a cute little boy, isn't he!'

3. **iyâ desu/kodomo**; 4. **yasásìi desu/gosyûziñ**; 5. **wakâi desu/ôkusañ**; 6. **taíheñ dèsu/kodomo**; 7. **muzúkasìi desu/okâasañ**; 8. **isóḡasìi desu/gosyûziñ**; 9. **suḡôi desu/bôttyañ**

L 1. **Señsèe ni gosyóokai-simasyòo kaˏ**
'Shall I introduce [you] to the teacher?'

Êe, syoókai-site kudasaimasèñ kaˏ
'Yes, would you (introduce)?'

2. **Señsèe ni okíki-simasyòo kaˏ**
'Shall I ask the teacher?'

Êe, kiíte kudasaimasèñ kaˏ
'Yes, would you (ask)?'

3. **ohánasi-simasyòo**; 4. **okári-simasyòo**; 5. **odêñwa-simasyoo**; 6. **omíse-simasyòo**

Application Exercises

A1. Complete your imaginary family tree, adding the family relationships listed at the end of the Breakdowns. Follow the procedures described in Lesson 10A, Application Drills.

2. Have one group member describe in Japanese the makeup of his/her extended family, with other group members diagramming the family tree as details are provided.

3. Practice introducing members of your group to each other, using real names and appropriate style. For further practice, assign new identities to group members, establishing a variety of differences of rank.

B. Core Conversations: Substitution

In this section, only limited substitutions in the CC are possible. CC1 does not permit any variation beyond stylistic changes. In CC2 and CC3, substitutions should be restricted to names, relationships, and affiliations. Practice until you can produce these ritualized conversations smoothly, convincingly, and with appropriate timing and gestures. Be sure to stand up when performing introductions and being introduced.

SECTION C

Eavesdropping

(Answer the following on the basis of the accompanying audiotape. In each conversation, A = the first speaker and B = the second speaker.)

1a. What kind of weather is it?
 b. What seems appealing to B?
2a. What is A looking for?
 b. According to B, where is it located?
3a. How much has A completed?
 b. What is B's reaction?
4a. What is A's concern?
 b. What is B's explanation?
 c. Where is Mr/s. Carter?
5a. What does A want to know?
 b. What is the total number? In what categories?
6a. What surprised A?
 b. What two explanations does B offer?
7a. Who is being discussed?
 b. Where is that person? Since when?
 c. What was B unaware of?
8a. What is A trying to locate?
 b. Where is it?
 c. What does B offer to do?
 d. What is A's reaction?
9a. What does A want to do? With whom?
 b. What is B's reaction?
 c. What does B request?
10a. Who is A?
 b. Who is B?
 c. What does A seem to think might be in the vicinity?
 d. What actually is close by?
 e. Who is there today?
 f. What day is today?

11a. How is today's temperature?
  b. What had B expected?
  c. What month is it?
  d. What does A find unpleasant?
12a. What is B studying? Why? Give details.
  b. What is A's warning?
13a. How far from Shinjuku are A and B?
  b. What does A suggest?
  c. Why does B think this is a good idea?
  d. When does A want to leave?
14a. Whom did A meet? When?
  b. What are A's two comments about that person?
  c. What is B's explanation for one of those comments?
 15. How many more people are expected? Identify who is still to come.
16a. In what country does this conversation take place?
  b. Who is coming? When? From where?
  c. What two places will they visit?
  d. How long will the visitors stay in the first place?
  e. When are they going to the second place mentioned? Who is there?
17a. Who is A?
  b. What does B wonder about A's possible identity?
  c. What is the actual situation?
  d. What rituals are exchanged?
18a. What request does A make of B?
  b. Who is B?
  c. How does B react to the request?
  d. What suggestion does B make? Who is involved? When? At what place?
19a. Where does this conversation probably take place?
  b. Who outranks whom?
  c. What does A invite B to do?
  d. Why does B refuse?
  e. What does B invite A to do?
  f. When do A and B expect to meet again?
20a. Where is B going for vacation?
  b. What is the apparent reason?
  c. Where would B prefer to go?
  d. Where is A going?
  e. Who will accompany A?

Utilization

(Refer to the instructions for Utilization in Lesson 10 as a guide for procedures to be followed. This section should be given serious attention. It is really the lesson's 'show and tell': it provides an opportunity to *show* everything you have learned, and at the same time, *tells* you where—if anywhere—your weaknesses lie.)

  1. Tell your supervisor (humble-politely!) that you met his son at Tokyo University yesterday.
  2. Tell the secretary that you would like to meet with Professor Ono next week. (Be polite!)
  3. Comment on what a nice person Mrs. Hashimoto is.
  4. Express your amazement at how good Mr. Yamanaka is in foreign languages.
  5. Tell an associate that you were amazed at how convenient the new computer is.

6. Complain to an associate that the new teacher is a terribly difficult person; and what is more, you were amazed at how poor his English is.

7. Tell an associate that you thought you wanted to buy a new car but they've become terribly expensive so you've given up [the idea].

8. Exclaim on how hot; cold; warm; cool it's become.

9. Suggest to a colleague that you go to Ueno Park together on Sunday—your family and his.

10. Tell a close friend that you and your wife are going to Europe together next month.

11. Ask a colleague what she's going to do for vacation.

12. Tell a close friend that four of you—you, Hayashi, Hayashi's (younger) brother, and your (younger) sister—are going to Kyoto next week.

13. You've just made a suggestion. Ask a colleague what he thinks.

14. Tell a colleague that you think the computer has probably broken down again.

15. You've been asked when you will return to Japan from your trip abroad. Say that you think (a) you'll return on about December 1; (b) you'll (already) be back on December 1 (at least); (c) you will not return until December 1; (d) you'll return by December 1 (at least).

16. Tell a close friend you've been thinking you'd like to study Italian. Ask her what she thinks.

17. Find out if Ms. Kubota has any brothers and sisters.

18. Tell a colleague that since you hate the rush hour you're going to stay in your office until late.

19. Compliment a colleague on his great idea.

20. Ask a close friend why he supposes Ms. Matsuda is waiting at the reception desk.

21. You've been asked about the availability of an apartment in a building your (older) brother owns. Reply that you will consult with your brother and telephone (again) later.

22. You've been looking for Mr. Yamamoto's office. Tell your friend that you thought it was on the second floor but . . . (you're not sure).

23. Ask Mr. Hayashi if he has come here for the first time.

24. Explain that since your American friend is extremely proficient in Japanese, he usually speaks Japanese.

25. Explain that since your Japanese friend is extremely proficient in English, you usually speak English with him.

26. Announce that you are about to perform an introduction.

27. Introduce (a) your father to Mr. Hayashi from the Ministry of Education; (b) Mr. Kubota from the Foreign Ministry to Professor Tanaka of Kyoto University; (c) your wife to Mr. Nakamura of the Finance Ministry.

28. You have just been introduced. Perform!

29. Express your obligation for help your son is always receiving from the person addressed.

30. In response to the preceding, insist on *your* obligation.

31. Greet a colleague you haven't seen for a while. Ask if things are as usual.

32. In response to the preceding, ask if things are the same for your addressee's in-group.

33. Tell an associate to give your regards to his parents.

34. Express your request for help and assistance and generally favorable treatment.

Check-up

1. Describe the difference between the use of the polite family terms as compared with that of the generic or 'plain' forms. Give examples of the use of Japanese family terms without any notion of familial connection. (A-SP1), (B-SP2)

2. How would a Japanese *address* his mother; his aunt; his brother Takashi (older); his brother Yukio (younger); his uncle? How would he *refer* to these individuals in talking to an associate? How would he refer to the comparable family members of his associate? (A-SP1), (B-SP2)

3. How are people counted? Distinguish between the Japanese equivalents of 'those twelve children' and 'those twelve-year-old children.' (A-SP1)

4. What is the meaning of a /predicate (imperfective, perfective, or tentative) + **kara**/? Describe the occurrence of distal- and direct-style before **kara**. (A-SP2)

5. What is the implication of minor sentences ending in **kara**? (A-SP2)

6. How does the Japanese language distinguish between 'Tanaka became ill, so he (= Tanaka) came late' and 'Tanaka became ill, so I came late'? (A-SP2)

7. What is meant by a 'manner' expression? How is manner expressed in Japanese? Give examples. (A-SP3)

8. How are opinions expressed in Japan? Areas of wondering? (A-SP4)

9. What determines the form of the quoted thought, in terms of whether it is imperfective, perfective, etc.? (A-SP4)

10. What is the direct-style equivalent of **desyoo**? Where does it occur? (A-SP5)

11. What is meant by ritual language? Give examples. (B-SP1)

12. In performing an introduction, what is the preferred order of presentation of the individuals being introduced? (B-SP1)

13. What is regularly included in addition to the ritual statements made by a person being introduced in Japanese that has no parallel in a comparable English-language situation? (B-SP1)

14. In being introduced to someone to whom one is obliged even indirectly, what ritual statement is included? (B-SP1)

15. Describe the Japanese attitude toward introductions. (B-SP1)

Lesson 12

SECTION A

Core Conversations

1(J)a. **Kaísya no deñwabàñḡoo wa?**

b. **Kamáimasèñ. Kakímàsu kara, iťte kudasài.**

c. **Zyâa, yoñ·nàna·rêe no yoñ·ròku·nií·ìti, matâ wa nií·nìi desu neʕ Naiseñ wa?**

2(J)a. **Watakusi, oókuràsyoo no Kodáma to moosimàsu. Dôozo yorosiku.**

b. **Sôo desu ka. Dê wa, mata izure.**

3(N)a. **Nakada-sañ ni deñwa o kaketài ñ desu kedo, deñwabàñḡoo gozôñzi desyoo ka.**

b. **Kaísya nò desu.**

c. **Moo iti-do yuḱkùri ośsyàtte kudasaimaseñ kaˇ Bôku, suuzi ni yowâi desu kara . .**

d. **Wakárimàsita. Dôo mo arîḡatoo.**

(N)a. **Ainiku, kyôo wa, meesi no motiawase ḡa nâi ñ desu kedo . .**

b. **Hâi. Yoñ·nàna·rêe no yoñ·ròku·nií·ìti, matâ wa nií·nìi.**

c. **Nâi ñ desu.**

(N)a. **Koñtineñtaru·gìñkoo no Kâataa de gozaimasu. Moósiwake gozaimasèñ ḡa, meesi o kirâsit(e) orimasite . .**

b. **Moósiwake arimasèñ.**

(J)a. **Otáku nò desu kaˇ—kaísya nò desu kaˇ Dôtira mo zôñzite (i)masu kara . .**

b. **Hâi. Sañ·ḡòo·nâna no nií·hà-ti·marú·màru; naiseñ wa, yoñ·-sàñ·kyûu-bañ desu.**

c. **Sañ·ḡòo·nâna no neʕ Nií·hà-ti·marú·màru. Sore kara, naiseñ wa, yoñ·sàñ·kyûu-bañ desu.**

English Equivalents

1(J)a. Your company telephone number?

(N)a. Unfortunately, (it's that) today (at least) I don't have my cards with me, but . . . (I can give you my number).

b. That's all right. I'll write it down, so [just] tell me.

c. (Well then,) that's 470–4621 or 22—right? Your extension?

b. Certainly. 470–4621 or 22.

c. (It's that) I don't have one.

2(J)a. My name is Kodama, from the Finance Ministry. How do you do?

(N)a. I'm Carter from Continental Bank. I'm terribly sorry, but having run out of cards . . . (I can't give you one).

b. Oh. Well, some other time.

b. I'm sorry.

3(N)a. I'd like to telephone Mr/s. Nakada; would you know the (telephone) number?

(J)a. The home one, or the office one? I know both, so . . . (I can give you either one).

b. The office one.

b. Certainly. It's 357–2800, extension 439.

c. Would you please say it again slowly? I'm terrible (*lit.* weak) at numbers, so . . . (I need a repetition).

d. I have it. Thanks very much.

c. 357 (OK?) 2800. And the extension is 439.

Breakdowns
(and Supplementary Vocabulary)

1. **baṅġòo** — (assigned) number
    deṅwabàṅġoo — telephone number
    ainiku — unfortunate; unfortunately
    meesi — name card, calling card
    motiawase — things on hand
    meesi no motiawase — cards on hand
    meési no motiawase ġa nài — have no cards on hand
    iu /-u; itta/ (SP1) — say; be called
    rêe *or*
    +**zêro** (SP2) — zero
    matâ wa — or on the other hand
    naiseñ — extension

2. **Kodama**   (family name)

môosu ↓ **/-u; môosita/** (SP1)	say; be called /humble-polite/
Koṅtineñtaru-gìñkoo	Continental Bank
moosiwake	excuse, explanation
moósiwake nài	I'm very sorry (*lit.* there is no excuse)
kirâsu /-u; kirâsita/	exhaust the supply
kirâsite (i)ru	have exhausted the supply
kirâsite (o)rimasite ↓ **. .** (SP3)	having exhausted the supply . . . /humble-polite; distal/
izure	someday, sometime

3. **Nakada**   (family name)

/question X, question Y/ (SP4)	is it X, or is it Y?
dôtira mo	both
mâru	zero
iti-do	one time
moo iti-do	one more time
yuḱkùri	slowly; leisurely
ośsyàru ↑ **/-aru; ośsyàtta/** (SP1)	say; be called /honorific-polite/
+**yômu /-u; yôñda/**	read
suuzi	number(s)
yowâi /-katta/	is weak
+**tuyôi /-katta/**	is strong
+**zyoobu /na/**	strong, rugged, sturdy
suuzi ni yowâi	is weak in numbers

MISCELLANEOUS NOTES

1. CC1 is an essentially careful-style conversation between two business acquaintances who have just met. Most predicates are neutral distal-style; but there are also a number of minor sentences, including fragments. The overall style suggests a meeting on a comparatively informal level.

When members of the business community meet in Japan, they immediately exchange business cards on which are printed name and business information—company name, address, telephone number, and position. This information is crucial in order for the new acquaintances to know how to interact with each other—to know who outranks whom, and what speech style is appropriate. For (N) not to have a card in CC1 calls for an explanation—in this case, that he doesn't have his cards with him.

Professional women also use **meesi**, but housewives do not. Most academics exchange cards, but the practice among them is not as universal as among the business community (cf. Lesson 11B). Since **meesi** received from other people are sometimes used as a demonstration of association with the cards' owners, some Japanese—particularly eminent members of the society—are deliberately sparing in their distribution of cards.

Meesi are handed over, and accepted, with a certain amount of ceremony. Upon receiving a card, it is polite to look at it with interest before putting it away.

(N)a. **Ainiku**, contrary to the fact that its final mora is **-ku**, is a nominal: this is its only form. It links up with a predicate as a manner construction, describing *how* the predicate occurs, i.e., 'unfortunately,' or it becomes part of a nominal-predicate: **ainiku desu** 'it is unfortunate.' Note the extended predicate: 'it's that I don't have cards with me' (that explains my not giving you one). **Motiawase** is the nominal derivative of a vowel verbal **motiawaseru** 'have on hand.'

(N)b. **Matâ wa** occurs between nominals or between predicates or even as a link between the utterances of two different speakers, naming alternate possibilities. Here the alternate telephone numbers are 4621 or 4622.

(N)c. The extended predicate here explains that 'it's that I don't have an extension' (that explains why I didn't give you a number).

2. CC2 involves self-introduction, a ritualized situation of frequent occurrence. This example is extremely formal, in polite, careful-style: all predicates are in the distal-style, and most are polite as well. Minor sentences and fragments are either polite ritual expressions or sentence partials which are also distal-style (cf. SP3, following).

(J)a. It is common to begin a self-introduction with **wata(ku)si**, with no phrase-particle following. As in introductions in general, one's affiliation is included along with the family name. The presentation of the **meesi** would regularly accompany this self-introduction involving two business people: the card would be ceremoniously handed over, accepted, and usually read by the recipient before being put away. Mr. Carter's failure to be able to present his own card calls for an apology and explanation.

(N)a. **Kirâsu** is an operational verbal: its **-t(e) òru** form refers (in humble-polite style) to the continuing state that results from the action, i.e., 'I have exhausted my supply,' 'I am out of my supply.'

(J)b. Mr. Kodama responds politely to the apology and explanation offered by Mr. Carter, by suggesting that the problem can be cleared up at some future time. Note the use of uncontracted **dê wa** in place of **zya**, as an added indication of the formality of the situation. **Izure**, too, is a rather formal word.

(N)b. Mr. Carter's switch to **arímasèñ** reflects an avoidance of unrelieved polite-style in the given setting.

3. CC3 is a careful-style conversation, including several examples of polite vocabulary: **gozôñzi** and **zôñzite**, and **ossyàtte** (cf. SP1). Predicates—even those preceding **kara**—are distal-style. However, note that when (N) relaxes to the extent of confessing a personal weakness in (N)c, he does refer to himself as **bôku**. In (J)c, we find an example of an utterance that is broken down into shorter, readily understandable units and articulated slowly and explicitly in response to (N)'s request for a repetition. On the accompanying videotape, a young, foreign student (N) is speaking (carefully and politely!) with his Japanese guarantor[1] (J), who uses a similar style of speech in this type of encounter.

(N)a. The extended predicate here, in anticipation, accounts for the following question: 'it's that I want to telephone' (that explains what follows).

(J)a. **Dôtira mo** 'both' is another example of the pattern that underlies **îtu mo** and **dôo mo**. The pattern will be explained in detail in a later lesson.

(N)c. The **-do** of **iti-do** was previously encountered in **maido** 'every time.' This classifier,

---

1. Japanese law requires that foreigners holding student or work visas have guarantors resident in Japan.

which counts the number of occasions, occurs commonly only with low numerals: **iti-do,
ni-do, sâñ-do, yôñ-do**; and in the interrogative **nâñ-do.**

Yukkùri 'slowly (and deliberately)' is a nominal which occurs most commonly as a manner
expression, linking up with a predicate to describe 'how': **yukkùri hanâsu** 'talk slowly';
yukkùri 'sono siḡoto (o) suru 'take one's time doing that work.' **Yukkùri** also implies a
leisurely, unhurried manner: **yukkùri soodañ-suru** 'talk over at leisure,' **yukkùri otyá (o)
nòmu** 'have a leisurely cup of tea.' Note also **Dôozo goyúkkùri.** 'Take it easy!' a polite,
informal invitation to have a pleasant, relaxing time, or 'Take your time!' 'No need to rush!'
in what you are doing. The explicit mention of **bôku** makes clear that (N) is specifically
talking about himself, a shift from the operator of the preceding sentence.

Tuyôi and **yowâi** may refer to degrees of brute strength, or power, or persistence, or
dominance. They are also used in reference to the potency of medicine and to the alcoholic
content of drinks, as well as to an individual's capacity in that area—but *not* to strong/weak
coffee and tea. **Zyoobu**, a **na**-nominal, refers to ruggedness, sturdiness, and a capacity for
endurance.

Structural Patterns

1. **iu ~ ośsyàru** ↑ **~ môosu** ↓

The verbal **iu** has two basic meanings: 'say' and 'be named' or 'be called.' In the former
meaning, it refers to the uttering of a particular span of language, in contrast with **hanâsu**,
which refers to general speaking or talking. Compare: **hâyâku iu** 'say [it] fast' and **hâyâku
hanâsu** 'talk fast,' 'speak quickly.' Note: **soo itta** 's/he said so'; **sôo wa iwánàkatta** 's/he
didn't say so.' Further drills on quotation will be introduced later.

Iu is a **w**-consonant operational verbal (**itta; iwanai**). Its direct-style perfective (**itta**) and
its gerund (**itte**) are exactly the same as the corresponding forms of **iku.** Only context
distinguishes them in the spoken language.

In the pronunciation of the citation form, the coming together of **i-** and **-u** results in the
same pronunciation as that represented by the sequence **yuu.**[2]

In the sequence /name X + **to** + **iu**/ = 'be named or called X,' **to** is the quotative phrase-
particle previously encountered in /——— **to omôu**/ patterns. The corresponding question
is **nâñ to iu** 'be named or called what?' Thus:

Yamamoto-sañ no âkatyañ (no onamae) wa, nâñ to iimasu ka⤹

'What is the name of Mr/s. Yamamoto's baby?' (**Onamae** is optional.)

Kore wa, nihoñḡo de nâñ to iû ñ desu ka⤹

'What is it you call this in (i.e., by means of) Japanese?'

The honorific-polite ↑ equivalent of **iu** is **ośsyàru**, used in polite reference to members of
the out-group. In contrast, **môosu** (an **s**-consonant verbal) is the humble-polite ↓ partner,
used in polite reference to oneself or other in-group members in talking to the out-group.
Note that **ośsyàru** is a member of the special polite verbal class, along with **irássyàru,
kudásàru,** and *gozâru: stem **ośsyài.**

---

2. This is true throughout the language. For example, the name of Japan's largest newspaper is a combination
of two verbal stems: **yômi** 'reading' and **uri** 'selling.' At normal speed, the combination **Yomiuri** is pronounced
as if it were spelled **Yomyuuri.**

In polite self-introductions, two commonly occurring patterns are: **(Wata[ku]si)**,[3] /name/ **to moósimàsu**. *or* **(Wata[ku]si)**, /name/ **de gozaimàsu**. In such situations, Westerners often use their full name, in which case they regularly retain the original order.

In contacting a Japanese within a large organization where the family name alone is not sufficient, the full name—/last + given/—may be used. An alternative is identification by division of the organization, i.e., /division name + **no** + family name/. Remember that there are countless Tanakas and Satos and Nakamuras among the Japanese.

2. TELEPHONE NUMBERS

The Japanese telephone number system is extremely simple: each number is treated as an individual digit, represented by the appropriate numeral of the Chinese series. For 4, 7, and 9, **yôñ, nâna,** and **kyûu** are the preferred alternates. Zero may be **rêe, zêro,** or **mâru** (**maru** 'circle').

The use of the classifier **-bañ** (which names a number of a series) is optional in citing a telephone number, but required in the corresponding question: 'What is your telephone number?' is **Deñwa(bàñgoo) (wa) nâñ-bañ desu ka** Area codes, exchanges, and the final four-digit number are separated by **no: 813 no 560 no 3211**; but /**naiseñ** + number/ may directly follow the principal number without a connecting **no**. Area codes and exchanges may be two, three, or four digits.

In presenting a telephone number orally, the one-mora numerals, **nî** and **gô**, are often given a second mora through the lengthening of the final vowel. Compare the lengthening of **ka** and **do** as abbreviations for the days of the week (Lesson 8A). Starting from the beginning of a number, pairs of numerals are joined into single accent phrases, with the accent on the next-to-final mora. Example: **sañ·kyùu nií·yòñ**.

3. kirâsit(e) orimasite ↓ . .

Sentence-final **kirâsit(e) orimasite** is of special interest to us for two reasons:

a. In form, it is the gerund of a *distal-style* verbal. Compare

ik- /+ gerund formation/ > **it-te** *and*

ik- /+ stem formation/ > **iki** /+ **-màs**/ > **ikímàs**

/+ gerund formation/ > **ikímàsite**

It was previously noted that the distal-style marker **-màs-** is itself a verbal with typical derivative forms. However, until now, the gerund patterns that have been introduced have been only direct-style gerunds. But a distal-style alternate is also possible in the structural pattern we designated as /**-te,**/ (7B-SP5), thereby moving an utterance slightly higher on the casual–careful-style continuum. Example:

Tugî no kâdo made ikímàsite, migî e magatte kudasaimasèñ ka

'Would you be kind enough to go as far as the next corner, and turn right?'

b. We have already encountered a number of different minor-sentence types. Among the very common have been those ending in **kedo, ga,** and **kara**. Whenever they occur, the implication is that continuation is unnecessary: it is already understood by the listener, and often it is preferred—for various reasons—to leave the conclusion unstated. The gerund, too, may occur in sentence-final position, thus signaling a minor sentence. In this section,

---

3. In this context, **wata(ku)si** is *not* followed by a phrase-particle, unless contrast is to be indicated by the use of **wa**.

the gerund in this position is the gerund of the structural pattern described in detail in 8A-SP5, with the following predicate understood but unstated. In other words, the speaker is saying, 'This being the case—you know the rest.' (N) is explaining: 'Having run out of cards'—it's impossible for me to give you one. The meaning is perfectly clear, but the utterance seems gentler without the overt statement of the conclusion.

In this pattern, the gerund itself may be direct-style or distal-style. But since it is occurring in sentence-final position, it is more apt to be distal-style than are gerunds that occur within sentences.

We actually have encountered one ritual expression which is an example of this pattern, **Dôo itasimasite,** the humble-polite ↓ equivalent of **dôo site:** 'Doing what (on my part)'— do I deserve your thanks, apologies, etc.? More will be said about this utterance in Section B of this lesson.

4. ALTERNATE QUESTIONS

To offer a listener a choice between two alternatives—'is it X, or is it Y?'—the two yes-no questions are presented in the same form as independent questions; however, they become a single compound sentence, indicated by the intonation (lower pitch within the second part). Optionally, **matâ wa** may occur between the two alternates: it is particularly common between complex, lengthy alternates. Examples:

Îi desu ka⌣—damê desu ka⌣ 'Is it all right, or is it broken?'

Onîisañ desita ka⌣—otóotosañ dèsita ka⌣ 'Was it your older brother, or your younger brother?'

Kyôo kaérimàsu ka⌣—(matâ wa) asítà made kotíra ni imàsu ka⌣ 'Are you going home today, or are you staying here until tomorrow?'

Eeǧo wa, kotosi kara Nihôñ de beñkyoo-simàsu ka⌣—(matâ wa) Iǧirisu e itte, raíneñ kara beñkyoo-simàsu ka⌣ 'About English—are you going to study it in Japan starting this year, or are you going to England and study it starting next year?'

Drills

A 1. **Tomodati mo, kotíra ni kùru?**
'Is your friend coming here, too?'

Betu ni sôo wa iwánàkatta kedo, kûru ñ zya nai?
'S/he didn't especially say so, but don't you suppose s/he will (come)?'

2. **Mîyazi-sañ mo, kotíra ni mièru?**
'Is Mr/s. Miyaji coming here, too?'

Betu ni sôo wa iwánàkatta kedo, miêru ñ zya nai?
'S/he didn't especially say so, but don't you suppose s/he will (come)?'

3. **Suzuki-sañ/komâru;** 4. **onîisañ/kôñbañ tomaru;** 5. **kâre/zîsyo ǧa iru;** 6. **kânozyo/ eéǧo ǧa wakàru**

B 1. **Señsèe wa, kâre to oái ni nàru ñ desu ka⌣**

Ainiku sôo wa ossyaimasèñ desita. Oái ni nàru daroo to omôtta kedo . .

'(Is it that) the doctor is going to meet with him?'

'Unfortunately s/he didn't say so. I thought s/he probably would (meet) but . . .' (I'm not sure).

2. **Señsèe wa, uti o okári ni nàru ñ desu ka** ⤵
   '(Is it that) the doctor is going to rent a house?'

   Ainiku sôo wa ośsyaimasèñ desita. Okári ni nàru daroo to omôtta kedo . .
   'Unfortunately s/he didn't say so. I thought s/he probably would (rent) but . . .' (I'm not sure).

3. **asâtte omíe ni nàru**; 4. **deńwa o okake ni nàru**; 5. **konó ryokañ ni otomari ni nàru**; 6. **osókù made oíde ni nàru**; 7. **asíta no zèmi ni odé ni nàru**; 8. **gakusee o oyóbi ni nàru**

C 1. **Anô ko wa Tâkasi desita ne** ʃ
   'That child was Takashi—right?'

   Êe. Tâkasi to iû ñ desu.
   'Yes. (It's the case that) his name is Takashi.'

2. **Asoko wa Oókura-hòteru desita ne** ʃ
   'That (place) was the Hotel Okura—right?'

   Êe. Oókura-hòteru to iû ñ desu.
   'Yes. (It's the case that) the name [of the place] is the Hotel Okura.'

3. **anó àkatyañ/Yûkiko**; 4. **asoko/Toókyoo-dàiḡaku**; 5. **anó bìru/Paáku-bìru**; 6. **ano kooeñ/Uéno-kòoeñ**; 7. **asoko/Mêziro**; 8. **ano byooiñ/Toránomoñ-byòoiñ**; 9. **anó depàato/Pâruko**

D 1. **Kodáma-sañ de (i)rassyaimàsu ne** ʃ
   'You are Mr/s. Kodama—right?'

   Hâi. Kodáma to moosimàsu.
   'Yes, my name is Kodama.'

2. **Yamánaka-señsèe de (i)rassyaimasu ne** ʃ
   'You are Dr. Yamanaka—right?'

   Hâi. Yamánaka to moosimàsu.
   'Yes, my name is Yamanaka.'

3. **Hasimoto-sañ**; 4. **Kitamura-sañ**; 5. **Hayasi-sañ**

E 1. **Anó katà wa, Kodáma-sañ de (i)rassyaimàsu ne** ʃ
   'That (person) is Mr/s. Kodama—right?'

   Êe, Kodáma to ossyaimàsu kedo . .
   'Yes, his/her name is Kodama, but . . .' (why do you ask?)

2. **Anó katà wa, Yamánaka-señsèe de (i)rassyaimasu ne** ʃ
   'That (person) is Dr. Yamanaka—right?'

   Êe, Yamánaka to ossyaimàsu kedo . .
   'Yes, his/her name is Yamanaka, but . . .' (why do you ask?)

3. **Hasimoto-sañ**; 4. **Nîsida-señsee**; 5. **Matuda-sañ**

F 1. **Kâre wa, Tanaka Yukío dèsita ne** ʃ
   'That (lit. he) was Yukio Tanaka—right?'

   Êe, Tanaka Yukío to iù to omôu ñ desu kedo . .
   'Yes, (it's the case that) I think his name is Yukio Tanaka, but . . .' (I'm not sure).

2. **Kânozyo wa, Tanaka Yûkiko desita**
neʕ
'That (*lit.* she) was Yukiko Tanaka—
right?'

Êe, Tanaka Yûkiko to iû to omôu ñ desu
kedo . .
'Yes, (it's the case that) I think her name is
Yukiko Tanaka, but . . .' (I'm not sure).

3. **kâre/Kitamura Tâkasi**; 4. **kânozyo/Kitamura Tâkako**; 5. **kâre/Hayasi Yosîhiko**;
6. **kânozyo/Hayasi Yôsiko**

G 1. **Deńwabàñg̣oo wa neʕ**
Goó·nàna·'sañ no neʕ
Ití·rèe·nií·hatì-bañ desu.
'The telephone number (OK?) is
(number) 573 (OK?) 1028.'

Goó·nàna·'sañ no ití·rèe·nií·hàti desu neʕ
Wakárimàsita.
'That's 573–1028—right? Got it.'

2. **Deńwabàñg̣oo wa neʕ**
Naná·kyùu·rokû no neʕ
Goó·nìi·nií·gòo-bañ desu.
'The telephone number (OK?) is
(number) 796 (OK?) 5225.'

Naná·kyùu·rokû no goó·nìi·nií·gòo desu
neʕ Wakárimàsita.
'That's 796–5225—right? Got it.'

3. **sań·ròku·nî/yoń·nìi·hatí·hàti**; 4. **nií·gòo·rokû/rokú·yòñ·goó·nàna**;
5. **rokú·yòñ·gô/kyuú·nàna·sań·gòo**; 6. **sań·gòo·kyûu/goó·zèro·rokú·nàna**;
7. **sań·sàñ·rêe/reé·gòo·nií·ròku**; 8. **hatí·ròku·rokû/ití·nàna·yoń·nìi**;
9. **goó·ròku·itî/sań·ìti·marú·màru**; 10. **nií·ìti·rokû/yoń·nìi·ití·ìti**

H 1. **Naiseñ wa, rokú·nìi·sań dèsu ka**‿
'Is the extension 623?'

Iêie, rokú·sàñ·nî desu yo‿
'No no, it's 632.'

2. **Naiseñ wa, hatí·rèe·nî desu ka**‿
'Is the extension 802?'

Iêie, hatí·nìi·rêe desu yo‿
'No no, it's 820.'

3. **sań·kyùu·nâna**; 4. **kyuú·gòo·rokû**; 5. **naná·ìti·zêro**; 6. **nií·yòñ·gôo**;
7. **kyuú·sàñ·itî**; 8. **ití·hàti·kyûu**; 9. **hatí·màru·hatî**; 10. **naná·ìti·gôo**

I 1. **Arúbàito yamérù no?**
'You're going to give up part-time
work?'

Ñ, yamétài to omôtte . .
'Yeah, [I've been] thinking I'd like to
quit . . .' (and I may do it).

2. **Seńsèe to hanâsu no?**
'You're going to talk with the doctor?'

Ñ, hanásitài to omôtte . .
'Yeah, [I've been] thinking I'd like to have
a talk . . .' (and I may do it).

3. **goryôosiñ to 'soodañ-suru**; 4. **anó kàig̣i ni dêru**; 5. **ano gakusee to âu**; 6. **anó**
hòteru ni 'tomaru; 7. **anó bìru no zimûsyo 'kariru**

J 1. **Meesi o kirâsite (i)rassyaimasu ka**‿
'Have you run out of cards?'

Êe, kirâsit(e) orimasite . .
'Yes, I've run out, and . . .' (you know the
result).

2. **Kono deńwa o tukátte**
(i)rassyaimàsu ka‿

Êe, tukátt(e) orimàsite . .
'Yes, I'm using it, and . . .' (you know the

'Are you using this telephone?'   result).

3. **okyakusañ o mâtte**; 4. **konó zimùsyo o 'karite**; 5. **tyuuǧokuǧo o 'beñkyoo-site**;
6. **kono ryokañ ni 'tomatte**; 7. **doituǧo o 'osiete**; 8. **kono zassi o mîte**; 9. **ôkusañ
ǧa komâtte**; 10. **bikkûri-site**

K 1. **Moñbùsyoo e ikímàsu neʃ**   **Êe, moñbùsyoo e ikímàsite, soré kara uti
'You're going to the Education   e kaerimàsu.**
Ministry—right?'   'Yes, I'm going to the Education Ministry,
                                            and then I'm going home.'

2. **Anó kaisya no hitò to soódañ-   **Êe, anó kaisya no hitò to soódañ-
simàsu neʃ**   simàsite, soré kara uti e kaerimàsu.**
'You're going to consult with a person   'Yes, I'm going to consult with a person in
in that company—right?'   that company, and then I'm going home.'

3. **Yoóròppa e deñwa-simàsu**; 4. **ano teǧami o kakímàsu**; 5. **moó sukòsi matímàsu**;
6. **anó kyookàsyo o kaímàsu**

L 1. **Gaímùsyoo no 'Kodama-sañ,   **Gaímùsyoo no Kodáma-sañ dèsu ka** ...
gozôñzi desyoo ka.**   **Êe, zôñzit(e) orimasu kedo . .**
'Would you know Mr/s. Kodama from   'Mr/s. Kodama from the Foreign Office?
the Foreign Office?'   ... Yes, I know [him/her], but . . .' (why do
                                           you ask?)

2. **Koñtineñtaru-gìñkoo no Kâataa-sañ,   **Koñtineñtaru-gìñkoo no Kâataa-sañ desu
gozôñzi desyoo ka.**   ka** ... **Êe, zôñzit(e) orimasu kedo . .**
'Would you know Mr/s. Carter from   'Mr/s. Carter from the Continental Bank?
the Continental Bank?'   ... Yes, I know [him/her], but . . .' (why do
                                           you ask?)

3. **Toodai no Ôono-señsee**; 4. **moñbùsyoo no 'Nakamura-sañ**; 5. **Oókura-hòteru no
'Matuda-sañ**; 6. **Toránomoñ-byòoiñ no Kitámura-señsèe**

M 1. **Nâǧoya wa, gozôñzi zya arímasèñ   **Nâǧoya desu ka** **Êe, aíniku dèsu ga,
neʃ**   zôñzimasèñ nêe. Moósiwake arimasèñ.**
'You don't know Nagoya—right?'   'Nagoya? That's right, it's unfortunate but
                                           I don't know it. I'm sorry.'

2. **Toódai no deñwabàñgoo wa,   **Toódai no deñwabàñgoo desu ka** **Êe,
gozôñzi zya arímasèñ neʃ**   aíniku dèsu ga, zôñzimasèñ nêe.
'You don't know the Tokyo University   Moósiwake arimasèñ.**
telephone number—right?'   'The Tokyo University telephone number?
                                           That's right, it's unfortunate but I don't
                                           know it. I'm sorry.'

3. **Nakada-sañ no kaisya**; 4. **Matúda-sañ no òkusañ**; 5. **ano gaiziñ no namae**;
6. **Kodáma-sañ no otòosañ no siǧoto**

N 1. **Raísyuu no kàiǧi wa, getúyòobi ni   **Ie. Getúyòobi, matâ wa suíyòobi ni
mo suíyòobi ni mo arímàsu ka**   arímàsu yo**

'Will next week's conference(s) be on Monday *and* on Wednesday?'

'No. It will be on Monday *or* Wednesday.'

2. **Taípuràitaa mo 'waapuro mo tukáimàsu ka** 'Will you use a typewriter *and* a word-processor?'

Ie. Taípuràitaa, matâ wa waápuro o tukaimàsu yo 'No. I'll use a typewriter *or* a word-processor.'

3. **nihoñḡo/eeḡo/hanásimàsu;** 4. **tâkusii de/deñsya de/ikímàsu;** 5. **kañkokùziñ/tyuúḡokùziñ/simâsu**

O 1. **Biñseñ o kiràsite (i)ru ñ desu ka— huútoo o kiràsite (i)ru ñ desu ka** 'Is it stationery we've run out of, or envelopes?'

Dotíra mo kiràsite (i)ru to omoimasu. 'I think we've run out of both.'

2. **Eéḡo o osierù ñ desu ka— huráñsuḡo o osierù ñ desu ka** 'Is it English you're going to teach, or French?'

Dotíra mo osieru to omoimàsu. 'I think I'm going to teach both.'

3. **kaíḡìsitu ḡa samûi/kyoositu;** 4. **otóna ḡa kùru/kodomo;** 5. **uti o katta/kuruma;** 6. **eéwa-zìteñ ḡa iru/waée-zìteñ;** 7. **konó kèeki ḡa 'oisii/anó pài**

P 1. **Raisyuu Kyôoto e iťte kimàsu yo** 'I'm going to Kyoto next week (and coming [back]).'

Kyôoto desu ka. Îi desu nêe. Dôozo goyúkkùri. 'Kyoto? That's great. Have a good (i.e., relaxed) time!'

2. **Râiḡetu Hoḱkàidoo e iťte kimàsu yo** 'I'm going to Hokkaido next month (and coming [back]).'

Hoḱkàidoo desu ka. Îi desu nêe. Dôozo goyúkkùri. 'Hokkaido? That's great. Have a good time!'

3. **koñsyuu/Oósutorària** 4. **saraisyuu/Hukûoka;** 5. **saraiḡetu/Kânada;** 6. **si-ḡátù ni/Iḡirisu**

Q 1. **Matá àto de soódañ-simasyòo.** 'Let's talk it over again at a later time.'

Sôo desu ne! Izúre mata soodañ-simasyòo neʕ 'That's right. Let's talk it over again some time, shall we?'

2. **Matá àto de hanásimasyòo.** 'Let's talk again at a later time.'

Sôo desu ne! Izúre mata hanasimasyòo neʕ 'That's right. Let's talk again some time, shall we?'

3. **aímasyòo;** 4. **kimásyòo;** 5. **nomímasyòo**

Application Exercises

A1. Using a telephone book or any telephone list, practice asking and answering questions about the telephone numbers (and extensions) of particular individuals or organizations.

Expand the practice by asking for repetitions, confirming your understanding, and using explicit (**neʔ**) style.

2. Using pictures of familiar people, buildings, places, etc., ask members of the group (a) whether or not they know the item in question (using appropriate forms of **zoṅzìru**); and (b) the name (using appropriate forms of **X to iu**).

3. Setting up a model town once again, practice the naming pattern /**X to iu**/ and alternate question pattern /sentence X **ka**, sentence Y **ka**/, at the same time reviewing model town vocabulary. Examples:

> **Koṅna misè wa, nâñ to iimasu ka**⌇
>
> **Koko wa, hôñya desu ka**⌇—**buṅbooǧuya dèsu ka**⌇
>
> **Depâato no miǧídònari wa, giṅkoo dèsu ka**⌇—**yuúbìñkyoku desu ka**⌇
>
> **Hanâya wa, giṅkoo no temáe dèsu ka**⌇—**mukóo dèsu ka**⌇
>
> **Koko kara êki e ikítài ñ desu ǧa, tuǧî no kâdo de hidári e maǧarimasyòo ka— miǧî e maǧarimasyòo ka.**   ETC.

B. Core Conversations: Substitution

Practice CC1 and 3 with substitutions, until you can handle variations on the telephone numbers with facility. (In your listening practice, try to retain the original Japanese in your short-term memory so that you can repeat it subvocally as many times as you require for comprehension.) CC2 and 1(N)a provide important ritualized self-introduction language which should be practiced repeatedly—substituting your own name and affiliation—until you can handle it *comfortably*. Observe the participants in these exchanges on the videotape: remember that gestures and facial expressions also send out crucially important messages.

SECTION B

Core Conversations

(It is inevitable that interaction with native-speakers of Japanese will sooner or later involve the telephone. And if face-to-face conversation in a foreign language produces tension in a beginning student, the telephone can result in trauma—UNLESS there has been enough practice to result in confident control of the medium. It is very clear what must be done to prepare adequately!!!)

1(J)a. **Môsimosi. Suǧîura desu.**

    (N)a. **Môsimosi. Kotira, Suú·Buràuñ desu ǧa, Mîtiko-sañ irássyaimàsu ka**⌇

b. **Îma tyôtto rûsu desu kedo ..**

    b. **Zyâa, mêsseezi onéǧai-dekimàsu ka**⌇

c. **Hâi. Syôosyoo omáti-kudasài.**
  . . . Omátase-itasimàsita.

Burâuñ-sañ de (i)rassyaimasu
neˀ

    c. Hâi. Kôñbañ 'yoozi de Kyôoto e
       maírimàsite ne! Myôoniti wa,
       kotíra ni orimasèñ kara, soó
       ossyàtte kudasaimasèñ ka⤸

d. Kasíkomarimàsita.

    d. Zyâa, osôre-irimasu ğa, yorósiku
      oneğai-itasimàsu.

e. Hâi,

    e. Zyâa, sitûree-itasimasu. Goméñ-
      kudasài.

2(J)a. Hâi, Nihóñ-dàiğaku desu.

(N)a. Môsimosi. Yosída·Osamu-señsèe,
      irássyaimàsu ka⤸

b. Dôtira-sama de (i)rassyaimasu
   ka⤸

    b. Amerika no Nyuúyooku-dàiğaku
      no Sûmisu to moósimàsu ğa . .

c. Syôosyoo omáti-kudasài. . . .
   Môsimosi. Yosida wa, îma sêki o
   hazúsit(e) orimàsu ğa . .

    c. Zyâa, notihodo 'mata goréñraku-
      itasimàsu kara . .

d. Dôo mo sumímasèñ.

    d. Goméñ-kudasài.

e. Goméñ-kudasài.

3(N) |Anoo| Nôğuti-syotyoo ni
   reńraku-nasaimàsita ka⤸

    (J) Wasúretè (i)ta.[4]

English Equivalents

1(J)a. Hello. This is [the] Sugiura
    [residence].

(N)a. Hello. This is Sue Brown. Is
    Michiko there?

b. She's out just now, but . . . (can I
   help you?)

    b. Then can I ask you to take a
    message?

c. Yes. Just a moment. . . . I'm sorry
   to have kept you waiting. Ms.
   Brown—right?

    c. Yes. I'm going to Kyoto on business
    tonight—and tomorrow I won't be
    here, so would you tell her that?

d. I'll take care of your message.

    d. (Well then,) I'm sorry to bother you,
    but would you do that?

e. Certainly.

    e. Well, goodbye.

---

4. The accentuation, as usual in this pattern, applies to the contracted alternate, with /i/ deleted.

2(J)a. University of Japan.

b. Who's calling, please?

c. Just a moment, please. . . .
    [Professor] Yoshida is away from
    his desk (*lit.* seat) just now, but . . .
    (can I help you?)

d. I'm very sorry.
e. Goodbye.

3(N) Uh . . . Did you contact Institute
      Director Noguchi?

(N)a. Hello. Is Professor Osamu Yoshida
       there?

b. My name is Smith, from New York
    University in America, but . . . (is he
    in?)

c. Then I'll be in touch again later, so
    . . . (that's all now).

d. Goodbye.

(J) I forgot!!

BREAKDOWNS
(AND SUPPLEMENTARY VOCABULARY)

1. **môsimosi** (SP1)	hello (on the telephone)
Suḡîura	(family name)
Suú·Buràuñ	Sue Brown
Mîtiko	(female given name)
mêsseezi	message
onéḡai-dekìru ↓ (SP2)	can make a request /humble-polite/
itasu ↓ /-u; **itasita**/ (SP3)	do /humble-polite/
omátase-itasimàsita ↓	I've caused you to wait /humble-polite/
yoózi de màiru ↓	go/come on business /humble-polite/
myôoniti	tomorrow
+ **myôobañ**	tomorrow night
+ **myootyoo**	tomorrow morning
+ **myoógòniti**	day after tomorrow
osôre-irimasu	I'm sorry; thank you
onéḡai-itasimàsu ↓	I make a request /humble-polite/
sitûree /na/	rude; rudeness
sitûree-itasimasu ↓	excuse me (*lit.* I commit a rudeness) /humble-polite/
goméñ-kudasài(màse)	excuse me, pardon me
2. **Nihóñ-dàiḡaku**	University of Japan
+ **Tukúba-dàiḡaku**	University of Tsukuba
+ **Keéoo-dàiḡaku**	Keio University
+ **Waséda-dàiḡaku**	Waseda University
Yosida	(family name)
Osamu	(male given name)

dôtira-sama	who? /polite/
Nyuúyooku-dàiḡaku	New York University
Sûmisu	Smith
(o)sêki	seat, assigned place
hazusu /-u; hazusita/	let go; unfasten
hazusite (i)ru	have let go; have unfastened
sêki (o) hazusite (i)ru	have left one's seat
notihodo	later
(go)reñraku-suru	get in touch, make contact
goréñraku-itasimàsu ↓	get in touch /humble-polite/
3. **Nôguti**	(family name)
syotyoo	director of a research institute
nasâru ↑ /-aru; nasâtta/ (SP3)	do /honorific-polite/
syotyoo ni reñraku-nasàru ↑	get in touch with the institute director /honorific-polite/
wasureru /-ru; wasureta/	forget
+**obóèru /-ru; obôeta/**	commit to memory, learn by heart

MISCELLANEOUS NOTES

1,2. CC1 and CC2 are typical telephone conversations, containing many examples of ritual language, discussed in SP1, following. The situations represented by these two calls demand polite careful-style, with distal-style predicates. In CC1, (J) is probably a relative of Michiko's—perhaps her mother; and in CC2, (J) is undoubtedly an operator or secretary. In conveying her message, Sue Brown (1[N]c) uses explicit style, breaking down her message into two shorter units, the first ending in /**ne!**/.

1(J)a. The name **Suḡîura,** containing roots **suḡi** and **ura,** brings together /-**i** + **u**-/, and predictably, at normal speed, is usually pronounced **suḡyûura.**

(N)a. In calling the Sugiura household, it is necessary for Sue Brown to indicate which member of the family she wishes to speak with. One way is to use the given name alone, if the individual is young. Another method is to use the appropriate family term (example: **Suḡîura-sañ no gosyûziñ**).

(J)c. Here (J) asks Sue Brown to wait, undoubtedly to give her time to locate a pencil and paper.

(N)c. **Yoózi de mairimàsu:** compare **zîko de okureru.** This occurrence of **de** suggests a causal connection with what follows: 'because of business.'

Time words that include **myoo** are examples of vocabulary of Chinese origin, considered more learned and more formal than native Japanese equivalents. **Myôoniti** is an alternate for **asítà/asû; myôobañ** = **asita no bañ; myootyoo** = **asíta no àsa;** and **myoógòniti** = **asâtte.**

Note that Sue Brown uses distal-style even in the segment before /**ne!**/.

(N)d. **Osôre-irimasu,** which literally has to do with being 'filled with awe,' is a very formal ritual expression. It crosses the bounds between gratitude and apology: 'thanks for your trouble' and, at the same time, 'I'm sorry to bother you.' Compare **sumímasèñ**, which also covers these two areas.

Yorósiku oneĝai-itasimàsu is a polite request that the listener's actions be favorable to the speaker, as defined by the situation. This expression enjoys extremely frequent usage among Japanese.

(N)e. **Sitûree** is a **na**-nominal: **sitûree desu ĝa** is a commonly occurring introduction to a personal question which implies some rudeness on the speaker's part. **Sitûree-(ita)simasu** expresses an apology for what is about to occur, often the speaker's departure or withdrawal from the conversation. Literally, it means something like 'I am going to commit a rudeness,' but what constitutes a 'rudeness' among Japanese is not predictable on the basis of foreign patterns of behavior. For example, in Japanese society, initial contact with a stranger other than by a face-to-face meeting can be an example of **sitûree**, hence the occurrence of apologies like **odêñwa de sitûree-simasu, otêĝami de sitûree-simasu**. Literal English translations of these expressions used by Japanese when speaking or writing English can be surprising to native speakers of English.

2(J)a. The universities introduced in Lesson 11B—**Toodai, Kyoodai, Hokudai**, and **Kyuudai**—are all national universities, as is **Tukúba-dàiĝaku**. **Keeoo** and **Wâseda** are Japan's most prestigious private universities, and **Nihóñ-dàiĝaku** a particularly large one.

(J)b. Again the association of person with place becomes evident in this polite question regarding identity. Note also the use of **kotira** in self-reference, and **sotira** to indicate the person addressed, particularly common on the telephone.

(J)c. Here (J) is assumed to be the private secretary of a high ranking Professor Yoshida and in his in-group. If the person answering the telephone were part-time secretarial help— a common situation for lower ranking professors—Professor Yoshida would be referred to with honorific-polite / ↑ / forms.

Hazusu is an **s**-consonant operational verbal (perfective: **hazusita**). Its /gerund + **(i)ru**/ combination usually refers to the continuing state resulting from the action (cf. **tokee [o] hazusite [i]ru** 'I've taken off my watch').

(N)c. **Notihodo** is a more formal equivalent of **âto de**. **Goreñraku** implies 'contact with you,' and therefore occurs in humble-polite alternates.

3. In CC3, a foreigner (N) is checking on whether his/her supervisor remembered to make contact with a particular individual. The situation calls for not only politeness, but even some hesitation in raising the question. Accordingly, s/he introduces an honorific-polite, distal-style question with |anoo|. The supervisor's exclamatory reply is a brief, direct-style utterance. On the accompanying videotape, the exchange is between a foreign student and his professor.

(N) The use of phrase-particle **ni** in the sequence /person X + **ni** + **reñraku-suru**/ indicates that X is the *goal* of the contact. It is also possible to use /person + **to**/ with this verbal, implying contact with mutual involvement of the contactor and the contacted.

(J) Both **wasureru** and **obóeru** are operational vowel verbals—'commit to forgetfulness' and 'commit to memory.' Note the form (J) uses: the perfective of the /-**te** + **(i)ru**/ pattern indicates that at the time when he was supposed to get in touch with Noguchi, he *was* in a state resulting from his *already* having forgotten prior to that time. Compare: **Wasúremàsita.** 'I forgot' (i.e., in relation to the present); **Wasúrete (i)màsu kara . .** 'Since I have forgotten (and continue in that condition) . . .'; **Obôete (i)masu.** 'I remember (i.e., 'I have it memorized'). **Obóemàsita.** 'I committed [it] to memory.' **Obôete kudasai.** 'Please commit [it] to memory.'

Structural Patterns

1. TELEPHONE CONVERSATIONS

Japanese telephone conversations include a considerable amount of ritual language, which, once again, must be mastered through memorization. CC1 and 2 of this lesson section provide a number of examples:

(1) **Môsimosi**, a polite 'attention-getter,' is particularly common as a 'hello' on the telephone. **Hâi** is also used by the recipient of the call.

(2) Frequently the person answering the telephone in a private home identifies the family, immediately following a conversation opener. If a public organization of any kind is involved, identification of the organization is expected, often in addition to a conversation opener—**môsimosi, oháyoo gozaimàsu, maído arìḡatoo gozaimasu**, among others.

(3) The caller is next expected to identify him/herself. Failure to do so regularly results in a question as to who is calling (CC2[J]b). (That identification rarely seems to be passed on if the call is subsequently transferred to someone else.)

(4) If the call is interrupted for any reason (as when [J] goes for a pencil in CC1), the call is often resumed with **omátase-(ita)simàsita** 'I kept you waiting' (CC1[J]c). This is a humble-polite /**o-** + stem + **-suru**/ pattern, based on the vowel verbal **matásèru** 'cause to wait,' which in turn is derived from **mâtu** 'wait.' (More will be said about this verbal pattern in a later lesson.) Another way to resume a conversation after an interruption is with **môsimosi** (CC2[J]c). It is, of course, also possible to use both **môsimosi** and **omátase-(ita)simàsita**.

(5) One common pattern for giving a message is: /situation X + **kara** + **soó itte** (~**ossyàtte**) **kudasài**/ = 'the situation is X, so please say that.' (Cf. CC1[N]c.)

(6) If the message—or any utterance on the telephone—becomes at all long, it is normal to divide it into shorter, independent segments, each ending in /**ne!**~ʕ/. An occurrence of /**ne!**~ʕ/ requires acknowledgment by the listener—**hâi, êe, sôo, ñ**, etc.

(7) A request is usually followed by an apology (**sumímasèñ** or **osôre-irimasu**) followed by the ritual **yorósiku oneḡai-(ita)simàsu**, which in turn requests general consideration and favorable treatment.

(8) **Sitûree-(ita)simasu** in CC1(N)e indicates a withdrawal from the conversation.

(9) **Goméñ-kudasài**, literally a request to be excused or pardoned, is a very common 'goodbye' on the telephone. It is also used to attract attention when entering a home or shop when no one is in evidence.

In general, telephone calls tend to be careful-style and often polite—particularly the ritual portions—unless one is talking to a close friend. Formal words—**notihodo** instead of **âto de, myôoniti** instead of **asítà**—are also frequent. And on the telephone, gestures and facial expressions usually match the language that is being uttered, without regard to the fact that the speaker can't be seen. This includes bowing.

In asking whether an individual is in, no particle follows the designation of the individual:

Mîtiko-sañ irássyaimàsu ka↗

However, if a second individual were introduced contrastively, **wa** would, of course, occur:

(Zyâa,) Tâkasi-sañ wa irássyaimàsu ka↗

The Japanese telephone system is extremely efficient, with public phones to be found everywhere. Americans are usually struck by how reasonable local calls are, and conversely, how expensive long-distance is.

2. Onégai-dekimàsu ka↙

The affective verbal **dekîru** was introduced in the very first lesson. It was defined in terms of two different meanings:

1. **Dekîru** 'come into being,' 'become completed' occurs in the following kinds of patterns:

    dekîru daroo 'it will probably come into being,' 'it will probably become completed'

    dêkita 'it became completed,' 'it got finished'

    dêkite (i)ru 'it has become completed,' 'it has been finished'

    dêkite (i)ta 'it had become finished,' 'it was [already] finished as of some point in the past'

2. **Dekîru** 'be possible' never occurs in the **-te (i)ru** form, and in its citation form, it refers to a present, continuing condition; it occurs as a double-**ga** verbal. Examples: **dekîru daroo** 'it probably is or will be possible'; **nihóñgo ga dekìru** '[I] can handle *Japanese*'; **tomódati ga dekìru** '*my friend* is able to do it'; **dêkita** 'it was possible,' '[I] could do it.'

In its second meaning, **dekîru** functions as the *potential* (= 'can do') of **suru: suru** = 'do'; **dekîru** = 'can do.' This applies to **suru** not only as an independent verbal but also as part of compound verbals:[5] **beñkyoo-dekìru** 'can study'; **soódañ-dekìru** 'can consult'; **reñraku-dekìru** 'can get in touch.'

Consider now the humble-polite pattern /o- + stem + -suru/: in this pattern as well, **dekîru** may replace **-suru** to form a corresponding potential (= 'can do'):

    Onégai-dekimàsu ↓ ka↙ 'Can I request of you?'

    Oúkagai-dekimàsu ↓ ka↙ 'Can I ask you?'

    Okári-dekimàsu ↓ ka↙ 'Can I borrow [it] from you?'

These are humble-polite forms, and imply activity in some way connected with the person addressed or a third person to whom one is showing respect.

3. suru ~ nasâru ↑ ~ itasu ↓

Suru belongs to the small group of verbals which have special equivalents with unrelated roots as their polite equivalents. These polite verbals can replace **suru** both when it occurs as an independent verbal and when it is part of a compound like **beñkyoo-suru, kekkoñ-suru**, etc.

Nasâru ↑ is **suru**'s honorific-polite equivalent. This is another special polite **-aru** verbal, like **irássyàru, kudásàru, ossyàru** and *gozâru:[6] the stem is **nasâi**. There are alternate gerunds—both the regular form **nasâtte**, and an alternate form **nasûtte**. Examples:

    Raineñ mo beñkyoo-nasàru ↑ ñ desu ka↙ '(Is it that) you are going to study next year, too?'

    Ano kaisya ni reñraku-nasaimàsu ↑ ka↙ 'Are you going to contact that company?'

---

5. These combinations continue to be operational verbals if the **-suru** alternate was operational. This means that **dekîru** compounds, unlike **dekîru** alone, may be preceded by /nominal + o/ phrases: **Nihóñgo o beñkyoo-dekimàsu ka↙** 'Can you study Japanese?'

6. All five verbals in this category have now been introduced.

The humble-polite equivalent of **suru** is **itasu** ↓ , a regular **s**-consonant verbal. Examples:

Soó itasimasyòo ↓ ka. 'Shall I do it that way?'

Konó siḡoto (o) itasit(e) orimàsu ↓ . 'I am doing this work.'

Seńsèe ni goréñraku-itasimàsita ↓ . 'I contacted the professor.'

Given the implications of honorific and humble forms, consider these exchanges:

(a) **Nasáimàsita ka⌁ . . . Hâi, simâsita.**

(b) **Simâsita ka⌁ . . . Hâi, itásimàsita.**

(c) **Nasáimàsita ka⌁ . . . Hâi, itásimàsita.**

In (a), the questioner is showing more respect; probably the responder is of higher rank. In (b), the responder is showing greater respect than the questioner, who is probably of higher rank. In (c), both participants are showing respect to each other. This exchange would occur more commonly between women.

The ritual expression **dôo itasimasite** contains the distal-style gerund of **itasu**, making it a humble-polite equivalent of **dôo site**: 'Why'—do you thank me or make apologies? 'What have I done'—to deserve your thanks or apologies?

In /nominal + **-suru**/ compounds, the question as to (1) whether or not the nominal takes **go-** (or **o-**), and (2) whether the combination with **go-** (or **o-**) occurs as a humble-polite or as an honorific-polite must be learned for each verbal. In some cases, the **o-** or **go-** form refers to activity of the out-group and therefore becomes an honorific-polite form; but in other cases, the polite form indicates an in-group activity directed toward an out-group, thus becoming a humble-polite:

Honorific-polite	*Humble-polite*	*Plain*
reñraku-nasàru ↑	**goreñraku-suru** ↓	**reñraku-suru**
	goreñraku-itasu ↓	
syoókai-nasàru ↑	**gosyookai-suru** ↓	**syookai-suru**
	gosyookai-itasu ↓	
gokékkoñ-nasàru ↑	**kekkoñ-itasu** ↓	**kekkoñ-suru**

Alternates with two politeness indicators are more polite than those with only one, although both types are classified as polite-style.

Drills

A 1. **Seńsèe to hanásimasyòo ka.**
   'Shall I speak with the doctor?'

   Seńsèe to desu ka⌁ Onéḡai-dekimàsu ka⌁
   'With the doctor? Can I ask you to do that?'

2. **Teḡami o kakímasyóo ka.**
   'Shall I write a letter?

   Teḡámi ò desu ka⌁ Onéḡai-dekimàsu ka⌁
   'A letter? Can I ask you to do that?'

3. **deńwabàñḡoo o kikímasyòo**; 4. **kânozyo to soódañ-simasyòo**; 5. **kâre o gosyóokai-simasyòo**

B 1. **Mêsseezi onéḡai-dekimàsu ka⌁**

   Mêsseezi desu ka⌁ Îi desu yo⌁

'Can I ask you [to take] a message?'   'A message? Certainly.'

2. **Myôoniti oái-dekimàsu ka**   **Myôoniti desu ka Îi desu yo**
   'Can I see you tomorrow?'   'Tomorrow? Certainly.'

3. **kono deñwa okári-dekimàsu**; 4. **îma ohánasi-dekimàsu**; 5. **deñwabàñǧoo oúka-**
   ǧai-dekimàsu

C 1. **Señsèe to soódañ-simàsita ka**   **Sitâkatta ñ desu ǧa, soódañ-dekimasèñ**
   'Did you consult with the doctor?'   **desita.**
                                       'I did want to do it, but I wasn't able to
                                       (consult).'

2. **Kyôneñ 'tyuuǧokuǧo o beñkyoo-**   **Sitâkatta ñ desu ǧa, beñkyoo-dekimasèñ**
   simàsita ka   **desita.**
   'Did you study Chinese last year?'   'I did want to do it, but I wasn't able to
                                       (study).'

3. **kâre ni reñraku-simàsita**; 4. **kânozyo o syoókai-simàsita**; 5. **anô hito ni deñwa-**
   simàsita

D 1. **Kore o itásimasyòo ka**   **Êe. Nasâtte kudasaimaseñ ka**
   'Shall I do this?'   'Yes. Would you (do)?'

2. **Yosida-sañ o gosyóokai-itasimasyòo**   **Êe. Syoókai-nasàtte kudasaimaseñ ka**
   ka   'Yes. Would you (introduce him/her to a
   'Shall I introduce Mr/s. Yoshida?'   third person)?'

3. **Kodama-sañ ni goréñraku-itasimasyòo**; 4. **Mîyazi-señsee ni odéñwa-itasimasyoo**;
   5. **syotyoo to gosóodañ-itasimasyòo**

E 1. **Kore o simàsu neʕ**   **Êe. Sore kara, señsèe mo nasâru to**
   'You're going to do this—right?'   **omoimasu.**
                                       'Yes. And the professor is going to do it,
                                     too, I think.'

2. **Anó kaisya no hitò to reñraku-**   **Êe. Sore kara, señsèe mo reñraku-nasàru**
   simàsu neʕ   **to omoimasu.**
   'You're going to get in touch with a   'Yes. And the professor is going to get in
   person from that company—right?'   touch, too, I think.'

3. **ano kaisya ni deñwa-simàsu**; 4. **syotyoo to soódañ-simàsu**; 5. **okyákusàma o syoó-**
   kai-simàsu

F 1. **Anó katà ni reñraku-nasaimàsita**   **Êe, goréñraku-itasimàsita.**
   ka   'Yes, I did (contact).'
   'Did you contact him/her?'

2. **Onamae o oʼsyaimàsita ka**   **Êe, moósimàsita.**
   'Did you say his/her name?'   'Yes, I did (say).'

3. **kêsa mo biќkùri-nasaimasita**; 4. **anó kaisya no hitò to soódañ-nasaimàsu**;
   5. **Nakáda-sañ no zimùsyo e irássyaimàsu**; 6. **kokúǧo mo osiete (i)rassyaimàsu**

G 1. **Yoózi de ikù ñ desu ka⟍**   **Êe, yoózi ḡa arimàsite . .**
'(Is it that) you're going because of   'Yes, having things to attend to . . .' (I am
business?'   going).

  2. **Zisíñ de okuretà ñ desu ka⟍**   **Êe, zisíñ ḡa arimàsite . .**
'(Is it that) you were (*lit.* became) late 'Yes, there being an earthquake . . .' (I
because of an earthquake?'   became late).

  3. **kâzi de dekînai**; 4. **zîko de ikánàkatta**; 5. **kâiḡi de osóku nàtta**; 6. **siḡóto de dè-**
nakatta; 7. **zisíñ de bikkùri-sita**

H 1. **Myôoniti wa 'kotira ni orímasèñ**   **Asita 'kotira ni irássyarànai ñ desu neʃ**
kara neʃ Soó ossyàtte kudasaimaseñ **Kasíkomarimàsita.**
ka⟍   '(It's that) you won't be here tomorrow—
'Tomorrow I won't be here, so (OK?) right? Certainly.'
would you say that?' (i.e., pass on the
message)

  2. **Myootyoo wa Kyôoto e maírimàsu** **Asíta no àsa Kyôoto e irássyàru ñ desu**
kara neʃ Soó ossyàtte kudasaimaseñ **neʃ Kasíkomarimàsita.**
ka⟍   '(It's that) you're going to Kyoto tomorrow
'Tomorrow morning I'm going to   morning—right? Certainly.'
Kyoto, so (OK?) would you say that?'

  3. **myôoniti/zimûsyo de omáti-sit(e) orimàsu**; 4. **myoógòniti/sêki o hazúsit(e) ori-**
màsu

I 1. **Sitûree desu ḡa, Nôguti-sañ de**   **Tiḡáimàsu. Nôguti-sañ wa, ano mukóo**
(i)rassyaimasu ka⟍   **no katà desu.**
'Excuse me, but are you Mr/s.   'No, Mr/s. Noguchi is that person over
Noguchi?'   there.'

  2. **Sitûree desu ḡa, koko no syotyóo de** **Tiḡáimàsu. Koko no syotyoo wa, ano**
(i)rassyaimàsu ka⟍   **mukóo no katà desu.**
'Excuse me, but are you the institute 'No. The institute director here is that
director here?'   person over there.'

  3. **Watánabe-señsèe**; 4. **Kodama-sañ no bôttyañ**; 5. **Suḡîura-sañ no gosyûziñ**;
  6. **Matuda-sañ no 'musukosañ**

J 1. **Syotyóo ni reñraku-site kudasài.**   **Kasíkomarimàsita. Sûḡu goréñraku-**
'Please contact the institute director.' **itasimàsu.**
                                'Certainly. I'll get in touch right away.'

  2. **Señsèe ni karíte kudasài.**   **Kasíkomarimàsita. Sûḡu okári-itasimàsu.**
'Please borrow [it] from the teacher.' 'Certainly. I'll borrow [it] right away.'

  3. **syotyoo to soodañ-site**; 4. **anó katà to àtte**; 5. **anó gaiziñ to hanàsite**; 6. **señsèe**
ni kiite; 7. **syotyoo ni kasite**; 8. **anó katà ni osiete**

K 1. **Anô hito wa, Suḡîura-sañ desita neʃ** **Yôku obôete (i)nâi ñ desu ḡa, Suḡîura-**
'That (person) was Mr/s. Sugiura—   **sañ da to omóimàsu nêe.**

right?'

'I don't remember for sure, but I think it's Mr/s. Sugiura.'

2. **Anô hito wa, niǩkèeziñ desita neʕ**
'That (person) was of Japanese descent—right?'

Yôku obôete (i)nâi ñ desu ǧa, niǩkèeziñ da to omóimàsu nêe.
'I don't remember for sure, but I think s/he's of Japanese descent.'

3. **nîsee no hito**; 4. **Rôñdoñ no hito**; 5. **syotyoo**; 6. **tyuúǧokùziñ**

L 1. **Nôǧuti-sañ wa, Toódai o demàsita neʕ**
'Mr. Noguchi graduated from Tokyo University—right?'

Oniisañ wa Toódai o dèta kedo, kâre wa mukóo no daiǧaku o dèta to omóimàsu ǧa . .
'His (older) brother graduated from Tokyo University, but he graduated from a college abroad, I think, but . . .' (I'm not sure).

2. **Kyoodai**; 3. **Hokudai**; 4. **Keéoo-dàiǧaku**; 5. **Tukúba-dàiǧaku**; 6. **Waséda-dài-ǧaku**; 7. **Kyuudai**

M 1. **Kotira, Suǧiura desu. Notihodo 'mata odêñwa-itasimasu kara . .**
'This is Sugiura. I'll telephone again later, so . . .' (please pass on the message).

Suǧiura-sañ desu neʕ Wakárimàsita. Omáti-site orimàsu.
'That's Mr/s. Sugiura—right? I understand. We'll be waiting.'

2. **Kotira, Kodáma dèsu. Notihodo 'mata goréñraku-itasimàsu kara . .**
'This is Kodama. I'll get in touch again later, so . . .' (please pass on the message).

Kodáma-sañ dèsu neʕ Wakárimàsita. Omáti-site orimàsu.
'That's Mr/s. Kodama—right? I understand. We'll be waiting.'

3. **Matuda/ohánasi-itasimàsu**; 4. **Nakamura/oái-itasimàsu**; 5. **Hasimoto/maírimàsu**

N 1. **Kodáma-sañ o yobimasyòo kaↂ**
'Shall I call Mr/s. Kodama?'

Kodama-sañ, matâ wa Tanáka-sañ o yoñde kudasài.
'Please call Mr/s. Kodama or Mr/s. Tanaka.'

2. **Matúda-sañ to hanasimasyòo kaↂ**
'Shall I speak with Mr/s. Matsuda?'

Matuda-sañ, matâ wa Tanáka-sañ to hanàsite kudasai.
'Please speak with Mr/s. Matsuda or Mr/s. Tanaka.'

3. **Suǧîura-sañ ni kikímasyòo**; 4. **Nôǧuti-sañ ni deñwa-simasyòo**; 5. **Nisîzaka-sañ ni iímasyòo**; 6. **Nakámura-sañ ni reñraku-simasyòo**

Application Exercises

A1. Practice brief exchanges that use honorific-polite and humble-polite forms. Assign roles to make the style appropriate. Examples:

Huráñsuğo (o) beñkyoo-nasaimàsita ka✓ . . . Iie, Huráñsuğo wa beñkyoo-sit(e) orimasèñ ğa . .

Konó tèepu (o) okíki ni narimàsita ka✓ . . . Iie, kiít(e) orimasèñ.

Kinoo señsèe ni reñraku-nasaimàsita ka✓ . . . Êe, goréñraku-itasimàsita.

Asítà mo oái-dekimàsu ka✓ . . . Dôozo dôozo. Zyuú-zi-ğòro kara kotíra ni orimàsu kara . .

2. Practice telephone calls that involve leaving messages. Examples:
   You're going to Nagoya tomorrow and won't return until next week.
   You're going to Kyoto tonight, but you'll be back by tomorrow night.
   You're going to Hokkaido tonight and can't see X tomorrow.
   You'll be in your office until about 6 tomorrow.
   You'll be waiting [for X] in front of Mejiro Station at 5:30 P.M. this evening.
   Your father has become ill and you're going home early.
   You'll call again later.

B. Core Conversations: Substitution

Practice Core Conversations 1 and 2 with appropriate substitutions, until you are *confident* and *comfortable*. Keep in mind that these are conversation samples that you will have frequent occasion to utilize. Pay attention to your intonation and timing; and remember that it is more difficult to understand telephone conversation than face-to-face dialogue, and if your delivery is not reasonably accurate, your conversation partner may be hard-pressed to understand you.

If at all possible, use an actual telephone hook-up for this practice—either by calling in from another number or extension, or by using practice instruments borrowed from the telephone company. Simply pretending that you are talking on the telephone does not provide authentic practice in hearing the language with telephone-type distortion. Any cases of 'telephone-panic' should be treated *and cured* in the classroom before you venture out into the real world.

SECTION C

Eavesdropping

(Answer the following questions on the basis of the accompanying audiotape. For each conversation, A = the first speaker and B = the second speaker.)
  1a. What is A holding?
   b. Where did it come from?
  2a. What does A want to know?
   b. What problem does A encounter?
   c. What information does A finally acquire?
  3a. What information does A already have?
   b. What additional information does A want?
   c. What does A learn?
  4a. What is the situation?
   b. Who are the participants?
   c. What is the probable reason for their saying thank you?
  5a. Why does A apologize?

   b. Who is B?
   c. What does A ask for?
   d. Why can't B comply?
   e. What is A's alternate request?
6a. What information does A request from B?
   b. What further information does B require before answering?
   c. What does A learn?
7a. How much is the article A is looking at?
   b. Why doesn't A buy it immediately?
   c. What is A's hope?
   d. What is the problem with that solution?
   e. What solution does the shopkeeper propose?
8a. What is B's telephone number?
   b. In what city is this telephone?
   c. What telephone number is this?
   d. What is B's extension number?
9a. Who is B?
   b. Where is B going to go to college? Why?
   c. What is A's reaction?
10a. What does A want?
   b. What problem does A run into?
   c. How is it solved?
11a. What does A ask B to do? Why?
   b. Who is B?
   c. What does B tell A that is a surprise to A?
   d. What does A then decide to do?
12a. What request does A make of B?
   b. Who is B?
   c. To comply with the request, what does B require?
   d. Then what does B request? Why?
13a. What does A remind B of?
   b. How will B take care of the matter?
   c. What time is it now?
   d. Where is Michiko? Until when?
14a. Where is B going?
   b. Who is B?
   c. Why does A think B is particularly suited for such trips?
   d. What is A's specific question in this connection? And B's answer?
15a. Who is making this telephone call? To whom?
   b. What problem does B raise?
   c. How does A solve it?
16a. Whose suitcases does A think these may be?
   b. How many are there?
   c. Whose are they?
   d. Where is that person now?
   e. What does A offer to do?
   f. What does A need? Does A have it?
The following four examples (17–20) are telephone calls for which you will hear only one side of the conversation—the usual situation when one overhears a telephone call.
17a. Who is calling whom? Why?
   b. What person does the caller ask about?

  c. What is the caller going to do? Why?
18a. Who is receiving a call?
  b. Why does that person apologize?
  c. What request is apparently made by the caller?
19a. Who is calling whom?
  b. What ritual is exchanged?
  c. Why is the call being made?
  d. Why does the caller say **yokatta**?
  e. What will happen at about 5:30?
  f. In what connection is the caller's uncle mentioned?
20a. Who is taking the call? From whom?
  b. Who is it the caller wants to speak with?
  c. What is the problem?
  d. What request does the caller apparently make?
  e. What does the speaker check on?
21a. Describe A's invitation.
  b. Who is B?
  c. Why does B refuse? Give details.
  d. What accounts for the conditions of B's refusal?
  e. How does A respond?
22a. Who is calling whom?
  b. Who answers the telephone first?
  c. What is the relationship between the caller and the person called?
  d. Where is the caller at present?
  e. Why is the caller there?
  f. What does the person called want to do?
  g. To what extent is the time decided on?
  h. How and when will the final decision be made?

Utilization

(Follow the usual procedures, developing each item into a conversation to the extent appropriate—and possible.)

  1. Find out Mr. Nakada's office telephone number from a colleague.
  2. Ask a colleague if she knows Mr. Kodama's home phone number.
  3. A colleague is going to give you the name and telephone number of a Japanese teacher. Ask him to read it slowly, because you are going to write it down.
  4. Give a new acquaintance your home telephone number.
  5. Check with Ms. Kubota that her office number is 362–4288, ext. 579; 256–6457, ext. 103; 470–3711, ext. 400.
  6. Introduce yourself politely.
  7. Apologize for not having a business card with you.
  8. Apologize for being out of business cards.
  9. Tell the secretary that you are out of stationery *and* envelopes.
  10. Tell a colleague that you would like to telephone Ms. Nakamura. Ask him if he'd be kind enough to lend you ¥10.
  11. A visitor to your company is looking for Mr. Nakamura. Find out if he means Takashi Nakamura, or Osamu Nakamura.
  12. Find out if Mr. Kodama's daughter graduated from Tokyo University, or from Keio.
  13. Suggest to an acquaintance that you talk again some time, at leisure.
  14. Ask for a repetition (politely).

15. You were just given some numbers over the telephone. Confess to a friend that you didn't understand at all, because you're terrible at numbers.

16. Tell a colleague modestly that your Japanese (too) is poor because you're weak in foreign languages.

17. Your instructor has asked you something from an early lesson. Tell her you're sorry ('there's no excuse!') but you forgot.

18. Ask a colleague if he knows Mr. Nakada's wife.

19. You've been asked by your professor if that student over there is a friend of yours. Explain (politely) that he's not a friend but you do know his name (at least).

20. Warn a friend that this saké is very strong.

21. You've been offered some wine. Decline politely, on the grounds that you're not much of a drinker.

22. Find out if that building is (i.e., 'is named') the Park Building.

23. Find out the name of (a) Mr. Yoshida's daughter; (b) the institute director here.

24. You've been asked about a friend's children. Explain that they are both boys (sons), and both are studying in Europe.

25. Call Tokyo University and ask for Professor Osamu Nakamura.

26. Ask the secretary on the telephone to take a message (for X): (a) you'll come there at 10:30 tomorrow morning; (b) you're sick and will not attend today's conference; (c) you'll be waiting (for X) at the front entrance of the American Embassy at 2:30 tomorrow.

27. A call has come in for your colleague, Mr. Sugiura. Explain that he's away from his desk (*lit.* seat) just now.

28. Comment on how strong (i.e., sturdy) the Nakamura child is.

29. Ask a friend if he remembers the name of Mr. Yoshida's daughter.

30. Ask (a) a friend; (b) your supervisor: if s/he contacted the person at the Continental Bank.

31. Tell the part-time office worker to learn ('commit to memory') this (i.e., material you're handing over) by tomorrow.

32. Ask the secretary if you can see the institute director tomorrow morning.

33. Ask for favorable consideration of your request.

34. On the telephone: (a) answer; (b) begin a call that you have made; (c) ask who is calling; (d) ask if you can leave a message; (e) apologize for keeping the caller waiting; (f) say that you will call again later; (g) end the conversation.

35. You've been looking over something you studied in the past. Tell a friend that since you've forgotten all of it, you've been thinking you'd like to study it once more.

Check-up

1. What are the polite equivalents of the verbal **iu**? What are its two principal meanings? What is the difference in meaning between **iu** and **hanâsu**? (A-SP1)

2. How is **iu** pronounced? What rule covers its pronunciation? (A-SP1)

3. In stating that 'X is named Y,' what particle follows Y? (A-SP1)

4. How are telephone numbers expressed orally? What is the usually optional classifier? When is it not optional? What are the special alternate forms for 2 and 5? Which alternates for 4, 7, and 9 are regularly used? (A-SP2)

5. Explain one use of the gerund in sentence-final position. (A-SP3)

6. What is a distal-style gerund? Give an example. (A-SP3)

7. What is the pattern for asking a question that offers two choices? What is the optional linking word? (A-SP4)

8. Give four examples of ritual telephone language. What speech style is particularly common in telephone conversation? (B-SP1)

9. Explain the two basic meanings of **dekîru**. How do they differ in use? What is the connection between **suru** and **dekîru**? (B-SP2)

10. What is the difference in meaning among: (a) **aímasèñ**; (b) **oái-simasèñ**; (c) **oái-dekimasèñ**? (B-SP2)

11. What are the polite equivalents of **suru**? (B-SP3)

12. To what verbal class does **nasâru** belong? What is the special feature of that class? Name all the members of the class. (B-SP3)

Japanese–English Glossary

The following list contains all the vocabulary introduced in this volume—words occurring in the Miscellaneous Notes and Structural Patterns as well as those appearing in the Core Conversations. Only personal names are omitted. Numbers plus A or B following the entries refer to lesson and section; a number plus A or B alone means that the entry first occurs in the Core Conversations of that lesson and section; with a following plus sign it refers to a later part of that lesson. CI and GUP refer to Classroom Instructions[1] and Greetings and Useful Phrases, respectively.

Except in special cases, verbals and adjectivals are listed in their citation form only. Every verbal is assigned to the appropriate subclass;[2] its perfective form is also given. For example, **tabêru /-ru; tâbeta/** identifies **tabêru** as a verbal belonging to the **-ru** subclass (i.e., the vowel-verbal subclass), with perfective **tâbeta.**

Every adjectival is identified by **/-katta/**, the perfective ending, after the citation form. Thus, the adjectival meaning 'is big' appears as: **oókìi /-katta/.**

All forms of the copula which occur in the text are listed and identified.

Nominals occur with no special designation, except that the members of the subclass of **na**-nominals[3] are identified by a following **/na/.**

Particles and the quotative are identified as /ptc/ and /quotative/, respectively.

Pre-nominals are identified by the designation /+ nom/.

Classifiers are so identified and are listed with a preceding hyphen.

Except in a few special cases, words having a polite alternate that differs from the plain alternate only in the addition of the polite prefix **o-** or **go-** are listed only in the plain form.

For purposes of alphabetizing, hyphens and the macron of **ḡ** and **ñ** are ignored.

In most cases, combinations occurring as indented sublistings match the first occurrence of the pattern in the lessons; but a simpler, more generally occurring example of the pattern is cited in cases where the combination which occurs first seems less desirable as the model for a pattern of wide general use.

â(a) oh! 2A
abunai /-katta/ is dangerous 7B
aida interval; between-space 6A
  baiteñ to dêḡuti no aida between the stand and the exit 6A

âidea idea 11A
ainiku unfortunate; unfortunately 12A
aísukurìimu ice cream 3A+
akai /-katta/ is red 4A+
âkatyañ baby 10A+

1. Words designated as CI are those which occur only in the Classroom Instructions.
2. For a description of verbal subclasses, see Lesson 9A, Structural Pattern 1.
3. See Lesson 5B, Structural Pattern 1.

âme rain 4A
Amerika America 5B+
amérikàziñ an American 10B+
anâta you 2B+
ane older sister; my older sister 11A+
âni older brother; my older brother 11A+
a(ñ)mari /+ negative/ not much; not very 1B
añna that kind (of) 4B+
  añna ni to that extent; like that 9B+
ano /+ nom/ that —— over there; that ——
  (known to both of us) 3A
  anô hitò he; she 10A+
  anó kàtà he; she /polite/ 10A+
  |**anoo**| uh 4B
aôi /-katta/ is blue; is green 4A
are that thing over there; that thing (known to
  both of us) 2B
Arîgatoo (gozaimasu). Thank you. GUP
Arîgatoo (gozaimasita). Thank you (for what
  you did). GUP
âru /-u; âtta/ be located (of inanimate existence); have 4A
arúbàito part-time work, usually performed by
  students 10A
arûku /-u; arûita/ walk 7B
  arûite iku go on foot 7B
âsa morning 8B+
asâtte day after tomorrow 3B
asítà tomorrow 1A
asoko that place over there; that place (known
  to both of us) 6B+
asû tomorrow 1A+
asuko /casual alternate of **asoko**/ 9A
atárasìi /-katta/ is new; is fresh 1B+
at(á)takài /-katta/ is warm 11A
atira that side; that way; thereabouts; there;
  that alternative (of two) 6A+
aṫtì /casual alternate of **atira**/ 7B+
âto later; remaining 8A
  âto de later on 11A
  âto ití-zìkañ one hour left 8A
atûi /-katta/ is hot 11A+
âu /-u; âtta/ meet; see (a person) 11A
  X ni au meet person X; see person X 11A
  X to au meet (with) person X; see person
  X 11A+

baiteñ stand; concession; kiosk 6A
bañ night 8B+
-bañ /classifier for serial numbers/ 3A
bañğòo (assigned) number 12A

bâsu bus 7B+
Beekoku U.S.A. 5B+
beñkyoo study 9B+
beñkyoo-suru study 9B
bêñri /na/ convenient 4A
Bêruriñ Berlin 12B+
betu ni /+ negative/ not especially 9A
bîiru beer 5B+
biḱkùri-suru become surprised 11A
biñseñ stationery 4B+
bîru office building 6A
  Paáku-bìru the Park building 6A
bôku/boku I; me /M/ 2B+
booeki foreign trade 10A
  Oríeñtaru-bòoeki the Oriental Trading
  (Company) 10A
booeki-suru conduct foreign trade 10A+
boorupeñ ballpoint pen 4B
bôttyañ son; your son; young man /polite/
  10A+
buńbòoğu stationery; office supplies 7A+
buñbooğuya stationery store; stationery
  dealer 7A+
byooiñ hospital 6B+
byooki sick; sickness 9B

dà /copula: direct imperfective/ 9A
-dai /classifier for counting vehicles and ma-
  chines/ 7B+
daiğaku university; college 7A+
daiğakuiñ graduate school 7A+
daízyòobu /na/ all right; safe 2A
dakê just; only 5A
  soré dakè just that 5A
damê /na/ no good 2A
dâre who? 2B
daròo /copula: direct tentative/ 11A
dàtta /copula: direct perfective/ 9B
dè /copula: gerund/ 8A
  de gozaimàsu+ /neutral-polite equivalent of
  dèsu/ 10A
  de (i)rassyàru↑ /honorific-polite equivalent
  of **dà**/ 10A
  dê mo even so 8B
de /ptc/ in; at 7A; by means of 7B; because
  of 9B
  kiśsateñ de tabèru eat at a coffee shop 7A
  tâkusii de iku go by cab 7B
  zîko de okureru become late because of an
  accident 9B
dêğuti exit 6A

dekîru /-ru; dêkita/   become completed; can do; be possible   1A

deñsya/dêñsya   electric train   7B+

deñwa   telephone (call)   2A

  deńwa o kakèru   make a telephone call   9B

deńwabàñǧoo   telephone number   12A

deñwa-suru   telephone   11A

depâato   department store   7A+

dêru /-ru; dêta/   go out; come out; leave; attend   9B

dèsita   /copula: distal perfective/   2A

dèsu   /copula: distal imperfective/   1B; 2A

desyòo   /copula: distal tentative/   6B

-do   /classifier for counting occurrences/   GUP; 12A

Dôitu   Germany   5B+

doituǧo   German language   2A+

doítùziñ   a German   10A+

dôko   what place? where?   6B

  Toránomoñ no dòko   where in Toranomon? what part of Toranomon?   6B

  dôko no Toranomoñ   the Toranomon which is where?   6B

dônata   who? /polite/   2B+

dôñna   what kind (of)?   4B

  dôñna ni   to what extent? in what manner?   9B+

dôno /+ nom/   which ——?   3A

  dono-ǧurai   about how much?   8A

dô/do   /abbreviation for doyôo(bi)/   8A

  dôo·nîti/do·niti   Sat–Sun   8A

dôo   what way? how?   2A

  Dôo itasimasite.   Don't mention it.   GUP

  dôo mo   in every way; in many ways   GUP

  dôo suru   how will [you] act? what will [you] do?   11A

  dôo site   how come? how? why?   11A

Dôozo.   Please (speaker offering something).   GUP

Dôozo goyûkkuri.   Take it easy!   12A+

Dôozo yorosiku.   Please [treat me] favorably.   11B

dôre   which thing (usually of three or more)?   2B

-doru   /classifier for counting dollars/   3A+

dôtira   which side? which way? whereabouts? where? which alternative (of two)?   6A

  dôtira mo   both   12A

  dôtira no hôo   which alternative? which direction?   6A

  dôtira-sama   who? /polite/   12B

dôtti   /casual equivalent of dôtira/   7B+

doyôo(bi)   Saturday   8A

e   /ptc/ to; into; onto   7A

  hôñya e   to the bookstore   7A

êe   /affirmation/   GUP

eéǧàkañ   movie theater   6B+

eeǧo   English language   2A+

Eekoku   England   5B+

Eékokùziñ   English person   10B+

|eeto| uh   7B

eewa   English–Japanese   2B

eéwa-zìteñ   English–Japanese dictionary   2B

êki   station   6A

-eñ   /classifier for counting yen/   2B

eñpitu   pencil   4B+

ǧa   /ptc/   4A, 4B, 5A

gaikoku   foreign country   11B+

gaikokuǧo   foreign language   11B

gaíkokùziñ   foreigner   10A+

gaímùsyoo   Foreign Ministry   11B+

gaiziñ   foreigner (particularly Westerner)   10A

gakkoo   school   7A+

gakusee   student   2B+

gâñ-neñ   initial year of an era   8B+

-ǧatu   /classifier for naming months/   8B

gekizyoo   theater   6B+

gês·sûi·kîñ   Mon–Wed–Fri   8A

gêtu/gêk-/gês-   /abbreviation for getúyòo(bi)/   8A

getúyòo(bi)   Monday   8A

giñkoo   bank   7A

Giñza   (section of Tokyo)   7B+

gô   five   2B

Gobúsata-simàsita.   I've neglected to be in touch.   11B+

gôǧo   afternoon; p.m.   8B

Goméñ-kudasài.   Excuse me; Pardon me.   12B

-ǧòro   about (approximate point in time)   8A

  kono-ǧoro   these days, nowadays   8A+

gôruhu   golf   4A

Gotísoosama (dèsita).   It was delicious.   5B

gozáimàsu+   /neutral-polite equivalent of arímàsu/   5A

  de gozaimàsu+   /neutral-polite equivalent of dèsu/   10A

gôzeñ   A.M.   8B+

gozôñzi↑ da   /honorific-polite/ know   10B+

-ǧùrai   about, approximately   8A

  dono-ǧurai   about how much?   8A

gurêe gray 5B
gurîiñ green 5B+

hâa /polite affirmation/ GUP
hâha mother; my mother 11B+
hahaoya mother 11B+
hâi /affirmation/; here you are GUP, 1A
haiiro gray 5B+
hakkìri clearly CI
-hàñ one-half 8B
  hañ-zìkañ a half-hour 8B+
  yo-zí-hàñ 4:30 8B
  yo-zíkañ-hàñ four hours and a half 8B+
hanâ flower 7A+
hanâsu /-u; hanâsita/ talk; speak 10B
hanâya flower shop; florist 7A+
hañdobàggu handbag 5A+
hâtati twenty years of age 10A+
hatî eight 2B
hatu-ka twenty days; twentieth of the month 8A
hayâi /-katta/ is early; is fast 9A+
hayámè ni early; in good time 10A
Hazímemàsite. How do you do? 11B
hazimeru /-ru; hazimeta/ begin (something) 11B+
hazîmete the first time 11B
hazusu /-u; hazusita/ take off; let go; unfasten 12B
  sêki o hazusu leave one's seat 12B
hêe⤙ /exclamation of surprise/ 3B
Heesee the Heisei Era (1989–) 8B+
heñ area; vicinity 6A
hêñ /na/ strange 13A
hetâ /na/ unskillful; poor at 9B+
hî/hi day 10A+
hidari left 6B
  hidári no hòo the left side; the left direction 6B
hidáridònari next door on the left 6B
hikôoki airplane 7B+
hisasiburi after a long interval 11B
hitô/hito person 10A
  oñna no hitò woman 10A
  otóko no hitò man 10A
hitô-ri one person; alone; single (person) 11A
  hitô-ri de iku go alone (*lit.*, being one person) 11A
hitô-tu one unit 5A+
-hodo about as much as 5B
  itû-tu-hodo about five (units) 5B

hoka other 5A
  Hoká ni nàni ka? Anything else? 5A
Hokkàidoo Hokkaido (northernmost main island of Japan) 11A
Hokudai Hokkaido University 11B+
hôñ book 2B+
-hoñ /classifier for counting long, cylindrical objects/ 4B
Hôñsyuu Honshu (a main island of Japan) 11A+
hoñtoo true; truth 2B
hôñya bookstore; book dealer 7A
hôo direction; way; side; alternative 6A
  hidári no hòo left side; toward the left 6A
  miğí no hòo right side; toward the right 6A
hôteru hotel 6B
  Oókura-hòteru Hotel Okura 6B
hotôñdo almost; nearly; all but 3B
Hukûoka Fukuoka 8A+
-huñ /classifier for counting and naming minutes/ 8A
hûne boat, ship 8B+
-huñkañ /classifier for counting minutes/ 8A+
Hurañsu France 5B+
hurañsuğo French language 2A+
huráñsùziñ French person 10B+
hurosiki square wrapping cloth 4A
hurûi /-katta/ is old (i.e., not new) 1B+
hutá-tù two units 5A
hyakû one hundred 2B
-hyaku /counter for hundreds/ 2B

iê house, home; household 7B+
iêie /negation/ 1B
Iğirisu England 5B+
iğírisùziñ English person 10B+
ii /yôkatta/ is good, fine, all right; never mind 1B
  yôku dekîru can do well 1B
  yôku suru do often 1B
i(i)e /negation/ GUP
ikâğa how? /polite/ 4A
iku /-u; itta/ go 1A
îkura how much? 2B
îku-tu how many units? 5B; how old (of people)? 10A
îma now 7A
imôoto younger sister 11A
Îñdo India 5B+
iñdòziñ an Indian (from India) 10B+

irássyàru ↑ **/-aru; irássyàtta ~ irâsita/** be located (of animate existence) 7A; come 4B; go 8B /honorific-polite/

   de (i)rassyàru ↑ /honorific-polite equivalent of **dà**/ 10A

   Irássyài(màse). ↑ Welcome! 4B

iriǧuti entrance 6A+

irô color 5B

iru /-ru; ita/ be located (of animate existence) 7A

   Tookyoo ni iru be in Tokyo /animate/ 7A

   kekkoñ-sitè (i)ru be married 10B

   hanâsite (i)ru be talking 10B

iru /-u; itta/ need; be required 5A

îs-see first generation (used in reference to Japanese who have moved abroad) 10B+

isóǧasìi /-katta/ is busy 9A

issyo togetherness 11A

   issyo ni suru do together 11A

   tomodati to issyo together with a friend 11A

itadaku /-u; itadaita/ ↓ drink; eat; accept /humble-polite/ 1A

Itaria Italy 5B+

itariaǧo Italian language 2A+

itáriàziñ an Italian 10B+

itasu /-u; itasita/ ↓ do /humble-polite/ 12B

itî one 2B

itôko cousin 11B+

Itte (i)rassyài(màse). ↑ Goodbye (said to person leaving home). 7A

Itte kimàsu. Goodbye (said by person leaving home). 7A

Itte mairimàsu. ↓ Goodbye (said by person leaving home). /humble-polite/ 7A+

îtu when? 3B

   îtu mo always 11A

itû-tu five units 5A

iu /-u; itta/ say; be called, be named 12A

   X to iu be called or named X 12A

   Soó itte kudasài. Please say that. 12A

iya /negation/ 1A

iyâ /na/ unpleasant, disagreeable 11A

izure someday, sometime 12A

ka /question particle/ 1A

-ka/-niti /classifier for naming and counting days/ 8A

kâ(a) /abbreviation for **kayôo(bi)**/ 8A

   kâa·môku Tues–Thurs 8A

kabañ bag, suitcase 5A

kâdo street corner 7B+

kaérì a return 8A

kâeru /-u; kâetta/ return (home) 7A

   Okáeri-nasài(màse). Welcome back! 7A

-kaǧetu /classifier for counting months/ 8B

-kai /classifier for naming and counting floors/ 7A

kâiǧi conference, meeting 3B

kaíǧìsitu conference room 10B

kaisya a company, a firm 11A

-kakañ/-kaniti /classifier for counting days/ 8A+

kakâru /-u; kakâtta/ be required 8B

   zikáñ ǧa kakàru it takes time 8B+

kakêru /-ru; kâketa/ suspend (something) 9B

   deñwa o kakèru make a telephone call 9B

kâku /-u; kâita/ write; draw 7A

kamâu /-u; kamâtta/ mind; care; concern oneself about 10A

   kamáwànai /-katta/ it doesn't matter 10A

kamî paper 4B

Kânada Canada 5B+

kânai my wife 10B+

Kâñkoku South Korea 5B+

kañkokùziñ a South Korean 10B+

kânozyo she 10A

kara /ptc/ from; since; after 8B; because 11A

   gôǧo kara from the afternoon 8B

   koko kara from here 8B

   iyâ da kara because it's displeasing 11A

kâre he 10A+

kariru /-ru; karita/ borrow; rent (from someone) 10B

   tomodati ni (or kara) kariru borrow or rent from a friend 10B

kâsa umbrella 4A

Kasíkomarimàsita. Certainly. I'll do as you asked. 4B

kasu /-u; kasita/ lend; rent (to someone) 10B+

katâ person /polite/ 10A+

kau /-u; katta/ buy 1B

kawáìi /-katta/ is cute 10A

kawari a change 11B

kawaru /-u; kawatta/ undergo change 11B+

kayôo(bi) Tuesday 8A

kâzi a fire 9B+

kâzoku family; my family 11A

kedo /ptc/ 4B

kêeki cake 3A

Keeoo   Keio University   12B +
kekkoñ-suru   get married   10B
  kekkon-site (i)ru   be married   10B
-keñ   /classifier for counting buildings and shops/   7B
kêsa   this morning   9A +
kiiroi /-katta/   is yellow   4A +
kiku /-u; kiita/   ask   7B; hear; listen   10B
kimi   you /familiar/   9A +
kîñ   /abbreviation for **kiñyòo(bi)**/   8A
  gês·sûi·kîñ   Mon–Wed–Fri   8A
kinôo   yesterday   1A
kiñyòo(bi)   Friday   8A +
kirâsu /-u; kirâsita/   exhaust the supply   12A
  meési o kiràsite (i)ru   be out of business cards   12A
kîree /na/   pretty; clean   2A
kissateñ/kiśsàteñ   coffee shop; tearoom   7A
kisyâ   railroad train   7B +
ko   child   10A
  okosañ   child /polite/   10A +
  oñnà no ko   little girl; young girl   10A +
  otókò no ko   little boy; young boy   10A +
kodomo   child   10A +
kôe   voice   CI
koko   this place, here   6B
  kokó no tosyòkañ   the library here   6B
kokôno-tu   nine units   5A +
kokuǧo   the mother-tongue of the Japanese   2A +
komâru /-u; komâtta/   become upset; become a problem   1B
kôñbañ   this evening, tonight   9A +
Koñbañ wa.   Good evening.   GUP
koñǧetu   this month   9A +
koñna   this kind (of)   4B
  koñna ni   to this extent, like this   9B +
Koñniti wa.   Good afternoon.   GUP
kono /+ nom/   this ——   3A
  konó màe   (in) front of this   6A +
kono-ǧoro   these days, nowadays   8A +
koñpyùutaa   computer   3A
koñsyuu   this week   9A +
kôñya   this evening, tonight   10A +
koobañ   police box   6A +
Kôobe   Kobe   8A +
kooeñ   park   6B +
koóhìi   coffee   3A +
kookoo   high school   7A +
koósàteñ   intersection   7B
koósyuudèñwa   public telephone   6A
kootya   black tea   5B +

kore   this thing   2B
  kore kara   from this point, after this   8A
kòso /ptc/   11B
  Kotíra kòso.   *I'm* the one.   11B
kotáèru /ru; kotâeta/   answer   CI
kotira   this side; this way; hereabouts; here; this alternative (of two)   6A
  kotíra no hòo   this direction; this alternative   6A
kotosi   this year   8B
kottì   /casual alternate of **kotira**/   7B
kû   nine   2B
kudásài   /imperative of **kudásàru**/   give me   4A
  Koré o kudásài.   Please give me this one.   4A
  Kitê kudasai.   Please come.   4A
kudásàru ↑ **/-aru; kudásàtta ~ kudásùtta/** /honorific-polite/   give me   4A
  Kâite kudásaimasèñ ka⤹   Would (*lit.* won't) you be kind enough to write it for me?   7A
-kuñ   /suffix attached to male names; familiar/   9A
kuròi /-katta/   is black   4A
kûru /irreg; **kitâ**/   come   1A
  itte kùru   come, having gone (i.e., go and then come)   7A
  Itte kimàsu.   'So long!' (said leaving one's own quarters)   7A
kuruma   car   5B
kuukoo   airport   7B +
kyaku   guest; visitor; customer   10B
kyôneñ   last year   8B +
kyôo   today   1A
kyôodai   brothers and sisters, siblings   11A +
Kyoodai   Kyoto University   11B +
kyookai   church   6B +
kyoókàsyo   textbook   10B
kyoositu   classroom   10B
Kyôoto   Kyoto   2A +
kyûu   nine   3A
Kyuudai   Kyushu University   11B +
Kyûusyuu   Kyushu (a main island of Japan)   11A +

mâa   /expression of qualified agreement/   1B
mâa·mâa   so-so   1A
màde   /ptc/ as far as; up to and including   7A; until   8B
  giñkoo màde   as far as the bank   7A
  nâñzi made   until what time?   8B
  sâñ-zi made ni   by 3 o'clock   9A
mâe   front   6A; time before; past time   8A +
  toó-ka màe   ten days ago   10B

go-hûñ-mae five minutes before the hour 8A

maġaru /-u; maġatta/ make a turn 7B

-mai /classifier for thin, flat units/ 4B

mâiasa every morning 8B+

mâibañ every evening; every night 8B+

maido every time 4B

Maido arîġatoo gozaimasu. Thank you again and again. 4B

maiġetu every month 8B+

maineñ every year 8B+

mâiniti every day 8B

mâiru ↓ **/-u; mâitta/** come 7A; go 8B /humble-polite/

maisyuu every week 8B+

maitosi every year 8B+

maituki every month 8B+

maiyo every evening; every night 10A+

-mañ /counter for ten thousands/ 3B

maru circle; zero 12A

maśśùġu straight 7B

mata again 4B

matâ wa or on the other hand 12A

mâtu /-u; mâtta/ wait 8A

mazûi /-katta/ tastes bad 7A+

meesi calling card; business card 12A

meesi no motiawase cards on hand 12A

Mêezi the Meiji era (1868–1912) 8B+

mêsseezi message 12B

Mêziro (section of Tokyo) 7B

mîdori green 5B+

miêru /-ru; mîeta/ appear; show up 9B

miġi right 6B

miġí no hòo right side, right direction 6B

miġídònari next door on the right 6B

minâsañ everyone /polite/ 5B+, 11B

mi(ñ)nà all; everyone; everything 5B

mîru /-ru; mîta/ look at; see 5B

mîruku milk 5B+

misê store, shop 6A+

misêru /-ru; mîseta/ show 4A

miti street; road 6A+

mit́-tù three units 5A

mizíkài /-katta/ is short 9B+

mo /ptc/ also, too 4B

dôo mo in every way; in many ways GUP

dôtira mo both 12A

îtu mo always 11A

kore mo this one too 4B

kore mo sore mo both this one and that one 5B

mâe ni mo in the front too 6A

môku/môk- /abbreviation for **mokúyòo(bi)**/ 8A+

môku·dôo Thurs–Sat 8A+

mokúyòo(bi) Thursday 8A+

moñbùsyoo Ministry of Education 11B

moo /+ quantity expression/ more; additional 5A

moó mit-tù three more units 5A

moó sukòsi a little more; a few more 5A+

moosiwake excuse 12A

Moósiwake arimasèñ. I'm very sorry. (*lit.* There is no excuse.) GUP

môosu ↓ **/-u; môosita/** say; be called, be named /humble-polite/ 12A

X to môosu my name is X 12A

môsimosi hello (on the telephone); say there! 12A

Mosukuwa Moscow 8A

motiawase things on hand 12A

meési no motiawase ġa nài have no business cards on hand 12A

motiawaseru /-ru; motiawaseta/ have on hand 12A+

môtto more; a larger amount 5A

môtto yasûi no one that is cheaper 5A

mukôo/mukoo over there 6A; abroad 9B

mukooġawa opposite side, the other side 6B+

musuko son 10A+

musúmè daughter 10A+

mut́-tù six units 5A

muzukasii /-katta/ is difficult 3B

muzúkasii hitò a person hard to get on with 11A+

myôobañ tomorrow night 12B+

myoógòniti day after tomorrow 12B+

myôoniti tomorrow 12B

myootyoo tomorrow morning 12B+

ñ /casual-style affirmation/ 8A

ñ /contraction of nominal **no**/ 7B

abúnài ñ da it's that it's dangerous 7B

na /pre-nominal alternate of **da**/ 5B

naġâi /-katta/ is long 9B

Nâġoya Nagoya 8A

naiseñ extension 12A

nakanaka quite; rather; more than one might expect 4A

namae name 7A

nâñ what? 2A

nâna seven 3A
nanâ-tu seven units 5A
nâni what? 4A
  nâni ka something 5A
naniḡo what language? 2A+
naniiro what color? 5B
naniziñ what nationality? 10B+
nâru /-u; nâtta/ become; get to be 9A
  onári ni nàru ↑ /honorific-police equivalent
    of **nâru**/ 10A
  osóku nàru become late 9A
  rokú-syùukañ ni nâru get to be six weeks
    9B
naruhodo to be sure! of course! indeed! 9A
nasâru ↑ **/-aru; nasâtta/** /honorific-polite
  equivalent of **suru**/ do 12B
nâze why? 11A+
nê(e) /sentence-particle of confirmation, agreement, or deliberation/ 1A, 1B, 2A
-neñ /classifier for naming and counting years/
  8B
-neñkañ /classifier for counting years/ 8B+
nî two 2B
ni /ptc/ in; on; at 6A; into; onto; to 7A;
  from 10B
  hayámè ni kûru come early 10A
  hôñya ni iku go to the bookstore 7A
  Kimura-sañ ni deñwa o kakèru telephone
    Mr/s. Kimura 9B
  rokú-syùukañ ni nâru get to be six weeks
    9B
  soñna ni to that extent; like that 9B
  tomodati ni kariru borrow from a
    friend 10B
  usíro ni àru be located in back 6A
  zyûu-zi ni kûru come at ten o'clock 8B
Nihôñ/Níppòñ Japan 5B+
nihoñḡo/nippoñḡo Japanese language 2A
nihóñzìñ/nippóñzìñ Japanese person
  10B+
niḱkèeziñ person of Japanese ancestry 10B
-niñ/-ri /classifier for counting people/ 11A
nî-see second generation (used in reference to
  offspring of native Japanese who have moved
  abroad) 10B+
-niti-ka /classifier for counting days and naming dates/ 8A
nitíyòo(bi) Sunday 8A
n̂n̂↙ /casual-style negation/ 9A
no /nom/ 3B
  oókìi no a big one 3B

no /connective between nominals/ 5B
  gurêe no kuruma a gray car 5B
  kinoo no siñbuñ yesterday's newspaper 5B
  kokó no tosyòkañ the library here 6B
no /connective **no** + nominal **no**/ 5B
  kyôo no da it's today's (one) 5B
nômu /-u; nôñda/ drink 1A
nôoto notebook 4B
noótobùkku notebook 4B+
notihodo later 12B
Nyuúyòoku New York 8A

o /ptc/ 4A
  kore o iku go along this one (e.g., street) 7B
  kore o kau buy this one 4A
oba aunt; my aunt 11B+
obâasañ grandmother; old woman /polite/
  11B
obasañ aunt /polite/; woman 11B
obóèru /-ru; obôeta/ commit to memory; learn
  by heart 12B+
Oháyoo (gozaimàsu). + Good morning. GUP
oíde ni nàru ↑ go; come; be located (animate)
  /honorific-polite/ 10A+
oisii /-katta/ is delicious 5B
oitokosañ cousin /polite/ 11B+
okâasañ mother /polite/ 11B+
Okáeri-nasài(màse). Welcome back! 7A
okaḡesama de thanks to you; thanks for
  asking 11B
okosañ child /polite/ 10A+
okureru /-ru; okureta/ become late *or*
  delayed 9B
  okúrete kùru come late 9B
ôkusañ wife, your wife /polite/ 10B
Omátase-itasimàsita. ↓ I've caused you to wait
  /humble-polite/ 12B
omáti-kudasài please wait 4B
omâwarisañ policeman 7B+
omósiròi /-katta/ is interesting; is amusing; is
  fun 1B
omótè front side 7B+
omôu /-u; omôtta/ think 11A
  kâette (i)ru to omòu think [someone] is or
    will be back 11A
onazi same 5B
  onazi zassi same magazine 5B
(o)nêesañ older sister, your older sister
  /polite/ 11A+
Onéḡai-simàsu. ↓ I make a request of you.
  /humble-polite/ GUP

(o)nîisañ older brother, your older brother /polite/ 11A

oñnà female 10A

oñna no hitò woman 10A

oñna no katà woman /polite/ 10A+

oñnà no ko little girl 10A+

oókìi /-katta/ is big 1B+

Oókura-hòteru Hotel Okura 6B

oókuràsyoo finance ministry 11B+

Oosaka Osaka 8A+

Oósutorària Australia 5B+

oósutorariàziñ an Australian 10B+

ôru ↓ /-u; ôtta/ be located (of animate existence) /humble-polite/ 7A

Toókyoo ni òru ↓ be in Tokyo (animate) /humble-polite/ 7A

keḱkoñ-sit(e) òru ↓ be married /humble-polite/ 10B

hanâsit(e) oru ↓ be talking /humble-polite/ 10B

Osaki ni. (Excuse me for going) ahead of you. /polite/ 9B

Dôozo, osaki ni. Please go ahead. /polite/ 9B

Osewasama. (Thank you for) your helpful assistance. 6B

osieru /-ru; osieta/ teach; give instruction or information 7A

osoi /-katta/ is late; is slow 9A

osóku nàru become late; become slow 9A+

osókù late (time) 11A

osókù made until late 11A

Osôre-irimasu. I'm sorry; Thank you. 12B

ośsyàru ↑ /-aru; ośsyàtta/ say; be called /honorific-polite/ 12A

otaku home; household /polite/ 7B

otókò male 10A

otóko no hitò man 10A

otóko no katà man /polite/ 10A+

otókò no ko little boy 10A+

otona adult 10A+

otôosañ father; your father /polite/ 11B+

otôoto younger brother 11A+

otótòi the day before yesterday 3A

otótosi the year before last 10A+

ôtto husband; my husband 10B+

Otúkaresama (dèsita). (You must be tired!) GUP

oturi change (money returned) 4B

otya tea 3A+

oyâ parent 11B+

oyagosañ parent; your parent /polite/ 11B+

Oyásumi-nasài. Goodnight. GUP

ozi uncle; my uncle 11B+

ozîisañ grandfather; your grandfather; old man /polite/ 11B+

ozisañ uncle; your uncle; man /polite/ 11B+

ozyôosañ daughter; your daughter; young woman /polite/ 10A

Paáku-bìru the Park building 6A

pâi pie 3A+

Pâri Paris 8A

Pâruko Parco (name of department store) 7B

pêñ pen 4B+

pûriñ custard pudding 3A+

râiĝetu next month 9A+

raineñ next year 9A+

raisyuu next week 9A

rakú /na/ relaxed; comfortable; easy 8A

raśsyu-àwaa rush hour 11A

rêe zero 12A

reñraku-suru get in touch; make contact 12B

-ri/-niñ /classifier for counting people/ 11A

rikoñ-suru get divorced 10B+

rokû six 2B+

Rôñdoñ London 8A

rosiaĝo Russian language 2A+

rosíàziñ Russian person 10A+

rûsu absence from home 9B

ryokañ Japanese-style inn 6B

ryôosiñ both parents 11B+

ryoózìkañ consulate 6B

Amérika-ryoozìkañ American consulate 6B

sâa hmmm! 6A

-sai /classifier for counting years of human age/ 10A+

saki ahead 6A

samûi /-katta/ is cold (of atmosphere only) 11A+

sañ three 2B+

-sañ Mr.; Mrs.; Miss; Ms. /polite suffix/ 2A

Sañhurānsìsuko San Francisco 8A

sâñ-see third generation (used in reference to grandchildren of native Japanese who have moved abroad) 10B+

Sapporo Sapporo 8A+

saraiĝetu month after next 10A+

saraineñ year after next 10A+

saraisyuu   week after next   10A+
satôo   sugar   5B
-satu   /classifier for counting books, magazines, etc./   4B
Sayo(o)nara.   Goodbye.   GUP
seereki   Christian era; A.D.   8B
sêki   seat; assigned place   12B
   sêki o hazusite (i)ru   be away from one's seat   12B
señ   one thousand   2B
-señ   /counter for thousands/   2B
señḡetu   last month   10A
señsèe   teacher; doctor   2B
señsèñḡetu   month before last   10A
señsèñsyuu   week before last   10A
señsyuu   last week   10A
-señto   /classifier for counting cents/   3A+
sewâ   helpful assistance   11B
   sewâ ni nâru   become obliged for assistance   11B
sî   four   2B+
sibâraku   a while   11B+
siḡoto   work   8B
Sikôku   Shikoku (a main island of Japan)   11A+
siñbuñ   newspaper   2B+
siñḡoo   traffic light   7B
siñkàñseñ   bullet train   7B+
Siñzyuku   Shinjuku (section of Tokyo)   8B
sirôi /-katta/   is white   4A+
siru /-u; sitta/   get to know   10B
   sitte (i)ru   know   10B
sitî   seven   2B+
sitûree /na/   rude; rudeness   12B
Sitûree-simasita.   Excuse me (for what I have done).   GUP
Sitûree-simasu.   Excuse me (for what I am about to do).   GUP
sôba   nearby   6B
   êki no sôba   near the station   6B
Sobíeto   /see **Sôreñ**/   5B+
sôbo   (my) grandmother   11B+
sôhu   (my) grandfather   11B+
soko   that place (near you or just mentioned)   6B+
soñna   that kind (of)   4B+
   soñna ni   to that extent; like that   9B
sono /+ nom/   that —— near you; that —— just mentioned   3A
sôo   that way; like that   2A
soodañ-suru   consult; talk over   11A

Sôoru   Seoul   8A+
sore   that thing (near you or just mentioned)   2B
   sore kara   after that; and then   4B
   sore ni   onto that; on top of that; in addition   11A
Sôreñ   Soviet Union   5B+
soréñzìñ   Soviet citizen   10B+
sotira   that side; that way; thereabouts; there; that alternative (of two)   6A+
sottì   /casual equivalent of **sotira**/   7B+
-suḡi   past; after   8A
   go-hûñ-suḡi   five minutes after the hour   8A
suḡôi /-katta/   is awful, wonderful, weird, terrific   11A
   suḡôku zyoózù da   is awfully skilled/ skillful   11A
sûḡu   soon; immediate   5B
   sûḡu kûru   will come soon   5B
   sûḡu sôba   immediate vicinity   6B
sûi   /abbreviation for **suíyòo(bi)**/   8A
   gês·sûi·kîñ   Mon—Wed—Fri   8A
suíyòo(bi)   Wednesday   8A
sukôsi   a little; a few   5A
Su(m)ímasèñ.   I'm sorry; Thank you.   GUP
Su(m)ímasèñ desita.   I'm sorry (for what I did); Thank you (for the trouble you took).   GUP
Supêiñ   Spain   5B+
supeiñḡo   Spanish language   2A+
supéiñzìñ   Spaniard   10B+
supóotukàa   sportscar   5B
suru /irreg; **sita**/   do; play (of games)   1A
sûupaa suúpaamàaketto   supermarket   7B+
suútukèesu   suitcase   5A+
suuzi   number(s)   12A
suzúsìi /-katta/   is cool   11A+
syookai-suru   introduce   11B
syôosyoo   a little   4B
Syoowa   the Showa Era (1926–89)   8B+
syoppíñḡubàggu   shopping bag   5A+
syotyoo   institute director   12B
syuttyoo   business trip   9B
syuttyoo-suru   go away on a business trip   9B+
syuu   week   10A+
-syuukañ   /classifier for counting weeks/   8B+
syûziñ   husband; my husband   10B+

tabêru /-ru; tâbeta/   eat   1A
Tadaima.   Hello, I'm back.   7A
taiheñ /na/   awful; terrible; a problem   9B
taípuràitaa   typewriter   3A

taísìkañ embassy 6B
  Amérika-taisìkañ American embassy 6B
Taisyoo the Taisho Era (1912–26) 8B
taitee usually 8B +
Taíwàñ Taiwan 5B +
takâi /-katta/ is expensive; is high 1B
takúsàñ much; many 5A
tâkusii taxi 7B
tanósìmì a joy; a pleasure 8B
tanósìmu̞ /-u; tanósìñda/ take pleasure
  in 8B +
tatêmòno building 6B
teârai toilet 6A
têepu tape 3A
teğami letter 2A
temae this side (of) 7B
tênisu tennis 4A
terâ Buddhist temple 6B +
tiğau /-u; tiğatta/ be different; be wrong 1A
tiísài /-katta/ is small 1B +
tikâ underground 7A
tikatetu subway 7B +
titî father; my father 11B +
titioya father 11B +
tîzu map 7B
to /ptc/ and; with 3B
  kore to sore this and that 3B
  tomódati to hanàsu talk with a friend 10B
  tomodati to issyo together with a
    friend 11A +
to /quotative/ 11A
  îi to omôu think that it's good 11A
  Tanaka to iu be named Tanaka 12A
tôire toilet 6A +
tokee clock; watch 8A
tokórò place; location 10B
tomaru /-u; tomatta/ come to a halt; stop
  over 8A
tomeru /-ru; tometa/ stop (something); bring to
  a halt 7B
tomodati friend 2B +
tonari next door; adjoining place 6B
Tóńde mo nài. Heavens, no! 8B
tôo ten units 5A +
Toodai Tokyo University 11B
Tookyoo Tokyo 2A
Toranomoñ (section of Tokyo) 6B
tosî year 8B +
tosíyòrì old person 10A +
tosyôkañ library (a building) 6B
tosyôsitu library (a room) 8B

tot(t)emo very, extremely 1B
-tu /classifier for counting units and years of human age/ 5A, 10A
tuğî next 7B
tuítatì first day of the month 8A
tukau /-u; tukatta/ use 3A
tukî month; moon 8D +
tukiatari end of the street, corridor, etc. 7B +
Tukuba Tsukuba University 12B +
tukûru /-u; tukûtta/ make, construct 1A
tûma wife; my wife 10B +
tumárànai /-katta/ is boring; is trifling 1B
tuyôi /-katta/ is strong 12A +
tya tea 5B +
tyairo brown 5B +
-tyañ /polite suffix added to children's and
  young people's names/ 10A
tyoodo exactly 4B
tyôtto a bit; a little 1A
  Tyotto . . I'm afraid not . . . /polite refusal/
    1A
Tyûuğoku China 5B +
tyuuğokuğo Chinese language 2A
tyuúğokùziñ a Chinese 10B +

ukağau /-u; ukağatta/ ↓ inquire, ask /humble-
  polite/ 6A
uketuke receptionist 10B
urâ reverse side; rear 7B
usiro back; rear 6A
utî house, home; household; in-group 7B
  uti no /+ nominal/ our household's, our 7B

wa /assertive sentence-particle/ 9A
wa /ptc/ in regard to; at least; comparatively
  speaking 4A
  Tanáka-sañ wa wakarimàsu. Mr/s. Tanaka
    (at least) understands. 4A
  Síñbuñ wa kaimasèñ desita. A paper (in
    contrast) I didn't buy. 4A
  Konó heñ nì wa arímasèñ. It's not around
    here (at least) 6A
waapuro word processor 3A +
waee Japanese–English 2B
waée-zìteñ Japanese–English dictionary 2B
wâiñ wine 5B +
wakâi /-katta/ is young 10A +
wakâru /-u; wakâtta/ be(come) comprehensible; understand 1A
warûi /-katta/ is bad; is wrong 7A
Wâseda Waseda University 12B +

Wasîñtoñ Washington 8A
wasureru /-ru; wasureta/ forget 12B
wata(ku)si I; me 2B

yahâri /see **yappâri**/
yakusoku appointment; promise 10A
yakusoku-suru make an appointment;
    promise 10A+
yameru /-ru; yameta/ quit; give up 8B
yaoya vegetable store 7B+
yappàri after all 3B
yasasii /-katta/ is easy 3B+
    yasásii hitò a person who is gentle, kind,
    nice 11A
yasûi /-katta/ is cheap 1A
yasúmì vacation; holiday; time off 8A
yasûmu /-u; yasûñde/ rest; take time
    off 8A+
yat́-tù eight units 5A+
yo /informative sentence particle/ 1A
yobu /-u; yoñda/ summon, call 9A
yôi /-katta/ is good 1B+
Yokohama Yokohama 8A+
yôku /see **îi**/
yômu /-u; yôñda/ read 12A+
yôñ four 2B
Yoóròppa Europe 8B
yoozi matters to attend to 9B
    yoozi de iku go on business 12B
yorosii /-katta/ is good, fine, all right; never
    mind 5B
    Yorosiku. (May things go well.) 11B+
    Ôkusañ ni yorosiku. Regards to your
    wife. 11B+
yôru evening; night 8B+
yot́-tù four units 5A+
yowâi /-katta/ is weak 12A
    suuzi ni yowâi is poor at numbers 12A
yukî snow 4A+
yuḱkùri slowly; leisurely 12A

yuúbè last night 10A+
yuúbìñkyoku post office 6B
yuútàañ U-turn 7B
yuútàañ-suru make a U-turn 7B

zaǹnèñ /na/ regrettable; too bad; a pity 2A
zassi magazine 2B+
zêmi seminar 10A
zêñbu all; the whole thing 3B
zeñzeñ /+ negative/ not at all 3B
zêro zero 12A+
-zi /classifier for naming the o'clocks/ 8A
zikañ time 8A+
    zikáñ ğa àru have time 8A+
-zikan /classifier for counting hours/ 8A+
zîko accident 9B
zimûsyo office 11A+
zîñzya Shinto shrine 6B+
zisiñ earthquake 9B+
zîsyo dictionary 2B
zitêñsya bicycle 7B+
zoñzìru ↓ /-ru; zôñzita/ find out; get to know
    /humble-polite/ 10B+
    zôñzite (i)ru ↓ [I] know /humble-polite/
    10B+
    gozôñzi da ↑ [you] know /honorific-polite/
    10B+
zûibuñ awfully; very 8B
zutto by far 10B
    zut́to màe way before; long ago 10B
-zutu of each; for each; at a time 5B
zyâ(a) /contraction of **dê wa**/ 2A
    sôo zya nâi it's not so 2A
zyâ(a) well then; that being the case 2B
zyoobu /na/ strong; rugged; sturdy 12A+
zyoózù /na/ skillful; skilled 9B
    zyoózù ni nâru become skillful; become
    skilled 9B
zyûğyoo schooltime; classtime 8A
zyuğyoo-suru teach classes; give lessons 9B+
zyûu ten 2B

English–Japanese Glossary

This glossary, which includes only vocabulary introduced in this text, is intended as a reminder list for use when vocabulary items have been temporarily forgotten. It is not intended as a means of acquiring new vocabulary. On those occasions when both an item and the patterns in which it occurs have been forgotten, the Japanese equivalent should be located in this glossary and then further checked by using the Japanese–English glossary and the index.

Verbals are identified by a hyphen, the location of which identifies the verbal class: **X-u** = consonant verbal; **X-ru** = vowel verbal; **X-aru** = special polite verbal (cf. Lesson 9A-SP1).

Adjectivals are identified by a hyphen separating the root from **-i**, the imperfective ending: **X-i**.

Na-nominals are identified by /**na**/ immediately following the item: **X** /**na**/.

Polite alternates are included in cases where their use is particularly common and/or is in some way unusual or unpredictable in form.

A.M. **gôzeñ**
about (approximate amount) **-g̃ùrai**
about (approximate point in time) **-g̃òro**
about as much as **-hodo**
about how much? **dono-g̃urai**
absence from home **rûsu**
accident **zîko**
adjoining place **tonari**
after **kara** /ptc/
  after that; and then **sore kara**
after (past) **-sug̃i**
  ten after one **itî-zi zíppùñ-sug̃i**
after a long interval **hisasiburi**
after all **yáppàri**
afternoon **gôg̃o**
again **matâ**
ago **mâe**
ahead **saki**
  (Excuse me for going) ahead of you. **Osaki ni.**
airplane **hikôoki**
airport **kuukoo**

all right: is ~ **daízyòobu** /na/; **îi/yô-i; yorosi-i**
all **miñnà; zêñbu**
almost **hotôñdo**
alone **hitô-ri (de)**
also **mo** /particle/
alternative **hôo**
always **îtu mo**
America **Amerika**
American Consulate **Amérika-ryoozìkañ**
American Embassy **Amérika-taisìkañ**
American (person) **amérikàziñ**
answer **kotáèru**
appear **miê-ru**
appointment **yakusoku**
  make an ~ **yakusoku-suru**
area **heñ**
ask **kik-u; ukaga-u** ↓
attend **dê-ru**
aunt **oba; obasañ** /polite/
Australia **Oósutorària**
Australian (person) **oósutorariàziñ**
awful: is ~ **taíhèñ** /na/; **sug̃ô-i**

awfully   zûibuñ; taiheñ

baby   âkatyañ
back   usiro; urâ
bad: is ~   damê /na/; warû-i
bag   kabañ
ballpoint pen   boorupeñ
bank   giñkoo
be located (of animate existence)   i-ru; irássyàru ↑; ôr-u ↓
be located (of inanimate existence)   âr-u; go-
   zaru +
be possible   dekî-ru
because   kara /ptc/
become   nâr-u
beer   bîiru
before   mâe
between   aida
beyond   mukôo/mukoo
bicycle   zitêñsya
big: is ~   oókì-i
black: is ~   kurô-i
blue: is ~   aô-i
boat   hûne
book   hôñ
bookstore; book dealer   hôñya
boring: is ~   tumáràna-i
borrow   kari-ru
both   dôtira mo
   both parents   ryôosiñ; goryôosiñ /polite/
   both this one and that one   kore mo sore mo
boy   otókò no ko
brother: older ~   âni; (o)nîisañ /polite/
   younger ~   otóotò; otootosañ /polite/
brown   tyairo
Buddhist temple   terâ
building   tatêmòno; bîru
bullet train   siñkàñseñ
bus   bâsu
business card   meesi
   cards on hand   meesi no motiawase
business trip   syuttyoo
busy: is ~   isógasì-i
buy   ka-u
by far   zutto

cake   kêeki
call (summon)   yob-u
call on the telephone   deñwa o kakè-ru; deñwa-
   suru
   be called   i-u; ossy-àru ↑; môos-u ↓

car   kuruma
Certainly. I'll do as you asked.
   Kasíkomarimàsita.
change   kawari
change (money)   oturi
cheap: is ~   yasû-i
child   kodomo; ko; okosañ /polite/
China   Tyuuḡoku
Chinese language   tyuuḡokuḡo
Chinese (person)   tyuúḡokùziñ
Christian era, A.D.   seereki
church   kyookai
cigarette   tabako
cigarette shop   tabakoya
circle   maru
classifiers   See list at end of glossary
classroom   kyoositu
classtime   zyûḡyoo
clean   kîree /na/
clock   tokee
coffee   koóhìi
coffee shop   kiśsàteñ/kissateñ
cold: is ~ (of atmosphere only)   samû-i
college   daiḡaku
color   irô
   what color?   naniiro; dôñna irô
come   kû-ru /irreg/; irássy-àru ↑; mâir-u ↓
come out   dê-ru
comfortable   rakû /na/
company   kaisya
completed: become ~   dekî-ru
comprehensible: become ~   wakâr-u
computer   koñpyùutaa
conference   kâiḡi
conference room   kaíḡìsitu
consulate   ryoózìkañ
consult   soodañ-suru
contact   reñraku-suru
convenient   bêñri /na/
cool: is ~   suzúsì-i
corner: street ~   kâdo
cousin   itôko; oitokosañ /polite/
custard pudding   pûriñ
cute: is ~   kawáì-i

dangerous: is ~   abuna-i
daughter   musúmè; musumesañ, ozyôosañ
   /polite/
day   hî/hi
   day after tomorrow   asâtte; myoóḡòniti
   day before yesterday   otótòi

delicious: is ~ **oisi-i**
  It was delicious. **Gotísoosama (dèsita).**
department store **depâato**
dictionary **zîsyo**
  English–Japanese dictionary **eéwa-zìteñ**
different: be ~ **tiḡa-u**
difficult: is ~ **muzukasi-i**
direction **hôo**
disagreeable **iyâ** /na/
divorced: get ~ **rikoñ-suru**
do **suru** /irreg/; **nas-âru** ↑ ; **itas-u** ↓
  can do **dekî-ru**
doctor **señsèe**
Don't mention it. **Dôo itasimasite.**
draw **kâk-u**
drink **nôm-u; itadak-u** ↓

each: of ~; for ~ **-zutu**
early: is ~ **hayâ-i**
  early; in good time **hayámè ni**
earthquake **zisiñ**
easy: is ~ **yasasi-i**
eat **tabê-ru; itadak-u** ↓
eight **hatî**
  eight days; eighth of the month **yoo-ka**
  eight units **yaí-tù**
electric train **deñsya/dêñsya**
embassy **taísìkañ**
end of the street, corridor, etc. **tukiatari**
England **Eekoku; Iḡirisu**
English–Japanese **eewa**
  English–Japanese dictionary **eéwa-zìteñ**
English language **eeḡo**
English (person) **iḡírisùziñ; eékokùziñ**
entrance **iriḡuti**
Europe **Yoóròppa**
evening **bañ; yôru**
even so **dê mo**
every day **mâiniti**
every month **maituki; maiḡetu**
every morning **mâiasa**
every night **mâibañ; maiyo**
everyone **miñ́nà; minâsañ** /polite/
everything **miñ́nà; zêñbu**
every time **maido**
every week **maisyuu**
every year **maitosi; maineñ**
exactly **tyoodo**
excuse **moosiwake**
exhaust a supply **kirâs-u** '
exit **dêḡuti**

expensive: is ~ **takâ-i**
extension **naiseñ**
extent: to this ~; this much **koñna ni**

family **kâzoku; gokâzoku** /polite/
far: as ~ as **made** /ptc/
father **titî; titioya; otôosañ** /polite/
female **oñ́nà**
Finance Ministry **oókuràsyoo**
find out **sir-u; gozôñzi da** ↑ ; **zoñzì-ru** ↓
fine: is ~ **îi/yô-i; yorosi-i**
fire (conflagration) **kâzi**
first day of the month **tuítatì**
first generation **îs-see**
first time **hazîmete**
five **gô**
  five units **itû-tu**
  five days; fifth of the month **itu-ka**
flower **hanâ**
flower shop; florist **hanâya**
foreign country **gaikoku**
foreigner **gaiziñ, gaíkokùziñ**
foreign language **gaikokuḡo**
Foreign Ministry **gaímùsyoo**
foreign trade **booeki**
forget **wasure-ru**
four **sî; yôñ**
  four units **yoí-tù**
  four days; fourth of the month **yok-ka**
France **Hurañsu**
French language **hurañsuḡo**
French (person) **huráñsùziñ**
fresh: is ~ **atárasì-i**
Friday **kiñ́yòo(bi)**
friend **tomodati**
from **kara** /ptc/
front **mâe; omótè**
funny: is ~ **omósirò-i**

German language **doituḡo**
German (person) **doítùziñ**
Germany **Dôitu**
girl **oñ́nà no ko**
give to me/us **kudás-àru** ↑
give up **yame-ru**
go **ik-u; irássy-àru** ↑ ; **mâir-u** ↓
  go on foot **arûite iku**
golf **gôruhu**
good: is ~ **îi/yô-i; yorosi-i**
Good afternoon. **Koñniti wa.**
Goodbye. **Sayo(o)nara.**

Goodbye. (said by person leaving home) **Itte kimàsu; Itte mairimàsu.** ↓
Goodbye. (said to person leaving home) **Itte (i)rassyài(màse).**
Good evening. **Koñbañ wa.**
Good morning. **Oháyoo (gozaimàsu).**
Goodnight. **Oyasumi-nasai.**
go out **dê-ru**
grandfather **sôhu; ozîisañ** /polite/
grandmother **sôbo; obâasañ** /polite/
gray **gurêe; haiiro**
green **guríiñ; mîdori**
guest **kyaku; okyakusañ** /polite/

half **-hañ**
handbag **hañdobàggu**
hang (something) **kakê-ru**
hard (difficult): is ~ **muzukasi-i**
have **âr-u**
he **kâre; anô hitò; anó katà** /polite/
hear **kik-u**
Heavens, no! **Toñde mo nài.**
Heisei Era (1989–) **Heesee**
hello (on the telephone) **môsimosi**
    Hello, I'm back. **Tadaima.**
helpful assistance **sewâ**
    Thank you for your ~. **Oséwasama (dèsita).**
here **koko; kotira; kotti**
hereabouts **kotira; kotti**
high school **kookoo**
hmmm! **sâa**
holiday **yasúmì**
home **utî; iê; otaku** /polite/
hospital **byooiñ**
hot: is ~ **atû-i**
hotel **hôteru**
house; household **utî; iê; otaku** /polite/
how? **dôo; ikâga** /polite/
    How do you do? **Hazímemàsite.**
how many ——? **nañ-** + classifier
how many units? how old? (of people) **îku-tu**
how much? **îkura**
hundred **hyakû**
husband **syûziñ; otto; gosyûziñ** /polite/

I; me **wata(ku)si; bôku**
ice cream **aísukurìimu**
idea **âidea**
immediately **sûgu**
India **Îñdo**
Indian (person from India) **iñdòziñ**

inn (Japanese-style) **ryokañ**
inquire **ukaga-u**
institute director **syotyoo**
interesting: is ~ **omósirò-i**
intersection **koósàteñ**
interval **aida**
introduce **syookai-suru**
Italian language **itariaǧo**
Italian (person) **itáriàziñ**
Italy **Itaria**

Japan **Nihôñ/Níppòñ**
Japanese–English **waee**
Japanese language **nihoñǧo/nippoñǧo**
Japanese (person) **nihóñziñ/níppoñzìñ**
joy: a ~ **tanósìmì**
just now **tadâima**
just; exactly **tyoodo**
just **dakê**
    That's all (= It's just that.) **Soré dakè desu.**

Keio [University] **Keeoo**
kiosk **baiteñ**
know **sitte i(ru); gozôñzi da** ↑ **; zôñzite (i)ru** ↓
    come to know **sir-u**
Kyoto **Kyôoto**
Kyoto University **Kyoodai**

last month **sêñǧetu**
last night **yuúbè**
last week **señsyuu**
last year **kyôneñ**
late: is ~ **oso-i**
    become late **okure-ru**
    until late **osókù made**
later **âto de; notihodo**
leave **dê-ru**
leave one's seat **sêki o hazus-u**
left (direction) **hidari**
    left side **hidári no hòo**
left (remaining) **âto**
    one hour left **âto ití-zìkañ**
leisurely **yukkùri**
lend **kas-u**
letter **teǧami**
listen **kik-u**
library (a building) **tosyôkañ**
library (a room) **tosyôsitu**
little; is ~ **tiísà-i**
    a little **sukôsi; tyôtto**
located: be ~ (of inanimate existence) **âr-u; gozâr-u** +

(of animate existence) **i-ru; irássy-àru** ↑ ; **ôr-u** ↓
long: is ~ **naǧâ-i**
look at **mî-ru**

magazine **zassi**
make a turn **maǧar-u**
make an appointment **yakusoku-suru**
make **tukûr-u**
male **otókò**
man **otóko no hitò; otóko no katà, ozisañ** /polite/
many **takúsàñ**
map **tîzu**
marry **kekkoñ-suru**
matter **kamâ-u**
  it doesn't ~ **kamáwàna-i**
matters to attend to **yoozi**
meet **â-u**
meeting **kâiǧi**
Meiji Era (1868–1912) **Mêezi**
message **mêsseezi**
milk **mîruku**
Ministry of Education **moñbùsyoo**
Monday **getúyòo(bi)**
month; moon **tukî**
  last ~ **sêñǧetu**
  ~ before last **señsèñǧetu**
  this ~ **koñǧetu**
  next ~ **râiǧetu**
  ~ after next **saraiǧetu**
more **môtto**
  /+ quantity expression/ **moo**
  a little more **moó sukòsi**
morning **âsa**
  this morning **kêsa**
  tomorrow morning **asíta no àsa; myootyoo**
mother **hâha, hahaoya; okâasañ** /polite/
movie theater **eéǧàkañ**
Mr.; Mrs.; Miss; Ms. **-sañ** /polite suffix/
much **takúsàñ**

Nagoya **Nâǧoya**
name **namae**
  be named **i-u; ossy-àru** ↑ ; **môos-u** ↓
nearby **sôba**
need **ir-u**
never mind **îi/yô-i; yorosi-i**
new: is ~ **atárasì-i**
newspaper **siñbuñ**
next **tuǧî**

next door **tonari**
  ~ on the left **hidáridònari**
  ~ on the right **miǧídònari**
next month **râiǧetu**
next week **raisyuu**
next year **raineñ**
night **bañ; yôru**
  last ~ **yuúbè**
  tonight **kôñbañ**
  tomorrow ~ **asita no bañ; myooban**
nine **kû; kyûu**
  nine units **kokôno-tu**
  nine days; ninth of the month **kokóno-kà**
no **i(i)e; iya; iêie; ñ̂ñ**
no good **damê** /na/
not at all **zeñzeñ** /+ negative/
notebook **nôoto**
not especially **betu ni** /+ negative/
not much; not very **a(ñ)mari** /+ negative/
now **îma**
nowadays **kono-ǧoro**
number(s) **suuzi**
  assigned **bañǧòo**

obliged: become ~ for assistance **sewâ ni nâru**
of course; to be sure **naruhodo**
office **zimûsyo**
office building **bîru**
oh! **â(a)**
old: is ~ (not new) **hurû-i**
older brother **âni; (o)nîisañ** /polite/
older sister **ane; (o)nêesañ** /polite/
old man **ozîisañ** /polite/
old person **tosíyòri**
old woman **obâasañ** /polite/
one **itî**
  ~ day **ití-nitì**
  ~ person **hitô-ri**
  ~ unit **hitô-tu**
one hundred **hyakû**
opposite side **mukooǧawa**
or on the other hand **matâ wa**
other **hoka**
  Anything else? **Hoka ni nâni ka?**
our household's; our **uti no** /+ nominal/
out; be(come) ~ of **kirâs-u**
over there **asoko; atira; attì; mukoo**

P.M. **gôǧo**
paper **kamî**
parent **oya; oyaǧosañ** /polite/
  both parents **ryôosiñ; goryôosiñ** /polite/

park **kooeñ**
part-time work **arúbàito**
past **-suḡi**
   ten (minutes) past **zíp-pùñ-suḡi**
pen **pêñ**
pencil **eñpitu**
person **hitô; katâ** /polite/
person of Japanese ancestry **nikkèeziñ**
pie **pâi**
pity: a ~ **zañnèñ** /na/
place **tokórò**
Please (speaker offering something) **Dôozo.**
   (speaker requesting something) **Onéḡai-**
     simàsu.
pleasure: a ~ **tanósìmì**
police box **koobañ**
policeman **omâwarisañ** /polite/
post office **yuúbìñkyoku**
pretty **kîree** /na/
promise **yakusoku**
   make a ~ **yakusoku-suru**
public telephone **koósyuudèñwa**

quit **yame-ru**
quite **nakanaka**

rain **âme**
rather **nakanaka**
rear **usiro; urâ**
receptionist **uketuke**
red: is ~ **aka-i**
regrettable **zañnèñ** /na/
rent (from someone) **kari-ru**
   (to someone) **kas-u**
required: be ~ (of time and money) **kakâr-u**
   (need) **ir-u**
return: a ~ **kaérì**
return; go back **modôr-u**
   ~ (home) **kâer-u**
reverse side **urâ**
right **miḡi**
   ~ side **miḡí no hòo**
road **miti**
rush hour **rassyu-àwaa**
Russian language **rosiaḡo**
Russian (person) **rosìàziñ; soréñzìñ**

safe **daízyòobu** /na/
saké (rice wine) **sake**
same **onazi**
Saturday **doyôo(bi)**

say **i-u; ossy-àru** ↑ **; môos-u** ↓
school **gakkoo**
schooltime; classtime **zyûḡyoo**
seat (assigned place) **sêki**
   leave one's seat **sêki o hazus-u**
second generation **nî-see**
see (look at) **mî-ru**
   (meet with) **â-u**
seminar **zêmi**
seven **nâna; sitî**
   seven units **nanâ-tu**
   seven days; seventh of the month **nano-ka**
she **kânozyo; anô hito; anó katà** /polite/
ship **hûne**
shop **misê**
shopping bag **syoppiñḡubàggu**
short: is ~ **mizika-i**
show **misê-ru**
Showa Era (1926–89) **Syoowa**
sick; sickness **byooki; gobyooki** /polite/
side **hôo**
single (unmarried) **hitô-ri**
sister: older ~ **ane; (o)nêesañ** /polite/
   younger ~ **imôoto; imootosañ** /polite/
six **rokû**
   six units **mut-tù**
   six days; sixth of the month **mui-ka**
skillful; skilled **zyoózù** /na/; **ozyoozu** /polite/
slowly **yukkùri**
small: is ~ **tiísà-i**
so-so **mâa·mâa**
someday **izure**
something **nâni ka**
sometime **izure**
son **musuko; musukosañ, bôttyañ** /polite/
soon **sûḡu**
sorry: I'm ~ **su(m)ímasèñ; moósiwake**
   arimasèñ
South Korea **Kâñkoku**
South Korean (person) **kañkokùziñ**
Soviet Union **Sôreñ; Sobîeto**
Spain **Supêiñ**
speak **hanâs-u**
sportscar **supóotukàa**
stand (concession) **baiteñ**
station **êki**
stationery store; stationery dealer **buñbooḡuya**
stationery (writing paper) **biñseñ**
   writing supplies **buñbòoḡu**
stop; bring to a halt **tome-ru**
   come to a halt; stop over **tomar-u**

store **misê**
straight **maʹssùg̈u**
street **miti**
street corner **kâdo**
strong: is ~ **tuyô-i**
  sturdy **zyoobu /na/**
student **gakusee**
study **beñkyoo-suru**
sturdy **zyoobu /na/**
subway **tikatetu**
sugar **satôo**
suitcase **suútukèesu**
summon **yob-u**
Sunday **nitíyòo(bi)**
supermarket **sûupaa**
surprise: become surprised **biʹkkùri-suru**
suspend (something) **kakê-ru**

Taisho Era (1912–26) **Taisyoo**
take (require) **kakâr-u**
talk **hanâs-u**
tape **têepu**
taxi **tâkusii**
tea **otya**
  black tea **kootya**
teach **osie-ru**
teacher **señsèe**
telephone; make a telephone call **deñwa-suru;
    deñwa o kakè-ru**
telephone; ~ call **deñwa; odêñwa /polite/**
telephone number **deñwabàñg̈oo**
ten **zyûu**
  ten units **tôo**
  ten days; tenth of the month **too-ka**
tennis **tênisu**
terrible: is ~ **sug̈ô-i; taíhèñ /na/**
terrific: is ~ **sug̈ô-i**
textbook **kyoókàsyo**
thank you **arîg̈atoo gozaimasu + ;
    su(m)ímasèñ**
  thanks to you; thanks for asking **okag̈esama
    de**
that —— near you; that —— just men-
    tioned **sono /+ nom/**
that —— over there; that —— (known to both of
    us) **ano /+ nom/**
that being the case **soré dè wa**
that kind of —— **soñna, añna /+ nom/**
  to that extent, like that **soñna ni; añna ni**
that place **soko; asoko, asuko**
that side **sotira, soʹttì; atira, aʹttì**

that thing (near you or just mentioned) **sore**
that thing over there (or known to both of
    us) **are**
that way; like that **sôo**
theater **gekizyoo**
  movie ~ **eég̈àkañ**
there **soko; asoko, asuko; sotira, soʹttì; atira,
    aʹttì**
thereabouts **sotira, soʹttì; atira, aʹttì**
things on hand **motiawase**
  have no business cards on hand **meési no
    motiawase g̈a nài**
think **omô-u**
third generation **sâñ-see**
this —— **kono /+ nom/**
this kind of —— **koñna /+ nom/**
this place **koko**
this side **kotira, koʹttì**
this side (of) **temae**
this thing **kore**
thousand **sêñ**
three **sañ**
  three units **miʹt-tù**
  three days; third of the month **mik-ka**
Thursday **mokúyòo(bi)**
time **zikañ**
  have ~ **zikáñ g̈a àru**
  —— at a ~ **-zutu**
to be sure! **naruhodo**
today **kyôo**
together **issyo**
  together with a friend **tomodati to issyo**
  do together **issyo ni suru**
toilet **tôire; teârai**
tomorrow **asítà, asû; myôoniti**
touch: get in ~ **reñraku-suru**
traffic light **siñg̈oo**
train: (electric) ~ **deñsya/dêñsya**
  (steam) ~ **kisyâ**
true; truth **hoñtoo**
Tuesday **kayôo(bi)**
turn: make a ~ **mag̈ar-u**
twenty days; twentieth of the month **hatu-ka**
twenty years of age **hâtati**
two **nî**
  two units **hutá-tù**
  two days; second of the month **hutu-ka**
typewriter **taípuràitaa**

U-turn **yuútàañ**
  make a U-turn **yuútàañ-suru**

uh |anoo|; |eeto|
umbrella **kâsa**
uncle **ozi; ozisañ** /polite/
underground **tikâ**
unfasten **hazus-u**
unfortunate; unfortunately **ainiku**
university **daiḡaku**
unpleasant **iyâ** /**na**/
unskillful **hetâ** /**na**/
upset: become ~ **komâr-u**
use **tuka-u**
usually **taitee**

vacation **yasúmì**
vegetable store **yaoya**
very **tot(t)emo; taiheñ; zûibuñ**
vicinity **heñ; sôba**
visitor **kyaku; okyakusañ** /polite/

wait **mât-u**
walk **arûk-u**
warm: is ~ **at(á)takà-i**
watch; clock **tokee**
way (direction) **hôo**
way before; long ago **zuʹtto màe**
weak: is ~ **yowâ-i**
Wednesday **suíyòo(bi)**
week **syuu**
  this ~ **koñsyuu**
  last ~ **señsyuu**
  ~ before last **señsèñsyuu**
  next ~ **raisyuu**
  ~ after next **saraisyuu**
Welcome! **Irássyài(màse).**
Welcome back! **Okáeri-nasài.**
well then **zyâ(a); dê wa**
what? **nâñ, nâni**
what ——? **dôno** /+ nom/
what color? **naniiro**
what kind of ——? **dôñna** /+ nom/

what language? **naniḡo**
what nationality? **naniziñ**
when? **îtu**
where? **dôko; dôtira, dôtti**
which ——? **dôno** /+ nom/
which side? **dôtira (no hôo); dôtti (no hôo)**
which thing? (usually of three or more) **dôre**
  (of two alternatives) **dôtira (no hôo), dôtti (no hôo)**
white: is ~ **sirô-i**
who? **dâre; dônata, dôtira-sama** /polite/
whole: the ~ thing **zêñbu**
why? **dôo site; nâze**
wife **kânai, tûma; ôkusañ** /polite/
wine **wâiñ**
  rice ~ **sake**
woman **oñna no hitò; oñna no katà, obasañ** /polite/
wonderful **suḡô-i**
work **siḡoto**
wrapping cloth **hurosiki**
write **kâk-u**
wrong: be ~ **tiḡa-u**

yeah **ñ**
year **tosi**
  this ~ **kotosi**
  next ~ **raineñ**
  last ~ **kyôneñ**
  ~ before last **otôtosi**
  initial ~ of an era **gâñ-neñ**
yellow: is ~ **kiiro-i**
yes **hâi, êe; hâa** /polite/
yesterday **kinôo**
you **anâta; kimi** /familiar/
young: is ~ **wakâ-i**
younger brother **otóotò; otootosañ** /polite/
younger sister **imôoto; imootosañ** /polite/

zero **rêe, zêro, maru**

Classifiers

Counting		*Naming*		*Counting and Naming*	
bound volumes	**-satu**	months	**-ḡatu**	days and dates	**-ka/-niti**
buildings and		o'clocks	**-zi**	floors	**-kai**
shops	**-keñ**	serial		minutes	**-huñ**
cents	**-señto**	numbers	**-bañ**	years	**-neñ**
dollars	**-doru**				
hours	**-zikañ**				
long, cylindrical					
objects	**-hoñ**				
minutes	**-huñkañ**				
months	**-kaḡetu**				
occurrences	**-do**				
people	**-ri/-niñ**				
thin, flat					
objects	**-mai**				
vehicles and					
machines	**-dai**				
weeks	**-syuukañ**				
years	**-neñkañ**				
years of age	**-tu/-sai**				
yen	**-eñ**				

Index

References are to Lesson, Section, and Structural Pattern: for example, 11B-3 refers to Lesson 11, Section B, Structural Pattern 3. MN refers to Miscellaneous Notes; GUP refers to Greetings and Useful Phrases in the Introduction.

Items designated simply as particles are phrase-particles. /Ḡ/ and /ñ/ are alphabetized as /g/ and /n/.